The Rule of Metaphor

Multi-disciplinary studies
of the creation of meaning
in language

PAUL RICOEUR

Translated by
ROBERT CZERNY
with Kathleen McLaughlin
and John Costello, SJ

Routledge & Kegan Paul
London and Henley

This translation first published in Great Britain in 1978
by Routledge & Kegan Paul Ltd
39 Store Street,
London WC1E 7DD and
Broadway House,
Newtown Road,
Henley-on-Thames,
Oxon RG9 1EN
Printed in Great Britain by
Lowe & Brydone Printers Ltd
Thetford, Norfolk
Translated from La métaphore vive
French edition © Éditions du Seuil, 1975
English Translation © University of Toronto Press 1977

British Library Cataloguing in Publication Data

Ricoeur, Paul
    The rule of metaphor.
    1. Metaphor
    I. Title   II. Czerny, Robert   III. McLaughlin,
    Kathleen   IV. Costello, John
    808   PN228.M4

    ISBN 0 7100 8964 3

Contents

Translator's introduction

This translation was done from the author's manuscript. It diverges at several points from the first edition of *La Métaphore vive* (Éditions du Seuil, Paris 1975), where errors have been found in that edition, and where Professor Ricoeur has undertaken revisions.

In general, I have attempted to translate as literally as possible, in order not to obscure precise points of interpretation, but on the contrary to facilitate the interdisciplinary communication that Paul Ricoeur promotes. So too, to assist further study by readers restricted to English, I have used readily available translations of works originally in other languages wherever I could.

There are, of course, several exceptions to the pattern of literal translation. One exception is the title of the book. Uncomfortable with the more literal translations of *La Métaphore vive* that came to mind, I have offered *The Rule of Metaphor* because of its metaphorical suggestiveness. The primary reference is to Aristotle's assertion, quoted often by Ricoeur,[1] that 'the greatest thing by far is to be a master of metaphor. It is the one thing that cannot be learnt from others; and it is also a sign of genius, since a good metaphor implies an intuitive perception of the similarity in dissimilars.' And besides rule as mastery of metaphor, the reader will encounter the language rules that impinge on metaphor, and the domains of discourse in which metaphor holds sway. Perhaps this phrase will disclose other meanings as well.

Since many readers of *The Rule of Metaphor* may be unfamiliar with the development of Ricoeur's work, a broader overview than the author's own introduction is reprinted below as an appendix (pages 315-22). Although this address was given in May 1971, it is still relevant as a general introduction to Ricoeur's current work.[2] Nevertheless, it should be read with a few pointers in mind. First, etiquette demands that the many other authors to whom Ricoeur has turned appreciative and critical attention be assured that his list of citations was shortened and focused by the nature of the address and its locale, the University of Chicago. Second, Ricoeur might well present his orientations and projects differently now from six years ago. Third, Ricoeur does not allude here to his interests in the social sciences and political philosophy, and in many social issues.[3]

When first discussing this project with me, Professor Ricoeur requested that the final product read more like his own work than like that of someone else. If that and any other worthwhile standards have been met, it is due to his own great co-operation in checking the translation and answering specific queries; to Kathleen McLaughlin, who assisted in this checking and undertook the first draft of the translation of Study 8; and to John Costello, SJ, who corrected the entire translation. Many friends helped on particular sections; Michael Czerny, SJ, Geoffrey Williams, SJ, and Peter McCormick deserve special mention.

This book has been published with the help of a grant from the Humanities Research Council of Canada, using funds provided by the Canada Council, and with the help of the Publications Fund of the Universir of Toronto Press. The University of Toronto Research Fund supported tiน translation. The assistance of these institutions is gratefully acknowledged.

Besides the philosophical education it provided, I am thankful for the contribution of this experience to a coincident maturation over the past three years of my aesthetic and personal perspectives. The far greater debt, in all of this, is owed to my wife, Katharina.

Robert Czerny
Ottawa

THE RULE OF METAPHOR

Introduction

These eight Studies on metaphor grew out of a seminar course given at the University of Toronto in Autumn 1971, under the auspices of the Department of Comparative Literature. In this connection, I wish to express my very sincere thanks to Professor Cyrus Hamlin, who invited me to Toronto. These explorations progressed further during courses given subsequently at the University of Louvain, then at the University of Paris-X, within the framework of my Phenomenological Research Seminar, and finally at the University of Chicago, under the auspices of the John Nuveen professorship.

Each of these Studies develops one specific point of view and constitutes a complete whole. At the same time, each forms part of a unique path, which begins with classical rhetoric, passes through semiotics and semantics, and finally reaches hermeneutics. The progression from one discipline to the other corresponds to changes of the linguistic entity chosen for consideration: the word, the sentence, and then discourse.

The rhetoric of metaphor takes the *word* as its unit of reference. Metaphor, therefore, is classed among the single-word figures of speech and is defined as a trope of resemblance. As figure, metaphor constitutes a displacement and an extension of the meaning of words; its explanation is grounded in a theory of substitution.

The first two Studies correspond to this initial level. Study 1, 'Between Rhetoric and Poetics,' is devoted to Aristotle. It is he who actually defined metaphor for the entire subsequent history of Western thought, on the basis of a semantics that takes the word or the name as its basic unit. Furthermore, his analysis is situated at the crossroads of two disciplines – rhetoric and poetics – with distinct goals: 'persuasion' in oral discourse and the *mimêsis* of human action in tragic poetry. The meaning of this distinction is not developed until Study 7, where the heuristic function of poetic discourse is defined.

Study 2, 'The Decline of Rhetoric: Tropology,' is devoted to the last works on rhetoric in Europe, particularly in France. The work of Pierre Fontanier, *Les Figures du discours*, serves as the basis for discussion. Two principal points are to be demonstrated here. I wish to show, first of all, that rhetoric terminates in classification and taxonomy, to the extent that it focuses on the figures of *deviation*, or tropes, in which the meaning of a word departs from its lexically codified usage. Secondly, I wish to show that while a taxonomic viewpoint is adequate for a static account of figures, it fails to explain the production of meaning as such, of which deviation at the level of the word is only the effect.

The semantic and the rhetorical viewpoints do not begin to be differentiated until metaphor is transferred into the framework of the *sentence* and is treated not as a case of *deviant denomination*, but as a case of *impertinent predication*. The next three Studies belong to this second level of consideration.

Study 3, 'Metaphor and the Semantics of Discourse,' contains the decisive step of the analysis; it can, therefore, be considered the 'key' Study. Here a theory of the statement-metaphor and a theory of the word-metaphor are set provisionally in radical opposition. The confrontation is prepared by distinguishing (in the manner of the French linguist Émile Benveniste) between a semantics, where the sentence is the carrier of the minimum complete meaning, and a semiotics, where the word is treated as a sign in the lexical code. Corresponding to this distinction between semantics and semiotics I propose a parallel opposition between a tension theory and a substitution theory. The former theory applies to the production of metaphor within the sentence taken as a whole, the latter concerns the meaning effect at the level of the isolated word. The important contributions of three English-language authors – I.A. Richards, Max Black, and Monroe Beardsley – are discussed within this framework. I try first to show that the seemingly disparate points of view represented by each of them ('philosophy of rhetoric,' 'logical grammar,' 'aesthetics') can be arrayed together under the aegis of the semantics of the sentence introduced at the beginning of the Study. I then endeavour to delimit the problem that these authors leave unsolved: that of the creation of meaning, for which newly invented metaphors are the evidence. This question of semantic innovation will animate Studies 6 and 7.

Measured against the question.that emerges at the end of Study 3, the fourth and fifth Studies may appear to move backwards. But their essential aim is to integrate the semantics of the word, which the preceding Study seemed to have eliminated, with the semantics of the sentence. The definition of metaphor as transposition of the name is actually not wrong.

It allows metaphor to be identified and to be classed among the tropes. Above all, the traditional rhetorical definition cannot be eliminated because the word remains the carrier of the effect of metaphorical meaning. It should be remembered in this connection that, in discourse, it is the word that assumes the function of semantic identity: and it is this identity that metaphor modifies. What is vital, then, is to show how metaphor, which is produced at the level of the statement as a whole, 'focuses' on the word.

This demonstration is limited in Study 4, 'Metaphor and Semantics of the Word,' to works in the tradition of Saussurean linguistics, especially those of Stephen Ullmann. By stopping at the threshold of structuralism properly speaking, I show that a linguistics that does not distinguish between semantics of the word and semantics of the sentence cannot but assign the phenomena of meaning-change to the history of word usage.

The fifth Study, 'Metaphor and the New Rhetoric,' carries this same demonstration into the framework of French structuralism. This deserves a separate analysis inasmuch as it has produced a 'new rhetoric' that applies the rules of segmentation, identification, and combination to figures of speech, rules that already have been applied with success to phonological and lexical entities. The discussion is introduced by a detailed examination of the notions of 'deviation' and 'rhetoric degree zero,' by a comparison of the notions of 'figure' and 'deviation,' and then by an analysis of the concept of 'reduction of deviation.' This extended preparation prefaces the examination of neo-rhetoric properly speaking, where extremely careful consideration is given to its effort at reconstructing the set of figures systematically on the basis of the operations that govern the atoms of meaning at the infra-linguistic level. The essential aim of the demonstration is to establish that the undeniable subtlety of the new rhetoric is completely exhausted in a theoretical framework that overlooks the specificity of the statement-metaphor and limits itself to confirming the primacy of the word-metaphor. Nevertheless, I try to show that the new rhetoric hints from within its limits at a theory of statement-metaphor, which it cannot elaborate given the resources of its system of thought.

The transition from the semantic level to the hermeneutical level is provided by Study 6, 'The Work of Resemblance,' which takes up the problem left unresolved at the end of the third Study, that of semantic innovation or creation of a new semantic pertinence. The notion of resemblance is itself reintroduced for further examination in order to solve this problem.

The first step is to refute the view (which Roman Jakobson still holds) that the fate of resemblance is linked indissolubly to that of a substitution theory. I try to show that resemblance is no less required in a tension theory, for the semantic innovation through which a previously unnoticed 'proximity' of two ideas is perceived despite their logical distance must in fact be related to the work of resemblance. 'To metaphorize well,' said Aristotle, 'implies an intuitive perception of the similarity in dissimilars.' Thus, resemblance itself must be understood as a tension between identity and difference in the predicative operation set in motion by semantic innovation. This analysis of the work of resemblance suggests in turn that the notions of 'productive imagination' and 'iconic function' must be reinterpreted. Indeed, imagination must cease being seen as a function of the image, in the quasi-sensorial sense of the word; it consists rather in 'seeing as ...' according to a Wittgensteinian expression – a power that is an aspect of the properly semantic operation consisting in seeing the similar in the dissimilar.

The passage to the *hermeneutic* point of view corresponds to the change of level that moves from the sentence to discourse properly speaking (poem, narrative, essay, etc.). A new problematic emerges in connection with this point of view: the issue is no longer the *form* of metaphor as a word-focused figure of speech, nor even just the *sense* of metaphor as a founding of a new semantic pertinence, but the *reference* of the metaphorical statement as the power to 'redescribe' reality. The most fundamental support of this transition from semantics to hermeneutics is to be found in the connection in all discourse between sense, which is its internal organization, and reference, which is its power to refer to a reality outside of language. Accordingly, metaphor presents itself as a strategy of discourse that, while preserving and developing the creative power of language, preserves and develops the *heuristic* power wielded by *fiction*.

But the possibility that metaphorical discourse says something about reality collides with the apparent constitution of poetic discourse, which seems to be essentially non-referential and centred on itself. To this non-referential conception of poetic discourse I oppose the idea that the suspension of literal reference is the condition for the release of a power of second-degree reference, which is properly poetic reference. Thus, to use an expression borrowed from Jakobson, one must not speak only of split sense but of 'split reference' as well.

This theory of metaphoric reference is supported by a generalized theory of denotation close to that of Nelson Goodman in *Language of Art*; and I justify the concept of 'fictional redescription' by means of the kinship established by Max Black, in *Models and Metaphors*, between the functioning of metaphor in the arts and that of models in the sciences. This relationship on the heuristic level constitutes the principal argument of this hermeneutics of metaphor.

This brings the work to its most important theme, namely, that meta-phor is the rhetorical process by which discourse unleashes the power that certain fictions have to redescribe reality. By linking fiction and redescrip-tion in this way, we restore the full depth of meaning to Aristotle's discov-ery in the *Poetics*, which was that the *poiêsis* of language arises out of the connection between *muthos* and *mimêsis*.

From this conjunction of fiction and redescription I conclude that the 'place' of metaphor, its most intimate and ultimate abode, is neither the name, nor the sentence, nor even discourse, but the copula of the verb *to be*. The metaphorical 'is' at once signifies both 'is not' and 'is like.' If this is really so, we are allowed to speak of metaphorical truth, but in an equally 'tensive' sense of the word 'truth.'

This incursion into the problematic of reality and truth demands that the philosophy implicit in the theory of metaphorical reference be eluci-dated. The eighth and last Study, 'Metaphor and Philosophical Discourse,' is a response to that demand.

This Study is essentially a plea for the plurality of modes of discourse and for the independence of philosophical discourse in relation to the pro-positions of sense and reference of poetic discourse. No philosophy pro-ceeds directly from poetry: this is shown through what appears to be the most difficult case, that of Aristotelian and medieval analogy. Nor does any philosophy proceed indirectly from poetry, even under cover of the 'dead' metaphor in which the collusion between meta-physical and meta-phorical, denounced by Heidegger, could take place. The discourse that attempts to *recover* the ontology implicit in the metaphorical statement is a different discourse. In this sense, to *ground* what was called metaphorical truth is also to *limit* poetic discourse. Poetic discourse is justified in this manner within its own circumscription.

This, then, is how the work unfolds. It does not seek to replace rhetoric with semantics and the latter with hermeneutics, and thus have one refute the other, but rather seeks to justify each approach within the limits of the corresponding discipline and to demonstrate the systmatic continuity of viewpoints by following the progression from word to sentence and from sentence to discourse.

The book is relatively long because it takes pains to examine the metho-dologies proper to each point of view, to set out the detailed analyses be-longing to each, and always to relate the limits of a theory to that of the corresponding point of view. In this connection, it will be noted that the book sets out and criticizes only those theories that at one and the same time carry a viewpoint to its highest degree of expression and contribute to the progress of the overall argument. Blistering refutations, then, will not be found here – at most, a demonstration of the unilateral character of doctrines that proclaim themselves to be exclusive. With respect to their origins, some of the decisive doctrines are taken from English-language literature and some from the French. This is an expression of the double allegiance of my research as well as my teaching in recent years; and I hope by this to help reduce the mutual ignorance that persists among specialists in these two linguistic and cultural worlds. I propose to rectify the injustice this seems to do to German-language authors in another book on which I am working currently, which takes up the problem of hermeneutics in its full scope.

These Studies are dedicated to several of those with whom I sense a philosophical affinity, or who have welcomed me in the universities where the Studies took shape: Vianney Décarie, université de Montréal; Gérard Genette, École pratique des hautes études à Paris; Cyrus Hamlin, University of Toronto; Émile Benveniste, Collège de France; A.-J. Greimas, École pratique des hautes études à Paris; Mikel Dufrenne, université de Paris; Mircea Eliade, University of Chicago; and Jean Ladrière, université de Louvain.

Between rhetoric and poetics: Aristotle

For Vianney Décarie

1 / RHETORIC AND POETICS

The historical paradox of the problem of metaphor is that it reaches us via a discipline that died towards the middle of the nineteenth century, when it ceased to be part of the collegial *cursus studiorum*. This link between metaphor and a dead discipline is a source of great perplexity: does not the return of contemporary thinkers to the problem of metaphor commit them to the hopeless project of resurrecting rhetoric from its ashes?

Assuming for the present that such an undertaking is not entirely in vain, it seems appropriate to begin with Aristotle, since he is the one who first conceptualized the field of rhetoric.

A reading of Aristotle tells us that we must begin cautiously. First of all, a simple examination of the table of contents of Aristotle's *Rhetoric* shows that we have received the theory of figures of speech from a discipline that is not merely defunct but amputated as well. For Aristotle, rhetoric covers three areas. A theory of argumentation (*inventio*, the 'invention' of arguments and proofs) constitutes the principal axis of rhetoric and at the same time provides the decisive link between rhetoric and demonstrative logic and therefore with philosophy (this theory of argumentation by itself takes up two thirds of the treatise). Rhetoric also encompasses a theory of style (*elocutio*) and, finally, a theory of composition (*compositio*).

Compared to this, what the latest treatises on rhetoric offer us is, in G. Genette's fitting words, a 'restricted rhetoric,'[1] restricted first to a theory of style and then to the theory of tropes. The history of rhetoric is an ironic tale of diminishing returns.* This is one of the causes of the death

---

* 'L'histoire de la rhétorique, c'est l'histoire de la peau de chagrin.' Ricoeur is referring to the leather talisman in Balzac's *La Peau de chagrin*, which shrank each time it granted its possessor's wish. (Trans.)

of rhetoric: in reducing itself thus to one of its parts, rhetoric simultaneously lost the nexus that bound it through dialectic to philosophy; and once this link was lost, rhetoric became an erratic and futile discipline. Rhetoric died when the penchant for classifying figures of speech completely supplanted the philosophical sensibility that animated the vast empire of rhetoric, held its parts together, and tied the whole to the *organon* and to first philosophy.

This sense of irremediable loss increases all the more if we remember that the broad Aristotelian program itself represented the rationalization (if not reduction) of a discipline that in Syracuse, its birthplace, endeavoured to regulate all facets of public speech.[2] Because there was oratory [*éloquence*], public oratory, there was rhetoric. This remark implies a great deal. Originally, speech was a weapon, intended to influence people before the tribunal, in public assembly, or by eulogy and panegyric; a weapon called upon to gain victory in battles where the decision hung on the spoken word. Thus Nietzsche writes: 'Oratory is republican.' The old Sicilian definition 'Rhetoric is the master of persuasion' (*peithous dêmiurgos*)[3] reminds us that rhetoric was added to natural eloquence as a 'technique,' but that this technique is rooted in a spontaneous creativity. Throughout all the didactic treatises written in Sicily, then in Greece after Gorgias established himself in Athens, rhetoric was this *technê* that made discourse conscious of itself and made persuasion a distinct goal to be achieved by means of a specific strategy.

Thus, before taxonomy of figures of speech, there was Aristotle's far more embracing rhetoric; but even before the latter, there was undisciplined common speech [*l'usage sauvage de la parole*] and the wish to harness its dangerous power by means of a special technique. Aristotle's rhetoric is already a domesticated discipline, solidly bound to philosophy by the theory of argumentation, from which rhetoric, in its decline, severed itself.

Greek rhetoric did not just have a singularly larger program than modern rhetoric; from its relation to philosophy, it derived all the ambiguities of its position. The properly dramatic character of rhetorical activity is explained well by the 'savage' roots of rhetoric. The Aristotelian corpus presents us with just one possible equilibrium between such extreme tensions, an equilibrium that corresponds to the situation of a discipline that is no longer simply a weapon in the public arena but is not yet a mere botany of figures of speech.

Rhetoric is without doubt as old as philosophy; it is said that Empedocles 'invented' it.[4] Thus, rhetoric is philosophy's oldest enemy and its oldest ally. 'Its oldest enemy' because it is always possible for the art of 'saying it well' to lay aside all concern for 'speaking the truth.' The technique founded on knowledge of the factors that help to effect persuasion puts formidable power in the hands of anyone who masters it perfectly – the power to manipulate words apart from things, and to manipulate men by manipulating words. Perhaps we must recognize that the possibility of this split parallels the entire history of human discourse. Before becoming futile, rhetoric was dangerous. This is why Plato condemned it.[5] For him, rhetoric is to justice, the political virtue *par excellence*, what sophistry is to legislation; and these are, for the soul, what cooking in relation to medicine and cosmetics in relation to gymnastics are for the body – that is, arts of illusion and deception.[6] We must not lose sight of this condemnation of rhetoric, which sees it as belonging to the world of the lie, of the 'pseudo.' Metaphor will also have its enemies, who, giving it what one might call a 'cosmetic' as well as a 'culinary' interpretation, will look upon metaphor merely as simple decoration and as pure delectation. Every condemnation of metaphor as sophism shares in the condemnation of sophistry itself.

But philosophy was never in a position either to destroy rhetoric or to absorb it. Philosophy did not create the arenas – tribunal, political assembly, public contest – in which oratory holds sway, nor can philosophy undertake to suppress them. Philosophical discourse is itself just one discourse among others, and its claim to truth excludes it from the sphere of power. Thus, if it uses just the means that are properly its own, philosophy cannot break the ties between discourse and power.

One possibility remained open: to delimit the legitimate uses of forceful speech, to draw the line between use and abuse, and to establish philosophically the connections between the sphere of validity of rhetoric and that of philosophy. Aristotle's rhetoric constitutes the most brilliant of these attempts to institutionalize rhetoric from the point of view of philosophy.

The question that sets this project in motion is the following: what does it mean to persuade? What distinguishes persuasion from flattery, from seduction, from threat – that is to say, from the subtlest forms of violence? What does it mean, 'to influence through discourse'? To pose these questions is to decide that one cannot transform the arts of discourse into techniques without submitting them to a radical philosophical reflection outlining the concept of 'that which is persuasive' (*to pithanon*).[7]

A helpful solution was offered at this point by logic, one which, moreover, took up one of rhetoric's oldest intuitions. Since its beginnings, rhetoric had recognized in the term *to eikos*[8] ('the probable') a title to which the public use of speech could lay claim. The kind of proof appropriate to oratory is not the necessary but the probable, because the human affairs over which tribunals and assemblies deliberate and decide are not subject to the sort of necessity, of intellectual constraint, that geometry and first philosophy demand. So, rather than denounce *doxa* ('opinion') as inferior to *epistêmê* ('science'), philosophy can consider elaborating a theory of the probable, which would arm rhetoric against its characteristic abuses while separating it from sophistry and eristics. The great merit of Aristotle was in developing this link between the rhetorical concept of persuasion and the logical concept of the probable, and in constructing the whole edifice of a philosophy of rhetoric on this relationship.[9]

Thus, what we now read under the title of *Rhetoric* is the treatise containing the equilibrium between two opposed movements, one that inclines rhetoric to break away from philosophy, if not to replace it, and one that disposes philosophy to reinvent rhetoric as a system of second-order proofs. It is at this point, where the dangerous power of eloquence and the logic of probability meet, that we find a rhetoric that stands under the watchful eye of philosophy. It is this deep-seated conflict between reason and violence that the history of rhetoric has plunged into oblivion; emptied of its dynamism and drama, rhetoric is given over to playing with distinctions and classifications. The genius for taxonomy occupies the space deserted by the philosophy of rhetoric.

Hence, Greek rhetoric had not only a much broader program, but also a problematic decidedly more dramatic than the modern theory of figures of speech. It did not, however, cover all the usages of speech. The technique of 'saying it well' remained a partial discipline, bounded not only from above by philosophy, but laterally by other domains of discourse. One of the fields that remained outside rhetoric is poetics. This split between rhetoric and poetics is of particular interest to us, since for Aristotle metaphor belongs to both domains.

The duality of rhetoric and poetics reflects a duality in the use of speech as well as in the situations of speaking. We said that rhetoric originally was oratorical technique; its aim and that of oratory are identical, to know how to persuade. Now this function, however far-reaching, does not cover all the uses of speech. Poetics – the art of composing poems, principally tragic poems – as far as its function and its situation of speaking are concerned, does not depend on rhetoric, the art of defence, of deliberation, of blame, and of praise. Poetry is not oratory. Persuasion is not its aim; rather, it purges the feelings of pity and fear. Thus, poetry and oratory mark out two distinct universes of discourse. Metaphor, however, has a foot in each domain. With respect to structure, it can really consist in just one unique operation, the transfer of the meanings of words; but with respect to function, it follows the divergent destinies of oratory and tragedy. Metaphor will therefore have a unique *structure* but two *functions*: a rhetorical function and a poetic function.

This duality of function, which expresses the difference between the political world of eloquence and the poetic world of tragedy, represents a still more fundamental difference at the level of intention. This opposition has been concealed to a great extent for us, because rhetoric as we know it from the last modern treatises is amputated from its major part, the treatise on argumentation. Aristotle defines it as the art of inventing or finding proofs. Now poetry does not seek to prove anything at all: its project is mimetic; its aim (as will be elaborated later) is to compose an essential representation of human actions; its appropriate method is to speak the truth by means of fiction, fable, and tragic *muthos*. The triad of *poiêsis-mimêsis-catharsis*, which cannot possibly be confused with the triad *rhetoric-proof-persuasion*, characterizes the world of poetry in an exclusive manner.

Hence, it will be necessary to set the unique structure of metaphor first against the background of the mimetic arts, and then against that of the arts of persuasive proof. This duality of function and of intention is more radical than any distinction between poetry and prose; it constitutes the ultimate justification of this distinction.

2 / THE INTERSECTION OF THE *POETICS* AND THE *RHETORIC*: 'EPIPHORA OF THE NAME'

We will bracket provisionally the problems posed by the double insertion of metaphor in the *Poetics* and the *Rhetoric*. To do so is justified by the fact that the *Rhetoric* – whether it was composed or only revised after the *Poetics* was written[10] – adopts, pure and simple, the well-known definition of metaphor given in the *Poetics*:[11] 'Metaphor consists in giving the thing a name that belongs to something else; the transference being either from genus to species, or from species to genus, or from species to species, or on grounds of analogy' (*Poetics* 1457 b 6-9).[12] Furthermore, in both works metaphor is placed under the same rubric of *lexis*, a word difficult to translate for reasons which will appear later;[13] for the present, I will say simply that the word has to do with the whole field of language-expression. In fact, the difference between the two treatises turns on the poetic function of *lexis* on the one hand, and on its rhetorical function on the other, not on the position of metaphor among the elements of *lexis*. Thus, in each case *lexis* is the means by which metaphor is inserted, albeit in different ways, into the two treatises under consideration.

What is the nature of the link between metaphor and *lexis* in the *Poetics*? Aristotle begins by rejecting an analysis of *lexis* that would be organized according to 'modes of speech [*élocution*]' (*ta skhêmata tês lexeôs*) and would link up with notions such as command, prayer, simple statement, threat, question, answer, etc. (1456 b 10). Hardly has this line of analysis been alluded to when it is interrupted by the remark: 'Let us pass over this, then, as appertaining to another art, and not to that of poetry' (1456 b 19). This other 'art' can only be rhetoric. Then another analysis of *lexis* is introduced, one that no longer has to do with *skhêmata* but with *mérê* ('parts,' 'constituants') of diction: 'Diction viewed as a whole is made up of the following parts: the Letter ... the Syllable, the Conjunction, the Article, the Noun, the Verb, the Case, and the Speech [*logos*]' (1456 b 20-1).

The difference between these two analyses is important for our purposes. The 'modes' of *élocution* are obviously facts of speech; in Austin's terminology, these are the illocutionary forms of speech. On the other hand, the 'parts of diction' arise from a segmentation of discourse into units smaller than or as long as the sentence, divisions that today would arise from a properly linguistic analysis.

What is the result, for a theory of metaphor, of this change of level? Essentially, it is that the term common to the enumeration of parts of speech and to the definition of metaphor is the *name* or *noun* (*onoma*). Thus the destiny of metaphor is sealed for centuries to come: henceforth it is connected to poetry and rhetoric, not at the level of discourse, but at the level of a segment of discourse, the name or noun. It remains to be seen whether, because of examples used, a latent theory of metaphor at the level of discourse might not cause the breakdown of the explicit theory of metaphor at the level of the noun.

Let us look more closely, therefore, at how the noun functions in these two contexts – in the enumeration of the parts of speech and in the definition of metaphor.

If one considers first the analysis of speech into 'parts,' it is clear that the name or noun is the pivot of the enumeration. It is defined as 'a composite significant sound not involving the idea of time, with parts which have no significance by themselves in it' (1457 a 10-11). Accordingly, it is the first of the entities enumerated to be endowed with signification; in modern parlance, it is the semantic unit. The four preceding parts of *lexis* are situated below the semantic level and are presupposed by the definition of the noun. In fact, the noun is first of all a complex sound, so one must first define the 'indivisible sound.' This is the first part of speech, the 'letter' (today we would say 'phoneme'); it belongs to 'metrics' (which now would be phonetics, or better, phonology). This pattern is repeated with the second part of speech, the syllable, which is first defined negatively in relation to the noun – 'A syllable is a nonsignificant composite sound [*asêmos*]' – then positively in relation to the letter – it is 'made up of a mute and a Letter having a sound' (1456 b 34-5). So, too, the conjunction and the article are 'non-significant sounds.' Thus, it is in opposition to the 'indivisible' sound (letter) and the 'semantically meaningless [*asémique*]' sound (syllable, article, conjunction) that the noun is defined as a 'composite significant sound.' Onto this semantic stem of diction the definition of metaphor as a transfer of the meanings of nouns or names will presently be grafted. This is why the key position of the noun in the theory of diction is of such decisive importance.

The definition of the 'parts' of speech following the noun confirms this position. This point deserves attentive examination, because these are the parts of speech that connect the noun to discourse and subsequently could displace the centre of gravity of the theory of metaphor from the noun to the sentence or discourse. The sixth part of *lexis* is the verb; it differs from the noun only in its relation to time (Aristotle's doctrine here agrees completely with that of his treatise *On Interpretation*).[14] The definitions of noun and verb have one part in common – 'composite significant sound' – and one part different – 'not involving the idea of time' and 'involving the idea of time.' Whereas the noun 'does not imply *when*,' the verb implies 'time present or time past' (1457 a 14-18). Would their definition in relation to time, negatively as regards the noun and positively for the verb, imply that the verb has priority over the noun, and thus the sentence over the word (since *onoma* signifies both noun in opposition to verb and word in opposition to sentence)? Not at all; the eighth and last part of *lexis* – the 'phrase [*locution*]' (*logos*)[15] – takes its definition from the 'composite significant sound,' which, as we have seen, defines the noun; to this is added 'some of the parts of which have a certain significance by themselves' (1457 a 23-4). So it is not only a composite sound but also a composite meaning. Two species are thus included: the *sentence*, which is a compound of noun and verb, according to the definition of the treatise *On Interpretation*;[16] and the *definition*, which is a combination of nouns.[17] Therefore, one cannot translate *logos* as *sentence* or *statement*, but only as *locution*, in order to cover the two domains of sentence and definition. Consequently, the sentence has no special status whatsoever in semantic theory. The word, as noun and as verb, remains the essential unit of *lexis*.

However, I have two reservations with respect to this rather harsh conclusion. In the first place, the *logos* itself comprises a unity that does not appear to be derived from that of the word – witness 'A Speech [sentence or phrase, *locution*] is said to be one in two ways, either as signifying one thing, or as a union of several speeches made into one by conjunction' (1457 a 28-9). The remark is interesting on two counts. On the one hand, the unity of meaning referred to as *logos* could serve as the basis of a theory of metaphor that would be less dependent on the noun; on the other hand, it is a combination of phrases that constitutes the unity of a work, for example the *Iliad*. Hence, one should add a theory of discourse to a theory of the word. But it must be admitted that this double consequence is not to be taken explicitly from the remark on the unity of signification provided by *logos.*

My second reservation is this: can one not take the expression 'composite significant sound' as descriptive of a semantic unit common to the noun, the verb, and the locution, and consequently deny that this expression captures the definitional core of the noun alone? By means of this expression, Aristotle would then have designated, beyond the difference between noun, verb, sentence, and definition, the carrier of the semantic function as such – let us say, the 'semantic kernel.' The modern reader certainly has the right to isolate this 'semantic kernel' and, by the same token, to initiate a purely internal critique of the privileged status of the noun. It is important for the theory of metaphor that its link to the noun can be cut in this way. As we shall see, some examples of metaphor, even Aristotle's examples, follow this direction. However, even in the broadest of interpretations, the 'composite significant sound' would at the most designate the word and not the sentence. This kernel, common to the noun and to other things besides the noun, cannot really designate specifically the unity of meaning of statements, since *logos* covers composites of nouns as well as verb-noun composites, i.e. definitions as well as sentences. Accordingly, it is wiser to leave in abeyance the question of that element, common to noun, verb, and *logos,* called 'composite significant sound.' Finally, by its analysis into 'parts,' the explicit theory of *lexis* aims at isolating, not the kernel of meaningfulness (which eventually proves to be common to many of these parts), but the parts themselves, and one among them in particular. The noun is the pivot.

As a matter of fact, the noun is spoken of immediately after the analysis of *lexis* into parts and just before the definition of metaphor: 'A Noun must always be either (1) the ordinary word for the thing (*kurion*), or (2) a strange word, or (3) a metaphor, or (4) an ornamental word, or (5) a coined word, or (6) a word lengthened out, or (7) curtailed, or (8) altered in form' (1457 b 1-3). This textual bridge explicitly joins the theory of metaphor to that of *lexis* by means of the noun.

Let us turn now to the definition of metaphor cited above. I will draw particular attention to the following features:

The first characteristic is that *metaphor is something that happens to the noun.* As has been repeated since the introduction, in connecting metaphor to noun or word and not to discourse Aristotle establishes the orientation of the history of metaphor vis-à-vis poetics and rhetoric for several centuries. Aristotle's definition contains *in nuce* the theory of tropes, or figures of speech that focus on the word. Certainly, confining metaphor among *word-focused figures of speech* will give rise to an extreme refinement in taxonomy. It will, however, carry a high price: it becomes impossible to recognize a certain homogeneous functioning that (as Roman Jakobson will show) ignores the difference between word and discourse and operates at all the strategic levels of language – words, sentences, discourse, texts, styles.[18]

The second characteristic is that *metaphor is defined in terms of movement.* The *epiphora* of a word is described as a sort of displacement, a movement 'from ... to ...' This notion of *epiphora* enlightens at the same time as it puzzles us. It tells us that, far from designating just one figure of speech among others such as synecdoche and metonymy (this is how we find metaphor taxonomized in the later rhetoric), for Aristotle the word *metaphor* applies to every transposition of terms.[19] Indeed, its analysis paves the way for a global reflection concerning *the figure as such.* In the interests of a clearer glossary one might regret that the same term sometimes designates the genus (the phenomenon of transposition, that is, the *figure as such*) and sometimes a species (what later we will call the *trope of resemblance*). This equivocation is interesting in itself. Within it is hidden an interest distinct from the one that governs the taxonomies and culminates in the genius for classification, eventually becoming bogged down in the disaggregation of discourse. It is an interest in the transpositional movement as such, in processes more than in classes. We can formulate this interest as follows: what does it mean to transpose the meaning of words? This question could be set into the semantic interpretation proposed above. Indeed, to the extent that the notion of 'composite significant sound' simultaneously covers the domains of noun, of verb, and of locution (thus of the sentence), one could say that *epiphora* is a process that concerns the semantic kernel, not just of the noun and verb but of all meaningful linguistic entities, and that this process designates change of meaning as such. Let us keep in mind this extension of the theory of metaphor, supported by the homogeneous character of *epiphora*, beyond the limits imposed by the noun.

The counterpart of its indivisibility of meaning is the perplexity caused by *epiphora*. To explain metaphor, Aristotle creates a metaphor, one borrowed from the realm of movement; *phora*, as we know, is a kind of change, namely change with respect to location.[20] But we are anticipating the subsequent theory in saying that the word *metaphor* itself is metaphorical because it is borrowed from an order other than that of language. With the later theory, we are supposing: (1) that metaphor is a borrowing; (2) that the borrowed meaning is opposed to the proper meaning, that is, to the meaning that 'really belongs' to a word by virtue of being its original meaning; (3) that one resorts to metaphor to fill a semantic void; and (4) that the borrowed word takes the place of the absent proper word where such exists. What follows will show that none of these diverse interpretations is implied by *epiphora* as it appears in Aristotle himself. At least, though, the vagueness of this metaphor about metaphor gives free scope to such interpretations. Any wish to avoid prejudging the theory of meta phor by calling metaphor an *epiphora* would be shattered quickly by the realization that it is impossible to talk about metaphor non-metaphorically (in the sense implied by borrowing); in short, that the definition of metaphor returns on itself. Naturally, this warning applies to the subsequent pretension of rhetoric to the mastery and control of metaphor and of figures in general by means of classification – the word *figure* is itself obviously metaphorical. It takes in as well every philosophy that might wish to rid itself of metaphor in favour of non-metaphorical concepts. There is no non-metaphorical standpoint from which one could look upon metaphor, and all the other figures for that matter, as if they were a game played before one's eyes. In many respects, the continuation of this study will be a prolonged battle with this paradox.[21]

The third characteristic is that *metaphor is the transposition of a name* that Aristotle calls 'alien' (*allotrios*), that is, 'a name that belongs to something else' (1457 b 7), 'the alien name' (1457 b 31). This term is opposed to 'ordinary,' 'current' (*kurion*), which is defined by Aristotle as 'used by everybody,' 'in general use in a country' (1457 b 3). Metaphor accordingly is defined in terms of deviation (*para to kurion,* 1458 a 23; *para to eiôthos,* 1458 b 3); thus, as the enumeration quoted above indicates, the use of metaphor is close to the use of strange, ornamental, coined, lengthened, and shortened terms. In these characteristics of opposition or deviation and kinship are the seeds of important developments regarding rhetoric and metaphor:

(1) First, the choice of ordinary usage as point of reference foreshadows a general theory of 'deviations,' which becomes the criterion of stylistics for certain contemporary authors.[22] This character of deviation is emphasized by other synonyms given by Aristotle for *allotrios*: 'The perfection of Diction is for it to be at once clear and not mean. The clearest indeed is that made up of the ordinary words for things, but it is mean ... Diction becomes distinguished and non-prosaic by the use of unfamiliar terms [*xenikon*], i.e. strange words, metaphors, lengthened forms, and everything that deviates from the ordinary modes of speech [*para to kurion*]' (1458 a 18-23). In the same sense of deviation we have 'escapes banality' (*exallatousa to idiôtikon,* 1458 a 21). Hence all the other usages (rare words, neologisms, etc.) that metaphor approximates are themselves also deviations in relation to ordinary usage.

(2) Besides the negative idea of deviation, the word *allotrios* implies a positive idea, that of a *borrowing*. Herein lies the specific difference between metaphor and all the other *deviating* usages. This particular meaning of *allotrios* derives not only from its opposition to *kurios*, but also from its ties with *epiphora*. Thus, Ross translates, 'Metaphor consists in giving the thing a name that belongs to something else' (1457 b 7). The displaced meaning comes from somewhere else; it is always possible to specify the metaphor's place of origin, or of borrowing.

(3) Must one say that ordinary usage has to be 'proper,' in the sense of primitive, original, native,[23] in order for there to be deviation and borrowing? It is but one step from the idea of ordinary usage to that of proper meaning, a step that leads to the eventually customary opposition between *figurative* and *proper*. Later rhetoric takes this step, but there is no evidence that Aristotle took it.[24] That a name belongs properly, that is to say essentially, to an idea is not implied necessarily by the idea of current meaning; this is perfectly compatible with a conventionalism like that of Nelson Goodman, which we will talk about in due course.[25] The synonymy (referred to above) of 'current' (*kurion*) and 'usual' (*to eiôthos*), as also the proximity between 'clarity' and 'ordinary words' (1458 a 19), preserves the possibility of disconnecting the notion of ordinary usage from that of proper meaning.

(4) Another, contingent development of the notion of 'alien' usage is represented by the idea of *substitution*. We will see later that an *interaction* theory is readily contrasted with the *substitution* theory by English-language authors.[26] Now, the fact that the metaphorical term is borrowed from an alien domain does not imply that it substitutes for an ordinary word which one could have found in the same place. Nevertheless, it seems that Aristotle himself was confused on this point and thus provided grounds for the modern critiques of the rhetorical theory of metaphor. The metaphorical word takes the place of a non-metaphorical word that one could have used (on condition that it exists); so it is doubly alien, as a present but borrowed word and as substitute for an absent word. Although distinct, these two significations appear in constant association in rhetorical theory and in Aristotle himself. Thus, examples of the displacement of meaning quite often are treated as examples of substitution: Homer says of Ulysses that he performed '"ten thousand good deeds" ... *in place of* [*anti*] ... "a large number"' (1457 b 12) [emphasis added]; similarly, if the cup is to Dionysus what the shield is to Ares, one could use the fourth term 'in place of' (*anti*) the second, and vice versa (1457 b 18). Does Aristotle mean that the presence of a borrowed metaphorical word is always linked to substitution for an absent, non-metaphorical word? If so, the deviation involved would always be one of substitution, and metaphor would dwell under the sign of poetic licence.[27]

Thus, the idea of substitution appears to be bound up firmly with that of borrowing; but the former does not proceed from the latter by necessity, since it admits of exceptions. On one occasion Aristotle cites the case in which no current word exists that could substitute for the metaphorical word. So, for example, the expression 'sowing around a god-created flame' is analysed according to the rules of metaphor of proportion (B is to A what D is to C) – the action of the sun is to its light what sowing is to grain (1457 b 25-30). But there is no name for the B term (at least in Greek; French has *darder*).* In this manner Aristotle points to one of metaphor's functions, which is to fill a semantic lacuna. This function supplements that of ornamentation in the later tradition. So, if Aristotle does not dwell on this point,[28] it is because he is interested here only in the analogy itself, and the absence of a word for one of the terms of the analogy, which could be supposed to jeopardize the analogy, he finds in fact does not prevent the analogy from functioning: 'It may be that some of the terms thus related have no special name of their own, but for all that they will be metaphorically described in just the same way' (1457 b 25-6). Nevertheless, we can keep this exception in mind in anticipation of a modern critique of the idea of substitution.

In conclusion, the Aristotelian idea of *allotrios* tends to assimilate three distinct ideas: the idea of a *deviation* from ordinary usage; the idea of *borrowing* from an original domain; and the idea of *substitution* for an absent but available ordinary word. By contrast, the opposition between figurative and proper meaning, omnipresent in the later tradition, is not implied here. It is the idea of substitution that appears to bear the greatest consequences: for if the metaphorical term is really a substituted term, it carries no new information, since the absent term (if one exists) can be brought back in; and if there is no information conveyed, then metaphor has only an ornamental, decorative value. These two consequences of a purely substitutive theory characterize the treatment of metaphor in classical rhetoric. Rejection of these consequences will follow rejection of the concept of substitution; and this is itself tied up with a rejection of displacement or movement of names.

The fourth feature of this definition of metaphor is this: at the same time as the idea of *epiphora*, preserving the unity of metaphor's meaning, counterbalances the classificatory tendency that predominates in the later taxonomies, *a typology of metaphor is outlined in the continuation of the definition.* We are told that the transfer goes from genus to species, from species to genus, from species to species, or is made by analogy (or propor-

* And English the verb *beam* (Trans.)

tion). The outcome in subsequent rhetoric of the dismembering and counting out of *epiphora*'s domain as sketched here is that metaphor becomes
nothing more than a figure related to the fourth type in Aristotle's list. It
alone refers explicitly to resemblance – the fourth term in analogy is related to the third in the same way (*omoiôs ekhei*, 1457 b 20) as the second
is related to the first; old age is related to life *as* evening is related to the
day. We will reserve for later the question whether the idea of an identity
or a similarity between the relationships exhausts the idea of resemblance,
and whether the transfer from genus to species, etc. is not also grounded
on resemblance.[29] What interests us now is the relationship between this
embryonic classification and the concept of transposition, which constitutes the unity of meaning of the genus 'metaphor.'

Two facts should be noted. First, transposition operates between logical
poles. Metaphor occurs in an order already constituted in terms of genus
and species, and in a game whose relation-rules – subordination, co-ordination, proportionality or equality of relationships – are already given. Second, metaphor consists in a violation of this order and this game. In giving
to a genus the name of a species, to the fourth term of the proportional relationship the name of the second term, and vice versa, one simultaneously
recognizes and transgresses the logical structure of language (1457 b
12-20). The *anti*, discussed earlier, applies not just to the substitution of
one word for another, but also to the jumbling of classification in cases
that do not have to do only with making up for lexical poverty. Aristotle
himself did not exploit this idea of a categorial transgression, which some
modern authors compare to Gilbert Ryle's concept of 'category mistake.'[30]
Doubtless this was because he was more interested, within the perspective
of his *Poetics*, in the semantic gain attached to the transference of names
than in the logical cost of the operation. The reverse side of the process,
however, is at least as interesting to describe as the obverse. If pursued, the
idea of categorial transgression holds not a few surprises in store.

I propose three interpretative hypotheses. First, in all metaphor one
might consider not only *the* word alone or *the* name alone, whose meaning
is displaced, but *the pair* of terms or relationships between which the
transposition operates – *from* genus *to* species, *from* species *to* genus, *from*
species *to* species, *from* the second *to* the fourth term (and vice versa) of a
proportional relationship. This has far-reaching implications. As the English-language authors put it, it always takes two ideas to make a metaphor.
If metaphor always involves a kind of mistake, if it involves taking one
thing for another by a sort of calculated error, then metaphor is essentially
a discursive phenomenon. To affect just one word, the metaphor has to
disturb a whole network by means of an aberrant attribution. At the same
time, the idea of categorial transgression allows us to fill out that of devia-

tion, which seemed to be implied in the transposition process. 'Deviation' appeared to belong to a purely lexical order, but now it is linked to a kind of deviance that threatens classification itself. What remains to be puzzled out is the relationship between the two sides of the phenomenon, between logical deviation and the production of meaning that Aristotle calls *epiphora*. This problem will be solved in a satisfactory manner only when the statement-character of metaphor is fully recognized. The name-related aspects of metaphor can then become fully attached to a discursive structure.[31] As we shall see later, Aristotle himself invites us to take this path when, in the *Rhetoric*, he takes up the obviously discursive metaphor of comparison (*eikôn*), or simile.

A second line of reflection seems to be suggested by the idea of categorical transgression, understood as a deviation in relation to a pre-existing logical order, as a dis-ordering in a scheme of classification. This transgression is interesting only because it creates meaning; as it is put in the *Rhetoric*, metaphor 'conveys learning and knowledge through the medium of the *genus*' (1410 b 13). What is being suggested, then, is this: should we not say that metaphor destroys an order only to invent a new one; and that the category-mistake is nothing but the complement of a logic of discovery? Max Black's integration of model and metaphor,[32] in other words of an epistemological concept and a poetic concept, allows us to exploit thoroughly this idea, which is completely opposed to any reduction of metaphor to a mere 'ornament.' Pushing this thought to the limit, one must say that metaphor bears information because it 'redescribes' reality. Thus, the category-mistake is the de-constructive intermediary phase between description and redescription. The seventh Study will be devoted to this heuristic function of metaphor. However, this cannot be brought to light without prior recognition not only of the statement-character of metaphor, but also of its place within the orders of discourse and of the work.

A third, more venturesome hypothesis arises on the fringe of the second. If metaphor belongs to an heuristic of thought, could we not imagine that the process that disturbs and displaces a certain logical order, a certain conceptual hierarchy, a certain classification scheme, is the same as that from which all classification proceeds? Certainly, the only functioning of language we are aware of operates within an already constituted order; metaphor does not produce a new order except by creating rifts in an old order. Nevertheless, could we not imagine that the order itself is born in the same way that it changes? Is there not, in Gadamer's terms,[33] a 'metaphoric' at work at the origin of logical thought, at the root of all classification? This is a more far-reaching hypothesis than the others, which presuppose an already constituted language within which metaphor operates. Not only is the notion of deviation linked to this presupposition, but also the opposition between 'ordinary' language and 'strange' or 'rare' language, which Aristotle himself introduced, as well as, most definitely, the opposition introduced later between 'proper' and 'figurative.' The idea of an initial metaphorical impulse destroys these oppositions between proper and figurative, ordinary and strange, order and transgression. It suggests the idea that order itself proceeds from the metaphorical constitution of semantic fields, which themselves give rise to genus and species.

Does this hypothesis go beyond the boundaries of Aristotle's analysis? Yes, if one focuses on the explicit definition of metaphor as the *epiphora* of the name and if one's criterion of *epiphora* is the obvious opposition between ordinary usage and unusual usage. No, if one takes into account all that appears in Aristotle's own analysis outside of this explicit definition and this explicit criterion. One of Aristotle's observations (held in reserve until now) seems to justify the boldness of this rather extreme hypothesis: 'It is a great thing, indeed, to make a proper use of the poetical forms, as also of compounds and strange words. But the greatest thing by far is to be a master of metaphor [literally: to be metaphorical, *to metaphorikon einai*]. It is the one thing that cannot be learnt from others; and it is also a sign of genius [*euphuias*], since a good metaphor [literally: to metaphorize well, *eu metapherein*] implies an intuitive perception of the similarity [*to to homoion theôrein*] in dissimilars' (*Poetics* 1459 a 3-8; see also *Rhetoric* 1412 a 10).

Several things are notable in this text. (a) Metaphor becomes a verb, 'metaphorize'; this brings to light the problem of usage (*khrêsthai*, 1459 a 5) – process prevails over result. (b) Next, the problem of use brings up that of 'appropriate' use (*prepontôs khrêsthai*). It is a question of 'metaphorizing well,' of 'using in an appropriate way' the processes of *lexis*. The same strokes depict the user of this usage: he is the one called to this 'greatest thing,' to 'be metaphorical'; he alone, unaided, can learn it or not learn it. (c) For – and this is precisely the point – to metaphorize well cannot be taught; it is a gift of genius, of nature (*euphuias to sêmeion estin*). Are we not now back at the level of finding or inventing, of that heuristic that we said violates an order only to create another, that dismantles only to redescribe? All of modern creativity theory confirms that there are no rules for invention, no recipes for the concoction of good hypotheses, only rules for the validation of hypotheses.[34] (d) But still, why can we not learn to 'be metaphorical'? Because to 'metaphorize well' is to 'see *resemblance*.' This phrasing may seem surprising. Up to this point resemblance has not been mentioned, except indirectly through the particular nature of the fourth sort of metaphor, that by analogy, which, as we have seen, is analysed as an identity or similarity of two relations. But are we not forced to suppose resemblance at work in all four kinds of metaphor, as the positive principle of which 'categorial transgression' is the negative side? Is it not necessary that genus and species be brought together in terms of similarity, for the name of either to be given to the other? Metaphor – or, better, to metaphorize, that is, the dynamic of metaphor – would rest, therefore, on the perception of resemblance. This brings us very close to our most extreme hypothesis, that the 'metaphoric' that transgresses the categorial order also begets it. But that the finding or discovering peculiar to this fundamental metaphoric is that of resemblance calls for its own particular proof, which cannot be presented until much later.[35]

3 / AN ENIGMA: METAPHOR AND SIMILE (*EIKÓN*)

The *Rhetoric* presents an enigma of minor proportions. The *Poetics* contains nothing about simile or comparison; why then does *Rhetoric* 3·4 introduce a parallel between metaphor and comparison (*eikôn*),[36] when it claims to add nothing to the definition of metaphor given in the *Poetics*? This is a minor problem if one is dealing only with purely historical questions of priority and dependence within the Aristotelian *corpus*. On the other hand, it is extremely instructive for a study like this one, which is at pains to assemble all indications of an interpretation of metaphor in terms of discourse as against its explicit definition in terms of names and naming. Indeed, the essential feature of comparison is its discursive character. 'Achilles sprang up like a lion.' To make a comparison, one needs two terms that are both equally present in the discourse – 'like a lion' is not a comparison by itself. Let us say (anticipating the terminology of I.A. Richards) that one needs a *tenor* (Achilles springs up) and a *vehicle* (like a lion).[37] We can discern the implicit presence of this discursive moment in the notion of *epiphora* (the transposition from one pole to another). It is as present in the categorial transference (giving the name of a species to the genus, etc.) as in the transfer by analogy (replacing the fourth term of a proportion with the second). The modern authors who say that to make a metaphor is to see two things in one[38] are faithful to this feature, which simile brings to light and which the definition of metaphor as *epiphora* of the name could conceal. While it is true in a formal sense that metaphor is a deviation in relation to the ordinary use of words, from the dynamic point of view it proceeds from the encounter between the thing to be named and that foreign entity from which the name is borrowed. Simile makes explicit this mutual approach that underlies borrowing and deviation.

It may be objected that Aristotle's express purpose here is not to explain metaphor by means of simile, but simile by metaphor. And, true enough, in six spots Aristotle subordinates simile to metaphor.[39] The fact that later rhetorical tradition does not follow Aristotle here makes this point all the more remarkable.[40]

Several converging lines of argument serve to subordinate simile to metaphor. First, the realm of phenomena that come under simile is split up. One part, called *parabolê*, is connected to the theory of 'proof,' to which book 1 of the *Rhetoric* is devoted. This consists in illustration through example, which can be historical or fictitious.[41] The other part, under the title *eikôn*, is attached to the theory of *lexis* and falls into the special domain of metaphor.

Let us further note that it is the special kinship between simile and the proportional metaphor that guarantees its place within the field of metaphor: 'Successful similes also, as has been said above, are in a sense metaphors, since they always involve two relations [literally: they are said or made on the basis of two] like the proportional metaphor. Thus: a shield, we say, is the "drinking bowl of Ares," and a bow is the "chordless lyre" (1412 b 34-1413 a 2). Indeed, the proportional metaphor comes to give the name of the second term to the fourth by elision from the complex comparison that holds not between the things themselves but between the relations of the two pairs of things. In this sense, the proportional metaphor is not as simple as might appear when, for example, we call Achilles a lion. Therefore, the simplicity of simile, when contrasted with a proportion between four terms, is not the simplicity of a word but that of a relation between two terms[42] – that very relation, in fact, that proportional metaphor results in: 'The shield is the drinking-bowl of Ares.' In this manner, the metaphor by analogy tends to become identified with the *eikôn*; so the supremacy of metaphor over the *eikôn*, if not reversed, is in any case 'modified' (ibid.). But it is because *eikôn* 'always involves two relations'[43] – like metaphor by analogy – that the relation can be inverted so easily.

Lastly, the grammatical analysis of simile confirms its dependent status with regard to metaphor in general. They differ only by the presence or absence of a specific term of comparison: the particle *like* or *as* (*hôs*) in all the quotations in *Rhetoric* 3:4; in the example from Homer (whom Aristotle misquotes, incidentally), the verb (he compares) or adjective (similar) of comparison, etc.[44] In Aristotle's eyes, the absence of some term of comparison in metaphor does not imply that metaphor is an abbreviated simile, as was claimed from Quintilian onwards. Rather, simile is a metaphor developed further; the simile says 'this is *like* that,' whereas the metaphor says 'this *is* that.' Hence, to the extent that simile is a developed metaphor, all metaphor, not just proportional metaphor, is implicit comparison or simile.

Accordingly, the explicit subordination of simile to metaphor is possible only because the metaphor presents the polarity of the terms compared in an abridged form. 'When the poet says of Achilles that he "Leapt on the foe as a lion," this is a simile; when he says of him "the lion leapt," it is a metaphor – here, since both are courageous, [Homer] has transferred to Achilles the name of "lion"' (1406 b 20–3). Perhaps the best way to put it is that the element common to metaphor and simile is the assimilation that serves as foundation for the transfer of names. In other words, it is the apprehension of an identity within the difference between two terms. This apprehension of the genus by means of resemblance makes metaphor truly instructive: 'When the poet calls old age "a withered stalk," he conveys a new idea [literally: he has produced a knowledge] [*epoiêse mathêsin kai gnôsin*], a new fact, to us by means of the general notion [*dia tou genous*] of "lost bloom" ... ' (1410 b 13-15). And herein lies metaphor's superiority over simile, that it is more elegant (*asteïa*) (we will return later to metaphor's 'virtue' of urbanity, of brilliance): 'The simile, as has been said before, is a metaphor, differing from it only in the way it is put [*prothesei*]; and just because it is longer, it is less attractive. Besides, it does not say outright that "this" *is* "that," and therefore the hearer is less interested [*dzeteï*] in the idea. We see, then, that both speech and reasoning are lively in proportion as they make us seize a new idea promptly' (1410 b 17-21). Thus the chance to instruct and to provoke inquiry, contained in the abrupt subject-predicate confrontation, is lost by a too explicit comparison, which somehow dissipates that dynamism of comparison by including the comparative term. Beardsley's controversion theory[45] epitomizes the modern attempt to take the fullest possible advantage of this idea of semantic collision. And Aristotle saw that, underlying the *epiphora* of the alien name, a strange attribution operates: 'this is that' – an attribution whose grounds simile makes clear only by displaying them *in deliberate comparison*.

Herein lies the interest of the confrontation between metaphor and simile. At the very moment that Aristotle subordinates simile to metaphor, he sees within metaphor this paradoxical attribution. In the same vein, consider a suggestion made in passing in the *Poetics* and then abandoned: 'But a whole statement in such terms [deviations from ordinary modes of speech] will be either a riddle or a barbarism, a riddle, if made up of metaphors, a barbarism, if made up of strange words. The very nature indeed of a riddle is this, to describe a fact in an impossible combination of words (which cannot be done with the real names for things, but can be with their metaphorical substitutes)' (*Poetics* 1458 a 23-33). On the whole, then, this text tends to dissociate metaphor and enigma. But the problem would not even arise if they did not have a common feature, the common constitution that the *Rhetoric* always emphasizes under the heading of the 'virtue' of elegance, brilliance, urbanity: 'Liveliness is especially conveyed by metaphor, and by the further power of surprising the hearer; because the hearer expected something different, his acquisition of the new idea impresses him all the more ... Well-constructed riddles are attractive for the same reason; a new idea is conveyed, and there is metaphorical expression' (1412 a 18-24). We note once more the instructive and informative functions linked to a bringing-together of terms that first surprises, then bewilders, and finally uncovers a relationship hidden beneath the paradox. But is not the proximity between enigma and metaphor founded completely on the odd name-giving, 'this (is) that,' that simile develops and depletes at the same time but that metaphor preserves by the brevity of its expression?[46] Deviation in the use of names proceeds from deviation in attribution itself – from what the Greeks call *para-doxa*, that is, a divergence from pre-existing *doxa* (1412 a 26).[47] All this is a very clear lesson for the theoretician, but it remains an enigma to the historian.[48]

In conclusion, this close juxtaposition of metaphor and simile allows the question of *epiphora* to be taken up again. First, as simile, the transfer takes place between two terms; it is a fact of discourse before being a fact of name-giving. One could say of *epiphora*, too, that it is something involving two things or terms. Furthermore, the transfer rests on a perceived resemblance that simile makes explicit by means of its characteristic terms of comparison. The closeness of metaphor to simile brings to language the relationship that operates in metaphor without being articulated, and confirms that the inspired art of metaphor always consists in the apprehension of resemblances. We shall say that simile explicitly displays the moment of resemblance that operates implicitly in metaphor. The poet, as we read in the *Poetics*, is one who 'perceives similarity' (1459 a 8). 'In philosophy also,' adds the *Rhetoric*, 'an acute mind will perceive resemblances in things far apart. Thus Archytas said that an arbitrator and an altar were the same, since the injured fly to both for refuge. Or you might say that an anchor and an overhead hook were the same, since both are in a way the same, only the one secures things from below and the other from above' (1412 a 10-15). To apprehend or perceive, to contemplate, to see similarity – such is metaphor's genius-stroke, which marks the poet, naturally enough, but also the philosopher. And this is what remains to be discussed in a theory of metaphor that will conjoin poetics and ontology.[49]

4 / THE PLACE OF *LEXIS* IN RHETORIC

The definition of metaphor common to the *Poetics* and the *Rhetoric* and the very important variant introduced by the latter work have been established. The principal remaining task is to appreciate the difference in function that results from the different ways in which *lexis* is inserted in the *Rhetoric* and in the *Poetics*.

We begin with the *Rhetoric*, whose place in the Aristotelian *corpus* is easier to determine. As was noted at the beginning of this study, Greek rhetoric had an impressively larger scope and a conspicuously more articulated internal organization than rhetoric in its dying days. As the art of persuasion, the aim of which was the mastery of public speech, rhetoric covered the three fields of argumentation, composition, and style. The reduction of all of these to the third part, and of that to a simple taxonomy of figures of speech, doubtless explains why rhetoric lost its link to logic and to philosophy itself, and why it became the erratic and futile discipline that died during the last century. With Aristotle we see rhetoric in its better days; it constitutes a distinct sphere of philosophy, in that the order of the 'persuasive' as such remains the object of a specific *technê*. Yet it is solidly bound to logic through the correlation between the concept of persuasion and that of the probable. In this way a philosophical rhetoric – that is, a rhetoric grounded in and watched over by philosophy itself – is constituted. Our subsequent task will be to display the intermediary links between the rhetorical theory of metaphor and such an enterprise.

Rhetoric's status as a distinct *technê* poses no great difficulties. Aristotle was careful to define what he calls *technê* in a classical text of his *Ethics*.[50] There are as many *technai* as there are creative activities. A *technê* is something more refined than a routine or an empirical practice and in spite of its focus on production, it contains a speculative element, namely a theoretical enquiry into the means applied to production. It is a method; and this feature brings it closer to theoretical knowledge than to routine. The idea that there is a technique for producing discourse can lead to the sort of taxonomical project that we will consider in the next Study. Now, is not such a project the ultimate stage of the technicization of discourse? Without doubt this is so; however, in Aristotle, the autonomy of *technê* is less important than its linkage with other disciplines of discourse, especially that of proof.

This linkage is assured by the connection between rhetoric and dialectic. With undeniable genius, Aristotle makes a statement right at the beginning of his work that keeps rhetoric under the sway of logic and, through logic, of philosophy as a whole: 'Rhetoric is the counterpart [*antistrophos*] of Dialectic' (1354 a 1). Dialectic here refers to the general theory of argumentation as regards that which is probable.[51] So we now have the problem of rhetoric posed in terms of logic. Aristotle, we know, is proud to have invented that demonstrative argument or proof called the 'syllogism.' Now, to this corresponds the probable argument in dialectic called 'enthymeme.' Rhetoric is thus a technique of proof: 'Only proofs have this character of technique' (1354 a 12). And because enthymemes are 'the substance of rhetorical persuasion' (ibid.), rhetoric as a whole must be centred on the persuasive power attached to this kind of proof. A rhetoric dealing only with those methods likely to sway the judge's passions would not really be a rhetoric at all: 'About the orator's proper modes of persuasion they have nothing to tell us; nothing, that is, about how to gain skill in enthymemes'; and a bit further, 'Rhetorical study [*techné*] is concerned with the modes of persuasion. Persuasion is clearly a sort of demonstration ... The orator's demonstration is an enthymeme ... The enthymeme is a sort of syllogism' (1354 b 21-2; 1355 a 4-8).

This does not mean that there is no distinction between rhetoric and dialectic. Certainly rhetoric resembles dialectic in a number of ways: it deals with 'popular truths,' the accepted opinions of the majority of people;[52] it does not require special training, since anyone can discuss an argument, accuse another, and defend himself (*Rhetoric* 1:1. par. 1). But in other ways they are different. First, rhetoric comes into play in concrete situations – the deliberations of a political assembly, judgment by a tribunal, public orations that praise and censure. These three sorts of situations that discourse takes place in define the three genres of rhetoric – deliberative, judicial, and epidichtic. Whereas ancient rhetoric before Aristotle concentrated on the second (there the ways to influence a judge stand out), a rhetoric based on the art of argumentative proof will pay attention to all situations in which it is necessary to arrive at a judgment (*krisis, Rhetoric* 1:1. 12). This leads to a second point of divergence: such an art has to do with judgments regarding individual situations.

In addition, rhetoric cannot become absorbed in a purely 'argumentative' or logical discipline, because it is directed to 'the hearer' (1404 a 4). It cannot avoid taking into account the speaker's character and the mood of his audience. In short, rhetoric is a phenomenon of the intersubjective and dialogical dimension of the public use of speech. As a result, the consideration of emotions, of passions, of habits, and of beliefs is still within the competence of rhetoric, even if it must not infringe upon the priority of argument based on probability. So an argument that can properly be called rhetorical takes into account both the degree to which the matter under discussion seems to be true and the persuasive effectiveness it has, which depends on the quality of the speaker and listener.

This feature brings us to a final point. Rhetoric cannot become an empty and formal technique, because it is linked to what is contained in the most highly probable opinions, that is, what is admitted or endorsed by the majority of people. Now with this connection between rhetoric and non-critical subject matter goes the risk of turning rhetoric into a sort of popular science. This collusion with *accepted ideas* throws rhetoric into a scattered and dissipating pursuit of argument-motifs or 'positions,' which amount to so many recipes to protect the speaker from being taken by surprise in debate[53] – a collusion, then, between *Rhetoric* and *Topics*, which was doubtless one of the causes of the former's death. Perhaps rhetoric finally died of an excess of formalism in the nineteenth century; paraodoxically, however, it was already doomed by its overburdening content – witness book 2 of the *Rhetoric*, which abounds in what Kant would have called 'popular' psychology, 'popular' morality, 'popular' politics. This tendency of rhetoric to identify with a sub-science of man poses a formidable question that could reflect back on rhetoric itself: does not the solidarity between rhetoric and topics, and beyond this, between rhetoric and a sub-science of man, imply that the inclination to speak in parables, comparisons, proverbs, and metaphors arises from this same complex of rhetoric and the commonplace? We must keep this question in mind. But before heralding the death of rhetoric, this alliance at least assures it a cultural content. Rhetoric does not develop in some empty space of pure thought, but in the give and take of common opinion. So metaphors and proverbs also draw from the storehouse of popular wisdom – at least, those of them that are 'established.' This qualification is important, because it is this topology of discourse that gives the rhetorical treatment of *lexis* and metaphor a background and an aftertaste different from those of the *Poetics*.

All these distinctive features are reflected in the Aristotelian definition of rhetoric – 'the faculty of observing in any given case the available means of persuasion' (1355 b 25, 1356 a 19-20). It is a theoretical discipline, but without determinate theme. Its measure is the (neutral) criterion of *pithanon*, of '*the persuasive as such*.' This adjective transformed into a noun remains faithful to the primordial intention of rhetoric, namely persuasion, but it expresses rhetoric's movement towards a technique of arguments or proof. In this regard the relationship (lost in French and English) between *pithanon* and *pisteis* is very instructive. In Greek, *pisteis* (in the plural), i.e. 'proofs,' marks the priority of objective argument over the intersubjective aims of the project of persuasion. And yet the initial notion of persuasion is not abolished; it is merely set aright. In particular, the orientation of argument to a listener – evidence that all discourse is addressed to someone – and its adherence to contents defined by the *topics*, keep 'the persuasive as such' from turning into a logic of probability. Thus, rhetoric will remain at most the *antistrophos* ('counterpart') of dialectic, but will not dissolve into it.

It is now possible to sketch a truly rhetorical theory of *lexis*, and consequently of metaphor, since metaphor is one of its elements.

Let us note right away that the rhetorical and poetic functions of metaphor do not coincide: 'The language [*lexis*] of prose is distinct from that of poetry' (1404 a 28).[54] Unfortunately, notes Aristotle, the theory of *lexis* is further ahead in poetry than in the field of public discourse.[55] He has to close the gap, if not fill a void. The task is not easy. We noted earlier that *argumentation, style,* and *composition* are the three parts of rhetoric. But since rhetoric really cannot be identified at all with the theory of style, which is just one of its parts, we might ask ourselves whether rhetoric does not have a privileged relationship with the 'discovery' (*eurêsis*) of arguments by the orator, i.e. with the first part (of rhetoric). Was it not claimed that everything that does not concern proof is 'merely accessory' (1354 a 14, 1354 b 17)? And does not book 3 confirm this privileged position in saying that 'we ought in fairness to fight our case with no help beyond the bare facts: nothing, therefore, should matter except the proof of those facts' (1404 a 4-6)? So, it seems, it is only because of the 'defects of our hearers' that we need to linger over these external considerations (1404 a 8).

No one denies that the link is weak between *lexis* and the rest of the Treatise, which is centred on argumentation. Nevertheless, we must not turn what is possibly just an accident in the composition of the Treatise into an absence of logical connection between *pisteis* and *lexis*. 'For it is not enough,' says Aristotle, 'to know *what* we ought to say; we must also say it *as* we ought; much help is thus afforded towards producing the right impression of a speech' (1403 b 15-18). It is the link between the way discourse *appears* and discourse itself that we must examine here, for in it germinates the future course of the idea of figure of speech.[56] The 'how' of discourse is distinct from the 'what.' Taking the same distinction up again later, Aristotle opposes 'how ... these facts [are] set out in language' to 'the facts themselves' (*ta pragmata*) (1403 b 18-20). Now this 'appearance' is not external to discourse in the same way as is simple 'delivery' (*hupokrisis*, 1403 b 21-35), which has to do only with the way the voice is used, as in tragic plays (in the same way the *Poetics* distinguishes *lexis* from mere staging). Rather, one must search in the area of an 'appearance' more intimately connected to the dynamics of persuasion and to argument, which was said to be 'the stuff of proof.' In this case, *lexis* would rather be one kind of manifestation of thinking, linked to any kind of instruction (*didaskalia*): 'The way in which a thing is said does affect its intelligibility [*pros to dêlôsai*]' (1404 a 9-10). When the proof itself is the only thing of importance, we do not bother about *lexis*; but as soon as the relationship to our hearer comes to the foreground, it is through our *lexis* that we teach.

So the theory of *lexis* seems bound to the thematic mainstream of the *Rhetoric* quite loosely, although not in as loose a manner as to that of the *Poetics*, which, as we shall see later, sums it up neatly as one 'part of tragedy,' i.e. of the poem. Now one might hypothesize that in poetry, the form or 'figure' and the meaning of a message are integrated to form a unity similar to that of a sculpture.[57] But in oratorical delivery, the manner in which something is said retains an extrinsic and variable character. One might even venture to say that eloquence, or the public use of speech, involves precisely this tendency, to dissociate style from proof. By the same token, the lack of consistency in the link between a treatise on argumentation and a treatise on style reveals something of the instability of rhetoric itself, torn apart by the internal contradiction within the very project of persuasion. Set between two limits exterior to it – logic and violence – rhetoric oscillates between its two constitutive poles – proof and persuasion. When persuasion frees itself from the concern for proof, it is carried away by the desire to seduce and to please; and style itself ceases to be the 'face [*figure*],' that expresses and reveals the body, and becomes an ornament, in the 'cosmetic' sense the word. But this possibility was written into the origins of the rhetorical project, and moved within the very heart of Aristotle's treatise. To the degree that style is the external manifestation of discourse, it tends to separate the concern to 'please' from that of 'arguing.' It is doubtless because writing constitutes a second degree of exteriorization that the separation is particularly dangerous in this case: 'Speeches of the written or literary kind owe more of their effect to their diction [*lexis*] than to their thought' (1404 a 18-19).

What, now, is the present status of the properly rhetorical features of metaphor? Do they throw any light on this manifestational function of *lexis*? Reversing the question, does *lexis* reflect in any way the internal contradictions of public speech?

Since rhetoric remains the art of 'saying things well,' its special features are those of good usage and are related to those of public discourse in general; and these last constitute what Aristotle calls the 'virtues' (the merits or 'excellences') of *lexis*. They guide what one might call the strategy of persuasion in public discourse. This idea of 'virtues of *lexis*' is so important that it provides the guiding thread for the analysis in book 3 of the *Rhetoric*. Among these virtues, those that concern metaphor most directly are 'clarity' (chapter 2), 'warmth' (opposed to 'coldness,' chapter 3), 'facility' (chapter 6), 'appropriateness' (chapter 7), and, above all, 'urbanity or elegance' (chapter 10).[58]

Clarity is obviously a touchstone for the use of metaphor. The expression that 'points out' (*dêloi*) something is clear. Now, it is the use of words in their ordinary fashion (*ta kuria*) that makes for clarity of style. In deviating[59] from ordinary usage, metaphor, together with all the other unusual expressions, also abandons clarity and makes 'the language appear more stately' (1404 b 9). In the eyes of ordinary citizens, it is as if they were confronted with a foreign (*xenen*) language (1404 b 10), for these variations and turns in language give discourse an out-of-the-ordinary air: 'People like what strikes them, and are struck by what is out of the way' (1404 b 12). Actually, these remarks are more appropriate to poetry than to prose, where nobility and dignity befit only the more extraordinary subjects and personalities: 'In prose passages they [effects that give an unfamiliar air] are far less often fitting because the subject-matter is less exalted' (1404 b 14-15). Therefore, the ways in which poetic and rhetorical language operate are the same, but the latter is more subdued. Keeping this caveat in mind, one can say that 'the chief merit of rhetorical discourse' is to give discourse an 'unfamiliar' air, while not doing so in an obvious manner. Thus, rhetorical style combines clarity, embellishment, and the unusual, all in due proportion.

The interplay between distance and close kinship, to which I alluded earlier in connection with relationships of type in metaphorical transposition, contributes to this air of the 'unusual,' which finds itself set against the demand for clarity. It also gives rise to the enigmatic character of good metaphors (1405 b 3-5).[60]

The second quality or 'virtue' is treated negatively.[61] *Rhetoric* 3:3 deals with stylistic 'frigidity.' Among its causes it notes the inappropriate, even ludicrous, use of poetic metaphors in prose – style too grandiose or tragic, metaphors too far-fetched and thus obscure (as when Gorgias talks of 'events that are green and full of sap') (1406 b 9-10). Prose must not be 'too much like poetry' (ibid.). What, then, shall be our criterion? Aristotle does not hesitate: 'All these expressions fail ... to carry the hearer with them' (*apithana*) (1406 b 14).[62]

The quality of 'appropriateness' (chapter 7) is another occasion for underlining the difference between prose and poetry. It is significant that this characteristic of the 'appropriateness' of style to its subject-matter is called 'proportion' (*to analagon*) by Aristotle. That which is appropriate for prose is not appropriate for poetry, because 'poetry ... is an inspired thing [*entheon*]' (1408 b 18).

But the most interesting remarks on the rhetorical use of metaphor are occasioned by reflections on the elegance and liveliness of expression (literally: urbane style, *asteion*, as opposed to popular or vulgar speech) (*Rhetoric* 3:10).[63] And it is in this context that Aristotle first speaks of the *instructive* value of metaphor. This quality really concerns the pleasure of understanding that follows surprise. For this is the function of metaphor, to instruct by suddenly combining elements that have not been put together before: 'We all naturally find it agreeable to get hold of new ideas easily: words express ideas, and therefore those words are the most agreeable that enable us to get hold of new ideas. Now strange words simply puzzle us; ordinary words convey only what we know already; it is from metaphor that we can best get hold of something fresh. When the poet calls old age "a withered stalk," he conveys a new idea, a new fact, to us by means of the general notion (*genous*) of "lost bloom" ...' (1410 b 10-15). Furthermore, Aristotle attributes the superiority of metaphor over simile to this same virtue of elegance. More concentrated and shorter than simile, metaphor astonishes and instructs rapidly. Here surprise, in conjunction with hiddenness, plays the decisive role.

To this same characteristic Aristotle attributes another feature of metaphor that has not appeared before, and that seems somewhat disconcerting at first glance. Metaphor, he says, 'sets the scene before our eyes' (1410 b 33). In other words, it gives that concrete colouration – imagistic style, figurative style it is called now – to our grasp of genus, of underlying similarity. It is true that Aristotle does not use the word *eikôn* at all in the sense in which, since Charles Sanders Peirce, we speak of the iconic aspect of metaphor. But the idea that metaphor depicts the abstract in concrete terms is already present. How does Aristotle connect this power of 'placing things before our eyes' to the feature of spiritedness, elegance, urbanity? By appealing to the characteristic of all metaphor, which is to point out or show, to 'make visible.' And this feature brings us to the heart of the problem of *lexis*, whose function, we said, is to 'make discourse appear to the senses.' 'To place things before the eyes,' then, is not an accessory function of metaphor, but the proper function of the figure of speech. Thus, the same metaphor can carry both the logical moment of proportionality and the sensible moment of figurativity. Aristotle enjoys combining these two seemingly contrasting moments: 'Liveliness is got by using the proportional type of metaphor and by being graphic [literally: making your hearers *see* things]' (1411 b 21). This is true of all the examples listed in 3:10 (1411 a 25-b 10). But, pre-eminently among all the others, the metaphor that displays the inanimate by means of the animate has this power of making relationships visible. Following Heidegger and Derrida,[64] one might be tempted to detect here some shameful traces of Platonism. Does not the invisible appear to us through the visible in virtue of the supposed resemblance of one to the other? Whatever the verdict on Platonism may be, if metaphysics is joined here to metaphor, it is truly Aristotle's metaphysics and not Plato's: 'By "making them see things" I mean using expressions that represent things as in a state of activity [*hosa energounta sêmainei*]' (1411 b 24-5). Showing inanimate things as animate is indeed not relating them to something invisible, but showing these things themselves *as if* in act.[65] Taking some remarkable expressions from Homer, Aristotle comments: 'In all these examples the things have the effect of being active [*energounta phainetai*] because they are made into living beings' (1412 a 3). Now in all these examples the power of making things visible, alive, actual is inseparable from either a logical relation of proportion or a comparison (but as we already know, the backbone of simile with its two terms is the same as that of the four-termed analogy). Thus one and the same strategy of discourse puts into play the logical force of analogy and of comparison – the power to set things before the eyes, the power to speak of the inanimate as if alive, ultimately the capacity to signify active reality.

The objection might arise now that the frontier between prose and poetry has been erased. Is not Homer the author most frequently cited? And is it not said of Homer that 'he represents everything as moving and living; and activity is movement' (1412 a 8)? Might metaphor not be a poetical process extended to prose?

This objection cannot be dealt with completely without returning to Aristotle's *Poetics*.[66] Let us say provisionally that the difference lies not in the process but in the end that is envisaged. That is why figure-filled and enlivened presentation is treated in the same context as brevity, surprise, hiddenness, enigma, antithesis. Liveliness of speech serves the same purpose as all of these: persuasion of one's hearers. This purpose remains the distinguishing characteristic of rhetoric.

5 / THE PLACE OF *LEXIS* IN POETICS

Let us take up the other side of the problem of the inclusion of metaphor in both rhetoric and poetry via the medium of *lexis*. What is poetic *lexis*? In the course of my reply, I will connect the definition of metaphor, common to both treatises, with the distinct function that the project of the *Poetics* gives it.

The definition of metaphor led us into a descent from *lexis* towards its elements, and among these, to the *noun* or name, which is transposed by metaphor. An inquiry into the function of metaphor now demands that we rise above the level of *lexis* towards its conditions or terms.

The most immediate term is the poem itself – here Aristotle considers the tragic poem specifically, or tragedy – seen as a whole: 'There are six parts [*merê*] consequently of every tragedy, as a whole [that is] of such or such quality, viz. a Fable or Plot (*muthos*), Characters (*êthê*), Diction (*lexis*), Thought (*dianoia*), Spectacle (*opsis*) and Melody (*mélopoia*)' (1450 a 7-9). The plot is 'the combination [*sustasis*] of the incidents of the story' (1450 a 15). The character is what confers coherence upon action, by a sort of unique 'purpose' underlying the action (1450 b 7-9). The *lexis* is 'the composition of the verses' (1449 b 39). The thought is what a character says in arguing or justifying his actions (1450 a 7); thought is to action what rhetoric and politics are to discourse (1450 b 5-6). Hence the thought is the properly rhetorical aspect of the tragic poem (1456 a 34-6). Spectacle refers to the externally visible configuration (*cosmos*) (1449 b 33). Finally, melody is the 'greatest of the pleasurable accessories of tragedy' 1450 b 17).

In the same way, then, as the word was called a 'part' of *lexis*, in its turn *lexis* is a 'part' of tragedy. Once the poem itself is being considered, the strategic level changes. Though something that happens to words, metaphor, mediated by *lexis*, is attached to tragedy, or, as is said from the first lines on, to the 'poetry [*poiêsis*] of the tragic play' (1447 a 13).

Tragedy too is defined by one of its traits, 'the imitation of human action' (1448 a 1, 29). This will furnish a second-level condition for *lexis*. A later discussion will be devoted to the Aristotelian concept of *mimêsis*, which performs the same sort of guiding-concept function for poetry as *persuasion* does for prose in the public arena.

Staying now with the enumeration of the constituents of tragic poetry, we must, in order to understand the role of *lexis*, grasp how the relationships among all these elements are articulated. They form a network, as it were, in which everything centres on one dominant factor: the fable, the plot, the *muthos*. In fact, three factors together play an instrumental role: spectacle, melody, and *lexis* ('for these are, truly, the means used for imitation' [1449 b 33-4]). Two others, thought and character, are called the 'natural causes' of action (1450 a 1). Character gives action the coherence of purpose or valuation; and thought makes action coherent by arguing that its reasons are such-and-such. Everything links up within the factor called *muthos*, fable, plot. And here the sort of transposition of actions that Aristotle calls the *imitation of nobler actions* is achieved: 'Now the action [that which was done] is represented in the play by the Fable or Plot' (1450 a 3). So there is no longer just a means-end or natural cause-effect relationship between *muthos* and tragedy, but a link at the level of essence. This is why, from the first lines of the Treatise on, this inquiry is addressed to 'ways of composing plots' (1447 a 8). Thus, it is important for our purpose to have a keen sense of the proximity between the *muthos* of the tragic poem and the *lexis* of which metaphor is part.

The fundamental trait of *muthos* is its character of order, of organization, of arranging or grouping. This characteristic of order, in turn, enters into all the other factors: the arrangement of the spectacle, coherence of character, sequence of thoughts, and finally the ordering of the verses. Thus *muthos* is echoed in the discursive nature of action, character, and thought. Now it is essential that *lexis* also share in these traits of coherence – but how? Only once does Aristotle say that it originates *dia tês onomasias hermêneian* (1450 b 15), which I should like to translate as *language-istic interpretation* [*l'interprétation langagière*], and which Bywater renders as 'the expression of their thoughts in words.'[67] Here there is no issue of prose versus poetry; this interpretation or expression, says Aristotle, 'is practically the same thing with verse as with prose' (ibid. 16). This *hermêneia* or interpretation is by no means exhausted in what Aristotle has just termed *dianoia*; this latter, nevertheless, already contains all the rhetorical features that add to plot and character – and consequently it already belongs to the order of language (it is rhetorical like 'everything [that is] to be effected [*paraskeuasthênai*] by ... language,' [1456 a 37]). What this ordering *in* language still lacks is the coming *into* language, the fact of having been made manifest, of *appearing* in spoken words: 'What, indeed, would be the good of the speaker, if things appeared in the required light even apart from anything he says?' (1456 b 8).[68] Drawing these three traits together – arrangement of the verses, interpretation by words, manifestation in language – we see the function of *lexis* taking shape as that which exteriorizes and makes explicit the internal order of *muthos*. We might even say that there is a relationship between the *muthos* of tragedy and its *lexis* like that between interior and exterior form. This, then, is how, within the tragic poem, *lexis* (of which metaphor is one part) is bonded to *muthos* and becomes, in turn, 'one part' of tragedy.

Our investigation turns now to the relationship between the *muthos* of the tragic poem and the function of *mimêsis*. One must admit that very few modern critiques speak favourably about the definition in terms of imitation that Aristotle gives for tragic and (secondarily) epic poetry. Most of them see in this concept the original sin of Aristotelian aesthetics, perhaps of all Greek aesthetics. Richard McKeon and, more recently, Leon Golden and O.B. Hardison have tried to clear up the misunderstandings obscuring the interpretation of the Aristotelian concept.[69] But perhaps our translators were hasty in choosing as the equivalent of the Greek *mimêsis* a term that we think we understand better than we really do. They chose 'imitation,' which turns out to be easily accused of a naturalistic tendency. It is only since the exclusively modern opposition between figurative and non-figurative art that, ineluctably, we are really approaching the Greek *mimêsis*.[70] Furthermore, this development should not be mistaken for some desperate project of mustering those characteristics of *mimêsis* that distinguish it from a simple copy of nature.[71]

Let us note, to begin with, that the concept of *mimêsis* is narrowed down remarkably in passing from Plato to Aristotle.[72] Its extension with Plato is boundless; it applies to all the arts, to realms of discourse, to institutions, to natural entities which are imitations of ideal models, and thus to the very principles of things. The dialectical method, understood in the broad sense as the procedure of dialogue, assigns determinations to the meaning of the word that are contextual for the most part, confronting the semanticist with a discouraging plethora of meanings. The only reliable guideline is the very general relationship between something that *is* and something that *resembles*, where the resemblance can be good or bad, real or apparent. The reference to ideal models merely allows the construction of a scale of resemblance, marking the degree to which this or that appearance approximates being. Thus, a painting could be described as 'imitation of imitation.'

Aristotle will have none of this. First of all, definition occurs at the beginning of scientific discourse, not as the outcome of dialectical usage. Words may have more than one meaning, but their use in science permits just one. And it is the division of the sciences that defines this normative usage. Consequently, one and only one literal meaning of *mimêsis* is allowed, that which delimits its use in the framework of the *poetical* sciences, as distinct from theoretical and practical sciences.[73] There is *mimêsis* only where there is a 'making [*faire*].' So there could not be imitation *in* nature since, as opposed to making, the principle of its motion is internal. Moreover, there could not be imitation of ideas, since making is always production of an individual thing; speaking of *muthos* and its unity of composition, Aristotle remarks that 'one imitation is always of one thing' (1451 a 30-5).

A possible objection is that the *Poetics* 'uses' the concept of imitation but does not 'define' it. This would be true if the only canonical definition were by means of *genus* and *differentia*. Now the *Poetics* defines imitation in a perfectly rigorous manner by enumerating its species (epic poetry, tragedy, comedy, dithyrambic poetry, compositions for flute and lyre), and then by relating this division into species to the division according to the 'means,' 'objects,' and 'modalities' of imitation. If one notes further that the 'function' of imitation is to afford pleasure (we still have to learn what sort), one may hazard the interpretation[74] that imitation is defined in full by just this structure, which corresponds, point by point, to the distinction between material, formal, efficient, and final cause.

This non-generic definition provides a fourfold structure so strong[75] that, in fact, it determines the distribution of the six 'parts' of tragedy. That is, three of them have to do with the object of imitation (*muthos, êthos, dianoia*), two others concern the means (*melos, lexis*), and the last the manner (*opsis*). What is more, *katharsis*, although not a 'part' as such, can be linked to the fourth dimension of imitation, the 'function,' as the tragic variant of the pleasure associated with imitation. Accordingly, *katharsis* would be less dependent on the spectator's psychology than on the intelligible composition of the tragedy.[76] Imitation is thus a 'process,' the process of 'forming each of the six parts of the tragedy,'[77] from plot through to spectacle.

We will concentrate, within this logical structure of imitation, on the two traits likely to interest our philosophy of the metaphor. The first of these traits really belongs to the role of *muthos* in poetic creation. As I said above, this is what *mimêsis* is. More precisely, it is the 'structure' of plot that constitutes *mimêsis*. Now this is quite a strange brand of imitation, which composes and constructs the very thing it imitates! Everything said about the 'whole and entire' character of myth, of the ordering of beginning, middle, and end, and in general of the unity and order of action (1451 a 28, b 23), helps distinguish imitation from all duplication of reality. We have also noted that, in various degrees, all the other constitutive elements of the tragic poem display the same character of composition, order, and unity. So, in different ways, they are all factors of *mimêsis*.

It is this function of ordering that allows us to say that poetry is 'more philosophic ... than history' (1451 b 5-6). History recounts what has happened, poetry what could have happened. History is based on the particular, poetry rises towards the universal: 'By a universal statement I mean one as to what such or such a kind of man will probably or necessarily say or do' (1451 b 9). And through this universal 'kind' of man, the spectator 'believes in the possible' (ibid. 16).[78] In this manner a tension is revealed at the very heart of *mimêsis*, between the submission to reality – to human action – and the creative action which is poetry as such: 'It is evident from the above that the poet must be more the poet of his stories or plots than of his verses, inasmuch as he is a poet by virtue of the imitative element in his work, and it is actions that he imitates' (1451 b 27-9).

Further, it is this ordering function that explains why the pleasure that imitation gives us would be a variety of the pleasure that man finds in learning. What pleases us in the poem is the sort of clarification, of total transparency, that the tragic composition achieves.[79]

Therefore, it is only through a grave misinterpretation that the Aristotelian *mimêsis* can be confused with imitation in the sense of copy. If *mimêsis* involves an initial reference to reality, this reference signifies nothing other than the very rule of nature over all production. But the creative dimension is inseparable from this referential movement. *Mimêsis* is *poiêsis*, and *poiêsis* is *mimêsis*. A dominant theme in the present research,[80] this paradox is of the utmost import; and it was anticipated by Aristotle's *mimêsis*, which holds together this closeness to human reality and the far-ranging flight of fable-making. This paradox cannot but concern the theory of metaphor. First, though, let us finish describing the concept of *mimêsis*.

The second trait of interest to this investigation is expressed in the following manner: in tragedy, as opposed to comedy, the imitation of human action is an imitation that magnifies, ennobles. This trait, even more than the preceding one, is the key to understanding the function of metaphor. Of comedy and tragedy Aristotle says that 'the one would make its personages worse [*kheirous*], and the other better [*beltiones*], than the men of the present day' (1448 a 17-18). (This theme is repeated several times, cf. 1448 b 24-7; 1449 a 31-3; 1449 b 9.) Thus, *muthos* is not just a rearrangement of human action into a more coherent form, but a structuring that elevates this action; so *mimêsis* preserves and represents that which is human, not just in its essential features, but in a way that makes it greater and nobler. There is thus a double tension proper to *mimêsis*: on the one hand, the imitation is at once a portrayal of human reality *and* an original creation; on the other, it is faithful to things as they are *and* it depicts them as higher and greater than they are. With these two traits combined, we return to metaphor.

Relocated on the foundations provided by *mimêsis*, metaphor ceases to be arbitrary and trivial. If considered simply as a fact or element of language, it could be taken for a mere deviation in relation to ordinary usage, alongside the rare word, the newly coined, the lengthened, abbreviated, and altered. But the subordination of *lexis* to *muthos* already puts metaphor at the service of 'saying,' of 'poetizing,' which takes place no longer at the level of the word but at the level of the poem as a whole. Then the subordination of *muthos* to *mimêsis* gives the stylistic process a global aim, comparable to rhetoric's intention to persuade. Considered formally, metaphor as a deviation represents nothing but a difference in meaning. Related to the imitation of our actions at their best, it takes part in the double tension that characterizes this imitation: submission to reality *and* fabulous invention, unaltering representation *and* ennobling elevation. This double tension constitutes the referential function of metaphor in poetry. Abstracted from this referential function, metaphor plays itself out in substitution and dissipates itself in ornamentation; allowed to run free, it loses itself in language games.

Let us go further. Within the bounds of this second trait of *mimêsis*, is it not possible to apply a still more closely fitting relationship between the elevation of meaning proper to tragic imitation and operating in the poem taken as a whole, and the displacement of meaning proper to metaphor and taking place on the level of the word? Aristotle has a few remarks on the proper use of metaphor in poetry,[81] which are an exact counterpart of the expressions we assembled under the title of 'virtues' of metaphor in rhetoric. They tend towards a de-ontology of poetic language, which is not unlike the teleology of *mimêsis* itself.

What does Aristotle say on this point? 'The perfection [virtue, *aretê*] of *lexis* is for it to be at once clear and not mean' (1458 a 18). What is meant here by clarity and meanness? A poetic composition that is at once clear and base is precisely one that employs only the most familiar vocabulary in its most common usage. Here, then, is the right place for deviation. Two strands meet here, the strange and the noble (*semnê*); and we cannot avoid pushing this connection further. If the 'strange' and the 'noble' meet in the 'good metaphor,' is it not because the nobility of such language befits the grandeur of the actions being depicted? Now I readily admit that this interpretation goes beyond Aristotle's intentions, but it is permissible in terms of his text and arose from my reading of it. In any case, if this inter-pretation is valid, we are forced to ask whether the secret of metaphor, as a displacement of meaning at the level of words, does not rest in the eleva-tion of meaning at the level of *muthos*. And if this proposal is acceptable, then metaphor would not only be a deviation in relation to ordinary usage, but also, by means of this deviation, the privileged instrument in that up-ward motion of meaning promoted by *mimêsis*.

In this way we can discover a parallel between the elevation of meaning accomplished by *muthos* at the level of the poem, and the elevation of meaning by metaphor at the level of the word – a parallelism that really should be extended to *katharsis*, which one could consider an elevation of feeling like that of action and of language. Considered from a functional point of view, imitation constitutes a unitary whole in which mythic ele-vation, displacement of language by metaphor, and the purging of feelings of fear and pity work side by side.

It will be objected, however, that no exegesis of *mimêsis* based on its connection to *muthos* can suppress the important fact that *mimêsis* is *mimêsis phuseôs*. For it is untrue that *mimêsis* is the final concept attained in the climb towards the primary concepts of the *Poetics*. It would appear that the expression *imitation of nature* takes us out of the domain of the *Poetics* and into the *Metaphysics*.[82] Is the entire preceding analysis not subverted by restoring the connection between discursive creation and nat-ural production? In the last analysis, does not linking the fullness of mean-ing to natural abundance render the deviation of metaphor useless and im-possible?[83]

We will have to return, then, to the reference to nature, such a scanda-lous stumbling-block in an aesthetics that nevertheless wishes to make room for *muthos* and metaphor.

If it is true that imitation functions in the Aristotelian system as the differentiating characteristic that distinguishes the fine and the useful arts from nature, it follows that the function of the expression *imitation of nature* is as much to distinguish human making from natural production as to align them. The proposition that 'Art imitates nature' (*Physics* 2:2. 194 a 21-2; *Meteorology* 4:3. 381 b 6) introduces a discriminant as well as a connective element.[84] The precise meaning given by this thematic usage of the words cannot be outweighed by any simply operative usage, like that put into play by the different occurrences of the word *nature* or its cognates in the text of the *Poetics*.

It is because the aim of the expression *imitation of nature* is to distinguish the poetic from the natural that the reference to nature does not appear at all as a restriction on the composition of the poem. The poem imitates human actions 'either as they were or are, or as they are said or thought to be or to have been, or as they ought to be' (1460 b 7-11). An enormous range of possibilities is thus kept in play. On this basis one can understand how the same philosopher could have written '[The poet] is a poet by virtue of the imitative element in his work' (1451 b 28-9, 1447 b 1-5) *and* 'The action [that which is done] is represented in the play by the Fable or Plot' (1450 a 4). It is also because nature leaves space for the 'making' of imitation that human actions can be depicted as 'better' or 'worse,' according to whether the work is tragedy or comedy. Reality remains a reference, without ever becoming a restriction. Therefore, the work of art can be judged on purely intrinsic criteria, without any interference (*contra* Plato) from moral or political considerations, and above all, without the burdensome ontological concern for *fitting the appearance to the real*. In renouncing that Platonic use of *mimêsis* that allowed even the things of nature to be taken as imitations of eternal models and allowed a painting to be called imitation of imitation, Aristotle undertakes not to use the concept of imitation of nature except within the limits of a science of poetic composition that has won its full autonomy. It is in the composition of the fable or plot that the reference to human action, which is in this case the nature being imitated, must become apparent.

In ending, I would like to venture a last argument that goes beyond the resources of a semantics applied to the words of a philosopher of the past, an argument that puts into play his meaning reactivated in a contemporary context and therefore arises from a hermeneutic. The argument concerns this very term *phusis*, the ultimate reference of *mimêsis*.

We believe that we understand *phusis* when we translate it by *nature*. But is not the word *nature* as far off the mark with respect to *phusis* as is the word *imitation* concerning *mimêsis*? Certainly Greek man was far less quick than we are to identify *phusis* with some inert 'given.' Perhaps it is because, for him, nature is itself living that *mimêsis* can be not enslaving and that compositional and creative imitation of nature can be possible. Is this not what the most enigmatic passage of the *Rhetoric* suggests? Metaphor, it relates, makes one *see things* because it 'represents things as in a state of activity' (1411 b 24-5). The *Poetics* echoes that one may 'speak in narrative' or present 'personages as acting [*hôs prattontas*] and doing [*energountas*]' 1448 a 22, 28). Might there not be an underlying relationship between 'signifying active reality' and speaking out *phusis*?

If this hypothesis is valid, it can be understood why no *Poetics* can truly ever have done either with *mimêsis* or with *phusis*. In the last analysis, the concept of *mimêsis* serves as an index of the discourse situation; it reminds us that no discourse ever suspends our belonging to a world. All *mimêsis*, even creative – nay, *especially* creative – *mimêsis*, takes place within the horizons of a being-in-the-world which it makes present to the precise extent that the *mimêsis* raises it to the level of *muthos*. The truth of imagination, poetry's power to make contact with being as such – this is what I personally see in Aristotle's *mimêsis*. *Lexis* is rooted in *mimêsis*, and through *mimêsis* metaphor's deviations from normal *lexis* belong to the great enterprise of 'saying what is.'

But *mimêsis* does not signify only that all discourse *is* of the world; it does not embody just the *referential* function of poetic discourse. Being *mimêsis phuseôs*, it connects this referential function to the revelation of the Real as Act. This is the function of the concept of *phusis* in the expression *mimêsis phuseôs*, to serve as an *index* for that dimension of reality that does not receive due account in the simple description of that-thing-over-there. To present men '*as acting*' and all things '*as in act*' – such could well be the *ontological* function of metaphorical discourse, in which every dormant potentiality of existence appears *as* blossoming forth, every latent capacity for action *as* actualized.[85]

Lively expression is that which expresses existence as *alive*.

The decline of rhetoric: tropology

For Gérard Genette

The guiding thread of this work passes from rhetoric to semantics and from semantics to hermeneutics. The present Study deals with the passage from the first to the second. We hypothesized in the introduction, and will now try to prove, that a purely rhetorical treatment of metaphor is the result of the excessive and damaging emphasis put initially on the word, or, more specifically, on the noun or name, and on naming, in the theory of meaning; whereas a properly semantic treatment of metaphor proceeds from the recognition of the sentence as the primary unit of meaning. The first orientation makes metaphor a trope, that is, a change or deviation affecting the meaning of a word. In the second case, it is a phenomenon of predication, an unusual attribution precisely at the sentence-level of discourse (we will see whether, and to what extent, one can still speak of deviation at this level of analysis).

This change of approach could be accomplished by means of a direct analysis, which, bypassing the rhetoric of tropes, would be applied straight away on the level of propositional logic; in fact, this is the usual tactic of English-language authors since I.A. Richards. Instead, we have chosen the longer route of an indirect proof that argues basically from the failure of rhetoric on the wane. This gives us, in effect, a proof *a contrario* of the need to back up the theory of metaphor with that of discourse as sentence. We will pursue this path by examining one of the last treatises of rhetoric, *Les Figures du discours* by Pierre Fontanier.

1 / THE RHETORICAL 'MODEL' OF TROPOLOGY

Our hypothesis leads us to give an explanation of the decline of rhetoric which is palpably different from the one given by certain new-rhetoric theorists of structuralistic bent. They[1] give as its cause the progressive reduction of the domain of rhetoric, which we described above.[2] Indeed, since the Greeks, rhetoric diminished bit by bit to a theory of *style* by cutting itself off from the two parts that generated it, the theories of *argumentation* and of *composition*. Then, in turn, the theory of style shrank to a classification of figures of speech, and this to a theory of tropes. Tropology itself now paid attention only to the complex made up of metaphor and metonymy, at the price of reducing the first to resemblance and the second to contiguity.

This explanation, which is also a critique, aims at clearing the way for a new rhetoric, which would first reopen the rhetorical regions that had been progressively closed. Such a project would be opposed to the dictatorial position of metaphor. Nevertheless, it would not be any the less faithful to the taxonomical ideals of classical rhetoric; it would only pay greater attention to the multiplicity of figures. Its slogan could be 'Yes, figures of speech – but all of them!'

As I see it, the reduction of the domain of rhetoric is not the decisive factor. This is not to deny that an extremely significant cultural phenomenon is involved, and that we are warned thereby against overrating metaphor. But even this warning cannot be put to good use, unless one lays bare a deeper root that the neo-rhetoricians might not be prepared to recognize. The problem is not to restore the original domain of rhetoric – in any case, this may be beyond doing, for ineluctable cultural reasons – rather, it is to understand in a new way the very workings of tropes, and, based on this, eventually to restate in new terms the question of the aim and purpose of rhetoric.

The decline of rhetoric results from an error that affects the theory of tropes directly, independently of the place given to it within the field of rhetoric. This initial error has to do with the tyranny of the word in the theory of meaning. We now glimpse only the most distant effects of this error: the reduction of metaphor to a mere ornament. A whole series of postulates is at work between the point of departure – the primacy of the word – and the final outcome – metaphor as ornament. Step by step, they bring together the initial theory of meaning, whose axis is naming, and a purely ornamental theory of tropes, which finally proclaims the futility of a discipline that Plato had long before placed among the 'cosmetic arts.'

This series of postulates can be made explicit as follows; taken together, they constitute the implicit model of tropology.

(a) Certain names belong properly to certain kinds (genera and species) of things; the meaning of these terms can be called 'proper meaning.' By contrast, metaphor and the other tropes are improper or figurative meanings. This is the postulate of 'the proper versus the improper or figurative.'

(b) Certain sorts of things are called by an improper term, instead of the applicable proper word being used. This absence of the proper word in actual discourse may result from a stylistic choice or from some real lack. In either case, recourse to an improper term has as its purpose the filling of a semantic or, better, a lexical lacuna, in the actual message or in the code. Thus, the postulate of 'semantic lacuna.'

(c) The lexical lacuna is filled by borrowing an alien term – the postulate of 'borrowing.'

(d) The price paid for applying the borrowed term to the sort of thing being considered is the divergence between the improper or figurative meaning of the borrowed word and its proper meaning – the postulate of 'deviation.'

(e) The borrowed term, taken in its figurative sense, is substituted for an absent word (which is lacking, or which one does not wish to use) that, in its proper meaning, could be used in that place. This substitution is a matter of preference; one is not forced into it, when the proper word exists. In that case we speak of trope in its strict sense. When the substitution corresponds to a real gap in vocabulary, when it is forced, one speaks of catachresis. This gives us the 'axiom of substitution.'

(f) Between the figurative sense of the borrowed word and the proper meaning of the absent word, there exists a relationship that can be called the 'reason' (in the sense of rationale or basis) for the transposition. This reason constitutes a paradigm for the substitution of terms. In the case of metaphor, the paradigmatic structure is that of resemblance. This is the postulate of 'the paradigmatic character of the trope.'[3]

(g) To explain (or understand) a trope is to be guided by the trope's 'reason,' that is, the paradigm of substitution, in finding the absent proper word; thus, it is to restore the proper term for which an improper term had been substituted. In principle the restitutive paraphrase is exhaustive, so the algebraic sum of substitution and subsequent restitution is zero. Here we have the postulate of 'exhaustive paraphrase.'

Two last postulates, which characterize the properly rhetorical treatment of metaphor and of tropes in general, result from this chain of presuppositions:

(h) The figurative use of words does not provide any new information. This postulate is part and parcel of the preceding one: if restitution annuls the substitution, if an exhaustive paraphrase of the metaphor (and of tropes in general) can be given, then the metaphor says nothing new. Thus, the postulate of 'no new information.'

(i) The trope, teaching us nothing, has a merely decorative function. Its fate is to please by serving as the ornament of language, in giving 'colour' to discourse, in 'clothing' the naked expression of thought.

Such is the chain of presuppositions implicit in the purely rhetorical treatment of metaphor. There is no break between the point of departure, which makes metaphor an accident in naming, and the conclusion, which gives metaphor a simply ornamental function and confines rhetoric as a whole to the art of pleasing. These two assertions, that metaphor teaches or says nothing new and serves only to ornament language, proceed step by step from the initial decision to treat metaphor as an unusual way of naming things.

Aristotle's analysis viewed in this light seems to anticipate this model. Now this is not to say that Aristotle can be accused of having reduced the fuller scope of rhetoric to a theory of style, much less to a theory of figures of speech, nor that the vitality of his analysis is dissipated in purely taxonomical exercises. The four species that he distinguished are still species of metaphor, and metaphor itself has no counterpart, is opposed to no other figure. As for the distinction between metaphor and simile, his analysis is completely reductive, and the reduction is finally in metaphor's favour. If, then, Aristotle is the father of this model, it is not at all because of his definition of the field of rhetoric, and thus of the place of *lexis* in it, but solely because of the central position accorded the noun in the enumeration of the parts of *lexis* and the reference to noun in the definition of metaphor. This is why the Aristotelian theory of metaphor abounds in allusions that apply more or less directly to this or that postulate in our sequence above: the opposition between the 'ordinary' word and the 'strange' word, and the deviating character of the second when compared with the first; the transfer of the meaning of the 'borrowed' word to the thing to be named; the 'substitution' of one word for another that could have been used in the same place; the possibility of 'restoring' this other word; the ornate character of metaphorical style; and the pleasure one takes in this style.

It is true that there are other features of Aristotle's description which resist reduction to the model under consideration. But these features in no way recall, at the heart of the theory of *lexis*, the original extension of rhetoric; they point more towards a discursive, and no longer to a nominalistic, theory of metaphor. Let us recall some of these traits: first, the close connection between metaphor and simile – in which metaphor is the more important of the two only because it contains, in summary form, the attribution (Achilles is a lion) that simile spells out as if in a logical argument (Achilles is like a lion). The difference between metaphor and comparison or simile, therefore, is the difference between two forms of predication: 'to be' and 'to be like.' This is why metaphor is the more powerful: the direct attribution causes surprise, whereas simile dissipates this surprise. At the same time, the operation that consists in giving one thing's name to another reveals how closely related it is to the predicative operation. It is not just the proportional metaphor that is so akin to simile, but all the species of metaphor, by virtue of the polarity between two terms that the other three kinds of metaphor also presuppose. How, indeed, is one to give the name of the species to the genus, if the metaphor does not 'say' two things, the thing that lends its name and the thing that receives it? Accordingly, the *epiphora* of metaphor does not seem to exhaust its meaning in the notions of borrowing, of deviation, and of substitution. To the extent that it seems enigmatic, metaphor invokes a 'tension' theory more than a theory of substitution. This is certainly why Aristotle claims in addition that metaphor 'teaches through the genus'; this declaration undercuts the last two postulates that round out the rhetorical model.

Thus, even while being the originator of the model that will hold sway in the last days of rhetoric, Aristotle also provides some of the arguments that will put it in check. However, this is not because his rhetoric covers a greater area than a theory of diction, but because *lexis*, whose explicit centre is the noun, rests implicitly on a predicative operation.

2 / FONTANIER: THE PRIMACY OF IDEA AND OF WORD

Pierre Fontanier's treatise *Les Figures du discours* (1830) comes as close as any to the rhetorical model that we sketched systematically. It affirms unambiguously the pre-eminence of the word. This primacy is assured by the analytical method (related to the method of ideology, if not borrowed from it) which, before being applied to figures, is applied to 'the basic elements of thought and of expression: ideas and words' ('Preliminary Notions' 39). This is the place to begin, because the definition of trope is constructed on that of the idea-word pair: 'Tropes are *certain meanings more or less different from the primitive meaning, which words, when applied to new ideas, evince in the course of the expression of thought*' (ibid.). At the heart of the coupled terms 'idea-word,' idea is in the governing position: 'Thought is made up of ideas, and the expression of thought by speech is made up of words. Let us see, then, what ideas are in themselves ...' (41). So it is the primacy of idea that guarantees that of the word. Thus, rhetoric depends upon some extra-linguistic theory, an 'ideology' in the proper sense of the term [i.e., 'idea-logy'], that secures the passage from idea to word.[4]

Let us review the elements of this 'ideology,' thus set as a foundation beneath the theory of word and, by extension, the theory of tropes. Ideas are 'the objects which our mind sees' (41). All the distinctions between ideas are formed in relation to this direct vision: complex, simple ('none are truly simple except those that resist analysis' [42]), concrete, individual, and general ideas. This is also true of the way in which they 'link up, one to the other, and form chains in our minds, in a manner to form groupings there on the basis of association, by collection, or in other diverse ways' (43). The distinction between principal and secondary or accessory ideas is founded on these 'chains.' The principle of a grammar is contained here: before introducing the 'substantive,' one can define by itself the substantive idea (or idea of a substance); that is, 'If an idea relates immediately to such a given particular object that exists as a substance, it is an *individual* idea' (42). Before speaking of adjectives, one can likewise define the concrete idea, that is, the idea that 'points out some quality, action, or passion in the object of a complex idea' (ibid.). Finally, one must look among the accessory ideas for the ideas of relationship or circumstance that 'we can make known only through words, which are their signs' (44).

It follows that everything that can be said concerning words is the result of their 'correspondence with ideas' (44). To talk about ideas and about words is to talk twice about ideas: once about 'ideas in themselves,' and the second time about ideas as 'represented by words' (41).

The list of species of words, therefore, will reflect that of the kinds of ideas. Two broad classes of words are distinguished: signs for ideas of objects, and signs for ideas of relationship. Noun, adjective, participle, article, and pronoun belong to the first class. Nouns correspond to ideas of substances; and they are divided further into the proper noun, corresponding to an individual idea, and the common noun, which corresponds to general ideas. Adjectives correspond to concrete ideas of quality, and participles to concrete ideas of action, of passion, or of state of being. Articles define the extension of nouns, while pronouns take the place of nouns.

The second class is made up of the verb, preposition, adverb, and conjunction. Here, *verb* means just the verb *to be*; actual verbs are formed by combining the verb *to be* with a participle (I read, I am reading). The verb *to be* points to the coexistence of some idea of substance and a concrete idea, corresponding to a participle or an adjective. By dealing with the verb in this fashion, under the heading of 'ideas of relationship.' Fontanier not only brings the verb into the idea-word theory, that is, a theory of the elements of thought and of expression; he also makes it subject to the primacy of the first species of words, the noun. Considering the six species that can vary according to gender, number, person, time, and mood, Fontanier notes: 'But it is easy to see that they all converge more or less directly on the idea of substance, which subjects them to itself either by itself or through accessory ideas that it carries along with it' (46). Converge, subject, carry along: so many and so insistent are the ways in which the noun's position of pre-eminence – already assured by that of the idea of substance – is reinforced.

True, its rule is not undivided; a second point of departure is proposed, which is not the idea any more but thought itself. Thought was mentioned from the start, at the same time as the word: 'Thought is made up of ideas, and the expression of thought by speech is made up of words' (41). This was implied in the definition of trope as well: 'Tropes are certain meanings more or less different from the primitive meaning, which words, when applied to new ideas, evince in the course of the expression of thought' (39). Hence thought and word appear to be equally fundamental. Moreover, a specific theory of thought and its expression is prepared for by the distinction between the idea of an object and the idea of a relationship. While the verb is the sign of the coexistence of a substantive idea and a concrete idea, this coexistence can be affirmed or denied; for thought is nothing but 'the reunion of these two ideas, via the inner act of our mind that sets one inside the other or sets one outside the other' (49). Here, then, we have rhetoric established upon a dual-focus analysis, an analysis in terms of idea and judgment; correspondingly, from the point of view of expression, we have the duality of word and proposition, the latter being nothing but 'judgment projected outside our mind, as if *set before us*, as if *set in front of* the minds of others' (49).

Accordingly, it is possible to transcribe all the distinctions between kinds of words in terms of the function of their role in the proposition. Considered in judgment, the substantive idea becomes the propositional subject, the concrete idea becomes the so-called attribute, and the relationship of coexistence expressed by the verb *to be* is now called the copula.

The definition of the notions of meaning and of signification supports the view that word and proposition constitute two distinct poles of the expression of thought. Meaning is defined first of all in relation to the word: 'Relative to a word, *meaning* is what this word makes us understand, think, *feel* by means of its *signification*; and its *signification* is what it signifies, that is to say, that of which it is a sign, when it acts as a sign' (55). But 'the word *meaning* can also be used of a whole sentence, sometimes even of a whole discourse' (ibid.). Furthermore, 'a *proposition* is a *sentence* only when, because of a certain construction, it presents a complete and finished meaning' (52-3). And it is with reference to the proposition in its entirety that objective, literal, and spiritual or intellectual meaning can be distinguished. Objective meaning is not opposed to the two others; it is the basic meaning of the proposition: 'that which it has relative to the object to which it applies' (56). The broad categories subsumed under objective meaning are precisely the ones provided by the theory of ideas – substantive or adjectival meaning, active or passive meaning, etc. More important for our purposes is the distinction between literal meaning and spiritual or intellectual meaning; unlike objective meaning, these form a pair. Both of these meanings belong to the proposition, but they differ because of a trait that is peculiar to words: 'The literal meaning is that which is borne by words taken to the letter, by words understood according to the way they are accepted in common usage. Consequently, it is the meaning that suggests itself immediately to those who understand the language' (57). 'The spiritual meaning, the diverted or figurative meaning of a group of words, is that which the literal meaning causes to be born in the spirit by means of the circumstances of the discourse, by tone of voice, or by means of expressed connections with unarticulated relationships' (58-9).

It is most significant for us that the theory of the word prevails ultimately over the theory of the proposition. Indeed, the theory of tropes will be organized finally with reference to the word and not the proposition. The notion of tropological meaning is related immediately to that of literal meaning, but with the express restriction on literal that it is the literal meaning of a word in isolation that is meant: 'The literal meaning that belongs only to the isolated word is either primitive, natural and proper, or "derived" (if one must speak in this way) and tropological' (57). The notion of figure is itself placed in the same context, not primarily as the genus of which the trope would be the species, but as one of the two ways in which tropes take place: 'by choice and figuratively' versus 'as required and by extension' (ibid.). This second case, that of tropological meaning by extension, is one of 'stepping into the breach when the language lacks a word for a certain idea' (ibid.). The first case, figurative tropological meaning, involves 'presenting ideas through images that are more lively and more striking than their proper signs' (ibid.).

The hegemony of the word, which a theory of the proposition could have balanced, thus is reaffirmed even in the distinction between literal and spiritual meaning – just when the notion of meaning seemed to be assumed by the sentence in its entirety rather than by the word.

The distinction between one-word tropes, or 'tropes properly speaking,' and tropes consisting of several words is made on the same basis. And yet the very distinction between letter and spirit would seem to demand that the accent be on the other pole. For is the 'spiritual sense' not always to some degree the meaning 'of a collection of words,' and consequently linked to the more extended tropes? And is it not 'through the circumstances of the discourse, by the tone of voice or because of the ties between those ideas that are expressed and those that are not' – that is, by means of those traits that affect thought at the level of propositions – that the literal meaning gives rise to spiritual meaning in our minds? And does the very expression of spiritual meaning not remind us that it is 'spirit that forms it'? Surely the internal act in our mind is judgment, is it not?

As we see, the primacy of the word does not abolish entirely the bipolar organization of thought and its expression. But every time the examples seem to put discourse above the word, idea re-establishes the reign of the word.

3 / TROPE AND FIGURE

Even while calling in various places for a return to the polarity of idea and judgment, reflected in that of word and sentence – which alone presents a 'complete and finished meaning' (53) – the entire theory of tropes and figures is based upon this primacy of the word.

It might seem, however, that the foundation-stone of the taxonomical enterprise would not be the trope, whose dependence on word we have begun to see, but the figure, which refers equally to word, to statement, to discourse. For Gérard Genette, in his remarkable introduction to the 1968 reissue of Fontanier's treatise, the work's principal interest lies in the reunion of tropes and non-tropes under the notion of *figure*. To choose figure – which is neither word nor statement – as the basic unit is to take an intermediate course between that of Aristotle, who still took in the whole of the field of rhetoric (that is, argumentation, composition, style), and that of Dumarsais, who reduced rhetoric to grammar, the function of the latter being 'to make one understand the true signification of words and in what sense they are used in discourse' (cited by Genette 8). Fontanier's basic unit could not be discourse, nor yet the word, 'the unit for grammar more than for rhetoric' (ibid.). His intermediate course is expressed well by the maxim 'only the figures, but all the figures' (ibid.). The advantage of this third course is that it establishes rhetoric upon an entity that can sustain that ambition for complete enumeration and systematic classification that makes of Fontanier's work a 'chef-d'oeuvre of taxonomic intelligence' (Genette 13).[5] The figure can take on this architectonic role because it is coextensive with discourse in general: 'What are figures of discourse in general? They are these more or less remarkable forms, features or turns, varyingly successful, through which discourse, as expression of ideas, thoughts, or feelings, makes itself more or less different from what would have been the simple and common expression' (Fontanier 64, 179). Thus, figure can apply equally to word, to sentence, or to the traits of discourse that express the workings of feelings and passion.

But what is to be said of figure as such? It must be admitted that figure, like Aristotle's *epiphora*, is itself spoken of only metaphorically. Figures are to discourse what contours, characteristics, and exterior form are to the body: 'Even though it is not a body but an act of mind, discourse ... has, nevertheless, in its different ways of signifying and expressing, something analogous to the differences of forms and characteristics that are found in real bodies' (63).

We are reminded again of Aristotle's distinguishing the 'how' of discourse from its 'what,' and assimilating the 'how' to an 'appearing' of discourse.[6] (Perhaps the same metaphor exists germinally in the notion of expression.)

Fontanier does not appear to be bothered by this incipient circle (metaphor is a figure and the word *figure* is metaphorical).[7] He prefers to go directly to two traits of figure. The first is what the new rhetoric will call 'deviation' and what Fontanier uses in saying that 'discourse, as expression of ideas, thoughts or feelings, departs more or less from what would have been the simple and common expression' (64). It is true that to depart, deviate, or turn away from are still, like Aristotle's *epiphora*, metaphors of movement. However – and this is the essential point – at least the notion of deviation applies equally well no matter how extended the expression is, be it word, sentence, or discourse. Thus one of the basic postulates of our model, that of deviation, stands out from the rest.

The second trait brings with it a restriction; it has to do with application rather than with extension. The use of figure must remain free, even if it becomes habitual; a deviation that is imposed by the language, forced usage, no longer deserves the name of figure. Accordingly catachresis, the forced extension of the meaning of words, is excluded from the field of figures (213-19). The present trait calls to mind two other postulates of our model. First of all, free and unconstrained use implies that expressions are being diverted from their proper meaning, that is, taken 'in a sense that one gives them for the moment and that is merely borrowed' (66). Then too, free use supposes that the proper expression is available and that another is substituted for it as a result of free choice. To write 'flame' for 'love' is to form a figure; 'the figure exists,' comments Genette, 'only to the extent that one can oppose to it a literal expression ... the criterion of figure is the substitution of one expression (word, phrase, sentence, and even group of sentences) for another, which the rhetorician must be able to restore mentally in order to have the right to speak of figure ... So, with Fontanier, we see a clear and forthright affirmation of the essence of figure as *substitution*' (Genette, 10-12). Genette goes on to link this 'substitutive obsession' to a 'piercing and very precious awareness of the paradigmatic dimension of the units (small or large) of discourse' (12). This paradigmatic character is extended step by step from word to sentence and to discourse – that is, to ever larger syntagmatic units.[8]

Thus, the essence of the rhetorical model with which we began this chapter is to be found in Fontanier, at least at the level of the program as a whole. The only exception might be the primacy of the word, which we had believed was the fundamental postulate. Is it reasonable to suggest, then, that Fontanier was trying to found a rhetoric of figures that is not reducible to a tropology, to a theory of deviations in the significations of words?

This was beyond doubt Fontanier's aim. And it is also true that his ambition is partially realized in his treatise *Les Figures du discours.* His 'division' of figures[9] is truly imposing – in Genette's words, it establishes Fontanier as the 'Linnaeus of rhetoric' (13). Ancient tropology consists of just one class of figures among others: the figures of signification, or tropes properly speaking, that is single-word tropes. The rest of the field is divided up into five other classes: figures of expression, of construction, of elocution, of style, and of thought.

It is difficult to say as much for the detailed development of this work. One point certainly puts us on guard: the theory of metaphor is completely unaffected by the choice of figure as the characteristic unit of rhetoric. Metaphor remains classed among the single-word tropes, the tropes properly speaking. And the theory of tropes itself constitutes an autonomous whole; the notion of figure is superimposed on it pure and simple. In this way the rhetorical model, whose network of postulates we reconstructed, continues to function at the level of trope, oblivious to the addition of other classes of figures and to the superimposition of the concept of figure itself, which is more general than that of trope. As to the other figures, they are simply added to the trope-figures. More important, among all classes of figures, the trope is 'marked' for special duty. The treatise is composed so as to begin with 'tropes properly speaking,' which are single-word figures of signification. It then adds the 'tropes improperly speaking' or the longer figures of expression, and it ends with all the other figures which throughout are called 'non-trope figures.'[10] The key unit remains the trope because the foundation remains the word. This is what makes the treatise seem rather odd: the trope is at once both one class among others and the paradigm of all figures.[11]

Fontanier's treatise thus appears as if constructed according to two blueprints: one establishes figure as the basic unit; the other guarantees a key position to idea, therefore to word, and hence to the trope. While it is true that the first scheme is the floor-plan for the treatise as general taxonomy of the figures of discourse, the second determines the division of figures between tropes and non-tropes. The first would prevail over the second were discourse to have supplanted the word in the theory of 'first foundations' (39). But, in the spirit of ideology, this latter remains a theory of 'elements' (ibid.). This is why the key unit remains the simple idea, which alone can be called 'a simple element of thought' (453).

In spite of the theory of figures, then, the theory of tropes, and especially that of metaphor, verifies our model. Only the second signification of the notion of figure – the opposition to catachresis – is retained. Hence, this notion can be treated no longer as the higher genus, but as the specific difference: 'The tropological meaning is either *figurative* or purely an *extension*, according to whether the new signification of concern was given freely and as if playfully to the word, or whether it had become a forced,

habitual signification, almost as *proper* as the primitive signification' (75).
Hence the paradoxical consequence that the theory of tropes envelopes
the distinction between figure and catachresis ('But, whether *figure* or *catachresis*, in how many different ways do single-word tropes occur?' [77]).

True, Fontanier sustains the possibility that propositions, like words,
might offer 'a sort of tropological sense' (77). This possibility is written
right into the definition of primitive and tropological meaning, which, as
we recall, was applied from the start to the various meanings that the proposition can have. However, to be precise, this is only 'one sort' of tropological meaning, presented by 'figures of expression' that are only tropes
'improperly speaking' (109).

4 / METONYMY, SYNECDOCHE, METAPHOR

Systematically and exhaustively, Fontanier constructs the list of possible
kinds of tropes within the limits so set out, and based on the relationship
through which tropes 'occur' (77).[12]

This last expression is notable: tropes are indeed events, since the figures of signification 'occur through a new signification of the word' (ibid.).
The opposition between free and forced usage, essential to the figurative
character of the trope, makes of the trope a semantic innovation that
exists only 'for the moment' (66). Therefore, the trope is not the relationship itself; it is based on the relationship, which is recognizable as what, in
the fifth postulate, we called the 'reason' of the substitution. But relationship between what and what? The relationship through which tropes take
place is one between ideas. More specifically, it is a relationship between
two ideas: on the one hand, 'the primary idea attached to the word,' that
is, the primitive signification of the borrowed word; and on the other, 'the
new idea given to it' (77), or the tropological meaning substituted for some
other proper word that one did not wish to use in this particular situation.

Except for a few points of divergence, this relationship between a primary and a new idea corresponds to the Aristotelian *epiphora*. Let us look
at these differences for a moment. The first is that Fontanier's definition
does not appear to point explicitly to the movement of transference. Now
while this is true enough, the *'static' of relationships* provides the foundation for the *'dynamic' of transferences*, as the listing of the types of tropes
will show. Next, Aristotle treats metaphor as a genus, not as a species.
Aristotle's metaphor is a trope for Fontanier; and Fontanier's metaphor
corresponds approximately to the fourth species of metaphor in Aristotle's
scheme. This difference seems more serious than the preceding one; however, it can be treated, up to a certain point, as just a difference of glossary.
Another seeming difference is that, for Fontanier, relationship affects

'ideas' before it links words or names; but, as we saw, idea is the element of thought that underlies words (or names in the case of the 'substantive' ideas). With these few reservations, Fontanier's trope and Aristotle's *epiphora* mirror each other fairly well.

We are now able to say of the relationship through which the trope occurs what we said earlier of *epiphora*: the trope truly does consist *of* one word; however, if one may speak in this manner, it occurs *between* two ideas, by a transfer from one to the other. Hence, in a sense that will have to be clarified, the trope, like *epiphora* before it, occurs 'based upon a duality' (see above, page 25).

Next, while *epiphora* and trope correspond to a high degree, this cannot be said for Aristotle's four species of metaphor and Fontanier's three kinds of relationships. Herein lies Fontanier's profound originality compared to all his predecessors and also, as we shall see, in relation to his successors. Fontanier prides himself on having given an exhaustive theory of the relationships between ideas by distinguishing between *relations of correlation* or *correspondence, relations of connection*, and *relations by resemblance*. The three species of tropes – metonymies, synecdoches, and metaphors – 'take place' through these three kinds of relationships respectively.

What is remarkable in this system of paradigms is the breadth and fullness that Fontanier gives to each of these three relationships. By correspondence he understands something quite different from the contiguity to which his successors reduce the functioning of metonymy; he sees in it a relationship that brings together two objects each of which constitutes 'an absolutely separate whole' (79). This is why metonymy divides up in turn according to the variety of relationships that satisfy the general condition of correspondance: relationship of cause to effect, instrument to purpose, container to content, thing to its location, sign to signification, physical to moral, model to thing.

In the relationship of connection, two objects '*form an ensemble, a physical or metaphysical whole, the existence or idea of one being included in the existence or idea of the other*' (87). It follows that this relationship will also have many species: relations of part to whole, of material to thing, of one to many, of species to genus, of abstract to concrete, of species to individual. The inclusiveness of all these relationships varies, some being greater and some narrower, but according to a wider range than just numerical relation or even a simple generic extension.

Correspondence and connection thus designate two relationships as distinct as exclusion ('absolutely separate whole') and inclusion ('included in ...'). Furthermore, we should note that these two initial relationships connect objects prior to connecting ideas, so that alteration in the designating reference of names follows the objective relationship. (There is, however, a slight difference to be noted. In the relationship of connection, objects are said to belong to the same whole if the existence or idea of one object is contained in the existence or the idea of another.) From this arises the almost total symmetry between the definitions of metonymy and synecdoche. In both cases, one object is designated by the name of another; and in both cases, it is the objects (or, in the exception just noted, the ideas) that enter into a relationship of exclusion or inclusion.

It is in the play of resemblances that this symmetry is broken and metaphor is set somewhat apart. In the first place, its definition does not refer directly to a changing of the designations of things by names or nouns; it mentions only the relationship between ideas. This is not a chance omission; for while metaphor lacks species, as opposed to the other two tropes, 'it takes in far greater territory' than they, 'since not only the noun or name, but also the adjective, participle, verb, and actually all the species of words belong to its domain' (99). Now why does metaphor allude to every type of word, whereas metonymy and synecdoche affect only the designation of things by nouns? There is a strong suggestion here of an extremely important shift that will be recognized only by a properly predicative theory of metaphor. We can follow this up by considering the examples. What is the metaphorical use of a noun? To 'make a tiger of an angry man,' 'of a great writer a swan': is this not already something other than designating a thing by a new name? Is it not 'naming' in the sense of characterizing, of qualifying? And is this operation, which consists in 'carrying the name outside its species,' not a sort of attribution, which requires the whole sentence? The adjective, the participle (which is similar to it when acting as an epithet), the verb (which is analysed into participle and copula), and the adverb (which modifies the verb) lend themselves most readily to metaphorical usage. Is this not because they function only within a sentence that relates not just two ideas but also two words, namely one term taken non-metaphorically, which acts as a support, and the other taken metaphorically, which fulfils the function of characterization? This remark brings us close to the distinction made by I.A. Richards between *tenor* and *vehicle*.[13] Fontanier's examples already lean in this direction. When one says 'the *Swan* of Cambrai,' '*consuming* remorse,' 'courage *craving* for peril and praise,' 'his *seething* spirit,' and so on, these metaphors do not name, but characterize what has already been named.

This quasi-predicative character of metaphor is confirmed by another trait. Not only does the definition of metaphor make no direct reference to the noun or name, it does not even refer to objects. It consists '*in presenting one idea under the sign of another that is more striking or better known*' (99). Analogy operates between ideas; and idea itself is to be understood not 'from the point of view of the objects seen by the spirit' but 'from the point of view of the spirit that sees' (41). For it is in this sense only that an idea can be called 'more striking or better known'; even if one discovers objective relationships supporting the analogy (when one calls a man a tiger), 'the name is not transferred from one member of a species to another but from one species to another' (100). But it is important that the 'common opinion' recognizes such resemblance (ibid.). Hence, connection and correspondence are primarily relationships between objects, while resemblance is principally a relationship between ideas, between generally held beliefs. This is why the second trait confirms the first: characterization, as distinct from naming, is formed through comparisons of opinions, that is, within the realm of judgment.

Fontanier evidently was prevented from seeing these consequences by the preoccupation that dominates the conclusion of his analysis of metaphor. Perhaps to re-establish symmetry between metaphor and the two other figures, and despite his initial declaration that 'ordinarily we do not divide *metaphor* into species as we do *metonymy* and *synecdoche*' (99), he does attempt to divide metaphor into species. He finds his principle of classification in the nature of objects as they define either the domain from which they are borrowed or the place of their application. Did he not say, however, that metaphor takes place between ideas? But even when considered from the point of view of the spirit that sees, ideas remain images of the objects seen by the spirit (41). So it is always possible to invoke the ideas behind the words and the things beyond the ideas. Furthermore, since the resemblance has to do with the character that things are believed to have, it is possible to pass from this character to the realm of the things that possess it; Fontanier says that the 'transfer' (101) takes place between the things as characterized. But how are the regions of borrowing and application to be classified? After remarking that metaphors can be taken from everything that surrounds us, from all of the real and the imagined, from intellectual or moral as well as physical entities, and that they can be applied to all the objects of thought, no matter what they are, Fontanier somewhat arbitrarily chooses the dividing line to be between the animate and the inanimate. This is how he comes to preserve an old classification that saves him from the difficulty of infinite divisions. His five species of metaphor – 'transfer of something that belongs to an animate thing to some other animate thing,' 'of something inanimate but physical to something inanimate and usually purely moral or abstract,' 'from an inanimate thing to an animate,' 'physical metaphor going from the animate to the inanimate,' and 'moral metaphor going from the animate to the inanimate' – can be reduced ultimately to the pair made up of 'the physical metaphor, that is, one in which two physical objects (whether animate or inanimate) are compared'; and 'the moral metaphor, in which something abstract and metaphysical, something from the moral order, is compared with something physical, the meanings of both being affected whether the transfer is from the second to the first or from the first to the second' (103).

,The opportunity will arise later to report on the complicity between this principle of classification and the completely 'metaphysical' distinction between the physical and the moral.[14]

It seems reasonable to agree that this classification is more a concession to the past than a necessary implication of the definition of metaphor by resemblance. The division into species does not in any way proceed from a diversification of the resemblance relationship, as in the case of metonymy and synecdoche; it remains completely extrinsic to the definition. So we must return to this definition: nowhere is the distinction between animate and inanimate implied in *'presenting one idea under the sign of another that is more striking or better known'* (99). Far from having to reconstruct the interplay of resemblances beginning in the *real* domains of the borrowing and application, one would have to derive the domains from familiar and striking characteristics and these latter from popular opinion. Nelson Goodman will do this in treating the notion of 'realm' as a collection of 'labels' and defining metaphor as a redescription involving the transposition of labels.[15] Something of this theory is prefigured in Fontanier's initial formula, 'presenting one idea under the sign of another that is more striking or better known'; but the notion of the one-word trope kept him from seeing all that is implied in this notion of second-degree signification.

5 / THE FAMILY OF METAPHOR

The notion of trope taken as a single word not only snuffs out the potential meaning contained in the admirable initial definition of metaphor; it also breaks up the unity of the problematic of the analogy between ideas, which is thereby dispersed among all the classes of figures.

Among the 'tropes improperly speaking,' namely the *'figures of expression'* that 'concern the proposition's particular manner of expression' (109), *poetic fancy* (what Fontanier calls *fiction*) has a striking resemblance to metaphor. To give one thought 'the features or colours of another, in order to make it more tangible or more pleasant' (ibid.) – is this not the same as presenting one idea under the sign of another which is more striking and better known? Personification (the first sub-species of this poetic fancy) in turning an inanimate, non-sentient, abstract, or ideal entity into a living and feeling being, into a person, reminds us of the metaphorical transfer from the inanimate to the animate. It is true that personification does not take place only through metaphor but also by metonymy and synecdoche. But what distinguishes personification by means of metaphor and metaphor properly speaking, except the extension of the verbal entity?

It is tempting to say the same of *allegory* which also '*presents one thought in the image of another that is better suited to making it more tangible or more striking than if it were presented directly and without any sort of disguise*' (114). But another trait besides its connection to the proposition distinguishes allegory from metaphor. According to Fontanier, metaphor – even the extended metaphor that he calls 'allegorism' – has only one true meaning, the figurative meaning; whereas allegory 'consists *in a proposition with a double meaning, having a literal and a spiritual meaning together*' (114).[16] Is this to say that double meaning happens only with the figures of expression and cannot appear in figures of signification? It seems so, although the reason is far from clear. Perhaps to hold together the two meanings an act of spirit is necessary, thus a judgment, and thus a proposition. One wonders whether it was with an eye to this analysis of allegory that the notions of literal and spiritual meaning were defined in the context not of the word but of the proposition.

Poetic fancy bears an additional interest for our discussion. It highlights repeatedly a trait of the notion of figure that perhaps was already suggested in the definition of metaphor that has been referred to several times. To present an idea under the sign of another implies that the two ideas differ not only as to the species of the objects involved, but also in the vivacity and familiarity of the ideas. Now this difference is not studied as such by Fontanier; nevertheless, it implies a nuance in the meaning of the notion of figure that poetic fancy and allegory help isolate, namely, the presentation of a thought in a sensible or tangible form. This trait is very often called 'image.' Fontanier himself uses this term in saying that allegory 'presents one thought in the image of another that is better suited to making it more tangible or more striking' (114). Thus he says that Marmontel, 'comparing his spirit to a shrub, depicts the advantageous influences that he has drawn from his acquaintance with Voltaire and Vauvernagues, whom he presents in the image of two rivers' (116). So figure, picture, and image go hand in hand. A bit later, again, speaking of imagination as 'one of the causes that generate tropes' (161-2), Fontanier judges it to be at work 'in all the tropes that offer some image or some picture to the spirit' (162). And if there is 'something enchanting, something magical' (173, 179) in poetic language, it must be because a poet like Racine is 'so *figurative*; everything in him is, so to speak, in images, wherever this is appropriate to the subject and the genre' (173). Is this not the effect of all the tropes; not satisfied with just transmitting ideas and thoughts, 'they depict them in a more or less lively fashion, they clothe them in richer or

duller colours; like so many mirrors, they reflect the different faces of objects and show them off in their most advantageous light; they adorn the
ideas and thoughts, setting them into relief or giving them a new grace;
they trail, as if before our eyes, a train of images and scenes, whose nature
we long to know, as this nature presents itself with entrancing novelty'
(174). As this indicates, it is truly the figure that confers outward appearance on discourse by giving it contours, characteristics and exterior form,
similar to the traits of physical bodies (63). It must be said that all the
tropes are, 'like poetry, the children of fictive fancy' (180). For poetry,
less mindful of truth than of resemblance, gives itself over to 'creating figures, to colouring its language, to putting it into images and scenes, to
turning it into a living and speaking picture' (181). This is not to say that
the tropes that take after metaphor all present 'a sensible or tangible image,
one that could be formed by the eye and by the hand of a painter' (185).
Fontanier protests that this would be giving too much over to sight. His
reservation here anticipates a distinction exploited by Wittgenstein and
Hester, that between 'seeing' and 'seeing as.'[17] So we will say that *to figure*
is always *to see as*, but not always *to see or to make visible.*

We should still take our investigation beyond the tropes improperly
speaking, in order to see how analogy works within the 'figures of construction,' the 'figures of elocution,' and the 'figures of style.' Imitation is
brought up in this context, first in the 'figures of construction' (288) and
later in the 'figures of style' (390). The 'figures of thought' themselves,
although they 'have to do with thought alone,' come close to metaphor
and analogy; thus the 'figures of thought' by imagination (*prosopopée*)
and by development exhibit the general character of figure that we have
just explained, namely that of providing thought with a stage-setting. Indeed, one can say of 'description,' which in general covers the field of 'figures of development,' 'that it consists in setting an object before our eyes
and in making it known by presenting the detail of all its most interesting
aspects ... it gives rise to *hypotyoposis*, when the exposition is so lively and
emphatic that an *image*, a tableau, appears in the style' (420). This notion
of description is particularly interesting; it covers topography and chrono-
graphy (descriptions having to do with space or place and time), prosopo-
graphy, ethopy, and portrait (physical and moral personification of living
beings and their combination), and parallelism and tableau, which combine
the foregoing (422-33).

This vast domain of analogy could not be restructured except by a refusal to confine metaphor within the tropes of a single word and by pursuing
to its conclusion the action that detaches it from the linguistic activity of
naming in order to attach it to the central act of discourse, namely, predication.

6 / FORCED METAPHOR AND NEWLY INVENTED METAPHOR

I will end this analysis with a trait which, more than all the others, takes us in this direction. It concerns the distinction between the figurative and the catachretic character of each trope. Fontanier finds this distinction so important that he even claims that these 'principles concerning catachresis constitute a foundation for our entire tropological system' (213).

The difference has to do first with a fact of language, namely that certain ideas *lack* signs: '*In general, catachresis refers to a situation in which a sign, already assigned to a first idea, is assigned also to a new idea, this latter idea having no sign at all or no other proper sign within the language.* Consequently, every trope whose use is forced and necessitated, every trope that results in a pure *extension* of *meaning*, is a case of catachresis. This is a proper meaning of secondary origin, something between *primitive proper meaning* and *figurative meaning* but closer by nature to the first than the second, even though in principle it could itself have been used *figuratively*' (213). Thus one cannot call forced metaphors figures, be they nouns ('light' for spiritual clarity, 'blindness' for confusion and obscurity in understanding), adjectives (a 'ringing' voice), verbs ('grasp' in the sense of 'understand'), prepositions ('to' in connection with both destination and purpose), etc. This purely extensional trope, giving rise to a proper meaning of second degree, presents (or intends to present) one idea only; and it presents this idea 'completely naked and undisguised, as opposed utterly to *figurative tropes*, which always present two ideas, present them intentionally, and present one under the image of the other or beside the other' (219).

Hence, the thing that should draw our attention in the figure-trope is its characteristic of being *free*. This alone – its freely presenting one idea under the image of another – seems to indicate that the trope properly speaking, even though it takes place in one word, has the features of what Benveniste will call 'the instance of discourse.'[18]

What Fontanier says about newly invented metaphors (504) confirms the close relationship between the trope and the living event of actual speech. As the free-forced distinction applies to usage, all usage tends to become habitual, and metaphor tends to resemble catachresis. The metaphor still remains a figure, for its purpose is not to fill a gap in signs. However, it appears in a more and more fixed and standardized fashion, and, in this sense, can be said 'to be part of the foundation of language' (104) – that is, it begins to act like a literal meaning. This is why the conditions necessary for a good metaphor – realism, clarity, nobility, naturalness, coherence – 'apply only to the *newly invented metaphors* that one intends as figures and that have not yet received the sanction of general use' (104).

This point leads us to set up an internal distinction with regard to figure, parallel to that between figure and catachresis; this is a distinction between initial use and the eventual usage that can become 'forced in present-day speech' (213).

It is really this ordinary usage that rhetoric reflects. If we observe, with Boileau and Dumarsais, that 'there are more tropes used in the marketplace in a single day than in the entire *Aeneid*, or in several consecutive sessions of the Academy' (157), we must admit that most of these are examples of standardized tropes. One can be said to 'know them through regular use, like one's mother tongue, without being able to say when or how one learned them' (157). This is also why we can turn around and say that 'they are an essential part of spoken language' (157) and 'part of the very foundation of language' (164). To put it differently, standardized tropes are midway between the tropes of invention and catachresis. The boundary between forced tropes and catachresis tends to fade away all the more as the phenomenon of erosion, just as the tropes themselves, seems to go back to the beginnings of language. The reason for catachresis is found in the origin of tropes themselves, namely 'the failure of proper words, and the need, the necessity to supplement their deficiency and failure' (158). This is a deficiency and lack for which we should be grateful, for if we had as many words as ideas, 'what memory would be sufficient to learn so many words, and to retain them and reproduce them?' (158). In the same way that von Humboldt defines discourse as an infinite use of finite means, Fontanier attributes to memory 'a fairly restricted number of words [which] furnish the means to express an infinite number of ideas' (158). In this manner, at least at its origins, the figure-trope has the same extended function as the catachresis-trope. For this reason they tend to blend into one another in the course of normal use.

But besides being needed in view of the deficiency of vocabulary, the figure trope is occasioned by another cause, that is, pleasure. 'The chosen, the stylistic tropes, the *figure-tropes*, are also brought about by the delight and pleasure that, as if by a sort of instinct, we first anticipate and then experience in them' (160). So this pleasing quality acts as an incentive to invention, as opposed to just being necessary.

This invention forces us to distinguish between the occasional causes of tropes (necessity and also pleasure), and the properly generative causes: imagination, spirit, passion. To give colour, to astonish and surprise through new and unexpected combinations, to breathe force and energy into discourse – so many impulses express themselves only in the figure-tropes, which must be called 'writer's tropes' since they are the 'special creation of poets' (165). While the metaphor 'burdened with age' is obviously a standard part of the language, 'who before Corneille ever said *consume* a kingdom [*dévorer un règne*]?' (ibid.).

However, the consideration of tropes 'as to their use in discourse' (499) is not along the same lines. This use (which Fontanier investigates in the third section of the theory of tropes), though not constitutive for the trope as founded on a specific relationship, is at least constitutive for its character as figure. If the indirect meaning is one 'lent for the moment' (66) to the word, the most authentic tropes are the tropes of invention alone. Therefore, we must shift our focus from the word to discourse, because only the conditions proper to discourse can distinguish between the figure-trope and the catachresis-trope, and within the figure-trope, between constrained and free usage.

Metaphor and the semantics of discourse

For Cyrus Hamlin

In our first two Studies, the change of meaning constituting the trope and continually referred to as metaphor in ancient and classical rhetoric found its locus in the *word*. This allowed us to adopt, as an initial approximation, a definition of metaphor that identifies it with giving an unaccustomed name to some other thing, which thereby is not being given its proper name. But the investigation of the interrelationships of meaning that give rise to this transposition of the name also relentlessly forces open the frame of reference determined by the word, and *a fortiori* that determined by the name or noun, and imposes the *statement* as the sole contextual milieu within which the transposition of meaning takes place. The present Study is devoted to a direct examination of the role of the statement, as the carrier of 'complete and finished meaning' (according to Fontanier's own expression), in the production of metaphorical meaning. Hence, we will speak from now on of the *metaphorical statement*.

Does this mean that the definition of metaphor as transposition of the name is wrong? I prefer to say that it is nominal only and not real, using these terms as Leibniz does. The nominal definition allows us to identify something; the real definition shows how it is brought about. The definitions that Aristotle and Fontanier gave are nominal, in that they specify which tropes are metaphors. Restricting themselves to identifying metaphor, however, they also restrict themselves to classifying it. In this sense, the sort of taxonomy belonging to tropology cannot rise above the level of nominal definition. But as soon as rhetoric looks into generative causes, it is already considering discourse and not just the word. Thus, a theory of the metaphorical statement will be a theory of the production of metaphorical meaning.

Consequently, the nominal definition should not be abolished by the real definition. This Study may, however, seem to sanction such a choice, for we shall continually contrast a discursive theory of metaphor with a reduction of metaphor to an accident of naming. Several authors go somewhat further than this and take an *interaction* theory, which is intimately connected to a discursive conception of metaphor, to be incompatible with a *substitution* theory, where substitution, as we have seen, is inseparable from the definition of metaphor as a deviation in naming.

Foreshadowing an analysis to be undertaken in the fifth Study, let us establish now that the real definition of metaphor in terms of statement cannot obliterate its nominal definition in terms of word or name, because the word remains the locus of the effect of metaphorical meaning. It is the word that is said to take a metaphorical meaning. This is why Aristotle's definition is not abolished by a theory that no longer deals with the place of metaphor in discourse but with the metaphorical process itself. Using Max Black's terminology (which will be justified later), the word remains the 'focus' even while it requires the 'frame' of the sentence. And the reason why the word remains the locus of the effect of metaphorical meaning is that the function of the word within discourse is to embody the semantic identity. It is this identity that metaphor affects. But nothing is more difficult to appreciate than the function of the word, which at first sight seems to be divided between a semiotics of lexical entities and a semantics of the sentence. We must thus postpone any attempt to co-ordinate a theory of substitution and a theory of interaction, which are both valid though at different levels, until the end of our reflection on the function of the word as mediator in semiotics and in semantics.

In this Study, accordingly, we will adopt a provisionally disjunctive conception of the relationships between semiotics and semantics. First we will outline this conception. Then we will connect it to the interaction theory which is summoned to replace a purely substitutive theory of metaphor. Thus we will derive all the consequences of the opposition between the nominal definition and the genetic definition of metaphor.

1 / THE DEBATE BETWEEN SEMANTICS AND SEMIOTICS

The working hypothesis underlying the notion of metaphorical statement is that the semantics of discourse is not reducible to the semiotics of lexical entities. (A discussion of the word as such will occur in the fifth Study.)

In the theories of metaphor that arise more or less within the English-language tradition of linguistic analysis, the theory of discourse itself is not developed by linguists but by logicians and epistemologists, who occasionally pay some attention to literary criticism but more rarely to the linguistics that linguists themselves engage in. The advantage of a direct attack on the phenomenon of discourse, omitting the linguistic stage, is that the traits proper to discourse are recognized in themselves without any need to contrast them with anything else. But with the contributions that the linguistic study of language has made to the humanities, one cannot any longer simply disregard the relationship between discourse and language. Nowadays, whoever wants his research to be up-to-date in the good sense must take the indirect route of the contrast between the unity of discourse and the unity of language. The results that English-language philosophical semantics reaches directly and with greater elegance must be attained more laboriously by a semantics influenced by linguistics, via the indirect path of a confrontation with the linguistics of language. We will take this route here. Our guide will be the distinction between semiotics and semantics in the work of Émile Benveniste,[1] with which the results of English-language linguistic analysis will be compared.

Benveniste's choice of the word *discourse* is itself significant. To the extent that it is above all a *linguistics* of language, linguistics tends to turn speech into a mere residue of its analyses. Benveniste chooses the term *discourse* [*discours*], preferring it to *speech* [*parole*], in order to point out the consistency of the object of his study. In considering the different levels in the architecture of language, this great French Sanskritist introduces the distinction between the fundamental units of language and of discourse: the signs and the sentence respectively. The notion of level is itself integral, not external, to the analysis; it is incorporated into the analysis as an 'operator' (104). This is meant to indicate that any linguistic unit whatsoever can be accepted as such only if one can identify it within some higher-level unit – the phoneme in the word, the word in the sentence. In this way the word occurs in 'an intermediary functional position that arises from its double nature. On the one hand it breaks down into phonemic units, which are from the lower level; on the other, as a unit of meaning and together with other units of meaning, it enters into a unit of the level above' (104). We will return to this claim in the fifth Study.

And what of this higher-level unit? The reply is quite definite: 'This unit is not a longer or more complex word – it belongs to another class of notions; it is a sentence. The sentence is realized in words, but the words are not simply segments of it. A sentence constitutes a whole which is not reducible to the sum of its parts; the meaning inherent in this whole is distributed over the ensemble of the constituents' (105). Thus, not only does the sentence not derive from the word understood as lexeme, that is, the isolated word as it exists in the lexical code; but the word as meaning is itself a constituent of the sentence – 'a syntagmatic element, a constituent of empirical utterances' (105). Rather than there being a linear progression from one unit to the other, then, new properties appear, which derive from this specific relationship between units of different levels. Whereas distributional relationships hold between units of the same level, the elements of different levels are governed by integrative relationships.

The distinction between these two sorts of relationships governs that between form and meaning. Distributional analysis within one level exposes the formal segments, the 'constituents.' On the other hand, decomposition into units of a lower level results in 'integrators,' which have a meaning-relationship with those of the higher level: 'This is the point: the analysis discloses the formal constituents; the integration discloses meaningful units ... The *form* of a linguistic unit is defined as its capacity for being broken down into constituents of a lower level. The *meaning* of a linguistic unit is defined as its capacity to integrate a unit of a higher level' (107).

If we apply these distinctions to the passage from lexeme to discourse, we find, as we suspected, that 'with the sentence a boundary is crossed and we enter into a new domain' (108). Benveniste puts 'being a *predicate*' (109) at the forefront of the characteristics that belong to this level. It is, in his eyes, 'distinctive beyond all others and inherent in the sentence' (ibid.). The presence of even a grammatical subject is optional; a single sign suffices to constitute a predicate.

Now this unit is not defined in opposition to other units, as was the case with phonemes and lexemes (which is why the principle of phonematic analysis could be extended to lexematic analysis). There is no range of kinds of predication. One cannot set up contrasts between 'categoremes' (*categorema = predicatum*) or between 'phrasemes' (sentential units), as is done with lexemes and phonemes: 'It is thus necessary to recognize that the categoremic level contains only one specific form of linguistic utterance, the proposition, which does not constitute a class of distinctive units' (109). As a consequence, there is no unit of an order higher than the proposition, in relation to which the proposition would constitute a class of distinctive units. Propositions can be set one after the other in a consecutive relationship, but they cannot be integrated. Another consequence is that the proposition, though containing signs, is not itself a sign. A final consequence is that, as opposed to phonemes and morphemes, which have a distribution at their own levels and a use at higher levels, 'sentences have neither distribution nor use (as integrated in some higher level)' (110). Benveniste concludes: 'The sentence is the unit of discourse'; again; 'The sentence, an undefined creation of limitless variety, is the very life of human speech in action' (110).

This has considerable methodological implications. Two different kinds of linguistics refer respectively to the sign and to the sentence, to language and to discourse. They proceed in opposite directions, and their paths cross. Taking the smallest units that can be differentiated as its point of departure, the linguistics of language sees in the sentence its highest possible level. But the process it follows presupposes the inverse analysis, which is closer to the speaker's awareness. Starting with the infinite variety of messages, it works downward to that limited number of units that it uses and encounters, the signs. It is this procedure that the linguistics of discourse takes for its own. Its guiding conviction is: 'It is in discourse, realized in sentences, that language is formed and takes shape. There language begins. One could say, in imitation of a classical formula: nihil est in *lingua* quod non prius fuerit in *oratione*' (111).

A few years later,[2] Benveniste gave these two forms of linguistics the names 'semiotics' and 'semantics.' The sign is the unit of semiotics while the sentence is the unit of semantics. As these units belong to different orders, semiotics and semantics hold sway over different arenas and take on restricted meanings. To say with de Saussure that language is a system of signs is to characterize language in just one of its aspects and not in its total reality.

The consequences are considerable for the extension of the well-known distinction between the signifier and the signified. This analysis of the sign holds only in the semiotic, and not the semantic, order. For semiology, says Benveniste, what the sign signifies does not have to be defined. It is necessary and sufficient for a sign to exist that it be accepted. (Does 'sun' exist? Yes. 'Zun'? No.) The question of the signified calls only for a yes-or-no answer: does it signify or not? But if the signified does not call for an intrinsic definition, it is defined extrinsically by the other signs that delimit its position within the language: 'Proper to every sign is that which distinguishes it from other signs. To be distinctive and to be meaningful are the same thing' ('La forme' 35). Circumscribed in this manner, the order of the sign leaves out the order of discourse.

The fruitfulness of this distinction between the semiotic and semantic orders is seen in its capacity to support and lead to numerous other distinctions. Some of these were made by Benveniste himself; others crop up here and there in the linguistic analysis of English-language writers, whose disregard for linguistics was noted above. This conjunction of philosophical semantics and linguistics is particularly valuable.

I wish to synthesize these divergent descriptions; their respective, often disparate origins will be mentioned only in passing. Specifically, I offer the following enumeration of the distinctive traits of discourse. These traits readily permit a presentation in pairs, which gives discourse a pronounced dialectical character; and it emphasizes the need for a methodology different from that which applies to the operations of segmentation and of distribution appropriate to a purely taxonomic conception of language.

First pair: discourse always occurs as an event, but is to be understood as meaning.

To point out the event character of discourse, Benveniste creates the expression 'instance of discourse,'[3] which is meant to encompass 'the discrete and always unique acts by which the language is actualized in speech by a speaker' (217). The contrast between discourse and language finds sharp focus in this trait. A linguistic system, precisely because it is synchronic, has only a virtual existence within the passage of time. Language really exists only when a speaker takes it in his possession and actualizes it. But at the same time as the event of discourse is fleeting and transitory, it can be identified and reidentified as 'the same'; thus, meaning is introduced, in its broadest sense, at the same time as the possibility of identifying a given unit of discourse. There is meaning because there is sameness of meaning. As P.F. Strawson shows in *Individuals*, it is true to say of every individual entity that what can be identified can also be reidentified. Such, then, is the 'instance of discourse': an event which is eminently repeatable. This is why this trait can be mistaken for an element of language; but what we have here is the repeatability of an event, not of an element of a system.

To this first pair one can add the distinction introduced by Paul Grice, whose theory of meaning differentiates between utterance meaning, meaning of the uttering, and utterer's meaning.[4] It belongs to the very essence of discourse to allow these distinctions. Their foundation is to be found in Benveniste's analysis, in his speaking on the one hand of the instance of discourse (as we have just seen), and on the other hand, of the 'intended' of discourse. This is something completely different from the meaning of an isolated sign. Ferdinand de Saussure said quite rightly that this meaning, the signified, is only the counterpart of the signifier, a simple difference within the language system; whereas the intention or the intended is 'what the speaker wants to say' ('La forme' 36). The signified meaning belongs to the semiotic order, the intention to the semantic; Grice deals with the latter in his analysis.

A second pair distinguishes between identifying function and predicative function.

This familiar polarity has a long history. In the *Cratylus, Theaetetus*, and *Sophist*, Plato designates it as *logos* itself and pictures it as the 'interlacing' (*sumplokê*) of the noun and the verb;[5] and this recourse to articulated *logos* lets him escape the impasse to which the question of the 'correctness' of words led him. Indeed, at the level of word, there is no solution: 'conventionalism' is just as good as 'naturalism'; only the interlacing of discourse '*has to do with something.*'[6] Correctness and error belong to discourse alone. The stalemate reached in the *Cratylus*, which is the stalemate of a theory of naming (and which demands the creation of a theory of predication), finds an echo in the stalemate of a theory of metaphor that also dwells within the limits of a reflection on the designative property of names.

The pair of identification and predication has been described meticulously by P.F. Strawson.[7] By reduction after reduction, every proposition bears upon an individual (Peter, London, the Seine, this man, that table, the man who saw the man who saw the bear). *Individual* here means 'logically proper subject.' Language is constructed so as to permit singular identification. Among the means employed for this, four stand out: the proper noun; the demonstrative; the pronouns; and especially the most frequently used means – what since Russell is called 'definite description'[8] – the such-and-such (the definite article followed by a determinant). To specify one thing and one alone – such is the function of identifying expressions, to which the logical subjects are ultimately reducible. Associated with the predicate are the adjectives of quality (great, good) and their substantival counterparts (greatness, goodness); the classes to which individuals belong (minerals, animals); relations (X is beside Y); and actions (Brutus killed Caesar). What qualities, classes, relations and actions have in common is that they are universalizable (for example, running, as a type of action, can be said of both Achilles and the tortoise). This produces the fundamental polarity of language, which on the one hand is rooted in named individuals, and on the other hand predicates qualities, classes, relations, and actions that in principle are universal. Language works on the basis of this dissymmetry between two functions. The identifying function always designates entities that exist (or whose existence is neutralized, as in fiction);[9] when I speak of something, in principle I speak of something that exists. The notion of existence is linked to the singularizing function of language. Proper logical subjects are potentially existents. This is the point at which language 'sticks,' where it adheres to things. By contrast, in having the universal in view, the predicative function concerns the nonexistent. The unfortunate dispute over universals in the Middle Ages was possible only because of confusion between the singularizing and predicative functions: for it makes no sense to ask whether goodness exists, only whether some thing, which is good, exists. The dissymmetry of the two functions thus also implies the ontological dissymmetry of subject and predicate.

Benveniste remarks that the predicate is sufficient in itself to be the criterion of units of discourse, and it is tempting to oppose this to Strawson's analysis: 'The presence of a "subject" alongside the predicate is not indispensable; the predicative term of the statement is sufficient unto itself since it is in reality the determiner of the "subject"' (*Problems* 109). Perhaps this apparent disagreement is the result of the difference between the logician's point of view and that of the linguist. The latter can point out predicates without a subject; whereas the former can argue that the determination of a subject – which is the task of the predicate – is always the counterpart of a singularizing identification. The Strawsonian distinction actually has an equivalent, if not even a justification, in the distinction between semiotics and semantics. In effect, semiotics has the generic or universal function and semantics the view to the singular: 'The sign's value is always and only generic and conceptual. Therefore, it has nothing to do with any particular or contingent signified, and anything individual is excluded; circumstantial factors are to be regarded as irrelevant' ('La Forme' 35). This characteristic proceeds from the very notion of 'instance of discourse'; it is language, as used and in action, which can take circumstances into account and have particular applications. Benveniste goes further: 'The sentence, the expression that belongs to semantics, is only concerned with the particular' (ibid. 36). Thus we are brought back to Strawson's analysis, for only within discourse does a generic term take on a singularizing function. This was already established convincingly by Russell's theory of definite descriptions. Now, the predicate, which in itself has a universalizing function, only has this circumstantial character to the extent that it determines a proper logical subject.

An important difference does remain between Strawson's analysis and that of Benveniste if it is proposed that the predicate by itself characterizes the sentence. For in Strawson's analysis, predicates have a generic value in that they designate a class, a property, a relation, or a category of action. To resolve this remaining contradiction, it is necessary to make two points more precise. First, it is the sentence taken as a whole, that which is intended by discourse, that carries with it a particular application, even when the predicate is generic: 'A sentence is always embedded in the here and now ... Every verbal formation without exception, no matter what the idiom may be, is always linked to a particular present, thus to an always unique combination of circumstances, to which the language refers by means of a specific morphology' (ibid. 37). Second, as we shall see later, this sentence-as-a-whole itself has a sense and a reference. 'The king of France is bald' has a sense apart from any circumstances, and a reference that, in given circumstances, makes it sometimes true, sometimes false.[10] Here, linguistic analysis is more precise than the semantics of the linguists, who seem too dependent on the opposition between semiotics and semantics and hence pay too much attention to the sole trait that guarantees the difference between these two orders.

A third pair of traits has to do with the structure of acts of discourse.

Every such act can be considered with regard to its *locution* aspect and its *illocution* aspect (in addition, it has a *perlocution* aspect, which is not relevant in the context of the present discussion). It is easy to relocate this distinction, introduced by J.L. Austin,[11] in a further development of Benveniste's theory of the instance of discourse. What is one doing, in effect, when one speaks? One is doing several things at several levels. There is, first of all, the act of saying or the locutionary act. This is what we are doing when we bring the predicative and identifying functions together. But the same act of combining the action of 'closing' with the subject 'door' can be accomplished as a statement, command or wish, with regret, etc. These diverse modalities of the same propositional content have nothing to do with the propositional act itself, but with its 'force,' namely, what one does *in* saying (hence the prefix of *il*locution). *In* saying, I make a promise, or give an order, or submit a statement. The roots of this distinction are, in fact, quite old; the Sophists, with Protagoras, had already distinguished several forms of discourse – question and answer, prayer, order.[12]

What first interested Austin, the originator of this sort of analysis, is another difference (which later seemed to him to be a particular case of the one we are considering), namely, the difference between the constatives and the performatives, the model of the latter being the promise. In promising I *do* the very thing which is *said* in the promise: by saying, I commit myself, I place myself under the obligation of doing.[13] The performatives are first person singular statements in the present indicative, and they concern those actions that depend on the one who commits himself. The theory of speech acts progressed further when it was noted that the performative is not unique in *doing* something. In the constative, I commit myself in a way that is different from promising. I believe what I say. If I say, 'The cat is on the mat, but I do not believe it,' the contradiction exists not at the propositional level, but between the self-engagement implicit in the first proposition and the explicit denial that follows it. Accordingly, it is not just the performatives that present the complex structure of acts of discourse. It will be noted that the locutionary act allows one to anchor elements in language that are considered to be psychological – belief, desire, feelings, and in general, a corresponding 'mental act.'[14] This remark is important because it refers to the locutionary agent, the speaking subject, whom we will discuss later on.

Émile Benveniste did not find it difficult to integrate the speech act theory into his own views of the instance of discourse, as we see in his report of 'Analytical Philosophy and Language.'[15]

Our fourth pair concerns sense and reference.

These terms were introduced into contemporary philosophy by Gottlob Frege in 'Über Sinn und Bedeutung.'[16] It too, as we will see, finds a place in the concept of semantics according to Benveniste. It is really only the sentence that makes this distinction possible. Only at the level of the sentence, taken as a whole, can what is said be distinguished from that of which one speaks. This difference is implied already in the simple equational definition, A = B, where A and B have different meanings. But if one says that the one equals the other, one says at the same time that they refer to the same thing. One can expose the difference between sense and reference by looking at cases in which there are obviously two senses for one reference (Alexander's instructor and Plato's pupil), or cases in which no referent can be assigned empirically (the farthest thing from earth).

The distinction between sense and reference is a necessary and pervasive characteristic of discourse, and collides head-on with the axiom of the immanence of language. There is no reference problem in language: signs refer to other signs *within* the same system. In the phenomenon of the sentence, language passes outside itself; reference is the mark of the self-transcendence of language.

This trait, more than others perhaps, marks the fundamental difference between semantics and semiotics. Semiotics is aware only of intra-linguistic relationships, whereas semantics takes up the relationship between the sign and the things denoted – that is, ultimately, the relationship between language and world. Therefore, the definition of sign by the signifier-signified relationship and its definition by the relation to thing are not opposed to one another. The substitution of the first definition for the second simply means that semiotics is being taken as semiotics. But this does not abolish the second definition; it continues to be valid for language in use and in action, whenever language is taken in its mediatory function between man and man, between man and world, and so integrating man into society and assuring the correspondence between language and world.

It is also possible to link up the problem of reference with the notion of the intended, which was distinguished earlier from the notion of the signified. It is the intended, not the signified, whose reach goes outside language: 'In the sign we have reached the intrinsic reality of language, while with the sentence we connect up with things outside language; and whereas the constitutive counterpart of the sign is the signified, which is inherent to the sign, the sense of the sentence implies reference to the discourse situation and the speaker's attitude' ('La forme' 36). Leaving this last remark aside for the time being, it is clear that the transcendence-function of the intended captures perfectly the meaning of the Fregean concept of reference. At the same time, Husserl's phenomenological analysis based on the concept of intentionality is completely justified: language is intentional par excellence; it aims beyond itself.[17]

A fifth pair differentiates reference to reality from reference to the speaker.

Reference is itself a dialectical phenomenon. To the extent that discourse refers to a situation, to an experience, to reality, to the world, in sum to the extra-linguistic, it also refers to its own speaker by means of procedures that belong essentially to discourse and not to language.[18] On the first level of these procedures we find the personal pronouns, which are truly 'asemic': the word *I* has no signification in itself, but is an indicator of the reference of discourse to the one who is speaking. *I* means the one who can apply I to himself in a sentence, as being the one who is speaking. Thus the personal pronoun is the function of discourse essentially, and takes on meaning only when someone speaks and designates himself by saying 'I.' To personal pronouns can be added the tenses of verbs. These constitute very different grammatical systems, but they are anchored in the present. For the present, like the personal pronoun, is auto-designative. The present is the very moment at which the discourse is being uttered. This is the present of discourse. By means of the present, discourse itself qualifies itself temporally. The same is to be said of many adverbs (here, now, etc.), all of them connected to the instance of discourse. So too with the demonstratives, 'this one' and 'that one' [*ceci, cela*], whose oppositions are determined in relation to the speaker. In so far as it is auto-referential, discourse establishes an absolute this-here-now.

This auto-referential character is clearly implied in the very notion of instance of discourse. And it can also be linked up to the theory of speech acts. Indeed, 'the modalities of which the sentence is capable' (*Problems* 110) (that is, assertive, interrogative and imperative proposition), even though they are alike in their dependence on predication, express diverse ways in which the speaker is engaged in his discourse: 'Now these three modalities do nothing but reflect the three fundamental behaviours of man speaking and acting through discourse upon his interlocutor: he wishes to impart a piece of knowledge to him or to obtain some information from him or to give an order to him' (ibid.). Now what we have here are corollaries of the communication function, which itself depends on the auto-referential function of discourse. Indeed, 'these are the three inter-human functions of discourse that are implied in the three modalities of the sentence-unit, each one corresponding to an attitude of the speaker' (ibid.). Thus we find a good match established between the speech-act theory and the auto-referential character of discourse, itself implied in the notion of instance of discourse.

A last pair, very important for our study of metaphor, concerns the redistribution of the spheres of the paradigmatic and the syntagmatic, which the distinction between semiology and semantics brings along with it.

Paradigmatic relations (principally inflections, derivation, etc.) concern the signs in the system, and so belong to the semiotic order. The 'binary' law, cherished by Jakobson and the structuralists,[19] holds true for them. On the other hand, 'syntagma' is the name given to the specific formation in which the meaning of the sentence is achieved. The reason why this trait is so important for our investigation is that, if the paradigm is semiotic and the syntagma semantic, then substitution, a paradigmatic law, belongs on the side of semiology. Consequently, it will be necessary to say that metaphor as treated in discourse – the metaphorical statement – is a sort of syntagma. It follows that the metaphorical process can no longer be put on the paradigmatic side and the metonymic process on the syntagmatic side. As I shall show in Study 5, this does not prohibit the classification of metaphor, taken as a meaning phenomenon affecting words, among the substitutions; but, in return, this semiotic classification does not debar a properly semantic investigation into the form of discourse (therefore of syntagma) that is realized by metaphor. Indeed, it is as syntagma that the metaphorical statement must be considered if it is true that the meaning-effect results from a certain interaction of the words within the sentence. The place reserved for metaphor can be seen in this account by Benveniste: 'It is a consequence of their being set together, that words take on qualities they did not possess in themselves, which even contradict those they possess otherwise' ('La forme' 38).

2 / SEMANTICS AND RHETORIC OF METAPHOR

The pioneering job done by I.A. Richards' *The Philosophy of Rhetoric* cannot be overestimated. The theory of metaphor that we find in the fifth and sixth chapters of his book is connected to a new definition of rhetoric, and not initially to a semantics of the sentence. But it is not difficult to demonstrate that his idea of rhetoric[20] derives from a semantic conception close to the one that has just been articulated. Furthermore, he is aware that his is an attempt 'to revive an old subject' (3) on the basis of a new analysis of language.

Richards borrows his definition of rhetoric from one of the last great English treatises of the eighteenth century, that of Archbishop Whateley. Rhetoric, proclaims Whateley, is 'a philosophic discipline aiming at a mastery of the fundamental laws of the use of language' (7). It can be seen that the amplitude of Greek rhetoric is restored in each of the elements of this definition. By putting the accent on the use of language, the author situates rhetoric on the properly verbal plane of understanding and communication; rhetoric is thus the theory of discourse, of thought as discourse. By seeking the laws of this usage, furthermore, he submits the rules of competence to a disciplined reflection. By proposing that the goal of rhetoric is the mastery of these laws, he sets the study of misunderstanding on the same level as the study of understanding. (Following him, Richards calls rhetoric 'a study of verbal understanding and misunderstanding' [23].) Finally, the philosophical character of this discipline is assured in that its major concern is to remedy 'losses in communication' (3) rather than to assign to rhetoric the office of persuading, of influencing, and lastly, of pleasing – an office that in the past cut rhetoric off progressively from philosophy. And so, rhetoric will be called 'a study of misunderstanding and its remedies' (3).

In addition to its aims, the frankly anti-taxonomical bent of this rhetoric distinguishes it from its decadent relations. Not a single attempt at classifying figures is to be found in this short work. Metaphor holds sway here without a single allusion to features that might oppose it to metonymy or to synecdoche, oppositions that were already explored in Aristotle's *Poetics*. But it does not have this negative trait just by chance. Deviations are what one classifies; further, deviations exist in relation to fixed significations. And what elements of discourse are fundamentally the carriers of fixed signification, if not nouns or names? Now Richards mobilizes his whole rhetorical enterprise with the aim of re-establishing the rights of discourse at the expense of the rights of the word. From the start he attacks the cardinal distinction in classical rhetoric between proper meaning and figurative meaning, a distinction for which he blames 'the Proper Meaning Superstition' (11). Words have no proper meaning, because no meaning can be said to 'belong' to them; and they do not possess any meaning in themselves, because it is discourse, taken as a whole, that carries the meaning, itself an undivided whole. Hence, in the name of an undisguisedly contextual theory of meaning – a theory summed up in 'the context theorem of meaning' (40) – the author denounces the notion of proper meaning.

Richards constructs his contextual law on the following considerations. First of all, it is the fact of change that makes the context primary: 'We are things peculiarly responsive to other things' (29). The context of discourse, therefore, is itself one part of a larger context, which is constituted by the question and answer. Furthermore, in any segment of discourse, the words owe their meaning only to a phenomenon of '*delegated efficacy*' (32). This phenomenon is the key to the notion of context, which is the 'name for a whole cluster of events that recur together – including the required conditions as well as whatever we may pick out as cause or effect' (34). Consequently, words have meaning only through the abridgment of the context: 'What a word means is the missing parts of the contexts from which it draws its delegated efficacy' (35). So it remains true that the word 'holds true for,' 'stands for' – but not for a thing or an idea. The belief that words possess a meaning that would be proper to them is a leftover from sorcery, the residue of 'the magical theory of names' (71). Words are not at all the names of ideas present to the mind; they are not constituted by any fixed association with data, whatever that data might be. All they do is refer back to the missing parts of the context. Consequently, constancy of meaning is never anything but the constancy of contexts. And this constancy is not a self-evident phenomenon; stability is itself something to be explained. (Something more likely to be self-evident would be a law of process and of growth, like that which Whitehead postulated as the principle of reality.)

Consequently, nothing prevents a word from signifying more than one thing. Since it refers back to 'contextually missing parts,' these parts can belong to opposed contexts. By their 'overdetermination,' therefore, words express the 'large scale rivalries between contexts' (40). This critique of the superstition concerning the single, true meaning quite obviously paves the way for a positive appreciation of the role of metaphor. However, this observation holds true for all forms of double meaning that can be linked to intentions, mental reservations, and conventions conveyed by the missing parts of the context.

The relationship of priority between word and sentence is thus entirely reversed. We might recall the coincidence between idea and proposition in Fontanier, and the ultimate privileged position of the idea in *Les Figures du discours*.[21] With Richards, hesitation is no longer possible. The meaning of the sentence is not the result of the meaning of the words; rather, the latter meaning proceeds from breaking down the sentence and isolating one of its parts. The route taken by the *Theaetetus* prevails over that of the *Cratylus*. In a chapter significantly titled 'The Interanimation of Words' (47), Richards sets down his theory of the interpenetration of parts of discourse, upon which the theory of the interaction proper to metaphor will be built.

The modalities of this interpenetration are themselves the function of the degree of stability of the meanings of words, that is, of the contexts that have been abridged. According to this perspective, technical language and poetic language constitute the two ends of a single scale. One end is occupied by univocal meanings anchored in definitions. At the other end, no meaning stabilizes outside the '*movement* among meanings' (48). Certainly, the work of good authors tends to give words fixed values of usage – which is, without doubt, the origin of the false belief that words have a meaning, that they possess their meaning. So too, the theory of usage did not overthrow, but finally strengthened, the preconception of the proper meaning of words. But, as opposed to the usage that fixes their meanings, the literary use of words consists precisely in restoring 'the interplay of the interpretative possibilities of the whole utterance' (55). This is why the meaning of words has to be 'guessed' (53) every time; one can never build upon an acquired stability. The experience of translation is parallel to this. It shows that the sentence is not a mosaic, but an organism. To translate is to invent an identical constellation, in which each word is influenced by all the others and, bit by bit, profits from its relation to the whole language.

We said that Richards broke with the theory of word conceived as the name of the idea. It must be added that he goes further than Benveniste regarding the primacy of the instance of discourse over the word. Benveniste certainly subordinated the actual meaning of the word to the entirely circumstantial meaning of the sentence, but he did not dissolve the one into the other. The fact is that, with him, semantics remains in tension with a semiology that assures the identity of signs by means of their differences and oppositions. We will return in Study 5 to this conflict between a semiology founded on differential laws and thus allowing the establishment of a taxonomy, and a semantics that recognizes only one sort of operation, that of the predicate, and allows at most one enumeration (perhaps endless, as Wittgenstein suggests)[22] of 'acts of discourse.' With Richards we enter into a semantics of the metaphor that ignores the duality of a theory of signs and a theory of the instance of discourse, and that builds directly on the thesis of the interanimation of words in the living utterance.

This theory is a rhetoric, in that it teaches the mastery of contextual interplay by means of a knowledge of criteria of understanding other than those of simple univocity upon which logic is built. Such attention to criteria is a descendant of the ancient reflection on 'virtues of *lexis*'[23]; but those older criteria – precision, liveliness, expressiveness, clarity, beauty – remain locked in to the superstition concerning proper meaning. If rhetoric is 'a study of misunderstanding and its remedies' (3), the remedy is the 'command'[24] of the shifts of meaning that assure the effectiveness of language in communication. Ordinary conversation consists in following these shifts, and rhetoric should teach their mastery. A 'systematic' study (73) of the recurrent forms of ambiguity and transference, therefore, is the most urgent task of the new rhetoric. It is doubtful, however, whether such a study could be systematic in the sense treasured by the taxonomic spirit. It is more a question of 'a clarification ... a translation of our skills into comprehension' (73), in a spirit close to the linguistic analysis of English-language authors.

And, indeed, the two lectures devoted to metaphor (lectures 5 and 6) undertake just such a clarification. We learn, first of all, that the functioning of metaphor is to be detected within ordinary usage; for, contrary to Aristotle's well-known saying that the mastery of metaphor is a gift of genius and cannot be taught, language is 'vitally metaphorical,' as Shelley saw very well.[25] If to 'metaphorize well' is to possess mastery of resemblances, then without this power we would be unable to grasp any hitherto unknown relations between things. Therefore, far from being a divergence from the ordinary operation of language, it is 'the omnipresent principle of all its free action' (90). It does not represent some additional power, but the constitutive form of language. By restricting itself to the description of the ornaments of language, rhetoric condemned itself to treating nothing but superficial problems – whereas metaphor penetrates to the very depths of verbal interaction.

This pervading presence of metaphor results from the 'context theorem of meaning.' If the word substitutes for a combination of aspects that are themselves the missing parts of their diverse contexts, the principle of metaphor derives from this constitution of words. According to one elementary formulation, metaphor holds two thoughts of different things together in simultaneous performance upon the stage of a word or a simple expression, whose meaning is the result of their interaction. Or, to bring this description and the theorem of meaning into accord, we can say that the metaphor holds together within one simple meaning two different missing parts of different contexts of this meaning. Thus, we are not dealing any longer with a simple transfer of words, but with a commerce between thoughts, that is, a transaction between contexts. If metaphor is a competence, a talent, then it is a talent of thinking. Rhetoric is just the reflection and the translation of this talent into a distinct body of knowledge.

At this stage of the description, the danger would be in fact the inverse of that to which the excessive minutiae of tropology was exposed. Would not every pair of thoughts condensed in a single expression constitute a metaphor? Here Richards introduces a distinctive factor that plays the role of specific difference in relation to the generic concept of 'transaction between contexts.' The two thoughts in metaphor are somehow disrupted, in this sense, that we describe one through the features of the other. Fontanier perceived something of this in his definition of metaphor, 'to present one idea under the sign of the other'[26]; but without an adequate theory of discourse, he was unable to draw out all its consequences. Richards suggests that we call the underlying idea the 'tenor' and that 'vehicle' be the name of the idea under whose sign the first idea is apprehended.[27] It is very important to note, however, that the metaphor is not the vehicle alone, but the whole made up of the two halves.

No doubt this terminology is less familiar than another. Why not say 'the original idea' and 'the borrowed idea'? Or 'what is really being thought or said' and 'what it is compared to'? Or 'the principal subject' and 'what it resembles'? Or, better, 'the idea' and 'its image'? No: the advantage of this esoteric terminology is precisely that it combats every allusion to a proper meaning, every return to a non-contextual theory of idea, but also and above all, anything borrowed from the notion of mental image. (Richards' principal adversaries here are the eighteenth-century English rhetoricians, against whom he quotes the insightful Coleridge.)[28] Nothing is more misleading in this regard than the confusion between figure of style and image, if image is understood as the copy of a sensible perception. Tenor and vehicle are neutral terms with regard to all these confusions. But above all, they prevent one from talking about tenor apart from the figure, and from treating the vehicle as an added ornament. The simultaneous presence of the tenor and vehicle and their interaction engender the metaphor; consequently, the tenor does not remain unaltered, as if the vehicle were nothing but wrapping and decoration. (We shall see presently the use Max Black makes of this remark.)

What can we say now about 'The Command of Metaphor' (lecture 6) as a conscious reflection on the spontaneous talent at work in metaphor? We are in great danger of letting our theories, necessarily 'oversimplifying' and 'fallacious,' usurp the place of our talent, which in many respects is 'prodigious and inexplicable' (116). Perhaps every renewal of rhetoric must risk making this mistake, which William James called 'the Psychologist's Fallacy' (116): 'Very likely a new attempt must again lead into artificialities and arbitrariness' (115). (Perhaps this warning applies to the explorations that we will examine in Study 5.)

A first, critical problem that a reflective rhetoric cannot elucidate is the outcome of the distinction between literal and metaphorical meaning. As we saw, the tenor-vehicle pair completely ignores this distinction. But even though it was not the point of departure, we might still end up there. The sole criterion of metaphor, in effect, is that the word presents two ideas at once,[29] that it comprises at once both tenor and vehicle in interaction. By contrast, this criterion can serve to define literal meaning: a word in which tenor and vehicle cannot be distinguished can be taken provisionally to be literal. So this distinction is not wholly lost; however, it does not arise from a characteristic indigenous to words, but from the manner in which interaction functions, on the basis of the contextual meaning theorem. But then literal meaning has no connection any longer with proper meaning. Moreover, literal language becomes quite rare outside of the technical language of the sciences.

Reflective lucidity applied to metaphorical talent consists in good part in locating the 'ground' of the metaphor (117), its underlying 'rationale.' Whether the metaphor concerned be dead (the leg of the chair) or living (an author's metaphor), our procedure is the same: we look for its ground in some shared characteristic. But this characteristic does not necessarily lie in a direct resemblance between tenor and vehicle; it can result from a common attitude taken to them both (118). And a vast range of intermediary cases fans out between these two extremes.

This brings up another critical problem: does the relationship between tenor and vehicle belong necessarily to the order of comparison? And what is comparison? To compare can be to hold two things together in order to let them act together; it can also mean perceiving their resemblance; or, again, it can mean apprehending certain aspects of one thing through the co-presence of the other. Resemblance, then, on which the last examples of classical rhetoric based their definition of metaphor, is just one particular form of the approximation [*rapprochement*] through which we describe one thing in terms of another. The vehicle has many techniques for influencing the way in which the tenor is apprehended. But if we adopt a thesis that is the exact counter-position of the strict definition of metaphor as resemblance – replacing comparison, as does André Breton, by the juxtaposition of two dissimilar ideas 'in an abrupt and gripping manner'[30] – then all the good we do is to produce a negative image of classical rhetoric. To compare, maintains Richards, is always to connect things, and 'The mind is a connecting organ, it works only by connecting and it can connect any two things in an indefinitely large number of different ways' (125). Evidently, however hostile this 'philosophy of rhetoric' may be to proper meanings, it does not advocate calculated anarchy. The bow may be stretched to the limit, but the arrow keeps its aim. There is no language, then, that does not bestow meaning on that which first created tension in the mind. Sometimes a whole poem is needed for the mind to invent or find a meaning; but always the mind makes connections.

Thus, one and the same tensive theory gives equal status to dissimilarity and to resemblance. Perhaps the modification imparted by the vehicle to the tenor is even greater because of their dissimilarity than because of their resemblance.[31]

The last critical problem concerns the *ontological* bearing of metaphorical language. This problem is first alluded to in connection with spontaneous competence. In effect, according to the contextual meaning theorem, the context lets us understand the missing parts of discourse implied in the meaning of the words, and also the situations represented by these missing terms. Therefore, we readily assent to speaking of a metaphorical grasp of reality itself: 'Our world,' says Richards, 'is a projected world, shot through with characters lent to it from our own life ... the exchanges between the meanings of words which we study in explicit verbal metaphors are superimposed upon a perceived world which itself is a product of earlier or unwitting metaphor ...' (108-9). This is all written into the general theorem of meaning. But Richards' analysis lacks the orientation towards the problem of the relationships between metaphor and reality that we will consider later in Study 7 with the work of Philip Wheelwright. Indeed, we have to set this problem aside as we are unable at this stage of our research to differentiate between sense and reference.

A reflective rhetoric cannot settle this problem either. It can, at best, clarify it by tying it up with the problem of belief. Must we believe what an utterance says in order to understand it fully? Must we accept as true what the Bible or the *Divine Comedy* says metaphorically? A critical response involves discerning four possible modes of interpretation and thus also of belief: 'We can extract the tenor and believe that as a statement; or extract the vehicle; or, taking the tenor and vehicle together, contemplate for acceptance or rejection some statement about their relations, or we can accept or refuse the direction which together they would give to our living' (135). This last possibility of understanding a metaphorical statement seems really to increase, but in a critical way, the spontaneous action (cited above) of a metaphorical grasp of the world. (We will return to this mode of comprehension as the paradigm of a hermeneutical conception of metaphor.)[32] Then, as Richards himself suggests, the 'command of metaphor' will be 'the control of the world that we make for ourselves to live in' (135). But he goes no further in this direction; he is content to remind us of the case of psychoanalysis, where 'transference' – a precise synonym for metaphor – does not reduce to a verbal interplay, but operates between our 'modes of regarding, of loving, of acting' (135). Indeed, it is within the very density of living relationships that we decifer new situations in terms of figures – for example, the parental image – that play the role of 'vehicle' with respect to these new situations considered as 'tenor' (135-6). Thus, the process of interpretation takes place at the level of modes of existing. The example of psychoanalysis, although dealt with briefly, gives us a glimpse of the horizon of the rhetorical problem: if metaphor consists in talking about one thing in terms of another, does it not consist also in perceiving, thinking, or sensing one thing in terms of another?

3 / LOGICAL GRAMMAR AND SEMANTICS

Max Black's article entitled 'Metaphor' and published in *Models and Metaphor*[33] has become a classic in its field on the west side of the Atlantic. And justly so: in a somewhat nuclear fashion, he condenses the essential theses of a semantic analysis of metaphor at the level of the statement as a whole in order to account for a change in meaning that is centred in the word. Nevertheless, this brief essay does not eclipse Richards' work, despite the tentativeness and a certain lack of technical development in the latter. For Richards made the breakthrough; after him, Max Black and others occupy and organize the terrain.

At first sight, Black's purpose seems quite different from that of Richards. He is not at all concerned with the restoration of the old rhetoric. His aim is rather to work out a 'logical grammar' of metaphor, by which he understands the set of convincing answers to questions of the following sort: What features let one recognize an instance of metaphor? Are there criteria for the detection of metaphor? Is metaphor to be seen as a mere ornament, added to the pure and simple meaning? What are the relationships between metaphor and simile? What effect does the use of metaphor attempt to achieve? Evidently the task of clarification raised by these questions hardly differs at all from what Richards calls rhetoric, since for Richards acquiring the command of metaphor demands that one understand its workings and those of the whole of language. Reflective mastery and clarification are closely related. Moreover, the two authors share a conviction about the presuppositions of their work of clarification: for Richards, technical competence in the use of metaphor is presupposed; for Black, spontaneous agreement on a preliminary list of obvious metaphors. In the same way, then, that it is impossible to begin to bring off well-formed expressions without a foundation in the grammatical consciousness that speakers have, spontaneous usage guides the first steps of logical grammar. Hence, it covers the same territory as the reflective rhetoric of Richards, to which it adds more highly technical precision, thanks to Black's skills as a logician and epistemologist.

Black's work marks decisive progress in clarifying the field in at least three ways. The first concerns the very structure of the metaphorical statement, which Richards expressed through the tenor-vehicle relationship. Before being able to introduce this distinction and criticize it, one must begin with this point: an entire statement constitutes the metaphor, yet attention focuses on a particular word, the presence of which constitutes the grounds for considering the statement metaphorical. This balance of meaning between the statement and the word is the condition of its principal feature, the contrast within a single statement between one word that is taken metaphorically and another that is not. In 'The chairman *plowed* through the discussion,' the word *plowed* is taken metaphorically, the others not. We shall say then that metaphor is 'a sentence or another expression in which *some* words are used metaphorically while the remainder are used non-metaphorically' (27). This trait provides us with a criterion that distinguishes metaphor from the proverb, allegory, and riddle, in which all the words are used metaphorically. For the same reason, Kafka's symbolism in *The Castle* is not a case of metaphor.

This attempt at greater precision, besides allowing us to circumscribe the phenomenon, lets us correct the distinction between tenor and vehicle. The problem with these words is that they bear on 'ideas' or 'thoughts,' which are said to be 'active together,' and above all that the meaning of each of them is too ambiguous (47, note 23). The definition above allows us to isolate the metaphorical word from the rest of the sentence. The word *focus*, then, will designate this word, and *frame* will designate the rest of the sentence. The advantage of this terminology is that it directly expresses the phenomenon of focusing on a word, yet without returning to the illusion that words have meanings in themselves. Indeed, the metaphorical use of *focus* results from the relationship between *focus* and *frame*. Now Richards saw this perfectly well; metaphor, he said, arises from the joint action of the tenor and the vehicle. Black's more precise vocabulary allows us to get closer to the interaction that takes place between the undivided meaning of the statement and the focused meaning of the word.

The second decisive advance occurs at this point. A distinct boundary is set up between the interaction theory, which comes from the above analysis, and the classical theory, which Black divides into two groups: a substitution and a comparison conception of metaphor. He leads the interpretation in this connection to a clear alternative, which will provide the point of departure for our own inquiries in Studies 4 and 5; but first we must work our way through the alternative that Black institutes.

What Black calls the substitutive theory very exactly matches the model that we set up at the beginning of Study 2, to act as a touchstone for the classical rhetorical conception. Black concentrates his attack on what we called the fifth postulate: instead of using a given literal expression, the speaker chooses to replace it with an expression taken in a sense that is different from its proper, normal meaning. To this postulate Black adds (as we did earlier) the two others that conclude the model. If the metaphor is an expression substituted for an absent, literal expression, then these two expressions are equivalent, and the metaphor can then be translated by means of an exhaustive paraphrase. Consequently, the metaphor introduces no new information. And if the metaphor teaches nothing, then its justification must be sought elsewhere than in its cognitive function; perhaps, like the catachresis of which it is just a species anyway, it fills a gap in our vocabulary. But then it functions like a literal expression and disappears as metaphor; or rather, it is merely an ornament for discourse, giving the hearer the joy of surprise, of disguise, or of imagistic expression.

But Black does not stop at contrasting an interaction theory with a substitution theory. To the latter he joins a theory of comparison, which he sees as a particular case of substitution. However, it is not introduced in that fashion, but through a general reflection on the notion of 'figurative' language. Every figure implies a displacement, a transformation, a change of semantic order, which makes the figurative expression a function 'in the algebraic sense' of a prior literal expression. This prompts the question: what characterizes the transformative function that metaphor puts in play? The reply: the grounds of metaphor are analogy or similarity (the first holding between relationships, the second between things or ideas). Richards, it will be remembered, adopted an argument of this sort in the framework of his reflective rhetoric. But, for Black, the comparison theory is just a particular case of the substitution theory; to spell out the grounds of an analogy is in effect to produce a literal comparison, which is held to be equivalent to the metaphorical statement and could therefore be substituted for it.

One may doubt, however, whether the similarity at work in metaphor is simply spelt out, 'literalized' if one can use such a word, in the comparison. Our study of Aristotle demonstrated the complexity of the relationship between metaphor and comparison or simile; the idea that metaphor is a condensed, abbreviated, or elliptical simile is not self-evident. Besides, there is nothing that says that a simile, restored by the explication of its comparative term (as, like, etc.), constitutes a literal expression that can be treated as equivalent to the metaphorical statement substituted for it. Briefly, a theory in which similarity plays a role need not be a theory in which comparison or simile constitutes the paraphrase of metaphor. We will return to this in Study 6.

In addition, Black confronts the comparison theory with a series of objections that have nothing to do with its dependence on the substitution theory. It is well that he does so, since the comparison theory has a logic of its own, and is connected to the preceding theory only by its consequences. Actually, Black does not return to the notion of figure and figurative language, although it calls for a separate discussion (as is shown by Aristotle's remarks on 'setting before the eyes' and Fontanier's concerning the kinship between figurative and imagistic language). Black's attack centres on the explication of the metaphorical figure by similarity or by analogy. Similarity, he declares, is a vague notion, if not an empty one. Besides admitting of degrees and thus of indeterminate extremes, it owes more to subjective appreciation than to objective observation. Finally, in the cases where it is legitimate to invoke similarity, it is more enlightening to say that the metaphor creates the similarity than that the metaphor gives verbal form to some pre-existent similarity. We will return at length to these objections in Study 6. In the meantime, we will say that it has been established only that the fates of similarity and formal comparison or simile are linked, and not that the latter constitutes a case of interpretation by substitution.

No doubt the destruction of the primacy of analogy or of similarity has the most far-reaching consequences, for this also eliminates the entire tropological theory and the theory of transformative functions that constitute it and of which analogy is one kind. Turning his back on all taxonomy, Black accepts that all sorts of 'grounds' allow for changes of meaning according to context and indeed even the absence of any true ground (43): 'There is, in general, no simple "ground" for the necessary shifts of meaning – no blanket reason why some metaphors work and others fail' (45). It is claimed that this argument is formally incompatible with the comparison thesis.

Starting with Study 4, we will reconsider the legitimacy of such an entrenched opposition between a substitution theory and an interaction theory. Underlying this opposition is the dichotomy between semiology and semantics. We have adopted it as a working hypothesis in the present Study, but it will have to be reviewed at some suitable moment. Let us first emphasize the benefits of this entrenched opposition between the interaction theory and its rivals. The decisive point is that, since substitution for an interaction metaphor is impossible, it also cannot be translated without 'loss of *cognitive* content' (46). Being untranslatable, it carries new information; briefly, it tells us something.

Black's third major contribution concerns the very functioning of interaction. How does the 'frame,' the context, act on the focal term so as to give rise in it to a new meaning, irreducible at once to literal usage and to exhaustive paraphrase? This is the problem faced by Richards. But his solution either takes us into a comparison theory by invoking a common character, or sinks into confusion by speaking of the simultaneous activity of two thoughts. Nevertheless, he is on the right track with his suggestion that the reader is forced to 'connect two ideas.' But how?

Let our metaphor be 'Man is a wolf.' The focus, 'wolf,' operates not on the basis of its current lexical meaning, but by virtue of the 'system of associated commonplaces' (40) – that is, by virtue of the opinions and preconceptions to which a reader in a linguistic community, by the very fact that he speaks, finds himself committed. This system of commonplaces, added to the literal uses of the word, which are governed by syntactic and semantic rules, forms a system of implications that lends itself to more or less easy and free invocation. To call a man a wolf is to evoke the lupine system of associated commonplaces. One speaks then of the man in 'wolf-language.' Acting as a filter (39) or screen (41), 'The wolf-metaphor suppresses some details, emphasizes others – in short, *organizes* our view of man' (41).

In this way metaphor confers an 'insight.' Organizing a principal subject by applying a subsidiary subject to it constitutes, in effect, an irreducible intellectual operation, which informs and clarifies in a way that is beyond the scope of any paraphrase. (An adequate account of this could be drawn from Black's juxtaposition, in another essay,[34] of model and metaphor, which would also reveal very decisively the contribution that metaphor makes to a logic of invention. We will follow this line of thinking in Study 7, once the referential function of metaphor has been distinguished clearly from the properly significative function.) The present Study, taking only immanent elements of discourse into account – a principal subject and a subsidiary subject – cannot do justice to the *redescriptive* power that belongs to the model and, by reflection, the metaphor. Nevertheless, within the limits of the present Study it is possible to speak of the 'cognitive content of metaphor' in contrast to the non-informative nature of metaphor according to the substitution theory.

Black's theory, then, has great merits. Nevertheless, there are questions that remain unanswered. We have already spoken of some reservations concerning the elimination of the substitution theory and especially of the comparison theory. And the explication of interaction by reference to the system of associated commonplaces warrants particular attention.

The major difficulty (which, by the way, Black himself recognizes, 43-4) is that to return to a system of associated commonplaces is to address oneself to connotations that are already established. In one stroke, the explication is limited to trivial metaphors. (In this connection, it is significant that the 'man is a wolf' example is surreptitiously substituted for the richer examples in the initial list.) Now, is it not the role of poetry, and sometimes of stately prose, to establish new configurations of implications? This must be admitted: 'Metaphors can be supported by specially constructed systems of implications, as well as by accepted commonplaces' (43). This is a sizeable adjustment: it nearly ruins the very foundation of the explication. In his final resumé, given as a set of theses, Black maintains: 'These implications usually consist of "commonplaces" about the subsidiary subject, but may, in suitable cases, consist of deviant implications established *ad hoc* by the writer' (44). But how are we to think of these implications that are created on the spot?

This same question arises again in connection with the following, different perspective. The author acknowledges that the system of implications does not remain unchanged by the action of the metaphorical utterance. To apply the system is to contribute at the same time to its determination – the wolf appears more human at the same moment that by calling the man a wolf one places the man in a special light. But then the creation of meaning, which belongs to what Fontanier called newly invented metaphors, is dispersed and attributed to all metaphorical statements, and the analogy of the filter or the screen no longer amounts to very much. The emergence of metaphorical meaning remains just as enigmatic as before.

This question of the emergence of meaning is posed still more directly by what Black calls the *application* of the metaphorical predicate. This application is plainly something unusual and, in the proper sense of the word, paradoxical; 'The metaphor selects, emphasizes, suppresses, and organizes features of the principal subject by implying statements about it that normally apply to the subsidiary subject' (44-5). There is in this a sort of misapprehension, already suggested in Aristotle's saying that one gives the name of the species to the genus, of the genus to the species, and so on. (As we will see later, Turbayne[35] puts great emphasis on this trait, likening it to Gilbert Ryle's category-mistake.) Now this paradox, in which the very notion of *epiphora* is mired, is blurred by a theory that puts more weight on the implications of the focal term than on their application as such.

As far as the epistemological status of the present description is concerned, one can ask whether Black has kept his promise to write a 'logical grammar' of metaphor. He proposes 'semantics' as an equivalent term, opposing it on one hand to 'syntax' and on the other to '*physical* inquiry' into language (28). Now, the fact of translation – the same metaphor appearing in different languages – makes metaphor independent of its phonetic configuration and its grammatical form. Its analysis would be purely semantic if the rules of our language by themselves, independently of utterance-circumstances on the one hand and of the thoughts, actions, feelings, and intentions of speakers on the other, would permit us to say whether a predicate expression has metaphoric value. But it is rare, the author agrees (29), for the 'recognition and interpretation of a metaphor' to authorize this double abstraction. What is called the 'weight' or the 'emphasis' (29) attached to a particular use of an expression depends largely on the intention of the one who uses it. For instance, to what degree does a thinker speaking of 'logical forms' have containers and contours in mind, and how much would he want to insist on this relationship (30)? It must be admitted, then, that metaphor owes as much to 'pragmatics' as to 'semantics' (30).

This question with its methodological flavour rejoins our previous inquiry concerning the status of the 'system of associated commonplaces.' It is hard to call semantic such an explication by means of the non-lexical implications of words. No doubt it will be claimed that there is nothing psychological about this explication, since the implications are still governed by rules to which the speaking subjects of a linguistic community are 'committed.' But it is also emphasized that 'the important thing for the metaphor's effectiveness is not that the commonplaces shall be true, but that they should be readily and freely evoked' (40). Now this evocation of a system of associations seems truly to constitute a creative activity that is spoken of here only in psychological terms.

From every angle, consequently, the explication in terms of 'logical grammar' or of 'semantics' borders on an enigma that eludes it, the enigma of novel meaning beyond the bounds of all previously established rules.

4 / LITERARY CRITICISM AND SEMANTICS

On what discipline does the explication of metaphor depend? We have heard two replies – rhetoric and logical grammar. Now, with Monroe Beardsley's *Aesthetics*, we have the reply of literary criticism. How is it rooted in the common ground of the semantics of the sentence? What distinct path does it take? What benefit does the theory of metaphor derive from this change of axis?

I have turned to the *Aesthetics* of Beardsley for two reasons. First, Beardsley offers an explanation of metaphor that focuses again on the questions left unanswered by the analysis of Max Black. Secondly, the literary criticism within which his explanation takes place is based on a semantics similar to the one I presented at the beginning of this Study.

Before constituting its own level of distinct organization, the literary work is, in effect, a linguistic entity homogeneous with the sentence, which is itself 'the smallest complete unit of discourse' (Beardsley 115). It is at this level, therefore, that the principal technical concepts to which criticism will have recourse must be elaborated. A purely semantic definition of literature will take shape in terms of these concepts.

The aim of these concepts is to demarcate the phenomenon of signification, in sentences and in words, as brought to light by literature. Centring on this, the author stays far away from any emotivist definition of literature. For the distinction between cognitive and emotive language (which comes out of logical positivism), Beardsley substitutes a distinction internal to signification, one between primary and secondary signification. The first is what the sentence 'states,' the second is what it 'suggests.'

This distinction does not coincide with Austin's 'constative' and 'performative.' This is because an assertive statement can establish one thing and at the same time suggest something else, both these things being capable of being true or false. Consider the example from Frege: 'Napoleon, who recognized the danger to his right flank, himself led his guards against the enemy position.' The complex sentence 'states' that Napoleon recognized ... and led ... but it 'suggests' that the manœuvre took place *after* danger was recognized and *because of* this recognition, that is, that this was Napoleon's reason for deciding on the manœuvre. It could be established that the suggestion is wrong, for example if it is discovered that such was not the sequence of decisions. Hence, what a sentence 'suggests' is what we can infer concerning what the speaker probably believes, based on what it 'states.' The nature of suggestion includes the possibility of leading astray. It can be called 'secondary signification' because it is not experienced as being as central or fundamental as the primary signification; nevertheless, it is part of the signification. Let us reiterate that it is implicit and not explicit. To varying degrees, every sentence thus has an implicit, suggested, secondary signification.

Now we may transfer this distinction from the sentence to the word. The word has a meaning all by itself, and yet it remains a part of the sentence, a part which one cannot define and understand except in relation to real or possible sentences (115). The explicit signification or meaning of a word is its denotation, what it points to or designates; the implicit meaning, its connotation. In ordinary language, any particular context never brings a whole 'range of connotations' into play, but only one chosen part – the 'contextual connotation' of the word (125). In certain contexts, the other words eliminate the undesirable connotations of a given word; such is the case with respect to technical and scientific language, where everything is explicit. But 'in other contexts, [the] connotations are liberated; these are most notably the contexts in which language becomes figurative, and especially metaphorical' (ibid.). Such discourse can be said to involve a primary level and a secondary level of meaning at the same time. Its meaning is multiple; play on words, implication, metaphor, and irony are some particular cases of this polysemy. It is important here to say multiple meaning rather than ambiguity, because, properly speaking, we are confronted with ambiguity only when one meaning alone of two possible meanings is required, and the context does not provide us grounds for deciding between them. But literature precisely does confront us with discourse where several things are meant at the same time, without the reader being required to choose between them. Thus, a semantic definition of literature – that is, a definition in terms of meaning – can be deduced from the degree to which a discourse involves implicit or suggested secondary meanings. Be it fiction, essay, or poem, 'a literary work is a discourse in which an important part of the meaning is implicit' (126).

But the literary work is not only a linguistic entity homogeneous to the sentence, differing from it just with respect to length. It is a whole, organized at a level proper to the drawing of distinctions between several classes of works, between poems, essays, and prose fiction (we take it that these are the principal classes; between them they include all literary works).[36] This is why the work poses a specific problem of reconstruction, which Beardsley calls 'explication.' However, before getting into the 'logic of explication,' a most important refinement can be introduced concerning the notion of meaning. Unlike the preceding distinction between the implicit and the explicit, this can be seen only at the level of the work taken as a whole, even though its foundation lies in the semantics of the sentence; for it is the work, taken as a work, that reveals 'in retrospect' this property of discourse. There are two different senses in which 'the meaning of a work' can be understood. On the one hand, one can understand this to mean *the world of the work*. What story does it tell? What characters does it display? What feelings and attitudes? What, overall, is brought to light? These are questions that occur spontaneously to the reader; they concern what in the seventh Study I will call the *reference*, in the sense of the ontological import of a work. In this sense, meaning is the projection of a possible and inhabitable world. It is what Aistotle has in mind when he combines the *muthos* of tragedy with the *mimêsis* of human actions.[37]

On the other hand, the question that preoccupies literary criticism when it asks what a work is concerns only the verbal design, or discourse as an intelligible string of words (115). The decisive point is that this question proceeds from the suspension and adjournment of the preceding one (which Beardsley relegates to book 5, section 15 of his *Aesthetics*). In the language of Aristotle, criticism gives rise to this second acceptation of 'meaning' in dissociating *muthos* from *mimêsis* and reducing *poiêsis* to the construction of *muthos*. This duality in the notion of meaning is the work of literary criticism; in any case, its possibility rests on a constitution of discourse whose foundation lies in the semantics of the sentence that was laid out at the beginning of this chapter. We have acknowledged with Benveniste that what discourse intends, as opposed to what is signified at the semiotic level, relates to things, to a world. However, following Frege, we have claimed with equal force that it is possible, with respect to every statement, to distinguish its purely immanent sense from its reference, that is, from its transcending motion towards an extra-linguistic 'outside.' In spontaneous discourse, understanding does not stop at the sense, but passes by sense towards reference. This is Frege's principal argument in his article 'On Sense and Reference': in understanding the sense, we proceed to the reference.

Literary criticism takes an opposing position, by suspending this spontaneous motion, stopping at the sense, and taking the problem of reference up again only in light of the explication of sense: 'Since [the world of the work] exists as what is meant, or projected, by the words, the words are the things to consider first' (115). The program of literary criticism is expressed well by this statement. We see how a purely semantic definition of the literary work proceeds from splitting sense from reference and from reversing the priority between these two planes of meaning. An issue to be resolved is whether this split and this reversal are written into the nature of the work as a literary work, and whether criticism is here merely obeying the behest of literature as such. We will return to this question in the seventh Study. Whatever the answer, nevertheless, and however far one may be able to go in negating reference (at least for certain forms of literary work), what must never be lost sight of is that the question of sense is separated in advance from that of reference; and that the sort of purely verbal intelligibility that can be granted metaphor within the limits of this abstraction proceeds from suppressing, and perhaps from forgetting, another question that no longer concerns structure but reference – namely, the power of metaphor to project and to reveal a world.

Beardsley himself is not guilty of such forgetfulness: 'The essential thing that the literary creator does is to invent or discover an object – it can be a material object or a person, or a thought, or a state of affairs, or an event – around which he collects a set of relations that can be perceived as connected through their intersection in that object' (128). Thus, the creative writer indulges in multivocal discourse only because he bestows the characteristics brought into play by the secondary meanings of his discourse on the objects to which he refers. So literary criticism is really rebounding, it takes a second step, when it returns from these diversely robed objects to the purely verbal phenomenon of multiple meaning.

Such is the benefit of an approach through literary criticism rather than via logical grammar. In making the work the level of consideration, literary criticism brings into view a conflict, which was invisible at the level of the sentence alone, between two modes of understanding: the first (which becomes the ultimate) having to do with the world of the work, the second (and most immediate) concerning the work as discourse, i.e. as a configuration of words. The difference of outlook between literary criticism and the rhetoric of I.A. Richards is faint by comparison. Perhaps it is even just a purely formal difference, rhetoric being defined in terms of processes of discourse (thus of transpositions of meaning, among them the tropes of ancient rhetoric) and literary criticism being defined in relation to works (poems, essays, prose fiction).

It is within a field with boundaries marked off in this manner that the question of a purely semantic definition of literature, and of metaphor with it, is raised.

But why pose the problem of metaphor now where the viewpoint is not that of rhetoric? And why pose the problem if the level of consideration proper to literary criticism is the literary work taken as a whole – poem, essay, prose fiction? The somewhat oblique manner in which Beardsley introduces the problem of metaphor is in itself very interesting. The explication of metaphor is to serve as a test-case (134) for a larger problem, that of the method of explication that is to be applied to the work itself, taken as a whole. To put it in another way, the metaphor is taken as a *poem in miniature*. The proposed working hypothesis is that if a satisfactory account can be given of what is implied in this kernel of poetic meaning, it must be possible equally to extend the same explication to larger entities, such as the entire poem.

Before proceeding, though, let us point out what is at stake. The very choice of the word *explication* indicates a steadfast intention to combat relativism in literary criticism. Indeed, relativism finds some solid support in the theory of meaning. If it is true that 'to point out a meaning in a poem is to *explicate* the poem' (129), and if it is true that the meaning of the poem reveals a great depth, an inexhaustible reserve, then the very idea of stating the meaning of a poem seems to be condemned in advance. How is the truth of the explication to be spoken of, if all meanings are contextual? And how could there be a method for identifying a meaning that exists only for the moment, a meaning which may well be called 'emergent meaning' (131)? Even supposing that one could take the 'range of connotations' to constitute an objective part of verbal meanings, on the grounds that the way they are delimited corresponds to the way things appear in human experience, the major difficulty still would remain of deciding which of these connotations is brought into play in any given poem. Lacking the power to summon up the intention of the writer, is it not the reader's preference that ultimately makes the decision?

Hence, it is in order to solve a problem similar to that of E.D. Hirsch in *Validity in Interpretation*[38] that Beardsley turns to metaphor as a distilled model of the formidable difficulty delineated by relativistic criticism. How is one 'to produce a nonrelativistic logic of explication' (Beardsley 134)? To put it more precisely, how do we know which potential meanings should be attributed to a poem and which others should be disclaimed?

We will not delay over the polemical aspects of the theory of metaphor. Beardsley's adversaries are more or less those of Max Black. He fights with equal vigour against the reduction of metaphor to simile. Such a reduction is assimilated into a 'literalist' theory; in effect, once the grounds of a simile are known, the enigma of the metaphor is dissipated and all problems of explication vanish.[39]

Beardsley's contribution (138-47) differs appreciably from that of Max Black, as regards the positive role assigned to logical absurdity at the level of primary meaning, functioning as a means of liberating the secondary meaning. Metaphor is just one tactic within a general strategy, which is to suggest something other than what is stated. Another such tactic is irony, in which you suggest the contrary of what you say by withdrawing your statement at the very moment that you make it. In all the tactics within this strategy, the trick consists in giving indicators that point towards the second level of meaning; and 'in poetry the chief tactic for obtaining this result is that of *logical absurdity*' (138).

Thus, the point of departure is the same for Richards, Black, and Beardsley. Metaphor is a kind of attribution,' requiring a 'subject' and a 'modifier' – an obviously analogous pair to those others, 'tenor-vehicle' and 'focus-frame.' What is new here is the stress put on the notion of 'logically empty attributions' and – especially among all the possible forms of such attributions – on incompatibility, that is, on 'self-contradictory attribution,' attribution which cancels itself out (139-40). Among the logically empty attributions, one must place (besides self-contradiction) redundancies, which are self-implicative attributions in expressions shorter than the sentence (two-legged biped); and tautologies, that is, self-implicative attributions that are sentences (bipeds are two-legged beings) (139).

In the case of incompatibility, the modifier, by means of its primary meanings, points to characteristics incompatible with the corresponding characteristics designated by the subject at the level of its primary meanings. Accordingly, incompatibility is a conflict between designations at the primary level of meaning, which forces the reader to extract from the complete context of connotations the secondary meanings capable of making a 'meaningful self-contradictory attribution' from a self-contradictory statement. Oxymoron is the simplest sort of meaningful self-contradiction (to live a living death). Within the domain of what is normally called metaphor, contradiction is more indirect: in calling the streets 'metaphysical,' the poet invites us to draw various applicable connotations from the attribute *metaphysical*, despite the manifestly physical character of streets. Let us say, then, that 'whenever an attribution is indirectly self-contradictory, and the modifier has connotations that could be attributed to the subject, the attribution is a *metaphorical attribution*, or metaphor' (141). So oxymoron is just an extreme case of direct contradiction; it bears in most cases on the joint presuppositions of the ordinary designations.

The important point to be underlined in the subsequent discussion concerns what I will call the production of meaning [*le travail du sens*]. It is the reader, in effect, who works out the connotations of the modifier that are likely to be meaningful. A significant trait of living language, in this connection, is the power always to push the frontier of non-sense further back. There are probably no words so incompatible that some poet could not build a bridge between them; the power to create new contextual meanings seems to be truly limitless. Attributions that appear to be 'non-sensical' can make sense in some unexpected context. No speaker ever completely exhausts the connotative possibilities of his words.[40]

We now see in what sense 'the explication of a metaphor is a model of all explication' (144). An entire logic of explication is put into play in the activity of constructing meaning. Two principles regulating this logic can now be transposed from the microcosm to the macrocosm, from the metaphor to the poem. The first is a principle of 'fittingness,' of congruence: it has to do with 'deciding which of the modifier's connotations can *fit* the subject' (ibid.).

This first principle is, as it were, one of *selection.* As we read a poetic sentence, we progressively restrict the breadth of the range of connotations, until we are left with just those secondary meanings capable of surviving in the total context. The second principle counterbalances the first, being a principle of *plenitude.* All the connotations that can 'go with' the rest of the context must be attributed to the poem, which 'means all it *can* mean' (144). This principle is a corrective to the first in the sense that poetic reading, as opposed to that involved with scientific or technical discourse, is not obliged to choose between two meanings that are equally admissible in the context; what would be ambiguity in the one is honoured as the plenitude of the other.

Are these two principles sufficient to exorcise the demon of relativism? If reading is compared to playing a musical score, then one could say that the logic of explication shows one how to give the poem a *correct* performance, even though every performance is *individual* and stands alone. If it is kept in mind that the principle of plenitude complements the principle of congruence and that complexity counterbalances coherence, it becomes clear that the principle of economy that rules over this logic does not just eliminate impossibilities. It also tends towards 'maximizing' the meaning, that is, towards getting as much meaning out of the poem as possible. The only thing this logic must do is maintain a division between getting meaning out of the poem and reading (i.e. forcing) meaning into the poem (147).

Beardsley's theory partially resolves some of the difficulties left unresolved by Max Black. Giving logical absurdity such a decisive role accentuates the inventive and innovative character of the metaphorical statement. And this has two advantages. First of all, it gives the old opposition between figurative and proper meaning an entirely new foundation. 'Proper meaning' can be the name of that meaning of a statement that reflects only the catalogued, lexical meanings of a word, those that constitute its designation. 'Figurative meaning' is then not a deviant meaning of words, but that meaning of a statement as a whole that arises from the attribution of connotative values of the modifier to the principal subject. Consequently, if a 'figurative meaning of words' is still to be spoken of, it can only concern meanings that are wholly contextual, 'emergent meaning' that exists only here and now.

Secondly, the semantic collision that forces designation to give way to connotation gives the metaphorical attribution not only a singular but also a made-up character. The dictionary contains no metaphors; they exist only in discourse. For this reason, metaphorical attribution is superior to every other use of language in showing what 'living speech' really is; it is an 'instance of discourse' *par excellence*. Accordingly, Beardsley's theory is directly applicable to newly invented metaphor.

The revision of the controversion theory that Beardsley proposes in 'The Metaphorical Twist' attempts in fact to highlight the 'constructed' character of metaphorical meaning. The notion of 'potential range of connotations' is open to the same objections as the notion of 'system of associated commonplaces' in Max Black. Are not newly invented metaphors just those metaphors that add to this storehouse of commonplaces, this range of connotations? It is really not good enough to say that the properties of a word at a given moment in its history have perhaps not yet all been used, and that there are unrecognized connotations of words. We ought to say that there may be connotations that 'wait, so to speak, lurking in the nature of things, for actualization – wait to be captured by the word ... as part of its meaning in some future context' (300). If, indeed, one's intention is to draw a line within the domain of metaphor between the class of familiar metaphors and the class of new metaphors, one should say that the first time that a metaphor is made up, the modifier receives a connotation that it never had until then. Similarly, Max Black was forced to speak of 'specially constructed systems,' and to admit that in metaphorical attribution, the subsidiary subject is modified just as much as the principal subject to which it is being applied. To do justice to the way the use of metaphor disrupts the very order of connotations, Beardsley comes to claim that 'the metaphor transforms a *property* (actual or attributed) into a *sense*' (302). In other words, metaphor 'would not only actualize a potential connotation, but establish it as a staple one' (302).

This modification is very important. Beardsley is here expounding a 'Verbal-opposition Theory' of metaphor, which, as against the 'Object-comparison Theory,' foreswears all resources except those of language itself. Here we find 'properties' spoken of as seeking to be designated, 'properties' receiving, through the metaphorical attribution itself, new status as moments of verbal meaning. When a poet writes for the first time that 'virginity is a life of angels, the enamel of the soul,'[41] something develops in the language. There accrue to the language various properties of enamel that until then had never been clearly established as recognized connotations of the word: 'Thus this metaphor does not merely thrust latent connotations into the foreground of meaning, but brings into play some properties that were not previously meant by it' (303). And so, as the author recognizes, the object-comparison theory does have a role to play: it establishes that some 'properties are eligible to become part of the intention' of the word; 'what was previously only a property is made, at least temporarily, into a *meaning*' (ibid. my emphasis).

Thus, Beardsley's theory of metaphor takes us a step further in the investigation of the new metaphor. But it too in turn is caught short by the question that asks where the secondary meanings in metaphorical attribution come from. Perhaps the question itself ('From where do we get ...?') is wrong-headed. In this connection, the 'potential range of connotations' says nothing more than the 'system of associated commonplaces.' Of course, we enlarge the notion of meaning by including secondary meanings as connotations within the perimeter of the entire meaning; but we have not stopped relating the creative process of metaphor to a non-creative aspect of language. Is it sufficient to add the range of properties that are not yet part of the range of connotations of our language to this potential range of connotations, as Beardsley does in his 'revised theory of controversion'? At first glance this addition improves the theory; but to speak of still unsignified properties of things or objects is to admit that the new, emerging meaning is not taken from anywhere, at least not from anywhere within language (since 'property' belongs to the sphere of things, not of words). To say that a new metaphor is not taken from anywhere is to recognize it for what it is, namely, a creation of language that comes to be at that moment, a *semantic innovation* without status in the language as something already established with respect to either designation or connotation.

Now this statement is hard to accept. Indeed, one could ask how we can speak here of *semantic innovation*, or *semantic event*, as something that can be identified and reidentified. And was this not the first criterion of discourse, according to the model laid out at the beginning of this Study? Only one line of defence remains open: one must adopt the point of view of the hearer or reader and treat the novelty of an emerging meaning as his work within the very act of hearing or reading. If we do not take this route, we do not really get rid of the theory of substitution. Instead of substituting (as does classical rhetoric) a literal meaning, restored by paraphrase, for the metaphorical expression, we would be substituting (with Black and Beardsley) the systems of connotations and commonplaces. I would rather say that metaphorical attribution is essentially the construction of the network of interactions that causes a certain context to be one that is real and unique. Accordingly, metaphor is a semantic event that takes place at the point where several semantic fields intersect. It is because of this construction that all the words, taken together, make sense.

Then, and only then, the metaphorical *twist* is at once an event *and* a meaning, an event that means or signifies, an emergent meaning created by language.

Only a truly semantic theory that pushes the analysis of Richards, Black, and Beardsley to their limits satisfies the principal features of discourse noted at the beginning of this Study. Let us return once more to the first contrasting pair, event and meaning. In the metaphorical statement (we will not speak any longer of metaphor as word, but of metaphor as statement), the contextual action creates a new meaning, which truly has the status of event since it exists only in the present context. At the same time, however, it can be reidentified as the same, since its construction can be repeated. In this way, the innovation of an emergent meaning can be taken as a linguistic creation. And if it is adopted by a significant part of the linguistic community, it in turn can become a common meaning and add to the polysemy of lexical entities, thus contributing to the history of the language as code or system. But at this final stage, where the meaning-effect we call metaphor has become this shift of meaning that increases polysemy, the metaphor is then no longer living, but a dead metaphor. Only authentic metaphors, that is, living metaphors, are at once meaning and event.

In the same way, contextual action calls for our second polarity, between singular identification and general predication. A metaphor distinguishes some principal subject and, as modifier of this subject, operates like a sort of attribution. All the theories to which I referred earlier rest on this predicative structure, whether they oppose 'vehicle' to 'tenor,' 'focus' to 'frame,' or 'modifier' to 'principal subject.'

We began to spell out the necessity of the sense-reference polarity for metaphor in presenting the theory of Monroe Beardsley; yet we deliberately attended to a theory of meaning where the question of reference is bracketed. But this abstraction is only provisional. What use would we have for a language that satisfies the two principles of congruence and plenitude, if metaphor did not enable us 'to describe, to fix and preserve, the subleties of experience and change ... while words in their standard dictionary designations can only cope with

The weight of primary noon,
The ABC of being,
The ruddy temper, the hammer
Of red and blue ...'

according to Wallace Stevens' magnificent expression in his poem 'The Motive for Metaphor.'[42]

But the question of the reference of poetic discourse would take us from semantics into hermeneutics, which will be the theme of the seventh Study. We are not yet finished with the duality of rhetoric and semantics.

Metaphor and the semantics of the word

For Émile Benveniste

This Study has two objectives. One purpose is to portray the theoretical and empirical background that forms the point of departure for those works which the next Study groups under the name of New Rhetoric. The other purpose is to set in perspective – and eventually to set aside – certain concepts and certain descriptions of the semantics of the word that are not integrated entirely into the later works, which have a more deliberately formalistic character. On the other hand, they are more compatible with the concepts and descriptions of the semantics of the sentence set out in the third Study than is the conceptual apparatus of the New Rhetoric. This second project will come into its own only gradually, and will be clarified only in the last section, which will try to put to effective use the connection between semantics of the word and semantics of the sentence.

1 / MONISM OF THE SIGN AND PRIMACY OF THE WORD

What motivates this retrospective glance over more than a century's history of semantics is the astonishment we experience when we compare the most recent works on metaphor coming out of the semantics of the linguists – especially those in French, which will be discussed in Study 5 – with the works, principally English ones, explored in the preceding Study. In the former one finds highly technical analyses, and this sets them apart; but their fundamental hypothesis is exactly the same as that of classical rhetoric, namely, that metaphor is a figure of one word only. This is why the science of deviations and their reductions creates no shock in the rhetorical tradition comparable to that produced by the theory of metaphor presented above. It just makes the theory of metaphor as substitution one degree more scientific, and above all, what is more important, it strives to enclose this theory within a general science of deviations and the reductions of deviations. But here metaphor remains what it was, a one-word trope. Substitution, its distinguishing characteristic, has become just a particular case of a more general concept, that of deviation and reduction of deviation.

This permanence of the thesis of the word-metaphor and this fidelity of neo-rhetoric to the theory of substitution are less astonishing once one considers the difference in historical contexts. The analysis typical of English-language authors owes so much less to linguistics as practised by linguists – which it imperially ignores often enough – than to logic or, more precisely, to propositional logic, which focuses immediately on the sentence as the point of interest, and spontaneously suggests that metaphor be considered within the framework of predication. In opposition to this, the new rhetoric grows out of the groundwork of a linguistics that tended in several ways to reinforce the link between metaphor and word and (as a corollary) to consolidate the substitution thesis.

The new rhetoric inherits a conception of language that gradually became more entrenched during the course of half a century, due principally to the influence of the *Cours de linguistique générale* by Ferdinand de Saussure. According to this work, the fundamental units that characterize various levels of organization in language are homogeneous, and they all come under a single science, the science of signs or semiotics. This fundamental orientation towards a semiotic monism is the most decisive reason for the divergence in the explanation of metaphor. We observed that the most important analyses of metaphor in the English-language school show a strong kinship with a theory of language like that of Émile Benveniste, who sees language as resting on *two* kinds of units – those of discourse or 'sentences,' and 'signs,' the units of language [*langue*]. Structural semantics, on the other hand, developed progressively on the postulate of the homogeneity of all the units of language, in so far as they are 'signs.' This difference at the level of basic postulates becomes a divorce at the level of metaphor-theories. Furthermore, the examination of ancient and classical rhetoric had already demonstrated the link between the substitution theory of metaphor and a conception of language whose fundamental unit is the word. This primacy of the word, however, was not based upon an explicit science of signs, but on the correlation between word and idea. Since de Saussure, modern semantics is in a position to provide a new foundation for the same description of tropes, because it has at its disposal a new concept of the fundamental linguistic entity, the sign. Godel's publication of the manuscripts of the *Cours de lingistique générale* shows this truly to have been the overriding preoccupation of the master of modern semantics: to identify, to define, to demarcate the fundamental linguistic unit, the sign.[1]

With de Saussure, semiotic monism still had its limits and various challengers. After him, it continually became more radical.

This explains why the opposition at the level of metaphor, between a substitution theory and an interaction theory, reflects the deeper opposition at the level of basic linguistic postulates between a semiotic monism (which rules the semantics of the word and of the sentence) and a dualism of semiotics and semantics, where the semantics of the sentence is built on principles distinct from all operations with respect to signs.

Now, whereas this general orientation became explicit and exclusive only in the most recent phase of the development of structural linguistics, a second motivation must be mentioned, which was in full force right from the beginning of the history of semantics. Since the beginning – in fact, since the time of Bréal and Darmesteter – semantics understands itself to be the science of the meaning [*signification*] of words and of changes in the meaning of words.[2] The pact between semantics and the word is so strong that no one would dream of placing metaphor in any framework other than that of changes of meaning applied to words.

I call this a second motivation because later the theory of the sign will absorb that of the word. But this is a distinct motivation in that it precedes the Saussurean definition of the sign and even, to a great extent, governs it; indeed, the Saussurean sign is *par excellence* a word. For de Saussure, phonetics is as yet nothing but an accessory science, and its distinctive units do not yet have the dignity of the sign. A dominating, extremely rigid framework, which very sharply delimits a thematic field, is thus set in place. It forces metaphor to be placed within the conceptual network that the Swedish linguist Gustaf Stern characterizes very well with his title *Meaning and Change of Meaning*. The semantic fields theory of Josef Trier[3] confirms that the Saussurean conception of a synchronic and structural linguistics, for which all the elements of language are independent and take their meaning from the entire system considered as a whole, finds its application principally in the study of vocabulary.

If we bring together these two major tendencies – monism of the sign, primacy of the word – it appears that the *Cours de linguistique générale* constitutes not just a rupture but also a stage within a discipline whose contours had already been sketched before de Saussure, and whose fundamentally lexical preoccupations it reinforces. As we will discuss at greater length later, de Saussure introduces a methodological crisis into a discipline whose definition precedes and survives him. This crisis takes place within the context of the word. The great dichotomies that dominate the *Cours* focus exclusively on the word: dichotomies of signifier and signified, synchronic and diachronic, form and substance. Not that it ignores the sentence: the very first dichotomy, between language and speech, involves the message, which can only be a sentence. But this is the last mention of speech, and linguistics becomes a linguistics of language, that is, of its lexical system.[4] This is why the *Cours* tends ultimately to identify general semantics with lexical semantics. This identification is so strong that for most authors influenced by de Saussure the very expression 'lexical semantics' is a pleonasm.

The level of the word is not just the intermediary level between those of the phoneme and syntagma; it is the connecting layer. From one side the first-level distinctive units presuppose the significant units of the lexical level: the test of commutation cannot be used if a phonematic change does not lead to a change in the meaning of a word, even if the question has to do only with whether this word exists or not, and not with what it signifies. In this sense phonology is semantically conditioned. But the situation is the same with the syntagma: the relational units on which it rests presuppose as terms the signifying units of the mediating level.

Such is the primacy of the word in the structure of language units for a semantics of Saussurean inspiration. Strictly speaking, it is true that semantics and lexicology do not coincide. For one thing, the word responds to two disciplines, for its form and for meaning (so lexical semantics contrasts with a lexical morphology – composition, derivation, fusion, suffixation, etc.). At the same time, syntax itself also presents a morphology and a semantics (the study of functions corresponding to syntactic forms, as far as meaning is concerned).[5] All the more astonishing, then, is the decision that the adjective-turned-substantive, '*the* semantics,' should be called on to designate, through abbreviation, lexical semantics alone, that is the theory of the meaning of words. As for metaphor, it remains classed among the changes of meaning. It will be recalled that this was the place assigned it by Aristotle when he defined metaphor as *epiphora of the name*. Thus the most explicit aspect of the Aristotelian definition is taken up by the 'semantics of the word.'

2 / LOGIC AND LINGUISTICS OF DENOMINATION

Before considering the theories of metaphor that base the primacy of the word-metaphor on a purely *linguistic* analysis of the notions of signification and change of meaning, I would like to dwell on a French-language work which 'for more than twenty years,' according to a recent author, 'has justly been considered to be the best on the subject,'[6] namely, the study of metaphor by Hedwig Konrad.[7] Her description of metaphor considered as a modality of denomination is based on logico-linguistic considerations – this is Le Guern's expression, not the author's – rather than on linguistics properly speaking. Besides the considerable attraction of its many detailed analyses,[8] the work interests us because of the reinforcement that logic gives linguistics towards consolidating the primacy of the word and containing the theory of metaphor within the boundaries of denomination. This suggests a question for later: whether a componential analysis coming from the work of Pottier and Greimas (and serving as the foundation for works that we will study further on)[9] will succeed in freeing itself entirely from a logical theory and in clearly distinguishing the semic composition of words from the conceptual structure of their referents. In this sense, although it predates the current technical apparatus, this work has not aged at all. In fact, it anticipates real difficulties in contemporary semic analysis. But it is examined at this stage of our investigation not because of these factors, but in view of the primacy of denomination in its treatment of metaphor.

The author attaches her conception of the word and of metaphorical denomination to a theory of the concept and of the relationship between *linguistic* signification and the *logical* concept. This theory of concepts, which sees itself as a development of Cassirer and Bühler, is very original in many respects; and this originality extends to the explication of metaphor.

The author begins with a polemic against every conception that would oppose the vagueness of significations to the precision of the concept. Such conceptions sweep away the whole foundation of the difference between proper and figurative meaning and (as we will see later) of the difference that affects the operation of abstraction in both these cases. With a daring akin to Husserl's in the *Logical Investigations*, Konrad maintains that 'the normal value of the signification is equal to that of the concept' (49). But the concept does not have to be taken as a generality whose function would be to gather in a class (and thus to classify) some sensible objects; its function is to distinguish, to delimit, by assigning an order, a structure, to the object of reference. The prime function of the concept is to recognize the individual nature of the object, not to constitute general attributes.[10] This function is particularly suited to grounding the use of the substantive in language, prior to qualities or actions being brought to it by means of adjectives and verbs. It is of utmost importance to the theory of metaphor that the detection of structure by comparison with the context of objects precede the enumeration of species and the search for extension. The problems of classification are thus neatly subordinated to problems of structure. It is no less important that the role of the dominant trait or of the principal attribute itself be subordinated to the act of delimitation and systematic ordering of traits. The concept is thus nothing but the symbol at this fundamental level, that is, a system of relationships that relate the elements of a particular object.

A definition of *conceptual* abstraction (to which *metaphorical* abstraction will be opposed) can thus be given: conceptual abstraction is nothing but the illumination or setting-out of this complex of elements that the concept symbolizes. Partly because of the contrast with metaphorical abstraction, it is important to add that this conceptual abstraction does not consist in forgetting, ignoring, or eliminating the secondary attributes; it is a rule for completing and for differentiating structure (thus the concept of metal contains the representation of various possible colours).

These are the broad outlines of the theory of concept that underlies that of denomination. It has great advantages to offer for a *logico-linguistic* theory of metaphor.

First of all, a distinctive criterion of change of meaning is provided: metaphor 'does not take part in the normal use of the word' (80). But the price of this first advantage is high: it can be asked whether the specific problems of lexical semantics, especially that of polysemy, have not indeed been dismissed in favour of a logical theory of concept. This is something that Cassirer did not do, even if he teleologically related 'language' (the topic of the first volume of his *Philosophy of Symbolic Forms*) to conceptual thought (the subject of volume 3). What with Cassirer was still just teleological subordination of signification to concept becomes identification of the two.[11]

The second benefit, which will also have its negative side, is that the problem of metaphor is attached to that of the *delimitation* of objects. Both Bühler and Cassirer, and Geoffrey de Vinsauf[12] before them, saw that the problem of abstraction is indeed the central problem of metaphorical denomination.

Thus, changes of metaphorical meaning are not banished to psychology and sociology, as in the works of Wundt and Winkler, which place metaphor among individual transpositions of meaning, which, consequently, are willed and arbitrary transpositions. Rather, changes of metaphorical meaning are treated linguistically, which here means logico-linguistically. That these changes are involuntary and unconscious confirms that they obey universal laws of structure and proceed from a 'tendency' in language itself. In this regard, we are indebted to the author for her energetic and extensive subordination of other tendencies (irony, euphemism, ennoblement, disparagement) and other psycho-social factors (association, cultural influence) to the 'tendencies of denomination' (116) that come under the jurisdiction of the logico-linguistic method.

Metaphorical denomination (which is here called 'linguistic metaphor' to distinguish it from the 'aesthetic metaphor' that will be discussed later on) is based on a different abstractive procedure. It does not consist in perceiving the order of a structure, but in 'forgetting,' in eliminating – really, in 'making us abstract from' – several attributes that the metaphorized term evokes in us in its normal usage. Accordingly, to call a line of people a 'queue' [literally 'tail' in French] is to neglect all its conceptual traits except its length; to say 'The roses in these cheeks have paled' is to forget many attributes present in 'This rose is fresh.' This theory of metaphorical abstraction anticipates the contemporary theories (to be examined in Study 5) that attempt to explain metaphor as an alteration in the semic composition of a lexeme, and more particularly, as a semic *reduction*.

But Konrad has observed rightly that abstraction is simply a foundational mechanism. Three other factors must still be added. First of all, through abstraction, the word loses its reference to an individual object and again takes on a *general* value; this sets metaphorical abstraction on a course opposite to that of the concept, since the latter, as we have seen, aims at designating an individual object. One can speak in this sense of metaphorical generalization. Hence, more than any other substantive, the metaphorized substantive resembles the name of an attribute. Nevertheless, the metaphorical term does not become the symbol of a logical 'species,' because (and this is the second added trait) 'it has become the name of the carrier of a general attribute and thus can apply to all objects that possess the general quality expressed' (88). Generalization is thus balanced by a concretization. Consequently, the transposed term is the one that appears to be most suited to the attribute in question, or in other words, the representative of a dominant attribute (which can vary among cultures and individuals as regards its content of meaning).[13] In this fashion the substantive function is preserved, the general aspect being designated by its representative: 'The metaphorical term designates the new object totally, with its whole structure, just as formerly it designated the object that alone was involved when it first became extended' (89). But this is still not all: metaphor acts as a sort of *classification*, as it were. It is precisely here that resemblance comes in. In effect, the common attribute, issuing from the abstraction, is the foundation for the similitude between the transposed meaning and the proper meaning. Accordingly, 'the two terms of a metaphor behave like two species joined by the representation of a genus' (91).[14]

But metaphorical classification itself also has differential traits that locate it midway between logical classification based on a conceptual structure and classification based on isolated features like that which Cassirer still attributes to 'primitives' at the end of volume 1 of *The Philosophy of Symbolic Forms*, and which Durkheim and Mauss also describe in their study *Primitive Classification*.[15] Metaphorical classification is distinguished from the classification ascribed to primitive peoples by the role of abstraction, which established a generic scope entirely absent from classification based on isolated features. Rather, metaphorical classification manifests the intersecting of the two other classifications, that based on structure (the logical) and that based on isolated features.

A conception that connects the functioning of resemblance to the three other traits of abstraction, generalization, and concretization is evidently a particularly full one. The whole of this conception is summed up in the following definition: 'Metaphor names an object with the help of the most typical representative of one of its attributes' (106).

The counterpart of this logico-linguistic treatment of metaphorical denomination is the disjunction that results between *linguistic* and *aesthetic* metaphor, the latter being the stylistic effect of metaphor. Only some of the functions of aesthetic metaphor correspond to those of linguistic metaphor (creating new words, making up for poverty of vocabulary). Aesthetic metaphor is essentially different. Its aim is to create illusion, principally by presenting the world in a new light. Now, to a great extent this effect puts into play an entire operation of unusual relationships, of connections between objects governed by a personal point of view – in brief, a creation of relationships.[16] The author claims that 'it is not just the grammatical relationship that functions here; a second relationship is evoked with the help of identical domains to which all these objects belong' (137). What arises here is the ontological dimension (which will be the object of Study 7). Illusion itself as 'quasi-reality' has this ontological dimension. Let us say for the moment that it is difficult to co-ordinate this aim with a simple process of denomination, and more so even with a process of unusual attributions.

Thus this work, which is so powerfully synthetic, ends up splitting the field of metaphor into a denominative function, hence one of delimitation (147), and an aesthetic function that only emphasizes a trait of an object in order to give 'a new impression' of the object (147). The abstraction at work in the one and the other is insufficient to preserve their unity.

This first doubt, raised by the opposition between linguistic and aesthetic metaphor, should make us question seriously the way the author has marshalled the facts. Is denomination truly the pivot of the problem of metaphor?

Even within the logico-linguistic viewpoint the author has assumed, the case of the metaphor-adjective and that of the metaphor-verb pose interesting problems which shatter the strict framework of denomination. Konrad again refers explicitly to Geoffroy de Vinsauf (17-18), whom she acknowledges for having taken into consideration the metaphor-adjective or metaphor-verb in conjunction with the substantive (*Dormit mare, nudus amicis*). Following his lead, she proposes (49) to fill the gap that she detects in her predecessors. In particular she corrects Meillet, who brought the adjective too close to the substantive, whereas it ought to be assimilated to the verb. They are both, in effect, functions of the substantive, which alone independently designates an object. Besides, they do not involve any complexity of elements: certainly they admit of species (which moreover are themselves nothing but attributes and actions) (69-71), but these are dependent terms and simple terms. It follows that the adjective and the verb cannot support the same abstraction as can the substantive: 'Abstraction here means forgetting the relationship between the adjective or verb and a defined substantive' (89). But – taking full account of the logical simplicity of adjectives and verbs – is this not a notable case of *application* of a predicate, a case of interaction?

The problem of interaction arises once the question of resemblance is introduced and, in its wake, that of classification. The sub-title itself is revealing: 'Metaphorical joining as classification' (91). Suddenly it is decided that one needs 'two coupled significations in one metaphor' (91), that 'two species [are there] joined by the representation of a genus' (91). Resemblance operates precisely here between these 'coupled significations,' these 'joined species.' The author is so careful to formulate her description within the framework of denomination that she has not noticed the predicative character of the operation. The result of the operation, which is simply an act of classification, is in effect a new way of naming. But is this not an equivocation on 'to name or denominate [*dénommer*]'? When one says that metaphor names an object with the help of the most typical representative of its attributes, 'to name' can sometimes mean giving a new name, and sometimes it can mean giving X the name of Y.[17] The act of naming has the second of these meanings when the author says that 'the metaphorical term *indicates the group of objects under which another object is to be subsumed, due to a characteristic trait that belongs to it*' (107). Here classification is no longer absorbed into denomination, but is linked to predication.

This implicit role of predication is attested to by the two facts of language that the author classes in the 'family of metaphor' (149), namely, comparison and subordination.

The author grants that simile and metaphor share a perception of otherness [*altérité*] : 'In both cases we see an object compared to another, not on the basis of a simple resemblance, but because this other appears to represent *par excellence* the base of comparison concerned' (149). The difference, then, is not that the one is one word long and the other needs two words. The difference lies rather in the fact that, as Le Guern strongly emphasizes, bringing two concepts together in simile does not destroy their duality, whereas it is destroyed in metaphor (or more exactly, in metaphor *in absentia*); so the correlation is not as close as in metaphor, where the transposed term replaces the proper term (150, note 1).[18]

Does this not indicate that the duality (and the tension, as we shall say later) between the terms is more evident in metaphor *in praesentia* than in metaphor *in absentia*, where substitution hides the correlation from view?

Indeed, it is the metaphor *in praesentia* that is in question under the term of 'substitution' (the form with 'is,' for example, 'The tree *is* a king') (150). Konrad agrees that this is 'the most frequent form of metaphor' (ibid.). In this case as well, a term is not *replaced* but 'expressed in the sentence and *subordinated* to the metaphorical term' (ibid.). In this functioning the author sees only the confirmation of the *generic* value resulting from metaphorical abstraction, the common foundation of subordination as species and of complete replacement of one term by another. She does not draw any conclusion from it concerning the predicative operation at work in subordination. Is it to be understood that subordination is an imperfect form of substitution? But then sentence order is being confused with an operation affecting signs.

Finally – and this is perhaps the most serious objection that can be addressed to a logico-linguistic theory of metaphorical denomination – it can be asked whether an explication centred entirely on denomination can distinguish between living and worn-out [*usée*] metaphor. Outside of examples borrowed from poets, which illustrate aesthetic metaphor alone, all the examples involve metaphorical usage in a state of advanced *lexicalization*. Further, the theory clarifies above all the phenomenon of lexicalization of metaphor, its power to enrich our vocabulary by adding to polysemy (which the theory does not take into account). This process hides another, that of metaphorical production.

3 / METAPHOR AS 'CHANGE OF MEANING'

Because of its *logico-linguistic* character, the work of Hedwig Konrad has remained in many ways without successor. The unity of its perspective succumbed to the pressure of the postulates of Saussurean semantics, which no longer looked to the concept (henceforth considered to be extra-linguistic) for the measure of verbal meaning. But if the divorce between the semantics of the linguists and that of the logicians took place quite easily,[19] the dissociation of semantics from psychology has been much longer in taking hold.[20]

We will now locate our inquiry at a stage where semantics has not yet managed to dissociate itself from psychology; a stage where it is not the concept, in the German sense of *Begriffsbildung*, but association of ideas that provides semantics with a support of external origin.

I have chosen to take the semantics of Stephen Ullmann in its three successive versions[21] as principal witness, and a few related works as accessory evidence (Stern,[22] Nyrop[23]). There are many reasons for doing so. The general theses of semantics are supported here by a keen sense of empirical description, principally of the French language. Further, the long history of semantics since Bréal, Marty, and Wundt is not forgotten, although the Saussurean revolution provides the main axis of the description; but the linguistics of Bloomfield, of Harris, and of Osgood[24] are also taken into account. Finally, the most recent development of structuralism is looked at, without either hostility or over-enthusiasm. We look accordingly with special curiosity into the place and the role that might be assigned to metaphor in this firmly built as well as accommodating framework.

Metaphor is counted among the 'changes of meaning,' and thus figures in the 'historical' part of a treatise whose central axis is provided by the synchronistic constitution of states of language. Accordingly, metaphor brings into play the ability of synchronistic linguistics to take phenomena of meaning change into account. Our discussion of Ullmann's thought will accordingly be organized with reference to this specific problem.

The first thesis concerns the choice of the word as carrier of meaning. Of the four basic units within the purview of linguistics – phoneme, morpheme, word, locution (sentence) – it is the word that defined the lexical level of linguistics; and, at this level, semantics properly speaking is distinct from morphology in the way that meaning is from form.

This first thesis is not adopted without nuance or reservation. The definition of word according to Meillet, 'association of a given meaning with a given combination of sounds amenable to a given grammatical use,'[25] is taken rather as a concentration of all the accumulated difficulties surrounding the problem of the word. We will refer to some of them in section 4, especially those that concern the relationship between word meaning and sentence meaning. Diverse classical definitions of the word[26] testify that the separation of the word from the orbit of the sentence, at the very level of the identification of the word, is not accomplished without difficulty. The semanticist is always absolutely against any reduction of the meanings of words to their purely contextual values. For him the thesis that the word owes its semantic existence entirely to context is anti-semantic in principle. A lexical semantics is possible because the meaning of an isolated word can be understood (for example the title of a book – *La Peste, If, Nothing*); because one can learn the names of things and give their equivalents in another language; because dictionaries can be constructed; because a culture tends to understand itself by crystallizing its convictions in keywords (the 'honest man' of the seventeenth century).[27] It must be conceded, then, that whatever the importance of the various contexts (sentence, text, culture, situation, etc.), words have a permanent meaning by which they designate some referents and not others. It is the semanticist who contends that words have a hard core that contexts do not modify.

On the other hand, while it is possible to carry out the abstraction with respect to the word-sentence relationship in order to restrict study to individual isolated words as semantics demands, the problems attached to identifying the word prove to be considerable. Just the phonological demarcation of the word, that is, the steps taken by language to preserve the unity of the word at this level (Troubetzkoy's *Grenzsignale*), presents a wealth of problems that will not be explored here.[28] Similarly, it is very difficult to pinpoint the semantic core and the grammatical function that says what part of speech a word is (noun, verb, adjective, etc.), when, for example, the role of the word as part of speech is incorporated into its semantic core within the boundaries of the word as a lexical item. To this is added the problem of words that have meaning only in combination with other words (the 'asemic' words of the Greeks, the 'syncategorematics' of Marty, here called 'form-words'), as opposed to words that have meaning by themselves ('semic' words, the 'categorematics,' 'full words'). The semanticist evidently must hack his way through a forest of difficulties towards what he takes to be the word's unity of meaning, that is, the very object of his science.

The second thesis that such a semantics involves concerns the very status of meaning. Here Ullmann's position is deliberately Saussurean, except for two additions.

Following de Saussure, the third corner of the well-known triangle of Ogden and Richards[29] (symbol, thought or reference, referent or thing) is abandoned, and one stays within the boundaries of a two-sided phenomenon: signifier-signified (de Saussure), expression-content (Hjelmslev), name-sense (Gombocz).[30] Ullmann adopts the last-mentioned terminology, accentuating at the same time the phenomenon of naming. This is not unimportant for the later theory of changes of meaning, which, by prior rights, will be name-changes. The meaning of a word is the double unity of the name and the sense. In order to give the reciprocity of positions of speaker and hearer its due, the reciprocity and reversibility of the name-sense relation will be included within the definition of meaning. Meaning, then, will be defined as a 'reciprocal and reversible relationship between the name and the sense' (*Semantics* 67). It is because this two-fold access to the texture of the word is possible that both alphabetical and conceptual dictionaries can be compiled.

Ullmann makes two important additions to this nuclear thesis. First of all, except for the case of the highly codified vocabularies of science, technology, and administration, the name-sense relation is rarely a term-to-term relation, a name for a sense. Several names can correspond to one sense, the condition called synonymy; there can be several senses for one name, i.e. homonymy (although homonyms are really distinct words and not multiple senses of one and the same word); and above all, as we shall see later, there is the situation of polysemy.

Next, an 'associative field' must be added to every name as well as to every sense. This brings relationships of contiguity and resemblance into play, either in the sphere of the name, or in the sphere of the sense, or in both at once. This extension will allow us presently to distinguish four kinds of changes of meaning and to locate metaphor among them.

Such, then, is 'the infinite complexity of semantic relations' (*Semantics* 63). And this complexity will appear even greater if the 'emotive overtones' of words are added to what to this point is just a denotative value – that is, their expressive values with regard to the feelings and moods of the speaker, and at the same time the power of words to arouse the same states or processes in the hearer. A theory of meaning changes and especially of metaphor will not abandon contact with this emotive function, especially as metaphor could be one of the 'lexical devices' with regard to it (*Semantics* 136).

The third thesis that we extract from the semantics of Stephen Ullmann concerns the characteristics of meaning. These are accessible to a 'descriptive' linguistics, which the author always opposes to 'historical' linguistics; they can be retained within 'historical' linguistics under the heading of causes of change.

At the centre of all the descriptions and all the discussions reigns the key phenomenon of the entire semantics of the word, the phenomenon of *polysemy*; and the three works of Ullmann that we are considering abound with very emphatic statements on this point.[31] Polysemy is defined on the previously established base of the name-sense relation; it signifies that there is more than one sense for one name. The study of polysemy, however, is preceded by a more general commentary that includes it, and to which we will return in the next section. It speaks of a very general characteristic of language, called *vagueness* by Ullmann, which indicates the slight degree to which the lexical organization of a language is systematic. Vagueness is to be understood not exactly as that abstraction which is itself a phenomenon of order, a taxonomic feature, but in the 'generic' sense, that of not ordered, indefinite, and imprecise, which always demands that a further discrimination be made on the basis of actual context. We will return as well to this connection between vagueness and contextual discrimination. Let us say for the time being that most words in our ordinary language answer sooner to this feature, which Wittgenstein calls 'family resemblance,'[32] than to an implicit taxonomy within the lexicon itself. Polysemy is just an already more ordered and a more determinate characteristic of the more general phenomenon of lexical imprecision.

Another phenomenon comes into the understanding of polysemy, since it is its opposite. This is the phenomenon of synonymy, which is also of interest to a general reflection on the systematic and non-systematic features of language. It implies a partial semantic identity, which would be inadmissible in a system based only on oppositions; it points to overlapping of semantic fields, with the result that an acceptation of one word is synonymous with an acceptation of another word. The image of paving tiles or of a mosaic is deceptive in this regard: words are not just distinct from one another, that is, defined only by their opposition to other words, as are phonemes in a phonological system; they also trespass on one another. Certainly the art of speaking consists in distinguishing synonyms while applying them discriminatingly in appropriate contexts; but such contextual discrimination presupposes just this phenomenon of synonymy, as a descriptive trait of natural languages. To take the other side of the coin, so to speak, there would be no question of looking for the contexts in which synonyms are not interchangeable, if there were not contexts in which they are interchangeable. What defines synonymy is precisely the possibility of substituting words in given contexts without altering the objective and affective meaning. Inversely, the irreducible character of the phenomenon of synonymy is confirmed by the possibility of providing synonyms for the various acceptations of a single word (this is the commutative test of polysemy itself): the word *review* is the synonym sometimes of 'parade,' sometimes of 'magazine.' In every case a community of meaning is at the bottom of synonymy. Because it is an irreducible phenomenon, synonymy can play two roles at once: offering a stylistic resource for fine distinctions (*peak* instead of *summit, minuscule* for *minute*, etc.), and indeed for emphasis, for reinforcement, for piling-on, as in the mannerist style of Péguy; and providing a test of commutativity for polysemy. Identity and difference can be accentuated in turn in the notion of partial semantic identity.

So polysemy is defined initially as the inverse of synonymy, as Bréal was the first to observe: now not several names for one sense (synonymy), but several senses for one name (polysemy).

The case of homonymy must be set apart. Certainly homonymy and polysemy rest on the same principle of the combination of a single signifier with more than one signified (*Précis* 218). But while homonymy applies to a difference between two words and between their entire semantic fields, polysemy takes place within a single word whose several acceptations it distinguishes. Actually, although the boundary is easy to trace when homonyms by etymology are at issue (for example *locare* and *laudare* both give *louer* [laud]), it is more difficult to see in the case of semantic homonyms. These are explained in terms of the divergent evolution of senses of a single word beyond a point at which no community of meaning is to be perceived any longer, as in the case of the word *pupil*. Truly, notes Ullmann, 'there are border-crossings in both directions between polysemy and homonymy' (*Précis* 222).

The central phenomenon of descriptive semantics is polysemy (here also called lexical ambiguity, in order to distinguish it from grammatical ambiguity or amphibology). The theory of changes of meaning in historical semantics will deal essentially with the description of polysemy. This phenomenon signifies that in natural languages the identity of a word in relation to other words at the same time allows an internal heterogeneity, a plurality, such that the same word can be given different acceptations according to its contexts. This heterogeneity does not destroy the identity of the word (as does homonymy) because (1) these meanings can be listed, that is, identified by synonymy; (2) they can be classified, that is, referred to classes of contextual use; (3) they can be ordered, that is, they can present a certain hierarchy that establishes a relative proximity and thus a relative distance of the most peripheral meanings in relation to the most central meanings; (4) finally and above all, the linguistic consciousness of speakers continues to perceive a certain identity of meaning in the plurality of acceptations. For all these reasons, polysemy is not just a case of vagueness but the outline of an order and, for that very reason, a counter-measure to imprecision.

That polysemy is not a pathological phenomenon but a healthy feature of our language is shown by the failure of the opposite hypothesis. A language without polysemy would violate the principle of economy, for it would extend its vocabulary infinitely. Furthermore, it would violate the rule of communication, because it would multiply its designations as often as, in principle, the diversity of human experience and the plurality of subjects of experience demanded. We need a lexical system that is economical, flexible, and sensitive to context, in order to express the spectrum of human experience. It is the task of contexts to sift the variations of appropriate meanings and, with the help of polysemic words to devise discourse that is seen as relatively univocal – that is, giving rise to just one interpretation, that which the speaker intended to bestow on his words.[33]

On this foundation of 'descriptive' semantics (synchronistic in the Saussurean sense), Ullmann plants his study of changes of meaning, of which metaphor is one species.

Being placed among changes of meaning, metaphor accordingly is part not of 'descriptive' but of 'historical' semantics.[34] Thus a methodological line is being crossed, one which the *Cours de linguistique générale* had etched firmly between two points of view too often confused in the past. Semantic constitution and semantic change belong to 'two orders of facts ... disparate even while interdependent' (*Précis* 236). Ullmann remains faithful to de Saussure when he writes: 'One can surely *combine* the two points of view – one even has to in certain situations, for example in the integral reconstitution of a homonymic collision; but the combination must never result in a *confusion*. To forget this precept would be to falsify at once the present and the past, description and history' (ibid.). Even more, by putting his study of changes of meaning at the end of his works, the author asserts his distance from the first semanticists, who not only defined semantics in the same breath as the study of the meaning of words and as the study of their changes, but put the principal accent on these changes. The opposite holds true for structural semantics, where it is the descriptive point of view that provides the guiding thread in the study of changes.

It is true that, as such, changes of meaning are innovations, and so phenomena of speech. Most often these innovations are individual and even intentional; unlike phonetic changes, which in general are hardly conscious, 'semantic modifications are often the work of a creative intention' (*Précis* 238). Furthermore, the blossoming of new meaning is sudden, without intermediate gradations: 'What intermediate stage can there be between a man's throat [*gorge*] and a mountain gorge [*gorge*] ?' (*Précis* 239). Like Minerva springing forth from Jupiter's head, metaphor issues wholly formed from an 'act of immediate apperception' (ibid.). Possibly its social diffusion will be slow; the innovation itself is always sudden.

But while changes of meaning are always innovations, the foundation of the explication of innovations lies in the descriptive point of view.

First of all, what allows changes of meaning is the nature of the lexical system, namely the 'vague' character of meaning, the indeterminacy of semantic boundaries, and, above all, the cumulative character proper to the meanings of words (a feature of polysemy that we have not yet highlighted). Indeed, it is not enough that a word should have several acceptations at a given moment in a state of a system, that is, variants belonging to several contextual classes. It should also be able to acquire a new meaning without losing its earlier meaning. This cumulative capability[35] is essential for understanding metaphor, in that it possesses the character of double or stereoscopic vision described in an earlier Study. More than anything else, this cumulative character of the word opens language to innovation. We will return later to the implications of this notion of meaning-accumulation for a discussion of Saussurean postulates. Let us now establish just one key characteristic: polysemy, the descriptive fact *par excellence*,

makes change of meaning possible; and within polysemy, it is the phenomenon of accumulation of meaning that does this. Polysemy attests to the
quality of openness in the texture of the word: a word is that which has
several meanings and can acquire more. Thus it is a descriptive trait of
meaning that leads into the theory of change of meaning – namely, that
there can be more than one sense for a name and more than one name for
one sense.

The theory of changes of meaning receives a new application in a 'descriptive' trait presented above, the union of each 'sense' and each 'name'
with 'associative fields' that permit shifts and substitutions at the level of
the name, at the level of the sense, or at both levels at once. Since these
substitutions by association take place on the basis of contiguity or of resemblance, four possibilities present themselves: association by contiguity
and association by resemblance in the realm of the name; and association
by contiguity and association by resemblance at the level of the sense. The
last two cases define metonymy and metaphor.[36]

Recourse within a semantic theory to psychological explanation should
not be surprising. Within the purely Saussurean tradition, this interference
presents that much less difficulty to the degree that both signifier and signified have a psychological status, as acoustic image and as concept.[37] Accordingly, no problem arises when the principle of a classification of
semantic changes is borrowed from the tradition of Wundt[38] and these
changes are incorporated into the Saussurean theory of the sign in such a
way that the explication of innovations remains in line with the broad articulations of the linguistic structure. Besides, there is a precedent right in
the *Cours de linguistique générale*, in the famous chapter on 'Mechanism
of Language,' for this marriage between associationist psychology and
structural linguistics. There, the syntagmatic and paradigmatic operations
are interpreted in terms of combination. Fifty years later, Roman Jakobson sees no difficulty in principle in these interchanges between semantics
and psychology, since he grafts his distinction between metaphorical process and metonymic process directly on to the Saussurean distinction, itself
interpreted in terms of association by resemblance and by contiguity.[39]

Hence a psychological mechanism regulates semantic innovations, and
that principle is association. Léonce Roudet in 1921[40] and Z. Gombocz in
1926[41] were the first to show how one can derive an explication of semantic changes – one that returns to the broad rhetorical categories – from a
purely psychological explication. Ullmann completes this movement to
bring the rhetorical classes into semantics by tightly linking the theory of
associative fields to the definition of meaning as correlation of name and
sense. Following a suggestion of Léonce Roudet in this procedure, he suggests that it is during the effort of expression, such as Bergson described in

the famous essay on 'L'effort intellectuel,'[42] that interference occurs between the two systems of senses and of names. The usual association between such a meaning and such a word is found wanting; the idea seeks expression through another word associated with the first, sometimes by resemblance, sometimes by contiguity; what results is sometimes metaphor, at other times metonymy. Ullmann notes judiciously that psychic associations do not 'set up' the change but only determine its 'direction'; in fact, the effort of expression remains the efficient cause (*Précis* 276).

This psychological mediation between semantics and rhetoric deserves attention. It carries very positive benefits, no matter what our later reservations might be. In the first place, a bridge is constructed between the individual activity of speech and the social character of language. The associative fields provide this mediation. They belong to the language, and they present the same character of latency as the 'storehouse of language' in de Saussure; at the same time, they demarcate a field of play for an activity that remains individual since it is an effort at expression: 'Whether it has to do with filling a real void, avoiding a verbal taboo, giving free play to the emotions or to the urge to express oneself, the associative fields are what will provide the primary material for innovation' (*Précis* 276-7).

Next, the psychology of association opens the door to uniting a classification with an explication, that is, a taxonomic principle with an operative principle. Dumarsais and Fontanier tried to do this by means of the distinction of tropes according to different sorts of relationships between objects or their ideas. The resemblance relationship of Fontanier is preserved unchanged. Only the two relationships of inclusion and exclusion are contracted into the idea of contiguity, as much on the plane of operations as on that of figures; thus, metonymy and synecdoche are reduced to metonymy.

Another advantage is that metaphor and metonymy derive their similarity from association itself. The only differentiating factor is the nature of the association. The distinction between figures is reduced to a psychological difference within a single general mechanism.

As for metaphor itself, it owes the preservation of its close kinship with the two-term comparison of simile to its rapprochment with association by resemblance. In other words, a psychologizing semantics gives metaphor *in praesentia* precedence over metaphor *in absentia* (as we shall see, this will not be the case any longer with a semantics that breaks all ties with psychology). In effect, the primacy of simile is properly psychological. Esnault[43] had emphasized this point: 'Metaphor is a condensed simile by which the spirit affirms an intuitive and concrete identity' (quoted in *Précis* 277). Ullmann remarks subsequently: 'In the final analysis, metaphor is an abridged simile. Rather than explicitly spelling out analogies,

one compresses them into an image that has the air of an identification'
(ibid.). Truly the key to metaphor is the perception of a resemblance between two ideas – in Aristotle's words *to homoïon theôrein.*[44]

On the other hand, the marriage with associationist psychology is not
without grave complications. Besides the overall dependence of linguistics
on another discipline (a dependence that subsequent linguistics will no
longer tolerate), the mélange of the two disciplines carries harmful effects
for the very analysis of figures of discourse. What is damaged primarily is
its complexity. At first the distinction between two sorts of association
might appear to be a simplification, and would thus satisfy the concern for
economy. This is revealed quite quickly to be an impediment. By boxing
the relationships of inclusion and exclusion together under the heading of
contiguity, the associationist principle impoverishes the operations as well
as the figures that result from it. Further, the reduction of synecdoche to
metonymy is a flagrant case of reducing a logical difference (co-ordination
versus subordination) into a single psychological procedure, that of contiguity. What survives this operation is a rhetoric of two figures, a 'restricted rhetoric' par excellence.[45]

The analysis of metaphor itself suffers from the psychological explication. One might have thought that the idea of 'abridged simile' would have
introduced a description in terms of statement and of predication. Ullmann (*Semantics* 213) explicitly likens the conception of metaphor exposed here to that of I.A. Richards. The two compared terms that the
associative fields bring into proximity are in the same relationship as Richards' tenor and vehicle. Instead of explicitly comparing two things, metaphor contrives a verbal short-circuit: instead of comparing a certain part of
the anatomy to a little mouse, one says 'muscle' (the transference having
occurred in the Latin origins of these words, cf. *Semantics* 213). Moreover,
Ullmann accepts Richards' valuable idea that the greater the distance between tenor and vehicle[46] and the more unexpected their combination, the
more striking and surprising is the metaphor.

But these remarks do not contribute to overthrowing the very principle
of a description that remains within the boundaries of the word. Recourse
to the process of association tends rather to strengthen these limits: in
fact, operating as it does only with individual elements – meanings and
words – associationism never confronts the truly predicative operation.
(We will return later to this decisive point for the relationship between the
semantics of the word and the semantics of the statement at the very heart
of metaphor.) This is why the analysis is quick to reduce simile to substitution, which indeed takes place between psychic atoms, elements, or terms.
The double play of association between senses and between names finally
includes only substitutions resulting in novel naming: 'Instead of stating

precisely that [the] elements [of a comb] are *like* teeth, one will simply call them the *teeth of the comb*. In doing this one will have transposed the name of a human organ in order to designate an inanimate object' (*Précis* 277). The resemblance between the two senses is what permits one to give the name of one to the other.

Confined thus within the realm of naming, the study of metaphor does not regain the breadth it used to have with the rhetoricians until the enumeration of its *species* is begun. Association is still the guiding thread. The innumerable borrowings that metaphor brings into play can indeed be assembled into broad classes that are themselves divided up according to which associations are the most typical, that is, the most usual; associations not only between senses, but between domains of sense, for example that of the human body and that of physical objects. Hence we again come upon the broad classes of Fontanier, where pride of place is held by the transposition of the animate to the inanimate and, less frequently, of the inanimate to the animate. Transposition from the concrete to the abstract forms another large group (for example, from *velum* 'veil' to 'reveal' [*Semantics* 215]). The 'sensorial transpositions,' joining two different perceptual domains (a *warm* colour, a *clear* voice), fit without difficulty into the great family of metaphors. The synaesthetics constitute a case of spontaneous perception of resemblances, which is nevertheless a function of the mental dispositions of speakers. Sensorial correspondences harmonize neatly with substitutions of names since both are cases of resemblance between 'senses.' The difference of level between sensorial and semantic resemblance is diminished by the fact that, as the famous sonnet 'Correspondances' by Baudelaire shows, the synaesthetic transpositions themselves become recognizable thanks to the mediation of language.

4 / METAPHOR AND THE SAUSSUREAN POSTULATES

At first glance, the theory of metaphor in the work of Ullmann and in that of post-Saussurean semanticists close to him appears to be nothing more than an application of the fundamental postulates of structural linguistics to a sector of historical linguistics, that of changes of meaning. In a second and more critical approximation their analysis is really something other than an application: it initiates, virtually at least, a correction of the postulates through consideration of their consequences. This rebounding of the consequences on the principle deserves attention, because it is the index of a certain latitude in a semantics that pretends to be solely a semantics of the word. To explore this further, an attempt will be made in the next section to co-ordinate the metaphor of the word, to which this Study and the following are restricted, with the statement-metaphor of the preceding Study.

The post-Saussurean treatment of metaphor shows after the fact that the *Cours de linguistique générale* constituted as much a stage as a disruption in the program of the semantics of the word. This trait is explained well enough by the nature of the methodological crisis that the *Cours* initiated at its heart.

It is really a two-fold crisis. On the one hand, the *Cours* eliminated confusions and equivocations in an essentially simplifying and purifying action. On the other hand, through the dichotomies that it instituted, it left a legacy of perplexities, ones for which the problem of metaphor, even if confined to lexical semantics, continues after de Saussure to be a good touch-stone. Indeed metaphor straddles most of the divisions instituted by de Saussure and reveals at what point these dichotomies today constitute antinomies to be reduced or to be mediated.

For de Saussure, accordingly, the gap between *language* and *speech* makes of language a completely homogeneous object contained within a single science, with the two faces of the sign – signifier and signified – falling on the same side of the gap.[47] But this dichotomy creates as many problems as it resolves; as Roman Jakobson observes in his synthesis of modern linguistics, 'although this restrictive program still finds its theoretical adherents, in fact the absolute separation of the two aspects turns into a recognition of two different hierarchic relations: an analysis of the code with due regard for the messages, and vice versa. Without a confrontation of the code with the messages, no insight into the creative power of language can be achieved.'[48] In addition to the examples of interchange between code and message that Jakobson proposes (the role of sub-codes freely chosen by the speaking subject on account of the communication situation, construction of personal codes supporting the speaking subject's identity, etc.), metaphor constitutes a magnificent example of exchange between code and message. As we saw, metaphor is to be classified among the changes of meaning; for 'it is within speech, the concrete realization of language, that the changes proclaim themselves' (Ullmann *Précis* 237). Moreover, the discrete character of these changes has been noted: however numerous the intermediary stages recorded by the history of semantic changes in a word, each individual change is a leap that attests to the dependence of innovation on speech. But on the other hand, metaphor depends on a characteristic of the code, namely polysemy. This is what metaphor will augment to some degree, when, having ceased to be an innovation, it enters into standard usage and then becomes a cliché; the circle is then completed between language and speech. The circle can be described in the following manner. Initial polysemy equals 'language,' the living metaphor equals 'speech,' metaphor in common use represents the return of speech towards language, and subsequent polysemy equals 'language.'

This circle is a perfect illustration of the untenability of the Saussurean dichotomy.

The second large dichotomy, which opposes the synchronistic and the diachronistic points of view,[49] was no less beneficial than the first. It not only put an end to a confusion by dissociating two distinct relations of linguistic fact to time (that of simultaneity and that of succession), it also put an end to the hegemony of the historical perspective precisely at the level of the principles of intelligibility, by imposing a new priority of system over evolution.

But the trouble created is as great as the advantages gained. A phenomenon like metaphor has some systematic aspects and some historical aspects. For a word to have more than one meaning is, strictly speaking, a synchronistic fact – it is *now*, in the code, that it signifies several things. Consequently, we must align polysemy with synchrony. But the alteration of meaning that adds to the polysemy and in the past had contributed to building up current polysemy is a diachronistic fact. Thus, as innovation, metaphor is to be set among changes of meaning, and thus among diachronistic facts; yet as accepted deviation, it is aligned with polysemy, and thus belongs in the synchronistic realm.[50] Once again, then, it is necessary to mediate too severe an opposition and to interrelate the structural and historical aspects. The word seems truly to stand at the crossroads of two orders of consideration, thanks to its capacity for acquiring new meanings and for retaining them without losing the old meanings. In its two-fold character, this cumulative process seems to call for a panchronistic point of view.[51]

Quite apart from the consideration of changes of meaning, the complete description of polysemy demands some such panchronistic point of view. It would appear to be rather difficult to describe polysemy without alluding to its origin; Ullmann, accordingly, despite his declarations to which I referred, discusses in the chapter on polysemy the 'four principal sources' on which it 'feeds.'[52] Now these four 'sources' have a more or less obvious diachronistic character. 'Shifts in meaning' are developments in divergent directions. 'Figurative expressions' grow out of metaphor and metonymy, which, acting in the present instant, are no less events of speech that engender polysemic series. 'Popular etymology,' a sort of popular semantic wisdom endorsing or conjuring connections that are frequently philologically unsound, leads to a situation of polysemy. And as the words themselves indicate, 'foreign influences' belong in the group of evolutions that create their situations by means of semantic imitation. The very notion of 'semantic copying' introduced here implies a return to analogy, itself treated as a factor in semantic change. Thus, despite every effort at partitioning description and history, the very description of polysemy makes reference to the possibility of semantic change. Polysemy as such, that is, regarded apart from consideration of its 'sources,' refers to possibilities of a diachronistic character: polysemy is simply the possibility of adding a new meaning to the previous acceptations of the word without having these former meanings disappear. Thus the open structure of the word, its elasticity, its fluidity, already allude to the phenomenon of change of meaning.[53]

If polysemy is so difficult to contain within the limits of synchronistic description, conversely changes of meaning that arise from the historical perspective cannot be identified completely until they are written into the synchronistic domain and show themselves to be a variety of polysemy. Thus Ullmann himself considers stylistic 'ambiguity' in the chapter on polysemy. Now this expression points out very precisely the rhetorical level of figures: 'dreaded by the foreigner, denounced by the logician, battled by the need for clarity that dominates everyday speaking, ambiguity is sometimes sought by the writer for stylistic purposes.[54] This assignment of stylistic ambiguity to the same division as polysemy is perfectly legitimate, since at a given time it will be inscribed into the current state of the language as a double meaning. Therefore, the synchronistic projection of a change of meaning is truly a phenomenon of the same order as polysemy.

In its turn, moreover, equivocation can be treated as one of the conditions of semantic changes.[55] By figuring in an ambiguous sentence, for which two interpretations remain possible, words receive new values. Thus the ambiguity of discourse clears the way for equivocity of the word, which can result in established changes of meaning that add to polysemy.

Nothing would be more accurate than to say that the Saussurean dichotomies create as many problems as they solve. Not even his most firmly fixed distinctions avoid being a source of perplexity. We know how insistently de Saussure contrasted the relation between signifier and signified (which is purely immanent to meaning) with the external sign-thing relation, which he repudiated. Henceforth, 'thing' is excluded from the factors involved in meaning; the linguistic sign does not unite a thing and a name, but a concept and an accoustic image.[56]

But even this disjunction, which has been adopted by all the post-Saussurean linguists, leads to an aporia. This is because discourse, through its referential function, sets signs fully into relation with things. Denotation is a sign-thing relation, whereas signification is a relation between signifier and signified.[57] What this leads to is an ambiguity within the very notion of meaning. As the Saussurean 'signified,' meaning is nothing other than the counterpart of the signifier; what defines one defines the other, as both sides of a sheet of paper are cut by the same motion of the scissors. But in relation to the reality denoted, meaning stands as mediator between words and things, i.e. it is that through which words relate to things – *vox significat mediantibus conceptis.*[58] This rift cuts across semantics, taken in its broad sense, and separates the semantics of Saussurean-school linguists from that of philosophers like Carnap, Wittgenstein, and so on, for whom semantics is fundamentally the analysis of the relationships between signs and the things denoted.

By holding the meaning-thing relationship at bay, linguistics emancipates itself with regard to the normative logico-grammatical sciences; and it establishes its autonomy by guaranteeing the homogeneity of its object, with the signifier and signified falling within the frontiers of the linguistic sign. All this has its unfortunate consequences, however. It becomes very difficult, if not impossible, to give an account of the denotative function of language within the framework of a theory of the sign that acknowledges only the internal difference between signifier and the signified. This denotative function, on the other hand, presents no problem in a conception of language that distinguishes from the start between signs and discourse and defines discourse, as opposed to the sign, by its relation to extra-linguistic reality. Thus the semantics of the English-language philosophers, which is a semantics of discourse, finds itself from the start in the territory of denotation, even when it is discussing words. This is because for it, words, as parts of discourse, are equally carriers of a part of the denotation.[59]

It is quite true that a semantics of the Ullmann variety succeeds in defining most of the phenomena it describes – synonymy, homonymy, polysemy, etc. – within the limits of a theory of the sign that does not involve any concession to extra-linguistic reality. But the denotative relationship, which puts the relation of sign to thing into play, is required as soon as the focus is concentrated on the operation of these differences within discourse. A purely virtual characteristic in the lexical sense, polysemy is screened in discourse. The same contextual mechanism (verbal or nonverbal) serves to separate the polysemic equivocations and determines the genesis of new meanings: 'It is the *context*, verbal and non-verbal, which makes deviations possible, the use of unusual acceptations.'[60] One really has to return to contextual uses to define the diverse acceptations of one and the same word, whether they be usual or unusual acceptations; so these are actually nothing but the contextual variations that can be classed according to their families of occurrence. And once one embarks on this mission, it is immediately apparent that the classes of these conceptual variations are dependent on the different possibilities of analysing objects, that is, things or their representatives. As the *Rhétorique générale* itself admits,[61] the material analysis of objects into their parts and the rational analysis of concepts into their elements both appeal to models of description from the universe of representations. Thus the consideration of deno-tation interferes necessarily with that of the signified as such when it takes account of the classes into which the polysemic variations of a single word are arranged, once they are characterized as contextual meanings. The ad-jective *contextual* reintroduces discourse, and with it the denotative pur-pose of language.

If polysemy as a synchronistic fact has such implications, so all the more does metaphor as change of meaning. Innovation properly speaking is a fact of speech, as Ullmann reminds us.[62] We have seen its consequences for the language-speech relation and the synchronistic-diachronistic rela-tion; the implications are no less important for the signified-denotated relation. A semantic innovation is a way of responding in a creative fashion to a question presented by things. In a certain discourse situation, in a given social milieu and at a precise moment, something seeks to be said that demands an operation of speech, speech working on language, that brings words and things face to face. The final outcome is a new descrip-tion of the universe of representations. We will return to this problem of redescription in a later Study.[63] What had to be shown right now was its insertion into a semantic theory that nevertheless wishes to restrict itself to changes of meaning, that is, to the study of the signified alone. Every change implicates the entire debate between man speaking and the world.

But no bridge can be laid directly between the Saussurean signified and the extra-linguistic referent; one must detour through discourse and pass through denotation of the sentence in order to arrive at denotation of the word. This detour alone allows one to interrelate the denotative operation at work in metaphor and the predicative operation that gives it the frame-work of discourse.

5 / BETWEEN SENTENCE AND WORD:
THE INTERPLAY OF MEANING

Rendering the broad methodological decisions of the theory problematic once again is not the only effect of applying the fundamental principles of Saussurean linguistics to metaphor. It reveals an uncertainty at the very heart of the semantics of the word, a stirring, a space for moving about, thanks to which it again becomes possible to forge a link between the semantics of the sentence and the semantics of the word, and correspond-ingly, between the interaction theory and the substitution theory of meta-phor. If this extension should prove to be practicable, then the real loca-tion of metaphor in the theory of discourse would begin to define itself *between* the sentence and the word, *between* predication and naming.

I wish first to refer to three clues, within a semantics as deliberately given over to the word as that of Stephen Ullmann, that indicate the point of connection between this semantics and the semantics of the sentence discussed in the preceding Study.

(a) The first of these indications is given by the non-systematic aspects of the lexical system (if one can say such a thing). Let us go no further than the quantitative viewpoint: the lexical code bears features that distinguish it emphatically from the phonological code (45,000 words in the Oxford Dictionary against 44 or 45 phonemes!) as well as from the grammatical system (even if the lexical morphology of suffixes, prefixes, inflexions, compounds, etc., are included in it). The code is certainly beyond the capacity of the individual memory, and the lexical level does not need to be comprehended entirely within an individual consciousness in order to function. But the number of units in the two other codes is also not unrelated to the capacity of human memory. If one adds that this code is such that it is always possible to add new entities to it without changing it fundamentally, this absence of closure suggests the thought that the structure of vocabulary consists in 'a loose aggregate of an infinitely larger number of units'[64] than the other systems. If one considers given segments of this code, like those that have occasioned the most brilliant 'semantic field' analyses in the mode of J. Trier, it is evident that these sectors present extremely variable degrees of organization. Some present a subdivision of meaning such that each element exactly delimits its neighbours and is determined by them as if in a mosaic – colour names, kinship terms, military ranks, and some groups of abstract ideas like the triad *Wisheit-Kunst-List* in Middle High German of about 1200, as studied by Trier.[65] Other sectors are much less well ordered. These are most often 'incomplete patterns' with 'half-finished designs' (Ullmann here adopts Entwistle's phrases) where the overlapping of senses overrides neat delimitation. De Saussure himself saw in a given term, 'teaching' for instance, 'the centre of a constellation; it is the point of convergence of an indefinite number of co-ordinated terms.'[66] Obviously the idea of a twofold associative field, which continues this image of the constellation, does not take one in the same direction as the idea of mutual delimitation, which is rather a continuation of the mosaic image; thus the idea of an open system imposes itself a second time.

If one finally considers isolated words, all that was said above about synonyny and about polysemy comes together and points to the same notion of open texture. It repeats itself on the level of the lexical whole, on the regional level of semantic fields, and on the local level of the single word. The vague character of the word, the indecision about its frontiers, the combined action of polysemy, which disseminates the meaning of the word, and of synonymy, which discriminates the polysemy, and above all the cumulative power of the word, which allows it to acquire a new meaning without losing its previous meanings – all these traits indicate that the vocabulary of a language is 'an unstable structure in which individual words can acquire and lose meanings with the utmost ease.'[67] This renders meaning 'of all linguistic elements ... [the one which] is probably the least resistant to change.'[68]

In the words of an author cited by Ullmann, language *in toto* is 'neither systematic nor completely non-systematic.' This truly is why it is at the mercy not only of change in general, but of non-linguistic causes of change, among whose various effects is the prevention of the establishment of lexicology on an entirely autonomous base. The appearance of new natural and cultural objects in the field of naming; the deposit of beliefs in keywords; the projection of social ideals in emblematic words; the reinforcement or lifting of linguistic taboos; political and cultural domination by a linguistic group, by a social class, or by a cultural milieu – all these influences leave language, at least at the level of semantics of the word, which our authors have chosen, to the mercy of social forces whose effectiveness underlines the non-systematic character of the system.

At the limit, this character would lead one to doubt that the term *code* applies rigorously at the lexical level of language. In a text that we have already cited,[69] Jakobson suggests that the word *code* be put in the plural, so entangled are the sub-codes among which we learn to orient ourselves in order to speak in an appropriate manner, according to the milieux, the circumstances, and the situations where these sub-codes have currency. Perhaps one ought to go further and refuse to call 'code' a system about which, after all, so little is systematic.

(b) A second index of the opening of the semantics of the word towards the semantics of the sentence is provided by the properly contextual characteristics of the word. The predicative functioning of language is imprinted to some extent on the word itself; and this takes place in several ways.

First of all, the delimitation of the word cannot be done without reference to its eventual occurrence as a complete statement. To call the word the 'minimum free form' (Bloomfield) is to refer it ineluctably to the sentence, the model of the free form. That form is free that can constitute a complete statement ('Are you happy? ' – 'Very!').

Furthermore, in many languages the class of forms of discourse to which a word belongs (noun, verb, etc.) is announced within the perimeter of the word as entered in the dictionary. In any case, the word has the power of figuring in at least one class, for together the semantic kernel and the class define the word. In brief, the word is grammatically determined.[70]

Finally, the distinction reported earlier between categorematic and syn-categorematic words cannot be made without reference to the function of the word in discourse.

This imprint of the predicative operation on the word is so strong that certain authors define meaning in a way that is frankly contextual or, as Ullmann puts it, 'operational.'[71] Wittgenstein's theory in the *Philosphical Investigations* – to the extent that it is still valid to speak here of theory – is the most 'provocative' example of this conception: 'For a *large* class of cases – though not for all – in which we employ the word "meaning" it can be defined thus: the meaning of a word is its use in the language.'[72] The comparison of language to a toolbox from which one sometimes takes a hammer, sometimes pliers[73]; then the comparison (very Saussurean, at least in appearance) of the word to a piece in a chess set[74] – all these analogies tend to reduce lexical meaning to a simple function of the meaning of the sentence taken as a whole. This at least is the most general tendency in the semantics of English-speaking philosophers. Thus Ryle declares in a celebrated article: 'Understanding a word ... is knowing how to use it, i.e. make it perform its rôle in a wide range of sentences. But understanding a sentence is not knowing how to make it perform its rôle ... It has not got a rôle ...'[75]

These many reroutings of the word towards discourse do not in any way imply that the word has no semantic autonomy at all. The reasons listed earlier in favour of its independence still hold: I can say what something is called and look for an equivalent of its name in a foreign language; I can say the key-words of the tribe; I can point out the dominant elements of this or that moral code, the fundamental concepts of this or that philosophy; I can endeavour to name exactly the qualitative nuances of emotions and feelings; I can define a word by means of other words; and for purposes of classification, I must define genera, species, and sub-species, which is still to name them. In short, naming is an important 'language game,' which fully justifies the compiling of dictionaries and authorizes in large part the defining of meaning by the reciprocal relationship between name and sense. But, although naming is an important 'language game,' the overestimation of the word and even fascination with words, pushed to the point of superstition, reverence, or terror, are due perhaps to a basic illusion that Wittgenstein attacks at the beginning of the *Philosophical Investigations* – namely, the illusion that the naming game is the paradigm of all language games.[76]

When we begin to examine this naming-game in itself, context reappears within the very perimeter of the word. What we call the diverse accepta-tions of a word are contextual classes, which emerge from the contexts themselves after patient comparison of samples of usage. So the many meanings of a word can be identified as types of contextual values. Hence the semanticist is forced to make room for the contextual definition of meaning beside the properly analytical or referential definition; or rather, the contextual definition becomes a phase of the properly semantic definition: 'The relation between the two methods, or rather between the two phases of the inquiry, is ultimately the same as that between language and speech: the operational theory is concerned with meaning in speech, the referential with meaning in language.'[77] It would be hard to affirm more strongly that the definition of the word cannot appear except where speech and language intersect.

(c) The dependence of word-meaning on the meaning of the sentence becomes even more obvious when, no longer considering the word in isolation, we take up its actual, effective functioning in discourse. Taken in isolation, the word still has only a potential meaning, made up of the sum of its partial meanings, themselves defined by the types of contexts in which they can participate. They have actual meaning only in a given sentence, that is to say, in an instance of discourse, in Benveniste's sense. While the reduction of potential meaning to use is still open to discussion, that of actual meaning to use is completely beyond debate. This was noted by Benveniste: 'The meaning of a sentence is its idea, the meaning of a word is its use (always in the semantic acceptation). Based on the idea, which is particular in every case, the speaker assembles words which, in *this* employment, have a particular "meaning."'[78]

A consequence of this dependence of the actual meaning of the word on the actual meaning of the sentence is that the referential function that attaches to the sentence taken as a whole distributes in some fashion over the words of the sentence. In the language of Wittgenstein,[79] which in this instance is close to that of Husserl,[80] the referent of the sentence is a 'state of affairs' and the referent of the word is an 'object.' In a closely related sense, Benveniste calls the referent of the word 'the particular object to which the word corresponds in the concrete actuality of circumstance or of use.'[81] He distinguishes this from the sentence reference: 'If the meaning of the sentence is the idea it expresses, the "reference" of the sentence is the state of affairs it provokes, the discursive or factual situation to which it relates and which we can never foresee nor guess.'[82]

Taking this to its limit, if one puts the accent on the actual meaning of the word, to the point of identifying the word with this actual meaning in discourse, one comes to doubt that the word is a lexical entity; and one is led to say that the signs in the semiotic repertory stand this side of the threshold of what is properly semantic. The lexical entity is at most the lexeme, that is, the semantic kernel separated by abstraction from the mark indicating the class to which the word belongs as an element of discourse. This semantic kernel is what earlier we called the potential meaning of the word or its semantic potential; but this is nothing real or actual. The real word, the word as an occurrence in a sentence, is already something entirely different; its meaning is inseparable from 'its capacity to integrate a particular syntagma and to fill a propositional function.'[83]

It is not by chance, therefore, that earlier we had to incorporate the effect of context into the potential meaning itself, that is, into the word in isolation. As Benveniste remarks, 'what one calls polysemy is nothing but the institutionalized sum, let us say, of these contextual values, always instantaneous, continually apt to enrich, to disappear – in brief, without permanence, without constant value.'[84]

We are brought thus to picture discourse as a reciprocal interplay between the word and the sentence. The word preserves the semantic capital constituted by these contextual values deposited in its semantic treasury. What it brings to the sentence is a potential for meaning. This potential is not formless: the word does have an identity. Certainly, this is a plural identity, an open texture, as we said; but this identity is nevertheless sufficient for it to be identified and reidentified as the same in different contexts. The game of naming discussed just above is possible only because the semantic 'diversity' that the word consists in endures as a limited, rule-governed, and hierarchical heterogeneity. Polysemy is not homonymy. But this plural *identity* is also a *plural* identity. This is why, in the game of the word and of the sentence, the 'initiative of meaning,' as it were, passes over again to the sentence. The passage from the potential to the actual meaning of a word requires the mediation of a new sentence, just as the potential meaning issues from the sedimentation and institutionalization of previous contextual values. This trait is so important that Roman Jakobson unhesitatingly makes 'sensitivity to context' a criterion of natural languages as opposed to artificial languages, together with the two other criteria of plurivocity and mutability of meaning.[85]

This mediation of the new sentence is required especially if one considers (again with Ullmann) the 'vague' character of words and above all the phenomenon of polysemy. The word receives from the context the determination that reduces its imprecision. This is true even of proper names: Ullmann notes that while proper names have several aspects – 'Queen Victoria' as a young woman, the same person at the time of the Boer War – only one is appropriate to a given situation.[86] In like manner, Strawson notes that the proper name identifies one and only one person only if it is the abbreviation of some anterior descriptions present in the rest of the context (verbal or non-verbal) in which the name is mentioned.[87]

But, above all, it is the function of context to sift out polysemy by means of a 'conspiracy' (Firth) or 'coaptation' (Benveniste) effect of words on each other. This mutual selection of acceptations of semantically compatible meaning is most often effected so inconspicuously that, in a given context, the other inappropriate acceptations do not even cross one's mind. As Bréal remarked already about this, 'one does not even go to the trouble of suppressing the other meanings of the word: these meanings do not exist for us, they do not cross the threshold of our consciousness.'[88]

This action of the context – sentence, discourse, work, discourse situation – to reduce polysemy is the key to the problem that motivated this entire Study.

What takes place in a metaphorical statement can be understood perfectly in terms of the above phenomenon. If it is true that metaphor adds to polysemy, then the operation of discourse set in motion by metaphor is the inverse of that which we have just described. For a sentence to make sense it is necessary (it was claimed just above) that all the acceptations of the semantic potential of the word under consideration be eliminated except one, that which is compatible with the meaning, itself appropriately reduced, of the other words of the sentence. In the case of metaphor, none of the already codified acceptations is unsuitable; it is necessary, therefore, to retain all the acceptations allowed *plus one*, that which will rescue the meaning of the entire statement. The theory of the statement-metaphor puts the accent on the predicative operation. It seems now that it is not incompatible with the theory of the word-metaphor. The metaphorical statement achieves its statement of meaning by means of an *epiphora* of the word. A little while ago we said with Stephen Ullmann that the 'analytical' definition and the 'contextual' definition of the word are compatible with each other to the extent that the perspectives of language and of speech call for and complete each other. Now it must be said that the theory of the word-metaphor and the theory of the statement-metaphor relate to each other in just the same way.

The complementary value of the two theories can be demonstrated in the following manner, which cuts short any accusation of eclecticism. The theory of the statement-metaphor refers back to the word-metaphor through an essential trait that the preceding Study set into relief. Recalling the distinction proposed by Max Black between 'focus' and 'frame,' this trait can be called the *focalization* on the word. The 'focus' is a word, the 'frame' is a sentence. It is to the 'focus' that the 'system of associated commonplaces' is applied in the manner of a filter or a screen. It is, again, through a focalizing effect that interaction or tension polarizes on a 'vehicle' and a 'tenor'; they relate to each other within the statement, but it is the word that assumes each of the two functions. In the same vein I will strive in the next Study to show that deviation at the level of the word – through which, according to Jean Cohen,[89] a deviation at the predicative level, i.e. a semantic impertinence, comes to be reduced – is itself also an effect of focalization on the word. Its origin is in the establishment of a new semantic pertinence at the very level where the impertinence takes place, that is at the predicative level. In various ways, consequently, the dynamism of the statement-metaphor condenses or crystallizes into an operation of meaning whose focus is the word.

But the reverse is no less true. The changes of meaning for which the semantics of the word tries to give an account demand the mediation of a complete expression. To the focalization of the statement by the word corresponds the contextualization of the word by the statement. One can be led astray in this regard by the role played by associative fields in the semantics of Ullmann. Recourse to the association of ideas is even an effective way of avoiding the properly discursive aspects of change of meaning and of operating only with the elements – names and senses. In particular, in the case of metaphor, the operation of resemblance is carried on at the level of the elements, without quarter being given to the idea that this resemblance itself results from the application of an unusual and impertinent predicate to a subject that 'yields while protesting' (in the words of Nelson Goodman,[90] who will be discussed later).

The argument is not limited to proposing a different formulation in which predication would replace association. On at least two points, to my mind, the marriage between semantics and associationist psychology has ruinous results.

I hold first that the psychologizing interpretation of figures is responsible for the false symmetry between metaphor and metonymy that prevails in the 'restricted rhetoric' inspired by associationism. This symmetry is very deceptive. Only metonymy can be treated purely as a phenomenon of denomination, one word in place of another. In this sense, it alone satisfies a substitution theory, because it alone is located within the limits of naming. Metaphor does not differ from metonymy in that the association takes place by resemblance in this case instead of by contiguity. It differs by the fact that it takes place on two planes, that of predication and that of naming; and it takes place on the second only because it takes place on the first. This is what the English-language authors have perceived so well: words change meaning only because discourse must confront the threat of an inconsistency at the properly predicative level, and it re-establishes its intelligibility only at the price of what looks, in the framework of semantics of the word, like a semantic innovation. The theory of metonymy makes no appeal to such an exchange between discourse and the word. This is why metaphor has a role in discourse that metonymy never equals; their difference in fecundity brings into play more complex factors than the simple difference between two sorts of associations. Metaphor prevails over metonymy not because contiguity is less fruitful a relationship than resemblance, or again because metonymic relationships are external and given in reality whereas metaphorical equivalences are created by the imagination, but because metaphorical equivalences set predicative operations in motion that metonymy ignores.[91]

The psychologizing interpretation of figures has the even more serious drawback of impeding the full recognition of the interchange between word and sentence in the constitution of the figure. The role attributed to associative fields lets metaphor and metonymy be kept in the domain of denomination; and this helps reinforce the substitution theory, basing it on the psychological mechanism of the association by contiguity or by resemblance, which occurs sometimes between name and name, sometimes between sense and sense, and sometimes between both at once. On the other hand, if, like Max Black, one sees in association an aspect that envisages the 'application' of a strange predicate to a subject which itself consequently appears in a new light, then the association of ideas requires the framework of a complete expression.

Once this obstacle is cleared away, the same mechanism of exchange between the word and the sentence that was seen to be at work in the case of polysemy can be brought into play again to explain metaphor. Finally it becomes possible to formulate this mechanism first in terms of statement and then in terms of word. The two analyses become not just complementary but also reciprocal. Just as the statement-metaphor has as 'focus' a word whose meaning is changing, the change of meaning of the word has as 'frame' a complete expression whose meaning is in tension.

We can now state, at this point where our third and fourth Studies converge, that metaphor is the outcome of a debate between *predication* and *naming*; its place in language is between words and sentences.

Metaphor and the new rhetoric

For A.-J. Greimas

The common aim of the works of the new rhetoric to which this Study is devoted is to renovate the essentially taxonomic enterprise of classical rhetoric by founding the *species* of classification on the *forms* of the operations that take place at all levels of articulation in language. In this respect the new rhetoric is dependent on a semantics taken to its own highest degree of structural radicalism.

Because the period is too short and the works too recent, I will concentrate less on the historical succession of theses than on their major theoretical articulations, taking as immediate reference the *Rhétorique générale* published by Groupe μ (Centre d'études poétiques, Université de Liège).[1] This is not to say that all the partial analyses to be examined along the way are considered exhaustively here; nevertheless, all the problems that have given rise to special analyses are taken up in the synthesis of the *Rhétorique générale*.

The semantics of the word discussed in the preceding Study provides the background from which this ongoing investigation stands out. It inherits from this semantics the two foundational postulates set out at the beginning of Study 4: metaphor belongs in the semantics of the word; and the semantics of the word fits into the framework of a semiotics for which all the units of language are varieties of the sign – that is, negative, differential, oppositive entities – all of whose relations with the other homologous units are immanent within language itself.

But the structural semantics on which the new rhetoric is based is not a simple outgrowth of the semantics set out above. It proceeds from a revolution within the revolution, which confers a sort of crystalline purity on the postulates of Saussurism. In the first place, the definition of the sign is detached from its matrix, both psychological (acoustic image, mental content) and sociological (the societal storehouse of the language inscribed in the memory of each individual); the relation between signifier and signified is held to be a relation *sui generis*. Furthermore, all the consequences are drawn from the Saussurean distinction between form and substance (whether this be the sound-substance of the signifier or the psycho-social substance of the signified); the operations to be defined later all take place at the level of the form of language. Phonology, which de Saussure still held as a subsidiary science, provides the purest model of the oppositions, disjunctions, and combinations that allow linguistics to pass beyond the stage of description and of classification to that of explanation. But above all, the analysis of the signified finds itself pushed in a direction that assures the parallelism between the two planes of the signified and the signifier. Just as the analysis of the signifier since Troubetskoy has proceeded essentially as its decomposition into distinctive traits that no longer belong as such to the linguistic domain, the analysis of the signified with Prieto[2] and Greimas[3] is pursued beyond the distinct lexical type, beyond the semantic kernel of the word, to the level of *semes*, which are to the signified (that is, the lexical units of the preceding chapter) what distinctive traits are to the phoneme. Thus, the strategic level of structural semantics shifts from the word towards the seme in a step that is exclusively linguistic, for there is no speech-related consciousness, on the part of either the sender or the receiver of messages, accompanying the constitution of the word as a collection of semes. At the same time, it becomes possible to define not only entities at the semic level, but also operations at a purely semic level. These are principally binary oppositions, thanks to which one can display collections of semes as a hierarchy of disjunctions that give the form of a 'tree' or a 'graph' to all the repertories language offers at the properly linguistic level, the level at which speakers express themselves, signify, and communicate.

I will not consider here the results that semantics properly speaking has drawn from the application of the strictly structural method to semic analysis (just as the preceding Study did not consider in itself the 'semantic fields' theory of Josef Trier, which would be to semic analysis what the description of the phenotype is to the reconstruction of the genotype in the biological conception of organisms). I shall simply refer for an exposition of these works to the *Sémantique structurale* of Greimas, and shall focus essentially on the attempts at a redefinition of the domain of rhetoric on the basis of this purely structural semantics.

As indicated in the introduction to the preceding Study, one ought not to expect from neo-rhetoric a reshaping of the problematic of metaphor comparable to that which English-language authors have achieved in this domain. The radicalization of the semiotic model results rather in reinforcing the privilege of the word, in forging an even tighter pact between metaphor and the word, and in consolidating the substitution theory of metaphor. Furthermore, by changing the strategic level, structural semantics makes it more difficult to see the point where a bond is possible between semiotics of the word and semantics of the sentence, and at the same time obscures the locus of the exchange between naming and predication, which also serves as the anchorage of the word-metaphor in the statement-metaphor.

For all these reasons, the new rhetoric at first glance is nothing but a repetition of classical rhetoric, at least that of tropes, only at a higher level of technicity.

But this is just a first impression. The new rhetoric is far from being a reformulation of the theory of tropes in more formal terms; it proposes instead to restore the entire breadth of the theory of figures. We have alluded several times to the protest of modern writers against 'restricted rhetoric,'[4] that is, to put it more exactly, against the reduction of rhetoric to tropology and of tropology eventually to the pair of metonymy and metaphor, for the greater glory of metaphor, the pinnacle of the tropological edifice. Fontanier wanted to include the theory of tropes in a theory of figures; but, lacking an adequate instrument, he had to be content with reorganizing the entire field of the rhetoric of figures as a function of that of tropes and with giving the name *non-trope figures* to all other figures. Thus, trope survived as the strong concept and figure as the weak. The new rhetoric proposes explicitly to construct the notion of trope on that of figure, not the other way around, and to build up a rhetoric of figures directly. The trope will then be able to remain what it was in the ancient rhetoric, a substitution figure at the level of the word. At least it will be enframed by a more general concept, that of *deviation*.

This concept took shape first in Aristotle's *Rhetoric*, where metaphor is defined, among other uses of words – rare word, shortened word, lengthened word, etc. – as a deviation in relation to the norm of the 'standard' meaning of words. Gérard Genette shows easily in his introduction to *Les Figures du discours* by Fontanier that deviation is the telling trait of the figure.[5]

But it is contemporary stylistics that has paved the way for a generalized concept of deviation. Jean Cohen provides this reminder in his *Structure du langage poétique*: 'Deviation is the very definition that Charles Bruneau, reviving Valéry, gave for the fact of style ... [style] is a deviation in relation to a norm, and so a fault, but, as Bruneau also said, a voluntary fault' (13).

The whole effort of neo-rhetoric, therefore, is directed towards incorporating deviation among the other operations that take place, as structural semantics shows, at all the levels of articulation of language – pho-

nemes, words, sentences, discourse, etc. Hence, deviation at the level of
the word, i.e. the trope, appears somewhat as a local item in the general
table of deviations. This is why, on the one hand, one can see in the new
rhetoric a rather uninstructive repetition of classical rhetoric as far as the
actual description of metaphor is concerned (which remains what it was,
namely a substitution of meaning at the level of the word); and on the
other hand, one can see in it a highly clarifying explanation resulting from
the integration of the trope into a general theory of deviations. It is worth
the effort to grant full scope to these new aspects of the theory of figures
in general, before returning to the problems posed by the purely repetitive
aspect of the theory of metaphor in particular.

I propose to order the problems posed by a general theory of figures in the
following manner:

(1) First, deviation from what? Where is the 'rhetoric degree zero' from
which the distance could be felt, appreciated, even measured? Did not
classical rhetoric die from (among other mortal weaknesses) having left
this preliminary question unanswered?

(2) Next, what does one mean by 'deviation'? Can the corporeal metaphor of *figure* and the spatial metaphor of *deviation* clarify each other,
and, taken together, what do they say?

(3) And if deviation and figure are to mean something together, what
are the rules of the meta-language in which one can speak of deviation and
of figure? Put differently, what are the criteria of deviation and of figure
in rhetorical discourse? This third question will bring to light a new factor,
that of reduction of deviation, which does not limit itself to specifying the
concept of deviation, but which rectifies it to the point of inverting it.
This raises the question of what is important in the figure: is it deviation
or the reduction of deviation?

(4) The search for the criterion leads to problems that set one outside
the consciousness of speakers, since from this point onwards one operates
with infralinguistic units, the semes. How, then, is the effect of meaning at
the level of discourse linked to the operations applied to atoms of meaning
at the infralinguistic level? This fourth question will lead us back to our
initial problem, that of the insertion of the word-metaphor into discourse-
metaphor.

A problem pertaining to the object of further investigation will be left
on the border of this inquiry. One can ask why language in operation has
recourse to the play of deviations. What defines the rhetorical intention of
figurative language? Is it the introduction of new information that would
enrich the referential function of discourse, or rather, must the apparent

surplus of meaning be referred to another non-informative, non-referential function of discourse? This last question will be answered only in Study 7, which is devoted more specifically to the referential scope of discourse.

1 / DEVIATION AND RHETORIC DEGREE ZERO

The first question is a considerable one just on its own. Properly speaking, it governs the demarcation of the rhetorical object.[6] Perhaps classical rhetoric died through not having resolved this question; but neo-rhetoric has not arrived at its complete answer. Everyone agrees in saying that figurative language exists only if one can contrast it with another language that is not figurative. There is even agreement on this point with the English-language semanticists. As we saw, a metaphorical word functions only when it is contrasted and combined with other non-metaphorical words (Max Black);[7] the self-contradiction of literal interpretation is necessary for the unfolding of metaphorical interpretation (Monroe Beardsley).[8] What, then, is this other language, unmarked from the rhetorical point of view? One must first admit that it cannot be found. Dumarsais identified it with etymological meaning; but then all derivative meanings (which is to say, all actual usage) are figurative, and rhetoric is confused with semantics or, as was said then, with grammar.[9] Or, to put the same thing in another way, an etymological and thus diachronic definition of the non-figurative tends to identify figures with polysemy itself. This is why Fontanier contrasts figurative meaning with proper meaning and no longer with primitive meaning, by giving 'proper' a value derived from use, and not from origin. Figurative meaning contrasts with proper meaning within current usage. The line of separation falls between two levels of meaning. Rhetoric says nothing about 'the ordinary and common manner of speaking' – that is about meanings to which single words alone correspond – a feature that makes the path of usage forced and necessary. Rhetoric will be concerned with the non-proper alone, that is, with borrowed, circumstantial, and freed meanings. This line, unfortunately, cannot be drawn within current usage: neutral language does not exist. The upcoming examination of criteria will confirm this fact.

Must one then just note this impasse and bury the question alongside rhetoric itself? The new rhetoric has to be given credit for refusing to capitulate in the face of this question which is, in some ways, the watchdog at the threshold of rhetoric.

Three answers have been proposed, ones which, moreover, are not mutually exclusive. With Gérard Genette[10] it will be said that the opposition of figurative and non-figurative is that of a real language to a virtual language, and that the evidence for the reference of one to the other is the self-awareness of the speaker or the listener. Consequently, this interpretation links the virtuality of language of rhetorical null degree to its mental status. The deviation is between what the poet thought and what he wrote, between meaning and letter. Unfortunately, the author identifies the detection of this virtual meaning with the idea that every figure can be translated, and therefore with the theory of substitution; what the poet thought can always be re-established by another thought that translates the figurative expression into a non-figurative expression. The best way to put it is to say that this recourse to an absent term is completely dependent on a substitutive conception of metaphor and of the figure in general, and consequently is at one with the thesis according to which 'every figure is translatable' (*Figures I* 213). The real word is *put in for* an absent word, which, however, can be restored by translation.[11]

This manner of linking the consciousness of deviation to translatability in fact condemns the very thing one wants at least to describe, if not to save. The non-translatability of poetic language is not just a pretension of romanticism, but an essential trait of the poetic. It is true that one can save the thesis by saying, with Genette himself, that the figure is translatable with respect to meaning, and not translatable with respect to signification, that is, with respect to the 'more' that the figure entails; and one assigns the study of this increase to another theory, not now of denotation but of connotation. We will come back to this point further on. What creates difficulty here is the idea that 'every figure is translatable,' an idea that is inseparable from that of a deviation between actual signs and virtual or absent signs. I wonder whether one ought not to dissociate the postulate of deviation from the postulate of implicit translation, and to say with Beardsley[12] that what the figure contrasts with is a literal interpretation of the sentence as a whole, the impossibility of which motivates the constitution of the metaphorical meaning. This impossible virtual interpretation is in no way the translation of a present word by an absent word, but a way of making sense with the words present, and a way that destroys itself. I shall say, then, that a theory of interaction and of metaphor as a phenomenon of discourse resolves the problem of the status of the non-figurative better than a substitution theory with its continual fealty to the primacy of the word ('sail' in place of 'ship'!). The idea prevails, because it is profoundly right, that figurative language seeks to be opposed to a non-figurative, purely virtual language. However, this virtual language cannot be restored by a translation at the level of words, but only by an interpretation at the level of the sentence.

A second manner of resolving the paradox of the undiscoverable degree zero of rhetoric is that of Jean Cohen, whose work will be explored at greater length in the third section from the viewpoint of the notion of reduction of deviation. It consists in choosing as point of reference not absolute degree zero, but a relative degree zero, i.e. that stratum of language usages that would be the least marked from the rhetorical point of view, and thus the least figurative. This language exists; it is the language of science.[13]

The advantages of this working hypothesis are numerous. First, one avoids having to go back to the consciousness of the speaker in order to measure the deviation between the sign and the meaning. Next, one takes account of the fact that the rhetorical point of view is not without form. It already has a grammatical form, which the preceding theory acknowledges; and above all, it has a semantic form, which the preceding theory presupposes but does not thematize. For there to be deviation between the virtual sign and the actual sign, there must also be semantic equivalence, or, as was said, there must be a meaning that stays the same while significations alter. Thus, one must be able to point, if not to an absolutely neutral language (which Todorov considers 'colourless and dead'), at least to the closest approximation of this neutral language; this is what permits the choice of scientific language as relative degree zero. Finally, the adoption of this level of reference allows one to give a quantitative value to the notion of deviation and to introduce statistical instrumentation into rhetoric. Instead of metaphorizing the spatial aspect of deviation, let us measure it. What one measures in this way will be not only the deviation of all poetic language in relation to scientific language, but also the relative deviation of some poetic language systems in relation to others. By such means a diachronic study of the evolution of deviation, for example from classical to romantic and then to symbolist poetry, can avoid impressionism and subjectivism and achieve scientific status.[14]

Perhaps the theoretical difficulties are not resolved, but they are neutralized. They are unresolved, in that the style of scientific prose already marks a deviation: 'Deviation is not absent from its language, but it certainly is minimal' (*Structure* 22). Where can the 'natural language' be found, that is, the negative pole of null deviation? (23) What defines this minimum of deviation, and how are we to speak of the frequency of deviation proper to this style? The difficulty is merely neutralized by the affirmation that deviation is not at the zero level in scientific language but tends toward zero, and thus that such a language offers the best approximation of a 'writing degree zero' (23). A bit later, dealing with the content, i.e., with the signified, Jean Cohen returns from another angle to the notion of degree zero of style. Absolute prose is content, as distinct from expression. Translatability, whether into another language or in the same language, permits the definition of the semantic equivalence of two messages, that is, identity of information. On this basis, translatability can be taken as the criterion that differentiates the two types of language. 'Abso-

lute prose' is the substance of the content, the signification that guarantees the equivalence of the messages in the 'before' and the 'after' languages. The zero degree is the signification defined by identity of information (16). Now is the difficulty eliminated? Not entirely, if one considers
that absolute translation is itself an ideal limit.

To my mind, the merit of the method is undeniable; its results speak
for it. But I would not say that the measurement of deviations replaces the
consciousness of deviation possessed by speakers; it only provides an equivalent. Moreover, Jean Cohen asks only that his method 'verify an hypothesis,'[15] one which supposes a prior identification of the poetic fact and
its consecration by the 'vast public called posterity' (17). It is not a replacement because the term of comparison is taken outside of the poetic
statement itself, in another discourse belonging to other speakers, to scientists. At the same time the rhetorical consciousness vanishes with the internal tension between two lines of meaning. This is why it seems more
legitimate to me to preserve Gérard Genette's idea of a virtual, filigreed
language, and to pay the price of a correction eliminating the idea of word-
for-word translation in favour of that of an inconsistent literal interpretation of the entire statement. In order that the dynamism of the tension between two interpretations remain immanent within the statement itself,
what Genette says of translation must be said of literal interpretation,
namely that the figure brings about 'visibility in transparency, like a filigree or a palimpsest, beneath its apparent text.'[16] A theory of the figure
must not lose the valuable idea of this 'duplicity of language.'[17]

This is why I say that the calculation of the deviation of poetic language
in relation to another language offers only an equivalent, with respect to
an internal term of reference, of what takes place in the statement between
two levels of interpretation. And the elaboration of this objection is not
all that unjust to Jean Cohen's enterprise in that his most interesting contribution is elsewhere, in the relation between deviation and its reduction.
Moreover, this relation resides within the poetic statement, and consequently it too leads on to a comparison between an actual level and a virtual level of reading at the heart of the poetic statement itself.

Another way to give an account of rhetoric's degree zero is to take it as
a metalinguistic construction – neither virtual in the sense of Genette, nor
actual in the sense of Cohen, but constructed. This is the position adopted
by the authors of the *Rhétorique générale*.[18] Just as decomposition into
smaller and smaller units reveals components on the side of the signifier,
the distinctive traits, that have no explicit and independent existence in
language, so too the decomposition of the signified reveals entities, the
semes, that do not belong to the level where discourse manifests itself. In
both cases, the end-state of the decomposition is infra-linguistic: 'The

units of signification, as they manifest themselves in discourse, begin at the immediately higher level' (*Rhétorique générale* 30). One should not be restricted then to the manifest lexical level, but should transfer the analysis to the semic level. Genette's virtual is not to be linked to some speaker-consciousness but to a construction of the linguist: 'Degree zero is not contained in the language as it is given to us' (35). 'Accordingly, degree zero would be a discourse brought down to its essential semes' (36). However, since these are not distinct lexical types, this reduction is a metalinguistic step (36). It supports the distinction of two parts in figurative discourse: that which has not been modified, or the 'base,' and that which has undergone rhetorical deviation (44). In turn, the latter conserves with its degree zero a certain relation, not gratuitous but systematic, which entails that invariants can be discerned in this other part. While the base has the structure of the syntagma, these invariants have the constitutive structure of a paradigm: that in which degree zero and the figured degree exist together at the same time.

We will leave discussion of the fundamental theses of the *Rhétorique générale* for a later investigation (section 4). Let us just note here that, as concerns the practical determination of degree zero, the problems are the same as in the preceding interpretations. In effect, deviation as such belongs to the level of the manifestation of discourse: 'In the rhetorical sense, we will understand deviation as the detected alteration of degree zero' (41). This definitely is as it should be, if the reduction of deviation (section 3) is more important than deviation; for this is what makes deviation a 'meaningful alteration' (39). Besides, in all discourse, the essential semes are enrobed by lateral semes that carry supplementary, inessential information. This fact is what prevents the practical degree zero – that which can be registered in discourse – from coinciding with the absolute degree zero that a semic analysis could eventually recognize and to which it assigns the 'place outside of language' (37). Recourse to subjective probabilities – fulfilled expectation, etc. – also implies a return to the plane of manifestation. The same holds for the notion of isotopy in Greimas,[19] taken as the semantic norm of discourse: in effect, this notion implies the rule that every message seeks to be taken as a meaningful whole.

Hence, the solution of the problem of deviation at an infralinguistic level does not substitute for its description at the level where discourse manifests itself. At this level, rhetoric needs to note a practical degree zero in language itself. It is in relation to this that deviation is a 'detected alteration'; for 'without doubt it is impossible to decide at what degree of accumulation of inessential semes a deviation begins to be perceived' (42). These difficulties concern precisely the domain of word figures – the metasememes – to which metaphor belongs.

In addition, only those deviations are disclosed by the reader or hearer that have some warning *mark*; this is a greater or lesser departure from the normal level of redundancy, which 'is something known implicitly by every user of a language' (41). Thus, we are brought back to the virtual of the previous interpretation. The characterization of deviation and of its reduction in terms of base and invariant leads back to it ineluctably. Base, it was said, is a particular form of syntagma; as for the invariant, it belongs to the order of the paradigm. Now 'the syntagma is actual and the paradigm is virtual' (44).

2 / THE SPACE OF THE FIGURE

But what does deviation mean? The word itself is a metaphor on the road to extinction, and a spatial metaphor at that. Rhetoric battles valiantly with this metaphoricity of metaphor, which leads it to remarkable discoveries about the actual status of the literal in discourse and thus about 'literature' as such.

We faced this problem already once with the Greek expression *epiphora*.[20] *Epiphora* 'spatializes' in many ways: it is a transfer of meaning 'from (*apo*) ... to (*epi*)'; it runs alongside (*para*) standard usage; it is a replacement (*anti*, in place of). Furthermore, if one compares these spatializing values of transfer of meaning with other properties of metaphor – for example, that it 'sets (something) before the eyes'[21] – and if one also adds the remark that *lexis* makes discourse 'appear,'[22] one constructs a converging cluster that calls for the unifying thread of an enquiry into the figure as such.

A passing remark by Fontanier concerning the word *figure* itself comes very close to wrapping up this issue: 'It appears that, originally, the word *figure* was to be said only of bodies, or, equivalently, of man and of animals considered as physical and with respect to the limits of their extension. And, in this first acceptation, what does it signify? Contours, features, the exterior form of man or of an animal or of any palpable object whatsoever. Addressed only to the intelligence of the soul, discourse is not, properly speaking, a body, even when considered in terms of the words that transmit it through the spirit and the senses. Therefore it has no *figure*, properly speaking; but still, in its different ways of signifying and expressing, it has something analogous to the differences in form and features to be found in real bodies. Without doubt, it was on the basis of this analogy that the *metaphor* "the figures of discourse" was coined. But this *metaphor* ought not be considered a true *figure*, because we have no other words in the language for the same idea.'[23]

Two ideas of space are suggested here, a quasi-corporeal exteriority, and contour, feature, form. The expression *exterior form* unites them in the suggestion of something like a milieu of spatiality overlaid by a design. And these two values of spatiality seem to be implied jointly, if figures are to be defined as 'the features, forms, or contours [second value] by which means discourse, in the expression of ideas, thoughts, or sentiments, assumes a more or less distant position [first value] from what would have been the simple and common expression.'[24]

Roman Jakobson's interpretation of the poetic function in language, in his famous remarks to an Interdisciplinary Conference on Style,[25] provides the bridge between these fleeting remarks and the more concentrated investigations of the neo-rhetoricians. After having enumerated the six factors of communication – addresser, message, addressee, context (which is or can be verbalized), common code, contact (physical or psychic) – Jakobson enumerates functions in parallel fashion, according to which factor dominates. In this way he defines the poetic function as the function that puts the accent on the message for its own sake, and he adds: 'This function, by promoting the palpability of signs, deepens the fundamental dichotomy of signs and objects' (356). The two spatial values brought out above are interpreted here in a completely original fashion. On the one hand, the notion of a contour, of a configuration of the message, rising to top rank, is attached to a precise functioning of the signs in messages of poetic quality, namely, a very particular interlacing of the two fundamental modes in which signs are arranged – selection and combination.[26] Accordingly, with the introduction of two orthogonal axes in place of the simple linearity of the spoken chain endorsed by de Saussure, it is possible to describe the poetic function as a certain alteration in the relation between these two axes. The poetic function projects the principle of equivalence, which belongs to the selection axis, onto the axis of combination. In other words, in the poetic function equivalence is promoted to the rank of constitutive procedure of the sequence. Thus, recurrence of the same phonic figures, rhymes, parallels, and other related procedures in some way introduce a semantic resemblance.

It is evident in what new sense the quasi-corporeality of the message is interpreted – as an adherence of meaning to sound. At first this idea seems to be opposed to that of deviation between letter and meaning; but if one remembers that this meaning is virtual, one can say that sound and real meaning intermingle in the letter of the poem, giving rise to figure according to the process described by Jakobson.

On the other hand, no longer occupying a place between the tonal form and the semantic content, the very notion of a spatiality of deviation is directed elsewhere, and takes up a position between the message accentuated for itself and things – what Jakobson calls the dichotomy of signs and objects. This point is spelled out, following the communication model that is its framework, as a different division of the functions: 'Poeticalness is not a supplementation of discourse with rhetorical adornment but a total re-evaluation of the discourse and of all its components whatsoever' (377). The message is accentuated at the expense of the referential function. Because the message is centred on itself, the poetic function prevails over the referential function; prose also produces this effect ('I like Ike') once the message begins to exist for itself instead of being crossed by the purpose that carries it towards the context it verbalizes. I shall reserve for a separate discussion the question whether the referential function is abolished in poetry or whether, as Jakobson himself suggests, it rather is 'split.'[27] This is a huge question in itself; it involves a properly philosophical decision about what 'reality' signifies. It could be that the everyday reference to the real must be abolished in order that another sort of reference to other dimensions of reality might be liberated. This, when the time comes, will be my thesis. The idea of a shrinking of the referential function – in the form, at least, that ordinary discourse makes use of it – is entirely compatible with the ontological conception that will be set out in the last Study. Hence, we may retain it for our reflection on the spatiality of the figure. The 'conversion of a message into an enduring thing' (371) is what constitutes the quasi-corporeality suggested by the metaphor of the figure.

Taking advantage of Jakobson's breakthrough, neo-rhetoric attempts to reflect on the *visibility* and *spatiality* of the figure. Expanding Fontanier's remark on the metaphor of the figure, Todorov proclaims figure to be what makes discourse appear by making it opaque: 'Discourse that simply brings thought to our cognition is invisible and, by the same token, nonexistent.'[28] Instead of disappearing in its mediating function and making itself 'invisible' and 'nonexistent' as 'thought,' discourse points to itself as discourse: 'The existence of figures equals the existence of discourse' (102).

The remark is not without its difficulties. Firstly, 'transparent discourse,' which would be the rhetoric degree zero of which we spoke earlier, would not be formless from another point of view, for it is said that it 'would be what allows signification to be visible' and that its only purpose is 'to make itself heard' (102). It must be possible, then, to speak of signification quite apart from figure. But in a semiotics that does not turn to the description of the operation as such of the discourse sentence, the very notion of signification remains suspended. Further, the opacity of discourse is identified too quickly with its lack of reference. In opposition to transparent discourse, it is said that 'there is opaque discourse so well covered with "designs" and "figures" that it lets nothing be seen behind it;

this would be a language that does not refer to reality at all, that is complete in itself' (102). The problem of reference is dismissed without a theory of the relations of sense and reference in discourse at the sentence level. It is entirely conceivable that the opacity of words implies some *other* reference and not *no* reference at all (Study 7).

What remains, however, is the very valuable idea that one function of rhetoric is to 'make us take notice of the existence of discourse' (103).

Gérard Genette claims to push to the limit the spatial metaphor of figure, according to its two aspects of distantiation and configuration.[29] There are really two ideas, then: deviation between sign and virtual meaning, which constitutes 'the inner space of language'; and the contour of the figure ('the writer draws the limits of this space'), which here is opposed to the absence of form, at least of rhetorical form, of virtual language. In these two aspects, spatiality is defined here, in the tradition of ancient rhetoric, in relation to virtual language, which would be rhetoric degree zero ('the simple and common expression has no form, the figure does have one,' 209). In this manner, justice is done to Roman Jakobson's idea of an accentuation of the message centred on itself.

But why stay with the metaphor of space instead of translating it, in line with Genette's own stand that every metaphor is translatable? The reason is, essentially, to leave in play the surplus of meaning that constitutes the connotation of the metaphor but does not belong to its denotation (that is, the meaning common to the figure and its translation). Accordingly, the metaphor of a space of discourse is partially translatable. Its translation is the very theory of denotation. What is untranslatable in it is its power to evoke an affective tone, a literary dignity. By calling a ship a sail, my connotation indicates the desire (in the case of synecdoche) to designate the thing by means of a sensible detail, or (in the case of metaphor) to designate it by means of a similarity – in both cases, therefore, by a detour through the sensible. This motivation is 'the very soul of figure' (219). In this sense Genette contrasts the 'surface' of rhetorical form, 'that which the two lines of the present signifier and the absent signifier demarcate,' with the simple linear form of discourse, which is 'purely grammatical' (210). In its first sense, space is a void; in its second sense, it is a design.

To exhibit this motivation, and thus to 'signify poeticalness,' is the connotative function of the figure. Here again we encounter Roman Jakobson's idea of the message centred on itself. What deviation brings to light, beyond the meaning of words, are the values of connotation. These are what the old rhetoric codified: 'Once outside the living speech of personal invention and within the code of the tradition, the sole function of every figure is to hint, in its particular way, at the poetic quality of the discourse that contains it' (220). In the *emblem* that the classical 'sail of the ship' has become for us, we can read at once both '*This* is a *ship*' and 'Look: poetry!' (220).

Thus, the theory of figures blends into a whole current of thought for which literature is auto-significative. The code of literary connotations, which the rhetoric of figures joins, is to be linked to the codes under which Roland Barthes puts the 'signs of literature.'[30]

The metaphor of the interior space of discourse, then, must be treated like every figure. It denotes the distance between the letter and virtual meaning; it connotes a whole cultural orientation, that of a person who highlights in contemporary literature its self-signifying function. Because of these untranslatable connotations, Genette is in no hurry to translate the metaphor of the space of language and is happy to stay with it. The space of language, in effect, is a connoted space, 'connoted, manifested more than pointed to, speaking rather than spoken of, which betrays itself in metaphor like the surfacing of the unconscious in a slip or a dream.'[31]

Is it unfair to apply to this declaration what the author just said about the symbolic value of the word 'sail'? – and to cry 'Look: modernity!'? Genette's discourse on the spatiality of discourse connotes the preference of contemporary man for space, following the Bergsonian inflation of duration ('man prefers space to time' [107]). On this basis, when the author writes 'one could almost say that it is space that speaks' (102), his own speaking is to be interpreted more in terms of what it connotes than in terms of what it denotes: 'Today, literature – thought – no longer articulates itself except in terms of distance, horizon, universe, surroundings, place, area, routes, and home-ground: naive figures, but characteristic, figures *par excellence*, in which language *spatializes itself* in order that space, having become language, may speak and inscribe itself in it' (108). In fashioning this brilliant maxim, the author produces the sign of his allegiance to the school of thought for which the meaning of literature is found in literature.

I should like to ask whether what is really denoted by this meditation on space, and not only what is connoted, is entirely satisfactory. What seems to me to be gained is the idea of an opacity of discourse centred on itself, the idea that figures render discourse visible. What I question are the two consequences drawn from it. It is supposed, first, that the suspension of the referential function, as it operates in ordinary discourse, implies the abolition of all referential function; this leaves literature to signify itself. Once again, we are faced with a decision concerning the signification of 'reality' that goes beyond the resources of linguistics and rhetoric and belongs properly to the philosophical order. The affirmation of the opacity of poetic discourse and its corollary, the obliteration of ordinary reference, are merely the starting-point of an immense inquiry on the topic of reference, one which cannot be dismissed so summarily.

The second reservation has to do with the very distinction between denotation and connotation. Can one say that figurative language signifies poetry alone, that is, the particular quality of discourse that possesses figure? The surplus of meaning would then remain generic, as is moreover the alarm 'Look: poetry!.' If one wanted to preserve the notion of connotation, it would be necessary in any case to treat it in a more specific fashion, in terms of the uniqueness of each poem. One might reply that this generic quality can be analysed in turn into epic quality, lyric quality, didactic quality, oratorical quality, and so on. Would this mean then, that to call something literature is to point to the multiple, distinct qualities – the figures – that rhetoric lists, then classifies and orders in systems? But this is again designation of species, of types. Genette says so himself: rhetoric cares little about the originality or the novelty of figures, 'which are qualities of individual speech, and which, as such, do not concern it' (220). What interests it are the codified forms whose system would make a second language out of literature. What is to be said, then, of the singular connotations of this or that poem? Northrop Frye is closer to the truth when he says that the structure of a poem articulates a 'mood,' an affective value.[32] However (as I will argue in Study 7), this 'mood' is quite a bit more than a subjective emotion. It is a way of being rooted in reality; it is an ontological index. With it the referent returns, but in a radically new sense in comparison to ordinary language. This is why the denotation-connotation distinction has to be maintained to be entirely problematic and linked to a properly positivistic presupposition according to which only the objective language of scientific prose would be able to denote. To deviate from it would be to no longer denote anything. This presupposition is a prejudice that must be exposed to direct interrogation.

Unable to carry out this process here, we will note only that the affirmation that the figure's surplus of meaning depends on connotation is the exact counterpart of the affirmation discussed earlier that the figure is translatable with regard to its sense – in other words, that it carries no new information. Now this thesis is eminently debatable. I believe that, with the English authors, I have shown that it is of a piece with a substitutive conception of metaphor, which in turn remains restricted to a word-focused conception of metaphor. But if metaphor is a statement, it is possible that this statement would be untranslatable, not only as regards its connotation, but as regards its very meaning, thus as regards its denotation. It teaches something, and so it contributes to the opening up and the discovery of a field of reality other than that which ordinary language lays bare.

3 / DEVIATION AND REDUCTION OF DEVIATION

Is figure nothing but deviation? With this question we enter into a criteriology of properly rhetorical deviations. This question cannot be dissociated from the one dealt with in the first section, about the rhetoric degree zero in relation to which deviation takes place. Instead of returning to this problem, we will concentrate on one of a different sort: are there criteria of figurative language? The ancients, Todorov remarks, were unable to give any meaning to the idea of a 'deviation towards the alogical,'[33] not having defined the logical character of everyday discourse and not having explained the rule of infractions in which usage sets limits on the overly indeterminate boundaries of logic. The criterion of 'frequency' (101) falters before the same paradox. Figure is opposed to the common and usual ways of speaking. But figures are not always rare; moreover, the most unusual of all discourses would be one devoid of figure. More interesting is the remark of ancient and classical authors that figures are what render discourse describable by making it appear in discernible forms. I spelt out above the idea that figure makes discourse 'perceptible.' Let us now add: makes it 'describable.'

But the author says himself that this third criterion, of 'describability,' is only a weak criterion. Figure here is not contrasted with a rule but with a discourse that one does not know how to describe. This is why, to the extent that this weak criterion is applicable to it, a good part of the classical theory of figures is really just an anticipation of linguistics and of its four domains – sound-meaning relation, syntax, semantics, sign-referent relation (113). We will return to this point in the fifth section.

A strong criterion is not provided by the idea of describability but by that of rule-breaking. Subsequently, however, if transgression itself is to be regulated, the idea of deviation understood as violation of a code must be completed by the idea of reduction of deviation, in order to give form to deviation itself, or, in the language of Genette, to mark off the space opened up by deviation.

It was Jean Cohen who introduced – in decisive fashion, to my mind – the notion of reduction of deviation. His identification of metaphor with all reduction of deviation is more debatable, but it does not affect the substance of his discovery. Nowhere is the confrontation with the interaction theory more illuminating or fruitful.

I shall not return to Jean Cohen's stylistic definition of deviation, nor its statistical treatment (cf. section 1). I shall take up his work at the point where the notion of deviation allows him, at the very core of the signified, to distinguish the signified substance (that is, the information produced) from the 'form of the meaning' (38), in the words of Mallarmé. 'The *poetic fact* is born the moment Valéry calls the sea "roof" and boats "doves." That constitutes a violation of the language code, a linguistic deviation, which (with ancient rhetoric) can be called "figure" and which alone gives the poetic its true object' (44).

Two methodological decisions are made at this point. The first concerns distribution in levels and functions, and the second the introduction of the notion of reduction of deviation, which is of more particular interest to us.

Through the first methodological decision the theorist can claim to assume again the task of the old rhetoric at the point where the latter stopped. It is necessary, after having classified the figures, to extract their common structure. The old rhetoric had identified only the rationale proper to each figure, whereas 'structural poetics is located at a superior level of formalization. It seeks a form of forms, a general poetic operator of which all the figures would just be so many particular virtual realizations, specified according to the level and the linguistic function in which the operator actualizes itself' (50). The analysis of figures (setting aside the second theme, the reduction of deviation) will first be accomplished according to levels – the phonic level and the semantic level – and then according to functions. Thus rhyme and meter are two distinct phonic operators, the one relating to the function of diction, the other to the function of contrast. At the semantic level, the identification of the three functions of predication, determination, and co-ordination permits the distinction of a predicative operator, metaphor; a determinative operator, epithet; and an operator of co-ordination, incoherence. Accordingly metaphor is opposed on the one hand to rhyme, as semantic operator versus phonic operator, and on the other hand to epithet among the semantic operators. In this way poetics rises from a simple taxonomy to a theory of operations.

The second methodological decision must now be taken. The notion of deviation as it has been defined up until now, that is as a systematic violation of the language code, is in effect nothing but the other side of another process: 'Poetry destroys ordinary language only to reconstruct it on a higher level. The "de-structuring" done by the figure is followed by a "re-structuring" of another order' (51).

By joining the two rules of method, it is possible to come up with a theory of figure that would not be a mere extension of the theory of tropes. Here, in its deep structure, the verse is a figure like others. But is the phenomenon of reduction of deviation to be seen there as well as the phenomenon of deviation? The latter is strongly evident, represented first in versification by the contrast between phonic and semantic segmentation (divisions of the verse and of the sentence respectively); the insertion of a metric pause without semantic value constitutes a disruption of the phono-semantic parallelism. Now does versification offer at the same time something like a reduction of deviation that subdues the conflict between meter and syntax? The quantitative analysis of Jean Cohen claims only that, from classical to romantic and then to symbolist poetry, 'versification did not stop increasing the divergence between meter and syntax; *it has always gone further in the direction of agrammaticalism*' (69). Verse, concludes Cohen, is the anti-sentence. But it is not apparent where the reduction of deviation is located. The comparative study of rhyme presents the same phenomenon of increase of deviation, calculated in terms of the frequency of non-categorial rhymes (85). The same holds for meter, and for the split it creates between homometry (and homorythmics) at the level of the signifier and a homosemy that does not exist in the poem: 'By this the parallelism of sound and sense is broken, and it is within this rupture that verse fulfils its true function' (93).

Truly, then, it seems that at the phonic level deviation operates alone, without reduction of deviation. Must one conclude that the counterpart is treated only by omission – 'we have ... examined in this study only the first phase of a mechanism which, we feel, entails two phases' (51) – or that reduction of deviation is a semantic phenomenon *par excellence*? This sort of conclusion will be particularly interesting for the later discussion of the phenomena of semantic impertinence and pertinence.[34]

Now the author himself remarks that the resistance of intelligibility is what prevents the total destruction of the message by the phonic figure. So prose is present at the very heart of poetry: 'In fact, the verse is constituted by antimony. For it is not unidirectional;* it doubles back. If it were, it would not be able to carry meaning. Because it signifies, it remains linear. The poetic message is at once verse and prose' (101). Accordingly, I do not think it is forcing the author's thought to conclude that what reduces the phonic deviation is the meaning itself – that is, what at the semantic level reduces another sort of deviation that itself is properly semantic. Therefore, the phenomenon of reduction of deviation should be sought essentially at the semantic level.

The conception of a deviation – and a reduction of deviation – proper to the semantic level of discourse depends on the elucidation of a code of pertinence [meaningfulness or relevance, *pertinence*] governing the interrelationships of signified entities. It is this code that the poetic message violates. Syntactically correct sentences can be absurd, that is incorrect with respect to meaning, through impertinence [calculated error, *impertinence*] of the predicate. A law exists demanding that in every predicative

---

* 'L'antinomie constitue le vers. Car il n'est pas tout entier vers, c'est-à-dire retour.' The English does not capture the pun on *vers* the noun (verse) and the adverb (towards). (Trans.)

sentence the predicate must be pertinent in relation to the subject, that is, should be semantically capable of fulfilling its function. Plato called on this law when, in the *Sophist*,[35] he noted that communication of 'kinds' rests on the distinction between genera that are entirely incompatible with each other and those that can accommodate each other partially. This law is more restrictive than the general condition of 'grammaticality' defined by Chomsky, at least before the properly semantic developments of his theory since 1967.[36] The law of semantic pertinence, according to Jean Cohen, designates the combinatory permissions that the *signified* must satisfy among themselves if the sentence is to be received as intelligible. In this sense, the code governing semantic pertinence is properly a 'code of speech' (109).

On this basis it is possible to characterize Mallarmé's expression 'The sky is dead' as flagrant predicative impertinence, since the predicate *is dead* is compatible only with individuals belonging to the category of living beings.

We turn now to metaphor, which has not yet been mentioned, but supposedly embodies the fundamental characteristic of poetic language – that is, metaphor is not deviation itself, but the reduction of deviation. Deviation exists only if words are taken in their literal meaning. Metaphor is the process through which the speaker reduces the deviation by changing the meaning of one of the words. As the rhetorical tradition established, metaphor is truly a trope, that is, a change of the meaning of words; but the change of meaning is the answer of discourse to the threat of destruction represented by semantic impertinence. And this answer in turn consists of the production of another deviation, namely in the lexical code itself. 'Metaphor intervenes in the interests of reducing the deviation created through impertinence. The two deviations are complementary, but precisely because they are not situated on the same linguistic plane. Impertinence is a violation of the code of speech, and is located on the syntagmatic level; metaphor is a violation of the language code, and belongs to the paradigmatic level. There is a sort of dominance of speech over language, with the latter agreeing to change in order to give meaning to the former. The totality of the procedure comprises two inverse and complementary phases – (1) situation of deviation: *impertinence*; (2) reduction of deviation: metaphor' (114).

This conception of a counterbalanced operation, bringing the two domains of speech and of language into play, is applied in the three adjoining regions of predication, determination, and co-ordination, which functional analysis distinguishes at one and the same semantic level. Predication and determination actually overlap, since the attribution of a characteristic to a subject in the name of a property is studied, for 'the convenience of the analysis' (119), in the epithet form. The essence of the study of the first function is an inquiry into *impertinent epithets* ('the clenched-fist wind of morning,' 'he ascended the ruthless stairs').

According to the second function, determination, the epithet has the precise meaning of a quantification and a localization that cause the epithet to apply only to a segment of the subject's extension. Rhetorical, and so impertinent, use of the epithet will be that which violates this rule of determination – in other words, redundant epithets; for example, 'pale death.' At first sight redundancy is the opposite of impertinence (the 'verte émeraude' of Vigny, the 'azur bleu' of Mallarmé). This would be the case were determination not a function distinct from predication. If, on the other hand, the two figures are distinct, they each have their own type of deviation and (in this broad sense) of impertinence. The rule that the redundant epithet breaks is that it should bear new information in determining its subject. The violation of this rule through redundancy results in absurdity, since it makes the part equal to the whole. Where, then, is the reduction of deviation? It can consist in a change in grammatical function (the detached epithet becomes apposition, it loses its determinative function to resume a predicative function); the trope is then grammatical. But the reduction can also consist in a change in word meaning; the tautology in 'azure blue' disappears if 'the blue, on account of the metaphor, takes on a meaning that is no longer that of the code' (155). And this leads back to explanation in terms of impertinent epithets.[37]

The function of co-ordination takes the analysis beyond the sentence and to the level of the succession of sentences in discourse. It is grounded in the semantic level, to the extent that the constraints that codify it borrow from the semantic homogeneity of ideas 'set together.' In violating this demand for thematic unity, nonsense, as well as disconnected or incoherent style, refers back to the rules of semantic pertinence that govern the first predicative function. One can speak of deviation through inconsequence. Consider, for example, nature's unexpected invasion of the human drama in Victor Hugo's famous verse in *Booz endormi* ('Asphodels breathed a fresh perfume; / Whispers of night brushed o'er Galgala'), and every unexpected combination of the physical and the spiritual ('Here are fruit, flowers, leaves and branches. And then here is my heart which beats only for you' – Verlaine, quoted p. 177). Discovery of a homogeneity, therefore, will reduce the deviation caused by terms not all belonging to the same universe of discourse; the procedure here is the same as in the case of predication.

Thus, the same two-phase process rules in the three regions of predication, determination, and co-ordination. Each time 'the figure is the conflict between syntagma and paradigm, discourse and system ... Poetic discourse runs counter to the system, and in this struggle it is the system that backs down and agrees to transform' (134).

The critical remarks that follow aim at situating the analysis by Jean Cohen in relation to the interaction theory set out in the third Study. This comparison brings out a convergence, then a divergence, and finally a possible co-ordination.

Let us begin with the convergence. Nowhere is the structural treatment of metaphor as close to the interaction theory. To start with, the properly semantic aspect of metaphor is fully recognized here as a phenomenon of the predicative order. In this connection, the concept of semantic impertinence in Cohen and that of self-contradictory statement in Beardsley correspond perfectly. Cohen's analysis even has the advantage over that of Beardsley of distinguishing absurdity from contradiction, by distinguishing the code of semantic pertinence from the codes of grammaticality and of logical coherence.

Moreover, the theory addresses itself directly to newly invented metaphor, since metaphor in common use is not a case of poetic deviation.[38]

Finally, the breadth of the problem of *epiphora* in Aristotle is restored by a theory that propounds the universality of the double process of production and reduction of deviation. Given that, one may well quarrel with the author's terminology. Was it necessary to reserve the word *metaphor* to designate those changes of meaning where the relationship is one of resemblance, or to give it the generic meaning of 'change of meaning'? This, though, is a peripheral issue: Jean Cohen is in good company with Aristotle.[39]

And yet Cohen's theory, despite its extraordinary merit in comparison to the rest of French-language writing on the subject, is significantly inferior in relation to the corresponding English-language work. As was noted, the only phenomenon of the syntagmatic order is impertinence, the violation of the code of speech. Metaphor properly speaking does not belong to the syntagmatic order; as a violation of the language code, it is situated on the paradigmatic plane. With this bias, we remain within the rhetorical tradition of the one-word trope and under the sway of the theory of substitution. It seems to me that the theory contains a serious omission, that of the new pertinence, which is properly syntagmatic and of which the paradigmatic deviation is but the reverse side. Jean Cohen writes: 'The poet plays upon the message in order to change the language' (115). Should he not also write: 'The poet changes the language in order to play upon the message'? Does he not come close to doing so when he adds: 'If the poem transgresses the code of speech, it is in order that the language re-establish it by transforming it' (115)? But then, it is untrue that 'the goal of all poetry' is to 'establish an alteration in language that at the same time, we shall see, is a mental metamorphosis' (115). Rather, it seems that the goal of poetry is to establish a new pertinence by means of an alteration in the language.

The force of the interaction theory lies in keeping together the two stages of the process, production and reduction of deviation, on the same level, namely that of predication. In changing the lexical code, the poet 'makes sense' with the entire statement containing the metaphorical word. The metaphor as such is a case of application of the predicate. The structural theory of Jean Cohen rids itself of such a concept, in order to operate with just two sorts of deviations. It succeeds through this conceptual economy in shepherding metaphor into the fold of the word and under the care of the substitution theory; the problem posed by the initiation of a new pertinence is thus avoided.

Yet it seems to me that Cohen's own analysis calls for this absent term. The production of deviation brings to light impertinent epithets (Cohen is justified in bringing predication itself into the 'epithetic form' (119), that is, the attribution of a characteristic in the guise of property of a logical subject), without as a consequence giving epithet properly speaking a distinct function of determination (137 ff.). Should he not have set up the new compatibility as epithet face to face with the paradigmatic deviation, i.e. lexical deviation – and thus, have spoken of a metaphorically pertinent epithet?

It is true that Cohen himself states that poetry creates 'a new linguistic order founded on the ruins of the old, through which ... a new type of signification is built' (134). But the author, as we shall see, like Genette and others, seeks this order not in the area of objective information but in that of affective values of a subjective character. Can one not hypothesize that it is because he has not reflected on the new pertinence at the very level of predication that the author joins the idea of a new type of signification lacking referential import to the idea of a paradigmatic deviation?

In this fashion the author confronts (only to dismiss it immediately) the properly semantic treatment of co-ordinative deviation (the third type at the semantic level): 'Between heterogeneous terms, homogeneity must be discovered' (178). Will the new pertinence be considered? No: this case was assimilated immediately into that of predicative deviation; and all that is pointed out in addition is the 'affective resemblance' that takes us completely outside the semantic domain, to the conclusion that 'emotional unity is the obverse side of notional inconsequence' (179).

Nevertheless, the missing term is sighted several times. The author holds that poetry, like all discourse, must be intelligible for its reader; like prose, poetry is a discourse that the author offers to his reader. Cannot then reduction of deviation unfold on the same plane on which deviation arose?

'Poetizing is a process with two correlative and simultaneous faces: deviation and reduction, destruction and restructuring. For the poem to function poetically, it is necessary that in *the consciousness of the reader, the signification be at once lost and recovered*' (182, author's emphasis). But must one then assign to other disciplines, 'psychology or phenomenology,' the task of determining the nature of this 'transmutation' (182) that draws meaning out of non-sense?

After having created a place for predicative pertinence and impertinence, Cohen's theory realigns with the other structural theories that operate with signs or collections of signs alone and ignore the central problem of semantics: the constitution of meaning as a property of the undivided sentence.

This omission of the properly predicative moment of metaphor is not without consequences. Since the theory thematizes just the lexical mutation, the study of the function of poetic language will be deprived of its essential support, namely the mutation of meaning at the same level at which the semantic impertinence takes place. It is not surprising, then, that one falls back into a theory of connotation and, at the same time, to an emotionalist theory of poetry. Recognition of the new semantic pertinence achieved through the lexical mutation is the only thing that could lead to an investigation of the new referential values attached to the innovation in meaning and open the way to an examination of the heuristic value of metaphorical statements.

But I would not want to end on this critical note. The addition of the predicative moment, which I call the *new pertinence*, at the same time allows one to say at what level a theory of paradigmatic deviation acquires meaning and validity. My critique will have been misunderstood if the conclusion is drawn from it that the notion of paradigmatic deviation is to be rejected.

On the contrary, it is invested with its full value if it is attached to the term missing from the theory, to the new pertinence. Indeed, Cohen proposes to show how the syntagmatic and the paradigmatic planes, far from being opposed, complete each other. Now, only the inception of a new pertinence within the metaphorical statement clears the way for linking a lexical deviation with a predicative deviation.

Returned thus to its place, paradigmatic deviation recovers its full value. It corresponds, in the interaction theory, to the phenomenon of *focalization* on the word described at the end of the previous Study.[40] Metaphorical meaning is an effect of the entire statement, but it is focused on one word, which can be called the metaphorical word. This is why one must say that metaphor is a semantic innovation that belongs at once to the predicative order (new pertinence) and the lexical order (paradigmatic deviation). In its first aspect it depends upon a 'dynamics' of meaning; under the second, upon a 'stasis' or non-dynamic state of a system. It is under this second aspect that it is addressed by a structural theory of poetry.

Accordingly, there is no conflict, properly speaking, between the theory of substitution (or of deviation) and the interaction theory. The latter describes the dynamics of the metaphorical statement; it alone deserves to be called a *semantic* theory of metaphor. The substitution theory describes the impact of this dynamic on the lexical code, where it sees a deviation; in doing so, it offers a *semiotic* equivalent of the semantic process.

The two approaches are grounded in the double character of the word. As a lexeme, the word is a difference in the lexical code. In this first guise it is affected by the paradigmatic deviation that Jean Cohen describes. As a part of discourse, it bears a part of the meaning that belongs to the entire statement. In this second role, it is affected by the interaction described by the interaction theory.

4 / THE FUNCTIONING OF FIGURES: 'SEMIC' ANALYSIS

The question of criteria of rhetorical deviation may still be posed at the level at which discourse appears. The question of operation or procedures calls for a change of level comparable to that which led to the decomposition of phonemes, the last distinctive units in the order of the signifier, into pertinent traits at the infralinguistic level. In the same way, the *signified* can be decomposed into semantic atoms, called semes, that do not belong to the surface level of discourse. The *Rhétorique générale* of the Liège group, and to a lesser degree the work of Le Guern,[41] will serve as my guide. We have already referred to this methodological decision in connection with the determination of the rhetoric degree zero, but we postponed examination of the problem posed by this strategy until later. We shall examine it now, at the same time as we pass from a simple criteriology to a theory of procedures.

At stake in this enterprise is the possibility of linking functional concepts (deviation, redundancy, etc.) to simple operations, such as *suppressing* and *adding*, that are at work at all the levels at which discourse is effected. In this way justice would be done to the universality of the notion of figure and to the generality of rhetoric itself.

But this involves the presupposition, which precedes all the other analyses and which the authors pass over very quickly (*Rhétorique générale* 37), that all the levels of decomposition (in the 'descending' sense) and of integration (in the 'ascending' sense) are homogeneous. We recognize in this what we have called the *semiotic postulate*.[42] Certainly this borrows from Benveniste's idea of the hierarchy of levels, but one destroys his point by depriving it of its fundamental corollary, the duality between semiotic units or signs and semantic units or sentences. The level of the sentence is just one among others (cf. table I, 31); the minimal complete sentence 'is defined by the presence of two syntagmas, the one nominal and the other verbal, by the relative order of these syntagmas, and by the complementarity of their markings' (68). But this order and this complementarity do not constitute a heterogeneous factor in a system where addition and suppression are to be the fundamental operations. These operations demand that one work only with collectivities. Phonemes, graphemes, words, and so on are collectivities (see the definitions, 33). So too the sentence; it is defined, at least in French, 'by the minimal presence of certain constituents, the syntagmas' (33); and these 'are defined in turn by morphemes that belong to them and divide them into classes' (33-4). As for morphemes, they subdivide into phonemes on the one hand, then into distinctive traits (which are infralinguistic); and on the other hand, into sememes (words) and then into (infralinguistic) semes. No discontinuity is allowed, either in the ascending or the descending scale. This is why all the units at all levels can be considered as 'collections of elements built upon pre-existing stocks' (31). The sentence is no exception; it is defined, as to its grammatical side, as a 'collection of syntagmas and of morphemes, endowed with an order and admitting of repetition' (34). This order is what Benveniste calls predicate and what breaks up the monotony of the hierarchy. From a semiotic point of view, order is just an aspect of collection.

The table of *metaboles* (that is, of all operations on language) presents the same homogeneous character. It is established on the basis of a double dichotomy, which on the one hand distinguishes the signifier from the signified (expression and content in the terminology of Hjelmslev), and on the other hand distinguishes entities smaller than or as large as the word from larger entities.

Four domains are distinguished in this way. The domain of *metaplasmes* covers figures that act on the sound or graphic aspect of words and of smaller units. That of *metataxes* contains figures that act on the structure of the sentence (as defined above). *The third domain contains metaphor.* The authors of the *Rhétorique générale* call it the domain of *metasememes*, which they define as follows: 'A metasememe is a figure that replaces one sememe by another, that is, modifies the groupings of degree-zero semes. This type of figure supposes that the word is equal to a collection of *nuclear semes*, without internal order and not admitting of repetition' (34). Finally we have the domain of *metalogismes*; these are figures that modify the logical value of the sentence (according to the second definition cited above).

It is granted from the outset that metaphor is to be sought among the metasememes, and so among the word-focused figures, as in classical rhetoric. With such a beginning, it will be difficult to connect its functioning to a predicative character of statements, since the metataxes constitute a distinct class and the sentence-structure they modify is considered from the perspective of the collectivity of its constituents (syntagmas or semes). The path of the statement-metaphor is thus blocked. It is granted at the same time that, as in classical rhetoric, the metasememes are substitutive phenomena, replacing one sememe with another. So the originality of the work, as it deals with metaphor, does not consist in the definition of metaphor as a word-focused figure, nor in the description of this figure as substitution; it lies in the explanation of substitution itself in terms of a modification bearing on the collectivity of nuclear semes. Put differently, all of its originality lies in the change in the level of analysis, in the descent to the infra-linguistic level of semes, which are to the signified what distinctive traits are to the signifier.

The whole apparatus of functional concepts and operations brought into play will not bring with it any essential change in the theory of metaphor, but only a higher level of technical finesse and the reduction of word-figures to a basic type of functioning common to all figures.

One can anticipate, nevertheless, that the framework adopted by the new rhetoric will break down in the same way as that of the old rhetoric, under the very pressure of the description that, whether we like it or not, reintroduces the predicative aspects of metaphor.

The change of strategic level permits the introduction of operative concepts and then of operations that act at all the levels where units of signification have managed to be brought together into collectivities of elements. Accordingly, one will come across them again at work in the four classes of metaboles.

We have already spoken of these operative concepts in connection with the notion of degree zero. The operative concepts are those of information theory (the concept of semantic information being that of Carnap and Bar-Hillel: the identification of a piece of information is determined by the number of binary choices one must make in order to arrive at it; thus, one will be able to give a numerical signification to the addition and suppression of units in which the transformations applied to units of signification consist). It then becomes possible again to take up the notions of deviation and its reduction, discussed in the two previous sections, as well as the notion of convention, which is a systematic deviation, and express these notions in terms of redundancy and self-correction. Deviation diminishes redundancy, and so predictability. Reduction of deviation is a self-correction that re-establishes the integrity of the message. Every figure alters the amount of redundancy in discourse whether by reducing it or by adding to it. From the point of view of redundancy, conventions operate in the reverse manner to deviation properly speaking, since they reinforce redundancy (38-45). As for reduction, it involves two conditions. (1) In figurative discourse one can distinguish on the one hand a part, or 'base,' that has not been modified and is a particular form of syntagma; and on the other hand, a part that has undergone rhetorical alterations. (2) The second part retains with its degree zero a certain relation that falls under certain paradigms of articulation of degree zero and of figurative degree. This point is important for the theory of metaphor. The invariant in the paradigmatic order will be the virtual term common to degree zero and the figurative degree. Here we encounter again a postulate that we have shown to belong to the same model as the other postulates of deviation and of substitution. Metaphor is a substitution within a sphere of selection that is here called the invariant and has the status of paradigm, whereas the base, which has the status of syntagma, remains unmodified. This amounts to saying that no information comes through the figure. That is why its positive function is consigned to the study of *ethos*, that is, of the specific aesthetic effect taken as the true object of aesthetic communication.

'In sum, rhetoric is a collection of *deviations* capable of *self-correction*, that is to say, modifying the normal level of *redundancy* of language, by breaking rules or by inventing new ones. The deviation created by an author is perceived by the reader thanks to a *mark* and subsequently is reduced thanks to the presence of an *invariant*' (45). (I am intentionally ending the quotation before the introduction of the notion of *ethos*, which, along with those of deviation, mark, and invariant, completes the list of 'operative concepts' [35-45].)

The operations that interest the whole of the field of figures and have provisionally been called transformations – the metaboles – divide into two large groups, according to whether they alter the units themselves or their position, that is, the linear order of units. Thus, they are either substantial or relational. Word-figures have an interest in the first type of transformation. The key idea – at which the notion of 'collection' hinted – is that the operations of this group reduce to additions and suppressions; that is, because of the operative concepts adopted, to an increase or decrease of information. The second kind of operation does not interest us, since the word is a collection of nuclear semes without internal order. Hence, metaphor will bring into play neither syntagmatic operation nor the concept of order implied by the sentence.

The theory of *metasememes* – a new name given to tropes or one-word figures to indicate symmetry with the 'metabole' and 'metaplasme' already adopted (33) and, further, in order to designate the nature of the operation in question – is the rigorous application of these operations of addition and suppression to the collection of semes or minimal units of meaning, which constitute the word. Classical rhetoric knew only the effect on meaning, namely, the fact that the figure 'replaces the *content* of one word by another' (93). General rhetoric takes this nominal definition as established; but it explains substitution as an arrangement of semes resulting from addition and suppression, with a portion of the initial meaning – the base – remaining unchanged.[43]

The enterprise encounters a major difficulty, however: how are figure and polysemy to be distinguished? A word is defined in lexicological terms, indeed, by the enumeration of its semantic variants or sememes. These are contextual classes, that is, types of occurrence in possible contexts. The dictionary word is the *corpus* constituted by these sememes. Now this field already includes the phenomenon of deviation, but internal to the corpus, between a principal meaning and peripheral meanings (the *Rhétorique générale* cites the semic analysis of the word *tête* ['head'] in *Sémantique structurale* by Greimas).[44] And so the word considered as paradigm of its possible uses appears as an area of substitution, in which all the variations have equal status (each use of the word *tête* is a metasememe equivalent to all the others). If the deviations that constitute word-figures are also substitutions, and if the lexicalized word carries deviations within itself, semantic process and rhetorical process become indistinguishable. Moreover, as we shall see, this is the direction of the notion of metaphorical process in Jakobson: all paradigmatic selection becomes metaphorical.[45]

The authors of the *Rhétorique générale* are conscious of this difficulty; but it seems to me that the answer they offer makes an implicit appeal to a theory of the figure of discourse that is foreign to their system.

In order 'to restore to the rhetorical process its specificity in relation to the purely semantic process' (95), it is necessary first to introduce the idea of a tension between two variations of meaning. Figure occurs only if, through the change of meaning, 'a tension endures, a distance, between the two sememes, of which the first remains present, even if implicitly' (95). What is this tension? Let us grant that it can be contained within the boundaries of one and the same word. But what about its mark? (The figure, in fact, is a sensed deviation; the word must be 'felt' to be filled with a new meaning [96].) It is here that a syntagmatic factor, a context, must necessarily intervene: 'If it remains true to say that the metasememe can be reduced to modification of the contents of a single word, one must add for the sake of completeness that the figure will not be perceived except in a sequence or sentence' (95). Is this really only 'for the sake of completeness'? Is the sentence merely the condition of the mark's perception, or is it involved in the very constitution of the figure? We have reiterated that there are no metaphors in the dictionary; even though polysemy is lexicalized, metaphor, at least newly created metaphor, is not; and when it does become lexicalized, it means that the metaphor in common use has become part of polysemy. Now it certainly seems that a syntagmatic factor from the order of the sentence should be at the origin of the figure, and not just of its mark. Within the figure, the message is perceived to be linguistically incorrect. Now this incorrectness is immediately a fact of discourse; if this is not granted, one cannot (as do the authors of the *Rhétorique générale*) integrate Jean Cohen's notion of semantic impertinence with the theory of metasememes ('Here we join Jean Cohen, who very neatly formulated the complementarity of these two operations, perception and reduction of deviation. The first is clearly located on the syntagmatic plane, the second on the paradigmatic plane' [97].) But how is it not seen that this 'dissonance ... of a semantic order' (96) is a fact of predication that corrupts the very notion of metasememe? The *Rhétorique générale* dismisses the difficulty by rejecting among the 'extrinsic conditions' (96) those that are manifestly intrinsic to the production of the meaning effect. I would account in the following manner for the ease with which the authors proceed to this reduction of the syntagmatic conditions of word figures to a simple extrinsic condition: it could be that synecdoche, to which metaphor presently will be reduced, lends itself better to this reduction than metaphor itself and that the dissymmetry between the two figures resides precisely in a difference at the level of operation of the sentence. We will come to this later.

So, as Jean Cohen says as well, it is reduction of deviation, unfolding (it is granted) only on the paradigmatic level, that carries the entire burden of explanation. How do addition and suppression operate?

The reply to this question cannot be given directly; it requires that the question of semantic segmentation first be resolved. Now the latter passes via the detour of the *object* and its linguistic counterpart, the *concept*. This perambulation is foreshadowed from the beginning of the work: 'One can equally take the view that certain words refer mediately to an object = collection of co-ordinated parts, and that this decomposition of the object into its parts (at the level of the referent) has its linguistic counterpart (at the level of concepts), the one like the other being designable by words ... the results of these two decompositions are completely different' (34).[46] Later these two decompositions are called 'models of representation,' that is 'models capable of aiding the description of the universe of representations' (97). Material analysis of the object and notional analysis of the concept do not coincide; the first results in a parcelling up of classes, its analysis resting on similarities, while the second results in a tree of disjunctions with its analysis resting on differences.

It certainly seems that the properly linguistic model (the endocentric series described on pages 99-100) is not independent of these 'purely cognitive' models (97), since the descending linear itineraries that the series of words follow are 'traced in the pyramid of nested classes or in the disjunctive tree' (99). Furthermore, the authors affirm this clearly: 'It is always the semantic universe itself that is at the bottom of this structuring of vocabulary' (99).

The two types of semantic *decomposition* considered, accordingly, are copied from the nesting of classes and from decomposition on the model of the disjunctive tree. The conceptual mode and the material mode of decomposition give two different statuses to the notion of an individual: a given tree will be either 'poplar' *or* 'oak' *or* 'willow,' but it will also be 'branches' *and* 'leaves' *and* 'trunk' *and* 'roots.' The semic analysis is thus dependent on the laws that 'govern the collective whole of the semantic universe.' This dependence particularly affects the theory of the noun, placed at the centre of the word figures. In effect, the distinction between concrete nouns and abstract nouns can be equated with the two modes of decomposition: the concrete 'tree' is the empirical conjunction of all its parts, the abstract 'tree' is the rational disjunction of all its modalities.[47]

It is to these two modes of decomposition that the two operations of suppression and of addition apply. The classification of tropes (synecdoche, metaphor, metonymy) undergoes a profound alteration due to this fact. The guiding thread is no longer to be sought at the level of effects of meaning but of operations: the notions of suppression of semes, of addition, and of suppression *plus* addition will now guide.

The principal result – the one that concerns our investigation directly – is that *synecdoche* takes first place and metaphor is reduced to synecdoche through an addition and a suppression making metaphor the product of two synecdoches.

This outcome could have been foreseen at the point at which the metasememe was considered within the limits of the word and its activity restricted to a modification of the collection of semes. Indeed, the partial suppression of semes gives us directly the generalizing synecdoche, most often of type Σ: species to genus, particular to general (e.g. when one says 'mortals' for 'men'). Total suppression would lead to asemy – 'stuff,' 'thing' for anything and everything. Simple addition gives us the particularizing synecdoche, most often of type π (e.g. 'sail' for 'vessel'). Synecdoche, in fact, is the figure that best verifies the theory, because of (1) the conservation of a foundation of essential semes whose suppression would render discourse incomprehensible; (2) the operation of simple addition and suppression; (3) the application of these operators in mode Σ and mode π; and (4) the extrinsic status of contextual factors.

The reduction of metaphor to a product of two synecdoches demands very close and detailed examination.

Three factors are brought into consideration in connection with these operators of suppression and addition. First, they are not mutually exclusive; they can be cumulative. Next, their combination can be partial or total. Partial combination gives us metaphor, and total combination metonymy. This analysis, accordingly, puts the two figures in the same class, as opposed to Jakobson.[48] Finally, the combination has 'degrees of presentation': in metaphor *in absentia* (true metaphor according to the Ancients), the substitutable term is absent from discourse; in metaphor *in praesentia*, the two terms are present together, as well as the mark of their partial identity.

So to discuss metaphor properly speaking is to consider (1) suppression-addition, (2) partial, and (3) *in absentia*.

According to the foregoing presentation, it is metaphor *in absentia* that is analysed as a product of two synecdoches.

But the proof of this thesis reveals immediately that only the reduction of deviation, Jean Cohen's second operation, is taken into consideration. In fact, the production of deviation brings the entire statement into play. The authors readily agree: 'Formally, metaphor reduces to a syntagma in which, contradictorily, the identity of two signifiers and the non-identity of the two corresponding signified things appear together. This affront to (linguistic) reason gives rise to a reduction procedure through which the reader seeks to validate the identity' (106-7). But once again, the initial operation is relegated to 'conditions extrinsic to rhetorical consciousness' (107). Thus reduced to the operation of validating identity alone, the explanation focuses on the stage that Cohen had placed on the paradigmatic plane.

And so the problem presents itself as follows: 'To find a limit class such that the two objects are both counted in together, but are separate in all inferior classes'; or again, 'to establish the shortest route by which two objects can reconnect' (107). Therefore, metaphorical reduction is the search for a virtual, hinge-like third term; the reader conducts this search 'by exploring any tree or any pyramid whatever, speculative or realistic' (ibid.).

The discovery of this zone of intersection can be broken down into two synecdoches, from the starting term to the intermediary term and from this latter to the destination term. The sought-for invariant is the narrow path; the rest of the semantic areas that lie outside the intersection maintain the consciousness of deviation. The only constraints are, on the one hand, that the synecdoches be complementary, that is that they function in opposite directions with respect to the level of generality so that the common term is at the same level on both sides (generalizing *plus* particu-

larizing and vice-versa); and on the other hand, that the two synecdoches
be homogeneous as to mode of decomposition, whether by semes or by
parts. The interaction takes place in a conceptual metaphor or in a referential metaphor.

It goes without saying that the reader of a metaphor is not conscious of
these two operations. He is conscious only of the transfer of meaning from
the first term to the second; it is for the semic analysis that this transfer consists of 'the attribution, to the combination of the two collections of semes,
of properties that strictly apply only to their intersection' (109). This is
why the reader of metaphor does not sense the impoverishment involved
in passing through 'the narrow path of the semic intersection,' but on the
contrary feels a sense of enlargement, an opening up, an amplification.

The same theory that demonstrates the close relationship between
synecdoche and metonymy also shows that the difference between metaphor and metonymy reduces to a difference between the partial and the
total character of the self-same addition-suppression operation.

Indeed, the difference between metaphor and metonymy is not a difference of operation, as is the case between resemblance and extrinsic relation. There is a movement in both of them from a starting term to a destination term via an intermediate term. In metaphor, this intermediate term
constitutes a semic intersection of the two classes; therefore, it belongs to
the semantic field of each of them. This is why the supplementary addition of semes is partial. In the well-worn case of contiguity, there is no
such semic intersection. From this point of view, metonymy 'rests on a
void' (117); one can speak of a null intersection. Nevertheless, there is a
common inclusion, but of the two terms in a larger domain, whether of
semes in the case of conceptual decomposition or of things in the case of
material decomposition. In short, 'in metaphor the intermediate term is
encompassed, whereas in metonymy it is encompassing' (118). To put
it differently, the third, absent term is to be sought in a contiguous region
of semes and of things. One can say, in this sense, that metaphor calls
upon only denotative semes, that is, nuclear semes, included in the definition of the terms, while metonymy calls upon connotative semes, that is,
'contiguous to the array of a larger grouping and combining to define this
grouping' (118).

It seems to me that this theory leaves out what constitutes the specificity of metaphor, namely the reduction of an initial semantic impertinence.
Synecdoche, indeed, lacks this function completely; there is no need, in
accounting for synecdoche, to diverge from a predicative character of discourse. The status of the impertinent epithet, essential to metaphor, is of
no concern whatsoever to synecdoche, which confines itself within the
bare limits of a substitutive operation applied to the word.

Having dismissed the predicative condition of impertinence, the theory can dismiss the properly predicative status of the new pertinence more easily than does Jean Cohen. The whole interplay of 'focus' and 'frame' that dominates the investigation of intersection is also dispersed, along with everything that arises from the predicative plane. All that is noted is the result of this attributive dynamic that *produces* the intersection. It is this implied product as *given* (with its 'virtual' status) that is decomposed after the fact into two synecdoches. The only function of this activity is to submit metaphor to the system that admits of additions and suppressions alone and omits predicative operations. To this extent it is utterly valid: it ensures the simplicity of the system, that is, in one stroke, the homogeneous character of the hierarchy among the levels of units of signification (from phoneme to sentence and to text), and the applicability of the same operative concepts (deviation, redundancy, correction, etc.) and the same operators (addition, suppression) at all the levels. Now, it is certainly possible to decompose a *given* metaphor into two synecdoches; but one cannot *produce* a metaphor with two synecdoches. The 'double logical operation' (111) is only the reformulation, in the terms of the semic arithmetic, of an operation whose dynamism puts into play the predicative operation of the sentence.

My objections are confirmed by an examination of metaphor *in praesentia* and of oxymoron. Their reduction to metaphor *in absentia* is an important condition of the success of the theory: 'We did justice at the appropriate point to the illusion created by the figures *in praesentia* and those which appear to involve several words: it is always possible to reduce them to a figure *in absentia* (cf. metaphor and oxymoron)' (132). The authors introduce the difference between metaphor *in absentia* and metaphor *in praesentia* under the title of 'degrees of presentation,' that is, of the extension of the units considered. In the case of metaphor *in absentia*, the semic intersection is between the absent degree zero and the figurative term, thus within the word. With metaphor *in praesentia*, the semic intersection is a mutual approach of two equally present terms: a simile, with or without the grammatical mark of comparison.

One might have thought that the precisely predicative structure of metaphor *in praesentia* would have turned attention towards the equally predicative conditions of metaphor *in absentia*, and consequently to the intersection of the metaphorical term with the other terms equally present in the metaphorical statement. One sees, indeed, that metaphors *in praesentia* reduce to syntagmas in which two sememes are assimilated improperly, whereas metaphor properly speaking does not manifest assimilation (114). The opposite is the case: 'We know that tropes, in Fontanier's sense, involve one word alone. In our category of metasememes, which encompasses all of the tropes of Fontanier, metaphor *in praesentia* would constitute an exception to this rule. In fact, this figure can equally be analysed as a figure by addition that involves a single word, that is, as synecdoche' (112). In the passage taken from Edmund Burke, 'l'Espagne – une grande baleine échouée sur les plages d'Europe (Spain – a great whale stranded on the beaches of Europe),' introduction of an absent degree zero, the swollen outline on the map, is all one needs in order to have a particularizing synecdoche (whale – swollen outline). In this way one eliminates the operation of the metaphor as impertinent predicate (or epithet). The authors have no trouble admitting that here the description bows to the imperatives of the system: 'Despite the undeniable metaphorical functioning of the example cited, we think that the synecdochic reduction is to be preferred, for reasons of method and of generality. It has the advantage, moreover, of insisting on the strict relation, discussed earlier, between metaphor and synecdoche' (112).

One may doubt that metaphorical comparison (discussed again on page 114) can be equated in this way with synecdochic reduction. In effect, what it presents is first and foremost a deviation that itself is of the predicative order, namely the incompatibility of a term with the rest of the message. The same holds for the rest of the message, the term of comparison re-establishing compatibility by reducing the degrees of identity, that is, by asserting a weak equivalence. This is why the term of comparison belongs to the order of the copula, as the authors also agree (114-16). There is even the case where the comparison contracts into an 'is' of equivalence: 'Nature is a temple where living columns ...' In the face of this example, the authors concede that 'this use of the verb to be is distinct from the "is" of determination: "the rose is red" is a process that is synecdochic and not metaphorical in nature" (115). How then are we to understand the reduction of metaphor *in praesentia* to metaphor *in absentia* and of the latter to a double synecdoche? Must not the reverse also be said, that metaphor is a syntagma contracted into a paradigm (substitution of a figurative meaning for an absent degree zero)? It is quite apparent to me that metaphor *in praesentia* requires one to modify the categorical affirmation that 'the definition of paradigm is, structurally, identical with that of metaphor: as a result, it is permissible to consider this last as a paradigm deployed as a syntagma' (116).

The theory confronts an analogous difficulty in oxymoron ('This obscure clarity that falls from the stars' [120]). Oxymoron is an impertinent epithet par excellence, where impertinence is heightened to the point of antithesis. Reduction, for this figure, consists in a contradiction being assumed in full, according to the expression of Léon Cellier.[49] The economy of the *Rhétorique générale* prescribes a search for the degree zero that allows one to consider the figure as *in absentia*: 'There is real question whether oxymoron is actually a figure, that is, whether it has a degree zero' (120). In the example quoted, the degree zero would be 'luminous clarity' and the transition to the state of figure would be accomplished through *negative* suppression-addition. But what is a negative suppression-addition? This operator on an operator (itself already complex: suppression-addition) is all the more unusual as it operates on an expression, luminous clarity, 'that already constitutes a figure: i.e., epithet, as understood by J. Cohen' (120). Does not this remark also lead us back to predication? It would be necessary to study the parallels in metalogisms, irony, and paradox.

At the end of this discussion, it might seem that the predication theory of metaphor of the English-language authors and the theory of the word-metaphor are equal in force and differ only in the choice of a different system of fundamental axioms, in the one case regulating the activity of 'bizarre' predicates and in the other case governing purely arithmetical operations applied to semic collections. Nevertheless, the theory of the statement-metaphor seems to me to have an undebatable advantage on two counts.

First of all, it alone gives an account, through the interaction of all the terms present at the same time in the same statement, of the *production* of the intersection that the theory of the word-metaphor postulates. The crucial phenomenon is the *augmentation* of the initial polysemy of words by means of an instance of discourse. What compels the addition of a semantic variant that did not exist before is the recoil shock where the predicative structure and the semantic field meet. The *Rhétorique générale* does well to say that 'the reader of poetry elaborates ... seeks ... traverses ... finds ...' – so many words attesting to a certain invention; but this no longer finds a place in the concept of semic intersection, which operates only with semantic fields that are already completely constituted.

One can question whether semic analysis, which, by definition, applies to terms already lexicalized, can give an account of the augmentation of polysemy by means of discourse.

Here the present doubt mingles with those of Jean Cohen, who nevertheless sets great store by this procedure.[50] Can one say that 'fox' analyses into 'animal' *plus* 'sly' in the same way as 'mare' analyses into 'horse' *plus* 'female'? The parallel is misleading, because the example is that of a metaphor in common use and the predicate *sly* is practically a part of the already lexicalized network of contextual significations (which, with Max Black, I have called the 'system of associated commonplaces'). Jean Cohen, from whom I borrow the example of the sly fox, which he treats according to the rules of semic analysis, notes himself: '"Fox" could signify "sly" [*ruse*] only because "cunning deceit" [*la ruse*] was, in the minds of speakers, one of the semantic components of the term' (127). There is, of course, no clearly marked border between the lexical code and the cultural code: expressions which are called figurative register the partial inscription of the latter in the former. But this semi-lexicalized status of common-places is not ignored by linguistic consciousness, which, even in the case of metaphor in common use, still distinguishes between literal meaning and figurative meaning.[51] This is certainly why the trope alone provides the cri-terion of extension of meaning: 'Perhaps the study of tropes would pro-vide – let us say in passing – the linguistic criterion required by structural semantics' (127).

With newly invented metaphor, uncertainty is no longer possible. In relation to the lexical code, the new value constitutes a deviation that semic analysis cannot contain. Even the cultural code of commonplaces is insufficient, according to Max Black.[52] Indeed, one must call forth a sys-tem of *ad hoc* references that comes into existence only with the meta-phorical statement itself. Neither the lexical code nor the code of clichés contains the new constituent trait of the signified, which is deviatory in relation to the two codes. If it was true that the metaphor rests on a com-mon seme already present at the infralinguistic level, even if in a virtual state, then not only would there be no new information, no invention, but there would not even be any need for a paradigmatic deviation in order to reduce a syntagmatic deviation. A simple subtraction of semes – which is precisely what synecdoche does – would be enough. It is clear why it was necessary at all costs to reduce metaphor to synecdoche: the latter is truly the one-word figure that completely satisfies the rules of semic analysis.

The newly invented metaphor is not alone in resisting semic analysis. Jean Cohen, of whose partial agreement with componential analysis we just spoke, raises the case of indecomposable predicates, like colours (the 'bleus angelus' of Mallarmé), to which he adds synaesthetic metaphors and affective resemblances. These metaphors, he notes, constitute deviations of second degree in relation to those (which he calls first-degree) whose im-pertinence can be submitted to semic analysis and reduced by simple sub-traction of inappropriate elements of the signified. With deviations of sec-ond degree, it is necessary to look *outside* the signified for the reason for the metaphorical usage, for example among the subjective effects (appease-ment, or others) produced by the figure. The evocation of this subjective effect would serve to diminish impertinence. Now, this value or effect 'in no way constitutes a pertinent trait of signification' (129). This acknowl-edgment is important if it is true that 'the fundamental resource of all poetry, the trope of tropes, is the synaesthetic metaphor, or affective res-semblance' (178). Is it not necessary, then, to return to the case of first-degree deviations? Is it true that 'sly' is an objective characteristic of 'fox' just as 'green' is of 'emerald,' and that we derive one from the other by a simple subtraction of inappropriate semes? In my opinion, the deviations of first degree must be reinterpreted as a function of second-degree deviations. If not, the explanation of reduction breaks down into two parts: on one side, a type of reduction motivated by internal relations; on the other side, a type motivated by an external relationship. It is not enough to say that the distance increases from the first to the second degree and that the first metaphors are 'closer' and the second more 'distant' (130); interiority and exteriority in relation to a semic collection designate two different statuses of the metaphorical use of a word in relation to semic analysis.

This is why I prefer to say, precisely in order to save the idea of code violation and paradigmatic deviation, that in the first place the impertinent predicate is outside the code. Let us repeat: there are no metaphors in dictionaries. Metaphor is not polysemy. Semic analysis produces a theory of polysemy directly, and only indirectly a theory of metaphor, to the extent that polysemy attests to the open structure of words and their capacity to acquire new significations without losing their old ones. This open structure is only the condition of metaphor and not yet the reason for its production. The appearance, with the impertinent predicate, of extra-code values that the prior polysemy could not contain by itself requires an event in the realm of discourse.

The second aspect of superiority of the theory of statement-metaphor over a theory of word-metaphor lies in the fact that it takes into account the kinship of the two domains of metasememes and metalogisms, which the *Rhétorique générale* dissociates.

The *Rhétorique générale* has ample reason to characterize metalogism as a deviation, not between words and meanings, but between the meaning of words and reality, the reality term being taken in the most general sense of extra-linguistic referent of discourse: 'Whatever its form, the metalogism necessarily has reference to something extra-linguistically given as its criterion' (125). Hence, a rhetoric aspiring to generality cannot operate merely in the 'interior' space that (according to the metaphor of Gérard Genette) lies deep between sign and meaning. It must also consider the 'exterior' space between sign and referent in order to account for figures such as litotes, hyperbole, allegory, and irony, which disturb not only the lexicon but also the referential function.

Now, one may be surprised to see Gilbert Ryle's famous 'category mistake' (presentation of certain facts arising in one category in the terms of a category that is not their own) appearing under the rubric of metalogisms, and to read the following: 'In particular, it is not an accident that the theories of Ryle serve as foundation for the study of metaphor by several English-language authors. His "category mistake," which is used to denounce the absurdity of cartesianism, is rebaptized "category-confusion" by Turbayne, who opposes it to "category-fusion," in which he sees the process by which metaphor is elaborated' (129-30). If 'it is not an accident,' then truly there must be a method for passing from trope to metalogism.

The *Rhétorique générale* itself demands this, and not just the historical rapprochement with the English-language theories: 'Doubtless the metaboles do not always present themselves in the predicative format, but it is always possible to reduce them to it. In this case, the metasememe is always a "pseudo-proposition," because it presents a contradiction to which logic objects and that rhetoric accepts. This is true of metaphor, it is also true of the other metasememes' (131). This belated admission is an important one, and reinforces our thesis. In fact, only this reduction to the predicative form allows a bridge to be laid between metasememe and metalogism. We saw the necessity of this recourse to the predicative form when we discussed the 'is' of equivalence in 'nature is a temple where living columns ...' (115). This is certainly what the authors have in mind when they remark: 'Under the predicative form, the metasememe uses the copula in a way that the logician judges illicit, because in this case "to be" signifies "to be and not be" ... In this manner, one can reduce all metasememes to ... the formula of contradiction, with the difference that this is not a contradiction' (131). But then metaphor is no longer a trope in one word only. The necessity of this reduction to the predicative form results again from this remark, that the constitution of the referent is quite often necessary for the identification of a metaphor: 'Metaphor *in absentia* especially does not appear as a metaphor unless its referent is known' (128).

Certainly the distinction in principle that the authors establish between metasememe and metalogism is not abolished, but their relatedness demands that one compare them as different types of statements (131).

This kinship is particularly close when one compares metaphor and *allegory* (137-8).[53] The former is a trope for these authors, the latter a metalogism. The first changes the meaning of words, the second enters into conflict with reality. Thus 'bateau ivre' [drunken boat], as a metaphor of Rimbaud, is a one-word trope; only the lexicon is upset. But the expression 'the drunken boat has rejoined the great and lonely sailor' is an allegory because the referents (Malraux and de Gaulle) are neither boat nor sailor. But if, as was just admitted, metaphor can be reduced to a statement, 'drunken boat' will have to enter into a composition with some other expression – for example, 'the drunken boat finally ended its days in Ethiopia.' The difference between metaphor and allegory, therefore, will not be between word and sentence, as is proposed here, but will consist in the fact that the metaphorical statement incorporates non-metaphorical terms ('end its days in Ethiopia') with which the metaphorical term ('the drunken boat') interacts, whereas allegory is made up only of metaphorical terms. Hence, the tension is not in the proposition but in the context. This is what leads to the belief that metaphor concerns words alone and only allegory is in conflict with a referent. But the structural difference between the two statements does not keep the reduction of absurdity from following the same path: when a reading of the complete sentence does not offer an acceptable or interesting meaning at the literal level, one investigates, provoked by this deception, 'whether a second, less banal isotopy might not perhaps exist' (137).

This is the direction in which the English-language authors have advanced their research. They say of metaphor and allegory, parable and fable as a group what the *Rhétorique générale* says only of allegory and the neighbouring figures: 'When the first isotopy appears to us to be insufficient, this is due to the impertinence of the relationships in relation to the elements to which they are connected (absence, for example, of Court or a tribunal among animals)' (138). But it is because metaphor has been separated from the complete statement that it appears to be another sort of figure, and that only its incorporation into a metalogism lets it participate in the referential function recognized in allegory, fable, and parable, while the metasememe as such remains a transformation operating at the level of every element of discourse, of every word (figure 16, page 138).

The theory of the statement-metaphor is more suited to display the profound relationship, at the level of statements, between metaphor, allegory, parable, and fable. For this very reason, it allows one to open up, for this entire set of figures – metasememes and metalogisms – the problematic of the referential function that the *Rhétorique générale* reserves for metalogisms alone.[54]

What remains true in the distinction between metasememes and metalogisms is that the metasememe designates the deviation at the level of the word through which the metaphorical statement re-establishes meaning. But if one admits, with the conclusion of the preceding Study, that this deviation is only the impact on the word of a semantic phenomenon that concerns the entire statement, then one must call 'metaphor' the entire statement with its new meaning, and not just the paradigmatic deviation that focuses the mutation of meaning of the whole statement on one word.

The work of resemblance

For Mikel Dufrenne

This Study is devoted to the examination of a problem that seems to be the counterpart of the very success of the semantic theory set out in the preceding Studies. This problem concerns the role of resemblance in the explanation of metaphor. There is no doubt surrounding this role in classical rhetoric. On the other hand, it seems to be progressively obscured as the discursive model becomes more refined. Does this imply that resemblance is linked exclusively to a theory of substitution and is incompatible with an interaction theory? Such is the question to be taken up in this Study, which I will preview by saying that I propose to dissociate the fate of resemblance from that of the substitution theory and to reinterpret the role of resemblance within the guidelines of the theory of interaction set out in the third Study. But before attempting this, we must test the common bonds between substitution and resemblance and measure the obstacles to a new pact between interaction and resemblance.

1 / SUBSTITUTION AND RESEMBLANCE

In the tropology of classical rhetoric, the place assigned to metaphor among the figures of signification is defined specifically by the role that the relationship of resemblance has in the transference from initial idea to new idea. Metaphor is the trope of resemblance *par excellence*. This pact with resemblance is not just an isolated trait; in the model underlying the theory of classical rhetoric, it is intimately connected to the primacy of naming or denomination and to the other traits that follow from this primacy. Now resemblance operates first between the ideas named by words. Subsequently, in the model, the theme of resemblance is closely united with those of borrowing, deviation, substitution, and exhaustive paraphrase. Indeed, resemblance first of all motivates the borrowing; next, it is the positive side of the process whose negative side is deviation; further, it is the internal link within the sphere of substitution; finally, it guides the paraphrase that annuls the trope by restoring the proper meaning. To the extent that the postulate of substitution can be taken to be representative of the whole chain of postulates, resemblance is the foundation of the substitution that is set in motion in the metaphorical transposition of names and, more generally, of words.

This pact between metaphor and resemblance is reinforced by an initial argument. The relation that Aristotle saw between metaphor and simile was subsequently reversed; simile is no longer a sort of metaphor, but metaphor a sort of simile, namely an abbreviated simile. Only the elision of the term of comparison distinguishes metaphor from simile. Now the latter brings resemblance itself into discourse, and by this means points out the grounds of metaphor.[1]

We will dwell on a more modern argument that consolidates the pact. In its binarist zeal, structural linguistics has been extreme in its tendency to simplify the complicated table of tropes, to the point where metaphor and metonymy alone remain in play – that is, it is alleged, contiguity and resemblance. We explained while discussing the rhetoric of Fontanier how far the ancient rhetoricians were from identifying metonymy and synecdoche (to speak only of tropes that can be set in opposition to metaphor). Even more, with Fontanier, 'correspondence' (which underlies metonymy) brings together ideas of objects each of which forms an absolutely separate whole. But the variety of relations satisfying this general condition of correlation cannot in any way be reduced to contiguity. As for the 'connection' relation, which involves the idea of inclusion of two things in a whole, it is opposed directly to the relationship of correlation, which implies a certain mutual exclusion of related terms. Only with contemporary neo-rhetoricians is tropology restricted to the opposition of metaphor and metonymy. At the same time, the role of resemblance is confirmed and amplified by a simplifying operation that makes it the sole counterpart of a single opposite, namely contiguity. But this is not all, nor is it the most important thing. Thanks to his famous article of 1953, 'Two Aspects of Language and Two Types of Aphasic Disturbances,' the coupling of metaphor and metonymy has been linked permanently with the name of Roman Jakobson. It was his stroke of genius to have connected this properly tropological and rhetorical duality with a more fundamental polarity that concerns the very functioning of language and not just its figurative use. Henceforward, metaphor and metonymy do not merely define figures and tropes; they define general processes of language. The analysis of Roman Jakobson is referred to at this stage of the investigation because, by generalizing the distinction between metaphor and metonymy far beyond tropology, and so the change in meaning of words, the famous linguist has

strengthened the idea that substitution and resemblance are two inseparable concepts, since they rule together over processes that work on the
numerous levels at which language is effected. It is this reinforcement of
the link between substitution, resemblance, and metaphor that will be at
stake in the following discussion.

The new linkage of the metaphorical and the metonymic in Jakobson
builds on a distinction (to be found in the *Cours de linguistique générale*
of Ferdinand de Saussure) between two ways in which signs are arranged –
combination and selection.[2] According to Jakobson, however, Saussure
would have sacrificed the second of these to the old prejudice that regards
the signifier as having a purely linear character. Nevertheless, the kernel of
the theory remains Saussurean. The primary mode of arrangement unites
in praesentia two or more terms *in absentia* in a virtual mnemonic series.
Hence, this concerns entities associated in the code but not in the given
message, whereas in the case of combination the entities are associated in
both places or only in the actual message. Now, where there is selection
between alternative terms, there is the possibility of substituting one for
the other, which is equivalent to the first in one aspect and different from
it in another. Selection and substitution, accordingly, are the two faces of
a single operation. All that remains is to link up combination and contiguity, substitution and similarity – which Jakobson does not hesitate to
do. Indeed, contiguity and similarity characterize the status of the constituents, in the context of a message on the one hand, within a substitution group on the other. From this point on, the correlation with tropes
presents no difficulty, if it is granted that metonymy rests on contiguity
and metaphor on resemblance. Thanks to this series of correlations, one
can for short call combination itself the metonymic pole and selection the
metaphoric pole of linguistic operations. These operations can be represented only with the help of orthogonal axes, of which only one, that of
combination, corresponds to the linearity of the signifier.

In this manner, the tropological distinction provides the vocabulary,
but not the key. Indeed, the two tropes are reinterpreted in the light of a
distinction that prevails on the most abstract plane conceivable by linguistic analysis – that of *any and all* linguistic identities or units. 'Any linguistic sign,' it is stated, 'involves two modes of arrangement: (1) combination
... (2) selection ...' (243). The distinction is thus profoundly semiological.

This point deserves to be dwelt upon for a moment. Jakobson's analysis
completely bypasses the distinction introduced by Benveniste between
semiotics and semantics, between signs and sentences. This monism of the
sign is characteristic of a purely semiotic linguistics. It confirms the fundamental hypothesis of this work, that the model to which a substitution
theory of metaphor belongs is one that ignores the difference between

semiotics and semantics and takes the word and not the sentence as the basic unit of tropology. This is a model that recognizes in the word only its character as a lexical sign, and in the sentence only the double characteristic of combination and selection, which it has in common with all signs from the distinctive trait, through phonemes, words, expressions, and sentences, right up to the text. The combination of these linguistic units truly presents an ascending scale of freedom, but it does not contain any discontinuity in kind like that which Benveniste sees between the order of the sign and that of discourse. The word is simply the highest among the linguistic units that must be encoded, and the sentence is just more freely composed than words. Hence, the notion of context can be used to designate equally the relationship of morpheme to phoneme and the relationship of sentence to morpheme. As a result, metaphor will characterize a general semiotic process and definitely not a form of attribution whose prerequisite is the distinction between discourse and sign.

The confirmation of the universally semiotic character of the polarity under consideration lies in the fact that the notion of semantics, which is not only recognized but vigorously defended against the attempts of a faction of American linguists to exclude meaning from the linguistic field, in no way constitutes an order distinct from the one, semiotic order. Semantics is incorporated into the bipolar schema at the same time as it receives its justification from it. Indeed, by adding new linkages to the preceding ones, it is possible to superimpose the pair 'syntax-semantics' onto the pair 'combination-selection,' therefore onto the pair 'contiguity-similarity,' and so also onto the pair comprising the metonymic and metaphorical poles. Indeed, the facts of combination within a message are facts of syntax, or syntagmatic facts (so as not to reduce syntax to grammar nor to include in it the composition of words or even phonematic sequences for instance). Contextual combination and syntagmatic combination overlap. The bonds between selection and semantics, on the other hand, are just as tight: 'For years and decades we have fought for the annexation of speech sounds to linguistics, and thereby established phonemics. Now we face a second front – the task of incorporating linguistic meaning into the science of language ... Let us, within the framework of synchronic linguistics, examine: what is the difference between syntax and semantics. Language entails two axes. Syntax is concerned with the axis of concatenation, semantics with the axis of substitution.'[3] This link between semantics and selection had already been perceived by de Saussure. In the constitution of a message, one word is chosen among other similar words within a group that constitutes a paradigm based on similarity. So it is possible to replace the Saussurean pair of the syntagmatic and the paradigmatic with that of syntax and semantics, and to arrange these on the orthogonal axes of combination and selection.

Some new correlations are revealed by the divergence of the two functional modes that characterize aphasia. Indeed, these disorders can be divided into those having to do with similarity and those related to contiguity. With regard to the latter, characterized by its agrammaticality (loss of syntax, inflections, derivations in the formation of words, etc.), the word survives the obliteration of syntax. Selection operations continue even while the contextual structure disintegrates; metaphorical shifts proliferate. On the other hand, in the case of disorders in similarity, connective chains are preserved while substitutive operations are destroyed. Metaphor disappears together with semantics; the aphasic fills the gaps left by metaphor with metonymies, thereby extending the drift of the context over that of substitution and selection. But the metaphorical use of language is not alone in being affected; other operations suffer the same fate, and their kinship with metaphor is thus revealed. For example, consider the power to define words, that is, to provide an equational definition, projecting a substitution group from the lexical code of the language into the context of a message. Consider also the capacity to give a name for an object that one can point to or manipulate, hence the power to give a linguistic equivalent for a gesture. This twofold approximation enriches our concept of metaphorical process: definition, naming, synonymy, circumlocution, and paraphrase are metalinguistic operations through which I designate elements of my code by means of equivalent elements within the same code. Even code-changing operations depend upon equivalence of terms from one code to another. All these operations are related profoundly to the capacity of words to receive additional, displaced, and associated meanings on the basis of their resembling the fundamental meaning. The same characteristic resides in the construction of paradigmatic series, of inflections or of tenses, in that the same semantic content is presented here from different points of view associated by their similarity. The same holds for the semantic unity common to the root word and its derivations.

Other interesting correlations add still more to the richness of the polarity of metaphoric process and metonymic process. Personal styles and verbal behaviour themselves also evince a preference for one type of arrangement or the other. Poetic forms also show a predominance sometimes of metonymy, as in realism, and sometimes of metaphor, as with romanticism and symbolism. The correlation is even more striking when the artist shows indications of the sort of pathological problems described above. The polarity is also so general that it finds a parallel in non-linguistic sign systems. In painting, one can speak of metonymy in connection with cubism, of metaphor with surrealism. In film, the synecdochic close-ups and the metonymic montage of D.W. Griffith contrast with the metaphorical montage of Charlie Chaplin. The same polarity can be found again in unconscious symbolic processes, such as those that Freud described in dreaming. Jakobson suggests that displacement (which would be metonymic) and condensation (synecdochic) be put on the side of contiguity, and identification and symbolism on the side of similarity.[4] Finally, in the area of the unconscious use of symbolism, we may find in *The Golden Bough* Sir James Frazer's two types of magic, the one working by contagion, and the other by imitation.

The article ends with an interesting remark that refers back to something noted earlier in connection with disorders concerning similarity. It is due to the fact that the same relation of similarity is at work in the trope *metaphor* where one term substitutes for another, and in metalinguistic operations where the symbols of a second-order language resemble those of the object language, that tropology, which itself is also a metalanguage, has favoured metaphor regularly over metonymy and has given a special place to symbolism in poetry. This remark could be read as a plea for metonymy, although such an interpretation would run counter to the criticism of de Saussure for favouring combination over selection in the name of the linearity of the signifier.

The strength of Jakobson's schema[5] is also its weakness. The strength of the bipolar scheme lies in its extreme generality and its extreme simplicity. The last correlations demonstrated its validity, since it extends beyond the sentence into the realm of style, beyond intentional use of linguistic signs into dreaming and magic, and beyond linguistic signs themselves into the use of other semiotic systems. The gains appear to be immense as far as metaphor is concerned. Formerly confined to rhetoric, the procedure itself is generalized beyond the sphere of the word and even beyond tropology.

But a heavy price must be paid. First of all, when applied to the domain of rhetoric, the binarism of the schema needlessly restricts its field to two figures. It is true that synecdoche is mentioned several times, but as a case of contiguity, sometimes in parallel with metonymy (metonymic displacement and synecdochic condensation in Freud), and sometimes as a species of metonymy (the Russian novelist Uspenski is said to have 'had a particular penchant for metonymy, and especially for synecdoche' ['Two Aspects' 257]). Now, the most extreme restriction that tropology seems previously to have undergone involved at least three figures: metonymy, synecdoche, and metaphor. (Dumarsais allowed a fourth fundamental figure, irony.) In a tripartite schema, resemblance is opposed not to contiguity but to the pair formed by inclusive and exclusive relations. Paradoxically, therefore, the generalization of the concept of metaphor beyond the linguistic field is paid for by the restriction of this field to two tropes.

But above all, those differences that derive from the cleft between discourse and the sign in the hierarchy of linguistic entities are obliterated in vague resemblances and in equivocations affecting the concept of combination as much as that of selection. As to the first, it can be doubted whether the logical operations that preside over the syntax of predication, and consequently over that of the co-ordination and subordination of statements, come from the same sort of contiguity as, for example, the concatenation of phonemes within morphemes. In one sense, predicative synthesis is the opposite of contiguity. Syntax represents the order of the necessary, ruled by completely formal laws concerning the condition of the possibility of well-formed expressions. Contiguity stays in the order of the contingent, and moreover, of the contingent at the level of objects themselves, where each thing forms a completely independent whole. So metonymic contiguity appears to be quite different from syntaxic liaison.

Regarding the notion of metaphorical process, it is not only equivocal, and in that sense too wide; in addition, it is cut off paradoxically from an essential trait – so that, despite its extremely general character, it remains too narrow.

The notion is too wide when one considers the heterogeneity of substitution and selection operations from one level to another. The linking of metaphorical procedure and meta-linguistic operations has been noted in passing. The first makes use of a virtual resemblance inscribed in the code and applies it in a message, whereas the equational definition, for example, talks only about the code. Can the use of resemblance in discourse and a totally different operation requiring a hierarchy of levels be put into the same class?

The notion of metaphorical process is even more emphatically too narrow if one considers that there is no place for the phenomenon of interaction, specifically of metaphorical statements, in the orbit of the selection-substitution phenomenon, even though this orbit is excessively extended. What is left out, ultimately, is the predicative character of metaphor.

In the end, metaphor settles into the status of substitution of one term for another, just as in classical rhetoric: 'Similarity connects a metaphorical term with the term for which it is substituted.'[6] It is legitimate to ask whether metonymy is not a substitution, more precisely a substitution of names, rather than metaphor. Fontanier triggered this thought earlier with his definition of 'metonymy, that is, changes of names, or names for other names.'[7] If the essence of metaphor is to 'present an idea under the sign of another idea that is more striking or better known,' does not the procedure consist as much in combining as in substituting? Let us go further: is it legitimate to reduce the semantic aspect of language to substitution? One is reminded of Jakobson's declaration, inspired by Peirce, that 'the meaning of a sign is the sign it can be translated into ... in all these cases we substitute signs.'[8] Is that not a semiotic definition where the central problem of predication has vanished? And if, with Benveniste, one defines semantics by predication, must it not be sought in the area of combination as well as in that of substitution, or better, outside this purely semiological distinction?

Finally, the fundamental problem of the difference between newly invented metaphor and metaphor in common use vanishes with the omission of the predicative character of metaphor, to the same extent that the degrees of freedom in combination affect the syntagmatic and not the paradigmatic side of language. In this connection, one should remember the force with which Fontanier contrasted catachresis with metaphor. One is constrained to use the former, one is free to use or not use the latter. It appears to be very difficult to do justice to this important difference if one cannot contrast phenomena of discourse with phenomena of language – indeed, catachresis is ultimately an extension of denomination and, by virtue of that, a phenomenon of language. Metaphor, and above all newly invented mataphor, is a phenomenon of discourse, an unusual attribution. Jakobson's generalized model cannot but completely obliterate this difference because, in a semiological monism, the difference between sign and discourse is itself minimized. It should be noted that for Jakobson, combination takes place in the code or in the message, whereas selection operates between entities associated in the code. In order that selection itself be free, it must result from an original combination created by the context and therefore distinct from pre-formed combinations within the code. In other words, it is in the region of unusual syntagmatic liaisons, of new and purely contextual combinations, that the secret of metaphor is to be sought.

We must now ask whether Michel Le Guern's reformulation[9] of Jakobson's theses is better able to meet the foregoing criticisms of the initial model. I have already made many separate references to this important work, but the time has now come for a systematic analysis.

Le Guern offers at once both a reinterpretation of the categories of Jakobson and two important additions, which, more than the reinterpretation itself, set forth a partial reply to our recent objections to Jakobson's analysis.

The reinterpretation concerns the very definition of the two processes of selection and combination. If one is based on 'internal' relations and the other on 'external' relations, then 'internal' must be understood in the sense of intralinguistic and 'external' in the sense of a relationship to the extra-linguistic order of reality. If this is so, it is possible to superimpose a Fregean distinction between sense and reference on the distinction, borrowed from Jakobson, between selection-substitution and combination-structure. Metaphor concerns only the substance of the language, i.e. meaning (sense) relations, while metonymy modifies the referential relation itself (44). The advantage of this reinterpretation is that it completely liberates an analysis in terms of sense from the yoke of the logic that holds sway in the order of the referent. The changes of meaning that the mechanism of metaphor puts into play concern only the internal groupings of the constitutive *semes* of the *lexeme* employed. Once the hold of the referent is broken, the semic analysis given by Greimas[10] can be applied directly to the operation of selection, whose close relationship with operations of a metalinguistic character applied to the code was demonstrated by Jakobson. It is on this basis that metaphor can be construed as the 'suppression, or more exactly as the *bracketing of one portion of the constitutive semes of the lexeme employed*' (*Sémantique* 15; my italics). In contrast, metonymy calls upon a syntagmatic choice that goes outside the limits of the paradigmatic structures internal to language. Let us recall the difference between the two orders: to say 'eating cake' rather than 'eating fruit' is to establish a connection between a linguistic entity and an extra-linguistic reality that cannot here be distinguished easily from the mental representation of the material object as perceived (14). Such is the level at which metonymy operates; indeed, it consists in 'a shift of reference between two objects connected by an extra-linguistic relation, which is brought to light by a common experience that is not linked to the semantic organization of a particular language' (25). The role of the reference is verified in the activity of interpreting a message that contains a metonymy. In order to understand it, one must always return to information furnished by the context and interpolate this information into the message, which then takes on the appearance of an ellipsis. If metonymy is regarded as a deviation, in the same way as other tropes, this deviation is nothing other than an ellipsis of the very relation of reference.

Introduction of the notion of reference into the explanation of metonymy provides a solid foundation for the reduction of synecdoche to metonymy. This reduction was implicit in Jakobson; it is explicit in Le Guern. However, a necessary prelude is th dismembering of synecdoche into two figures: synecdoche of the part and the whole (*sail* for ship); and synecdoche of the species and genus (eating *an apple* for eating a fruit). Only the first involves the same shift of reference and the same ellipsis of the statement as does metonymy. There is the important reservation, however, that in metonymy the shift of reference prevails over the ellipsis process.

In this manner, the bipolarity of metaphor and metonymy required by Jakobson's schema is safeguarded.

I would argue that this reinterpretation adds new difficulties without really resolving those raised by Jakobson's drastic reduction to a bipolar scheme. One is left perplexed by the liaison perceived between syntactic combination and referential function. The author asserts that what he calls here 'referential relation' has a 'bivalent' character, since 'at one and the same time it calls into play combination, interior to language, which links the elements on the syntagmatic axis, and correspondence, which is established between one element of the spoken chain and a reality exterior to the message itself' (24). Thus, we are further removed than the author imagines from the Fregean distinction between sense and reference, since reference in Frege's scheme coincides only with the second aspect of this bivalent relation. A certain ambiguity results with respect to the relationship between syntagmatic combination and the referential relation.[11]

If one must divide in this manner what is here called referential function, why could not the same bivalent character be found on the side of the metaphorical operation? Why would the latter not call into play simultaneously a semic composition internal to language and correspondence with a reality external to the message? In this same vein, the authors of the *Rhétorique générale* were seen to introduce consideration of the object in semic constitution.[12]

Le Guern's analysis, therefore, clarifies that of Jakobson only at the price of a supplementary difficulty concerning the work of reference in a semantic analysis. On the other hand, the objections addressed to Jakobson's analysis of metaphor still stand. To a purely lexematic analysis, metaphor is just a phenomenon of abstraction. But this points merely to the culmination of a process that involves the dynamics of the entire statement. Indeed, there would not be any metaphor if no deviation were detected between the figurative meaning of a word and the isotopy of the context, that is, in the language of Greimas, the semantic homogeneity of a statement or part of a statement. Le Guern is forced at once to connect the two phenomena of semic abstraction and deviation in relation to isotopy by relating them to two different moments of the theory. It is from the perspective of producing the message that the mechanism of metaphor is explained as the 'bracketing of one portion of the constitutive semes of the lexeme employed.' But it is 'from the perspective of interpretation of this message by the reader or hearer' (15-16) that consideration of the context imposes itself. Indeed, interpretation of metaphor is not possible unless one first perceives the incompatibility of the non-figurative meaning of the lexeme with the rest of the context. The author considers this to be an important difference from metonymy. The lexeme constituting metonymy is not generally perceived to be foreign to the isotopy: 'Metaphor, on the other hand, on condition that it be a living and image-triggering metaphor, strikes one immediately as being foreign to the isotopy of the context in which it is inserted' (16). Consequently, in order to interpret a metaphor, one must purge the proper meaning of traits that are incompatible with the context.

If this is the case, can one confine the function of deviation in relation to the isotopy of the context to *interpretation* of the message and keep the mechanism of semic abstraction for the *production* of the message? If something is essential to interpretation of the message, was not the same thing already essential for its production? Everything indicates that by distinguishing between production and interpretation in this way, the author has avoided the problem of the relationship between the dynamic of the statement and its meaning-effect at the level of the word. Eliminated from the purely semantic definition of the production of figure, semantic incompatibility at the level of the entire statement is spurned by an explanation of the mechanism of interpretation, which by that very fact becomes simply psychological: 'Semantic incompatibility plays the role of a signal that invites the receiver to select, among the constitutive meaning elements of the lexeme, those not incompatible with the context' (16). Yet the most remarkably detailed analyses by Le Guern suggest that semantic incompatibility is more than a signal for interpretation, and is in fact a component of the production itself.

Extension of the nuclear analysis of the *noun*-metaphor to the *adjective*-metaphor and *verb*-metaphor heralds the first consideration of context in the production of the figure (16-20). When the verb and adjective constitute one and the same metaphor with the substantive (*light* ... a *fire*), the effect of the verb-metaphor and adjective-metaphor is to attenuate the abruptness of the logical disruption produced by the substantive-metaphor. Therefore, semantic incompatibility is here an essential moment of the metaphor's production. (This is suggested by the author himself: 'Its specific character in relation to the substantive-metaphor is then a lesser degree of autonomy in relation to the context' [19].) Given this, suppression of semes is only one moment in a process that brings the entire statement into play. Jean Cohen describes this moment as reduction of deviation, which itself presupposes production of the deviation, or, as is said here, abrupt change of isotopy. It is this prior moment that is ignored in the definition of metaphor as semic reduction.

The excellent analysis of the difference between metaphor and comparison (52-65), to which we will return later from the point of view of the role of analogy, again necessitates incorporation of the disruption of isotopy into the very definition of metaphor. Indeed, it is impossible to discuss the relationship between metaphor and comparison without bringing the role of isotopy into play. Quantitative comparison, or comparison properly speaking (is *more* than, is *as much* as), is based in the isotopy of the context (only comparable things are compared). Qualitative comparison or simile (is *like*) shows the same deviation with regard to isotopy as does metaphor; the role of isotopy is fundamental in both cases, with the difference between metaphor and simile (as we shall see) lying elsewhere. It is best put by saying that deviation in relation to the context is not only a signal that orients the interpretation, but a constitutive element of the metaphorical message. It is hard to maintain the specificity of semantics in relation to logic with the same force as Le Guern displays (63 ff.), if semantics, within its own structure, does not retain the incompatibilities and compatibilities proper to its level and irreducible to those that bring the logic of comparison into play.

The relation between *denotation* and *connotation*, which constitutes the first important addition by Le Guern to Jakobson's thesis, provides a final reason for incorporating change of isotopy into the definition of metaphor. For Le Guern, metaphor combines a purely *denotative* aspect, the very one that was defined by semic reduction, and an aspect of *connotation*, which is external to the properly logical or informative function of the statement. This connotative function is expressed, in metaphor's case, by the role of the *associated image*, thus, a *psychological* connotation and, in addition, a connotation that is not free but *demanded* (21). The author emphasizes that this factor adds nothing to the information, properly speaking, of the message.[13] Indeed, the link between semic abstraction and evocation of an associated image is effected by 'the introduction of a foreign term into the isotopy of the context' (22). But how is this known, if the isotopy as such is not taken into account within the definition of metaphor?

Thus, the reinterpretation of Jakobson's dichotomizing model by Le Guern and his first important addition to it have brought us to the same issue as did the critique of Jakobson's own work, namely, the need to reintroduce the phenomenon of semic reduction at the end of a fundamentally syntagmatic process that affects the entire statement.

A second addition to Jakobson's theory calls for some separate remarks.

Over and above delimiting the language facts described by rhetoric and adding the distinctions between sense and reference, connotation and denotation, a semantics of metaphor and metonymy has the task of situating metaphor in relation to the set of procedures founded on similarity – symbol and synaesthesis on the one hand, comparison on the other. Now, as opposed to Jakobson, Le Guern does not consider the question of resemblance to be settled by the analysis of selection procedures. Moreover, the notion of similarity is not introduced at the point where semic selection is studied; the reason no doubt is that this consists less in a selection within a sphere of similarity, as was the case already with de Saussure, than in an alteration of the semic composition, as the structural semantics of Greimas suggests. The question of resemblance is put better in the context of the positive procedure that offsets the more exactly negative phenomenon of semic abstraction, namely, the operation of the *associated image*, which (as we just said) is based on connotation and not on denotation.

The way in which the workings of resemblance are incorporated into the dynamism of the statement as a whole will be explored later. Nevertheless, numerous traits of this analysis are anticipated in the framework of a substitution theory, by the interplay of denotation and connotation. But the important point for the present discussion is that analogy be introduced at the same time as the associated image, as a relationship between a term belonging to the isotopy and another, the image, that does not belong to it. Indeed, the basis for ordering the set of language facts related to similarity is provided by the manner in which the image operates in relationship to the logical or denotative kernel of significance (it will be noted that the author's word *analogy* is what we mean here by 'similarity'). Le Guern's contribution to semantics on this point is novel and invaluable.

First, three phenomena are compared – symbol, metaphor, and synaesthesis. In the symbol ('Faith is a great tree' writes Péguy), the analogical correspondence through which the symbol represents something else depends upon an extra-linguistic relationship that, to develop this correspondence, brings into play the mental representation of 'tree.' It is this very perception of the image that sustains the logical information of the statement. In other words, the symbol is an intellectualized image. What is meant here is that the image provides the basis for a 'reasoning by analogy, which remains implicit, but which is necessary to the interpretation of the statement' (45). I should say that the symbol according to Le Guern corresponds to Aristotle's metaphor by analogy or proportional metaphor. The situation is completely different in the case of metaphor properly speaking. The semic selection does not depend here on the image being evoked ('the metaphorical image does not intervene in the logical texture of the statement' [43]). This is the sense in which the image is an *associated* entity. No appeal is made to the conscious logic of reasoning by analogy. For this reason, the image, which is not part of the denotation, tends to become attenuated to the point where it is no longer perceived, as the metaphor enters into common usage. Finally, as for synaestheses, they depend upon purely perceptual analogies between the qualitative contents of the different senses (as in Rimbaud's 'Sonnet of the Vowels' with its analogies between vowels and colours). Accordingly, we are presented with three modalities of analogy. The semantic analogy of the metaphor is to be situated between the logical and extra-linguistic analogy of the symbol and the perceptual and infra-linguistic analogy of synaesthesis.

The specificity of semantic analogy in relation to 'analogy that is grasped intellectually' (47) is clarified once more by another distinction, between metaphor and comparison, where the latter is taken in the qualitative sense of *similitudo* or simile (like ...) and not as the quantitative *comparatio* (more, less, as much ...). Metaphor is not an abbreviated simile, as a formal analysis of surface structures may lead one to believe. Simile is related to metaphor rather than to quantitative comparison, since both disrupt the isotopy of the context. But simile and metaphor do not restore that isotopy in the same way. No transfer of meaning takes place in the case of comparison as simile (Jim is *as stubborn as a mule*); all the words retain their meaning, and the representations themselves remain distinct and coexist with fairly equal degrees of intensity. This is why 'no semic incompatibility is detected' (56). Since the terms remain distinct, they also retain their essential features, obviating the need for further semic abstraction. For the same reason, the imagistic accompaniment can remain very rich and the images themselves highly coloured. On the other hand, as we have already seen, perception of incompatibility is essential to the interpretation of the message in the case of metaphor. The incompatibility is expressed in metaphor *in praesentia* (Jim *is an ass*), and implicit in metaphor *in absentia* (*what an ass!*); but, even if implicit, it is still the grounds for figurative interpretation. Formally, then, analogy constitutes the common ground of metaphor, symbol, and simile, but the intellectualization involved increases as one passes from metaphor to symbol and from symbol to simile. The analogical relation is a logical tool in comparison; it belongs to the semantic and not the logical order when it is presented in an image.

However, a suggestion that I find even more important than this ordering of the vast and complex domain of analogy is the one that brings semantic analogy into view as the counterpart of semantic incompatibility. It is 'imposed ... as the only means of suppressing semantic incompatibility' (58). As opposed to logical comparison, which by definition does not break out of the isotopy of the context – only what is comparable is compared quantitatively – semantic analogy institutes a relationship 'between an element belonging to the isotopy of the context and an element that is foreign to this isotopy and for this reason produces an image' (58).

I consider this to be the most important observation of the entire work. But it is my feeling that its full value can be exercised only in a theory of statement-metaphor and not one of lexeme-metaphor. As the rest of this

Study will show, the image does not receive its properly semantic status unless it is attached not only to the perception of deviation but also to its reduction, that is, to the initiation of the new relevance, of which reduction of deviation at the level of the word is but an effect. This is what the last quotation from Le Guern suggests.

To follow this lead, however, one must further clarify the very status of the image and of the notion of associated image, as the fifth and sixth sections of this Study will attempt to do. With Le Guern, the image is defined above all by its negative relationship with isotopy; it is called 'an element that is foreign to this isotopy and for this reason produces an image' (58). 'Strangeness vis-à-vis the isotopy of the context' is, therefore, 'a typical feature of the image' (ibid.). The role of the image is assimilated to 'the use of a lexeme that is foreign to the isotopy of the immediate context' (53). But this negative definition of image leaves the very *iconicity* of the image in suspense. Is the image a 'mental representation that is alien to the informational purpose motivating the statement,' or rather 'a lexeme that is foreign to the isotopy of the immediate context' (ibid.)? In brief, in what sense is the image at once both representation and lexeme?

By the same stroke, the 'associated' character of the image itself remains in suspense. Is it a psychological trait or a semantic trait? If, as a factor belonging to the realm of connotation, it designates a characteristic that is extrinsic from the perspective of logical information, then the image is externally linked to the content of signification. In this position, however, how can it assist in suppressing semantic incompatibility? In short, how can it be outside the isotopy *and* semantic? But this asks twice how an analogy can 'produce an image.' Indeed, what aspect of the analogy at work in metaphor warrants the name *semantic*? For it to be convincing, Le Guern's analysis needs to be rounded out at this point by another analysis that will incorporate the role of the image more thoroughly into the reduction of deviation. With Le Guern, the associated image as image runs the risk of remaining an extra-linguistic fact; and if it is recognized as a fact of language, it runs the risk of remaining an extrinsic factor with regard to the statement, in that it is only associated. This extrinsic position concerns only the first phase, the perception of deviation; it no longer holds for the second, that of the reduction of deviation. Nevertheless, it is this second phase that holds the solution of the problem and justifies the terminology of semantic analogy when defining the role of the associated image.[14]

2 / THE 'ICONIC' MOMENT OF METAPHOR

Can the pact forged in the course of the history of rhetoric between substitution and resemblance be broken? The possibility of dissociating resemblance from a substitution theory and associating it with one of interaction seems to be denied by the brief history of this doctrine. To my knowledge, only one important author has attempted to do so. That author is Paul Henle,[15] whose influence in English-language circles has been substantial, although it has not equalled that of I.A. Richards. But since Henle, in the interaction theories put forward by Richards, notions of tension and then of logical absurdity seem to supplant resemblance, which by the same stroke is banished in an apparently unequivocal manner from the realm of substitution. So it is interesting to return to Paul Henle's analysis in order to ascertain the scope and the import of the refutation that it later suffers.

Henle begins by reformulating the definition of Aristotle in a way that, without expressly constituting a predicative theory of metaphor, nevertheless presents all the features that force it to be detached from naming and attached to predication.

Let us call any 'shift from literal to figurative sense' a metaphor. If the general sweep of this definition is to be preserved, it is necessary, first, that the notion of change of meaning be not restricted to names, or even to words, but extended to all signs. Furthermore, one must dissociate the notion of literal meaning from that of proper meaning. Any lexical value whatsoever is a literal meaning; thus, the metaphorical meaning is non-lexical: it is a value created by the context. It remains necessary to conserve the generic amplitude of Aristotle's definition, which also encompasses synecdoche, metonymy, irony, and litotes, that is, all shifts from literal meaning to figurative meaning that occur through discourse and in discourse. An implicitly discursive trait follows, which at the same time prepares for the entrance of resemblance: every metaphorical meaning is mediate, in the sense that the word is 'an *immediate sign* of its literal sense and a *mediate sign* of its figurative sense' (175). To speak by means of metaphor is to say something different 'through' some literal meaning. This trait says more than 'shift,' which could still be interpreted in terms of deviation and substitution. In turn, this intermediacy lays the foundation for the possibility of paraphrasing a metaphor by means of other words, some taken literally and others not. Not that the paraphrase could exhaust its meaning: for it is not necessary that a paraphrase be finalized for it to begin. The difference between trivial metaphor and poetic metaphor is not that one can be paraphrased and the other not, but that the paraphrase of the latter is without end. It is endless precisely because it can always spring back to life. If metaphor engenders thought throughout a long discourse, is this not because it is itself a brief discourse?

It is at this point that Henle introduces the iconic character that, according to him, specifies metaphor among all the tropes. One is thus undertaking to describe the fourth species of metaphor in Aristotle's breakdown, metaphor by analogy or proportional metaphor. But this trait too must be generalized well beyond the four-term proportion; it has to do with a parallel between two thoughts, such that one situation is presented or described in terms of another that is similar to it.[16] The author borrows the concept of *icon* from Charles Sanders Peirce to signal this very general analogical character. The essential role of the icon is to contain an internal duality that at the same time is overcome. In Keats' verse 'When by my solitary hearth I sit, / And hateful thoughts enwrap my soul in gloom'[17] the metaphorical expression *enwrap* consists in presenting sorrow as if enveloping the soul in a cloak. Thus, 'we are led [by figurative discourse] to think of something by a consideration of something like it, and this is what constitutes the iconic mode of signifying' (177). There is a danger here, which Henle clearly sees, that the theory of metaphor may be led into the impasse of a theory of the image, in the Humean sense of a weakened sensorial impression. This danger is coped with by the remark that 'if there is an iconic element in metaphor, it is equally clear that the icon is not presented, but is merely described' (ibid.). Nothing is displayed in sensible images, therefore; everything, whether associations in the writer's mind or in that of the reader, takes place within language. Henle continues very cautiously: 'What is presented is a formula for the construction of icons' (178). This calls to mind the 'productive' imagination that Kant distinguishes from the 'reproductive' in order to identify it with the schema, which is a method for constructing images.

Metaphor is analysed, therefore, in accordance with two modalities of semantic relationship. In effect, the expression first functions literally. It is (to continue with the description of symbol in the restricted sense of Peirce) a rule for pinpointing an object or situation. Subsequently, it functions iconically, by indirectly designating another, similar situation. Precisely because the iconic representation is not an image, it can point towards original resemblances, whether of quality, structure or locality, of situation or, finally, of feeling. In every case, the thing in focus is thought of as what the icon describes. Thus, the iconic representation harbours the power to elaborate, to extend the parallel structure.

This tendency towards further development distinguishes metaphor from the other tropes, which are exhausted in their immediate expression. On the other hand, metaphor is capable in the first place of extending vocabulary, whether by providing a guide for naming new objects or by offering concrete equivalents for abstract terms (thus the word *cosmos*, after having signified 'a pleasing sort of array such as a woman's headdress or the trappings of a horse's harness' [188], came to designate the disposition of an army and, finally, the order of the universe). Extension of vocabulary, however, is but the least effect of this penchant for development.

It is resemblance that allows us to function in new situations. If metaphor adds nothing to the description of the world, at least it adds to the ways in which we perceive; and this is the poetic function of metaphor. This still rests upon resemblance, but at the level of feelings. In symbolizing one situation by means of another, metaphor 'infuses' the feelings attached to the symbolizing situation into the heart of the situation that is symbolized. In this 'transference of feelings,' the similarity between feelings is induced by the resemblance of situations. In its poetic function, therefore, metaphor extends the power of double meaning from the cognitive realm to the affective.

It is regrettable that, by opposing feeling and description in this manner, the author gives in ultimately to an emotionalist theory of metaphor and loses part of the benefit of an analysis that had nevertheless recognized perfectly the connection between the workings of resemblance and the capacity for further development on the cognitive plane itself.[18]

However one regards this final interpretation of the role of metaphor, the major interest of Henle's analysis is that it does not force us to choose between a predicative theory and an iconic theory. This is, to my mind, the essential point of the present Study. Moreover, it is difficult to see how an iconic theory could be articulated, if not in terms of predication. Henle perceives clearly that metaphor as trope is a species of 'metaphoric statement' (181). In effect, only a complete statement can refer to a thing or a situation 'by symbolizing its icon' (as above, symbolizing is taken in the sense of Peirce, that is, in the sense of conventional sign). In such a statement, 'some terms symbolize the icon and others symbolize what is iconized' (ibid.).[19] (Max Black says nothing different: metaphor requires a complex of words in which some terms are taken literally and others metaphorically.) So important is this contrastive constitution that it suffices to distinguish metaphor from simile on the one hand (in which no term is taken in a figurative sense and where the parallelism operates between two sequences of literal terms) and allegory on the other (in which all of the terms are taken figuratively, giving rise accordingly to two parallel interpretations, each equally coherent).

This analysis also does not force a choice between a theory of logical absurdity and an iconic theory. It is the 'clash' (183) on the literal level that leads one to seek out a meaning beyond the lexical meaning; while the context allows one to maintain the literal sense of certain terms, it prevents one from doing so for others. However, metaphor is not quite the clash itself, but rather its resolution. One must decide, on the basis of various 'clues' (ibid.) provided by the context, which terms can be taken figuratively and which cannot. One must therefore 'work out' (185) the parallelism between situations that will guide the iconic transposition of one to the other. This activity has become useless in the case of conventional metaphors, where cultural usage decides on the figurative sense of certain expressions. It is only in living metaphors that one sees this activity at work.

We are not far from recognizing that semantic clash is just one side of a process whose other side is the iconic function.

3 / THE CASE AGAINST RESEMBLANCE

Despite the penetrating suggestions contained in the article by Paul Henle, the later history of the predicative theory of metaphor reflects an obliteration of interest in the problem of resemblance and the development of an explanation in which it plays no decisive role. The brief against resemblance can be drawn up as follows.

The keystone of the case is the long association between substitution and resemblance in the history of the problem of metaphor. The brilliant generalization by Roman Jakobson only confirms this assessment: every substitution of one term for another takes place within a sphere of resemblance. On the other hand, interaction is compatible with any sort of relation. The tenor-vehicle relationship still refers to resemblance between 'what is really thought or said' and 'that to which it is compared'; but the broader idea of 'transaction between contexts' does not require this reference.[20] Max Black follows this direction. By strongly opposing theory of interaction to substitution theory, and by connecting the outcome of the latter with that of the theory of comparison, he leads up to the conclusion that there are 'all kinds of "grounds" for shifts of meaning with context – and even no ground at all, sometimes.'[21] As for the application of the system of associated commonplaces to the principal subject, it can be described without recourse to analogy of terms. With Monroe Beardsley, the withdrawal of resemblance is complete. Everything takes place as if logical absurdity had replaced analogy in the explanation of metaphor. It is logical absurdity that forces one to leave the plane of primary meanings and seek, in the network of connotations, the one that can give rise to a meaningful attribution.[22]

A second argument can be stated thus: even though analogy is the relation metaphorical statement puts into play, it explains nothing, since it is more the result of the statement than its cause or reason. A resemblance suddenly becomes visible between two things that previously one had never dreamed of juxtaposing and comparing. This is why the interaction theory is forced to take account of resemblance itself, but does so without including it in its explanation for fear of falling into a vicious circle. Rather, the application of the metaphorical predicate to the principal subject is compared to a screen or a filter that selects, eliminates, and organizes meanings in the principal subject; and analogy is not involved in this application.

Thirdly, it can be argued that resemblance and analogy are equivocal terms, which cannot help introducing confusion into the analysis. Their use in Aristotle appears to confirm this criticism of the logical weakness of resemblance.[23] At least three uses of the term can be found in Aristotle – four even, if one considers the supplementary meaning that will be set out in the fourth argument. The one rigorous use of the term corresponds to what Aristotle continually calls analogy, which is a relationship of proportionality. It is defined in the *Nichomachean Ethics* (5 : 6) as 'equality of ratios, and involves four terms at least' (1131 a 31). But proportional metaphor does not define metaphor generically, but only the fourth type. Comparison of simile (*eïkôn*) comes close to this first meaning; *Rhetoric* 3 : 4 (1407 a 17-20) mentions this kinship specifically, despite the fact that the relationship in comparison is simple and not two-fold. But simile is not the foundation of metaphor: the *Poetics* ignores it, and the *Rhetoric* subordinates it to metaphor.

Without any detectable allusion to the logic of proportion and comparison, Aristotle states at the end of the *Poetics*: 'But the greatest thing by far is to be a master of metaphor. It is the one thing that cannot be learnt from others; and it is also a sign of genius, since a good metaphor implies an intuitive perception of the similarity in dissimilars' (1459 a 5-8). This general statement encompasses the four species of metaphor and therefore covers the entire domain of *epiphora.* But what is it to perceive similarity? There seems to be a hint in *Rhetoric* 3 that 'similar' is 'same,' that is, generic identity: 'Metaphors should be drawn ... from objects closely related [*apo oïkeïôn*] but not obvious to every one at first sight [*mê phanerôn*]; just as in philosophy also, to observe the resemblance [*to homoïon*] in widely distant things is characteristic of a sagacious penetrating intellect: like Archytas' saying, that arbitrator and altar were the same thing [*tauton*]; because both are the refuge of the injured or wronged' (1412 a 11-14). How is this universal role of resemblance to be squared with the specific reasoning of analogy or simile? And how are 'similar' and 'same' to be reconciled at the level of this universal role?

The focus of a fourth argument is a more serious equivocation that affects if not *resemblance* itself, then one term that is most often associated with it. To resemble is, in a sense, to be the image of. Do we not say interchangeably that a portrait or photograph 'is the image of' or 'resembles' the original? This connection between resemblance and image is reflected in a certain approach to literary criticism – a former approach, to be sure – for which to enquire into an author's metaphors is to hunt down his typical images, by which is understood his visual, auditory, and generally sensorial images. The resemblance here moves from the abstract to the concrete, with the concrete image resembling the abstract idea it illustrates. Resemblance, therefore, is precisely the property of that which depicts, of the portrait broadly speaking. This new equivocation would appear to find some support in Aristotle himself. Does he not say that a vivid metaphor is one that 'sets something before the eyes'? As it happens, this property is mentioned in the same context as proportional metaphor, without the author indicating any link whatsoever between these two traits. Now, what is there in common between positing an equality of relationships and setting something before the eyes, in other words, between calculating and making visible? It would be fair to ask whether this equivocation does not also underlie the description Paul Henle gives of the iconic character of metaphor. Is not the presentation of one thought in terms of another always, in one way or another, to make visible, to show the first in the light of the more vivid appearance of the second? Going further, is it not the property of figure as such to convey visibility, to make discourse appear?[24] If this is the case, what link remains between the two extremities of the range thus opened, between the logic of proportionality and the imagery of iconicity?

All these ambiguities seem to converge on a central point: what constitutes the metaphoricity of metaphor? Does the notion of resemblance have the power to encompass proportion, comparison or simile, the bond of similarity (or sameness), and iconicity, without destroying itself? Or must one rather admit that it just hides the initial embarrassment of a definition and an explanation that can produce nothing but a metaphor of metaphor – metaphor of transference in Aristotle, of vehicle with Richards, of screen, filter, and lens with Max Black? Do all these metaphors not bring us back ironically to our point of departure, to the metaphor of displacement, of change of location?[25]

4 / IN DEFENCE OF RESEMBLANCE

I propose to demonstrate:

(a) that the factor of resemblance is of even greater necessity in a tension theory than in a substitution theory;

(b) that resemblance is not only what the metaphorical statement fashions, but also what guides and produces this statement;

(c) that resemblance can accommodate a logical status capable of overcoming the equivocity criticized above; and

(d) that the iconic character of resemblance must be reformulated such that imagination becomes itself a properly semantic moment of the metaphorical statement.

(a) The first mistake on the part of the reasoning directed against including resemblance in the logical status of metaphor is to believe that the notions of tension, interaction, and logical contradiction make every possible role of resemblance superfluous. Let us turn to the strategy of language at work in a metaphorical expression as simple as an oxymoron (a *living* death, *obscure* clarity). In its literal sense, the expression constitutes an enigma to which the metaphorical meaning offers the solution. Now, the tension and contradiction point only to the form of the problem within the enigma, what one could call the semantic challenge or, in Jean Cohen's terms, the 'semantic impertinence.' The metaphorical meaning as such is not the semantic clash but the new pertinence that answers its challenge. In the language of Beardsley, the metaphor is what forms a meaningful self-contradictory statement from a self-destructive self-contradictory statement. It is in this mutation of meaning that resemblance plays its part. But this role cannot come to light unless one turns away from the alliance between resemblance and substitution, which is purely semiotic in character, towards a properly semantic aspect of resemblance – I mean, towards a functioning that is inseparable from the instance of discourse constitutive of the sentence (or from the complex expression at play in oxymoron). In other words, if it serves some purpose in metaphor, resemblance must be a characteristic of the attribution of predicates and not of the substitution of names. What constitutes the new pertinence is the kind of semantic 'proximity' established between the terms despite their 'distance' apart. Things that until that moment were 'far apart' suddenly appear as 'closely related.'[26] Aristotle was aware of this strictly predicative effect of resemblance when he considered, among the 'virtues' of good metaphors, that of being 'appropriate' (*Rhetoric* 3: 1404 b 3). He saw in this a sort of 'harmony' (1405 a 10). On guard against 'far-fetched' metaphors, he recommends that metaphors be derived from material that is 'kindred' (*sungenôn* and 'of like form' (*homoeïdôn*), such that once the expression is produced, it will appear clearly that the 'names' involved are 'near of kin' (*hoti sungenes*) (1405 a 37).[27]

This notion of generic relatedness is valuable; and since we acknowledge that metaphors instruct, there is no great drawback in the fact that it is expressed metaphorically. Besides, the metaphor of 'far' and 'near' merely continues that of 'transfer' or 'conveyance' [*transport*]; to transfer is to ap-proximate, to suppress distance [*dés-éloigner*]. In a preconceptual fashion, the notion of generic relatedness points towards the idea of a 'family resemblance,' to which the logical status of resemblance in the metaphorical process could be linked.

The following paragraphs will capitalize on this breakthrough. A first point at least has been made: namely, that tension, contradiction, and controversion are nothing but the opposite side of the reconciliation in which metaphor 'makes sense.' And a second point is established as well: that resemblance is itself a fact of predication, which operates between the same terms that contradiction sets in tension.[28]

(b) The objection here is that resemblance is not a good candidate to serve as the reason or cause of the new pertinence, because it is what results from the statement and from the rapprochement it effects. The reply to this objection takes us into a sort of paradox that is quite capable of shedding new light on the theory of metaphor. Phillip Wheelwright comes very close to this paradox in his work *Metaphor and Reality*[29] (to which I will devote more time in Study 7). The author proposes to distinguish between *epiphor* and *diaphor*. *Epiphora*, we recall, is Aristotle's term. It is transposition, transference as such, that is, the unitive process, the sort of assimilation that occurs between alien ideas, ideas distant from one another. As such, this unitive process arises from an apperception – an insight – that belongs to the order of *seeing*. Aristotle was pointing to this apperception when he said: 'To metaphorize well is to see – to contemplate, to have the right eye for – the similar.' *Epiphora* is this glance and this genius-stroke, unteachable and impregnable.[30] But there is no epiphor without diaphor, no intuition without construction. Indeed, the intuitive process, bringing together what is disparate, contains an irreducibly discursive moment. The same Aristotle who 'contemplates the similar' is also the theoretician of that proportional metaphor in which resemblance is more constructed than seen (even though the similar is at work there is some fashion, as the Greek expression *homoïôs ekheï*, to behave in a similar way, indicates [*Poetics* 1457 b 20]). Max Black captures this discursive moment again in another metaphor, that of the screen, filter, or lens, in order to express the way the predicate chooses and organizes certain aspects of the principal subject. There is no contradiction, therefore, in giving an account of metaphor now in the language of apperception, that is, of vision, and then in the language of construction. It is at once the 'gift of genius' and the skill of the geometer, who sees the point in the 'ratio of proportions.'

Perhaps this constitutes a divorce from semantics and remarriage to psychology. In the first place, however, there is no shame in being taught by psychology, especially when it is a psychology of process and not of elements. Gestalt psychology is very instructive in this respect, when, dealing with the phenomenon of invention, it shows that every change of structure passes through a moment of sudden intuition in which the new structure emerges from the obliteration and modification of the prior configuration. Furthermore, this paradox of psychological attraction between genius and calculation, between intuition and construction, is really a purely semantic paradox, which has to do with the unusual character of allocation of predicates in the instance of discourse. Nelson Goodman provides an interesting apologue in this connection (again a metaphor of metaphor!): metaphor, he says, is the 'reassignment of labels,' but a reassignment that fashions its figure from 'an affair between a predicate with a past and an object that yields while protesting.'[31] To yield while protesting is, in metaphorical form, our paradox. The protest is what remains from the former marriage, the literal assignation, destroyed by contradiction; the yielding is what finally happens thanks to the new rapprochement. Diaphor of the epiphor is this very paradox. It underlies the 'glance' that perceives the similar beyond the divorce.

(c) This last paradox may contain the key for a reply to the objection concerning the logical status of resemblance. That is, what holds for the operation of assimilation can hold for the relation of similarity, but only if it can be shown that the relation of similarity is another name for the operation of assimilation described earlier.

The argument accusing resemblance of logical weakness is, we know, that anything resembles anything else ... except for a certain difference!

The solution that remains is to construct the relationship on the model of the operation and relate the paradox of the operation to the relation. It then becomes apparent that the conceptual structure of resemblance opposes and unites identity and difference. It is not due to oversight that Aristotle assimilates 'similar' to 'same': to see sameness in what is different is to see similarity.[32] Now, metaphor reveals the logical structure of 'the similar' because, in the metaphorical statement, 'the similar' is perceived *despite* difference, *in spite of* contradiction. Resemblance, therefore, is the logical category corresponding to the predicative operation in which 'approximation' (bringing close) meets the resistance of 'being distant.' In other words, metaphor displays the work of resemblance because the literal contradiction preserves difference within the metaphorical statement; 'same' and 'different' are not just mixed together, they also remain opposed. Through this specific trait, enigma lives on in the heart of metaphor. In metaphor, 'the same' operates *in spite of* 'the different.'

This feature has been seen in one way or another by various authors,[33] but I would like to take the idea a stage – or rather, two stages – further.

If, in metaphor, resemblance can be construed as the site of the clash between sameness and difference, cannot this model serve as basis for an account of the diversity of species of metaphor, from which the alleged equivocity seems to be derived? We should ask in what sense transference from genus to species, from species to genus, and from species to species are all forms of *epiphora*, reflecting the same polemical unity of the similar.

Turbayne broaches the answer in *The Myth of Metaphor*.[34] He observes that what takes place in the metaphorical statement is comparable to what Gilbert Ryle calls 'category mistake,' which consists in the 'presentation of facts belonging to one category in the idioms appropriate to another.'[35] Indeed, the definition of metaphor does not differ radically from this; metaphor consists in speaking of one thing in terms of another that resembles it. It is tempting to say that metaphor is a planned category mistake. According to this perspective, the four Aristotelian species are brought together again. This is clear for the first three (giving the name of the genus to the species, etc.) – they manifestly transgress the conceptual boundaries of the terms considered. Moreover, proportional metaphor involves the same sort of error, because for Aristotle the metaphor is not the analogy itself (i.e. equivalence of the relations) but rather the transference of the name of the second term to the fourth and vice versa, on the basis of the proportional relationship. Aristotle's four types, therefore, are planned category mistakes.

The same structure allows us to understand the primacy of metaphor over simile in Aristotle. In effect, metaphor says 'this is that' directly (*Rhetoric* 3: 1410 b 19). This application of a predicate despite the incompatibility involved constitutes the instruction that metaphor provides. Simile is already something more; it is a paraphrase, which dissipates the force of the unusual attribution. This is why the attack on simile by Max Black and Monroe Beardsley does not reach metaphor, which is not merely the abridged form of simile, but on the contrary, its dynamic principle.[36]

The idea of category mistake brings us close to our goal. Can one not say that the strategy of language at work in metaphor consists in obliterating the logical and established frontiers of language, in order to bring to light new resemblances the previous classification kept us from seeing? In other words, the power of metaphor would be to break an old categorization, in order to establish new logical frontiers on the ruins of their forerunners.

Advancing still another step, can we not hypothesize that the dynamic of thought that carves its way through already established categories is the same as that which engenders all classification? (I speak here of hypothesis because we have no direct access whatsoever to any such origin of genera and classes. Observation and reflection always arrive too late. So it is by means of a sort of philosophical imagining, proceeding by extrapolation, that one can propose that the figure of speech we call metaphor, and that appears first of all as a phenomenon of deviation in relation to an established usage, is homogeneous with a process that has given rise to all the 'semantic fields,' and thus to the very usage from which metaphor deviates.) The same operation that lets us 'see the similar' also 'conveys learning and knowledge through the medium of the *genus*.' This too is in Aristotle. But if it is true that one learns what one does not yet know, then to make the similar visible is to produce the genus within the differences, and not elevated beyond differences, in the transcendance of the concept. This is what Aristotle signified through the idea of 'generic relationship.' Metaphor allows us to intercept the formation of the genus at this preparatory stage because, in the metaphorical process, the movement towards the genus, which is checked by the resistance of difference, is captured somehow by the rhetorical figure. In this manner, metaphor reveals the dynamic at work in the constitution of semantic fields, the dynamic Gadamer calls the fundamental 'metaphoric,'[37] which merges with the genesis of concepts through similarity. A family resemblance first brings individuals together before the rule of a logical class dominates them. Metaphor, a figure of speech, presents in an *open* fashion, by means of a conflict *between* identity and difference, the process that, in a *covert* manner, generates semantic grids by fusion of differences *into* identity.

This last generalization allows us to take up our suspended discussion of the concept of metaphorical process in Roman Jakobson. Like Jakobson, indeed, but in a different sense from his, we form a concept of 'metaphorical process' for which the rhetorical trope plays the role of agent of revelation. But we part ways with Jakobson in that what can be generalized in metaphor is not its substitutive essence but its predicative essence. Jakobson generalized a semiotic phenomenon, the substitution of one term for another. We are generalizing a semantic phenomenon, assimilation to each other of two networks of signification by means of an unusual attribution. At the same time, being properly predicative or attributive in essence, the 'metaphorical pole' of language does not have a metonymic pole as its counterpart. The symmetry of the two poles is broken. Metonymy – one name for another name – remains a semiotic process, perhaps even the substitutive phenomenon *par excellence* in the realm of signs. Metaphor – unusual attribution – is a semantic process, in the sense of Benveniste, perhaps even the *genetic* phenomenon *par excellence* in the realm of the instance of discourse.

(d) The same paradox of vision and discursiveness that served as a model in constructing the relation of resemblance can now serve as a guide in answering the fourth objection. This concerns the status of resemblance as a figurative presentation, as an image depicting abstract relationships. The issue, we remember, comes from a remark by Aristotle concerning the power of metaphor to 'set before the eyes'; and it is posed in its full scope by the iconic theory of Paul Henle and by the notion of 'associated image' of Michel Le Guern. For, as we also saw, the more a semantic analysis surrenders to a logical grammar, the greater its reluctance to return to the notion of image, which is considered too enmeshed with bad psychology.

The question then is whether the iconic moment of metaphor stands outside every semantic approach, and whether it is not possible to account for it starting from the paradoxal structure of resemblance. Would not imagination have something to do with the conflict between identity and difference?

We should make clear that we are not yet speaking here of imagination in its sensible, quasi-sensual aspect, which we will consider in the following section. It is advisable first to bracket this *non-verbal* kernel of imagination, that is, imagery understood in the quasi-visual, quasi-auditory, quasi-tactile, quasi-olfactory sense. The only way to approach the problem of imagination from the perspective of a semantic theory, that is to say on a verbal plane, is to begin with productive imagination in the Kantian sense, and to put off reproductive imagination or imagery as long as possible. Treated as a schema, the image presents a verbal dimension; before being the gathering-point of faded perceptions, it is that of emerging meanings. In the same way, therefore, that the schema is the matrix of the category, the icon is the matrix of the new semantic pertinence that is born out of the dismantling of semantic networks caused by the shock of contradiction.

Integrating this new viewpoint with those we have already accepted, I would suggest that the iconic moment involves a verbal aspect, in that it constitutes the grasping of identity within differences and in spite of differences, but based on a preconceptual pattern. Aristotelian seeing – 'to see the similar' – does not appear to be different from the iconic moment, when clarified in this way by the Kantian schema: for to teach the genus, to grasp the relatedness of terms that are far apart, is to set before the eyes. Accordingly, metaphor is established as the schematism in which the metaphorical attribution is produced. This schematism turns imagination into the place where the figurative meaning emerges in the interplay of identity and difference. And metaphor is that place in discourse where this schematism is visible, because the identity and the difference do not melt together but confront each other.

Furthermore, this notion of a schematism of metaphorical attribution allows us to take up again a question that was left in abeyance. It will be recalled that Aristotle said that *lexis* makes discourse appear, and that Fontanier compared the figure to the face of the body. Now, the idea of a

schematism of metaphorical attribution does proper justice to this phenomenon, since the schema is what makes the attribution appear, what gives
it body. This predicative process '*creates image*' and is itself the carrier of
the semantic analogy. In this way, it helps to resolve the semantic incompatibility perceived at the level of the literal meaning.

Does this mean that the problem posed by the image has been completely solved? To tell the truth, we have incorporated only the verbal
aspect of the image, in the guise of schema of the synthesis of the identical
and the different. What is the status of the *making-seen* as such? Of 'setting
before the eyes'? Of the figurative ability of the figure? We must admit
that, after this analysis, the residue left behind is the image itself!

Nevertheless, it may be possible, by concentrating on the schematism of
productive imagination, at least to explore the frontier between semantics
and psychology where one finds the junction of verbal and non-verbal, if
not to incorporate the image as such into semantic theory.[38]

5 / PSYCHOLINGUISTICS OF METAPHOR

A radical way of exploring the frontier between semantics and psychology
is to set up a combined discipline, *psycholinguistics*, at that boundary. The
need for this move is not shown only by the concern that the image be incorporated into the properly semantic operation of metaphor. The very
notion of transposition, the constant theme of a theory of tropes, brings
operations into play that legitimate a mixed approach involving psychology *and* linguistics. We will deal with this motif in the present section,
leaving till later the psycholinguistic consideration of the *image* itself.

The very principle of a psycholinguistic approach to operations involved
in metaphor deserves examination. Will we not fall again into just that
style of description and explanation from which linguistics with very great
effort freed itself? Not at all: the psycholinguistics to be encountered is
not pre-linguistic but post-linguistic; its aim is, in fact, to join in a new discipline the componential analysis of semic fields and the mental operations
that traverse these fields. Hence, this discipline would not be subject to the
former, justified criticism of a psychology whose two faults were to concentrate more on contents (image, concept) than on operations, and to
provide a mechanical representation of the relationships between contents
(thus the successive versions of association of ideas). It is a new discipline
born from the contribution of an entirely specific semic analysis and from
a description of operations investigated at their sublinguistic level.

As far as figures are concerned, Gaston Esnault was a forerunner.[39] He
saw that the operations brought into play by figures reduce to the capacity
to increase or restrict extension (i.e., the number of entities to which a

notion applies) or comprehension (i.e., the number of characteristics that make up a notion). According to him, synecdoche is nothing but a modification of extension, and metaphor and metonymy a variation in comprehension. The difference between these two figures is that metonymy follows the order of things and proceeds analytically, whereas metaphor plays on comprehension in a synthetic and intuitive manner, by means of a reaction that begins and ends in imagination. This is why the imaginative equivalence instituted by metaphor does more violence to the real than does metonymy, which respects the links inscribed in the facts. But Esnault lacked the methodological tool of psycholinguistics, which is (as stated above) the combination of a theory of operations and of a theory of fields.

Métonymie et Métaphore by Albert Henry attempts to satisfy this twofold requirement (at the same time, it addresses a properly stylistic concern which is outside our sphere of interest). Indeed, he considers 'the psycholinguistic foundations' that he proposes to be the 'indispensible basis for a sound stylistic analysis' (21). This work, accordingly, is to the psycholinguistics of metaphor what that of Hedwig Konrad was to the logico-linguistics of metaphor. For Henry, a single mental operation is at work in the synecdoche-metonymy-metaphor triad; and this operation appears in its first degree in metonymy (and synecdoche), and in its second degree in metaphor. This is why one must study it first in metonymy.

As Esnault saw, this operation is the perceptive synthesis that allows the mind to focus or to diffuse its inquiring searchlight (23). Figures are only the various ways in which the meaning-results of this unique operation are institutionalized on the linguistic plane.

What is to be said now of metonymy, if it is true that it exemplifies the simple level of the operation? The semic analysis of Pottier[40] and Greimas[41] is relevant at this point. If 'semic field' is the name we give to the collection of elementary constituents of a concept-entity, then a semic field is something that can be traversed. 'In the case of metonymy, the mind, traversing a semic field, focuses on one of its semes and labels the concept-entity that is the object of its contemplation with the word that, in pure linguistic reality, would name this seme, were it itself considered as a concept-entity' (25). Accordingly, we call a certain coin a *Louis* because it bears the portrait of a king by that name. Three aspects are to be considered, therefore: articulation of the semic field as a state of language, 'more or less free and more or less felicitous mental inspection' (25), and the naming of the object considered by the seme on which the mind focuses.[42]

This perspective is interesting for our present research because, by approaching the phenomenon from the operational side and not only from that of structure, one can distinguish from dead figures other figures in the process of being born, new metonymies that bring into play an 'active, selective perception' (30) – as in the expression of the Marquis de Brinvilliers, who said of her locket of poisons that 'many successions were contained in that box' (ibid.). Stylistics has much to expect from this differentiation based on the difference of operations.[43]

At the same time, the role of predication in the operation can be noted in passing, for example, when the figurative word is in the adjectival position ('to have a *lively* wine'): 'Predication is the linguistic process that allows the semantic phenomenon called metonymy to affirm itself' (33). Our critique will not lose sight of this trait.[44]

Semic focalization, then, is the fundamental 'creative mechanism.' And metonymy, furthermore, is the simple expression of this mechanism on the level of figures.

In what sense is metaphor a variant, as Esnault saw, of the same capacity for altering the understanding? Here again, this forerunner lacked technical means, and that is why he could not overcome the purely psychological opposition between the analytical mode and a synthetic, intuitive, imaginative mode. The linguistic shift permits the construction of metaphor on the basis of metonymy as a double and superimposed metonymy.[45]

To take this route is to pass up another, the traditional one in rhetoric, which identifies metaphor with an abbreviated simile. On this point, the author precedes Le Guern by developing the argument that simile is not a figure because it presents neither deviation nor substitution; that it results in no new naming; and lastly that it is a *bona fide* intellectual operation which leaves the compared terms intact (59-63).

If metaphor is not an abbreviated simile, how can it be considered to be 'the synthesis of a short-circuited double metonymy' (66)?

In order to show how this can be, let us begin with Aristotle's fourth class of metaphor, metaphor by analogy, which the author holds to be fundamental (whereas Konrad, with her logico-linguistic point of view, gave first place to the relationship of species to species). When Victor Hugo writes: 'Malta's armour was threefold [*trois cuirasses*], its fortresses, its ships, and the valour of its knights,' he achieves a first metonymy by crossing the semic field of *fortress* and focalizing on the seme *to protect.* He proceeds to a second metonymy with the word *armour*, and then posits the equivalence of the two retained characteristics. Finally, the intended equivalence is expressed in the name of the object (armour), that is, by the symbol of the entire semic field that possesses the common characteristic (to protect).

But where does the synthesis lie? At this point, the author offers a set of synonyms, themselves metaphorical as were the 'screen,' 'filter,'

'lens,' and 'stereoscopic vision' of the English-language critiques. He will
speak in like fashion of 'metonymic superposition creating a subjective
synonymy in discourse' (66). This superposition is to be represented
graphically by two planes (the semic fields) showing two centres of focalization, and by an arrow piercing the two planes through their two centres.
The author's comment on this diagram is that 'in metaphor, there is a double focalization and precision of vision along the longitudinal perspectival
axis' (68). This is exactly the same as the 'stereoscopic vision' of W.B.
Stanford.[46] The image can be completed by saying that the metaphorical
term 'loads down the metaphorized term with all of its own *connotation* –
some of it clear and precise, some of it vague and fuzzy' (67); and the
image of overload leads to that of 'metaphoric density' (67). This is the
dominant image in the formula that neatly summarizes the entire thesis:
'The sole fundamental figure is the figure of contiguity: at its first degree,
it is realized in metonymy and in synecdoche; at the second degree, it
multiplies and thickens into metaphor' (69).

Before proposing several critical thoughts specifically concerning the
psycholinguistic foundation of the work, I should admit that I have not
done enough justice to this work, which does not just lay these psycholinguistic foundations but builds a genuine stylistic edifice on them. I must
explain why I thus cut away the work's crowning feature and its incompar-
ably rich analyses concerning 'the stylistic status of metaphor' (115-39).
Once a stylistic point of view is adopted, a new unit of discourse is taken
as reference point, the literary *work*. Now, our whole discussion has been
located between the word and the sentence; new problems are linked specifically to this change of level, and we will discuss them in Study 7. This
is why I restrict my view to the analyses that support the transition from
the semantic level to the stylistic level (although actually the work talks
about the relationship between psycholinguistics and stylistics).

As with metonymy, the stylistic point of view puts the focus on combinations of figures. Along with those of contrasts and redundancies, one
finds twinnings, concatenations, rings, and plaitings, such as in Saint-John
Perse. This takes one close to Riffaterre's analysis of metaphoric series
(121). The integration of these metaphoric complexes into a work is mediated either by a narrative structure or, more simply, by a vast, metaphorically detailed semic field. So it is at the level of the work that one can
understand that metaphor belongs to 'a complex stylistic organism' (139).
At this level too, the value of metaphor as personal expression and its properly poetic function of indirect language (132) are made precise, without
overlooking its purely intellective and dialectical function (132). Accordingly, a whole metaphorical complex is required so that, in the two quat-
rains of *Les Fleurs du Mal* (superbly analysed on page 135), the conjunc-

tion of two figures (*sea / mane-like hair* and *ship / soul*) achieves 'cosmic opening from these waving tresses up to the over-arching sky' (135). An entire poem is needed in order to open up a world and create, 'in convergence, the harmony of a universe in motion' (135). We will come across this sort of problem again in Study 7.

My criticism is not directed at all against the principle of a psycholinguistics of metaphor. To repeat, the mixed method is perfectly justified, on the one hand by the operation constituted by transposition, and on the other hand by the conjunction of this operation and the image. The work under analysis provides almost no occasion at all for considering the latter side; but it is perfectly suited to a discussion of the former.

I am inclined to say that, in the mixture of psychology and linguistics, only one part of the resources of linguistics is exploited, namely, semic analysis; and another part is neglected, the very aspect that Jean Cohen recognized, i.e. the domain of semantic impertinence and pertinence. The reduction of metaphor to metonymy is the outcome of this unequal mingling of a theory of operations and a theory of semic fields in which a properly semantic aspect is missing.

Let us begin with a preliminary remark, which may only be a quibble over words but will receive greater weight in the remainder of the discussion: does the name *metonymy* apply strictly speaking to the two partial operations of focalization on a seme, on which the constitutive equivalence of metaphor is built? If one relies on the definition given above, metonymy is a figure only if the focalization results in a name change. Without that change, there is no longer deviation, nor figure. Now, this is not the case here: metonymy is not incorporated into metaphor as a figure, but only as focalization, which is an abstraction performed on the new naming. So the metaphor itself is a figure only when it is the outcome of the entire process. One can speak of course of metonymic focalization (76), as a reminder that this focalization is the same as that which gives rise to the figure called metonymy; nevertheless, metaphor and metonymy remain two distinct figures.

But the principal difficulty concerns the status of the equivalence itself, that central phenomenon which we saw bounded by a series of expressive metaphors: superposition, overloading, thickening. On one occasion, it is called, in a more direct manner, an 'integrating identification' (71). One would expect a psycholinguistic analysis (that is, psychological and linguistic at the same time) of this integrating identification. In fact, the linguistic aspect would not reduce to the naming, by application to the thing considered, of 'the linguistic sign that designates the whole semic field' (69). As Vinsauf and later Konrad both saw, substitution at the level of expression is only the final phase, itself grounded in the equivalence that is the essential phase. Nor would the linguistic aspect reduce to double metonymy. Equivalence arises of itself when the double metonymy is given, whereas the whole art of metaphor is to achieve the rapprochement that motivates the search for semes capable of identifying what was 'alien.' Thus, it is the operation of equivalence that summons the two partial operations imprecisely called metonymies. If the mind scans various semic fields and focalizes on this or that seme, it is because the entire process is stretched (as Jean Cohen perceived) between an impertinence to be neutralized and a new pertinence to be instituted. The two 'metonymies' are merely abstract phases of a concrete process, ruled by the interplay of distance and proximity. Their status here is not that of figures, therefore, but of segments in a process whose unity belongs to the semantic order (in the sense that we give to this word opposing it to the semiological).

The above suggests that the semantic character of the integrating identification comes to light if it is set in relation to the semantic character of the 'distance' that rapprochement overcomes. In this sense, a psycholinguistics of metaphor would have to include the concept of semantic impertinence in its theory of operations. But just as the theory of Jean Cohen lacks a correspondingly semantic analysis of the establishment of pertinence (a lack not satisfied by the idea of a deviation of language reducing a deviation in discourse),[47] the 'integrating identification' of Albert Henry, as it happens, is capable of filling in for the concept of new pertinence missing in Cohen's work.

Now, although this psycholinguistic node of equivalence is not a conscious target of the study of the 'mechanism' of metaphor, it is approached indirectly in the study of its 'morphology,' the topic of a separate chapter (74-114). Indeed, this study shifts the accent quite sharply from double metonymy towards the equivalence itself of the two metonymic relationships. There could be legitimate apprehension that morphology – precisely because it is morphology and not just a mechanism – might enclose itself in an algebra that retains only a trace of operations, especially if its guide is the 'number of terms expressed' (85). Indeed, the equation

$$\frac{a}{b} = \frac{a'}{b'},$$

where the metaphorizing term properly speaking is always placed in position a, is taken by the author as 'a prelinguistic or sublinguistic representational schema, which the expression will actualize and flesh out' (82). With this groundwork, all the theoretical possibilities are exhausted by the successive examination of metaphor in four terms, in three terms, in two terms (and even in one term). There is great danger that this schema will contain nothing but the formula of the resolved problem.

And yet the detail of the analysis lets through several less formal operational traits. Thus, metaphor in two terms reveals something concerning the scope of equivalence that distinguishes it from mathematical equality – as verified consistently, moreover, by our remarks on metaphor *in praesentia*. Formally, metaphor in two terms involves the ellipsis of two terms from the complete relationship. If these terms are a and a', then in *burning bush (a) of your lips (a')*, the terms to be restored are *flicker of flames (b)* and *red (b')*. The terms can be a and b', as in the genitive forms, the verbal or adjectival metaphors, as seen in the example *the sea smiled on him*. Here, too, the four terms can be completed: *to smile (a)* is to *man (b)* as *to shine (a')* is to *sea (b')*. However, even if formally the formula is that of metaphor in four terms, there is something specific in the way metaphor in two terms functions because of the link created between the two terms brought into each other's presence. In this way, the predicative value that a' acquires from a is not that of identification but that of subordination (91). In the case of b', it receives a specifically different signification of identification from a: identity, fundamental characterization of identity, belonging, etc. Above all, it is notable that 'no identification is possible between the substantive and the verb or adjective' (93); the nominal metaphor of a based on b' itself must be assimilated to verbal and adjectival metaphors (94). Now, it is insufficient here to invoke linguistic servitude, which demands that the verb apply to a substantive taken according to its proper meaning – with the result that the verb metaphorizes alone – in order to conclude that the verbal or adjectival metaphor does not constitute a particular category of metaphor (95). This deep linguistic structure accounts only for the normal type of such a metaphor being ab'; it does not explain why the predicative relation is not an identification. This is the trait that sets it apart. Generally speaking, neither 'is,' nor 'to call,' nor 'to name,' nor 'to do,' nor 'to have in the place of,' nor 'to stand for' is an identification. The nature of these relations is that of the copula.

Ultimately, 'properly metaphorical semantic fusion' (108) is revealed to be more highly singular than the algebraic identity of two relationships.

One last comment will orient us along the axis of the second psycholinguistic problem mentioned at the beginning of this section. Henry sees three aspects in 'the central problem of metaphoric expression: double metonymic operation, identification, and imaginative illusion' (82). We have discussed the relation of the second to the first aspect. We must still touch on the relation of the third to the second, a relation that is not the object of any special observations in the fundamentally psycholinguistic stylistics of Albert Henry.

6 / ICON AND IMAGE

Is a psycholinguistics of imaginative illusion possible? If, as the analysis of section 4 shows, semantics goes no further than the verbal aspect of imagination, could psycholinguistics perhaps cross over this line and join the properly *sensual* aspect of the image to a semantic theory of metaphor? This is the aspect that was bracketed in order to integrate the aspect of image closest to the verbal plane, namely (in quasi-Kantian language) the 'metaphoric schematization.'

I propose to examine this problem in the light of the interesting contribution of Marcus B. Hester.[48] True, this work does not claim to be 'psycholinguistic.' It is linguistic in the Wittgensteinian sense of the word, and psychological in the Anglo-American tradition of philosophy of mind. Nevertheless, the problem it addresses, the intersection between *'saying'* and *'seeing as ...'*, is psycholinguistic in the terms set out at the beginning of the preceding section.

At first sight, the orientation of this exploration is opposite to that of the semantic theory set out in Study 3. That theory opposed not only any reduction of metaphor to mental imagery, but also any intrusion of the image, considered as a psychological factor, into a semantic theory conceived as logical grammar. This was the price for containing the interplay of resemblance within the limits of the predicative operation, and therefore of discourse. But, ruling out a passage from the imaginary to discourse, the question remains whether one cannot or ought not to attempt the reverse, and *proclaim the image to be the final moment of a semantic theory* that objected to it as a starting point.

This question is called for by the preceding analysis, which, on an essential issue, suffers from a fundamental shortcoming that may well identify the gap that the image is to fill. What remains to be explained is the *sensible* moment of metaphor. This moment is designated in Aristotle by the lively character of metaphor, by its power to 'set before the eyes.' In Fontanier, it is implicit in the very definition of metaphor as something that presents one idea under the sign of another, better known idea. Richards also approaches it with his idea of the *tenor-vehicle* relationship. The relationship of resemblance between vehicle and tenor is not like the relationship of one idea to another, but like that of an image to an abstract meaning. The moment of the image is recognized more succinctly by Paul Henle in connection with the iconic character of metaphor. In the French-language literature on the subject, Le Guern is the one who has gone furthest in this direction with his notion of 'associated image.'

On the other hand, it is precisely this concrete, sensible side of the *vehicle* and *icon* that is eliminated in the interaction theory of Max Black. All that remains from Richards' distinction is the predicative *focus-frame* relationship, which itself is analysed into 'principal subject' and 'auxiliary subject.' Finally, neither Black's notion of 'system of associated common-places' nor that of 'network of connotations' in Beardsley necessarily involves reference to any use of images. All these expressions designate aspects of *verbal* meaning.

Now, it is true that my plea on behalf of resemblance ended with a certain rehabilitation of the iconic moment of metaphor. But this rehabilitation does not go beyond the verbal aspect of the icon, nor beyond a purely logical concept of resemblance, conceived as the unity of identity and difference. It is true as well that a certain concept of imagination returns with the iconic moment, but this concept of imagination is restricted prudently to the Kantian productive imagination. In this sense, the notion of *schematism of metaphoric attribution* does not violate the boundaries of a semantic theory, that is, of a theory of *verbal* meaning.

Can one go further and affix to a semantic theory that sensible element without which the productive imagination itself would not be imagination? The resistance to this proposal is understandable: by doing so, will one not be opening the gate of the semantic sheepfold to the wolf of psychologism? This is a significant objection. But must one not also ask the inverse question – must there remain indefinitely a moat between semantics and psychology? Now, the theory of metaphor would seem to provide the perfect instance for recognizing their common frontier. Indeed, a logical moment and a sensible moment, or if one prefers, a *verbal* moment and a *non-verbal* moment co-operate in it in the unique manner shortly to be discussed. Metaphor owes to this liaison its seemingly essential concreteness. So fear of psychologism should not impede a search, in the transcendental manner of Kantian critique, for the point where the psychological is inserted into semantics – the point in language itself where meaning and sensibility are articulated. My own working hypothesis is that the idea elaborated above of a schematism of attribution constitutes the point on the frontier of semantics and psychology where the imaginary is anchored in a semantic theory of metaphor. It is with this hypothesis in mind that I approach the theory of Marcus B. Hester.

This theory draws support from analyses relating to English-language literary criticism and applied more to poetic language in general than to metaphor in particular. The common characteristic of these analyses is an exaltation of the sensible, sensorial, even sensual aspect of poetic language – the very aspect that the logical grammar of metaphor removes from its purview. Hester retains three principal themes from this mass of analyses.

First of all, poetic language presents a certain 'fusion' between meaning or sense and the senses. This distinguishes it from non-poetic language, where the arbitrary and conventional nature of the sign separates meaning from the sensible as much as possible. This first trait constitutes in Hester's eyes a refutation, or at least a correction, of the Wittgensteinian concept of meaning contained in the *Philosophical Investigations* (this theory, laid out in detail in Hester's first chapter, accentuates the distance between meaning and its carrier and between meaning and object). Hester claims that Wittgenstein constructed a theory of ordinary language alone, to the exclusion of poetic language.

The second theme is that, in poetic language, the pairing of sense and the senses tends to produce an object closed in on itself, in contrast to ordinary language and its thoroughly referential character. In poetic language, the sign is looked at, not through. In other words, instead of being a medium or route crossed on the way to reality, language itself becomes 'stuff,' like the sculptor's marble. We might note here, foreshadowing a longer treatment in the next Study, that this second theme is close to the characterization of the 'poetic' in Jakobson, for whom the poetic function consists essentially in accentuating the message as such at the expense of the referential function.

The third characteristic, finally, is that this closure of poetic language allows it to articulate a fictional experience. As Susanne Langer says,[49] poetic language 'presents an experience of virtual life.' This feeling, which is given form by a centripetally, non-centrifugally oriented language, and which is precisely what this language articulates, is called mood by Northrop Frye.[50]

These three traits – fusion of sense and senses, density of language that has become 'stuff,' virtuality of the experience articulated by this non-referential language – can be summed up in a notion of icon palpably different from that of Paul Henle (on which W.K. Wimsatt lavished praise in *The Verbal Icon*). Like the icon of the Byzantine cult, the verbal icon consists in this fusion of sense and the sensible. It is also that hard object, similar to a sculpture, that language becomes once it is stripped of its referential function and reduced to its opaque appearance. Lastly, it presents an experience that is completely immanent to it.

Hester adopts this point of departure, but his purpose is to lodge the notion of the sensible firmly within the meaning of imagery. The context of this modification is a very original conception of reading, applied to the poem as a whole as well as to the somewhat localized metaphor. The poem, he says, is a 'read object' (117). The author compares reading to the Husserlian *epoché*, which restores the original claim of all the data by suspending any position with respect to natural reality. Reading is also a suspension of all reality and 'an active openness to the text' (131). It is this concept of reading as suspension and openness that introduces the complete rearrangement of the previous themes.

With respect to the first theme, the act of reading shows that the essential trait of poetic language is not the fusion of sense with sound, but the fusion of sense with a wave of evoked or aroused images. This fusion constitutes the true 'iconicity of sense.' Hester fully accepts an understanding of images as sensorial impressions evoked in memory or, as Wellek and Warren put it, as various 'vestigial representations of sensations.'[51] Poetic language is that language game (to use Wittgenstein's terms) in which the aim of words is to evoke, to arouse images. Not only do sense and sound function iconically in relation to each other, but the sense itself is iconic through this power of developing in images. The two traits of the act of reading, suspension and opening, are presented truly by this iconicity. On the one hand, the image is the achievement *par excellence* of neutralization of natural reality; on the other hand, the deployment of images is something that 'occurs' and towards which the sense opens indefinitely, giving unlimited scope to interpretation. One can say truly, in connection with the flux of imagery, that to read is to grant original right to all the data. In poetry, openness to the text is openness to the imagery as liberated by the sense.

Correction of the first theme, borrowed from what can be called the sensualist conception of *verbal icon*, brings with it correction of the second and third themes. This object that Wimsatt, Frye, and others describe as closed in on itself and non-referential is the meaning clothed in imagery. For nothing is obtained from the world except imagery unchained by meaning. From this point of view, not only must the metaphorical be identified with the iconic, but the iconic must also be interpreted as the fictive as such, before a non-referential theory of poetic language can be complete. Once again, it is *epoché*, the suspension proper to the imaginary, that withdraws all reference to empirical reality from the verbal icon. It is also imagery, through its quasi-observational character, that grounds the characteristic of quasi-experience or virtual experience – in short, the *illusion* attendant to reading a poetic work.

In the discussion that follows, I will set aside altogether the two themes of non-referentiality and the aspect of virtual experience. They concern the problem of reference, reality, and truth, which we decided to bracket when making a thoroughgoing distinction between the problem of sense and the problem of reference.[52] Furthermore, Hester's denial of the referential character of poetry is not as free from ambiguity as may appear. The notion of virtual experience indirectly brings back a 'relatedness' to reality, which paradoxically offsets the difference and the distance from reality that characterize the verbal icon. Hester is even seduced in passing by the distinction proposed by Hospers between truth about and truth to.[53] When, for example, Shakespeare likens time to a beggar, he is faithful to the profoundly human reality of time. Therefore, we must reserve the possibility that metaphor is not limited to suspending natural reality, but that in opening meaning up on the imaginative side it also opens it towards a dimension of reality that does not coincide with what ordinary language envisages under the name of natural reality. This is the perspective that I will try to develop in Study 7. Accordingly, following a suggestion by Hester himself,[54] we will restrict ourselves here to the problem of meaning, to the exclusion of the problem of truth. This delimitation of the problem puts us back by the same stroke inside the limits of the first theme: the fusion of 'sense' and 'sensa,' understood from now on as an iconic unfurling of sense in imagery.

The fundamental question posed by the introduction of image or imagery (Hester uses the two terms interchangeably) into a theory of metaphor concerns the status of a sensible, thus non-verbal, factor inside a semantic theory. The difficulty is amplified by the fact that image, as opposed to perception, cannot be related to any 'public' realities, and seems to reintroduce the sort of 'private' mental experience condemned by Wittgenstein, Hester's chosen master. So the problem is to bring to light a liaison between sense and sensa that can be reconciled with semantic theory.

A first trait of the iconicity of meaning seems to facilitate this accord. Images evoked or aroused in this way are not the 'free' images that a simple association of ideas would join to meaning. Rather, to return to an expression of Richards in The Principles of Literary Criticism (118-19), they are 'tied' images, that is, connected to poetic diction. In contrast to mere association, iconicity involves meaning controlling imagery. In other words, this is imagery involved in language itself; it is part of the game of language itself.[55] It seems to me that this notion of imagery tied by meaning is in accord with Kant's idea that the schema is a method for constructing images. The verbal icon in Hester's sense is also a method for constructing images. The poet, in effect, is that artisan who sustains and shapes imagery using no means other than language.

Does this concept of 'tied' image entirely escape the objection of psychologism? That can be doubted. The manner of Hester's detailed explanation of the fusion of sense and sensa, even when understood as tied images rather than as real sounds, leaves the sensible moment very much outside the verbal moment. In order to account for the aura of images surrounding words (143), he invokes, in turn, association in memory between words and the images of their referents; historical and cultural conventions (for example, determining that the Christian symbol of the Cross develops such and such a sequence of images); and the stylization that the author's intention imposes on diverse images. All these explanations remain more psychological than semantic.

The most satisfying explanation, and in any case the only one that can be reconciled with semantic theory, is the one that Hester links to the notion of 'seeing as' (which is Wittgensteinian in origin). *This theme constitutes Hester's positive contribution to the iconic theory of metaphor.* It is because he expressly brings resemblance into play that it seemed possible to discuss him at the end of this Study.

What is 'seeing as'?

The factor of 'seeing as' is exposed through the act of reading, even to the extent that this is 'the mode in which such imagery is realized' (21). The 'seeing as' is the positive link between vehicle and tenor. In poetic metaphor, the metaphorical vehicle is *as* the tenor – from one point of view, not from all points of view. To explicate a metaphor is to enumerate all the appropriate senses in which the vehicle is 'seen as' the tenor. The 'seeing as' is the intuitive relationship that makes the sense and image hold together.

With Wittgenstein,[56] the 'seeing as' concerns neither metaphor nor even imagination, at least in its relationship to language. Considering ambiguous figures (like the one that can be seen as a duck or a rabbit), Wittgenstein remarks that it is one thing to say 'I see this ...' and another to say 'I see this as ...'; and he adds: 'seeing it as ...' is 'having *this* image.' The link between 'seeing as' and imagining appears more clearly when we go to the imperative mood, where, for example, one might say 'Imagine this,' 'Now, see the figure as this.' Will this be regarded as a question of interpretation? No, says Wittgenstein, because to interpret is to form a hypothesis which one can verify. There is no hypothesis here, nor any verification; one says, quite directly, 'It's a rabbit.' The 'seeing as,' therefore, is half thought and half experience. And is this not the same sort of mixture that the iconicity of meaning presents?[57]

Following Virgil C. Aldrich,[58] Hester proposes to have the 'seeing as' and the imaging function of language in poetry clarify each other. The 'seeing as' of Wittgenstein lends itself to this transposition because of its imaginative side; conversely, as Aldrich puts it, thinking in poetry is a picture-thinking. Now this 'pictorial' capacity of language consists also in 'seeing an aspect.' In the case of metaphor, to depict time in terms of the characteristics of a beggar is to see time as a beggar. This is what we do when we read the metaphor; to read is to establish a relationship such that X is like Y in some senses, but not in all.

It is true that the transfer from Wittgenstein's analysis to metaphor introduces an important change. In the case of the ambiguous figure, there is a *Gestalt* (B) that allows a figure A or another figure C to be seen. Thus the problem is, given B, to construct A or C. In the case of metaphor, A and C are given in reading – they are the tenor and vehicle. What must be constructed is the common element B, the *Gestalt*, namely, the point of view in which A and C are similar.

Whatever the case with this reversal, 'seeing as' proffers the missing link in the chain of explanation. 'Seeing as' is the sensible aspect of poetic language. Half thought, half experience, 'seeing as' is the intuitive relationship that holds sense and image together. How? Essentially through its selective character: '*Seeing as is an intuitive experience-act by which one selects from the quasi-sensory mass of imagery one has on reading metaphor the relevant aspects of such imagery*' (180). This definition contains the essential points. 'Seeing as' is an experience and an act at one and the same time. On the one hand, the mass of images is beyond all voluntary control; the image arises, occurs, and there is no rule to be learned for 'having images.' One sees, or one does not see. The intuitive talent for 'seeing as' (182) cannot be taught; at most, it can be assisted, as when one is helped to see the rabbit's eye in the ambiguous figure. On the other hand, 'seeing as' is an act. To understand is to do something. As we said earlier, the image is not free but tied; and, in effect, 'seeing as' orders the flux and governs iconic deployment. In this way, the experience-act of 'seeing as' ensures that imagery is implicated in metaphorical signification: 'The same imagery which *occurs* also *means*' (188).

Thus, the 'seeing as' activated in reading ensures the joining of verbal meaning with imagistic fullness. And this conjunction is no longer something outside language, since it can be reflected as a relationship. 'Seeing as' contains a ground, a foundation, that is, precisely, resemblance – no longer the resemblance between two ideas, but that very resemblance the 'seeing as' establishes. Hester claims emphatically that similarity is what results from the experience-act of 'seeing as.' '*Seeing as* defines the resemblance, and not the reverse. This priority of 'seeing as' over the resemblance relationship is proper to the language-game in which meaning functions in an iconic manner. That is why the 'seeing as' can succeed or fail. It can fail as in forced metaphors, because they are inconsistent or fortuitous, or on the contrary, as in banal and commonplace metaphors; and succeed, as in those that fashion the surprise of discovery.

Thus, 'seeing as' quite precisely plays the role of the schema that unites the *empty* concept and the *blind* impression; thanks to its character as half thought and half experience, it joins the light of sense with the fullness of the image. In this way, the non-verbal and the verbal are firmly united at the core of the image-ing function of language.

Besides this role of bridging the verbal and the quasi-visual, 'seeing as' ensures another mediative service. Semantic theory, as we remember, puts the accent on the tension between the terms of the statement, a tension grounded in contradiction at the literal level. In the case of banal, even dead, metaphor, the tension with the body of our knowledge disappears. (This may also be the case with myth, if one agrees with Cassirer that myth represents a level of consciousness where tension with the body of our knowledge has not yet appeared.) In living metaphor, on the other hand, this tension is essential. When Hopkins says 'Oh! The mind has mountains,' the reader knows that, literally, the mind does not have mountains; the literal *is not* accompanies the metaphorical *is*. (We will return to this theme at length in Study 7.) Now, a theory of fusion of sense and the sensible, adopted prior to the revision proposed by Hester, appears to be incompatible with this characteristic, of tension between metaphorical meaning and literal meaning. On the other hand, once it is re-interpreted on the basis of 'seeing as,' the theory of fusion is perfectly compatible with interaction and tension theory. 'Seeing X *as* Y' encompasses 'X is *not* Y'; seeing time *as* a beggar is, precisely, to know also that time is *not* a beggar. The borders of meaning are transgressed but not abolished. Barfield[59] pictures metaphor well as 'a deliberate yoking of unlikes by an individual artificer.' Hester therefore is justified in saying that '*seeing as*' permits harmonization of a tension theory and a fusion theory. I should personally go further; I should say that *fusion* of sense and the imaginary, which is characteristic of 'iconized meaning,' is the necessary counterpart of a theory of interaction.

Metaphorical meaning, as we saw, is not the enigma itself, the semantic clash pure and simple, but the solution of the enigma, the inauguration of the new semantic pertinence. In this connection, the interaction designates only the *diaphora*; the *epiphora* properly speaking is something else. It cannot take place without fusion, without intuitive passage. The secret of *epiphora* then appears truly to reside in the iconic nature of intuitive passage. Metaphorical meaning as such feeds on the density of imagery released by the poem.

If this is how things really stand, then 'seeing as' designates the *nonverbal* mediation of the metaphorical statement. With this acknowledgment, semantics finds its frontier; and, in so doing, it accomplishes its task.

If semantics meets its limit here, a *phenomenology of imagination*, like that of Gaston Bachelard,[60] could perhaps take over from psycholinguistics and extend its functioning to realms where the verbal is vassal to the nonverbal. Yet it is still the semantics of the poetic verb that is to be heard in these depths. Bachelard has taught us that the image is not a residue of impression, but an aura surrounding speech: 'The poetic image places us at the origin of the speaking being.'[61] The poem gives birth to the image; the poetic image 'becomes a new being in our language, expressing us by making us what it expresses; in other words, it is at once a becoming of expression, and a becoming of our being. Here expression creates being ... one would not be able to meditate in a zone that preceded language.'[62]

If, then, the phenomenology of imagination does extend beyond psycholinguistics and even beyond the description of 'seeing-as,' this is because it follows the path of the 'reverberation'[63] of the poetic image into the depths of existence. The poetic image becomes 'a source of psychic activity.' What was 'a new being in language' becomes an 'increment to consciousness,' or better, a 'growth of being.'[64] Even in 'psychological poetics,' even in 'reveries on reverie,' psychism continues to be directed by the poetic verb. And so, one must attest: 'Yes, words really do dream.'[65]

Metaphor and reference

For Mircea Eliade

What does the metaphorical statement say about reality? This question carries us across the threshold from the *sense* towards the *reference* of discourse. But does the question itself have any meaning? This must be established first.

1 / THE POSTULATES OF REFERENCE

The question of reference can be posed at the two different levels of semantics and of hermeneutics. At the first level, it deals only with entities belonging to the order of the sentence. At the second level, it addresses entities that are larger than the sentence. It is at this level that the problem reaches its full amplitude.

As a postulate of semantics, the requirement of reference takes as given the distinction between semiotics and semantics, which the preceding Studies have already introduced. As we saw, this distinction first sets in relief the essentially synthetic character of predication, the central operation of discourse, and opposes this operation to the mere interplay of differences and oppositions among signifiers and among the signified in the phonological code and in the lexical code of a given language. Moreover, it means that what is *intended* by discourse [*l'intenté*], the correlate of the entire sentence, is irreducible to what semiotics calls the signified, which is nothing but the counterpart of the signifier of a sign within the language code. The third implication of the distinction between semiotics and semantics that concerns us here is the following: grounded on the predicative act, what is intended by discourse [*l'intenté*] points to an extra-linguistic reality which is its referent. Whereas the sign points back only to other signs immanent within a system, discourse is about things. Sign differs from sign, discourse refers to the world. Difference is semiotic, reference is semantic: 'One is never concerned in semiotics with the relation between the sign and the things denoted, nor with relationships between language and the world.'[1] But we must go beyond the simple opposition between the semiotic and the semantic viewpoint, and clearly subordinate the former to the latter. Not only are the two planes of the sign and of discourse distinct, but the first is an abstraction of the second; in the last analysis, the sign owes its very meaning as sign to its usage in discourse. How would we know that a sign *stands for ...* if its *use* in discourse did not invest it with the scope that relates it to that very thing *for which* it stands? To the extent that it restricts itself to the closed world of signs, semiotics is an abstraction from *semantics*, which relates the internal constitution of the sign to the transcendent aims of reference.

This distinction between sense and reference, which Benveniste establishes in all its generality, had already been introduced by Gottlob Frege, but within the limits of a logical theory. Our working hypothesis is that the Fregean distinction holds in principle for all discourse.

Let us recall the distinction that Frege proclaimed between *Sinn* (sense) and *Bedeutung* (reference or denotation).[2] The sense is *what* the proposition states; the reference or denotation is *that about which* the sense is stated. So what must be grasped, says Frege, is 'the regular connexion between a sign, its sense, and its reference' (58). This regular connection is 'of such a kind that to the sign there corresponds a definite sense and to that in turn a definite reference, while to a given reference (an object) there does not belong only a single sign' (ibid.). Accordingly, 'the reference of "evening star" would be the same as that of "morning star," but not the sense' (57). This lack of a one-to-one relationship between sense and reference is characteristic of common languages and distinguishes them from a system of perfect signs. The possibility that no reference corresponds to the sense of a grammatically well-formed expression does not weaken the distinction; rather, not to have a reference is another trait of reference that confirms that the question of reference is always opened by that of sense.

One might object that Frege, as opposed to Benveniste, applies his distinction initially to words and more precisely *to proper names*, not to the entire proposition – in Benveniste's terminology, to what is intended by the entire sentence. Indeed, what Frege first defines is the reference of the proper name, which 'is the object itself which we designate by its means' (60). The entire statement, considered from the point of view of its reference, plays the role of a proper name with regard to the state of affairs it 'designates.' Hence it can be said that 'a proper name (word, sign, sign combination, expression) *expresses* its sense, *stands for* or *designates* its reference' (61). Indeed, when we use a proper name ('the moon') we do not restrict ourselves to talking about our idea (that is, about a specific mental event); however, 'nor are we satisfied with the sense alone' (that is, the ideal object irreducible to any mental event); 'We presuppose besides a reference' (ibid.). It is precisely this presupposition that causes us to err; but if we are wrong, it is because a reference is demanded by 'our intention in speaking or thinking' (61-2). This intention is 'the striving for truth,' which 'drives us always to advance from the sense to the reference' (63). This striving for truth suffuses the entire proposition, to the extent that it can be assimilated to a proper name; but it is via the proper name as intermediary that, for Frege, the proposition has a reference: 'For it is of the reference of the name that the predicate is affirmed or denied. Whoever does not admit the name has reference can neither apply nor withhold the predicate' (62).

There is less than total opposition, therefore, between Benveniste and Frege. For Frege, the reference is communicated from the proper name to the entire proposition, which, with respect to reference, becomes the proper name of a state of affairs. For Benveniste, the reference is communicated from the entire sentence to the word, by subdivision within the syntagma. Through its *use*, the word takes on a semantic value, which is its particular sense in *this* use. In this manner the word has a referent, 'which is the particular object to which the word corresponds in the concrete situation of circumstance or of usage.'[3] Word and sentence are thus the two poles of the same semantic entity; it is in conjunction that they have sense (always in the semantic acceptation) and reference.

The two conceptions of reference are complementary and reciprocal, whether one rises by synthetic composition from the proper name towards the proposition, or whether one descends by analytic dissociation from the sentence down to the semantic unit of the word. At their intersection, the two interpretations of reference make apparent the polar constitution of reference itself, which can be called the *object* when the referent of the name is considered, or the *state of affairs* if one considers the referent of the entire statement.

Wittgenstein's *Tractatus Logico-Philosophicus* gives an exact presentation of this polarity of the referent. He defines the world as 'the totality of facts (*Tatsachen*), not of things (*Dinge*)' (1.1), and then defines fact as 'the existence of states of affairs (*das Bestehen von Sachverhalten*)' (2); next, he proposes that a state of affairs is 'a combination of objects (things) (*eine Verbindung von Gegenständen, Sachen, Dingen*)' (2.01). Thus, the pair of object and state of affairs corresponds, on the side of the world, to the noun-statement pair in language. On the other hand, Strawson returns in *Individuals*[4] to the strict Fregean position. Reference is linked to the function of singular identification, itself *carried by* the logically *proper* name. The predicate, which does not identify but characterizes, does not refer as such to anything that exists; to accord existential value to predi-

cates would be to make the same mistake as the realists make in the argument over universals. The identifying function and the predicative function
are totally asymmetrical: only the first poses a question of existence; the
second does not. In this way, then, the proposition refers globally to something via the function of singular identification of one of its terms. In
Speech Acts,[5] John Searle postulates without hesitation the thesis that
something must be in order that something may be identified. In the last
analysis, this postulate of existence as the foundation of identification is
what Frege had in mind when he said that we are not satisfied with a
sense, we presuppose a reference.

The postulate of reference requires a separate discussion when it
touches on those particular entities of discourse called texts, that is, more
extensive compositions than the sentence. The question henceforth arises
in the context of hermeneutics rather than of semantics, for which the
sentence is at once the first and the last entity.

The question of reference is posed here in terms that are singularly
more complex; for certain texts, called literary, seem to constitute an exception to the reference requirement expressed by the preceding postulate.

The text is a complex entity of discourse whose characteristics do not
reduce to those of the unit of discourse, or the sentence. By text I do not
mean only or even mainly something written, even though writing in itself
poses original problems that bear directly on the outcome of reference; I
mean principally the production of discourse as a work. With the work, as
the word implies, new categories enter the field of discourse. Essentially
these are pragmatic categories, categories of production and of labour. To
begin with, discourse is the arena of a work of composition or arrangement, 'disposition' (to echo *dispositio*, the term in ancient rhetoric), which
makes of a poem or novel a totality irreducible to a simple sum of sentences. Next, this 'disposition' obeys formal rules, a codification that belongs no longer to language but to discourse, and fashions from discourse
what we have just called a poem or a novel. This code is the one of literary
'genres,' that is, of genres that regulate the praxis of the text. Finally, this
codified production ends in a particular work: this poem, that novel. Ultimately this third trait is the most important. It can be called style, where
this is understood (with G.G. Granger)[6] as what makes the work a singular,
individual thing. It is the most important trait because it distinguishes
practical categories in an irreducible manner from theoretical categories.
Granger refers in this connection to a famous text in Aristotle according
to which to produce is to produce individual things;[7] conversely, an individual thing, opaque to theoretical consideration that stops at the last species, is the correlate of a making.

Such, then, is what the labour of interpretation addresses. It is the text as work. Arrangement, belonging to genres, achievement in a particular style, are the categories proper to the production of discourse as work.

This specific realization of discourse calls for an appropriate reformulation of the postulate of reference. It would seem enough at first glance to reformulate the Fregean concept of reference just by substituting one word for another: instead of saying that we are not satisfied with the sense and so presuppose reference besides, we would say that we are not satisfied with the structure of the work and presuppose a world of the work. The structure of the work is in fact its sense, and the world of the work its reference. This simple substitution of terms is sufficient as a first approximation. Hermeneutics then is simply the theory that regulates the transition from structure of the work to world of the work. To interpret a work is to display the world to which it refers by virtue of its 'arrangement,' its 'genre,' and its 'style.' In another publication, I contrast this postulate with the romantic and psychologizing conception of hermeneutics originating with Schleiermacher and Dilthey, for whom the supreme law of interpretation is the search for a harmony between the spirit of the author and that of the reader. To this always difficult and often impossible quest for an intention hidden behind the work, I oppose a quest that addresses the world displayed before the work. But the issue in the present discussion is not the quarrel with romantic hermeneutics, but the right to pass from the structure (which is to the complex work what sense is to the simple statement) to the world of the work (which is to the work what the denotation is to the statement).

This passage requires a distinct postulate because of the specific nature of certain works, those called literary. The production of discourse as 'literature' signifies very precisely that the relationship of sense to reference is *suspended.* 'Literature' would be that sort of discourse that has no denotation but only connotations. This rejection is supported not only by an internal examination of the literary work (as we shall see later), but also by Frege's own theory of denotation (or reference). This theory includes, in effect, an internal principle of limitation that defines its own concept of truth. The desire for truth motivating the push from sense towards reference is ascribed expressly by Frege only to scientific statements, and seems quite clearly to be denied to poetic statements. Considering an example from epic poetry, Frege holds that the proper name *Ulysses* has no reference; 'We are interested,' he says, 'only in the sense of the sentences and the images and feelings thereby aroused' (63). In contrast to scientific inspection, therefore, artistic pleasure seems linked to 'senses' without any 'reference.'

My whole aim is to do away with this restriction of reference to scientific statements. Therefore, a distinct discussion appropriate to the literary work is required, and a second formulation of the postulate of reference, more complex than the first, which simply mirrored the general postulate that every sense calls for reference or denotation. The second formulation is stated as follows: the literary work through the structure proper to it displays a world only under the condition that the reference of descriptive discourse is suspended. Or to put it another way, discourse in the literary work sets out its denotation as a second-level denotation, by means of the suspension of the first-level denotation of discourse.

This postulate brings us back to the problem of metaphor. It may be, indeed, that the metaphorical statement is precisely the one that points out most clearly this relationship between suspended reference and displayed reference. Just as the metaphorical statement captures its sense as metaphorical midst the ruins of the literal sense, it also achieves its reference upon the ruins of what might be called (in symmetrical fashion) its literal reference. If it is true that literal sense and metaphorical sense are distinguished and articulated within an interpretation, so too it is within an interpretation that a second-level reference, which is properly the metaphorical reference, is set free by means of the suspension of the first-level reference.

Whether or not, in the course of this process, our concepts of reality, of world, and of truth vacillate is a question reserved for Study 8. Do we actually know what 'reality,' 'world,' and 'truth' signify?

2 / THE CASE AGAINST REFERENCE

The possibility that the metaphorical statement might aspire to truth value meets considerable objections that do not reduce to the pre-judgment originating in the rhetorical conception discussed in the earlier Studies, namely, that metaphor carries no new information and is purely ornamental. The strategy of language that characterizes the production of discourse in the form of 'poetry' seems in itself to constitute a formidable *counterexample* to the alleged universality of the referential relationship of language to reality.

This strategy of language does not appear distinctly until one stops considering units of discourse, or sentences, and moves to totalities of discourse, or works. Here the question of reference is located not at the level of each sentence, but at the level of the 'poem' considered on the lines of the three criteria of the work: 'arrangement,' subordination to a 'genre,' and production of a 'singular' entity. If the metaphorical statement is to have a reference, it is through the mediation of the 'poem' as an ordered, generic, and singular totality. In other words, metaphor says something about something to the extent that it is, to quote Beardsley,[8] a 'poem in miniature.'

The strategy of language proper to poetry, that is, to the production of the poem, does indeed seem to consist in constituting a sense that intercepts reference and, in the limiting situation, abolishes reality.

The proper level of argument is that of 'literary criticism,' that is, a discipline scaled to discourse realized as a work. However, literary criticism draws support from a purely linguistic analysis of the poetic function, which Roman Jakobson sets into the more general framework of linguistic communication. As we remember, Jakobson[9] attempts with a powerfully synthetic exactitude to embrace the totality of linguistic phenomena within the scope of six 'factors' that contribute to the process of verbal communication. These six 'factors' of communication – addresser, addressee, code, message, contact, context – are matched by six 'functions,' any one of which may predominate at any time ('The verbal structure of a message depends primarily on the predominant function' [353]). Thus, the emotive function corresponds to the addresser, the conative function to the addressee, the phatic function to contact, the 'metalingual' or metalinguistic function to the code, and the referential function to the context. As for the 'poetic' function, the one that interests us, it corresponds to the highlighting of the message for its own sake: 'This function, by promoting the palpability of signs, deepens the fundamental dichotomy of signs and objects' (356). This definition directly places the poetic function of language in opposition to the referential function through which the message is oriented towards the non-linguistic context.

Two observations are required at this point. First of all, it should be understood clearly that this analysis concerns the 'poetic function' of language and does not define the 'poem' as a 'literary genre.' Even isolated statements such as 'I like Ike' can interrupt the flow of a prosaic referential discourse and present this accentuation of the message and this obliteration of the referent that characterize the poetic function. Therefore, one must not identify 'poem' with 'the poetic' in Jakobson. Furthermore, the predominance of one function does not mean that others are abolished, only that their hierarchy is altered. To carry this further, the poetic genres themselves are distinguished by the way in which the other functions mix with the poetic function: 'The particularities of diverse poetic genres imply a differently ranked participation of the other verbal functions along with the dominant poetic function. Epic poetry, focused on the third person, strongly involves the referential function of language; the lyric, oriented toward the first person, is intimately linked with the emotive function; poetry of the second person is imbued with the conative function and is either supplicatory or exhortative, depending on whether the first person is subordinated to the second one or the second to the first' (357). Hence, this analysis of the poetic function constitutes only a preparatory stage in the determination of the poem as work.

The linguistics of Roman Jakobson does offer, it is true, a second analytical instrument that relates the theory of the poetic function to that of the strategy of discourse proper to the poem. The poetic function is distinguished by the manner in which the two fundamental arrangements, selection and combination, relate to each other. We referred already to this theory of Jakobson within the framework of the Study on 'The work of resemblance.'[10] It is taken up again here in the somewhat different context of the issue of reference. Let us recall the principal claim. The operations of language can be represented by the intersection of two axes at right angles to each other. The relations of contiguity, and consequently the operations that are syntagmatic in character, occupy the first axis, that of combinations. The operations grounded in resemblance, and constitutive of all paradigmatic organizations, are played out along the second axis, that of substitutions. The elaboration of every message depends upon the interplay of these two modes of arrangement.

What characterizes the poetic function, then, is the alteration of the relationship of the operations located on one or the other axis: '*The poetic function projects the principle of equivalence from the axis of selection into the axis of combination*' (358). In what sense? In ordinary language, the language of prose, the principle of equivalence plays no part in constituting the sequence but only in the choice of appropriate words within a sphere of resemblance. The anomaly of poetry is precisely that equivalence plays a part in connection as well as selection. In other words, the principle of equivalence serves to constitute the sequence. We can speak in poetry of a 'reiteration of equivalent units' (the role of rhythmic cadences, of resemblance and opposition between syllables, of metric equivalence, of periodic repetition of rhymes in rhymed poetry, of alternation of long and short feet in stressed poetry). As for relations of meaning, they are introduced somehow by this recurrence of phonic form. A 'semantic propinquity' (367) and even a 'semantic equivalence' (368) result from the sounding of rhymes: 'In poetry, any conspicuous similarity in sound is evaluated in respect to similarity and/or dissimilarity in meaning' (372).

What is the upshot of all this for reference? The question is not settled by the preceding analysis, whose topic might be called the strategy of sense. What has just been called semantic equivalence concerns the interplay of sense. But it is precisely this interplay of sense that ensures the accentuation of the message for its own sake (as Jakobson put it in 'Linguistics and Poetics') and thus the obliteration of reference. The projection of the principle of equivalence from the axis of selection onto the axis of combination is what ensures the highlighting of the message. So what was treated as effect of sense in the above-mentioned essay is treated as process of sense in Jakobson's 'Two Aspects of Language and Two Types of Aphasic Disorders.'

Literary criticism comes in at just this point.

But let us not leave Roman Jakobson without accepting a valuable suggestion from him, which will not reveal its whole meaning until the end of this Study. The semantic equivalence brought about by phonic equivalence brings with it an ambiguity that affects all the functions of communication. The addresser is split (the 'I' of the lyrical hero or of the fictitious narrator), and so too the addressee (the 'you' as supposed addressee of dramatic monologues, supplications, epistles). The most radical consequence of this is that what happens in poetry is not the suppression of the referential function but its profound alteration by the workings of ambiguity: 'The supremacy of poetic function over referential function does not obliterate the reference but makes it ambiguous. The double-sensed message finds correspondence in a split addresser, in a split addressee, and what is more in a split reference, as is cogently exposed in the preambles to fairy tales of various peoples, for instance, in the usual exordium of the Majorca storytellers: "Aixo era y no era" (It was and it was not)' (371).

Let us keep this notion of *split reference* in mind, as well as the wonderful 'It was and it was not,' which contains *in nuce* all that can be said about metaphorical truth. But first, the case against reference must be pressed to the limit.

The dominant current of literary criticism, European as well as American, does not have split reference in mind, but more radically the destruction of reference – a theme, indeed, that appears better attuned to the principal trait of poetry, namely 'this capacity for reiteration whether immediate or delayed, this reification of a poetic message and its constituents, this conversion of a message into an enduring thing ...' (371).

This last expression – conversion of a message into an enduring thing – could serve as the subtitle of a whole series of works on 'Poetics,' for which the essence of the strategy of discourse in poetry is the attainment of meaning within the haven of sound. The idea is an old one; Pope said 'The sound must seem an echo to the sense.' Valéry sees the dance, which travels nowhere, as the model of the poetic act. For the reflecting poet, the poem is a prolonged oscillation between sense and sound. Like sculpture, poetry converts language into matter, worked for its own sake. This solid object is not the representation of some thing, but an expression of itself.[11] Indeed, the mirror-play between sense and sound somehow absorbs the movement of the poem, which does not spend its energy externally but within itself. To capture this mutation of language, Wimsatt forged the very suggestive expression of *verbal icon*,[12] which recalls not only Peirce but also the Byzantine tradition for which the icon is a thing. The poem is an icon and not a sign. The poem is. It has an 'iconic solidity' (*The Verbal Icon* 231). Language takes on the thickness of a material or a *medium*. The sensible, sensual plenitude of the poem is like that of painted or sculptured forms. The combination of sensual and logical ensures that expression and impression coalesce within the poetic thing. Poetic signification fused thus with its sensible vehicle becomes that particular and 'thingy' reality we call a poem.

The fusion of sense and sound is not alone in presenting an argument against reference in poetry. An additional and perhaps even more radical attack lies in the fusion of sense and images, which at one and the same time proliferate from the sense as source and are ruled from within by it. We have already discussed the work of Hester[13] and praised it for the role it gives the image in the constitution of metaphorical meaning. His argument is taken up again at the point where reference is at issue. Poetic language, says Hester, is the language in which 'sense' and 'sound' function in an iconic manner, creating accordingly a fusion of 'sense' and 'sensa' (96). These 'sensa' are, essentially, the ebb and flow of images allowed to be by the *epoché* of the referential relation. Therefore, the fusion of sense and sound is no longer the central phenomenon, but occasion for an unfolding of the imaginary that is bound to the sense. Now with the image comes the fundamental moment of 'suspension,' of *epoché*, Husserl's notion borrowed by Hester and applied to the non-referential interplay of imagery in poetic strategy. The abolition of reference, which belongs to the achievement of poetic sense, is thus *par excellence* the work of the *epoché* that makes the iconic functioning of sense and of sensa possible, itself achieved by the iconic functioning of sense and sound.

It is Northrop Frye, however, who approaches the limit most radically. In *Anatomy of Criticism*, Frye generalizes his analysis of poetry to all works of literature. Whenever a sort of signification oriented in the opposite direction to the centrifugal orientation of referential types of discourse can be opposed to informative or didactic discourse, exemplified by the language of science, then we can speak of literary signification. In effect, centrifugal or 'outward' movement takes us outside discourse, from words towards things. Centripetal or 'internal' movement of words presses towards the broader verbal configurations that constitute the literary work in its totality.

In informative or didactic discourse, the 'symbol' (Frye's term for any discernible unit of meaning) functions as a sign that 'stands for,' 'points to,' 'represents' something. In literary discourse, the symbol represents nothing outside itself but links the parts to the whole within the discursive framework: 'Verbal elements understood inwardly or centripetally, as parts of a verbal structure, are, as symbols, simply and literally verbal elements, or units of a verbal structure' – compare the 'motifs' of a musical composition (73-4). As against the striving for truth of descriptive discourse, Frye asserts with Sir Philip Sidney that 'the poet affirmeth' (76). Metaphysics and theology affirm, assert; poetry ignores reality and limits itself to forging a 'fable' (Frye revives here the expression of Aristotle who, in the *Poetics*, characterizes tragedy by its *muthos*). Were it necessary to compare poetry with something other than itself, that other would be mathematics: 'The poet, like the pure mathematician, depends, not on descriptive truth, but on conformity to his hypothetical postulates' (ibid.). Thus, the appearance of the ghost in *Hamlet* corresponds to the hypothetical conception of the play. No claim is made concerning the reality of ghosts – yet there must be a ghost in *Hamlet*! To begin reading is to accept this fiction; any paraphrase that approximates a description of something misconstrues the rules of the game. In this sense, meaning in literature is literal; it says what it says and nothing else: 'Understanding a poem literally means understanding the whole of it, as a poem, and as it stands' (77). One's only task is to perceive its unitary structure through the concatenation of its symbols.

One encounters at this point an analysis in the same style as that of Jakobson. The literality of the poem is established by recurrence in time (rhythm) and in space (pattern). Literally, its meaning is its pattern or its integrity. The internal verbal relations absorb the variability of the sign's external meaning to some extent: 'So literature in its descriptive context is a body of hypothetical verbal structures' (79).

Frye, it is true, introduces a moderately different factor, onto which our own reflections will be grafted: 'The unity of a poem,' he says, 'is ... a unity of mood' (80); 'Poetic images ... express or articulate the mood' (81). Now the mood '*is* the poem, not something else still behind it' (ibid.) All literary structure is ironic in this sense: ' "What it says" is always different in kind or degree from "what it means" ' (ibid.).

Such, then, is poetic structure, 'a self-contained "texture" ' (82) – that is, a structure entirely dependent on its internal relationships.

I would be loath to leave this case against reference without pointing to the *epistemological argument*, which, while augmenting the linguistic argument (for example, Jakobson) and the argument of literary criticism (for example, Frye), at the same time reveals their hidden presupposition. Critiques shaped by the school of logical positivism state that all language that is not *descriptive*, in the sense of giving information about *facts*, must be *emotional*. Furthermore, the suggestion is that what is 'emotional' is sensed purely 'within' the subject and is not related in any way whatsoever to anything outside the subject. Emotion is an affect which has only an inside, and not an outside.

This argument – which thus has two sides to it – did not arise originally in the course of consideration of literary works; it is a postulate imported from philosophy into literature. And this postulate decides on the meaning of truth and reality. It says that there is no truth beyond the pale of possible verification (or falsification), and that in the last analysis all verification is empirical, as defined by scientific procedure. This postulate functions in literary criticism as a prejudgment. Besides the alternative between 'cognitive' and 'emotive,' it imposes the alternative between 'denotative' and 'connotative.' The 'emotivist' theories in ethics are an adequate demonstration that this prejudice is not restricted to poetics. It is so powerful that the authors who are most hostile to logical positivism often fortify it while fighting it. To say, with Suzanne Langer, that to read a poem is to grasp 'a piece of *virtual life*,'[14] is to remain within the verifiable-unverifiable dichotomy. To say with Northrop Frye that images suggest or evoke the mood that informs the poem is to confirm that the 'mood' is itself centripetal, like the language that informs it.

The new rhetoric in France confronts us with the same scene: literary theory and positivist epistemology support each other. For example, the notion of 'opaque discourse' in Todorov is identified immediately with that of 'discourse without reference': over against transparent discourse, he says, 'there is the discourse so well covered with patterns and figures that no vision can penetrate behind it. This would be a language that does not point to any reality, a language satisfied in itself.'[15]

The concept of 'poetic function' in Jean Cohen[16] proceeds from the same positivist convictions. It is self-evident to this author that cognitive response and affective response overlap: 'The function of prose is denotative, the function of poetry is connotative' (205). It is no accident that Cohen recognizes himself in his quotation of Carnap: 'The aim of a lyrical poem in which occur the words "sunshine" and "clouds" is not to inform us of certain meteorological facts, but to express certain feelings of the poet and to excite similar feelings in us' (cited 205).

Nevertheless, doubts arise. How is one to explain that the emotion in poetry is 'linked to the object' (205)? Indeed, poetic sadness is 'felt as a quality of the world' (206). Carnap is not the one to quote at this stage, but Mikel Dufrenne, who tells us: 'To feel is to experience a feeling as a property of the object, not as a state of my being.'[17] How can one reconcile with the positivist thesis the admission that poetic sadness is 'a modality of consciousness of things, an original and specific way of seizing the world' (206)? And how is a bridge to be built between the purely psychological and affectivist notion of connotation and this opening of language towards a 'poetics of things' (226)? Must not the expressivity of things (to take up a notion of Raymond Ruyer)[18] find in language itself, and specifically in its power of deviation in relation to its ordinary usage, a power of designation that escapes the alternative of denotative and connotative? Is the issue not closed if the connotation is held to be a substitute for the denotation ['the connotation takes the place of the denotation which defaults' (211)]? This stumbling block is admitted in the pages of Cohen's work. Pointing to this 'evidence of feeling,' which, for the poet, is 'as compelling as empirical evidence,' he notes: 'This evidence is surely well-grounded: subjectivity is linked up with the profound objectivity of being – but that question belongs to metaphysics, not to poetics' (213). This is why Cohen finally beats a retreat and returns to the dichotomy of subjective and objective, which projects the task of an 'aesthetics that would like to be scientific' (207). 'The poetic sentence,' he says, 'is objectively false, but subjectively true' (212).

The *Rhétorique générale* of the Groupe de Liège confronts the same problem under the title 'The Ethos of Figures.'[19] Although systematic study of this topic is reserved for another work, the present volume can provide a preliminary sketch. Moreover, this study in fact could not be put off entirely because the specific aesthetic effect of figures, 'which is the real object of artistic communication' (45), is part of the complete description of a rhetorical figure, together with the descriptions of its deviation, its sign, and its invariant (45). The sketch of the theory of Ethos (145-56) leads one to anticipate an investigation alligned essentially to the response of the reader or listener, putting the metaboles in the position of *stimuli*, of signals, engendering a subjective impression. Now among the effects achieved by figurative discourse, the primordial effect 'is to neutralize the perception of the literality (in the wide sense) of the text in which it appears' (148). We are here truly on terrain marked out by Jakobson with his definition of the poetic function and by Todorov with his definition of opaque discourse. Yet the authors of the *Rhétorique générale* proclaim: 'This is where it all stops; our work, indeed, demonstrates that there is almost no necessary relationship between the structure of a figure and its Ethos' (148).

As for Le Guern,[20] he does not differ at all from the authors just cited as far as this point is concerned. We saw earlier that the distinction between *denotation* and *connotation* is even one of the major axes of his semantics: semic selection is assigned to denotation, the associated image arises from connotation.

3 / A GENERALIZED THEORY OF DENOTATION

The thesis to be argued now does not deny the preceding thesis, but rather draws support from it. It proposes that the suspension of reference in the sense defined by the norms of descriptive discourse is the negative condition of the appearance of a more fundamental mode of reference, whose explication is the task of interpretation. At stake in this explication is nothing less than the meaning of the words *reality* and *truth*, which themselves must vacillate and become problematical.

There were meaningful clues for this search for another reference in the preceding analysis devoted to the poetic function in all its generality, quite apart from the particular role of metaphor. First let us take up the notion of 'the hypothetical' in Northrop Frye. The poem, he says, is neither true nor false; it is hypothetical. But 'the poetic hypothesis' is not the mathematical hypothesis; it is the suggestion or proposal, in imaginative, fictive mode, of a world. Hence, suspension of real reference is the condition of access to the virtual mode of reference. But what is a virtual life? Can there be a virtual life without a virtual world capable of being inhabited? Is it not the function of poetry to establish another world – another world that corresponds to other possibilities of existence, to possibilities that would be most deeply our own?

There are other indications in Frye that point in the same direction. As was said before, 'The unity of a poem ... is a unity of mood';[21] and again: 'Poetic images do not state or point to anything, but, by pointing to each other, they suggest or evoke the mood which informs the poem' (81). Under the name of mood, an extra-linguistic factor is introduced, which is the index of a manner of being (on condition that it is not treated psychologically). A mood or 'state of soul' [*état d'âme*] is a way of finding or sensing oneself in the midst of reality. It is, in the language of Heidegger, a way of finding oneself among things (*Befindlichkeit*).[22] Here again, the *epoché* of natural reality is the condition that allows poetry to develop a world on the basis of the mood that the poet articulates. It will be the task of interpretation to elaborate the design of a world liberated, by suspension, from descriptive reference. The creation of a concrete object – the poem itself – cuts language off from the didactic function of the sign, but at the same time opens up access to reality in the mode of fiction and feeling.

A last indicator concerns Jakobson. As we saw, he links the notion of split reference to that of ambiguous meaning: 'Poeticalness is not a supplementation of discourse with rhetorical adornment but a total re-evaluation of the discourse and of all its components whatsoever' ('Closing Statements' 377).

It is within the very analysis of the metaphorical statement that a referential conception of poetic language must be established, a conception that takes account of the elimination of the reference of ordinary language and patterns itself on the concept of split reference.

Initial support comes from the very notion of metaphorical meaning; the way in which metaphorical meaning is constituted provides the key to the splitting of reference. We can start with the point that the meaning of a metaphorical statement rises up from the blockage of any literal interpretation of the statement. In a literal interpretation, the meaning abolishes itself. Next, because of this self-destruction of the meaning, the primary reference founders. The entire strategy of poetic discourse plays on this point: it seeks the abolition of the reference by means of self-destruction of the meaning of metaphorical statements, the self-destruction being made manifest by an impossible literal interpretation.

But this is only the first phase, or rather the negative counterpart, of a positive strategy. Within the perspective of semantic impertinence, the self-destruction of meaning is merely the other side of an innovation in meaning at the level of the entire statement, an innovation obtained through the 'twist' of the literal meaning of the words. It is this innovation in meaning that constitutes living metaphor. But are we not in the same motion given the key to metaphorical reference? Can one not say that, by drawing a new semantic pertinence out of the ruins of the literal meaning, the metaphoric interpretation *also* sustains a new referential design, through those same means of abolition of the reference corresponding to the literal interpretation of the statement? A proportional argument, therefore: the other reference, the object of our search, would be to the new semantic pertinence what the abolished reference is to the literal meaning destroyed by the semantic impertinence. A metaphorical reference would correspond to the metaphorical meaning, just as an impossible literal reference corresponds to the impossible literal meaning.

We have posited this unknown reference through analogy (specifically, as the fourth term of a proportional argument); but can we do more? Can the reference itself be seen at work?

The semantic study of metaphor contains a second hint in this connection. As we saw, the interplay of resemblance, which we held within the strict limits of an operation of discourse, consists in the initiation of a *proximity* between formerly 'remote' meanings. 'To see the similar,' we said with Aristotle, 'is to metaphorize well.' Why would not this proximity of meaning be at the same time a proximity between the things themselves? Is it not from this proximity that a new way of seeing springs forth? Accordingly, it would be the category mistake that clears the way to a new vision.

This suggestion is not just added to the preceding, it is developed with it. The vision of the similar that produces the metaphorical statement is not a direct vision, but one which itself can also be called metaphorical. Using Hester's terms, metaphorical seeing is a 'seeing as.' Indeed, the former classification, linked to the previous use of words, resists and creates a sort of stereoscopic vision in which the new situation is perceived only in the depths of the situation disrupted by the category mistake.

Such is the schema of split reference. Essentially, it sets up a parallel between metaphorization of reference and metaphorization of meaning. This is the schema to which we will try to give some body.

Our first task is to overcome the opposition between denotation and connotation and to insert metaphorized reference into a *generalized* theory of *denotation*.

This general framework is developed in *Languages of Art* by Nelson Goodman. But Goodman does more than this; within that framework, he also designates the place of a frankly denotative theory of metaphor.

Languages of Art begins by situating all symbolic operations, verbal and non-verbal (including pictorial among others), within the boundaries of a single operation, the referential function by which a symbol 'stands for' or 'refers to.' The universality of the referential function is guaranteed by the universality of the organizing power of language and, more generally, of symbolic systems. This theory appears on the horizon of a general philosophy that has certain affinities with the philosophy of symbolic forms of Cassirer, but even more with the pragmatism of C.S. Peirce. Moreover, it draws the consequences, for a theory of symbols, of the nominalist positions taken in Goodman's *The Structure of Appearance* and *Fact, Fiction and Forecast.* The title of the first chapter, 'Reality Remade,' is very significant in this regard: symbolic systems 'make' and 'remake' the world. Beyond its imposing technicality, the entire work is a homage to a militant attitude, as the last chapter says,[23] of 'reorganizing the world in terms of works and works in terms of the world' (241). Work and world mirror each other. The aesthetic attitude 'is less attitude than action: creation and re-creation' (242).

We will return later to the nominalist and the pragmatist tone of the work. Let us focus for the moment on the important corollary, the refusal to distinguish between cognitive and emotive: 'In aesthetic experience the *emotions function cognitively*' (248). The rapprochement that occurs throughout the book between verbal and non-verbal symbols is grounded in an emphatic anti-emotionalism. This is not to say that the two sorts of symbols function in the same way. On the contrary, it is a matter for difficult argumentation, attempted only in the last chapter of the book, to distinguish between 'description' by language and 'representation' by the arts. What is important is that the four 'symptoms' of the aesthetic – syntactic density, semantic density, syntactic repleteness, role of exemplification (i.e. showing rather than saying) – are distinguished within a single, unique symbolic function. Distinguishing these traits concedes nothing to immediacy. Under one or another mode, 'Symbolization ... is to be judged fundamentally by how well it serves the cognitive purpose' (258). Aesthetic excellence is a cognitive excellence. One must even speak of the truth of art, if truth here is defined as 'fit with a body of theory' and between hypotheses and the facts at hand – briefly, as the 'appropriateness' of a symbolization (264). These traits hold for the arts as well as for discourse. 'My aim,' concludes the author 'has been to take some steps toward a systematic study of symbols and symbol systems and the ways they function in our perceptions and actions and arts and sciences, and thus in the creation and comprehension of our worlds' (265).

This enterprise is akin to that of Cassirer, therefore, although there is no progression from art to science. Only the use of the symbolic function is different; the symbolic systems coexist simultaneously.

Metaphor is an essential piece of this symbolic theory, inserted directly into the framework of reference. What must be shown is the difference, on the one hand, between what is 'metaphorically true' and what is 'literally true,' and, on the other hand, between metaphorical and literal truth together and 'mere falsity' (51). Broadly speaking, metaphorical truth concerns the application of predicates or of properties to something by a sort of transference, as for example the application of predicates borrowed from the domain of sound to something coloured (significantly, the chapter containing the theory of transference is entitled 'The Sound of Pictures' [45 ff.]).

But what is the literal application of predicates? The response to this question involves setting in place an important conceptual network comprising notions such as denotation, description, representation, and expression.[24] Reference and denotation coincide on first approximation. But later it will be necessary to introduce a distinction between two ways of referring, by denotation and by exemplification. Initially, then, we can regard reference and denotation as synonymous. Denotation must be defined fairly widely from the start, so as to subsume what art does – represent something – and what language does – describe. To say that representing is one way of denoting is to assimilate the relation between a picture and what it depicts to that between a predicate and that to which it is applied. At the same time, it says that representing is not imitating in the sense of resembling or copying. Therefore, the preconception that representation is imitation by resemblance should be carefully broken down and dislodged from one of its seemingly safest refuges, the theory of perspective in painting.[25] But if to represent is to denote and if our symbolic systems 'remake reality' through denotation, then representation is one of the modes through which nature becomes a product of art and discourse. So too, representation can depict a non-existant (the unicorn, Pickwick); in terms of denotation, this is a situation of null denotation, as distinct from multiple denotation (the eagle design in the dictionary to depict all eagles) and singular denotation (the portrait of so-and-so). Will Goodman draw from this distinction the conclusion that the non-existant also helps to fashion the world? Curiously, the author backs away from this consequence, which the upcoming theory of models will impel us to accept. To talk about the picture *of* the Unicorn is to talk about the unicorn-picture, that is, about a picture classified by the term associated with it. To learn to recognize a picture is not to learn to apply a representation (asking *what* it denotes) but to distinguish it from another (asking *which* species it is).

No doubt the argument carries the day against the confusion between characterizing and copying. However, if to represent is to classify, it is difficult to see how, in the case of null denotation, symbolization can make[26] what it depicts: 'The object and its aspects depend upon organization; and labels of all sorts are tools of organization ... a representation or description, by virtue of how it classifies and is classified, may make or mark connections, analyze objects, and organize the world' (32). By linking *fiction* and *redescription* very tightly, an analysis borrowed from the theory of models will allow us to correct an incompatibility, apparent at least in Goodman, between the theory of null denotation and the organizing function of symbolism.

Up until this point, denotation and reference have been treated as synonymous. This identification caused no inconvenience so long as the distinctions considered (description and representation) fell within the concept of denotation. A new distinction must be introduced concerning the orientation of the concept of reference, according to which its direction is from symbol to thing or from thing to symbol. As long as we identify reference and denotation, we take account only of the first direction, which consists in applying 'labels' to events. (Let us note in passing that the choice of the term *label* is appropriate to the conventionalist nominalism of Goodman – there are no fixed essences giving a tenor of meaning to verbal and non-verbal symbols. At the same time, the way of the theory of metaphor becomes smoother, for it is easier to replace a label than to reform an essence – habit is the only barrier!)

The second direction in which reference operates is no less important than the first. It consists in exemplifying, that is, in pointing out a meaning or property that something 'possesses.'[27] The reason why Goodman would appear to be so greatly interested in exemplification is that metaphor is a transference that affects the possession of predicates by some specific thing, rather than the application of these predicates to something. We arrive at metaphor in the midst of examples where it is said, for instance, that a certain picture that *possesses* the colour grey *expresses* sadness. In other words, metaphor concerns an inverted operation of reference plus an operation of transference. Close attention must be paid, therefore, to this series – reversed reference, exemplification, (literal) possession of a predicate, expression as metaphorical possession of non-verbal predicates (e.g. a sad colour).

Let us go back up the chain from (literal) possession[28] before descending towards (metaphorical) expression.

For a painted figure to possess greyness is to say that it is an *example* of greyness; but to say that this, here, is an example of greyness is to say that greyness *as such* applies to ... this thing, hence denotes it. Accordingly, the denotation relation is reversed. The picture denotes what it describes; but the colour grey is denoted by the predicate 'grey.' If, then, to possess is to exemplify, possession differs from reference only as to its direction.

The term symmetrical in this context to 'label' is 'sample' (for instance, a sample of fabric). The sample 'possesses' the characteristics (colour, texture, etc.) designated by the label. It is denoted by that which it exemplifies. The sample-label relation, if it is well understood, holds for non-verbal as well as verbal systems; predicates are labels in verbal systems, but non-linguistic symbols can also be exemplified and function as predicates. Thus, a gesture can denote or exemplify or do both: the motions of the orchestral conductor denote the sounds to be produced without being sounds themselves; sometimes they exemplify the speed or cadence of the sounds; the gymnastics instructor provides samples that exemplify the movement called for that denotes the movement to be produced; dance denotes the motions of everyday life or of a ritual and exemplify the prescribed stance that in turn reorganizes experience. The opposition between representing and expressing will not be a difference of domain (for example the domain of objects or events and the domain of feelings, as in an emotionalist theory), since representing is a case of denoting, and expressing is a variant by transference of possessing, which is a case of exemplifying; and since exemplifying and denoting are cases of making reference, with only a difference of direction. A symmetry by inversion replaces an apparent heterogeneity, by means of which the ruinous distinction of the cognitive and the emotive – from which that of denotation and connotation is derived – could creep back in again.

What has been gained with respect to the theory of metaphor?[29] We find it bound solidly to the theory of reference, linked by transference of a relation, which itself is the inverse of denotation, of which representation is a species. Indeed, if one acknowledges what will be shown later, that metaphorical expression (the sadness of the grey picture) is transference of possession; and if it is proven already that possession, which is nothing other than exemplification, is the inverse of denotation, of which representation is a species, then all the distinctions fall within the bounds of reference, with the proviso that their orientations differ.

But what is a transferred possession?

Let our starting point be the suggested example – the painting is literally grey, but sad metaphorically. The first statement concerns a 'fact,' the second a 'figure' (whence the title of chapter 2, section 5, 'Facts and Figures,' which contains the theory of metaphor). But 'fact' must be taken in the sense of Russell and Wittgenstein, where fact is not to be confused with a given but understood as a state of affairs, that is, as the correlate of a predicative act. For the same reason, 'figure' is not the ornament of a word but a predicative usage in a reversed denotation, that is, in a possession-exemplification. 'Fact' and 'figure,' therefore, are different ways of applying predicates, of using labels as samples.

Metaphor is an unusual application for Goodman, that is, application of a familiar label (whose usage consequently has a past) to a new object that resists at first and then gives in. Goodman's droll formulation states that 'applying an old label in a new way ... is a matter of teaching an old word new tricks ... metaphor is an affair between a predicate with a past and an object that yields while protesting' (69); later, it is 'a happy and revitalizing, even if bigamous, second marriage' (73). (Metaphor is again being spoken of in terms of metaphor – but this time the screen, filter, grill, and lens give way to carnal union!)

Here, within a theory of reference and no longer just of sense, we rediscover the essential points of the semantic theory of metaphorical statement of Richards, Beardsley, and Turbayne. Ryle's idea of category-mistake is retained as well, which moreover was also referential; I say that the painting is sad rather than gay, *even though* only sentient beings are gay or sad. Nevertheless, there is a metaphorical truth here, for the mistake in label application is equivalent to the reassignment of a label, such that 'sad' is more appropriate than 'gay.' The literal falsity, through misassignment of a label, is transformed into metaphorical truth through reassignment of the label.[30] I will show later how the intermediary of the theory of models allows one to interpret this reassignment in terms of redescription. The heuristic device of fiction must be inserted between description and redescription, and this will be accomplished by the theory of models.

But first, an interesting extension of metaphor must be considered. Metaphor does not cover just what we have called 'figure,' that is, ultimately, transference of an isolated predicate operating in opposition to another (the alternative 'red' or 'orange'). It also covers what must be called 'schema,' which stands for a group of labels with the characteristic that a corresponding group of objects, a 'realm,' is picked out by it (for example, colour).[31] Metaphor's power of reorganizing our perception of things develops from transposition of an entire 'realm.' Consider, for example, sound in the visual order. To speak of the sonority of a painting is no longer to move about an isolated predicate, but to bring about the incursion of an entire realm into alien territory. The well-worn notion of 'transporting' becomes a conceptual migration, if not an armed and luggage-laden overseas expedition. The interesting point is that the organization brought about in the adopted region is *guided by* the use of the entire network in the region of origin. This means that even if the territory to be invaded is chosen arbitrarily (whatever closely resembles whatever else), the usage of the labels in the new field of application is governed by the previous practice. In this vein, the use of the expression *high numbers* may guide the use of 'high sounds.' The use of schemata is governed by the law of 'precedence.' Here again, Goodman's nominalism will not allow him to look for affinities in the nature of things or in an eidetic constitution of experience. Nothing is explained in this regard by etymological geneologies or reappearances of animistic confusions (for example, between the animate and the inanimate), because the application of a predicate is metaphorical only if it conflicts with an application governed by present practice. Ancient history and repressed memory can break through to the surface. Still, an expatriate according to the present laws remains an alien even when back in his homeland. A theory of application comes to life in the present.[32]

It is fruitless, therefore, to look for something to justify the metaphorical application of a predicate. The difference between literal and metaphorical can introduce dissymmetry in any way at all into compatible combinations. Are a person and a picture alike in being sad? Yet one is sad literally, the other metaphorically, according to the established usage of our language. If one still wishes, nevertheless, to speak of resemblance, one must join Max Black in saying that metaphor creates the resemblance rather than finding and expressing it.[33]

For a nominalist perspective, the problem posed by metaphorical application of predicates is no different from that posed by their literal application: 'The question why predicates apply as they do metaphorically is much the same as the question why they apply as they do literally' (78). Metaphorical sorting under a given schema conveys information just as a literal sorting does. Application in both cases 'is fallible and thus subject to correction' (79). Literal application is simply the one that has been endorsed by usage. This is why the question of truth is not restricted or peculiar. Only metaphorical application is peculiar; for extension in the application of a label or a schema must satisfy opposed demands – it must be new but fitting, strange but evident, surprising but satisfying. A simple 'labeling' does not equal a 're-sorting'; new discriminations, new organization must result from emigration of a schema.[34]

Finally, if all language, all symbolism consists in 'remaking reality,' there is no place in language where this work is more plainly and fully demonstrated. It is when symbolism breaks through its acquired limits and conquers new territory that we understand the breadth of its ordinary scope.

Two questions then occur with respect to the boundaries of the metaphorical phenomenon. The first concerns enumeration of 'modes' at the level of discourse. For Goodman as for Aristotle, metaphor is not one figure of discourse among others, but the transference principle common to all of them. If one's guideline is the notion of 'schema' or 'realm' rather than that of 'figure,' a first group will include all transfers from one realm to another, non-intersecting realm – thus, personification, from person to thing; synecdoche, from whole to part; antonomasia, from thing to property (or label). All transfers between intersecting realms will be put in a second group: upward displacement or hyperbole, downward displacement or litotes. A last group is kept for transfers that do not alter extension; here we have the reversing of irony (81-3).

Thus, Goodman takes the same route as other authors who, like Jean Cohen, subordinate taxonomy to functional analysis. Transference as such occupies the first level of consideration. Now it is merely an option of naming whether the general function or one of the figures is called metaphor. We saw earlier that everything that diminishes the role of resemblance also diminishes the singularity of metaphor the figure and reinforces the generality of metaphor as function.

The second question relative to the delimitation of the phenomenon of metaphor concerns the operation of the metaphorical function outside of verbal symbolism. We return here to our initial example, the sad expression of a painting. We find it at the end of a series of distinctions and linkages: (1) exemplification as the inverse of denotation, (2) possession as exemplification, (3) expression as the metaphorical transference of possession. Now this same series, denotation-exemplification-possession, must be considered not only in the order of verbal symbols and so in the order of description, but also in the order of non-verbal symbols (pictures, etc.), and thus in the order of representation. *Expression* is the name of a metaphorical possession of the representational order. In our example, the sad painting is a case of metaphorical possession of a representational 'sample,' which exemplifies a representational 'label.' In other words, 'what is expressed is metaphorically exemplified.'[35] The expression (sad), therefore, is no less real than the colour (blue). The fact that it is neither verbal nor literal, but representational and transferred, does not make the expression any less 'true,' so long as it is appropriate. Expression is not constituted by the effects on the spectator, for I can perceive the sadness of a picture without being made sad by it. 'Metaphorical importation' is able to make this predicate an acquired property; the expression is truly the possession of the thing. A painting expresses properties that it exemplifies metaphorically in virtue of its status as pictorial symbol: 'Pictures are no more immune than the rest of the world to the formative force of language even though they themselves, as symbols, also exert such a force upon the world, including language' (88).

In this way, *Languages of Art* solidly links verbal metaphor and nonverbal metaphorical expression to the plane of reference. Goodman succeeds in arranging the governing categories of reference in orderly fashion: denotation and exemplification (label and sample), description and representation (verbal and non-verbal symbols), possession and expression (literal and metaphorical).

I suggest the following assessment of Goodman's categories in application to the poetics of discourse:

(1) The distinction between denotation and connotation is not a fruitful principle of differentiation with respect to the poetic function, if connotation is understood as a set of associative and emotional effects without referential value. As a symbolic system, poetry has a referential function just as much as does descriptive discourse.

(2) The *sensa* – sounds, images, feelings – that adhere to the 'sense' are to be treated on the model of expression in Goodman's sense. These are representations and not descriptions, which exemplify instead of denoting and which transfer possession instead of retaining it by primordial right. Qualities in this sense are no less real than the descriptive traits that scientific discourse articulates; they belong to things over and above being effects subjectively experienced by the lover of poetry.

(3) Poetic qualities, through their status as transferred, add to the shaping of the world. They are 'true' to the extent that they are 'appropriate,' that is, to the extent that they join fittingness to novelty, obviousness to surprise.

On these three points, however, the analysis of Goodman calls for complements that will progressively turn into far-reaching alterations, in that they will affect his foundations in pragmatism and nominalism.

(1) Insufficient account is given of the strategy proper to poetic discourse, that of the *epoché* of descriptive reference. Goodman does proclaim the notion of a longstanding marriage that resists the initiation of a new and bigamous union, but he sees nothing in it except the resistance of habit to innovation. It seems to me that one must go further, up to the eclipse of one referential mode as the condition for the emergence of another referential mode. It is this eclipse of primary denotation that the theory of connotation had in view, without realizing that what it called connotation was still referential in its fashion.

(2) Poetic discourse faces reality by putting into play *heuristic fictions* whose constitutive value is proportional to their power of denial. Here again, Goodman offers a first step with his concept of null denotation, but he is too concerned to show that the *object* of null denotation serves to classify labels to see that precisely in this way, it helps redescribe reality. The theory of models will allow us to tighten the link between fiction and redescription.

(3) The 'appropriateness' of metaphorical as well as literal application of a predicate is not fully justified within a purely nominalist conception of language. Although such a conception has no trouble explaining the choreography of labels, since there is no essence to block re-labelling, it has greater difficulty accounting for the air of *rightness* that certain more fortunate instances of language and art seem to exude. To my mind, this is the place to part ways with Goodman's nominalism. Does not the fittingness, the appropriateness of certain verbal and non-verbal predicates, indicate that language not only has organized reality in a different way, but also made manifest a way of being of things, which is brought to language thanks to semantic innovation? It would seem that the enigma of metaphorical discourse is that it 'invents' in both senses of the word: what it creates, it discovers; and what it finds, it invents.

What must be understood, therefore, is the interconnection of three themes. In the metaphorical discourse of poetry referential power is linked to the eclipse of ordinary reference; the creation of heuristic fiction is the road to redescription; and reality brought to language unites manifestation and creation. This Study can explore the first two themes; it will be up to the eighth and final Study to clarify the conception of reality postulated by our theory of poetic language.

4 / MODEL AND METAPHOR

A detour through the theory of models constitutes the decisive stage in this Study. The idea of a kinship between model and metaphor is so fruitful that Max Black took it as the title of the collection containing 'Models and Archetypes,' the essay devoted specifically to this epistemological problem (the introduction of the concept of archetype will be explained later).[36]

The central argument is that, with respect to the relation to reality, metaphor is to poetic language what the model is to scientific language. Now in scientific language, the model is essentially a heuristic instrument that seeks, by means of fiction, to break down an inadequate interpretation and to lay the way for a new, more adequate interpretation. In the language of Mary Hesse,[37] another author close to Black, the model is an instrument of redescription. I will retain this expression for the duration of my analysis. Further, it is important to understand its meaning in its primitive epistemological usage.

The model belongs not to the logic of justification or proof, but to the logic of discovery. Again, it must be understood that this logic of discovery does not reduce to a psychology of invention without authentic epistemological interest but rather involves a cognitive process, a rational method with its own canons and principles.

The properly epistemological dimension of scientific imagination does not appear unless models are first distinguished according to their make-up and their function. Black arranges the hierarchy of models into three levels.

'Scale models' occupy the lowest level; examples are a model of a ship, enlargement of something very small (a limb of a mosquito), a slow-motion sketch of a manœuvre, simulation in miniature of social processes, etc. These are models in that they are models *of* something to which they refer in an asymmetrical relationship. Their purpose is to show how something looks, how it works, what laws govern it. It is possible to decode the model and, by reading off its properties, arrive at the properties of the original. Finally, only some features are relevant in a model, others are not. The model purports to be faithful only in respect to its relevant features. It is these relevant features that distinguish the scale model from other models. They are the counterparts of rules of interpretation that specify the way they are to be read. For everything with a spatial or temporal dimension, these conventions rest on partial identity of properties and invariance of proportions. For this reason, the scale model imitates its original, reproduces it. Black claims that the scale model corresponds to the 'icon' in Peirce. The scale model, through its sensible quality, adjusts what is too large or too small to our level and size.

At the second level Black situates *analogue models*: 'hydraulic models of economic systems, or the use of electrical circuits in computers,' etc. Two aspects are to be considered – change of medium, and representation of structure, that is, the 'web of relationships in an original.' Rules of interpretation determine the translation in this case from one system of relationships into another. The pertinent correlative traits of this translation constitute what in mathematics is called 'isomorphism.' The model and the original resemble each other in their structures and not through sensible features.

Identity of structure also characterizes *theoretical* models, which constitute the third level. However, one cannot point at them, nor are they to be constructed. They are not things at all; rather, they introduce a new language, like a dialect or idiom, in which the original is described without being constructed. An example would be Maxwell's 'representation of an electrical field in terms of the properties of an imaginary incompressible fluid.' The imaginary medium is here nothing more than a mnemonic device for grasping mathematical relationships. The important thing is not that one has something to view mentally, but that one can operate on an object that on the one hand is better known and in this sense more familiar, and on the other hand is full of implications and in this sense rich at the level of hypotheses.

The great interest of Black's analysis is that it escapes the alternative relative to the existential status of the model that seems to be imposed by the variations of Maxwell himself, the concretizing interpretations of ether by Lord Kelvin, and the savage rejection of models by Duhem. The issue is not whether and how the model exists, but what are the rules for interpretation of the theoretical model and, correspondingly, what are its pertinent features. The important point is that the model's only properties are those assigned to it by language convention, beyond any influence of a real construction. This is what the opposition between description and construction emphasizes: 'The heart of the method consists in *talking* in a certain way' (229). Its fruitfulness consists in our knowing how to make use of it; its 'deployability' – the expression is Stephen Toulmin's[38] – is its *raison-d'être*. To speak of intuitive grasp is only a shorthand way of indicating ease and rapidity in mastering the far-reaching implications of models. Recourse to scientific imagination in this regard does not signal a deflection of reason, distraction by images, but the essentially verbal power of trying out new relationships on a 'described model.' This imagination mingles with reason by virtue of the rules of correlation governing the translation of statements concerning the secondary domain into statements applicable to the original domain. Once more, it is the isomorphism of relationships that grounds the translatability of one idiom into another and, in so doing, provides the 'rationale' of the imagination (238). But the isomorphism does not hold now between the original domain and something constructed, but between that domain and something 'described.' Scientific imagination consists in seeing new connections via the detour of this thing that is 'described.' To remove the model from the logic of discovery, or even to reduce it to a provisional measure as the best substitute available for direct deduction, is ultimately to reduce the logic of discovery itself to a deductive procedure. The scientific ideal underlying this tendency, says Black, is finally that of 'Euclid as reformed by Hilbert' (235). The logic of discovery, let us say, is not a psychology of invention, because investigation is not deduction.

This epistemological outcome is highlighted well by Mary Hesse when she says that 'the deductive model of scientific explanation should be modified and supplemented by a view of theoretical explanation as metaphoric redescription of the domain of the *explanandum*' (249). This thesis incorporates two special emphases. The first applies to the word *explanation*. If the model, like metaphor, introduces a new language, its description equals explanation. This implies that the model operates precisely on the deductivist epistemological plane, modifying and completing the criteria of deductibility of scientific explanation as spelled out, for example, by Hempel and Oppenheim.[39] According to these criteria, it must be possible to deduce the *explanandum* from the *explanans*, which must contain at least one general law that is not redundant for the deduction; it must not yet have been empirically falsified; it must be predictive. Recourse to metaphorical redescription is a consequence of the impossibility of obtaining a strictly deductive relationship between *explanans* and *explanandum* – one can hope at most for an 'approximate fit' (257). This condition of acceptability is closer to the interaction at work in the metaphorical statement than is deductibility pure and simple. So too, the insertion of rules of correspondence between the *theoretical explanans* and the *explanandum* fits in with criticism of the ideal of deductibility; to have recourse to models is to interpret rules of correspondence in terms of extension of the language of observation through metaphorical usage. As for predictability, it cannot be conceived on a deductive model, as if general laws already present in the *explanans* were to incorporate events that are not yet observable, or as if the set of rules of correspondence were to need no addition. According to Mary Hesse in *Models and Analogies in Science*, there is no rational method for complementing the correspondence rules in a purely deductive way and for formulating new observational predicates. Prediction of new observational predicates requires a displacement of meanings and an extension of primitive observational language; so only the domain of the *explanandum* can be redescribed in the terminology transferred from the secondary system.

The second emphasis of the thesis of Mary Hesse focuses on the word *redescription*. This signifies that the ultimate problem posed by the use of models is 'the problem of metaphoric reference' (254-9). Things themselves are 'seen as'; they are *identified*, in a way that remains to be specified, with the descriptive character of the model. The *explanandum* as ultimate referent is itself changed by adoption of the metaphor. One must be willing, therefore, to reject the idea of an invariance of meaning with respect to the *explanandum* and move towards a 'realistic' view (256) of the theory of interaction. Not just our conception of rationality, but at the same time that of reality, is thrown open to question: as Hesse says, 'rationality consists just in the continuous adaptation of our language to our continually expanding world, and metaphor is one of the chief means by which this is accomplished' (259).

We will return later to the implications for the verb *to be* itself of this affirmation that things *are* 'as' described by the model.

What benefit does this detour through the theory of models bring to the theory of metaphor? The authors cited devote greater care to extending their original theory of metaphor to models than to considering the impact of their epistemological application to poetry. It is this reaction, the theory of models reflecting back on the theory of metaphor, that interests me here.

Extension of the theory of metaphor to that of models has other consequences besides confirmation of the principal traits of the original theory – interaction between secondary predicate and principal subject, cognitive value of the statement, production of new information, nontranslatability, inexhaustibility through paraphrase. The reduction of model to a psychic aid parallels the reduction of metaphor to a mere decorative process – misconception and recognition follow the same course in both cases. The procedure they possess in common is 'analogical transfer of a vocabulary' (Black 238).

The reflection of model back on metaphor results in exposure of new traits of metaphor not discovered in the foregoing analysis.

First of all, what on the poetic side corresponds exactly to the model is not precisely what we have called the 'metaphorical statement,' that is, a short bit of discourse reduced most often to a sentence. Rather, as the model consists in a complex network of statements, its exact analogue would be the extended metaphor – tale, allegory. What Toulmin calls the 'systematic deployability' of the model finds its equivalent in a metaphoric network and not in an isolated metaphor.

This first observation takes up the one made at the beginning of this Study, to the effect that it is the poetic work as a whole, the poem, that projects a world. The change of scale separating metaphor as a 'poem in miniature' (Beardsley) from the poem itself as an expanded metaphor calls for an examination of the constitution of the metaphoric universe as a network. The article by Max Black should be read in this context. The isomorphism that constitutes the 'rationale' of imagination in the use of models has its equivalent only in one kind of metaphor, which Black calls archetype (hence the title of the article, 'Models and Archetypes'). With this choice of terms, Black points out two aspects of certain metaphors, their 'radical' character and their 'systematic' character. Furthermore, these two aspects are linked; 'root metaphors,' to borrow the term of Stephen C. Pepper,[40] are also those that organize metaphors into networks (for example, in the work of Kurt Lewin, the network that inter-relates words like *field, vector, phase-space, tension, force, boundary, fluidity,* etc. – Black 241). By virtue of these two characteristics, the archetype has a less local, less pin-point existence than does metaphor; it covers an 'area' of experience or of facts.

The observation is excellent. We saw the need, with Nelson Goodman, to subordinate isolated 'figures' to 'schemas' that govern 'regions,' like that of sounds transferred in a group together to the visual order. It is to be expected that the referential function of metaphor should be carried by a metaphoric network rather than by an isolated metaphorical statement. (I prefer to speak of 'metaphoric network' rather than of 'archetype' because of the use of the latter term in Jungian psychoanalysis.) The paradigmatic power of these two kinds of metaphor comes as much from their 'radical' character as from their 'inter-connections.' To the simple idea of 'to see new connections,' a philosophy of imagination must add that of a breakthrough that is both profound and far-reaching, thanks to 'radical' and 'inter-connected' metaphors respectively (Black 237, 241).[41]

The second benefit of the detour via models is that it throws into relief the connection between heuristic function and description. This linkage suddenly takes us back to the *Poetics* of Aristotle. We recall how Aristotle linked *mimêsis* and *muthos* in his concept of tragic *poiêsis.*[42] Poetry, he said, is an imitation of human actions; but this *mimêsis* passes through creation of a plot, a tale, which shows signs of composition and order lacked by the dramas of everyday life. On these grounds, should not the relationship between *muthos* and *mimêsis* in tragic *poiêsis* be understood in the same way as that of heuristic fiction and redescription in the theory of models? In fact, tragic *muthos* evinces all the traits of 'radicality' and 'organization into a network' that Max Black accords to archetypes, that is, to metaphors with the same standing as models. Metaphoricity is a trait not only of *lexis* but of *muthos* itself; and, as in the case of models, this metaphoricity consists in describing a less known domain – human reality – in the light of relationships within a fictitious but better known domain – the tragic tale – utilizing all the strengths of 'systematic deployability' contained in that tale. As for *mimêsis,* it stops causing trouble and embarrassment when it is understood no longer in terms of 'copy' but of redescription. Both directions of the relationship between *muthos* and *mimêsis* must be appreciated: if tragedy achieves its effect of *mimêsis* only through the invention of the *muthos*, *muthos* is at the service of *mimêsis* and its fundamentally denotative character. In the terms used by Mary Hesse, *mimêsis* is the name of the 'metaphoric reference.' What Aristotle himself emphasized through this paradox is that poetry is closer to essence than is history, which is preoccupied with the accidental. Tragedy teaches us to 'see' human life 'as' that which the *muthos* displays. In other words, *mimêsis* constitutes the 'denotative' dimension of *muthos*.

This conjunction of *muthos* and *mimêsis* is not the work of tragic poetry alone. It is just easier to detect it there because, on the one hand, the *muthos* takes the form of a 'story' and the metaphoricity is attached to the plot of the tale, and because, on the other hand, the referent consists in human action which, due to its motivational course, has a certain affinity to the structure of the story. The conjunction of *muthos* and *mimêsis* is the work of all poetry. Let us recall Northrop Frye's linking of the poetic and the hypothetical. Now what is this 'hypothetical'? According to his perspective, poetic language, with its 'internal' and not 'outward' turn, constructs a mood, which has no existence outside the poem itself: this is what receives form from the poem as an arrangement of signs. Must we not say, first of all, that the mood is the hypothetical created by the poem, and that, as such, it occupies the place in lyric poetry that *muthos* occupies in tragic poetry? And ought we not to add that this lyric *muthos* is joined by a lyric *mimêsis*, in the sense that the mood created in this fashion is a sort of model for 'seeing as' and 'feeling as'? I will speak in this sense of lyric redescription, in order to introduce the fictive element highlighted by the theory of models into the heart of expression (in Goodman's sense). The feeling articulated by the poem is no less heuristic than the tragic tale. The 'internal' movement of the poem, therefore, could not be opposed purely and simply to 'outward' movement. What it signifies is only the disconnection of customary reference, the elevation of feeling to the hypthetical, and the creation of an affective fiction. But lyric *mimêsis*, which can be taken if desired as an 'outward' movement, is the very work of the lyric *muthos*; it is the consequence of the fact that the mood is no less heuristic than fiction in the form of a story. The paradox of the poetic can be summed up entirely in this, that the elevation of feeling to fiction is the condition of its mimetic use. Only a feeling transformed into myth can open and discover the world.

If this heuristic function of mood is so difficult to recognize, it is doubtless because 'representation' has become the sole route to knowledge and the model of every relationship between subject and object. Yet feeling has an ontological status different from relationship at a distance; it makes for participation in things.[43]

This is why the opposition between exterior and interior ceases to be valid here. Not being internal, feeling in like measure is not subjective. Metaphorical reference links rather with what Douglas Berggren calls 'poetic schemata of inner life' and 'the objectivity of poetic textures.'[44] By potetic schema he understands 'some visualizable phenomenon, whether actually observable or merely imagined, which serves as a vehicle for expressing something about the inner life of man, or non-spatial reality in general' (248); thus, for example, the 'lake of ice' at the bottom of Dante's *Inferno*.[45] To say with Frye that the poetic statement has a 'centripetal' direction is only to say how not to interpret the poetic schema, namely, in a cosmological fashion; but something is said about the sort of being of some spirits which, *in truth*, are of ice. Later I will discuss the meaning of the expression *in truth*, and will propose a *tensional* conception of metaphorical truth itself. It is enough for now to say that the poetic verb metaphorically 'schematizes' feelings or emotions only in depicting 'textures of the world,' 'non-human physiognomies,' which become actual portraits of our inner life. What Berggren calls 'textural reality' supports 'the schema of inner life,' which would be equivalent to those 'moods' that, for Northrop Frye, substitute for every referent. The 'joyous undulation of the waves' in Hölderlin's poem[46] is neither an objective reality in the positivist sense nor a mood in the emotivist sense. Such a contrast applies to a conception in which reality is first reduced to scientific objectivity. Poetic feeling in its metaphorical expressions bespeaks the lack of distinction between interior and exterior. The 'poetic textures' of the world (joyous undulations) and the 'poetic schemata' of interior life (lake of ice), mirroring one another, proclaim the reciprocity of the inner and the outer.

Metaphor raises this reciprocity from confusion and vagueness to bipolar tension. The intropathic fusion that precedes the conquest of subject-object duality is something different, as is the reconciliation that overcomes the opposition of subjective and objective.

The question of metaphorical truth has thus been raised. The meaning of the word *truth* is in question. The comparison of model and metaphor at least shows us the direction: as the conjunction of fiction and redescription suggests, poetic feeling itself also develops an experience of reality in which invention and discovery cease being opposed and where creation and revelation coincide. But what then does reality mean?

5 / TOWARDS THE CONCEPT OF 'METAPHORICAL TRUTH'

The discussion at hand has the following conclusions in view (the first and second merely record the advances made by the preceding discussion, whereas the third bears a consequence that calls for its own justification):

(1) The poetic function and the rhetorical function cannot be fully distinguished until the conjunction between fiction and redescription is brought to light. Each function now appears to be the other's inverse. The second seeks to persuade men by adorning discourse with pleasing ornaments; it is what emphasizes discourse in its own right. The first seeks to redescribe reality by the roundabout route of heuristic fiction.

(2) In service to the poetic function, metaphor is that strategy of discourse by which language divests itself of its function of direct description in order to reach the mythic level where its function of discovery is set free.

(3) We can presume to speak of metaphorical truth in order to designate the 'realistic' intention that belongs to the redescriptive power of poetic language.

This last conclusion needs clarification. In effect, it implies that the theory of tension (or of controversion), which has been the constant guiding thread of this investigation, might be extended to the referential relationship of the metaphorical statement to reality.

Three applications have in fact been given to the idea of tension:

(a) tension within the statement: between tenor and vehicle, between focus and frame, between principal subject and secondary subject;

(b) tension between two interpretations: between a literal interpretation that perishes at the hands of semantic impertinence and a metaphorical interpretation whose sense emerges through non-sense;

(c) tension in the relational function of the copula: between identity and difference in the interplay of resemblance.

These three applications of the idea of tension remain at the level of meaning immanent to the statement, even while the second involves a function external to the statement and the third already concerns the copula (but in its relational function). Our new application concerns reference itself and the claim of the metaphorical statement to reach reality in some particular manner. In the most radical terms possible, tension must be introduced into metaphorically affirmed being. When the poet says that 'nature is a temple where living columns ...' the verb *to be* does not just connect the predicate *temple* to the subject *nature* along the lines of the threefold tension outlined above. The copula is not only relational. It implies besides, by means of the predicative relationship, that *what is* is redescribed; it says *that* things really are this way. This is something we learned from Aristotle's treatise *On Interpretation.*

Are we now falling into a trap prepared for us by language, which, as Cassirer reminds us, does not go so far as to distinguish between two senses of the verb *to be*, the relational and the existential?[47] This would be the case if we were to take the verb *to be* itself in its literal sense. But is there not a metaphorical sense of the verb *to be* itself, in which the same tension would be preserved that we found first between words (between 'nature' and 'temple'), then between two interpretations (the literal and the metaphorical), and finally between identity and difference?

In order to elucidate this tension deep within the logical force of the verb *to be*, we must expose an 'is not,' itself implied in the impossibility of the literal interpretation, yet present as a filigree in the metaphorical 'is.' Thus, the tension would prevail between an 'is' and an 'is not.' This tension would not be marked grammatically in the example above. In any case, even if not marked, the 'is' of equivalence is distinct from the 'is' of determination ('the rose is red,' which is synecdochic in nature). That distinction, characteristic of the metaphorical process, issues from the *Rhétorique générale* of the Groupe de Liège.[48]

So it is not just the compared terms that are affected by this process, nor even the copula in its referential function, but the existential function of the verb *to be*. The same must be said of the 'to be like (or as)' of explicit metaphor or simile, which ancient rhetoric, in a departure from Aristotle, took to be the canonical form of which metaphor would be the abbreviation. 'To be like/as' must be treated as a metaphorical modality of the copula itself; the 'like/as' is not just the comparative term among all the terms, but is included in the verb *to be*, whose force it alters. In other words, the 'like/as' must be brought alongside the copula, as in 'her cheeks *are-like* roses' (one of the examples of the *Rhétorique générale*, 114). In this way, we would remain faithful to the tradition of Aristotle, which was not followed by later rhetoric. As we recall, for Aristotle metaphor is not an abbreviated simile, but simile is a weakened metaphor. Our primary focus, therefore, must truly be on the 'is' of equivalence. And my reason for trying to pinpoint within the very force of the verb *to be* that tension given three other applications by the preceding analysis is to distinguish its use from the 'is' of determination.

The question may be formulated in the following manner: does not the tension that affects the copula in its relational function also affect the copula in its existential function? This question contains the key to the notion of *metaphorical truth.*

In order to demonstrate this 'tensional' conception of metaphorical truth, I will proceed dialectically. First, I will point out the inadequacy of an interpretation that gives in to ontological *naïveté* in the evaluation of metaphorical truth because it ignores the implicit 'is not.' I will then portray the inadequacy of an inverse interpretation that, under the critical pressure of the 'is not,' loses the 'is' by reducing it to the 'as-if' of a reflective judgment.

The legitimation of the concept of metaphorical truth, which preserves the 'is not' within the 'is,' will proceed from the convergence of these two critiques.

Prior to any properly ontological interpretation, like the one we will try to initiate in the eighth Study, we will restrict ourselves to a dialectical discussion of opinions, as Aristotle does at the beginning of his analyses of 'first philosophy.'

(a) The first tendency – naïve and uncritical – is that of ontological *vehemence*. I will not renounce it, I will only mediate it. Without it, the critical moment would be weak. To state 'that is' – such is the moment of *belief*, of *ontological commitment*, which gives affirmation its 'illocutionary' force. There is no better testimony to this affirmative vehemence than the poetic experience. Along one of its dimensions, at least, this experience expresses the *ecstatic* moment of language – language going beyond itself. It seems, accordingly, to attest that discourse prefers to obliterate itself, to die, at the confines of the being-said.

Can philosophy take account of the non-philosophy of ecstasy? And at what price?

In a mélange of non-philosophy and Schellingian philosophy, Coleridge proclaims the *quasi-vegetal* power of imagination, concentrated in the symbol, to draw us to the growth of things: 'While it enunciates the whole, [a symbol] abides itself as a living part of that unity of which it is the representative.'[49] Thus, metaphor accomplishes an exchange between poet and world, thanks to which individual life and universal life grow together. In this way, the growth of plants becomes the metaphor for metaphorical truth, being itself 'a symbol established in the truth of things' (Coleridge in Richards 111). Just as the plant reaches towards the light and into the earth and draws its growth from them, and just as 'it becomes the visible *organismus* of the whole silent or elementary life of nature and therefore, in incorporating the one extreme becomes the symbol of the other; the natural symbol of that higher life of reason' (ibid.), so too the poetic verb enjoins us to participate in the totality of things via an 'open communion.' And all this moves I.A. Richards to repeat a question posed much earlier by Coleridge: 'Are not words parts and germinations of the plant?' (112).

Thus, the price that philosophy pays for countenancing poetic ecstasy is the reintroduction of philosophy of nature into philosophy of spirit,

along the lines of Schelling's philosophy of mythology. But then imagination, according to the vegetal metaphor, is no longer the fundamentally
discursive blending of identity and difference that we discussed earlier
(Study 6). The ontology of 'correspondences' seeks support in the 'sympathetic' attractions of nature, prior to the interposition of dissecting understanding.

Coleridge combined philosophy with non-philosophy. With Bergson,
the unity of vision and life is carried to the pinnacle of philosophy. The
philosophical character of his enterprise is preserved by the critique of critique, through which understanding reflecting back on itself creates its
own process. Thus, the status of the image is established by a proof *a contrario*, through the interconnection between conceptual atomization, spatial dispersion, and pragmatic interest. So too, the superiority of image
over concept, the priority of undivided temporal flux over space, and the
disinterestedness of the vision turned towards life's concerns are to be restored together. And it is in a philosophy of life that the pact between
image, time, and contemplation is sealed.

There is one particular theory of literary criticism, influenced by Schelling, Coleridge, and Bergson, that tries to give an account of this ecstatic
moment of poetic language.[50] We owe several romantic pleas focused specifically on metaphor to this critique. One of the most worthy is that of
Wheelwright in *The Burning Fountain* and *Metaphor and Reality*. The
author does not limit himself to connecting his ontology to generalized
considerations concerning the power of imagination; he ties it closely to
traits privileged by his semantics. These traits call directly for expression
in terms of life. Language, says the author, is 'tensive' and 'alive.' He plays
on all the contrasts between perspective and openness, designation and
suggestion, imagery and significance, concreteness and plural signification,
precision and affective resonance, etc. More particularly, this 'tensive'
character of language is focused in metaphor, as opposed to 'epiphor' and
'diaphor': epiphor juxtaposes and fuses terms by means of immediate assimilation at the level of the image, whereas diaphor proceeds mediately and
through combination of discrete terms. Metaphor is the tension between
epiphor and diaphor. This tension guarantees the very transference of
meaning and gives poetic language its characteristic of semantic 'plus-value,'
its capacity to be open towards new aspects, new dimensions, new horizons of meaning.

Hence, all these traits call for expression directly in terms of life – 'living,' 'alive,' 'intense.' In the expression *tensive aliveness*[51] (which I will put
to my own use, but in a rather different sense), the accent is put on the
vital rather than the logical aspect of tension; 'connotative fullness' and
'tensive aliveness' are opposed to the rigidity, the coldness, the deadening

effect of 'steno-language.'[52] 'Fluid-language' contrasts here with 'block-language,' which triumphs with the abstractions shared by several minds due to habit or convention. This is a language that has lost its 'tensional ambiguities,' its 'fluid uncaptured meanings.'[53]

These are the semantic marks of the affinity of 'tensive' language with a reality that presents corresponding ontological traits. Indeed, Wheelwright has no doubt that man, given that he is alert, has a constant concern for 'What Is.'[54] The reality brought to language by metaphor is termed 'presential and tensive'; 'coalescent and interpenetrative'; 'perspectival and hence latent'; in brief, 'revealing itself only partially, ambiguously, and through symbolic indirection' (154). Indistinctness bathes all these traits – presence is inflamed by a 'responsive-imaginative' act (156) and itself responds to this response in a sort of encounter. The author allows, it is true, that this sense of presence does not go unchallenged; but he adds right away that these contrastive elements are subordinated to the totality in view. As for 'coalescence,' Wheelwright opposes it to the selectivity of intelligence, which leads to the dichotomies of objective and subjective, physical and spiritual, particular and universal. The 'plus-value' of poetic expression causes each term to participate in its opposite, to metamorphose into it. Language itself, through the passage achieved in this way from one meaning to another, evokes 'something of a metaphorical character in the world which it [the poem] salutes' (169). Finally, the 'perpectival' character of poetic language evokes the excess that surpasses the angle of vision. Is this not what Heraclitus suggests when he says: 'The Lord whose oracle is at Delphi neither speaks nor conceals, but gives signs'? With the Hindu *guru* of the Upanishads, must we not whisper '*neti-neti*,' 'not quite that, not quite that'? Lastly, broaching the 'poeto-ontological question,' the author is quite agreeable to see his 'metapoetics' as an 'ontology not so much of concepts as of poetic sensitivity' (152, 20).

It is astonishing that Wheelwright should be brought quite close to a tensional conception of truth itself by his semantic conception of the tension between diaphor and epiphor. But the dialectical inclination of his theory is dissipated by the intuitionist and vitalist tendency that takes him finally into the metapoetics of the 'What Is.'

(b) The dialectical counterpart of ontological *naïveté* is presented by Turbayne in *The Myth of Metaphor*. He attempts to delimit the valid 'use' of metaphor by taking 'abuse' as his critical theme. Abuse is the 'myth' of his title, in a more epistemological than ethnological sense, scarcely differing from what we just called ontological *naïveté*. The myth, in fact, is 'believed poetry' – metaphor taken literally, I would put it. Now, there is something in the use of metaphor that inclines it towards abuse, and so towards myth.

What is this? Let us look back at Turbayne's semantic foundations (discussed above, Study 4). Metaphor is close to what Gilbert Ryle calls category mistake, which consists in presenting facts belonging to one category in idioms appropriate to another. Metaphor too is a calculated error, a 'sort-crossing.' The author builds his referential theory on this semantic base, where the inappropriateness of metaphorical attribution is underlined more strongly than the new semantic pertinence. Turbayne alleges that belief is led by a spontaneous movement from a 'pretence' that something is so, although such is not the case (13), to the corresponding 'intention' – I *in*tend what I *pre*tend (15) – and thence, from the intention, to 'make-believe' (17). Thus sort-crossing becomes a sort-trespassing, category-fusion becomes category-confusion (22); and belief, taken up in its pretending, is converted subtly into 'make-believe.'

Therefore, what earlier we called heuristic fiction is not an innocent pretence. It tends to lose sight of its nature as fiction and take on the dimensions of perceptual belief (this is close to how Spinoza described belief in countering Descartes: so long as imagination has not been limited and denied, it is indistinguishable from true belief). It is notable that the absence of grammatical markings serves here as a warning regarding this shift in belief. There is no grammatical feature that distinguishes metaphorical attribution from literal attribution. For example, grammar makes no distinction between Churchill's calling Mussolini 'That utensil!' and the use of the same phrase in a frying-pan advertisement (14); only the impossibility of taking the algebraic sum of the two statements raises our suspicion. Not marking the difference, and, in this sense, hiding it, is precisely the trap that grammar sets. This is why a critical instance must be applied to the statement in order to flush out the unmarked 'as if,' that is, the virtual mark of the 'pretence' immanent within the 'believe' and the 'make-believe.'

This dissimulative trait – one might almost say 'bad faith,' except that Turbayne does not use those terms – calls for a critical rejoinder. A line of demarcation should be drawn between 'to use' and 'to be used,' lest we fall victim to metaphor, mistaking the mask for the face. In brief, we must 'expose' metaphor, unmask it. This proximity between use and abuse leads to a correction of the metaphors about metaphor. We have spoken of transference or transporting. That is true: facts are reallocated by metaphor; but such reallocation is also a misallocation. Metaphor has been compared to a filter, a screen, and a lens, in order to say that it places things under a perspective and instructs us to 'see as ...' Yet it is also a mask that disguises. It was said that metaphor integrates diversity; but it also leads to categorial confusion. It was said that it 'stands for ...'; it must be said as well that it is 'taken for.'

But what is it to 'ex-pose' metaphor (54-70)? It must be noted that Turbayne is more inclined to reflect on scientific models than on poetic metaphors. This certainly does not disqualify his contribution to the concept of metaphorical truth, since, as we ourselves agreed above, the referential function of models is itself a model for the referential function of metaphor. But there is a strong possibility that the nature of critical vigilance differs from one situation to the other. Indeed, the examples of epistemological 'myths' are scientific theories where the index of the heuristic fiction has always been lost to view. Accordingly, Turbayne discusses at length the reification of mechanical models in Descartes and Newton, that is, their immediate ontological interpretation. The tension between metaphorical and literal, therefore, is absent from the very start. On this basis, 'to explode a myth' is to expose the model as metaphor.

Turbayne thus takes up the old tradition that began with Bacon denouncing the 'idols of the theatre' 'because in my judgment all the received systems are but so many stage-plays representing worlds of the creation ... which by tradition, credulity, and negligence have come to be received.'[55]

Nevertheless, this does not abolish metaphorical language. Quite the contrary, it confirms it, while adjoining to it the critical index of the 'as if.' It is not in fact possible to present 'the literal truth,' to say 'what the facts are,' as logical empiricism demands; every 'attempt to re-allocate the facts by restoring them to where they "actually belong" is vain' (64). 'We cannot say what reality is, only what it seems like to us' (ibid.). If there can be a non-mythic state, there can be no non-metaphorical state of language. So there is no other issue than to 'replace the masks,' but to do so consciously. We will not say 'non fingo hypotheses' but 'I feign hypotheses.' In brief, critical consciousness of the distinction between use and abuse leads not to disuse but to re-use of metaphors, in the endless search for other metaphors, namely a metaphor that would be the best one possible.

The limitations of Turbayne's thesis have to do with the specificity of his examples, which concern precisely that which is least transposible from models to metaphor.

In the first place, the author installs himself in an order of reality homogeneous with that of the positivism criticized by his thesis. The concern is always with 'facts' and therefore also with truth in a verificationist sense, and this is not fundamentally altered. There is no escaping this ultimately neo-empiricist character of the thesis, if we consider that the examples of model-metaphors are borrowed not from restricted areas of physics but from the order of meta-scientific world views, where the border between model and scientific myth tends to be erased, as we know since the *Timaeus* of Plato. The mechanicism of Descartes and that of Newton are cosmological hypotheses that are universal in character. The question is precisely whether poetic language does not break through to a pre-scientific, ante-predicative level, where the very notions of fact, object, reality, and truth, as delimited by epistemology, are *called into question* by this very means of the vacillation of literal reference.

Furthermore, the author speaks of a mastery of models that is not to be found in poetic experience, where something other than the poet speaks even as he speaks, and where, beyond the control of the poet, a reality comes to language. Turbayne's metaphor still belongs to the order of the manipulable. It is something we choose to use, to not use, to re-use. This power to decide, coextensive with the absolute hold of the 'as if,' is without analogue on the side of poetic experience, in which imagination is 'bound' (according to the description by Marcus Hester). It is difficult to harmonize this experience of being seized, instead of seizing, with the deliberate mastery of the 'as if.' The problem afflicting Turbayne is that of demythologized myth: does it still have its power as speech? Is there something like metaphor-faith beyond demythologization? A second *naïveté* beyond iconoclasm? The question requires different replies for epistemology and for poetry. A lucid, mastered, concerted employment of models may be conceivable, even though it seems difficult to maintain the ontological abstinence of the 'as if' without believing in the descriptive and representative value of the model. The experience of creation in poetry seems truly to ignore the lucidity required for any philosophy of the 'as if.'

These two limits appear truly to be related. The kind of vision that, *a parte rei*, penetrates beyond 'facts' dissected by methodology, and the kind of self-implication that, *a parte subjecti*, escapes the vigilance of the 'as if,' together designate the two faces of an experience of creation in which the creative dimension of language is consonant with the creative aspects of reality itself. Can one create metaphors without believing them and without believing that, in a certain way, 'that is'? So it is the relationship itself, and not just its extremes, that is at issue: it is still the correspondence concept of truth that rules between the 'as if' of self-conscious hypothesis and the facts 'as they seem to us.' It is only modulated by the 'as if,' without being altered in its basic definition.

(c) My twofold critique of Wheelwright and Turbayne is very close to that of Douglas Berggren in 'The Use and Abuse of Metaphor,' to which my own owes a great deal. No other author to my knowledge has gone as far in the direction of the concept of metaphorical truth. Not content, indeed, with recapitulating the principal theses of the theory of tension, Berggren tries to arbitrate (as I do too) between ontological *naïveté* and the critique of mythified metaphor. Thus he carries the tensional theory of the internal semantics of the statement forward to the subject of truth and dares to speak of the tension between metaphorical truth and literal truth (245). Earlier I used his combined analysis of 'poetic schemata' and 'poetic textures,' the first offering the portrait of interior life and the second the physiognomy of the world. What I did not say then is that for Berggren, these tensions affect not only the meaning but also the truth-value of poetic assertions concerning 'inner life' schematized in this way, and concerning 'textural reality.' Poets themselves, he says, 'often seem to think that they are making what are in some sense true assertions' (249). In which sense? Wheelwright is not wrong to speak of 'presential reality,' but he neglects to distinguish poetic truth from mythic absurdity. He who does so much to have the 'tensional' character of language recognized misses the 'tensional' character of truth, by simply substituting one notion of truth for another; accordingly, he goes over to the side of abuse by approximating poetic textures simply to primitive animism.

But the poet himself does not commit this error; he 'preserves the ordinary differences between the principal and subsidiary subjects of his metaphors, even while such referents are also being transformed by the process of metaphorical construing' (252). Again, 'unlike the child and the primitive native, the poet does not mythically confuse the textural feel-of-things with actual things-of-feeling' (255). 'It is only by the use of textural metaphor that the poetic feel-of-things can in a sense be liberated from prosaic things-of-feeling, or be properly discussed' (ibid.). This is why the phenomenological objectivity of what commonly is called emotion or feeling is inseparable from the tensional structure of the truth of metaphorical statements that express the construction of the world by and with feeling. The possibility of textural reality is correlative to the possibility of a metaphorical truth of poetic schemata; the possibility of one is established at the same time as that of the other (257).

And so the convergence of the two internal critiques, that of ontological *naïveté* and that of demythologization, culminates in a reiteration of the thesis of the 'tensional' character of metaphorical truth and of the 'is' that carries affirmation. I do not say that this twofold critique proves the thesis. The internal critique only helps us recognize the assumptions and commitments of one who speaks and uses the verb *to be* metaphorically. At the same time, it underlines the inescapably paradoxical character surrounding a metaphorical concept of truth. The paradox consists in the fact there there is no other way to do justice to the notion of metaphorical truth than to include the critical incision of the (literal) 'is not' within the ontological vehemence of the (metaphorical) 'is.' In doing so, the thesis merely draws the most extreme consequence of the theory of tension. In the same way that logical distance is preserved in metaphorical proximity, and in the same way as the impossible literal interpretation is not simply abolished by the metaphorical interpretation but submits to it while resisting, so the ontological affirmation obeys the principle of tension and the law of 'stereoscopic vision.'[56] It is this tensional constitution of the verb *to be* that receives its grammatical mark in the 'to be like' of metaphor elaborated into simile, at the same time as the tension between *same* and *other* is marked in the relational copula.

Now, what are the repercussions of such a concept of metaphorical truth on the very definition of reality? This question, constituting the ultimate horizon of the present Study, will be the object of the next inquiry. For it falls to speculative discourse to articulate, with its own resources, what is assumed spontaneously by the storyteller who, according to Roman Jakobson,[57] 'marks' the poetic intention of his tales by saying 'Aixo era y no era.'

Metaphor and philosophical discourse

For Jean Ladrière

The final Study in this collection sets out to explore the philosophical confines of an investigation that, in its passage to the plane of hermeneutics, has seen its centre of gravity shift from rhetoric to semantics and from problems of sense to problems of reference. The last shift involved, in the form of postulates, a certain number of philosophical presuppositions. Now, no discourse can claim to be free of presuppositions for the simple reason that the conceptual operation by which a region of thought is thematized brings operative concepts into play, which cannot themselves be thematized at the same time. No discourse can be radically stripped of presuppositions; nevertheless, no thinker is dispensed from clarifying his presuppositions as far as he is able. We began to do this at the beginning of the preceding Study, when we put forward the semantic and the hermeneutic postulates functioning in the theory of metaphorical reference. At the end of the same Study, these postulates justified our carrying the ontological aim of metaphorical utterance back to the copula, understood in the sense of *being-as*. These postulates have still to be thematized in themselves. The question, therefore, is this: *what* philosophy is *implied* in the movement that carries the investigation from rhetoric to semantics and from sense towards reference? The question appears simple; actually it is twofold. We are asking, in fact, both whether a philosophy is *implied* – and *which one*. The strategy of the present Study will be to pursue our inquiry into both questions simultaneously. The question of the *ontology* to be made explicit will accompany the question of the *implication* at work in the interplay of implicit and explicit.

The second question, more deeply hidden from us, requires a global decision concerning the collective unity of modes of discourse as modes of use, such as poetic discourse, scientific discourse, religious discourse, speculative discourse, and so on. Taking the notion of discursiveness as such as our theme, I should like to plead for a relative pluralism of forms and levels of discourse. Without going as far as the notion, suggested by Wittgenstein, of a radical heterogeneity of language games – which would exclude the very cases of interaction with which the closing part of this Study will be concerned – it is important to recognize 'in principle the *discontinuity* that assures the autonomy of speculative discourse.

It is only on the basis of this difference in discourse, established by the philosophical act as such, that we can elaborate the modalities of interaction or, more precisely, of interanimation between modes of discourse required for the task of making explicit the ontology that underlies our investigation.

The first three sections argue for discontinuity between speculative discourse and poetic discourse, and are a refutation of some of the ways in which, in our opinion, the implication binding metaphorical and speculative discourse is misunderstood.

(1) A philosophy could be said to be *brought about* by metaphorical functioning, if one could show that it simply reproduced the semantic workings of poetic discourse on the speculative plane. We shall take as our touchstone the Aristotelian doctrine of the analogical unity of the multiple meanings of being, ancestor of the medieval doctrine of the analogy of being. Aristotle's doctrine will provide the occasion for showing that there is no direct passage from the semantic functioning of metaphorical expression to the transcendental doctrine of analogy. On the contrary, the latter furnishes a particularly striking example of the autonomy of philosophical discourse.

(2) If categorial discourse leaves no place for any transition from poetic metaphor to transcendental equivocalness, is it the union of philosophy and theology in a composite discourse that creates the conditions for a confusion between analogy and metaphor, and therefore the conditions for an implication that would be only a *subreption*, to borrow Kant's expression? The Thomist doctrine of the analogy of being is an excellent counter-example for our thesis of the discontinuity of modes of discourse. If it can be shown that the composite discourse of onto-theology allows no confusion with poetic discourse, the way is opened for an examination of figures of intersection that presuppose the difference in modes of discourse, primarily a difference between the speculative mode and the poetic mode.

(3) A completely different – even inverse – manner of involving philosophy in the theory of metaphor must also be considered. It is the inverse of that investigated in the two earlier sections in so far as it establishes philosophical presuppositions at the very source of the distinctions that make a discourse on metaphor possible. This hypothesis does more than reverse the order of priority between metaphor and philosophy: it reverses the

pattern of philosophical argumentation. Our earlier discussion will be seen to have been situated at the level of the stated intentions of speculative – even onto-theological – discourse, and thus to have had at issue only the order of its argumentation. For another 'reading,' it is the undeclared movement of philosophy and the unseen play of metaphor that are in complicity. Instructed by Heidegger's assertion that '*the metaphorical exists only inside the metaphysical,*' we shall take Jacques Derrida's essay 'White Mythology' as our guide in this 'second navigation.' This is indeed a second navigation: the pivotal point of the discussion will shift in fact from living metaphor to *dead metaphor*, metaphor that is not declared but hidden in the 'elevation' of the concept that is expressed as such. Basing my analysis on the preceding Studies, I hope to show that the problematic of the dead metaphor is derivative, and that the required response is to climb back up the slope of this sort of entropy of language by means of a new act of discourse. Only revivifying the semantic aim of metaphorical utterance in this way can recreate the conditions that will permit a confrontation that is itself enlivening between the modes of discourse fully recognized in their difference.

(4) It is to this interanimation of philosophical and poetic discourse that I should like to contribute in the two final stages of this investigation. Taking first the perspective of the phenomenology of semantic aims, I shall attempt to show that the possibility of speculative discourse lies in the semantic dynamism of metaphorical expression, and yet that speculative discourse can respond to the semantic potentialities of metaphor only by providing it with the resources of a domain of articulation that properly belongs to speculative discourse by reason of its very constitution.

(5) We can hope to clarify the postulates of reference assumed in Study 7 only through a labour of speculative discourse turned back upon itself and spurred on by metaphorical utterance. I shall try to say in what way the concepts of truth and reality, and ultimately the concept of being, have to be reworked in order to respond to the semantic claim of metaphorical utterance.

1 / METAPHOR AND THE EQUIVOCALNESS OF BEING: ARISTOTLE

The first *counter-example* opposing our initial hypothesis – that philosophical and poetic discourse are different – is provided by the type of speculation that Aristotle was the first to apply to the anological unity of the multiple meanings of being. The question can be put this way: whenever philosophy tries to introduce an intermediate modality between *univocity* and *equivocalness*, is speculative discourse not forced to reproduce, on its own level, the semantic functioning of poetic discourse? If this were the case, speculative discourse would be brought about or *induced* in some way by poetic discourse. The very vocabulary used supports the hypothesis of an initial confusion of kinds. The word *analogy* seems to belong to both discourses. In poetics, analogy in the sense of 'proportion' is at the root of the fourth class of metaphor, which Aristotle termed metaphor 'by analogy' (or, in some translations, 'proportional' metaphor). To this day, some theorists do not hesitate to subsume metaphor and simile under the generic term of analogy, or to place the family of metaphor under this common heading. In philosophy, this same word is at the centre of a certain discourse that claims its source in Aristotle and continues through the neo-Thomists.

I should like to show that, contrary to appearances, the intellectual labour that later crystallized in the concept of the analogy of being stems from an initial divergence between speculative and poetic discourse. I shall reserve for the second stage of the discussion the question whether it was possible to preserve this initial difference in the mixed forms to which discourse on God gave rise in philosophy and theology.

It is necessary therefore to begin at the greatest point of divergence between philosophy and poetry, the position established by Aristotle in the treatise on the *Categories* and in books Γ, E, Z, and Λ of the *Metaphysics*.

The *Categories*, in which the term *analogy* does not actually appear, produces a non-poetic model of equivocalness and thus suggests the necessary conditions for a non-metaphorical theory of analogy. Since Aristotle, through the neo-Platonists and the Arab and Christian medieval philosophers, down to Kant, Hegel, Renouvier, and Hamelin, this act of ordering that the *Categories* represents has remained the perennial signal task of speculative discourse. But the *Categories* raises its question of the connection between the meanings of being only because the *Metaphysics* poses the question that breaks with poetic discourse just as with ordinary discourse – what is being?

This question is entirely outside the bounds of all language games. For this reason, when the philosopher is confronted by the paradox that 'being is said in several ways' and when, in order to rescue the diverse meanings of being from dispersal, he establishes between them a relation of reference to a first term that is neither the univocity of a genus nor the mere chance equivocalness of a simple word, the plurivocity that is thus brought to philosophical discourse is of a different order than the multiplicity of meaning produced by metaphorical utterance. It is a plurivocity of the same order as the very question that opened up the speculative field. The first term – *ousia* – places all the other terms in the realm of meaning outlined by the question: what is being? For the moment, it is of little importance whether these other terms are in a relation to the first term that could, justly or not, be called analogy. What is important is that a connection be identified among the multiple meanings of being, one which, though not proceeding from the division of a genus into species, nevertheless constitutes an order. This order is an order of categories, to the extent that it is the necessary condition for the ordered extension of the sphere of attribution. The regulated polysemy of being orders the apparently disordered polysemy of the predicative function as such. In the same way that categories other than substance can be 'predicated' of substance and thus add to the first meaning of being, so too, for every given being, the sphere of predication presents the same concentric structure extending progressively farther from a 'substantial' centre, and the same expansion of meaning through the addition of determinations. This ordered process has nothing in common with metaphor, not even with analogical metaphor. The ordered equivocalness of being and poetic equivocalness move on radically distinct levels. Philosophical discourse sets itself up as the vigilant watchman overseeing the ordered extensions of meaning; against this background, the unfettered extensions of meaning in poetic discourse spring free.

The lack of a common point of contact between the ordered equivocalness of being and poetic metaphor is attested to indirectly by the charge Aristotle levelled at Plato. Ordered equivocalness is to be substituted for Platonic participation, which is only metaphorical: 'And to say that [the Forms] are patterns and the other things share in them is to use empty words and poetical metaphors' (*Metaphysics* A 9, 991 a 19-22). Thus philosophy must neither use metaphors nor speak poetically, not even when it deals with the equivocal meanings of being. But can it help doing what it must not do?

It has been argued that the Aristotelian treatise on the *Categories* forms a self-contained position only to the extent that it is supported by a concept of analogy that is itself compelled to draw its logical force from a domain other than the speculative order. But it can be shown that these objections prove at most that the *Categories* should be reworked, doubtless on a basis other than that of analogy; however, they do not prove that the semantic aim guiding the treatise is borrowed from a field other than the speculative.

First, one may object that the alleged categories of thought are only categories of language in disguise. This is the contention of E. Benveniste.[1] Beginning with the general claim that 'linguistic form is not only the condition for transmissibility, but first of all the condition for the realization of thought' (56), the author attempts to demonstrate that Aristotle, 'reasoning in the absolute, is simply identifying certain fundamental categories of the language in which he thought' (57).[2]

The correlation established by Benveniste is irrefutable as long as one is considering only the passage from Aristotle's categories as enumerated by him to the categories of language. But what about the inverse path? For Benveniste, the entire table of the categories of thought is merely 'transposed from categories of language' (61), 'the conceptual projection of a given linguistic state' (ibid.). As for the notion of *being* 'which envelops everything,' this concept 'reflects' (ibid.) the wealth of uses of the verb *to be*.

Evoking 'the magnificent images of the poem of Parmenides as well as the dialectic of *The Sophist*' (61), however, the linguist is forced to concede that 'the language did not, of course, give direction to metaphysical definition of "being" – each Greek thinker has his own – but it made it possible to set up "being" as an objectifiable notion that philosophical thought could handle, analyze and define just as any other concept' (62). And again: 'All we wish to show here is that the linguistic structure of Greek predisposed the notion of "being" to a philosophical vocation' (63).

The problem is then to understand what principle of philosophical thought, applied to grammatical being, produces the series of meanings of the term *to be*. Between what would be merely a list and what would be a deduction in the Kantian sense, there is room for an ordering, which in the post-Aristotelian tradition – and even in a few rare suggestions by Aristotle himself – came to be thought of as analogy.

Jules Vuillemin demonstrates in the second study of his work *De la logique à la théologie: Cinq études sur Aristote*[3] that the Aristotelian treatise on the *Categories* has a logical construction and that in grasping this, 'one will perhaps find the thread of Aristotelian deduction, which up to now seems to have escaped analysis' (77).

It is not without importance that the treatise on the *Categories* begins with a semantic distinction that, instead of marking a dichotomy, makes room for a third class. In addition to things that have only the name (*onoma*) in common but not the notion (*logos*), which Aristotle calls homonyms, and those that share both a common name and a notional identity – synonyms – there are also paronyms, that is, those things that derive their name from some other name, but differ from it in termination (*ptôsis*). Thus the grammarian derives his name from the word *grammar*, and the courageous man from the word *courage* (*Categories* 1 a 12-15). Here for the first time an intermediate class is inserted between homonymous and synonymous items, and consequently between expressions that are merely equivocal and expressions that are absolutely univocal. The entire following analysis will attempt to widen the gap opened up by paronyms in the solid front of equivocalness and to lift the general ban on equivocalness laid by one of Aristotle's own theses, namely that 'to mean more than one thing is to mean nothing at all.'

There would be no point to this distinction, which still refers to things named and not directly to meanings, if it did not shed light on the formal organization of the table of categories. In fact, the decisive distinction, introduced in the second paragraph of the treatise, is the one that opposes and combines two senses of the copula is: namely, *being-said of* (thus man, secondary substance, is said of Socrates, primary substance) and *being-in* (for example, musician, accident of the substance Socrates). This key distinction, around which the rest of the treatise is organized, makes the distinction between synonyms and paronyms functional: only the relation *said-of* allows synonymous attribution (the particular man is identically man).[4]

We said above that the two senses of the copula involved in the relations *being-said-of* and *being-in* are both opposed and combined. Indeed, by arranging these two features in a table noting absence and presence, one can derive four classes of substantives, two concrete (Socrates, man) and two abstract (a certain white, science). Aristotelian morphology is thus based on the intersection of two fundamental oppositions: the opposition of particular to general, which permits predication in the strict sense (*being-said of*) and that of concrete to abstract (which permits predication in the broad sense). The first opposition, understood in the realist sense, founds the irreducible obscurity of the copula, bound to the materiality of individual substances (with the exception of separate beings). The second opposition, understood in a conceptualist sense, replaces the alleged participation of Platonic ideas, which Aristotle denounced as simply metaphorical. The abstract is in the concrete potentially; its inherence too is tied to the obscure ground of individual substances.

How does analogy enter into this, if not explicitly (since the word is never mentioned), at least implicitly? Its avenue is this, that as the modalities of the copula become more varied, they progressively weaken the sense of the copula in the passage from primordial, essential predication – which alone is held to have a synonymous sense – towards derived, accidental predication.[5] A correlation suggests itself, therefore, between the distinction made in the *Categories* on the level of morphology and predication, and the great passage of *Metaphysics* Γ on the reference of all categories to a first term, texts read by medieval thinkers within the framework of the analogy of being. This correlation is set forth in *Metaphysics* Z, the text *par excellence* on substance, which explicitly relates the various forms of predication – and hence the categories – to possible equivocation in regard to the first category, *ousia*.[6] But it is because 'predication can be interpreted neither as the relation of element to set nor as the relation of part to whole' that it remains 'an ultimate intuitive given, whose meaning moves from inherence to proportion and from proportion to proportionality.'[7] It is this outcome that we shall consider later when we examine the passage from the analogy of proportion to the analogy of attribution, which is achieved explicitly only with medieval philosophers.

Before this, however, it is important to show that within the limits traced by the distinction made in paragraph two of the *Categories*, the subsequent series of categories is constructed soundly (in paragraphs three to nine of this work) on the basis of a non-linguistic model. The text Z 4, referred to earlier, offers a key: 'For it must be either by an equivocation that we say [things] *are*, or by adding to and taking from the meaning of "are."' Substance, the primary category, is circumscribed by a set of criteria resulting from prolonged thought on the conditions of predication. A comparative study of the *Categories* and *Metaphysics* Z 3 renders no less than seven. Three are properly logical criteria of predication: as primary substance, it is not said-of and is not in; as secondary substance, it is the subject of synonymous and primordial attribution. Four are ontological criteria. Three of these are secondary – substance is a determined 'this,' it has no contrary, it does not involve degree. The last is essential: substance is capable of receiving contraries. On this foundation, the organization of Aristotle's *Categories* proceeds by weakening the criteria, as the deduction moves from that which resembles substance most to that which resembles it least.[8]

The entire problem of analogy (but not the word itself!) is contained *in nuce* in this derivation by means of diminishing criteria. Essence, taken as the first term in Z 4, is imparted by degrees to all the categories: 'Essence will belong, just as "what a thing is" does, primarily and in the simple sense to substance, and in a secondary way to the other categories also – not essence in the simple sense, but the essence of a quality or of a quantity' (*Metaphysics* Z 4, 1030 a 29-31; then follows the passage cited above, that opposes to mere homonymy the process of adding or subtracting various qualifications from being). This transcendental mode of predication can indeed be called paronym, by reason of its parallelism with *Categories* 1, and analogy, at least implicitly.[9] Analogy designates virtually this progressive weakening of the precision of the predicative function as one moves from primordial predication to derived predication and from essential predication to accidental predication (which is paronymous).[10]

What will later be termed analogy of attribution is precisely this relation of progressively extended derivation, which Aristotle bounds on one side by essential predication – which alone provides the exact or approximate forms of proportionality and for which, we shall see, Aristotle reserves the term *analogy* – and on the other side by homonymy pure and simple or equivocity.

It was therefore of critical importance to show that the tripartite division – homonym, synonym, paronym – did indeed mark the opening of the treatise, thereby providing an introduction to the problem of analogy.[11]

Yet Aristotle does not call analogy what we have just termed a relation of progressively extended derivation. What is more, if the table of categories formed 'by adding to and taking from the meaning of "are"'' does permit us to order the series of allegedly given terms, it does not show us why there must be other terms than the first nor why they are as they are. If we reread the canonical text of Γ 2,[12] we see that the other categories are so termed with reference 'to one central point (*pros hen*), one definite kind of thing (*kata mian phusin*)' (1003 a 33). But we do not see that the multiple meanings form a system. Aristotle may well declare that the lack of notional unity does not prevent there being a *single* science of the multiple senses of being. He may well affirm that terms that 'are related to one common nature' give rise to a *single* science, for 'even these in a sense have one common notion' (Γ 2, 1003 b 14). For, in this case, 'science deals chiefly with that which is primary, and on which the other things depend, and in virtue of which they get their names' (Γ 2, 1003 b 16-18). These statements do not prevent this enigmatic relation of dependence from being merely alleged, nor what Aristotle offers as a solution from being perhaps just a problem hypostatized in the form of a reply.

It might perhaps be a wise step, at this point in our study, to ignore the medieval interpretation and draw all we can from the fact that Aristotle did not call this *ad unum* reference 'analogy,' in order to lay bare what is thought under this term. An 'aporetic' reading of Aristotle, like that proposed by Pierre Aubenque,[13] combined with the logical and mathematical reading of Jules Vuillemin, permits us to isolate the operation by which medieval scholars, following a suggestion they found in other Aristotelian texts on analogy, tried to lessen the aporia of the 'many meanings of being.' From the perspective of my own inquiry into the heterogeneity of discourses in general and into the irreducibility of transcendental or speculative discourse to poetic discourse in particular, the aporetic interpretation applied to Aristotle's ontological discourse attests better than the medieval interpretation to the radical nature of the question, which for lack of a response is thus better exposed as a question.

Vuillemin has stated that primary attribution – that of a secondary substance to a primary substance – since it cannot be interpreted as the relation of element to set or as the relation of part to whole, is therefore 'an ultimate intuitive given, the meaning of which moves from inherence to proportion and from proportion to proportionality' (229). It is thus the very opacity of primary attribution that suggests analogy. For Aubenque, it is the absence of a generic unity – the sole support of Aristotelian science – and the resulting impossibility of generating categories other than *ousia*, which prevent attributing any determined meaning to *ad unum* reference. Discourse on being is the site henceforth of an unending investigation. Ontology continues to be the 'sought after science.'

Whatever the status of the arguments that finally develop all the reasons, well known from Aristotle, for which being is not a genus, and adding as well those reasons of which Kant made us aware, which determine that the table of categories cannot form a system but remains in a state of 'rhapsody';[14] it nonetheless remains that the aporia in question, if indeed this is an aporia, results from an aim, a requirement, an exigency, the original character of which ought to be recognized. It is because ontology aims at a non-generic science of being that even its failure is specifically its own. To develop the aporia – *diaporein* – as Aubenque wishes to do (221) is not to say nothing. For the effort that fails displays a particular structure, circumscribed by the very expression *pros hen, ad unum*. Something is required by the declaration even when it is put in the form of an aporia: 'But everywhere science deals chiefly with that which is primary, and on which the other things depend, and in virtue of which they get their names' (*Metaphysics* Γ 2, 1003 b 16). And a bit further: 'Therefore, since there are many senses in which a thing is said to be one, these terms also will have many senses, but yet it belongs to one science to know them all; for a term belongs to different sciences not if it has different senses, but if it has no one meaning *and* its definitions cannot be referred to one central meaning' (ibid. 1004 a 22-5). The search for this unity cannot be totally in vain for the very reason that the *pros hen* constitutes, 'in a certain sense,' one common notion, one definite kind of thing. If the science sought after were not structured in this way by the very form of the question, one could not even oppose, as Aubenque does, the reality of the failure to the 'ideal' of the investigation (240), or the actual analysis to the 'program.' The very disproportion between the analysis and its ideal attests to the semantic aim of this project, and it is on the basis of this aim that one could begin to look for something like a non-generic unity of being.

In this respect, the *rapprochement* between ontology and dialectic, which the aporetic character of the doctrine of being seems to impose (Aubenque 251-302), cannot, in the author's own opinion, be pursued very far. Between dialectic and ontology, the 'difference in intention' (301) is complete: 'Dialectic provides us with a universal technique of questioning, without concern for man's ability to answer; but man would not pose questions if he had no hope of answering them ... For this reason, the absence of prospective resolution required by the neutral character of the art of the dialectic is one thing; the actual incompletion of a project that by definition includes the very prospect of its accomplishment is something else again' (302).

One can pursue this point even further in an effort to understand the internal reasons why analogy presented itself as the solution to the central aporia of ontological discourse. If it is true, as Aubenque maintains, that this discourse receives its 'prospect,' its 'ideal,' and its 'program' from outside, namely from the theology inherited from Plato, it becomes even more urgent for ontology to reply to this external appeal with its own resources.

I am all the more willing to delve into this problem of the encounter between theological and ontological discourse, which Aubenque opposes to the hypothesis of a simple chronological succession between two states of Aristotle's system (an hypothesis first presented, as we know, by Werner Jaeger), as I find in it a compelling illustration of my own thesis regarding the plurality of spheres of discourse and the fecundity of the intersection of their semantic aims.

Let us therefore grant that what feeds the problematic of unity are properly theological considerations applied to 'separate realities' – the supralunar astral order, unmoved mover, thought of thought. It becomes all the more urgent to know how ontology responds to this appeal. At the same time, the encounter, in Aristotle, between an ontological problem of unity coming from a dialogue with sophistry and a theological problem of separation coming from a dialogue with Platonism provides a sort of paradigmatic example of the attraction between different spheres of discourse.[15]

It is therefore of little consequence that Aubenque exaggerates the heterogeneity of theological and ontological discourse and that he over-dramatizes the encounter between an 'impossible ontology,' one lacking a conceivable unity among the categories, and a 'useless theology' (331) lacking a fixed relation between the God who reflects upon himself and the world he ignores. On the contrary, by transforming once again into an aporia Aristotle's thesis in *Metaphysics* E 1 that the science of immovable substance is universal because it is primary, Aubenque makes problematical just what is at issue, namely the new semantic aim resulting from the encounter between the two orders of discourse.[16]

A new conceptual problem must be worked out, arising from the very interference between theology – even astral theology – which envisions not a hidden God, but a God presented as far away in astral contemplation, and our human discourse on being in the diversity of its categorial acceptations.[17]

Even if the conciliation proposed in E 1 – theology is 'universal ... because it is first' – is only the hypostasis of a problem in search of a solution, it remains that the denounced heterogeneity of ontological discourse on the multiple meanings of being and theological discourse on 'separate' being must not amount to total incommunicability between spheres of meaning. This would endanger the possibility of conceiving the interference required by the very thesis that aporetic ontology takes its perspective from unitary theology. I should even be tempted to see, in these arguments that tend to make this interference unintelligible at the very moment it is alleged, the profound reason that led Aristotle's successors, and perhaps even Aristotle himself, to appeal to analogy.

Let us consider these arguments. The divine, it is stated, being indivisible, cannot receive attribution and can give rise only to negations. In turn, the diversity of the significations of being can apply only to physical things, in which it is possible to distinguish substance, quality, quantity, etc. In the final analysis, motion is the difference making the unity of being impossible in principle, and is the reason why the division into essence and accident applies to being. In short, it is because of motion that ontology is not a theology but a dialectic of division and finitude (442). Wherever something is in a state of becoming, predication is possible: predication is based on physical dissociation introduced by motion. But if this is the final word, how can one speak of an interference between ontology and theology? One can indeed criticize the failure of this endeavour. But this is not the question here. We have still to think through the very topic that Aristotle assigned himself, that of conceiving the horizontal unity of the meanings of being together with the vertical unity of beings.[18]

Now, Aristotle indicated the point where the two problematics intersect. It is *ousia*, the first category in attributive discourse and the sole sense of divine being.[19] Beyond this point, the two discourses separate, since nothing can be said concerning a being that is *ousia* alone, and since, in regard to beings that are *ousia* and something else also, the unity of meaning is dispersed. In any case, the divergence between the impossible discourse of ontology and the futile discourse of theology, the twinning of tautology and circumlocution, of empty universality and limited generalization – all proceed from a common centre, *ousia*, which, in Aubenque's words, 'will signify nothing other than the act of that which is, the completion of what is given in the fulfilment of presence, or, to use a word we have encountered before, *entelechy*' (406). Ontology may indeed be only the human substitute for a theology that remains impossible for us; *ousia* is still the crossroads where these avenues meet.

If the two discourses thus intersect at a point at once common to both and localizable in each of them, should not the 'sought after' science, drawing upon its own resources, respond to the proposal of unity made by the other discourse? Is it not from this internal necessity that the problem of analogy arises? The textual evidence in this regard is *Metaphysics* Λ 5,

1071 a 33-5. It says first that 'the causes of all [things] are the same or analogous.' Secondly, it states that the primacy of divine *ousia* underlies the categorial unity of being: 'The causes of substances may be treated as causes of all things.' The thesis remains unchanged even if one takes the 'as' (*hôs*) in the weak sense of an *as if*.[20] In its third part, the text specifies (further, *eti*) that it is because the final cause is 'first in respect of complete reality (*entelechy*)' that it is 'the cause of all things.'[21]

It is in this way that an *aporetic* reading of Aristotle highlights by contrast the doctrine of analogy, to the very extent that this reading began by bracketing it. Even if one finds this notion to be nothing but a problem hypostatized into a reply, it nevertheless designates the conceptual labour by which the human, the too human, discourse of ontology attempts to respond to the entreaty of *another* discourse, which is itself perhaps only a non-discourse.

A question is in fact raised by the concept of reference *ad unum*. If there is no generic commonality among the many meanings of being, what can be the nature of the 'common notion' suggested by Aristotle in *Metaphysics* Γ 2, 1003 b 14? Can there exist a non-generic commonality to rescue the discourse on being from its aporetic state?

The concept of analogy, evoked at least once in this context by Aristotle, intervenes at this point. The problem it raises here is the result of a second-order reflection on the *Categories*. It arises from the question of whether, and to what extent, reference to a first term is itself a *conceivable* relation. We have seen how this order of derivation can be produced by reflecting on the conditions of predication. We must now ask what sort of relation is generated in this way. Here the mathematical notion of analogy of proportion provides a means of comparison. Its origin guarantees its scientific status. By the same token, one can understand the approximation of the relation *ad unum* and proportional analogy as an effort to extend to the transcendental relation the benefit of the scientific character that belongs to the analogy of proportion.

I am all the more disposed to recognize the heterogeneous character of this *rapprochement* in that the earlier analysis of the points of interference of theological and ontological discourse has prepared us to pose the problem of analogy in terms of the intersection of discourses. Indeed, application of the concept of analogy to the series of meanings of being is itself also an instance of the intersection of spheres of discourse. And this intersection can be understood without reference to theological discourse, even if theological discourse will employ analogy later on in an effort to annex ontological discourse – at the price, however, of greatly altering this concept.

In Aristotle, certainly, the pure concept of analogy has nothing to do with the question of categories. It is due to a shift in meaning that weakens the original criteria that this concept is joined to the theory of categories and that a tangential relation in Aristotle is turned into a clear intersection in medieval philosophers.

It is this conceptual exercise more than its admittedly disappointing results that is of interest here. Contemporary logicians and philosophers may be justified in claiming that this effort has failed and that the theory of analogy is nothing but a pseudo-science. It can even be stated that this pseudo-scientific character extends to the theological use of analogy as well, and that this in turn reflects upon the initial transcendental structure, enclosing onto-theology in a vicious circle. To my mind, this is not what is important. My express purpose is to show how, by entering the sphere of the problematic of being, analogy at once retains its own conceptual structure and receives a transcendental aspect from the field to which it is applied. Indeed, to the extent that it is marked by the domain in which it intervenes in its own distinct way, the concept of analogy assumes a transcendental function. By the same token, it never returns to poetry, but retains in regard to poetry the mark of the original divergence produced by the question, what is being? In what follows, we shall show that this inclination towards divergence is in no way weakened by the theological use of analogy. The rejection of metaphor as an improper analogy will attest to this.

It is not unimportant that the mathematical notion of analogy – far from being self-evident as a summary definition might lead one to believe (A is to B as C is to D) – crystallizes a prolonged exercise of thought. Its final definition expresses the solution to a paradox, namely how to 'master the "impossible relationships" between certain geometric dimensions and whole numbers, by reducing them indirectly to consideration of relations of wholes alone, or, more precisely, to inequalities of size.'[22]

Could one not say that it is the conceptual labour incorporated in the definition, rather than its result, that was taken as a model for philosophical thought? Here again, extension from a radically non-poetic pole occurs through the weakening of criteria.

The closest application is provided by the definition of distributive justice in the *Nicomachean Ethics* 5:3. The definition rests on the idea that this virtue implies four terms, two persons (equal or unequal) and two shares (advantages and disadvantages in the realms of honour or wealth); and that it establishes proportional equality in distribution between these four terms. But the application here of the idea of number, proposed by Aristotle,[23] concerns extension not of the idea of number to irrationals but of proportion to non-homogeneous terms, provided that they can be said to be equal or unequal in some particular relation.

In biology, the same formal conception of proportion permits not only classification (by saying, for example, that flying is to wings as swimming is to fins), but also demonstration (e.g., if certain animals have lungs and others do not, the latter possess an organ that takes the place of a lung). By lending themselves to proportional relationships such as these, functions and organs provide the outline of a general biology (*De Part. An.* 1:5).

The relation of analogy begins its migration towards the transcendental sphere when it is charged with expressing the identity of principles and elements that cut through the diversity of genera: thus, it is said, 'as sight is in the body, so is reason in the soul, and so on in other cases' (*Nicomachean Ethics* 1:4, 1096 b 28-9). Analogy still remains, formally, an equality of relations among four terms.[24]

The decisive step, the one that concerns us here, is taken in *Metaphysics* Λ 4 and 5, where analogy is applied to the problem of the identity of principles and elements belonging to different categories.[25] Its formulation certainly still allows an equality or similarity of relations to appear; thus, one can write that privation is to form, on the level of elements, as cold is to heat in sensible bodies, as black is to white in qualities, as darkness is to light in relatives. In this respect, the transition from proportional analogy to reference *ad unum* is more than hinted at in a text from the *Metaphysics*,[26] to which medieval philosophers will return relentlessly. 'Healthy,' Aristotle notes, is said analogously of the cause of health, of a sign of health, and of the healthy subject. 'Medical' is said analogously of the doctor, the scalpel, the operation, and the patient. Analogical extension is governed, then, by the order of the categories.

This formulation, however, cannot hide the fact that the analogy here concerns the categories, the very terms in which 'principles' (form, privation, and matter) come together through analogy. Not only is the number of these terms not specified by the relation itself, but the sense of the relation has changed. What is in question is the manner in which the terms themselves relate to one another, whereas the reference *ad unum* is limited to establishing dominance (the first term) and hierarchy (reference to the first term). This final weakening of the criteria results in a displacement from proportional analogy to the analogy of attribution.[27]

Modern logicians will be more sensitive than were medieval philosophers to the logical break that interrupts the extension of analogy as it moves from mathematics to metaphysics. To logicians, the unscientific features of analogy, taken in its final sense, add up to an argument against analogy.[28] The great text of *Metaphysics* A 9, 992 b 18-24 is turned against the philosopher and becomes the ultimate evidence of the unscientific character of metaphysics.[29]

Aristotle's failure, however, can have two meanings, between which a purely logical analysis cannot choose. According to the first, the transcendental project as such is stripped of all meaning; in line with the second, this project must be taken up again on some basis other than analogy and yet still remain faithful to the semantic aim that presided over the search for a *non-generic unity* for the meanings of being. It is this interpretation that we have tried to develop here, by stressing in each instance the conceptual labour crystallized in the logical result. Because the 'search' for a non-generic bond of being remains a task for thought, even after Aristotle's failure, the problem of a 'guide line' has continued to be raised down to modern philosophy. The reason the *Categories* has proved capable of continual consideration and reworking is that *once* the difference between the analogy of being and poetic metaphor was indeed thought.

In this respect, the first paragraph of the *Categories* remains highly significant. To say that there are not two classes of things to name – synonyms and homonyms – but three classes, with the insertion of paronyms, is to open up a new domain for philosophical discourse based on the existence of *non-accidental homonyms*. From this point on, there is a continuous chain formed from the paronyms in paragraph 1 of the *Categories* to the reference *pros hen, ad unum* in *Metaphysics* Γ 2 and E 1. The new possibility of thought opened up in this way was that of a non-metaphorical and properly transcendental resemblance among the primary significations of being. To say that this resemblance is unscientific settles nothing. It is more important to affirm that because it breaks with poetics, this purely transcendental resemblance even today attests, by its very failure, to the search that animated it – namely, the search for a relation that is still to be thought otherwise than by science, if thinking scientifically means thinking in terms of genus. But the primary task remains to master the difference between transcendental analogy and poetic resemblance. Based on this initial difference, the non-generic bond of being can be – and without a doubt must be – thought according to a model that will no longer owe anything to analogy as such. But this step beyond analogy was possible only because analogy itself had been a step beyond metaphor. It will thus have proved decisive for thought that a segment of equivocalness was wrested *once* from poetry and incorporated into philosophical discourse, just at the time when philosophical discourse was forced to disengage itself from the sway of pure univocity.

2 / METAPHOR AND *ANALOGIA ENTIS*: ONTO-THEOLOGY

The second counter-example that can be opposed to the thesis of the discontinuity between speculative discourse and poetic discourse is much more formidable. It is provided by a mode of discourse that itself is already a *composite* of ontology and theology. Following Heidegger, who himself follows Kant here,[30] we can call it simply *onto-theology*. In fact, the doctrine of *analogia entis* reaches its full development within the bounds of this composite discourse. For our own investigation, therefore, it is important to know if the initial split Aristotle established between speculative discourse and poetic discourse was preserved in the composite discourse of onto-theology.

The Thomist doctrine of analogy provides invaluable testimony in this respect.[31] Its express purpose is to establish theological discourse at the level of science and thereby to free it completely from the poetical forms of religious discourse, even at the price of severing the science of God from biblical hermeneutics.

And yet the problem here is singularly more complex than that of the ordered diversity of the categories of being in Aristotle. It concerns the possibility of speaking rationally of the creative God of the Judeo-Christian tradition. At issue, then, is the possibility of extending to the question of divine names the problematic of analogy to which the equivocal nature of the notion of being gives rise.

The new use of the concept of analogy might appear to be justified by the parallelism between the initial discourse situations. The problem in both cases is, in fact, to maintain a middle course between two impossibilities. For Aristotle, confronting the problem of the unity of the categories of being, the difficulty was to escape the dilemma of the generic unity of being and the pure and simple dispersion of its meanings. Reference to a primary term offered itself as a median solution. Now, theological discourse encounters a similar choice: to impute a discourse common to God and to his creatures would be to destroy divine transcendence;[32] on the other hand, assuming total incommunicability of meanings from one level to the other would condemn one to utter agnosticism.[33] It therefore seemed reasonable to extend the concept of analogy to theology by means of the invention (after Aristotle) of a third modality of attribution – analogous attribution – equidistant from univocal and equivocal attribution.[34] The doctrine of the analogy of being was born of this desire to encompass in a single doctrine the horizontal relation of the categories of substance and the vertical relation of created things to the Creator. This project defines onto-theology.

I shall not try to trace the history of the concept of *analogia entis* here. I only want to reappropriate the semantic aim of the conceptual enterprise which crystallized in the Scholastic debate: and I want to show further that, just when this semantic aim seems alligned completely with that of metaphorical statements (mainly because of a return to a Platonic and neo-Platonic type of participation), instead a new split is forged between speculative and poetic discourse.

What remains remarkable indeed, for us who come after the Kantian critique of this type of ontology, is the way in which the thinker deals with the difficulties inherent in his chosen solution. On the one hand, the Aristotelian solution to the categorial problem is retained in its general outline.[35] On the other hand, its application to the theological domain encounters such enormous obstacles that the very concept of analogy must continuously be redeployed and reshaped into new distinctions. The elaboration of these new distinctions is precisely the conceptual labour whose aim is what we are fundamentally interested in.

The main source of all the difficulties is the need to base analogical predication on an ontology of participation.[36] In fact, analogy functions at the level of names and predicates, and it belongs to the conceptual order. But the condition of the possibility of analogy lies elsewhere, in the very communication of being. Participation is the generic name given to the set of solutions tendered to this problem. To participate means, approximately, to have partially what another possesses or is fully. As a result, the struggle for an adequate concept of participation underpins the struggle for an adequate concept of analogy.[37] But then, is not participation evidence that metaphysics has turned to poetry through its lamentable recourse to metaphor, as Aristotle argues against Platonism?

It is significant, then, that Thomas did not stop with the solution closest to Platonic exemplarism, which was adopted in his *Commentary on Book I of the Sentences* when he was still influenced by Albert the Great. Two modalities were distinguished there. In addition to the order of priority (*per prius et posterius*) found in the series 'being, power and act' or in the series 'being, substance and accident,' it is necessary to conceive of an order of descendance (*a primo ente descendit*) and of imitation (*ens primum imitatur*) where 'one receives from the other *esse* and *rationem*' (Prologue, qu. 1, art. 2). *Distinctio* xxxv specifies (qu. 1, art. 4): 'There is a different analogy [than that of the order of priority] when a term imitates another as far as it can, but does not equal it perfectly, and this is the analogy we find between God and his creatures.' Of course, we must understand the reasons for this recourse to exemplary causality. It allows one to do away with a common term that would precede God and creatures: 'Between God and his creatures, there is no similarity by reason of something held in common but by imitation; whence we say the creature resembles God but not the inverse, as Dionysius says.'[38] So participation through deficient resemblance implies no common form that is possessed unequally. It is God himself who communicates his image. The diminished image ensures an imperfect and inadequate representation of the divine exemplar, halfway between fusion in a single form and radical heterogeneity. But the price to be paid is complete disjunction between attribution of divine names and categorial attribution. Theological discourse loses any basis in the categorial discourse on being.

Thomas did not stop at this solution for two opposing reasons that had to be developed in turn. On the one hand, direct resemblance is a relation still too close to univocity; on the other hand, in its formal character, exemplary causality must be subordinated to efficient causality, which alone founds the communication of being that underlies analogical attribution. The discovery of being as act then becomes the ontological keystone of the theory of analogy.

However, at the time of the *De Veritate*, St Thomas had first to test a distinction between two sorts of analogy, both capable of falling within the Aristotelian *analogia*. The distinction, borrowed from the Latin translation of Euclid (book 5, def. 3 and 5), is that between *proportio* and *proportionalitas*.[39] *Proportio* relates two quantities of the same kind in a direct relation of one to the other, where the value of one by itself determines the value of the other (for example, a number and its double). But St Thomas does not limit this first type of analogy to the order of magnitudes, any more than he will so limit *proportionalitas*. He extends *proportio* to any relation involving a 'determinate distance' (*determinata distancia*) and a strict relationship (*determinata habitudo*). This is why he is able to connect to *proportio* the relation of reference to a first term, as in the example of health, and thus the categorial relation of accidents to substance. What is essential is that the relation be direct and definite. *Proportionalitas*, on the other hand, contains no direct relation between two terms. It merely posits *similitudo proportionum*, a resemblance of relations (for example, 6 is to 3 as 4 is to 2). But just as *proportio* is not only mathematical, so *proportionalitas* posits a similarity of relations between any terms whatever; thus, we can say that the intellect is to the soul as sight is to the body. The advantages for theological discourse are evident. Between the created and God, the distance is indeed infinite: *finiti ad infinitum nulla est proportio*.[40] Now proportional resemblance establishes no determinate relation between the finite and the infinite since it is independent of distance. Yet this does not entail an utter absence of relationship. It is still possible to say: what the finite is to the finite, the infinite is to the infinite. In other words, divine science is to God as human science is to the created.[41]

In this way, exemplary causality, to the extent that it falls under the concept of *proportio*, still implied a relation that was too direct, thereby suppressing the infinite distance that separates beings from God. *Proportionalitas*, on the other hand, does not do justice to the communication of being that we conceive in the notion of creative causality. The formalism of *proportionalitas* impoverishes the abundant and complex network formed by participation, causality, and analogy.

The task is therefore immense. The relation of participation must be conceived in such a way as to imply no earlier term, and so no univocal attribution of perfection to God and to creatures. In addition, *proportio creaturae*, which always exists between the effect and its cause, must be given a sense that would make it compatible with the disproportion between the finite and the infinite.[42] Finally, the distance between the finite and the infinite must be conceived as a simple dis-semblance, without confusing this idea – which alone is essential – with that of a spatial exteriority, which is excluded in any case by the immanence of divine causality.[43]

It is to satisfy all these requirements that being is conceived in the works following the *De Veritate*, and particularly in the two *Summae*, less as form than as act, in the sense of *actus essendi*. Causality is then no longer the resemblance of copy to model but the communication of an act, the act being at once what the effect has in common with the cause and that by reason of which the effect is not identical to the cause.[44]

It is creative causality, therefore, that establishes between beings and God the bond of participation that makes the relation by analogy ontologically possible.

But what sort of analogy? The works subsequent to the *De Veritate* propose a new sort of split within the concept of analogy, a split which does not correspond to the distinction that preceded the *De Veritate*. In fact, the new break does not separate horizontal analogy, which governs the sequence of categories, from vertical analogy, which rules the hierarchy of the divine and the created. Instead, two manners of ordering a diversity are set in opposition, two manners that apply to horizontal and vertical analogy alike. The first analogy, we read in the *De Potentia*, qu. 7, art. 6, is that of two things to a third (*duorum ad tertium*); accordingly, quantity and quality relate to one another in relating to substance. This is not the manner in which God and the created relate to being. The second analogy is that of one thing to another (*unius ad alterum*, or again *ipsorum ad unum*). Accidents relate directly in this manner to substance. This is also the manner in which created being relates to the divine. The analogy goes directly from the set of secondary analogues to the principal analogue, without anything preceding God that might be established as a common genus. At the same time, this relation is capable of proceeding from the most eminent to the less excellent, following an asymmetrical order of perfection. Such is the mode of community half-way between the equivocal and the univocal.[45]

So the two uses of analogy are brought together once again, but at the price of a final correction to its definition.[46]

Yet the new price to be paid is higher than ever. To the very extent that thinking is no longer satisfied with the overly formal relation of *propor-*

tionalitas (now rendered problematic by the extrapolation beyond the sphere of mathematics), thinking is forced to base the diversity of names and concepts upon an ordering principle inherent in being itself and to assign the synthesis of unity and diversity required by discourse to efficient causality itself. In short, even causality has to be thought as analogical.[47] If indeed we can name God on the basis of the creature, it is 'accordingly as there is some relation of the creature to God as to its principle and cause, wherein all the perfections of things pre-exist excellently' (*Summa Theologiae* 1 a, qu. 13, art. 5). Here we see the distinction among univocity, equivocalness, and analogy carried from the level of meanings back to that of efficiency. If causality were single and undivided, it would engender only the same; if it were purely equivocal, the effect would cease to be like its agent. The most heterogeneous cause must therefore remain analogous cause. It is this structure of the real that prevents language in the final analysis from being completely dislocated. The likeness of causality resists the dispersal of logical classes that ultimately would force us to silence. In the interplay of Saying and Being, when Saying is at the point of being forced to silence by the force of the heterogeneity of being and beings, Being itself revives Saying by means of underlying continuities that provide an analogical extension of its meanings to Saying. But, at the same time, analogy and participation are placed in a mirror relationship, conceptual unity and the unity of the real corresponding exactly to one another.[48]

This circle of analogy and participation was forced to give way under a barrage of criticism. Not that the semantic intention animating the search for a continually more adequate concept of analogy was ever called into question. It is at the physical level, at the precise point where equivocal cause lends aid to analogical discourse, that the circular relation was broken by the combined blows of Galilean physics and the Humean critique. After this break, the full consequences of which are drawn out by the Kantian dialectic, the conceptual unity capable of encompassing the ordered diversity of the meanings of being remains to be thought.

Still, the battle for an ever more adequate concept of analogy remains telling on one count: the refusal to compromise in any way with poetic discourse. This refusal is expressed in the care always taken to distinguish between analogy and metaphor. I would call such concern the distinctive feature of the semantic aim of speculative discourse.

Does not the recourse to participation, however, imply a return to metaphor? Does not the passage from the *De Potentia* (qu. 7, art. 6, ad. 7) referred to above say that 'even the participatory form in the creature is inferior to its *ratio*, which is God, as the fire's heat is inferior to heat of the sun by which the sun engenders heat'? And does not the *Summa* say (1 a, qu. 13, art. 5): 'For example, the sun by the exercise of its one power produces manifold and various forms in these sublunary things. In the same way ... all perfections existing in creatures divided and multiplied pre-exist in God unitedly.'

Ah, the sun! Oh, the fire! The heliotrope – which heralds every trope of resemblance – cannot be far away![49]

Now it is precisely at the point of greatest proximity that the line between analogy and metaphor is most firmly drawn. When, in fact, is analogy closest to metaphor? When it is defined as proportionality. And this is precisely what, in turn, 'can happen in two ways' (*dupliciter contingit*) (*De Veritate* qu. 2, art. 11). On the one hand, the attribution is only symbolic; on the other, it is truly transcendental. In symbolic attribution (*quae symbolice de Deo dicuntur*), God is called 'lion,' 'sun,' etc.; in these expressions 'the name implies something belonging to the thing primarily designated,' and with it 'matter that cannot be attributed to God.' On the other hand, only the transcendentals such as 'being,' 'good,' 'true' can be attributed to God, because they 'include no defect nor depend on matter for their act of existence.' For this reason, during the Scholastic period of the analogy of proportionality, analogical attribution is not only opposed to univocal – that is, generic – attribution. It also introduces two splits within the sphere of analogy: a split within the relation of proportion, in so far as this relation still retains some common things that could precede and encompass God and creatures; and a split within symbolism, which assigns something belonging to what is principally signified to the name attributed to God. Such is the asceticism of denomination requiring the exclusion of poetry.

This purism in analogy does not waver when the communication of the act of being restores the ontological continuity that the relation of proportionality threatened to destroy. The question of metaphor is confronted head-on in the *Summa Theologiae* (1 a, qu. 13, art. 6) under the question: 'Whether names predicated of God are predicated primarily of creatures?' The answer distinguishes two orders of priority: a priority according to the thing itself, which begins with what is first in itself, that is, God; and a priority according to signification, which begins with what is best known to us, that is, creatures. The first type of priority governs analogy properly speaking, and the second, metaphor: 'All names applied metaphorically to God are applied to creatures primarily rather than to God, because when said of God they mean only similitudes to such creatures.' Metaphor indeed is based upon 'similarity of proportion'; its structure is the same in poetic and in biblical discourse. The examples given prove this: to call a meadow laughing and God a lion is to use the same sort of transposition – the meadow is pleasing when it is in flower, just as a man is when he laughs. By the same token, 'God manifests strength in His works, as a lion in his.' In both cases the meaning of the names issues from the domain from which they are borrowed. On the other hand, the name is said primarily of God, not of the creature, when we are dealing with names that aim at his essence: thus goodness, wisdom. The split, therefore, does not separate poetry from biblical language, but these two modes of discourse taken together from theological discourse. In theological discourse the order of the thing has precedence over the order of signification.[50]

Thus two predicative modalities intersect. Regarding the specific topic of the prescription of divine names, this intersection illustrates the union of Aristotelian reason with the *intellectus fidei* in the doctrine of St Thomas.[51]

This intersection of two kinds of transference, following the descending order of being and the ascending order of significations, explains the creation of *composite* modalities of discourse in which the meaning effects of proportional metaphor and transcendental analogy are added together. By means of this chiasmus, the speculative verticalizes metaphor, while the poetic dresses speculative analogy in iconic garb. This criss-crossing is especially noticeable whenever St Thomas states the relation of eminence that is both thought as analogy and expressed at the same time as metaphor.[52] This exchange constitutes a new case of intersection between various spheres of discourse. It is not surprising that the word and the meaning of words are found at the point of intersection. Just as the metaphorical process 'focuses' on the word to the extent of giving the impression that the transfer of meaning affects only the signification of names, so it is on a certain feature of the meaning of a word that the interplay between analogy and metaphor is focused. Thus the word *wise* can be applied analogously to God, even though it is not said in a univocal fashion of God and of men, because the signification presents different features in the two uses. In man, wisdom is a perfection 'distinct' from every other; it 'circumscribes' (*circumscribit*) and 'comprehends' (*comprehendit*) the thing signified. In God, wisdom is the same thing as his essence, his power, his being; the term therefore circumscribes nothing but leaves the thing signified 'as uncomprehended (*ut incomprehensam*) and as exceeding the signification of the name (*excedentem nominis significationem*).' Through this excess of meaning, the predicates attributed to God retain their power to signify without introducing any distinctions in God. It is therefore the *res significata* that is in excess in relation to the *nominis significatio*.[53] This splintering of the name and its signification corresponds to the extension of meaning by which words, in metaphorical statements, can satisfy unusual attribution. In this sense, one can speak of an effect of metaphorical meaning within analogy. If, however, this effect of meaning really originates in the predicative operation itself, it is at the level of predication that analogy and metaphor separate and intersect. One rests on the predication of trans-cendental terms, the other on the predication of meanings that carry their material content with them.

Such is the magnificent exercise of thought which preserved the differ-ence between speculative discourse and poetic discourse at the very point of their greatest proximity.

3 / META-PHOR AND META-PHYSICS

The dispute over *analogia entis* does not exhaust the possibilities of ex-change between speculative and poetic discourse. Up until now the discus-sion has involved only the semantic intentions of each type of discourse that are capable of being taken up in reflection, as is witnessed by this ter-minology, of intention or semantic aim, borrowed from Husserlian pheno-menology. It is indeed for a consciousness that means 'to justify itself,' 'to found itself completely,' and hence to hold itself to be 'entirely responsi-ble for itself,' that the reasons invoked by self-conscious thought are equi-valent to real motives.[54]

Now, a 'geneological' manner of questioning philosophers has emerged, thanks principally to Nietzsche, which does not limit itself to collecting declared intentions but holds them in suspicion and seeks the motives and self-interests behind their reasons. An entirely different sort of implication between philosophy and metaphor comes to light, which links them at the level of their hidden presuppositions rather than at the level of their stated intentions.[55] It is not only the order of the terms that is inverted, philo-sophy preceding metaphor; but the mode of implication is itself reversed, the 'un-thought' of philosophy anticipating the 'un-said' of metaphor.

In the introduction I mentioned Heidegger's celebrated saying: 'The metaphorical exists only within the metaphysical.' This saying suggests that the trans-gression of meta-phor and that of meta-physics are but one and the same transfer. Several things are implied here: first, that the onto-logy implicit in the entire rhetorical tradition is that of Western 'meta-physics' of the Platonic or neo-Platonic type, where the soul is transported from the visible world to the invisible world; second, that meta-phorical means transfer from the proper sense to the figurative sense; finally, that both transfers constitute one and the same *Über-tragung*.

How are these assertions arrived at?

In Heidegger himself the context considerably limits the import of this attack on metaphor, so that one may come to the conclusion that the con-stant use Heidegger makes of metaphor is finally more important than what he says in passing against metaphor.

In the first text in which metaphor is expressly mentioned, lesson 6 of *Der Satz vom Grund*,[56] the context is two-fold. The first context is formed by the very framework of the discussion, which refers back to an earlier analysis of the 'principle of sufficient reason,' that of *Vom Wesen des Grundes*. Heidegger notes that one can *see* (*sehen*) a situation clearly and yet not *grasp* (*er-blicken*) what is at issue: 'We see much and we grasp little' (85). This is true in the case of the principle 'Nothing is without a reason.' *Seeing* (*Sicht*) is not of the same order of penetration as insight (*Einblick*). Now, drawing nearer to what can be grasped means hearing (*hören*) more distinctly and retaining in the ear (*in Gehör behalten*) a certain determining emphasis (*Betonung*) (86). This emphasis makes us perceive a harmony (*Einklang*) between 'is' and 'reason,' between *est* and *ratio*. This is then the task: 'Our thought must grasp with insight what has been heard ... thinking is a grasping by the ear that grasps by sight' (86). In other words, 'thinking is a hearing and a seeing' (86).

The first context is thus formed by the network of the terms *seeing, hearing, thinking,* and *harmony*, which underlies thought as it meditates on the connection between *ist* and *Grund* in the formulation of the Principle of Sufficient Reason.

A second context is formed by introducing an interpretation in the form of an objection ('But we are called upon quickly to explain ...'). Someone says: 'Hearing and seeing can only (*nur*) be called thinking in a transposed sense (*übertragenen*) ...' (86). Indeed, in the earlier discussion 'sensible hearing and seeing were taken over and transferred (*hinübergenommen*) to the domain of non-sensible perception, that is thought. Such transference is μεταφέρειν in Greek; a transposition like this is called metaphor in scholarly language' (86-7). This, then, is the objection: 'It is only in a metaphorical, transferred sense that thought may (*darf*) be called a hearing and a grasping by the ear, a looking and a grasping by the sight' (87). But, Heidegger asks, who is saying 'may' here? He who asserts that hearing and seeing in the proper (*eigentlich*) sense are of the ear and the eye. To which the philosopher replies that there is not first sensible seeing and hearing, which would then be transposed to the non-sensible level. Our hearing and our seeing are never a simple reception by the senses. As soon as we call thought a listening and a seeing, we do not mean this only as (*nur als*) metaphorical transposition, 'but rather as (*nämlich als*) a transposition of the allegedly (*vermeintlich*) sensible into the non-sensible' (88).

It is in this twofold context that the equivalence of the two transfers is asserted: metaphysical transfer of the sensible to the non-sensible, metaphorical transfer of the literal to the figurative. The first transfer is determinative (*massgebend*) for Western thought, the second 'gives the standard for our representation of the nature of language' (89). Here, a statement is made in passing, but it is one we shall return to later: 'This is why metaphor is often used as an aid in the analysis of works of poetry and, more generally, of artistic creations' (ibid.). Then comes the saying: 'The metaphorical exists only within the bounds of the metaphysical' (ibid.).

The twofold context of the saying is significant. The first not only imposes an allusive and digressive tone, but also gives a type of example that circumscribes the field of discussion from the very outset. What kind of metaphors are these? As concerns their content, there are no poetic metaphors, just philosophical metaphors. Instead of being presented with a discourse other than his own, a discourse functioning in a manner different from his own, the philosopher straightaway confronts metaphors produced by philosophical discourse itself. In this respect, what Heidegger does when he interprets poets as philosophers is infinitely more important than what he says polemically, not against metaphor, but against a manner of casting metaphors as particular philosophical statements.

The second context reduces still more the eventual impact of a declaration that at first glance seemed quite impressive. Let us suppose an objection: metaphor to our objector not only is not a poem in miniature, but remains a mere transposition of meaning involving isolated words – seeing, hearing, etc. In order to interpret these single-word metaphors, our objector also introduces the twofold distinction of the proper and the figurative, the visible and the invisible. Finally, he asserts the equivalence (*nämlich*) of these two pairs of terms. So the metaphorical becomes 'merely' metaphorical; at the same time, the objection becomes a restriction (*darf*). It is therefore really the objector who comes under the aegis of Platonism, which then suffers Heidegger's wholehearted denunciation.

As far as I am concerned, I see no reason to recognize myself in this objector. The distinction between proper and figurative meaning applied to individual words is an obsolete semantic notion that does not have to be tacked onto metaphysics to be taken to pieces. An improved semantics is sufficient to unseat it as a 'determinative' conception of metaphor. As for its use in the analysis of poetry or of works of art, it is less a matter of metaphorical expression itself than of a very particular style of interpretation, an allegorizing interpretation that does go hand in hand with the 'metaphysical' distinction between the sensible and the non-sensible.

Let us now consider the remaining assertion, which holds that the separation of sensible and non-sensible is itself 'at the root of the meaning of the term *metaphysics*, and has become a determining norm for Western thought' (89). I am afraid that only a reading forced beyond any justification can make Western philosophy lie on this Procrustean bed. We have already indicated that an ontology other than a metaphysics of the sensible and the non-sensible can respond to the semantic aim of authentically poetic metaphors. And this is what we shall discuss in greater detail at the end of the present Study.

Moreover, Heidegger himself tells us how these 'remarks' (*Hinweise*) should be taken: 'their purpose is to warn us not to jump to the conclusion that the talk of thinking as (*als*) a hearing and a seeing is a mere metaphor, and thus take it too lightly' (89). Our own entire effort too is turned against this 'mere metaphor.'

Now this explicit warning has its positive counterpart in the non-thematized use of metaphor in the very text we have been analysing. True metaphor is not the 'learned theory' of metaphor; it is rather the very uttering that the objection reduced to mere metaphor, namely that 'thought looks in hearing and hears in looking' (89). By speaking in this way, Heidegger produces a deviation with respect to ordinary language, identified with representative thought. This 'leap,' Jean Greisch says, 'places language under the sign of the gift, connoted in the expression *es gibt*. Between "there is" and *es gibt* no passage is possible.'[57] Is not this divergence that of true metaphor?

Let us now consider what in fact makes this utterance a metaphor. It is, at the level of the utterance as a whole, the harmony (*Einklang*) between *ist* and *Grund* in 'nothing *is* without a *reason*.' This harmony is the very one that is seen-heard-thought. So the harmony belonging to the straightforward utterance – that of the principle of sufficient reason – is also the harmony of the second-level utterance, which understands thought as (*als*) the grasp by hearing and by seeing. As for this harmony, it is not a peaceful consonance; lesson 5 of *Der Satz vom Grund* teaches us instead that it is born of an earlier dissonance.[58] Actually, we find that two statements follow from the principle of sufficient reason. The rationalizing statement of representative thought proclaims: 'Nothing is without a why' (67). The statement borrowed from the spiritual poetry of Angelus Silesius says: 'The rose has no why; it flowers because it flowers, / It shows no self-concern, questions not, whether it is seen' (68). Nothing is without a why. And yet the rose is without a why. Without a why, but not without a because. By making the principle of sufficient reason more impenetrable, this vacillation forces the principle itself to be heard (*hören*): 'We must then be attentive to the tone (*Ton*) of its expression' (75). For now it resonates with 'two different tones (*Tonarten*)' (ibid.), one stressing *nothing* and *without*, the other stressing *is* and *reason*. The second, given priority in lesson 6, which was our starting point, must therefore be contrasted with the first emphasis, which is that of representative thought.

In *Unterwegs zur Sprache*,[59] the same struggle between representative thought and meditative thought produces true metaphor at the very point where metaphor in the metaphysical sense is challenged. Here, too, the context is important. Heidegger is attempting to break away from the concept of language formed by representative thought, when it treats language as *Ausdruck*, 'expression' – that is as the exteriorization of the interior, and hence as the domination of the outside by the inside, instrumental mastery attained by a subjectivity.

To help lead the philosopher's steps beyond this notion of representation, a line from Hölderlin is proposed. Here language is called *die Blume des Mundes*, 'the flower of the mouth' (99). The poet also says *Worte, wie Blumen*, 'words, like flowers' (100). The philosopher can welcome these expressions because he himself has called manners of saying *Mundarten*, 'modes of the mouth,' idioms, in which earth and sky, mortals and gods meet. An entire network is thus set vibrating and made to form intersignifying relations. The condemnation, identical to the one in *Der Satz vom Grund*, is then pronounced: 'It would mean that we stay bogged down in metaphysics if we were to take the name Hölderlin gives here in "words, like flowers" as being a metaphor' (100). What is more, protesting against Gottfried Benn's interpretation that reduces *wie* to the comparative 'like,' Heidegger accuses Benn of relegating this poetic expression to a 'herbarium, a collection of dried-up plants' (ibid.). Poetry indeed seems rather to climb back up the slope that language descends when dead metaphors are laid to rest in herbaria. What then is true poetry? It is, Heidegger says, that which awakens 'the largest view'; here 'the word is brought forth from its inception,' and it 'makes World appear in all things' (100, 101).

Now, is this not what *living* metaphor does?

Applying the 'flower' metaphor to language, however, can take us into an entirely different train of thought, one that Heidegger's remark on the interpretation of Gottfried Benn approaches. The flower that blossoms ends one day in a herbarium, just as 'using' does in 'used-up' [*usage, usure*].

In recognizing this we are led from Heidegger's restrained criticism to Jacques Derrida's unbounded 'deconstruction' in 'White Mythology.' Is not the entropy of language just what a philosophy of living metaphor wants to forget? Would not 'metaphysics' be more akin to a plant in a herbarium than to an allegorizing interpretation of metaphors already given in language? Would not a more subversive thought than Heidegger's be one that would support the universal suspicion of Western metaphysics with a more heightened suspicion directed at what in metaphor itself is left unsaid? Now the non-stated in metaphor is used, worn-out metaphor. Metaphoricity functions here in spite of us, behind our backs so to speak. The claim to keep semantic analysis within a metaphysically neutral area only expresses ignorance of the simultaneous play of unacknowledged metaphysics and worn-out metaphor.

Two assertions can be discerned in the tight fabric of Derrida's demonstration. The first has to do with the efficacy of worn-out metaphor in philosophical discourse, and the second with the deep-seated unity of metaphorical and analogical transfer of visible being to intelligible being.

The first assertion moves counter to our entire effort, which has been directed towards the discovery of living metaphor. The stroke of genius here is to enter the domain of metaphor not by way of its birth but, if we may say so, by way of its death. The concept of wearing away [usure][60] implies something completely different from the concept of abuse that English-language authors oppose (as we have seen) to use. This concept carries its own sort of metaphoricity with it, which is not surprising in a conception that aims precisely at demonstrating the limitless metaphoricity of metaphor. In its overdetermination the concept carries first the geological metaphor of sedimentation, of erosion, of wearing away by friction. To this is added the numismatic metaphor of wearing down the features of a medal or a coin. This metaphor in turn evokes the tie, perceived by de Saussure among others, between linguistic value and monetary value: a comparison that invites the suspicion that the using up or wearing away [usure] of things used and worn is also the usury of usurers. At the same time, the instructive parallelism between linguistic value and economic value can be pushed to the point where the *proper* sense and *property* are suddenly revealed as next of kin within the same semantic network. Following this assonance further, one may suspect that metaphor is a sort of 'linguistic surplus value' (7) functioning unknown to speakers, in the manner in which in the economic field the product of human labour is made at once unrecognizable and transcendent in economic surplus value and the fetishism of merchandise.

As we see, the task of reconstructing this network exceeds the resources provided by historical and diachronic semantics, just as it goes beyond the scope of lexicography and etymology. This work stems from a vaster 'discourse on figure' (14) that would measure economic effects and effects of language. A simple inspection of discourse in its explicit intention, a simple interpretation through the game of question and answer, is no longer sufficient. Heideggerian deconstruction must now take on Nietzschean geneology, Freudian psychoanalysis, the Marxist critique of ideology, that is, the weapons of the hermeneutics of suspicion. Armed in this way, the critique is capable of unmasking the *unthought* conjunction of *hidden* metaphysics and *worn-out* metaphor.

The efficacy of dead metaphor takes on its full meaning, however, only when one establishes the connection between the *wearing away* that affects metaphor and the ascending movement that constitutes the formation of the concept. The wearing away of metaphor is dissimulated in the 'raising' of the concept. (*Relève*, raising, is Derrida's very apt translation of the Hegelian *Aufhebung* [sublation, a transformation that partially cancels, a reinterpretation to a higher level].) Henceforth, to revive metaphor is to unmask the concept.

Derrida bases his work here on a particularly eloquent text in Hegel's *Aesthetics*.[61] It begins by stating that philosophical concepts are initially sensible meanings transposed (*übertragen*) to the spiritual order; and it adds that the establishment of a properly (*eigentlich*) abstract meaning is bound up with the effacement of what is metaphorical in the initial meaning and thus with the disappearance of this meaning, which, once proper, has become improper. Now, Hegel employs the term *Aufhebung* to describe this 'raising' of sensible and worn away meaning into the spiritual meaning, which has become the proper expression. Where Hegel saw an innovation of meaning, Derrida sees only the wearing away of metaphor and a drift towards idealization resulting from the dissimulation of this metaphorical origin: 'The movement of metaphorization (the origin and then the effacing of the metaphor, the passing from a proper sensible meaning to a proper spiritual meaning through a figurative detour) is nothing but a movement of idealization' (25). This movement of idealization, common to Plato and Hegel, brings into play all the oppositions that characterize metaphysics: nature/spirit, nature/history, nature/freedom, as well as sensible/spiritual, sensible/intelligible, sensible/sense or meaning. This system 'describes ... the possibility of metaphysics, and the concept of metaphor so defined belongs to [it]' (ibid.).

We must understand that here it is not a question of the genesis of empirical concepts but of the primary philosophemes, those that define the field of metaphysics: *theoria, eidos, logos,* etc. The thesis can be stated as follows: wherever metaphor fades, there the metaphysical concept rises up. We find a text from Nietzsche here to the effect that 'truths are illusions of which one has forgotten that they *are* illusions; worn-out metaphors which have become powerless to affect the senses, coins which have their obverse effaced and now are no longer of account as coins but merely as metal.'[62] Whence the title of the essay, 'White Mythology': 'It is metaphysics which has effaced in itself that fabulous scene which brought it into being, and which yet remains, active and stirring, inscribed in white ink, an invisible drawing covered over in the palimpsest' (11).

The final product of this effectiveness of worn-out metaphor, which is thus replaced by the production of a concept that erases its trace, is that discourse on metaphor is itself infected by the universal metaphoricity of philosophical discourse. In this regard, one can speak of a paradox of the auto-implication of metaphor.

The paradox is this: there is no discourse on metaphor that is not stated within a metaphorically engendered conceptual network. There is no non-metaphorical standpoint from which to perceive the order and the demarcation of the metaphorical field. Metaphor is metaphorically stated. The word *metaphor* and the word *figure* alike attest to this recurrence of metaphor. The theory of metaphor returns in a circular manner to the metaphor of theory, which determines the truth of being in terms of presence. If this is so, there can then be no principle for delimiting metaphor, no definition in which the defining does not contain the defined; metaphoricity is absolutely uncontrollable. The effort to decipher figures in philosophical texts is self-defeating; one is forced instead to 'recognize the *conditions which make it in principle impossible* to carry out such a project' (18). The layer of the first philosophical elements 'cannot be subsumed' (ibid.) because it is itself metaphorical. This layer, in the author's apt expression, 'is therefore self-eliminating every time one of its products (here the concept of metaphor) vainly attempts to include under its sway the whole of the field to which that product belongs' (ibid.). Were one successfully to establish order amid figures, still one metaphor at least would escape: the metaphor of metaphor, the 'extra metaphor.' And so the conclusion: 'The field is never saturated' (ibid.).

This perplexing tactic has proven to be only one episode in a much vaster strategy of deconstruction that always consists in destroying metaphysical discourse by reduction to aporias. Hence we may credit the 'conclusions' of the essay with being scarcely more than one groundwork for an enterprise that foments a good many other subversive manœuvres. We might attack the self-destruction of metaphor through assumption into the concept, that is, into the self-present idea. The other self-destruction (73) would still remain, that which would occur through the ruin of essential oppositions, first that of semantics and syntax, then that of figurative and proper, then, little by little, those of the sensible and the intelligible, convention and nature: in short, all the oppositions that found metaphysics as such.

We have thus returned, by way of an internal critique of worn-out metaphor, to the level on which Heidegger's declaration was located: 'The metaphorical exists only within the metaphysical.' Indeed, the movement of elevation and absorption or 'raising' by which worn-out metaphor is concealed in the figure of the concept is not just some fact of language. It is the pre-eminent philosophical gesture that, in a 'metaphysical' orientation, sights the invisible beyond the visible, the intelligible beyond the sensible, after having first separated them. There is thus only one such movement: the metaphorical 'raising' is also the metaphysical 'raising.'

According to this second assertion, true metaphor is vertical, ascending, transcendent metaphor. Characterized in this way, 'metaphor seems to bring into play the use of philosophical language in its entirety, nothing less than the use of what is called ordinary language *in* philosophical discourse, that is to say, of ordinary language *as* philosophical language' (6).

To grasp the full force of this assertion, we must go back to our own analyses of the interplay of resemblance. It is not uncommon for this play to be compared to analogy, whether analogy signifies quite specifically proportionality as in Aristotle's *Poetics*, or whether it designates in a less technical manner any recourse to resemblance in 'bringing closer' two 'distant' semantic fields.[63] The thesis we are now considering would allege that any use of analogy, although appearing to be neutral in regard to the 'metaphysical' tradition, rests unwittingly upon a metaphysical concept of analogy that points to the referential movement from the visible to the invisible. Primordial 'iconicity' would be encompassed here: everything visible would thus constitute what basically is capable of giving 'an image.' Its resemblance to the invisible would then constitute it as image. As a result, the very first transposition would be the transfer of meaning from the empirical to the 'intelligible place.' Using a method that in this case has no connection with Max Black's logical grammar, the task is then to unmask the metaphysics of analogy down to the seemingly most innocent uses of metaphor. Classical rhetoric continually gives itself away as well: is it by chance that regularly, in the guise of an example, the transfer of the inanimate to the animate reappears? Just so Fontanier eagerly falls back upon this dialectic of the animate and the inanimate to construct the species of metaphor, thereby re-establishing the parallel with the two other basic tropes (metonymy and synecdoche), whose species issued from the logical analysis of the relations of connection and correlation. With metaphor, the species belong no longer to the logical but to the ontological order.[64]

And so, whether we speak of the metaphorical character of metaphysics or of the metaphysical character of metaphor, what must be grasped is the single movement that carries words and things beyond, *meta*.

This privileged orientation of metaphysical metaphor explains the persistence of a few key metaphors that have a special capacity to receive and to concentrate the movement of the 'metaphysical raising.' In the forefront of these metaphors we find the Sun.

One might think that the Sun is simply an illustrative example. Precisely. It is 'the most illustrious, that which illustrates before all else, the most natural lustre that may be' (43). Already with Aristotle the Sun provided a quite unusual metaphor (*Poetics* 1457 b). The lack of a precise word to express the Sun's power to engender is filled by the metaphor of sowing. For Derrida, this is the symptom of a certain decisive characteristic: by its persistence, 'the movement which turns the sun into metaphor' proves to be that which 'turns philosophical metaphor towards the sun' (51). Why indeed is the heliotropic metaphor unique? Because it speaks of the 'paradigm of what is sensible *and* of what is metaphorical: it regularly turns (itself) and hides (itself)' (52). It follows that 'the orbit of the sun is the trajectory of metaphor' (52).

We can see the fantastic extrapolation involved here: 'With every metaphor, there is no doubt somewhere a sun; but each time that there is the sun, metaphor has begun' (53). Metaphor has begun, for with the sun come the metaphors of light, of looking or glancing, of the eye – pre-eminent figures of idealization, from the Platonic *eidos* to the Hegelian *Idea*. By virtue of this, '"idealizing" metaphor ... is constitutive of any element of philosophy in general' (56). More precisely, as the Cartesian philosophy of *lumen naturale* attests, light aims metaphorically at what is signified in philosophy: 'It is to that main item signified in onto-theology that the tenor of the dominant metaphor will always return: the circle of the heliotrope' (69). To this same network of dominant metaphors belong the metaphor of the ground-foundation and that of the home-return, metaphors *par excellence* of reappropriation. They also signify metaphoricity itself: the metaphor of the home is really 'a metaphor for metaphor: expropriation, being-away-from-home, but still in a home, away from home but in someone's home, a place of self-recovery, self-recognition, self-mustering, self-resemblance: it is outside itself – it is itself. This is philosophical metaphor as a detour in (or in view of) the reappropriation, the second coming, the self-presence of the idea in its light. A metaphorical journey from the Platonic *eidos* to the Hegelian Idea' (55).

And so, by reason of their stability, their perdurance, the dominant metaphors ensure the epochal unity of metaphysics: 'A presence disappearing in its own radiance, a hidden source of light, of truth and of meaning, an obliteration of the face of being – such would be the insistent *return* of that which subjects metaphysics to metaphor' (70).

By the same token, the paradox of metaphor's self-implication ceases to appear as a purely formal paradox. It is expressed materially by the self-implication of the dominant metaphors of light and home, where metaphysics signifies itself in its primordial metaphoricity. By being images for idealization and appropriation, light and sojourn are a figure for the very process of metaphorizing and thereby ground the return of metaphor upon itself.

The critical remarks I offer here cannot of course encompass the entire project of deconstruction and dissemination, but only touch upon the line of argument drawn from the collusion of worn-out metaphor with the metaphysical theme of analogy. Besides, this specifically polemical phase of my own argument is inseparable from the positive clarification of the concept of analogy implied in the theory of metaphor developed in the remainder of the present Study.

I should like to examine in its own right the thesis of an unstated effectiveness of worn-out metaphor and shall, for the moment, lay aside the thesis that identifies metaphorical 'raising' with metaphysical 'raising.' The hypothesis to the effect that worn-out metaphor possesses a specific fecundity is strongly contested by the semantic analysis developed in the preceding Studies. This analysis leans towards the position that dead metaphors are no longer metaphors, but instead are associated with literal meaning, extending its polysemy. The criterion of delimitation is clear: the metaphorical sense of a word presupposes contrast with a literal sense; as predicate, this contrasting sense transgresses semantic pertinence. In this respect, the study of the lexicalization of metaphor – for example in Le Guern[65] – greatly contributes to dispelling the false enigma of worn-out metaphor. Indeed, various traits that sustain the heuristic function of metaphor disappear with lexicalization: forgetting the customary meaning causes us to overlook the deviation in relation to the isotopy of the context. So it is only by knowing the etymology of the word that we can reconstruct the Latin *testa* ('little pot') in the French *tête* [head] and the popular metaphor from which the French word is derived. In current usage the metaphor has been lexicalized to such an extent that it has become the proper word; by this we mean that the expression now brings its lexicalized value into discourse, with neither deviation nor reduction of deviation. The phenomenon is thus less interesting than it seems at first. Le Guern even thinks that lexicalization 'involves only a very small number of metaphors among all those that the language creates' (82).

The effectiveness of dead metaphor can be inflated, it seems to me, only in semiotic conceptions that impose the primacy of denomination, and hence of substitution of meaning. These conceptions thereby condemn the analysis to overlook the real problems of metaphoricity, which, as we know, are related to the play of semantic pertinence and impertinence.

But if the problem of denomination is over-emphasized in this way, it is doubtless because one attaches to the opposition between the figurative and the proper a meaning that is itself metaphysical, one which a more precise semantics dispels. In fact, this shatters the illusion that words possess a proper, i.e. primitive, natural, original (*etumon*) meaning in themselves. Now nothing in the earlier analysis has authorized this interpretation. We did admit of course that the metaphorical use of a word could always be opposed to its literal use; but literal does not mean proper in the sense of originary, but simply current, 'usual.'[66] The literal sense is the one that is lexicalized. There is thus no need for a metaphysics of the proper to justify the difference between literal and figurative. It is use in discourse that specifies the difference between the literal and metaphorical, and not some sort of prestige attributed to the primitive or the original. Moreover, the distinction between literal and metaphorical exists only through the conflict of two interpretations. One interpretation employs only values that are already lexicalized and so succumbs to semantic impertinence; the other, instituting a new semantic pertinence, requires a twist in the word that displaces its own meaning. In this way, a better semantic analysis of the metaphorical process suffices to dispel the mystique of the 'proper,' without any need for metaphoricity to succumb along with it.

It is true that in its work of denomination philosophical language appears to contradict the semanticist's judgment concerning the rarity of lexicalized metaphors. The reason for this is simple. The creation of new meanings, in connection with the advent of a new manner of questioning, places language in a state of semantic deficiency; lexicalized metaphor must intervene to compensate for this lack. But, as Fontanier saw perfectly well, what we then require is a trope 'by necessity and by extension in order to supplement words lacking in language for certain ideas ...' (*Les Figures du discours* 90). In short, *catachresis* is called for, moreover, it can be metonymy or synecdoche as easily as metaphor.[67] Therefore, speaking of metaphor in philosophy, we must draw a line boldly between the relatively banal case of an 'extended' use of the words of ordinary language in response to a deficiency in naming and the case – to my mind singularly more interesting – where philosophical discourse deliberately has recourse to living metaphor in order to draw out new meanings from some semantic impertinence and to bring to light new aspects of reality by means of semantic innovation.

The result of this first discussion is that a reflection on the wearing away of metaphors is more seductive than earth-shaking. Perhaps its real fascination for so many minds is due to the disturbing fecundity of the oblivion that seems to be expressed here, but also to the capacity for revival that seems to persist in the most thoroughly extinguished metaphorical expressions. Here again, the semanticist is of great help. Contrary to what is often stated, Le Guern notes that 'lexicalization brings about the total disappearance of the image only under special conditions' (*Sémantique* 87).[68] In the other cases, the image is attenuated but still perceptible; this is why 'almost all lexicalized metaphors can recover their original brilliance' (88). The reanimation of a dead metaphor, however, is a positive operation of de-lexicalizing that amounts to a new production of metaphor and, therefore, of metaphorical meaning. Writers obtain this effect by various concerted and controlled procedures – substituting a synonym that suggests an image, adding a more recent metaphor, etc.

In philosophical discourse, the rejuvenation of dead metaphors is particularly interesting when these metaphors supply a semantic addition. Reanimated metaphor once again functions as fable and as redescription, which characterize living metaphor, and leaves behind its function of mere addition at the level of denomination. De-lexicalization is therefore in no way symmetrical to the earlier lexicalization. In philosophical discourse, moreover, the renovation of extinguished metaphors involves more complex operations than those evoked above. The most remarkable of these is the awakening of etymological motivations, pushed even to false etymology. This procedure, a favourite of Plato's, is common in Hegel and in Heidegger. When Hegel hears *taking-true* in *Wahrnehmung*, when Heidegger hears *non-dissimulation* in *a-lêtheia*, the philosopher creates meaning and in this way produces something like a living metaphor. The analysis of dead metaphor is thus seen to refer back to an initial foundation which is living metaphor.[69]

The baffling fecundity of dead metaphor is even less awesome when one takes true measure of its contribution to the formation of concepts. To revive dead metaphor is in no way to unmask concepts: first of all because revived metaphor functions differently than dead metaphor, but above all because the full genesis of the concept does not inhere in the process by which metaphor is lexicalized.[70]

In this respect the Hegelian text discussed above does not appear to me to justify the thesis of a collusion between metaphor and *Aufhebung*. This text describes two operations that intersect at one point – dead metaphor – but remain distinct. The first operation, which is purely metaphorical, takes a proper (*eigentlich*) meaning and transports it (*übertragen*) into the spiritual order. Out of this expression – non-proper (*uneigentlich*) because transposed – the other operation makes a proper abstract meaning. It is the second operation that constitutes the 'suppression-preservation' which Hegel calls *Aufhebung*. But the two operations, transfer *and* suppression-preservation, are distinct. The second alone creates a proper sense in the spiritual order out of an improper sense coming from the sensible order. The phenomenon of wearing away (*Abnutzung*) is only a prior condition allowing the second operation to be constituted on the ground of the first.

This pair of operations is not fundamentally different from what Kant considers to be the production of the concept in its schema. Thus, the concept of 'foundation' is symbolized in the schema of the 'earth' and of 'construction'; but the meaning of the concept is in no way reduced to its schema. What must be realized is precisely that giving up sensible meaning does not simply give us an improper expression but rather a proper expression on the conceptual level. The conversion of this process of wearing away into thought is not the wearing away itself. If these two operations were not distinct, we could not even speak of the concept of wearing away, nor of the concept of metaphor; in truth, there could be no philosophical terms. That there are philosophical terms is due to the fact that a concept can be active as thought in a metaphor which is itself dead. What Hegel precisely conceived was this life of the concept in the death of the metaphor. 'Comprendre' [comprehend, understand] can have a proper philosophical sense because we no longer hear 'prendre' [take, to take hold of] in it. So only half the work has been done when a dead metaphor beneath a concept is revived; it must still be proved that no abstract meaning was produced as the metaphor wore away. This demonstration belongs not to the metaphorical order but to the order of conceptual analysis. This analysis alone can prove that Hegel's Idea is not Plato's Idea, even though it is true to say with Derrida that its traditional metaphorical burden 'continues Plato's system into Hegel's' (57). But noting this continuation is not the same as determining the sense of Idea in each philosopher. No philosophical discourse would be possible, not even a discourse of deconstruction, if we ceased to assume what Derrida justly holds to be 'the sole thesis of philosophy,' namely, 'that the meaning aimed at through these figures is an essence rigorously independent of that which carries it over' (29).

Applying these remarks on the formation of the concept in its schema to the concept of metaphor is enough to dispel the paradox of the metaphoricity of all definitions of metaphor. Speaking metaphorically of metaphor is not at all circular, since the act of positing the concept proceeds dialectically from metaphor itself. Thus, when Aristotle defines metaphor as the *epiphora* of the word, the expression *epiphora* is qualified conceptually by its insertion in a network of intersignifications, where the notion of *epiphora* is bounded by the primary concepts *phusis, logos, onoma, sêmainein*, etc. *Epiphora* is thus separated from its metaphorical status and constituted as a proper meaning, although 'the whole surface of [this discourse],' as Derrida says, 'is worked by metaphor' (31). The subsequent determination of the concept of metaphor contributes to this conceptual conversion of dead metaphor underlying the expression *epiphora.* It does so either by the method of differentiation, which allows one to distinguish among various strategies of *lexis*, or by exemplification, which provides an inductive basis for the concept of the operation indicated. Let us add that the conceptualization of different metaphors is aided not only by the lexicalization of the metaphors employed, as in the case of the vocable 'transposition,' but also by the rejuvenation of worn-out metaphor, which places the heuristic use of living metaphor in the service of conceptual formation. This is true of other metaphors for metaphor evoked so frequently in the present work: screen, filter, lens, superimposition, overload, stereoscopic vision, tension, interanimation, change of labels, idyll and bigamy, etc. Nothing prevents the fact of language that metaphor constitutes from being itself 'redescribed' with the help of the various 'heuristic fictions' produced sometimes by new living metaphors, sometimes by worn-out metaphors that have been revived. Far from admitting the concept of metaphor to be only the idealization of its own worn-out metaphor, the rejuvenation of all dead metaphors and the invention of new living metaphors that redescribe metaphor allow a new conceptual production to be grafted onto the metaphorical production itself.

So we see that the abyss-like effect produced by 'this implication of what is to be defined in the definition' (55) is dispelled when we discern the proper hierarchy with respect to the concept of *epiphora* and its schema.

We can now consider the theoretical core common to Heidegger and Derrida, namely, the supposed collusion between the metaphorical pair of the proper and figurative and the metaphysical pair of the visible and invisible.

I myself hold this connection not to be necessary. The example of Fontanier, mentioned above, is instructive in this regard. His definition of metaphor – 'presenting an idea under the sign of another idea more striking or better known'[71] – in no way implies the division into species that he subsequently infers from the consideration of objects. Likewise, his initial definition is illustrated by innumerable examples that involve no transfer from the visible to the invisible: 'the *swan* of Cambrai, the brilliant *eagle* of Meaux,' '*consuming* remorse,' 'courage *craving* for peril and praise,' 'what is well conceived is expressed with *clarity*,' etc. These examples can all be interpreted in terms of tenor and vehicle, focus and frame. I should be inclined to think that the shift from a definition of metaphor drawn from the operation to a definition drawn from the kind of objects results in part from studying metaphor within the framework of the word (the kinds of object then serving as guide in identifying kinds of word), and in part from the substitution theory, which continually sacrifices the predicative (hence syntagmatic) aspect to the paradigmatic aspect (and so to classes of objects). This shift can be avoided if we carry the theory of metaphor from the level of the word back to the level of the sentence.

Consequently, if the substitution theory of metaphor presents a certain affinity to the 'raising' of the sensible into the intelligible, the tension theory eliminates every advantage that accrues to this latter notion. The play of semantic impertinence is compatible with all the calculated errors capable of making sense. So it is not metaphor that carries the structure of Platonic metaphysics; metaphysics instead seizes the metaphorical process in order to make it work to the benefit of metaphysics. The metaphors of the sun and the home reign only to the extent that they are selected by philosophical discourse. The metaphorical field in its entirety is open to all the figures that play on the relations between the similar and the dissimilar in any region of the thinkable whatsoever.

As for the position of privilege assigned to metaphysical discourse itself – a privilege that governs the partitioning of the narrow zone of metaphors where this discourse is schematized – this seems indeed to spring from the suspicion governing the strategy of deconstruction. The counter-example proposed in the Aristotelian philosophy of metaphor is valuable here. We shall call upon this counter-example one last time in concluding our inquiry.

4 / THE INTERSECTION OF SPHERES OF DISCOURSE

It is now possible to return to the question raised at the start of this Study: *what* sort of philosophy is *implied* in the movement that carries our inquiry from rhetoric to semantics and from sense towards reference? The earlier discussion has revealed the close connection between the question of the *content* of the implicit ontology and that of the *mode* of implication between poetic discourse and speculative discourse. What has only been suggested in the foregoing critical remarks remains to be stated in positive terms.

I shall therefore be undertaking two tasks at once: to erect a general theory of the intersections between spheres of discourse upon the difference we have recognized between modalities of discourse, *and* to propose an interpretation of the ontology implicit in the postulates of metaphorical reference that will fit this dialectic of modalities of discourse.

The dialectic outlined here considers self-evident the need to abandon the naïve thesis that the semantics of metaphorical utterance contains ready-made an immediate ontology, which philosophy would then have only to elicit and to formulate. From the perspective of this dialectic, it would appear equally disastrous for the dynamism of discourse as a whole if we were to lay down our arms too soon and agree to the thesis suggested by Wittgenstein's *Philosophical Investigations* – a tempting thesis due to its liberalism and its irenicism – to the effect that language games are radically heterogeneous. As Plato remarks in the *Philebus* – it is bad to arrive too quickly at the one or at the many. Philosophy's eminence lies in the art of arranging ordered manifolds. A general theory of interferences based on the phenomenology of the semantic aims of each discourse ought to be elaborated in this spirit. The particular intention that directs the system of language functioning in metaphorical utterances includes a demand for elucidation to which we can respond only by approaching the semantic possibilities of this discourse with a different range of articulation, the range of speculative discourse.

It can be shown that, on the one hand, speculative discourse has its condition of *possibility* in the semantic dynamism of metaphorical utterance, and that, on the other hand, speculative discourse has its *necessity* in itself, in putting the resources of conceptual articulation to work. These are resources that doubtless belong to the mind itself, that are the mind itself reflecting upon itself. In other words, the speculative fulfils the semantic exigencies put to it by the metaphorical only when it establishes a break marking the irreducible difference between the two modes of discourse. Whatever the subsequent relation of the speculative to the poetic may be, the first extends the semantic aim of the second at the cost of a transmutation resulting from its transfer into another zone of meaning.

The reference postulates stated at the beginning and end of Study 7 are truly at issue in this dialectic, which governs the passage to an explicit ontology where the meaning of being implicit in these postulates comes to reflection. Between the implicit and the explicit there is all the difference that separates two modes of discourse, and that cannot be eliminated when the first is taken up into the second.

(a) As could be seen by the end of Study 3, affirming the gain in meaning that results from founding a new semantic pertinence at the level of the metaphorical statement as a whole, the conceptual articulation proper to the speculative mode of discourse finds its condition of *possibility* in the semantic functioning of metaphorical utterance. But this gain in meaning is inseparable from the tension not just between the terms of the statement, but also between two interpretations – a literal interpretation restricted to the established values of words, and a metaphorical interpretation resulting from the 'twist' imposed on these words in order to 'make sense' in terms of the statement as a whole. The resulting gain in meaning is thus not yet a *conceptual* gain, to the extent that the semantic innovation is not separable from the switching back and forth between the two readings, from their tension and from the kind of stereoscopic vision this dynamism produces. We might say then that the semantic shock produces a conceptual need, but not as yet any knowledge by means of concepts.

This thesis is strengthened by our interpretation of the work of resemblance in Study 6. At that point we traced the gain in meaning back to a change in 'distance' between semantic fields, that is, to a predicative assimilation. Now, in saying that this is (like) that – whether the *like* is 'marked' or not – the assimilation does not reach the level of an identity of meaning. The 'similar' is not the 'same.' To see the similar, in Aristotle's words, is to apprehend the 'same' within and in spite of 'difference.' This is why we were able to refer this schematization of a new sense back to productive imagination. The gain in meaning is thus inseparable from the predicative assimilation through which it is schematized. This is another way of saying that the gain in meaning is not carried to the concept, to the extent that it remains caught in the conflict of 'same' and 'different,' although it constitutes the rough outline and the demand for an instruction through the concept.

A third suggestion results from the thesis developed in Study 7 to the effect that the reference of the metaphorical statement could itself be considered a split reference. For a split sense, we might say, a split reference. This is what we meant when we lodged metaphorical tension right within the copula of the utterance. Being as, we said, means being and not being. In this way, the dynamism of meaning allowed access to the dynamic vision of reality which is the implicit ontology of the metaphorical utterance.

The present task is thus made more specific. It will consist in showing that the passage to the explicit ontology called for by the postulate of reference is inseparable from the passage to the concept called for by the structure of meaning found in the metaphorical statement. Therefore, juxtaposing the results of the earlier Studies is no longer enough; instead these results must be linked more closely together by showing that every gain in meaning is at one and the same time a gain in sense and a gain in reference.

In a study on theological discourse and the symbol,[72] Jean Ladrière observes that the semantic functioning of the symbol – in our terms, of metaphor – is an extension of a dynamism of meaning that can be found in even the simplest utterance. The novelty of this analysis in relation to our own consists in its description of this dynamism as a criss-crossing of acts – acts of predication and acts of reference. Ladrière adopts Strawson's analysis of propositional acts, conceived as the combination of a singularizing operation of identification and a universalizing operation of characterization. Then, like John Searle in *Speech Acts*, he places this analysis within the framework of a theory of discourse and is thus able to speak of the relation between sense and reference as a commingling of operations. The dynamism of meaning is shown to be a dual and intersecting dynamism where any progress towards concepts has as its counterpart a more extensive exploration of the referential field.

Indeed, in ordinary language we master the predicative use of abstract meanings only by relating them to objects, which we designate in the referential mode. This is possible because the predicate is such that it performs its characteristic function only in the context of the sentence, when it targets this or that relatively isolable aspect within a determined referent. The lexical term is, in this respect, only a rule for use in a sentence context. So we master meaning by varying the conditions for use in relation to different referents. Conversely, we investigate new referents only by describing them as precisely as possible. Thus the referential field can extend beyond the things we are able to show, and even beyond visible, perceptible things. Language lends itself to this by allowing the construction of complex referential expressions using abstract terms that are already understood, i.e. definite descriptions in Russell's sense. In this way predication and reference lend support to one another, whether we relate new predicates to familiar referents, or whether, in order to explore a referential field that is not directly accessible, we use predicative expressions whose sense has already been mastered. So what Jean Ladrière has termed the power of signifying, in order to stress its operative and dynamic character, is the intersection of two movements. One movement aims at determining more rigorously the conceptual traits of reality, while the other aims at making referents appear (that is, the entities to which the appropriate predicative terms apply). This circularity between the abstractive phase and the concretizing phase makes this power of signifying an unending exercise, a 'continuing Odyssey.'[73]

This semantic dynamism, proper to ordinary language, gives a 'historicity' to the power of signifying. New possibilities of signifying are opened up, supported by meanings that have already been established. This 'historicity' is carried by the attempt at expression made by a speaker who, wanting to formulate a new experience in words, seeks something capable of carrying his intention in the network of meanings he finds already established. Thanks to the very instability of meaning, a semantic aim can find the path of its utterance. Therefore, it is always in a particular utterance – corresponding to what Benveniste calls the instance of discourse – that the sedimented history of assembled meanings can be recovered in a new semantic aim. Placed in the perspective of its use, meaning appears less like a determined content, to take or to leave, than (in Jean Ladrière's words) like an inductive principle capable of guiding semantic innovation. The act of signifying is an 'initiative that, as if for the first time, makes the syntactic elements coming from a syntactical history reappropriated in this effort produce truly new effects of meaning' (133).

This is the synthesis we can now make of the theory of the instance of discourse in Émile Benveniste, the speech act theory in Austin and Searle, and the theory of sense and reference in Strawson (which stems from Frege).

On this groundwork the tension theory we applied to three different levels of metaphorical utterance can then be located: the tension between the terms of the statement, the tension between literal interpretation and metaphorical interpretation, and the tension in the reference between is and is not. If it is true that meaning, even in its simplest form, is in search of itself in the twofold direction of sense and reference, the metaphorical utterance only carries this semantic dynamism to its extreme. As I tried to say earlier drawing upon a poorer semantic theory, and as Jean Ladrière says much better on the basis of the more subtle theory we have just summarized, the metaphorical utterance functions in two referential fields at once. This duality explains how two levels of meaning are linked together in the symbol. The first meaning relates to a known field of reference, that is to the sphere of entities to which the predicates considered in their established meaning can be attached. The second meaning, the one that is to be made apparent, relates to a referential field for which there is no direct characterization, for which we consequently are unable to make identifying descriptions by means of appropriate predicates.

Unable to fall back upon the interplay between reference and predication, the semantic aim has recourse to a network of predicates that already function in a familiar field of reference. This already constituted meaning is raised from its anchorage in an initial field of reference and cast into the new referential field which it will then work to delineate. But this transfer from one referential field to the other supposes that the latter field is already in some way present in a still unarticulated manner, and that it exerts an attraction on the already constituted sense in order to tear it away from its initial haven. It is therefore in the semantic scope of the other field that the energy capable of achieving this uprooting and this transfer resides. But this would not be possible if meaning were a stable form. Its dynamic, directional, vectoral character combines with the semantic aim seeking to fulfil its intention.

Two energies converge here: the gravitational pull exerted by the second referential field on meaning, giving it the force to leave its place of origin; and the dynamism of meaning itself as the inductive principle of sense. The semantic aim that animates the metaphorical utterance places these two energies in relation, in order to inscribe a semantic potential (itself in the process of being superseded) within the sphere of influence of the second referential field to which it relates.

But the metaphorical utterance, even more than plain utterance, provides only a semantic sketch without any conceptual determination. It is doubly sketchy. On the one hand, as regards its sense, the metaphorical utterance reproduces the form of a movement in a portion of the trajectory of meaning that goes beyond the familiar referential field where the meaning is already constituted. On the other hand, it brings an unknown referential field towards language, and within the ambit of this field the semantic aim functions and unfolds. At the origin of this process, therefore, there is what I shall call the ontological vehemence of a semantic aim, hinting at an unknown field that sets it in motion. This ontological vehemence cuts meaning from its initial anchor, frees it as the form of a movement and transposes it to a new field to which the meaning can give form by means of its own figurative property. But in order to declare itself this ontological vehemence makes use of mere hints of meaning, which are in no way determinations of meaning. An experience seeks to be expressed, which is more than something undergone. Its anticipated sense finds in the dynamism of simple meaning, relayed by the dynamism of split meaning, a *sketch* that now must be reconciled with the requirements of the concept.

(b) That speculative discourse finds something like the sketch of a conceptual determination in the dynamism described above does not bar it from beginning in itself and from finding the principle of its articulation within itself. By itself it draws on the resources of a conceptual field, which it offers to the unfolding of a meaning sketched metaphorically. The *necessity* of this discourse is not the extension of its possibility, inscribed in the dynamism of the metaphorical. Its necessity proceeds instead from the very structures of the mind, which it is the task of transcendental philosophy to articulate. One can pass from one discourse to the other only by an *epoché*.

But what are we to understand by speculative discourse? Must we see it as the equivalent of what above we repeatedly termed conceptual determination, in opposition to the semantic sketches of metaphorical utterances? I should reply that speculative discourse is the discourse that establishes the primary notions, the principles, that articulate primordially the space of the concept. Concepts in scientific language as well as in ordinary language can never actually be derived from perception or from images, because the discontinuity of the levels of discourse is founded, at least virtually, by the very structure of the conceptual space in which meanings are inscribed when they draw away from the metaphorical process, which can be said to generate all semantic fields. It is in this sense that the speculative is the condition of the possibility of the conceptual. It expresses the systematic character of the conceptual in a second-order discourse. If, in the order of discovery, the speculative surfaces as a second-level discourse – as meta-language, if one prefers – in relation to the discourse articulated at the conceptual level, it is indeed first discourse in the order of grounding. This discourse is at work in all the speculative attempts to order the 'great genera,' the 'categories of being,' the 'categories of understanding,' 'philosophical logic,' the 'principal elements of representation,' or however one wants to express it.

Even if one does not recognize that it can be articulated in a distinct discourse, this power of the speculative supplies the horizon or, as it has been called, the logical space on the basis of which the clarification of the signifying aim of concepts is distinguished radically from any genetic explanation based on perception or images. In this respect, Husserl's distinction[74] between the *Aufklärung* of 'acts of knowing' and any genetic-style *Erklärung* draws its source from the speculative horizon in which meaning is inscribed when it takes on conceptual status. If a sense that is 'one and the same' can be discerned in a meaning, it is not just because one sees it that way but because one can connect it to a network of meanings of the same order in accordance with the constitutive laws of the logical space itself.

The Husserlian-style critique, which is expressed in the opposition between *Aufklärung* and *Erklärung*, is possible only on the basis of this speculative horizon. The speculative is what allows us to say that 'to understand a (logical) expression' is something other than 'finding images.'[75] It allows us to say, further, that the scope [*visée*] of the universal is something other than the display of the images that accompany it, illustrate it, even coincide with the 'distinction' of speculative features and the 'clarification' of the tenor of meaning. The speculative is the very principle of the disparity [*inadéquation*] between illustration and intellection, between exemplification and conceptual apprehension. If the *imaginatio* is the kingdom of 'the similar,' the *intellectio* is that of 'the same.' In the horizon opened up by the speculative, 'same' grounds 'similar' and not the inverse. In fact 'wherever things are "alike," an identity in the strict and true sense is also present.'[76] What affirms this? Speculative discourse does, by reversing the order of precedence of metaphorical discourse, which attains 'same' only as 'similar.' By reason of the same founding principle, generic apprehension (*Auffassung*)[77] is rendered irreducible to the purely substitutive function of image-representation. Far from the concept's being reduced to an abbreviation, by reason of some principle of thrift and economy, some play of substitution, it is the concept that makes this play of re-presentation possible.[78] Signifying is always something other than representing. The same capacity of inscription in logical space enables the interpretation functioning in perception to become the seat of two distinct aims: one that tends towards individual things, and the other that tends towards logical signification, where interpretation at the perceptual or imaginative level plays nothing more than a 'supportive' role.[79]

The image no doubt introduces a moment of absence and, in this sense, an initial neutralization of the 'positing' inherent in perceptual belief.[80] But apprehending a sense that is one and the same is something else again.

This critique of 'the image' in Husserl is of the highest significance to us. It can be transposed easily into a critique of 'metaphor' in so far as the *imaginatio* includes not only so-called mental images but also, and especially, predicative assimilations and schematizations that underlie metaphorical utterance. *Imaginatio* is a level and an order of discourse. *Intellectio* is another level and another order. Here metaphorical discourse encounters its limit.

This containment of metaphorical discourse by speculative discourse can be restated as follows (the language is borrowed, as above, from Jean Ladrière). The signifying aim of the concept works free of interpretations, schematizations, and imaginative illustrations only if a horizon of constitution is given in advance, the horizon of speculative *logos*. By reason of this opening of horizon, the concept becomes capable of functioning semantically solely in terms of the configurational properties of the space in which it is inscribed. The resources of systematization involved simply in the play of articulation in speculative thought are substituted for the resources of schematization involved in the play of predicative assimilation. Because it forms a system, the conceptual order is able to free itself from the play of double meaning and hence from the semantic dynamism characteristic of the metaphorical order.

(c) But does this discontinuity of semantic modalities imply that the conceptual order abolishes or destroys the metaphorical order? My inclination is to see the universe of discourse as a universe kept in motion by an interplay of attractions and repulsions that ceaselessly promote the interaction and intersection of domains whose organizing nuclei are off-centred in relation to one another; and still this interplay never comes to rest in an absolute knowledge that would subsume the tensions.

The attraction that speculative discourse exerts on metaphorical discourse is expressed in the very process of interpretation. Interpretation is the work of concepts. It cannot help but be a work of elucidation, in the Husserlian sense of the word, and consequently a struggle for univocity. Whereas the metaphorical utterance leaves the second sense in suspension, while its reference continues to have no direct presentation, interpretation is necessarily a rationalization that at its limit eliminates the experience that comes to language through the metaphorical process. Doubtless it is only in reductive interpretation that rationalization culminates in clearing away the symbolic base. These interpretations are readily expressed as follows: such and such a symbol seemed to intend to say something new in regard to a referential field that was only intimated or anticipated; finally, after due consideration, the symbol signifies only this positing of desire, that class membership, such a degree of strength or weakness of fundamental will. In relation to this true discourse, symbolic discourse becomes synonymous with illusory discourse.

It must be granted that these reductive interpretations are consistent with the semantic aim characteristic of the speculative order. Every interpretation aims at relocating the semantic outline sketched by metaphorical utterance inside an available horizon of understanding that can be mastered conceptually. But destruction of the metaphorical by the conceptual in rationalizing interpretations is not the only outcome of the interaction between different modalities of discourse. One can imagine a hermeneutic style where interpretation would conform both to the notion of concept and to that of the constitutive intention of the experience seeking to be expressed in the metaphorical mode.

Interpretation is then a mode of discourse that functions at the intersection of two domains, metaphorical and speculative. It is a composite discourse, therefore, and as such cannot but feel the opposite pull of two rival demands. On one side, interpretation seeks the clarity of the concept; on the other, it hopes to preserve the dynamism of meaning that the concept holds and pins down. This is the situation Kant considers in the celebrated paragraph 49 of the *Critique of the Faculty of Judgment*. He calls 'the spirit (*Geist*) in an aesthetic sense,' 'the life-giving principle of mind (*Gemüt*).' The metaphor of life comes to the fore at this point in the argument because the *game* in which imagination and understanding engage assumes a task assigned by the Ideas of reason, to which no concept is equal. But where the understanding fails, imagination still has the power of 'presenting' (*Darstellung*) the Idea. It is this 'presentation' of the Idea by the imagination that forces conceptual thought to *think more*.[81] Creative imagination is nothing other than this demand put to conceptual thought.[82]

This sheds light on our own notion of living metaphor. Metaphor is living not only to the extent that it vivifies a constituted language. Metaphor is living by virtue of the fact that it introduces the spark of imagination into a 'thinking more' at the conceptual level.[83] This struggle to 'think more,' guided by the 'vivifying principle,' is the 'soul' of interpretation.

5 / ONTOLOGICAL CLARIFICATION OF THE POSTULATE OF REFERENCE

How will speculative discourse reply, given its resources, to the semantic aim of poetic discourse? Through an ontological clarification of the postulate of reference presupposed in the preceding Study.

This clarification is not a linguistic but a philosophical task. The relation of language to its counterpart, reality, concerns the conditions for reference in general, and thus the meaning of language as a whole. Now, semantics can only allege the relation of language to reality but cannot *think* this relation as such.[84] Perhaps it will venture a philosophical conclusion unawares, by positing language as a whole and in itself as mediation between man and the world, between man and man, within the self itself.

Language then appears as that which raises the experience of the world to its articulation in discourse, that which founds communication and brings about the advent of man as speaking subject. By implicitly assuming these postulates, semantics takes as its own a thesis of 'the philosophy of language' inherited from von Humboldt.[85] But what is this philosophy of language if not philosophy itself, to the extent that it thinks the relation between being and being-said?

It will be objected, before proceeding any farther, that it is not possible to speak of a relation like this because there is no standpoint outside language and because it is and has always been *in* language that men claim to speak *about* language.

This is certainly true. Yet speculative discourse is possible, because language possesses the *reflective* capacity to place itself at a distance and to consider itself, as such and in its entirety, as related to the totality of what is. Language designates itself and its other. This reflective character extends what linguistics calls meta-linguistic functioning, but articulates it in another discourse, speculative discourse. It is then no longer a function that can be opposed to other functions, in particular to the referential function;[86] for it is the knowledge that accompanies the referential function itself, *the knowledge of its being-related to being.*

This reflective knowledge allows language to know that it is installed in being. The usual relationship between language and its referent is reversed: language becomes aware of itself in the self-articulation of the being which it is about. Far from locking language up inside itself, this reflective consciousness is the very consciousness of its openness. It implies the possibility of stating propositions regarding what is and of saying that this is brought to language in our saying it. This knowledge articulates the reference postulates in a discourse other than semantics, even when the latter is distinguished from semiotics. When I speak, I know that something is brought to language. This knowledge is no longer intra-linguistic but extra-linguistic; it moves from being to being-said, at the very time that language itself moves from sense to reference. Kant wrote: 'Something must be for something to appear.' We are saying: 'Something must be for something to be said.'

This proposition makes reality the final category upon which the whole of language can be thought, although not known, as the being-said of reality.

We must now attempt an ontological clarification against the background of this general thesis, not only of the postulates of reference in general, but of the postulate of *split* reference in accordance with the semantic aim of poetic discourse.

It is first as a *critical* instance, directed against our conventional concept of reality, that speculative discourse in its own sphere of articulation
takes up the notion of split reference. The following question has arisen
repeatedly: do we know what is meant by world, truth, reality? At the
very heart of semantic analysis, this question anticipated the critical
moment of speculative discourse. But the logical space of this question had
not yet been opened. For this reason, it had to remain unarticulated, like a
doubt infecting the non-critical uses of the concept of reality by many theorists. Consequently, we were suspicious of the distinction, held to be self-
evident, between denotation and connotation. To the extent that this distinction amounted to one between cognitive and emotive values of discourse, we could see in it only the projection on the poetic level of a positivist prejudice holding that scientific discourse alone states reality.[87] We
were set on the path of a properly critical use of the concept of reality
by two more articulated themes. Poetic discourse, we said, is that in which
the *epoché* of ordinary reference is the negative condition allowing a
second-order reference to unfold. Furthermore, this unfolding is governed
by the power of redescription belonging to certain heuristic fictions, in the
manner of scientific models.[88]

Our task now is to work out the critical scope of the notions of secondary reference and redescription in order to insert them into speculative discourse.

One might be tempted to turn this critical function into a plea for the
irrational. And, indeed, upsetting customary categorizations has the effect
of a logical disordering through impertinent comparisons and incongruous
encroachments, as if poetic discourse were working for the step by step de-
categorization of our entire discourse. As regards second-order reference –
the positive counterpart to this disordering – it seems to mark the invasion
of language by the ante-predicative and the pre-categorial, and to require a
concept of truth other than the concept of truth-verification, the correlative of our ordinary concept of reality.

In this regard, the earlier analysis provides further suggestions. The discussion of the notions of appropriateness and accuracy in Nelson Goodman's nominalism[89] allowed us to see that the appropriate character of certain verbal and non-verbal predicates can be assumed by speculative discourse only at the price of remaking the correlative concepts of truth and
reality. The same question persistently returned in connection with what
we ventured to call lyrical *mimêsis*, to express the power of redescription
involved in the poetic articulation of so-called moods.[90] These poetical
textures, we said, are no less heuristic than fictions in narrative form; feeling is no less ontological than representation. Does not this generalized

power of 'redescription' explode the initial concept of 'description' to the extent that the latter remains within the limits of representation by objects? By the same count, must we not forgo the opposition between a discourse turned towards the 'outside,' which would be precisely descriptive discourse, and a discourse turned towards the 'inside,' which would portray only a mood and raise it to the hypothetical level? Is it not the very distinction between 'outside' and 'inside' that is shaken along with that between representation and feeling?

Other distinctions are shaken in turn, such as the distinction between discovering and creating and between finding and projecting. Poetic discourse brings to language a pre-objective world in which we find ourselves already rooted, but in which we also project our innermost possibilities. We must thus dismantle the reign of objects in order to let be, and to allow to be uttered, our primordial belonging to a world which we inhabit, that is to say, which at once precedes us and receives the imprint of our works. In short, we must restore to the fine word *invent* its twofold sense of both discovery and creation. It is because analysis had remained imprisoned within these familiar distinctions that the concept of metaphorical truth sketched at the end of Study 7 seemed caught in an insurmountable antinomy. The 'meta-poetics' of a Wheelwright, which we could call naïve, and the critical vigilance of a Turbayne, which did away with the ontological vehemence of poetic utterance through the concerted mastery of 'as if,' continued to oppose one another on the field of a verificationalist concept of truth, itself bound up with a positivist concept of reality.[91]

As we feared, it is here that the critical instance seems to turn into a plea for the irrational. When the reference to objects set over against a *judging* subject is suspended, is not the very structure of utterance shaken? When so many firmly recognized distinctions are erased, does not the notion of speculative discourse itself evaporate, and with this notion the dialectic of speculative and poetic?

This is the moment to recall the central contribution of Study 7: split reference, we said, signifies that the tension characterizing metaphorical utterance is carried ultimately by the copula *is*. Being-as means being *and* not being. Such-and-such was and was not the case. Within the framework of a semantics of reference, the ontological import of this paradox could not be seen; 'to be' operated there only as an affirmative copula, as being/apophansis. The distinction at the very centre of being as copula between the relational sense and the existential sense was at least an indication of a possible recovery by speculative discourse of the dialectic of being, of which the apophantic mark is this paradox of the copula *is*.

By what feature will the speculative discourse on being answer to the paradox of the copula, to the apophantic *is/is not*?

Going further back in our study, the interpretation of being-as reminds us in turn of an enigmatic remark made by Aristotle, a remark that to my knowledge is never taken up again in the body of his works. What does it mean for living metaphor 'to set (something) before the eyes'? Setting before the eyes, *Rhetoric* 3 replies, is to 'represent things as in a state of activity' (1411 b 24-5). And the philosopher specifies: when the poet infuses life into inanimate things, his verse 'represents everything as moving and living; and activity is movement' (1412 a 8).

By referring at this point in his reflection to a category of 'first philosophy,' Aristotle leads us to seek the key to ontological clarification of reference by reconsidering the meanings of being on the level of speculative thought. Yet it is worth noting that he does not refer again to the distinctions between the categorial significations of being but to an even more radical distinction, between being as potentiality and being as actuality.[92]

Extending the field of the polysemy of being in this way is of the greatest importance for our own viewpoint. It signifies, first of all, that the ultimate meaning of the reference of poetic discourse is articulated in speculative discourse: indeed, actuality has meaning only in the discourse on being. This signifies as well that the semantic aim of metaphorical utterance does intersect most decisively with the aim of ontological discourse, not at the point where metaphor by analogy and categorial analogy meet, but at the point where the reference of metaphorical utterance brings being as actuality and as potentiality into play. Finally, it signifies that this intersection of the poetic and the ontological does not concern tragic poetry alone,[93] since the remark in the *Rhetoric* cited above extends to poetry as a whole; it applies to lyrical *mimêsis* as well, what (to use an expression suggested in Study 7) we have termed the power 'to represent things as in a state of activity.'

But what indeed can this be interpreted to mean?

Do not these same difficulties that concern the ontology of power and act arise at the level of poetry as well? For, as we have been taught by Aristotle himself, ontology says hardly more than this: potency and actuality are defined correlatively, that is to say, in a circular fashion;[94] the corresponding discourse is not demonstrative but inductive and analogical.[95] Of course, we established above that analogy is not a lamentable metaphor. But to the difficulties of ontological discourse in general are added the difficulties proper to these two most radical meanings of being: did Aristotle really master the differing degrees of the concept of potency?[96] Did he order convincingly the closely related concepts of actuality, *praxis, poiêsis*, motion?[97]

As a result, it can only be in an exploratory and not in a dogmatic fashion, by questioning instead of asserting, that we can attempt to interpret the formula 'signifying things in act.' And this interpretation is inseparable from the ontological clarification of the postulate of metaphorical reference.

What, then, are we to understand by 'signifying things in act'?

This may mean seeing things as *actions*. This is certainly the case in tragedy, which shows men 'as acting, as in act.' And indeed, action has a special place in that the act inheres entirely in the agent, as vision does in the one who sees, life in the soul, and contemplation in the mind. In acting, the act is whole and entire in each of its moments and does not cease when the end is attained: 'At the same time we are living well and have lived well, and are happy and have been happy' (*Metaphysics* Θ 6, 1048 b 25-6). This vision of the world as a grand *gesture* might be that of a Goethe rewriting Saint John's Prologue: 'In the beginning was the Act.' And yet, to see all things as actions, is this not to see them as 'human, all too human,' and so to accord an improper prerogative to man himself?

Is seeing all things in act seeing them in the manner of a work of art, a result of technical production? Would reality then come to be seen in our eyes as some vast artifice engendered by an artist's will, provided 'nothing external hinders,' as it is stated in *Metaphysics* Θ 7? But does this not burden our gaze with an anthropomorphism even heavier than in the preceding interpretation?

Would seeing all things in act then be seeing them as naturally blossoming? This interpretation seems closer to the examples in the *Rhetoric* (seeing inanimate things as animate). Is this not what we ourselves suggested at the end of Study 1 – *lively* expression is that which expresses existence as *alive*? Signifying things in act would be seeing things as not prevented from becoming, seeing them as blossoming forth. But then would not signifying things in act also be signifying potency, in the inclusive sense that stands for every production of motion or of rest? Would the poet then be the one who perceives power as act and act as power? He who sees as whole and complete what is sketchy and in process, who perceives every form attained as a promise of newness? In short, he who reaches this 'source of the movement of natural objects, being present in them somehow, either potentially or in complete reality' (*Metaphysics* Δ 4, 1015 a 18-19), which the Greeks called *phusis*?[98]

For the modern philosopher, coming after the death of Aristotelian physics, this sense of *phusis* is perhaps empty once more, something that poetic language asks speculative discourse to consider. It is then the task of speculative discourse to seek after the place where appearance signifies 'generating what grows.' As this sense is no longer to be sought in the region of objects, that occupied by physical bodies and living organisms, it indeed seems to be at the level of appearance as a whole and as such that the poetic verb 'signifies things in act.' In relation to this open and unlimited acceptation, signifying actions, signifying artifice, and signifying movement are already determinations, that is to say, limitations and restrictions that miss something of what is indicated in the expression 'signifying the blossoming of appearing.' If there is a point in our experience where living expression states living existence, it is where our movement up the entropic slope of language encounters the movement by which we come back this side of the distinctions between actuality, action, production, motion.

So, once more, the task of speculative discourse is to seek after the place where appearing means 'generating what grows.' This project and this program lead us once more across the path of Heidegger. The final stages of his philosophy attempt to make speculative thought resonate with the poet's utterance. It is all the more appropriate to evoke Heidegger here in that, at the heart of his critique of the metaphysical interpretation of metaphor, the metaphor of blossoming forced itself upon him as the metaphor for metaphor. The 'flowers' of our words – *Worte, wie Blumen* – utter existence in its blossoming forth.[99]

In truth, as our investigation enters its next to last stage, Heidegger's philosophy steps forth as intermingled and inescapable attempt and temptation. It is an attempt from which we must draw inspiration whenever it manifestly contributes to clarifying speculative thought in accordance with the semantic aim that animated Aristotle's investigation into the multiple meanings of being; and it is a temptation we must shun when the difference between speculative and poetic threatens once again to disappear.

I agree with the principal commentators on Heidegger[100] that the core of his thought in its last stage is the belonging-together of *Erörterung* and *Ereignis*. The first term designates both the search for the 'place' and also the 'commentary' on this search. The second term designates the 'thing itself' that is to be thought. The belonging-together of *Erörterung* and *Ereignis* as the 'topology of being' is what typifies speculative thought in its 'constitutive gesture.'

That the meaning of *Ereignis* has the same aim as what was formerly thought as actuality/potency is confirmed negatively by the refusal to reduce its scope to event (*Geschehnis*) or to process (*Vorkommnis*). Furthermore, it is confirmed positively by the relation between *Ereignis* and the *es gibt* that announces every blossoming of appearing under the connotation of 'gift.' *Ereignis* and *es gibt* mark the opening and the unfolding by reason of which there are objects for a judging subject. The 'thing' that is given to thought in this way is called, in the vocabulary of topology, 'region,' the capacity for coming to a 'meeting,' the nearness of the 'near.' But have we not been prepared for these variations in distance by the play of resemblance?

That *Erörterung* in its turn marks the difficulty of saying that corresponds to the difficulty of being[101] should not surprise a reader who has already acknowledged the conceptual labour incorporated into the old doctrine of the analogy of being. When the philosopher fights on two fronts, against the seduction of the ineffable and against the power of 'ordinary speech' (*Sprechen*), in order to arrive at a 'saying' (*Sagen*) that would be the triumph neither of inarticulateness nor of the signs available to the speaker and manipulated by him – is he not in a situation comparable to that of the thinker of Antiquity or the Middle Ages, seeking his path between the powerlessness of a discourse given over to the dissemination of meanings and the mastery of univocity through the logic of genera?

By moving towards *Ereignis, Erörterung* moves towards a 'same,' an 'identical,' by which it is defined as speculative thinking.[102] And this 'same' is like analogy for the Ancients, to the extent that here, too, resemblance assembles [*ressembler ... c'est rassembler*].

Does this mean that once again speculative discourse threatens to merge with poetry? Not at all. Even if *Ereignis* is called a metaphor,[103] it is a philosopher's metaphor, in the sense in which the analogy of being can, strictly speaking, be termed a metaphor, but one which always remains distinct from a poet's metaphor. The very way in which Heidegger juxtaposes poetic discourse and philosophical discourse without confusing them, as in *Aus der Erfahrung des Denkens,*[104] confirms that the gulf cannot be bridged between the Same that is to be thought and poetic resemblance. What is remarkable, in this short text, is that the poem does not serve as an ornament to the philosophical aphorism, and that the latter does not constitute the poem's translation. Poem and aphorism are in a mutual accord of resonance that respects their difference. To the imaginative power of thought-full poetry, the poet replies with the speculative power of poeticizing thought.

Certainly the difference is infinitesimal when the philosopher approves a thinking poetry – that of poets who themselves write poetically on language, like Hölderlin – and when he responds in a thinking that poeticizes, 'semi-poetic thinking.' But even here, speculative thought employs the metaphorical resources of language in order to create meaning and answers thus to the call of the 'thing' to be said with a semantic innovation. A procedure like this has nothing scandalous about it as long as speculative thought knows itself to be distinct and responsive because it is thinking. Furthermore, the philosopher's metaphors may well resemble those of the poet – like the latter, they diverge from the world of objects and ordinary language – but they do not merge with the poet's metaphors.

The same must be said in regard to the well-known practice of etymologism, a practice already found in Plato and in Hegel. The philosopher has a perfect right to try and say what is strange and distant by rejuvenating some dead metaphor or by restoring some archaic meaning of a word. Our own investigation has prepared us to say that this language ploy involves no mystique of 'primordial meaning.' A buried sense becomes a new meaning in the present instance of discourse. This is all the more true when speculative thought adopts the new meaning in order to blaze a path to the 'thing' itself. The return of ancient metaphors – that of light, the ground, the home, the way or path – must be regarded in the same manner. Their use in a new context is a form of innovation. The same metaphors can contribute to a Platonism of the invisible or glorify the visibility of appearance. This is why if no metaphor is privileged, neither is any forbidden. So it is not surprising that the ancient meditation on the polysemy of being returns and that, in the manner of the theorists of the analogy of being, we meditate on signifying more – on a *Mehrdeutigkeit* – which is distinguished from pure and simple dissemination – from *Vieldeutigkeit*.[105] In confronting this new polysemy of being, philosophy confirms that thinking is not poeticizing.

It will be objected that this way of reading Heidegger takes into account neither his wish to break with metaphysics, nor the 'leap' outside its circle that poeticizing thought demands.

It is here, I admit, that I regret the position assumed by Heidegger.

This inclosure of the previous history of Western thought within the unity of 'the' metaphysical seems to me to express a sort of vengefulness – which this thinking, nevertheless, calls us to renounce – along with a will to power that seems inseparable from it.[106] The unity of 'the' metaphysical is an after-the-fact construction of Heideggerian thought, intended to vindicate his own labour of thinking and to justify the renunciation of any kind of thinking that is not a genuine overcoming of metaphysics. But why should this philosophy claim for itself alone, to the exclusion of all its predecessors, that it breaks through and innovates? It seems to me time to deny oneself the convenience, which has become a laziness in thinking, of lumping the whole of Western thought together under a single word, metaphysics.[107]

If one can say that Heidegger is part of the lineage of speculative philosophy, it is to the extent that he in fact pursues a task analogous to that of his predecessors by means of new thinking and new language, and in the interests of a new experience.

What philosopher worthy of the name prior to Heidegger has not meditated on the metaphor of the way and considered himself to be the first to embark on a path that is language itself addressing him? Who among them has not sought the 'ground' and the 'foundation,' the 'dwelling' and the 'clearing'? Who has not believed that truth was 'near' and yet difficult to perceive and even more difficult to say, that it was hidden and yet manifest, open and yet veiled? Who has not, in one way or another, linked the forward movement of thought to its ability to 'regress,' to take a step 'backward'? Who has not attempted to distinguish the 'beginning of thinking' from any chronological starting point? Who has not conceptualized his own task essentially as a labour of thought directed toward itself and against itself? Who has not believed that to continue one must make a break and 'leap' outside the circle of accepted ideas? Who has not opposed thinking based on a horizon to knowledge based on objects, opposed meditating thought to representative thought? Who has not known that ultimately the 'way' and the 'place' are the same, and 'method' and 'thing' identical? Who has not seen that the relation between thinking and being is not a relation in the logical sense of the word, that this relation presupposes no terms preceding it but, in one way or another, constitutes the belonging-together of thinking and being? Finally, what philosopher before Heidegger has not attempted to think identity other than as tautology, on the basis of this belonging-together of thinking and being?

This is why, in contrast to the interpretation Heidegger gives of his work, the value of his philosophy of *Erörterung-Ereignis* lies in its contribution to the continuous and unceasing problematic of thinking and of being. Let the philosopher write *Sein, Seyn,* ~~Sein~~ one after the other – it is still the question of being that is posed in what is crossed out. Nor is it the first time that being has had to be cancelled out in order to be recognized in its reserve and in its generosity, in its modesty and in its gratuitousness. Like the speculative thinkers who preceded him, Heidegger is seeking the key word, 'the one that decisively carries the whole movement.' For him, *es gibt* is this key word. It carries the mark of a determined ontology, in which the neutral is more expressive than the personal and in which the granting of being at the same time assumes the form of something destined. This ontology proceeds from a listening turned more attentively to the Greeks than to the Hebrews, more to Nietzsche than to Kierkegaard. So be it. It is appropriate that we in turn be attentive to this ontology without soliciting it. As such an ontology, however, it cannot assume the privilege of opposing all other ontologies by confining them inside the bounds of 'the' metaphysical. Its unacceptable claim is that it puts an end to the history of being, as if 'being disappeared in *Ereignis*.'

The price of this claim is the inescapable ambiguity of the later works, divided between the logic of their continuity with speculative thought and the logic of their break with metaphysics. The first logic places *Ereignis* and the *es gibt* in the lineage of a mode of thought that unceasingly rectifies itself, unceasingly searches for a *saying* more appropriate than ordinary *speech*, a *saying* that would be a *showing* and a *letting-be*; a mode of thought, finally, which could never leave discourse behind. The second logic leads to a series of erasures and repeals that cast thought into the void, reducing it to hermeticism and affectedness, carrying etymological games back to the mystification of 'primitive sense.' Above all, this second logic invites us to sever discourse from its propositional character, forgetting Hegel's lesson in regard to speculative propositions, which do not cease to be propositions.[108] This philosophy gives new life in this way to the seductions of the unarticulated and the unexpressed, even to a kind of despair of language resembling that found in the next to last proposition in Wittgenstein's *Tractatus.*

In concluding, I should like to retain only this excellent statement from the later works of Heidegger: 'Between these two [thinking and poetry] there exists a secret kinship because in the service of language both intercede on behalf of language and give lavishly of themselves. Between both there is, however, at the same time an abyss for they "dwell on the most widely separated mountains."'[109]

What is described here is the very dialectic between the modes of discourse in their proximity and in their difference.

On the one hand, poetry, in itself and by itself, sketches a 'tensional' conception of truth for thought. Here are summed up all the forms of 'tensions' brought to light by semantics: tension between subject and predicate, between literal interpretation and metaphorical interpretation, between identity and difference. Then these are gathered together in the theory of split reference. They come to completion finally in the paradox of the copula, where being-as signifies being and not being. By this *turn* of expression, poetry, in combination with other modes of discourse,[110] articulates and preserves the experience of belonging that places man in discourse and discourse in being.

Speculative thought, on the other hand, bases its work upon the dynamism of metaphorical utterance, which it construes according to its own sphere of meaning. Speculative discourse can respond in this way only because the *distanciation,* which constitutes the critical moment, is contemporaneous with the experience of belonging that is opened or recovered by poetic discourse,[111] and because poetic discourse, as text and as work,[112] prefigures the distanciation that speculative thought carries to its highest point of reflection. Finally, the splitting of reference and redescription of reality submitted to the imaginative variations of fiction strike us as specific figures of distanciation, when they are reflected and rearticulated by speculative discourse.

What is given to thought in this way by the 'tensional' truth of poetry is the most primordial, most hidden dialectic – the dialectic that reigns between the experience of belonging as a whole and the power of distanciation that opens up the space of speculative thought.

From existentialism to the philosophy of language*

Nineteen sixty-one was the year when I published *Fallible Man* and *The Symbolism of Evil*, and at that time a specific problem occupied my mind: how is it possible to introduce within the framework of a philosophy of the will, on which I had written ten years earlier, some fundamental experiences such as guilt, bondage, alienation, or, to speak in religious terms, sin? As such this problem could be expressed in terms of an existential philosophy. All existential philosophies of the forties and fifties had met this problem. We may speak of inauthentic life with Heidegger, or boundary situations (*Grenzsituationen*) with Jaspers, or of Being and Having and of despair with Gabriel Marcel. My problem belonged to the sphere of questions, with a somewhat more specific interest. My problem was to distinguish between finitude and guilt. I had the impression, or even the conviction, that these two terms tended to be identified in classical existentialism at the cost of both experiences, guilt becoming a particular case of finitude and for that reason beyond cure and forgiveness, and finitude, on the other hand, being affected by a kind of diffused sense of sadness and despair through guilt. This is why I chose *Finitude and Guilt* as a general title for the two volumes of which I spoke and the problem was that of their difference and of their connection.

But at the same time, a secondary problem emerged, which tended afterwards to pass to the forefront of my inquiries. This was the problem of language. Why? Because in order to introduce the dimension of evil into the structure of the will, a fundamental change in the method of description itself was required. In my first work I had relied heavily on a reflective method which came from both Husserl and the existentialist pair, Jas-

---

* Reprinted from *Criterion* 10, 3 (Spring 1971) by permission of the Divinity School, University of Chicago. Originally presented in address form before the Divinity School at a luncheon on 5 May 1971. Translated by David Pellauer.

pers and Marcel, to whom I had devoted two books. I may now call this kind of first description an existential phenomenology, although at the time I did not dare call it phenomenology for I did not wish to cover my own attempt with the authority of Husserl, whom I was translating into French. It was phenomenology, however, in the sense that it tried to extract from lived experience the essential meanings and structures of purpose, project, motive, wanting, trying, and so on.

I note in passing that phenomenology at that time had already attacked problems which now are in the forefront of the school of linguistic analysis with the philosophy of action. But if it was phenomenology, it was existential phenomenology in the sense that these essential structures implied the recognition of the central problem of embodiment, of *le corps propre*. Anyhow, whatever might be the relation between phenomenology and existentialism in this first attempt, this kind of philosophizing did not yet raise any particular problem of language, for a direct language was thought to be available. This direct language was ordinary language in which we find words like purpose, motive, and so on. This is why I now believe that there is an intersection of the philosophy of ordinary language and phenomenology at this first level.

Now the consideration of the problem of evil brought into the field of research new linguistic perplexities which did not occur earlier. These linguistic perplexities were linked to the use of symbolic language as an indirect approach to the problem of guilt. Why an indirect approach? Why symbolic language when we have to pass from a philosophy of finitude to a philosophy of guilt? This was the question that intrigued me. The fact is that we have a direct language to say purpose, motive, and 'I can,' but we speak of evil by means of metaphors such as estrangement, errance, burden, and bondage. Moreover, these primary symbols do not occur unless they are embedded within intricate narratives of myth which tell the story of how evil began: how at the beginning of time the gods quarrelled; how the soul fell into an ugly body; or how a primitive man was tempted, trespassed a prohibition, and became an exiled rebel.

It seemed, therefore, that direct reflection on oneself could not go very far without undertaking a roundabout way, the detour of a hermeneutic of these symbols. I had to introduce a hermeneutical dimension within the structure of reflective thought itself. In other words, I could speak of purposive action without symbolic language, but I could not speak of bad will or of evil without a hermeneutic. This was the first way in which the problem of language appeared in a kind of philosophy which was not at first a philosophy of language, but a philosophy of the will. I had been compelled by my initial subject to inquire into the structure of symbolism and myth, and this inquiry by itself led me to the more general problem of hermeneutics. What is hermeneutics if there is something like an indirect language, a metaphorical language, if there are symbols and myths?

But I must now say that at that time I was not aware of the real dimension of the hermeneutical problem. Perhaps because I did not want to be drawn into the immensity of this problem, I tried to limit the definition of hermeneutics to the specific problem of the interpretation of symbolic language. I still held this position in my book on Freud which I shall come to in a moment. In the last chapter of *The Symbolism of Evil* and in the first part of *Freud and Philosophy*, I defined symbolism and hermeneutics in terms of each other. On the one hand, a symbolism requires an interpretation because it is based upon a specific semantic structure, the structure of double meaning expressions. Reciprocally, there is a hermeneutical problem because there is an indirect language. Therefore I identified hermeneutics with the art of deciphering indirect meanings.

Today I should be less inclined to limit hermeneutics to the discovery of hidden meanings in symbolic language and would prefer to link hermeneutics to the more general problem of written language and texts. (I shall come to this at the end.) Nevertheless, such was the way I was introduced to the hermeneutical problem.

At the same time, or maybe somewhat later, I felt compelled to shift my interest from the original problem of the structure of the will to the problem of language as such, which had remained subsidiary even at the time when I was studying the strange structures of the symbolism of myths. I was compelled to do so for several reasons which I will now try to explain. First, my reflection on the structure of psychoanalytic theory; secondly, the important change in the philosophical scene, at least in France, where structuralism was beginning to replace existentialism and even phenomenology; thirdly, my continuing interest in the problem raised by religious language, and, more specifically, by the so-called theologies of the Word in the post-Bultmannian school; and finally, my increasing interest in the British and American school of ordinary language philosophy, in which I saw a way both of renewing phenomenology and of replying to the excesses of structuralism.

My interest in psychoanalysis was in a sense the result of my interest in the problem of will, bad will, and guilt. I could not go very far indeed in a reflection concerning guilt without encountering the psychoanalytic interpretation of guilt. But psychoanalysis was also directly linked to linguistic perplexities due to its own use of symbolic structures. Not only the problem of guilt, therefore, compelled me to consider the problem of psychoanalysis, but also the general structure of language according to psychoanalysis. Are not dreams and symptoms some kind of indirect language? What is more, psychoanalysis claims to give not only a specific interpretation of dreams and symptoms, but also of the whole fabric of cultural symbols and of religious myths, which I had previously approached with a merely descriptive method similar to that used in comparative history of religions and especially by Mircea Eliade. Therefore, I had to consider something which had escaped my reflections until then, the fact that there was not only one hermeneutic, but two hermeneutics, since psychoanalysis claimed to interpret symbols by reducing them. The idea of a reductive hermeneutic could no longer be overlooked. In fact, I had to understand that Freud was only one of the exponents of the reductive hermeneutic, and that Marx and Nietzsche, and before them Feuerbach, had to be understood as the fathers of this reductive method. The claim of psychoanalysis to explain symbols and myths as fruits of unconscious representations, as distorted expressions of the relation between libidinal impulses and the repressive structure of the super-ego, compelled me to enlarge my first concept of hermeneutics beyond a mere semantic analysis of double meaning expressions.

Hermeneutics appeared henceforth as a battle field traversed by two opposing trends, the first tending toward a reductive explanation, the second tending toward a recollection or a retrieval of the original meaning of the symbol. My problem was to link these two approaches and to understand their relation as dynamic and as moving from first *naïveté* through critique toward what I called at the time a second *naïveté*. Therefore, without giving up my earlier definition of hermeneutics as the general theory of symbolic language, I had to introduce into the theory the polarity between these two hermeneutical requirements and to link philosophical reflection not only to a semantics of indirect language, but to the conflictual structure of the hermeneutical task. In this way a dramatic element was added to the previous recognition of the necessity of the detour through obscure and hidden meaning.

My book on Freud, published in 1965, reflects this double recognition, first of the necessity of the detour through indirect signs, and secondly of the conflictual structure of hermeneutics and thus of self-knowledge. Self-knowledge is a striving for truth by means of this inner contest between reductive and recollective interpretation.

Now a word about the second reason for shifting from existential phenomenology to a more linguistically concerned kind of philosophizing. I spoke of a general change in the philosophical scene in France, chiefly due to the emergence of structuralism as the main trend in philosophy. This new model of philosophizing came from linguistics; more precisely, it was an effort to extend to semantics and to all semiological disciplines the model which had succeeded in phonology. Inasmuch as there are signs in human life, the structural model was to be utilized. As you know, this structural model relies mainly on the affirmation that language, before being a process or an event, is a system, and that this system is not established at the level of the speaker's consciousness, but at a lower level, that of a kind of structural unconscious. Structuralism as a philosophy draws radical consequences from this epistemological model which directly affect the presuppositions of existentialism. First of all, the primacy of subjectivity which was so strongly emphasized by existentialism is overthrown by this displacement of analysis from the level of the subject's intentions to the level of linguistic and semiotic structures.

Hermeneutics is also called into question along with existential phenomenology and existentialism. The idea that language is a closed system of signs, within which each element merely refers to the other elements of the system, excludes the claim of hermeneutics to reach beyond the 'sense' – as the immanent content of the text – to its 'reference,' i.e., to what it says *about* the world. For structuralism, language does not refer to anything outside of itself, it constitutes a world for itself. Not only the reference of the text to an external world, but also its connections to an author who *intended* it and to a reader who *interprets* it are excluded by structuralism. This twofold reference to a subject of the text, whether author or reader, is rejected as psychologism or 'subjectivism.'

Confronted by this situation, I tried to react in the following way. First, I tried to become more competent in linguistic problems. Secondly, I tried to incorporate within hermeneutics as much as I could of this structural approach by means of a better connection between the stage of objective explanation and the stage of subjective appropriation. My discussions about and with Lévi-Strauss reflect this effort.

The kind of hermeneutics which I now favour starts from the recognition of the objective meaning of the text as distinct from the subjective intention of the author. This objective meaning is not something hidden behind the text. Rather it is a requirement addressed to the reader. The interpretation accordingly is a kind of obedience to this injunction starting from the text. The concept of 'hermeneutical circle' is not ruled out by this shift within hermeneutics. Instead it is formulated in new terms. It does not proceed so much from an intersubjective relation linking the subjectivity of the author and the subjectivity of the reader as from a connection between two discourses, the discourse of the text and the discourse of the interpretation. This connection means that what has to be interpreted in a text is what it says and what it speaks about, i.e., the kind of world which it opens up or discloses; and the final act of 'appropriation' is less the projection of one's own prejudices into the text than the 'fusion of horizons' – to speak like Hans-Georg Gadamer – which occurs when the world of the reader and the world of the text merge into one another.

This shift within hermeneutics from a 'romanticist' trend to a more 'objectivist' trend is the result of this long travel through structuralism. At the same time, I had to depart from my previous definition of hermeneutics as the interpretation of symbolic language. Now I should tend to relate hermeneutics to the specific problems raised by the translation of the objective meaning of written language into the personal act of speaking which a moment ago I called appropriation. In that way, the broader question, What is it to interpret a text? tends to replace the initial question, What is it to interpret symbolic language? The connection between my first definition and the new emerging definition remains an unsolved problem for me, which will be the topic of my forthcoming work. The course which I gave at this university last year represented the first attempt to overcome this difficulty.

I want now to say a few words concerning the third field of inquiry in which I found an impulse and a help for my effort to co-ordinate phenomenology and the philosophy of language. The post-Bultmannian schools of theology, especially those of Ebeling and Fuchs, seemed to me to be following a parallel evolution. Bultmann had imposed two fundamental limitations upon the theory of religious language. On the one hand, myth was taken to be the opposite of Kerygma. In that way, demythologization became the central problem and this prevented grasping the question of religious language as a unique problem. On the other hand, understanding had to be opposed to objectification in a manner similar to the opposition between *Verstehen* and *Erklären* inherited from Dilthey. Thus Biblical theology remained trapped in the perplexities of romanticist hermeneutics. The recognition of this led post-Bultmannian exegetes and theologians to subordinate the problem of demythologizing and the problem of existential interpretation to the broader problem of the 'linguisticality' of human experience which makes possible both the emergence of texts and the response of interpretation to this emergence. The polarity between myth and Kerygma, on the one hand, and between interpretation and explanation, on the other hand, appeared to be only partial solutions to the more general question of how religious language functions.

Therefore studies devoted to the word *God* and in general to 'God-talk' appear from this broader standpoint to be more fruitful than the studies of myth and of demythologizing. These inquiries intersect the linguistic and semantic question of how a word functions in different contexts. They also intersect the question of how a form of discourse – such as a narrative, an oracle, a psalm, or a parable – is linked to a specific theological content. This is why I am so interested in what Donald Evans, John Macquarrie, and Langdon Gilkey are doing in the field of the semantics of religious discourse. And I am just as interested in what Gerhard von Rad,

Joachim Jeremias, Daniel Via, and Norman Perrin are saying concerning the relation between the narrative form or the form of the parable and specific kinds of confession of faith.

What we need now is a new framework which would allow us to connect Biblical hermeneutics to general hermeneutics conceived as the question of what is understanding in relation to text-explanation. It is the function of general hermeneutics to answer problems such as: What is a text? i.e., what is the relation between spoken and written language? What is the relation between explanation and understanding within the encompassing act of reading? What is the relation between a structural analysis and an existential appropriation? Such are the general problems of hermeneutics to which a Biblical hermeneutics has to be submitted.

On the other hand, the problem of the specificity of Biblical hermeneutics is perfectly legitimate: but it could only be raised, in a consistent manner, against the background of a general hermeneutics. Questions like these would arise: What do we mean by the Kerygmatic kernel of 'preaching'? What are the connections between faith and Word, between the character of 'disclosure' belonging to all religious texts and even to non-religious texts (tragedy, poetry, novels, etc.) and what is intended by the concept of revelation? What is the contribution of a general theory of discourse and of texts to the traditional notion of inspiration? All these classical problems may be renewed when related in some dialectical way to the topics and methods of a general hermeneutics.

I finish this survey of the problems and methods which contributed to my present concern for a philosophical hermeneutics with a few words concerning the growing influence of the British and American school of ordinary language philosophy on my inquiries. I do not think that this philosophy has the last word, but I do think that it is at least a necessary first stage in philosophical inquiry. To my mind, the contribution of ordinary language philosophy is twofold. First, it has proved that ordinary language does not, cannot, and must not function according to the model of ideal languages constructed by logicians and mathematicians. The variability of semantic values, their sensitivity to contexts, the irreducibly polysemic character of lexical terms in ordinary language, these are not provisory defects or diseases which a reformulation of language could eliminate, rather they are the permanent and fruitful conditions of the functioning of ordinary language. This polysemic feature of our words in ordinary language now appears to me to be the basic condition for symbolic discourse and in that way, the most primitive layer in a theory of metaphor, symbol, parable, etc.

Secondly, ordinary language now appears to me, following the work of Wittgenstein and Austin, to be a kind of conservatory for expressions which have preserved the highest descriptive power as regards human experience, particularly in the realms of action and feelings. This appropriateness of some of the most refined distinctions attached to ordinary words provides all phenomenological analysis with linguistic guidelines. Now the recapturing of the intentions of ordinary language experiences may become the major task of a linguistic phenomenology, a phenomenology which would escape both the futility of mere linguistic distinctions and the unverifiability of all claim to direct intuition of lived experience. Thanks to this grafting of linguistic analysis to phenomenology, the latter may be cured of its illness and find its second wind. (I surmise that the same thing may be said of ordinary language philosophy; that its conjunction with phenomenology could also enhance and renew it.)

Not only phenomenology, but also hermeneutics may draw some benefit from an accurate inquiry into the functioning of ordinary language. I have already alluded to the connection between the functioning of symbolic discourse and the polysemic structure of our ordinary words. We may extend the parallelism further: understanding, in the most ordinary sense of the word – let us say, in conversation – is already an intersubjective process. Inasmuch as ordinary language differs from an ideal language in that it has no fixed expressions independent of their contextual uses, to understand discourse is to interpret the actualizations of its polysemic values according to the permissions and suggestions proposed by the context. What happens in the far more intricate cases of text-interpretation and what constitutes the key problem of hermeneutics is already foreshadowed in the interpretive process as it occurs in ordinary language. Thus the whole problem of text-interpretation could be renewed by the recognition of its roots in the functioning of ordinary language itself.

Such are the problems I am now working and reflecting on.

Notes

Full bibliographical information for publications identified in the notes by author and title may be found in the list of works cited.

TRANSLATOR'S INTRODUCTION

1 Aristotle *Poetics* 1459 a 5-8, Ingram Bywater, trans. in *The Basic Works of Aristotle*
2 For other English language introductions to Ricoeur's thought, see Don Ihde *Hermeneutic Phenomenology: The Philosophy of Paul Ricoeur.* Northwestern University Press, Evanston, Ill. 1971; David M. Rasmussen *Mythic-Symbolic Language and Philosophical Anthropology: a Constructive Interpretation of the Thought of Paul Ricoeur.* Nijhoff, The Hague 1971; and Patrick Bourgeois *The Extension of Paul Ricoeur's Hermeneutic* Nijhoff, The Hague 1975. Ihde's book contains a selective but extensive Ricoeur bibliography.
3 Translations of many of Ricoeur's important contributions in these areas have appeared in *Political and Social Essays* Joseph Bien and David Stewart, trans., Ohio University Press, Athens, Ohio 1974.

STUDY 1

1 Gérard Genette 'La rhétorique restreinte'
2 Concerning the beginnings of rhetoric, see E.M. Cope *An Introduction to Aristotle's Rhetoric* I: 1-4; A.É. Chaignet *La Rhétorique et son histoire* 1-69; O. Navarre *Essai sur la rhétorique grecque avant Aristote*; R. Barthes 'L'ancienne rhétorique, aide mémoire' 175-6; G.A. Kennedy *The Art of Persuasion in Greece.*
3 Socrates attributes this formula to Gorgias in the course of the dialogue that pits him against the Athenian master of rhetoric (*Gorgias* 453 a). Its germ, however, was discovered by Corax, a student of Empedocles, and the first author (followed then by Tisias of Syracuse) of a didactic treatise (*techné*) on the oratorical arts. The expression itself conveys the idea of a governing and sovereign operation (Chaignet *Rhétorique* 5).
4 Diogenes Laeartius 8: 57; 'in the *Sophist* Aristotle reports that "Empedocles was the first to discover (*eurein*) rhetoric"' (cited in Chaignet *Rhétorique* 3, n.1).
5 The *Protagoras, Gorgias,* and *Phaedrus* lay out Plato's uncompromising condemnation of rhetoric: 'But we won't disturb the rest of Tisias and Gorgias, who realized

that probability deserves more respect than truth, who could make trifles seem important and important points trifles by the force of their language, who dressed up novelties as antiques and vice versa, found out how to argue concisely or at interminable length about anything and everything' (*Phaedrus* 267 a-b, trans. Hackforth; see also *Gorgias* 449 a-458 c). Finally, 'true' rhetoric is dialectic itself, i.e. philosophy (*Phaedrus* 271 c).

6 'To be brief, then, I will express myself in the language of geometricians – for by now perhaps you may follow me. Sophistic is to legislation what beautification is to gymnastics, and rhetoric to justice what cookery is to medicine' (*Gorgias* 465 b-c, trans. W.D. Woodhead). The generic term for these simulations of art – cookery, cosmetics, rhetoric, sophistic – is 'flattery' (*kolakeia*, ibid. 463 b). The underlying argument of which this polemic presents the negative side, is that the mode of being called 'health' in the order of the body has a counterpart in the order of the spirit. This homology of the two 'therapies' regulates that of the two pairs of authentic arts, gymnastics and medicine on the one hand and justice and legislation on the other (*Gorgias* 464 c).

7 '... to discover the means of coming as near such success [in persuading] as the circumstances of each particular case allow' (*Rhetoric* 1, 1355 b 10); '... it is the function of one and the same art [rhetoric] to discern the real and the apparent means of persuasion, just as it is the function of dialectic to discern the real and the apparent syllogism' (1355 b 15); 'Rhetoric may be defined as the faculty of observing in any given case the available means of persuasion' (1355 b 25); 'But rhetoric we look upon as the power of observing the means of persuasion on almost any subject presented to us' (1355 b 32).

8 In book 2, chapter 24 of the *Rhetoric* (1402 a 17-20), Aristotle credits Corax with inventing the rhetoric of the probable: 'It is of this line of argument that Corax's *Art of Rhetoric* is composed. If the accused is not open to the charge – for instance if a weakling be tried for violent assault – the defence is that he was not likely to do such a thing.' Nevertheless, Aristotle cites Corax in the context of 'apparent enthymemes,' or paralogisms. Plato before him had given the honour of fathering probabilistic argumentation to Tisias 'or whoever it really was and whatever he is pleased to be called after [Corax, the crow?]' (*Phaedrus* 273 c). Regarding the use of such *eikota* arguments in Corax and Tisias, see Chaignet *Rhétorique* 6-7, and J.F. Dobson *The Greek Orators* chapter 1, section 5.

9 The enthymeme, the 'rhetorical syllogism' (*Rhetoric* 1356 b 5), and 'the example,' which belongs to the inductive order (1356 b 15), are frameworks for arguments that 'deal with what is in the main contingent' (1357 a 15). Now a contingency or a 'probability is a thing that usually happens; not, however, as some definitions would suggest, anything whatever that usually happens, but only if it belongs to the class of the "contingent" or the "variable." It bears the same relation to that in respect of which it is probable as the universal bears to the particular' (1357 a 34-5).

10 For the various hypotheses concerning the order of composition of the *Rhetoric* and the *Poetics*, see Marsh McCall *Ancient Rhetorical Theories of Simile and Comparison* 29-35.

11 References to the actual wording of the *Poetics* are to be found in *Rhetoric* 3: 2, 1; 3: 2, 5; 3: 2, 7; 3: 10, 7. The development of *eikôn* in the *Rhetoric*, which has no counterpart in the *Poetics*, poses a separate problem; for this, see section 3 of this Study, below.

12 Ingram Bywater, trans. in *The Basic Works of Aristotle*

13 The problem of translating the greek *lexis* has inspired a variety of solutions. Among French translators, Hatzfeld and Dufour (*La Poétique d'Aristote* Lille-Paris 1899) employ 'discours'; J. Hardy says 'élocution'; and Dufour and Wartelle (Éditions Les Belles Lettres 1973) use 'style' for *lexis* in *Rhetoric* 3. Among English translators, W.D. Ross says 'diction,' as does Bywater; E.M. Cope says 'style' and calls the *Aretai Lexeôs* the 'various excellences of style.' D.W. Lucas translates *lexis* by 'style' (*Aristotle's Poetics* 109), and says (*ad* 1450 b 13): '*lexis* can often be rendered by *style*, but it covers the whole process of combining words into an intelligible sequence.'

14 *On Interpretation* chap. 2: 'By a noun we mean a sound significant by convention, which has no reference to time, and of which no part is significant apart from the rest' (16 a 19-20); chapter 3: 'A verb is that which, in addition to its proper meaning, carries with it the notion of time. No part of it has any independent meaning, and it is a sign of something said of something else' (16 b 6, trans. Edghill).

15 Ross translates *logos* by 'speech' (*ad. loc.*).

16 *On Interpretation* chapter 4: 'A sentence (*logos*) is a significant portion of speech, some parts of which have an independent meaning, that is to say, as an utterance, though not as the expression of any positive judgment' (16 b 26-8). 'Yet every sentence is not a proposition; only such are propositions as have in them either truth or falsity. Thus a prayer is a sentence, but is neither true nor false' (17 a 1-5). Chapter 5: 'Let us, moreover, consent to call a noun or a verb an expression only (*phasis*), and not a proposition, since it is not possible for a man to speak in this way when he is expressing something, in such a way as to make a statement, whether his utterance is an answer to a question or an act of his own initiation ... of propositions one kind is simple, i.e. that which asserts or denies something of something' (17 a 17-21).

17 The definition is the unity of meaning of a thing: 'Therefore there is an essence only of those things whose formula (*logos*) is a definition (*orismos*). But we have a definition not where we have a word (*onoma*) and a formula (*logos*) identical in meaning (for in that case all formulae or sets of words would be definitions; for there will be some name for any set of words whatever, so that even the *Iliad* will be a definition), but where there is a formula of something primary,' i.e. of a substance as opposed to accidents (*Metaphysics* Z 4, 1030 a 6-11 trans. Ross). See also *Metaphysics* H 6, 1045 a 12-14. A unity of meaning of this sort has absolutely no need for the sentence as its foundation.

18 See below, Study 6, section 1.

19 D.W. Lucas makes the following remark in *Aristotle's Poetics* 204: '*Metaphora*: the word is used in a wider sense than English "metaphor," which is mainly confined to the third and fourth of Aristotle's types.' The generic notion of transposition is assumed by the use of the terms *metaphora* and *metapherein* in diverse contexts in Aristotle's work. For example the *Eudemian Ethics* makes use of species in place of an unnamed genus (1221 b 12-13), transfers a quality of one part of the soul to the entire soul (1224 b 25), and claims that we 'metaphorize' in naming intemperance *akolasia* (1230 b 12-13). Note the parallel text in the *Nicomachean Ethics* 3: 15 (1119 a 36-b 3). Thus, metaphorical transposition serves to fill the gaps in common language.

20 *Physics* 3: 1, 201 a 15; 5: 2, 226 a 32-b 1

21 This paradox is the core of the argument of the article 'La mythologie blanche' by Jacques Derrida: 'In every rhetorical definition of metaphor is implied not just a philosophical position, but a conceptual network within which philosophy as such is constituted. Each thread of the net in addition forms a turn of speech (we might say a metaphor, but that the notion is too derivative in this case). Thus the definiens presupposes the definiendum' ('White Mythology' 30). This recurring theme is particularly striking in Aristotle, whom Derrida explores at length (18 ff.): The theory of metaphor 'seems to belong to the great unmoving chain of Aristotelian ontology, with his theory of the analogy of being, his logic, his epistemology, and more precisely with the basic organisation of his poetics and his rhetoric' (36). A detailed exegesis and a discussion of Derrida's thesis as a whole are to be found in Study 8, section 3 below. I will mention here just some technical points concerning the interpretation of Aristotle: (1) The name is never so tightly bound to the being of things, in Aristotle, that things could not be named differently, or that one could not vary their names in the diverse ways enumerated under the heading of *lexis*. Of course, *Metaphysics* Γ asserts that 'not to have one meaning is to have no meaning' (1006 a 30-b 15). But this univocity does not exclude the possibility of a word having more than one meaning; it prevents only, in Derrida's own words, 'a spread which cannot be controlled' (49). Hence, a limited polysemy is permitted. (2) As for the analogy of being, this is strictly speaking a medieval doctrine, founded moreover on an interpretation of the relationship of the entire series of categories to its first term, substance (*ousia*). There is nothing to justify this short-circuit between proportional metaphor and the analogy of being. (3) As we shall see later, there is no link between the notion of 'current' (*kurion*) meaning and 'proper' meaning, if by the latter one understands a primitive, original, indigenous meaning. (4) The ontology of metaphor which seems to suggest the definition of art in terms of *mimêsis* and its subordination to the concept of *phusis* is not necessarily 'metaphysical,' in the sense that Heidegger has given to this word. At the end of this first Study I will propose an interpretation of the implicit ontology of Aristotle's *Poetics* that in no way employs the transition from the visible to the invisible; see below, 34.

22 Concerning the notion of deviation, see below, Study 5, sections 1 and 3.

23 Rostagni, it is true, translates *kurion* by *proprio* (*Index* 188 *ad proprio*); cf. *ad* 1457 b 3 (125).

24 This point is crucial for Derrida's interpretation. It constitutes one link in the demonstration of the close connection between the theory of metaphor and Aristotelian ontology. Even though the *kurion* of the *Poetics* and *Rhetoric* and the *idion* of the *Topics* do not coincide, Derrida says that 'this whole "metaphorology" seems to be sustained by the notion of the *idion*, though it does not occupy the forefront' ('White Mythology' 48). Now, a study of the *Topics* offers encouragement neither to the assimilation of *kurion* and *idion*, nor especially to the interpretation of *idion* as being original, primitive, indigenous in the 'metaphysical' sense. The manner in which the *Topics* deals with *idion* is based on considerations completely outside the theory of *lexis*, and foreign in particular to the theory of ordinary or unusual denominations. The 'proper' (or 'Property,' trans. Pickard-Cambridge) is one of the four foundational notions that the tradition has called the 'predicables,' to distinguish them from the 'predicaments,' which are the categories (cf. Jacques Brunschwig, introduction to the French translation of the *Topics*). It is with this in mind that the 'proper' ('property') is distinguished from

'accident,' 'genus,' and 'definition.' Now what does this mean, that the 'proper' should be a predicable? It means that every proposition (every concrete focus of reasoning) and every problem (every subject with which discourse is concerned) 'indicates either a genus or a peculiarity or an accident' (101 b 17). In turn the peculiarity, or proper or property, is divided into two parts, one signifying 'the essential of the essence' (Brunschwig's translation of *to ti ên einai*; often called quiddity) and the other not signifying it. Now the first of these parts is called 'definition' in the *Topics*, while the second is the 'proper' ('Property') in its strict sense. Thus we have four predicables, 'property or definition or genus or accident' (101 b 25). From these notions all propositions are formed, because every proposition must assign its predicate in terms of one of these predicables. Accordingly and henceforth, it appears that in setting the 'proper' among the predicables, Aristotle situates it on a level distinct from that of denomination, to which alone belongs the opposition among ordinary words and metaphorical words, lengthened, abbreviated, and coined words, etc. On the other hand, the 'proper' belongs to a logic of predication. This latter builds upon a double polarity: essential and non-essential, coextensive and non-coextensive. Definition is at once both essential and coextensive, while accident is neither essential nor coextensive. The proper is located midway between these two poles, as something which is not essential, but coextensive: 'A "property" is a predicate which does not indicate the essence of a thing, but yet belongs to that thing alone, and is predicated controvertibly of it' (102 a 18-19). Thus, to be capable of reading and writing is a property (is proper) with respect to being human. By contrast, to sleep is not proper to man, since this predicate can be applied to another subject and, conversely, cannot be substituted for the predicate 'man'; although nothing prevents it being implied that a given subject happens to be a man. Thus, the proper is somewhat less than the definition, but much more than an accident which may or may not belong to one and the same subject. Since it does not point to essence, I should say that the criterion retained for the proper is the commutability of subject and predicate, what Aristotle calls convertibility. As we see, no metaphysical abyss reveals itself here. It suffices that the predicate should be coextensive without being essential, according to the 'crossed dichotomy' detailed above in the manner of J. Brunschwig. Furthermore, this criterion of coextensiveness finds its true function within argumentation itself: to show that a predicate is not coextensive is to refute a proposed definition. An appropriate method corresponds to this strategy, the *topic of the proper*, which applies to the good use of non-definitional predicates that are neither generic nor accidental. Finally – and above all – the location of the theory of the proper within the *Topics* is enough to remind us that we are not here in a fundamental, or constitutive, order, but in the order of dialectic. 'The formal objects' of dialectic, points out Brunschwig, are 'the discourses about things and not the things themselves' (introduction 50); like 'games based on a contract ... each predicable corresponds to a particular type of contract' (ibid.). The partial topic of the 'proper' is not exempt in this regard; it regulates the workings of discourse relative to the application of coextensive but non-essential predicates. Aristotle devotes book 5 of the *Topics* to it; there we find the 'proper' defined again, in chapter 2 (129 b 1 ff.) and chapter 4 (132 a 22-6). So Aristotle would only have had to make a 'proper' meaning of this notion, in order to oppose the series of deviations of denomination to it; but he needed the notion of 'current' meaning, which defines its use in denomination.

25 Study 7, section 3
26 See Study 3 on the opposition between interaction theory and substitution theory.
27 Concerning the vocabulary of substitution in Aristotle, see 1458 b 13-26: 'To realize the difference one should take an epic verse and see how it reads when the normal words are introduced [*epithemenôn*].' He proceeds to use verb forms of 'substitution' four times in succession: *metatitheis, metathentos, metathêken, metatitheis* (1458 b 16, 20, 24, 26 respectively). Substitution works in both directions, from the current word to the rare or metaphorical, and from the latter to the former: 'The same should be done with the strange word, the metaphor, and the rest; for one has only to put the ordinary words in their place to see the truth of what we are saying' (1458 b 18). But see the following note for the major exception, which occurs when metaphor names an 'anonymous' genus.
28 We have already pointed to this use of metaphor as the transfer of naming in the case of an 'anonymous' genus, or of a thing that has no name. Examples abound; cf. *Physics* 5, the definition of growth and decay, the definition of *phora*. The problem is dealt with explicitly in the first chapter of *On Sophistical Refutations*, concerning ambiguity: 'For names are finite and so is the sum-total of formulae (*logoi*), while things are infinite in number. Inevitably, then, the same formulae, and a single name, have a number of meanings' (165 a 10-13, trans. Pickard-Cambridge).
29 Concerning the relationship between analogy and resemblance, see Study 6, section 4.
30 Gilbert Ryle *The Concept of Mind* 16 ff., 33, 77-9, 152, 168, 206
31 See below, Study 4, section 5.
32 Max Black *Models and Metaphors.* On model and redescription, see below, Study 7, section 4.
33 H.-G. Gadamer *Wahrheit und Methode*; on *metaphoric*, see 71, 406 ff.
34 E.D. Hirsch *Validity in Interpretation* 169 ff.
35 On the workings of resemblance, see Study 6, *passim*; sections 3 and 4 of this Study take up the interpretation and discussion of the Aristotelian theory once more, this time from a less historical and more systematic point of view.
36 McCall devotes a whole chapter to *eikôn* in Aristotle (*Ancient Rhetorical Theories* 24-53). See also Cope *Introduction* 290-2.
37 On vehicle and tenor in I.A. Richards, see Study 3, section 2.
38 See below, Study 3, note 1.
39 McCall *Ancient Rhetorical Theories* 51, cites 3: 4, 1406 a 20, 1406 b 25-6, 1407 a 14-15; 3: 10, 1410 b 17-18; 3: 11, 1412 b 34-5, 1413 a 15-16.
40 Whereas E.M. Cope saw a perfect correspondence between the definition of simile as an 'extended metaphor' and the definition, coming from Cicero and Quintillian, of metaphor as a 'contracted simile' (*Introduction* 290), McCall insists that the later tradition 'reverses' matters (*Ancient Rhetorical Theories* 51). The case of Quintillian (ibid. 178-239) is particularly striking. He states: *in totum autem metaphora brevior est similitudo* ('on the whole metaphor is a shorter form of *similitudo*') (ibid. 230, from *De Institutione Oratoria Libri Duodecim* 8: 6, 8-9). McCall remarks that Quintillian has put the matter more strongly than if he had just said *brevior est quam similitudo*, or *brevior est similitudine*, expressions 'which would put metaphor and *similitudo* on an equal footing' (230). It is true that Le Guern disputes this interpretation (*Sémantique de la métaphore et de la metonymie* 54, note 1), invoking the Paris edition of 1527, which gives *brevior quam similitudo.* If this were so, 'the classical explanation of metaphor would have its origin in a corruption of the text of Quintillian' (ibid.). The consistency

of the post-Aristotelian tradition lends little credibility to this hypothesis. We
will take this discussion up again when we look at the works of Le Guern and
examine the fundamental relationships between metaphor and simile or comparison (Study 6, section 1).

41 As we saw earlier (note 9), *paradeigma* is distinct from *enthumêma* as a probable
induction is from a probable deduction. There are two kinds of *paradeigma* or
example, actual (or historical) parallels and invented parallels. The latter can be
either 'illustrations' (*parabolê*) or 'fables' (*logoi*), such as Aesop's fables (*Rhetoric* 2: 20, 1393 a 28-31). Ultimately, the heart of the opposition is between
historical example, to which *paradeigma* reduces, and the illustrative parallel,
which is the essence of *parabolê*. The unity of historical example and fictive
comparison is purely epistemological, in that both are forms of persuasion or
proof. On all this, see McCall *Ancient Rhetorical Theories* 24-9.

42 This adjective, *haploun* ('simple'), raises various problems of interpretation and
also of translation. To call comparison simple, when one says on the other hand
that it 'speaks, or is made, on the basis of two,' seems to be contradictory. Certainly one must agree that comparison, made up of only two terms and one relationship, is 'simple' compared with proportional metaphor, which is composed
of four terms and two relationships (see McCall's discussion of Cope's and
Roberts' interpretations, ibid. 46-7). For my part, I do not see any contradiction in calling simple the expression 'a shield is a cup,' from which the terms
'Arès' and 'Dionysius' are absent. This does not prevent its being composed of
two terms. By contrast, McCall uses the translation 'involves two relations' (45),
the reason actually being its closeness to proportional metaphor. He refers to
Rhetoric 3: 4 (1407 a 15-18), which makes a point of the reversibility of proportional metaphor; if one can give the fourth term the name of the second, one must
be able to do the opposite – for example, if the cup is the shield of Dionysius, it is
quite appropriate to call the shield the cup of Arès.

43 E.M. Cope (*The Rhetoric of Aristotle with a Commentary*) translates 3: 10, 11 as
follows: 'Similes ... are composed of (or expressed in) two terms, just like the proportional metaphors' (137). And he comments: 'The difference between a *simile*
and a metaphor is – besides the greater detail of the former, the simile being a
metaphor *writ large* – that it always *distinctly expresses* the two terms that are
being compared, bringing them into *apparent* contrast; the metaphor, on the
other hand, *substituting* by *transfer* the one notion for the other of the two compared, identifies them as it were in one image, and expresses both in a *single* word,
leaving the comparison between the object illustrated and the analogous notion
which throws a new light upon it, to suggest itself from the manifest correspondence to the hearer' (137-8).

44 It is the same in 3: 10, 7: the example borrowed from Pericles contains the explicit
marks of comparison (*houtôs ... hôsper*); on the other hand, that taken from Lep-
tines displays metaphor's brevity – 'he would not have the Athenians let Greece
"lose one of her two eyes"' (1411 a 2-5). The examples of 3: 11, 12 and 3: 11, 13
are also to be considered from this point of view (1413 a 2-13). It is true that Aristotle's quotations are generally inexact. Among those that can be verified (*Repub-
lic* 5: 469 d-e; 6: 488, a-b 10: 601 b), the first two contain neither the conjunction
nor the verb nor the adjective of comparison ('Do you see any difference between
...?' 'Conceive this sort of thing happening ...'); only the third contains a term of
comparison ('resemble'). The grammatical mark can vary, however, without affecting the general meaning of the comparison. This is noted by McCall, who speaks of

an 'overall element of comparison' in connection with 'stylistic comparison' (36), as opposed to the illustrative comparison whose purpose is to prove.

45 See below, Study 3, section 4.

46 A similar relationship underlies the suggested affinity between proverbs (*paroimiai*) and metaphors (1413 a 14-16). These are metaphors, it is suggested, that relate species to species. The proverb is, in effect, a comparison pursued between two orders of things (the man abused by the guest whom he has received into his house and the rabbit eating the crop of the peasant who brought him onto his land) (ibid.). The 'like' of comparison can be omitted here just as in metaphor, and with the same result: the relationship is that much more striking to the extent that it is unexpected, even paradoxical and bewildering. This same paradox, which is connected to explicit or implicit comparison, is also the kernel of hyperbole, which is nothing but an exaggerated comparison that is developed in the face of obvious differences. Thus, Aristotle can say, 'Successful hyperboles are also metaphors' (1413 a 19).

47 In this sense, 'new' metaphors (to use a name borrowed from Theodorus), which Aristotle likens to 'paradoxical' metaphors, are not exceptions to a rule, but rather are metaphors *par excellence.*

48 Why does Aristotle say the *eikôn* is 'of the nature of poetry' (1406 b 25) when the *Poetics* ignores it? (The sole mention of the word *eikôn* in the *Poetics* has nothing to do with comparison – 1448 b 10, 15.) Is the opening not provided when the *Poetics* extols 'the art of metaphorizing well' and links it to the ability to perceive similarities (1459 a 5-8)? All we can do is note this strange neglect: 'the odd absence of *eikôn* from the *Poetics* must be left unresolved' (McCall *Ancient Rhetorical Theories* 51).

49 Study 8, section 5

50 'Now since architecture is an art and is essentially a reasoned state of capacity to make, and there is neither any art that is not such a state nor any such state that is not an art, *art* is identical with a state of capacity to make, involving a true course of reasoning. All art is concerned with coming into being, i.e. with contriving and considering how something may come into being which is capable of either being or not being, and whose origin is in the maker and not in the thing made; for art is concerned neither with things that are, or come into being, by necessity, nor with things that do so in accordance with nature (since these have their origin in themselves)' (*Nicomachean Ethics* 1140 a 6-16, trans. Ross).

51 It would be impossible to over-emphasize the humbling – the 'loss of prestige,' says Jacques Brunschwig in his introduction to Aristotle's *Topics* – that dialectic suffers in passing from Plato's hands into those of Aristotle. Sovereign and synoptic science in Plato, it is only the theory of probabilistic argumentation with Aristotle (cf. Pierre Aubenque *Le Problème de l'être chez Aristote; Essai sur la problématique aristotélicienne* 251-64; M. Gueroult 'Logique, argumentation et histoire de la philosophie chez Aristote').

52 The *endoxa* of *Rhetoric* 1: 11 (1355 b 17) are defined precisely in *Topics* 1: 10 (104 a 8): 'Now a dialectical proposition consists in asking something that is held [*endoxos*] by all men or by most men or by the philosophers, i.e. either by all, or by most, or by the most notable of these, provided it be not contrary to the general opinion; for a man would probably assent to the view of the philosophers, if it be not contrary to the opinions of most men' (trans. Pickard-Cambridge). The *endoxa* are ideas taken up into the 'inter-play' [*jeu à deux*] that constitutes dialectical discussion (Brunschwig *Topiques* xxiii). This characteristic of propositions

is the signature of dialectical syllogism, whose premises are 'assented to in reality' (ibid. xxiv), as opposed on the one hand to demonstrative syllogism, whose premisses are intrinsically true, and on the other hand to 'apparently endoxal' propositions, which make reasoning materially eristic.

53 Brunschwig relates the question of *topoi* to that of dialectical reasoning in the following way: 'As a first approximation, the *topoi* can be described as rules, or if one prefers, as recipes for argumentation, arranged to supply effective tools to a very precisely laid out activity, that of dialectical discussion' (ibid. ix). The author adds: 'Closely bound up with the activity which they pretend to take from the level of blind practice and advance to that of methodic art, the *Topics*, the *vademecum* of the perfect dialectician, run the risk of appearing to be an art of winning at a game that no one plays any longer' (ix). But then, why speak of *topoi* to designate this 'machinery for constructing premises on the basis of a given conclusion' (xxxix)? One can emphasize the fact that the *topoi* are scattered about, or the fact that each has an assembling function. On the one hand, stress can be put on the 'non-systematic and seemingly headless [character] of logical thought' in the dialectical order (xiv), and on the closed nature of the isolated units located in this fashion. But one can also draw attention to the fact, as does *Rhetoric* 2: 26 (1403 a 17), that each *topos* 'embrac(es) a large number of particular kinds of enthymeme.' This unifying function is exercised in succession by the topics of accident, genus, proper or property (book 5), and definition.

54 I. During, in *Aristoteles, Darstellung und Interpretation seines Denkens*, sees grounds in this opposition between prose and poetry for calling *Rhetoric* book 3 'die Schrift "von der Prosa"' (149 ff.). While mindful of the definition in the *Poetics* (1450 b 13), which identifies *lexis* with the verbal expression of thought, During notes that in the context of the *Rhetoric, lexis* tends to become more and more like 'die literarische Kunstprosa' (150), yet without reducing to a theory of kinds of style (*charaktêres* or *genera dicendi*), which is a hellenistic creation.

55 It is interesting to note the reasons for this superiority: 'It was naturally the poets who first set the movement going; for words represent things, and they had also the human voice at their disposal, which of all our organs can best represent other things' (*Rhetoric* 3: 1, 1404 a 20-2).

56 On figure, see Study 5, section 2.

57 On the adherence of meaning to the sensible in poetry, see Study 6, section 2.

58 Cope observes that while the overall outline was already familiar in Aristotle's time, the division into four 'excellences' – purity, perspicuity, ornament, and propriety – 'is not accurately made, nor the order regularly followed' (*Introduction* 279). Moreover, the line is broken frequently, by the study of similitude for instance (see above), or by considerations that do not fit easily into an enumeration of the virtues of *lexis*, like the remarks concerning the 'form' of *lexis* (rythm, free-running and periodic style, 3: 8 and 9).

59 The verb that designates deviation – *exallattô, exallaxai* – comes up twice: 'Such variation from what is usual' (1404 b 8) and 'They depart from what is suitable, in the direction of excess' (1404 b 30). In each instance, an unusual usage is opposed to one that is customary and commonplace (*to de kurion kai to oikeion*, ibid. 32) or suitable (*prepon*, ibid. 30).

60 It is more difficult to relate to the theme of 'clarity' what is said immediately after in regard to the 'beauty' words should have: 'The beauty, like the ugliness, of all words may, as Licymnius says, lie in their sound or in their meaning' (3: 2, 12, 1405 b 6-7). And a bit further on: 'The materials of metaphor must be beautiful

to the ear, to the understanding, to the eye or some other physical sense' (ibid. 1405 b 17-18). It seems that the function of pleasing prevails here over that of indirect signification. The polarity of clarity and beauty might reflect something of the tension at the heart of eloquence or style, which was spoken of earlier.

61 For Cope, this disquisition on errors of style or bad taste does not imply the introduction of a specific excellence or virtue that would be 'warmth' in style (*Introduction* 286-90).

62 The same argument – avoidance of what would be too poetic – is applied to metaphors intended as euphemisms, and in general to circumlocutions (3: 6, 4, 1407 b 32-5).

63 Cope's commentary is particularly brilliant and *asteïon*! (*Introduction* 316-23).

64 See Study 8, section 3.

65 The ontological implications of this claim of Aristotle's will be taken up again below, 42-3, and Study 8, section 5.

66 See below, 40-1.

67 Ross gives the same rendering; Lucas opts for 'communication by means of words.'

68 J. Hardy remarks, 'The text and the meaning of this sentence are very much in doubt.' The French translation – 'car quelle serait l'œuvre propre du personnage parlant, si sa pensée était manifeste et ne résultait pas de son langage' – is less clear than Bywater's, which emphasizes that language in general, like the figure in particular (as mentioned earlier), functions as the manifesting, the 'making-it-appear,' of discourse. Hence, what 'thought' still lacks in order to become *poem* is the 'appearing.' In this regard, Derrida observes: 'If there were no difference between *dianoia* and *lexis* there would be no room for tragedy ... The difference is not restricted to the possibility that a character may think one thing and say another. He exists and acts in the tragedy only on condition that he speak' ('White Mythology' 32).

69 Richard McKeon 'Literary Criticism and the Concept of Imitation in Antiquity,' and 'Imitation and Poetry' 102-223

70 In the second text cited in the preceding note, McKeon points to the *aesthetics of genius* as the source of the pejorative interpretation of *mimêsis.*

71 For our conciliation of *mimêsis* and redescription, see Study 7, section 4.

72 On all this see McKeon, to whom, in large part, the development of what follows is owed. He insists on the necessity of always recreating the philosophical contexts in which a concept acquires meaning, and of relating every definition to the philosopher's own methodology.

73 McKeon writes: 'Imitation functions in that system as the *differentia* by which the arts, useful and fine, are distinguished from nature' (*Critics and Criticism* 131).

74 Leon Golden and O.B. Hardison *Aristotle's Poetics, a Translation and Commentary for Students of Literature* 68-9, 79, 87, 93, 95-6, 115; and the epilogue, 'On Aristotelian Imitation,' 281-96. Similarly, Gerald F. Else (*Aristotle's Poetics: The Argument*) is justified in dwelling on the paradox of defining *poiêsis* as *mimêsis.* He notes, with reference to 1451 b 27-33: 'What the poet "makes," then, is not the actuality of events but their logical structure, their meaning' (321). It is in this manner that creating and imitating can coincide. In this way also, the feeling of terror itself can be caused 'by imitation' (1453 b 8), in that the plot itself *is* the imitation (410-11, 447-50).

75 It constitutes, according to Hardison (*Aristotle's Poetics* 96), the 'first logical unit' of the *Poetics.* At the same time it adds to the significance of Aristotle's introduc-

tory remark, 'Let us follow the natural order and begin with the primary facts' (1447 a 13).

76 Ibid. 115. Hardison depends here on a Leon Golden article, 'Catharsis.'

77 'Tragic imitation, then, can be understood as a six-part process that begins with plot' (Hardison *Aristotle's Poetics* 286).

78 Hardison goes so far as to say that the tragic poem 'universalizes' history or nature (ibid. 291 ff.). History as such proffers nothing but the singular, nothing but undifferentiated individuals. Now the story is an intelligible interpretation of history, in a broad sense including or embracing a collection of single things. An action thus 'universalized' would obviously not be a copy.

79 The interpretation of tragic *katharsis* proposed by Golden acquires a certain measure of plausibility at this point, to the extent at least that the purification of pity and terror is mediated by the clarification effected by the intelligibility of the plot, spectacle, characters, and thought.

80 See Study 7, sections 4 and 5.

81 See the words 'perfection' or 'virtue' (*aretê*, 1458 a 18), 'rule of moderation' (*metrion*, 1458 b 12), 'improper' (*aprepôs*, ibid. 14), 'proper use' (*to harmottom*, ibid. 15, and *prepontôs khrêsthai*, 1459 a 4).

82 It is worth noting the occurrences of the word *phusis* in the *Poetics*, as these constitute a network replete with allusion pointing beyond that work. *Mimêsis* is the first thing to be mentioned if one is to follow 'the natural order' (1447 a 12): here, 'nature' designates the division of knowledge according to the order of things, in virtue of which imitation is to be found in the orbit of the sciences of 'making.' The concept of *telos* occasions an indirect allusion to nature: 'It is the action in it, i.e. its Fable or Plot, that is the end and purpose of tragedy' (1450 a 22). In a slightly less allusive fashion it is said that 'the first essential [*arkhê*], the life and soul [*psukhê*], so to speak, of Tragedy is the Plot' (1450 a 38), whereas thought and character are the 'natural causes' of the actions (1450 a 1). As for imitation itself, it is linked to nature in that 'Imitation is natural [*sumphoton*] to man' (1448 b 5); moreover, man is distinct from the animals in that 'he is the most imitative of creatures' (ibid. 7). It is nature again that among men distinguishes the most gifted artists (mastery of metaphor 'is a sign of genius [*euphuias*],' 1459 a 7); indeed, poets take up comedy or tragedy as their own natures dictate (1449 a 15). Finally, among all the poetic genres, the development of tragedy, which is born in improvisation and is thus in continuity with nature, culminates at a certain point when it attains 'its natural form' (1449 a 15). Furthermore, the characteristics of order, of completeness (*teleion*), of symmetry – in brief, everything that makes of a tragedy a perfect composition, something whole in itself – at the same time reveal 'the limit ... set by the actual nature of the thing' (1451 a 9). Thus the concept of nature, although not *thematized* as such in the *Poetics*, returns repeatedly as an *operational* concept (in E. Fink's sense of this opposition).

83 For Derrida ('White Mythology' 36-7), the tightly drawn agreement linking *mimêsis* and *phusis* constitutes one of the most penetrating indices of the dependence of metaphorology with respect to onto-theology. One could say that this partnership reveals the 'gesture constitutive of metaphysics and of humanity' (37). The preceding note owes much to Derrida, in both its substance and its tone of analysis.

84 The formula 'art imitates nature' pervades Aristotle's work. Vianney Décarie (*L'Objet de la métaphysique selon Aristote*) notes it already in the *Protrepticus*, where it contrasts with a Platonic formulation (*Laws* 10: 888 e-890 d): 'And nature's product always has an end and it is always constituted in view of a higher

end than that of the product of art; for art imitates nature, not nature art' (23 and note 3). The formula does not serve here to distinguish, nor even to co-ordinate; it seeks to subordinate. But the context shows us why: the exhortation to philosophize, which is the object of the treatise, is based upon 'the will of nature' (ibid.). It is necessary, therefore, to move from the teleology of art to an even *higher* teleology. In a different way, Aristotle's *Physics* (2: 2. 194 a 21-7) argues from what is seen in art to what must be demonstrated in the case of nature, namely, composition of form and of matter, and teleology. The argument reads as follows (trans. Hardie and Gaye): '*If ...* art imitates nature ... it would be the part of physics also to know nature in both its senses [form and matter].' And the text continues, 'nature is the end or "that for the sake of which"' (194 a 28). The same formula evidently could be read in the opposite sense and would thus distinguish art from nature on the grounds that art receives the characteristic of having an end from nature. This is the very source of the autonomy of art: for it is not the things produced, there to be copied, which are imitable in nature, but production itself and its teleological order, which remains to be understood and which the plot may reconstruct. On imitation in Aristotle, see Aubenque *Le problème de l'être chez Aristote* 487-508. (Study 8, section 1 contains a detailed discussion of this work.)

85 This interpretation will be taken up again and extended at the end of Study 8.

STUDY 2

1 Gérard Genette 'La rhétorique restreinte' 158-71
2 See Study 1, section 1.
3 Certain neo-rhetoricians contrast the rhetoric of style with the rhetoric of the invention of proofs and arguments and with that of composition (following Aristotle's tripartite plan in his *Rhetoric*), and they treat this as a contrast between the paradigmatic and the syntagmatic (Roland Barthes 'L'ancienne rhétorique, aide-mémoire' 175-6). A properly discursive theory of metaphor, like the interaction or the controversion theory, will deprive this distinction of much of its force.
4 Rhetoric implies even a theology: 'But it is given only to God to be able to embrace, in one single view, all individuals, whatever kind they may be, and to see them all together and singly at the same time' (*Les Figures du discours* 42).
5 Fontanier's 'Forewords,' 'Prefaces,' and 'Preambles' (21-30) (271-81) are of great interest in this connection. There he praises his 'system,' 'undeniably the most reasoned-out and the most philosophical, as well as the most complete, yet to appear in our language, and perhaps in any other' (23), 'a rational and philosophical system, all of whose details have been sorted out and interconnected in such a way that, in their collectivity, they form an absolutely coherent whole' (28).
6 Aristotle *Rhetoric* 3: 1, 2; cf. above, Study 1, 31 and 37.
7 Fontanier simply observes that 'this metaphor ought not be looked upon as a true figure, because we have no other word in the language for the same idea' (63).
8 I cannot resist quoting these wonderful lines by Gérard Genette: 'To identify a unit of discourse is quite necessarily to compare and oppose it implicitly to what could be, in such a situation and in its stead, another "equivalent" unit, that is, something at once similar and different ... To perceive a language is, quite necessarily, to imagine a silence or another language in the same place or at the same

point in time ... Where keeping silent or saying something else are impossible, there the fullness of speech is lacking: this is what Fontanier's monumental argument with catachresis symbolizes and brings out ... Speaking that is obligated does not oblige; speech that was not chosen from among other possible ways of speaking says nothing – it is not speech. If there were no figure, would there even be language?' ('Introduction' 12-13).

9 *Les Figures du discours* 66-7; 221-31; 279-81; 451-9
10 281, 451 ff., 461 ff., and passim. The ascendancy of the word can still be seen even in the definition of these figures (283, 323). Only the figures of style and of thought are less subservient to the word: the former because they are obviously features of discourse; the latter because they are 'independent of words, of expression, and of style' (403), although this puts them in danger of not being figures at all ('Perhaps it is unfortunate that these are called figures in this way, when they have to do only with thought alone, with thought considered abstractly and without regard for the form that it can borrow from language – they consist in nothing, so to speak, but a certain twist of spirit and imagination ... [403]).
11 How different the figures of signification are from all the others, exclaims Fontanier, 'for, unlike these last, they consist not in several words but in a single word; and what they present through an unaccustomed image is not a whole thought, a collection of ideas, but a single and unique idea, a simple element of thought!' (453).
12 With respect to the nomenclature, consult Henri Morier *Dictionnaire de poétique et de rhétorique.*
13 I.A. Richards *The Philosophy of Rhetoric* 96 ff.; see below, Study 3, section 2.
14 Jacques Derrida 'White Mythology'
15 Nelson Goodman *Languages of Art*
16 It seems that, for Fontanier, the possibility of double meaning gives the advantage to allegory: 'Instead of transforming the object and modifying it to a greater or lesser extent, as metaphors do, allegories leave the object in its natural state and only reflect it, like some kinds of transparent mirrors' (205).
17 Marcus B. Hester *The Meaning of Poetic Metaphor*
18 Émile Benveniste *Problems in General Linguistics*

STUDY 3

1 Émile Benveniste *Problems in General Linguistics*
2 Émile Benveniste 'La forme et le sens dans le langage'
3 *Problems in General Linguistics* 217-22
4 Paul Grice 'Meaning,' 'Utterer's Meaning, Sentence-Meaning and Word-Meaning,' and 'Utterer's Meaning and Intentions'
5 Plato *Cratylus* 425 a, 431 b-c ('the statement is a synthesis of name and verb,' trans. Jowett); *Theaetetus* 206 d; *Sophist* 261 d-262 d
6 '... there could not be a statement that was a statement about nothing' (*Sophist* 263 c, trans. Cornford).
7 Strawson *Individuals* part 2
8 Bertrand Russell 'On Denoting.' Cf. L. Linsky *Referring.*
9 On the ontological postulate connected to the identifying function, cf. John Searle *Speech Acts*. The axiom of existence is formulated thus: 'Whatever is referred to must exist' (77).

10 P.F. Strawson 'On Referring.' See also Linsky *Referring*.

11 J.L. Austin *How to Do Things With Words*

12 Aristotle *On Interpretation* paragraph 1

13 Austin *How to Do Things* lecture 1

14 Peter Geach *Mental Acts*. On the 'commitment' proper to every act of discourse and on the psychological factor of 'desire' and 'belief' implied by this 'commitment,' cf. Searle *Speech Acts* 64-71; Paul Ricoeur 'Discours et Communication.'

15 Benveniste *Problems in General Linguistics* chapters 13 and 14

16 Gottlob Frege 'On Sense and Reference'

17 Edmund Husserl *Logical Investigations* Investigation 1, Investigation 5

18 Benveniste *Problems in General Linguistics* part 5 'Man and Language'

19 Roman Jakobson 'Linguistics'

20 It is not without interest to note that of three studies brought together in this chapter, one is put under the aegis of 'rhetoric,' the second under that of 'logical grammar,' and the third under 'literary criticism.' There could be no more striking sign of the uncertain character of the boundaries of these disciplines. This makes the attempt to root all three in a single semantics all the more significant.

21 Study 2, section 2

22 Ludwig Wittgenstein *Philosophical Investigations* §23 'But how many kinds of sentence are there? Say assertion, question, and command? – There are *countless* kinds ...'

23 Study 1, 32

24 The expression *command* (which inspires the title of the sixth lecture, 'The Command of Metaphor' *Philosophy of Rhetoric* 115 ff.) is suggested by Aristotle's famous statement in the *Poetics* (1459 a 8), which Richards translates as follows: 'The greatest thing by far is to have a command of metaphor. This alone cannot be imparted to another: it is the mark of genius, for to make good metaphor implies an eye for resemblances' (ibid. 89).

25 'Language is vitally metaphorical, that is, it marks the before unapprehended relations of things and perpetuates their apprehension, until words, which represent them, become, through time, signs for portions or classes of thought instead of pictures of integral thoughts: and then, if no new poets should arise to create afresh the associations which have been thus disorganized, language will be dead to all the nobler purposes of human intercourse' (quoted in ibid. 90-1).

26 Study 2, 57

27 Richards *Philosophy of Rhetoric* 96. The fundamental meaning of the term *tenor* is captured in the following passage by Berkeley, quoted by Richards (4-5): 'I do ... once for all desire whoever shall think it worth his while to understand ... that he would not stick on this or that phrase, or manner of expression, but candidly collect my meaning from the whole sum and tenor of my discourse, and laying aside the words as much as possible, consider the base notions themselves ...' In *The New Rhetoric: A Treatise on Argumentation*, Ch. Perelman and L.O. Olbrechts-Tyteca introduce the two expressions *thème* and *phore*, which might be good translations for tenor and vehicle. However, the authors limit the application of their pair of terms to analogy, that is, to the relationship of proportionality: 'We propose that *thème* refer to the terms A and B taken together, on which the conclusion bears ... and that *phore* refer to the terms C and D taken together, which provide the basis for the reasoning ...' (501).

28 In this text borrowed from appendix C of the *Statesman's Manual*, Coleridge compares the growth of the imaginary to vegetal growth. Or, more precisely, it is in

meditating on the changes between individu:¹ and cosmic life, through which the part becomes the 'visible organism' of the whole, that at the same time the meaning of every symbol is, metaphorically, produced. Indeed, a symbol, 'while it enunciates the whole, abides itself as a living part of that unity of which it is the representative' (Richards *Philosophy of Rhetoric* 109). On metaphor according to Coleridge, see I.A. Richards *Coleridge on Imagination.*

29   Richards (*Philosophy of Rhetoric* 116) cites Johnson's statement that every word that 'gives us two ideas for one' is a metaphor.

30   A. Breton *Les Vases communicants* (cited in ibid. 123)

31   The problem of resemblance is discussed below, in Study 6.

32   Study 7

33   Chapter 3. See also chapter 13 of *Models and Metaphors* entitled 'Metaphor and Archetypes.'

34   'Metaphor and Archetypes,' ibid.

35   Colin M. Turbayne *The Myth of Metaphor.* Cf. below, Study 7.

36   'All literary works fall into three main classes: poems, essays, and prose fiction' (126).

37   See Study 1, section 5.

38   Cf. especially chapters 4 and 5.

39   Beardsley adds an important argument to the present critique of the theory of metaphor in 'The Metaphorical Twist.' There he states that comparison takes place between objects whereas opposition exists between words. The 'twist' is brought about by tensions within discourse itself. Consequently, a theory of verbal opposition is distinct from object comparison theory as the order of words is distinct from the order of things. The connotations to which a purely semantic theory has recourse are to be found in the realm not so much of objects as of everyday beliefs concerning these objects. A second argument is that looking for a motif of comparison leads almost inevitably to the imagination as a matter of individual psychology. In effect, one must interpolate not only the term that completes the comparison but also the meaning it carries; in conjuring an absent term, explication is at the mercy of the reader's idiosyncratic imagery as much as that of the poet. Beardsley's final argument is that to invoke a comparison is also to ask whether it is appropriate or too far-fetched. As the 'controversion' theory abundantly proves, there is practically no limit to the 'fit' between a metaphorical attribute and a given subject.

40   In 'The Metaphorical Twist,' directed as much against psychologism as against realism, Beardsley strongly emphasizes that 'the opposition that renders an expression metaphorical is ... within the meaning-structure itself' (299). The logical opposition that compels the reader to pass from central to marginal meanings can be defined independently of any intentionality. The distinction between two levels of meaning (primary and secondary) as well as logical opposition within a single level (that of attribution) are semantic and not psychological facts. The passage from designation to connotation can be described entirely with the resources of a semantic analysis of the sentence and the word.

41   Jeremy Taylor *Of Holy Living* London 1847; see ibid. 302, note 20.

42   *Collected Poems of Wallace Stevens* 286 (cited in ibid. 304, note 22)

STUDY 4

1   Robert Godel *Les Sources manuscrites du Cours de linguistique générale de Ferdinand de Saussure* 189 ff.

2 In an 1883 article, 'Les lois intellectuelles du langage' (*Annuaire de l'Association pour l'encouragement des études grecques en France*), Michel Bréal confers the name of semantics on the 'science of meanings [*significations*]'; he pledges to turn his wits no longer 'to the flesh and form of words' but to 'the laws that preside over the transformation of meanings, the choice of new expressions, the birth and death of expressions.' Accordingly, changes in the meanings of words are inserted at the first level of this new science. This fundamental orientation is confirmed in Arsène Darmesteter's work *La vie des mots étudiée dans leurs significations* and later in that of Bréal *Essai de sémantique: Science des significations.*

3 Josef Trier *Der deutsche Wortschatz im Sinnbezirk des Verstandes*

4 The proper level of the sentence seems about to be recognized when the distinction is made between associative and syntagmatic relations, whose interplay constitutes the 'mechanism of language' (*Course in General Linguistics* part 2, chapters 5 and 6). In fact it is 'outside discourse' (123) that words associate *in absentia*, and it is 'in discourse' (ibid.) that words combine *in presentia* in a syntagmatic relation. It seems, then, that the theory of relations between signs would find reference to discourse essential. Even more than the associative relation, the syntagmatic relation appears bound to appeal to a theory of the discourse-sentence: is it not said that 'the sentence is the ideal type of syntagma' (124)? There is no hint, nevertheless, of anything of this sort. Syntagmas do not depend on speech but on language, for they are 'pat phrases in which any change is prohibited by usage' (ibid.). It is clear that de Saussure recognizes only a psychological difference (constraint versus freedom) between language and speech, itself founded on a sociological difference (speech is individual, language is social) (14). As a 'part of the inner storehouse that makes up the language of each speaker' (123), the syntagma depends thus on language and not on speech. Hence, the *Course* ignores entirely the properly logical difference between discourse and language, that is to say, the difference between the predicative relation in discourse and the opposition-relation between signs in the language system. In this fashion one can say that de Saussure has a theory of speech in the individual and psychological sense, but not a theory of discourse in the properly semantic sense defined at the beginning of the third Study. He also never gives the sentence a status comparable to that of the entities about which the essence of the *Course* is organized.

5 Reference is made here to the schema proposed by Stephen Ullmann in *The Principles of Semantics* 31-42. A good deal of time will be spent on this in the second section of this Study.

6 Michel Le Guern *Sémantique de la métaphor et de la métonymie* 121

7 Hedwig Konrad *Étude sur la métaphore*

8 The discussion of the work of Michel Le Guern (Study 6, section 1) will occasion a return to Hedwig Konrad's treatment of synecdoche (113), simile (150), symbol (151), and ellipsis (116). Further, examination of the 'metaphysical implications' of metaphor in Derrida (Study 8, section 3) will provide the opportunity to speak of the notes on personifications (139). And the notion of semantic impertinence in Jean Cohen (Study 5, section 3) will remind us of what is said here about enigma (148).

9 The *Rhétorique générale* of the Groupe de Liège in Study 5, and the *Sémantique de la métaphore et de la métonymie* by Le Guern in Study 6

10 'Hence, the role of the concept of a substantive is to symbolize a unique and individual structure, and to determine in our minds the special place that each of

the object's representations should have in relationship to the others. Those among the ensemble of attributes that are possessed *par excellence* and in a unique way play a special demarcative role. We call this specific interrelation of attributes the fundamental order of the concept' (66). The author refers specifically (51) to the notion of *Gegenstandsbezug* in the second *Logical Investigation* of Edmund Husserl. And it is not overdone to draw a parallel as well between this analysis and what P.F. Strawson says in *Individuals: An Essay in Descriptive Metaphysics* about the identifying function of logical subjects. But Strawson shows that the concept cannot fulfil the function of identifying singular things without the addition of demonstratives and of indicators of place and time. In this sense, it is doubtful whether the concept, if completely unaided, would be able to enframe an individual.

11 'The word that serves to designate concrete objects must itself in every instance evoke a single and unique structure. The word *rose* evokes the particular structure of the rose; the word *tree*, that of a tree. In order to designate several objects, a word would have to evoke an amorphous sum of general attributes. But then the word would no longer be the symbol of precise objects and would not produce the borrowed effect immediately upon being transposed from its standard use ... Thus, in its normal use, the *meaning* is a concept' (72). And further on: 'The word does not change meaning with a partial change in the partial representation of an object. The word does not change meaning as long as it applies to one of the logical species' (79).

12 Geoffroy de Vinsauf *Poetria Nova*

13 This was also seen by Geoffroy de Vinsauf: according to him, metaphor is based on a privileged analogy. One can take as the transposed term the thing that stands forth as *the most obvious representative of the attribute* - milk and snow for whiteness, honey for sweetness, etc. (cited by Konrad *Étude sur la métaphore* 18).

14 Aristotle was aware of this, for he defined three of the classes of metaphor in terms of a relation that brings genus and species into play. The author endeavours to show that in reality the four classes are defined in relation to the transposition from species to species (ibid. 100 ff.).

15 For the same reason the author stays clear of assimilations between myth and metaphor, which are found in Cassirer among others (ibid. 154-62).

16 Of special note is the study of *celestial metaphors* in Victor Hugo (131-6). The author concludes her discussion in the following fashion: 'All his comparisons have the effect of taking us into an atmosphere of illusion and of dreams; for Victor Hugo develops and justifies his analogies as much as possible, so that he gives the impression of having discovered a new truth, of having perceived more profound relationships existing in reality between beings and things' (136).

17 Discussing the concept of *ascription* in a context different from our own (to ascribe the act X to A), Peter Geach notes that the question of opposing *ascription* and *description* would not be posed, were it not for the fact that 'what is regularly ignored is the distinction between calling a thing "P" and predicating "P" of a thing' ('Ascriptivism' *Phil. Review* 69, 2 [1960] reprinted in Geach *Logic Matters*).

18 Recognizing that naming is not the function of simile, the author rather curiously sets simile on the side of the aesthetic (149), encouraged in this view, it seems, by the hyperbolistic character, the intentional exaggeration of literary comparisons. The argument is not incisive.

19 In appearance only, as the difficulties of the componential analysis will show (Study 5, section 4).

20 Perhaps in its turn this second divorce will call for a revision, in particular in the domain of metaphor, which offers especially strong justifications from the *psycholinguistic* point of view; see below, Study 6, section 6.

21 Stephen Ullmann *The Principles of Semantics, Précis de Sémantique française, Semantics: An Introduction to the Science of Meaning*

22 Gustaf Stern *Meaning and Change of Meaning*

23 K. Nyrop *Grammaire historique de la langue française*

24 L. Bloomfield *Language*, Z.S. Harris *Methods in Structural Linguistics*, C.E. Osgood 'The Nature and Measurement of Meaning'

25 A. Meillet *Linguistique Historique* 1: 30, cited in Ullmann *Principles of Semantics* 54. The old definitions, from an era when anti-psychologism was not so marked, did not hesitate to make the word correspond to a mental entity, the identity of the same notion in the spirit. Thus Meillet writes: 'To each notion there is attached a phonic compound called *word*, giving body to this notion in the subject's thought and raising the same notion or a similar notion in his interlocutor' (*Linguistique historique* 2: 1 and 71, quoted in Ullmann 51). Similarly L.H. Gray, 'the smallest thought-unit vocally expressible' (*Foundations of Language* [New York 1939] 146, quoted in Ullmann 51).

26 Let us recall here the definition of L. Bloomfield, 'minimum free-form' (*Language* 178; Ullmann *Principles of Semantics* 51). Similar is J.R. Firth's definition of the word as 'lexical substitution-counter,' which in addition brings in the test of communication, transposed from phonology to lexicology ('The Technique of Semantics' cited in Ullmann 56).

27 Here Ullmann cites the works of G. Matoré (*Le Vocabulaire et la société sous Louis-Philippe* and *La Méthode en lexicologie*), which he compares to Trier's research on semantic fields (see Ullmann *Semantics* 252).

28 André Martinet 'Le mot.' We will retain his definition: 'Segment of the spoken chain or of the written text, such that one can separate it from its context by saying it by itself or by separating it with a white space from the other elements of the text and attribute a meaning or a specific function to it' (40). See also *Eléments de linguistique générale* and *A Functional View of Language*.

29 C.K. Ogden and I.A. Richards *The Meaning of Meaning* 11

30 Z. Gombocz *Jelentéstan*

31 On polysemy see *Principles of Semantics* 114-25, *Précis* 199-218, *Semantics* 159-75.

32 L. Wittgenstein *Philosophical Investigations* par. 67

33 Cf. Roman Jakobson 'Linguistics.' We will refer especially to 453 ff. concerning the 'Essentials and goals of contemporary linguistics.'

34 *Principles of Semantics* part 4, 'Historical Semantics' 171-258, *Précis* chapter 10 'Why Words Change Meaning' (236-69), chapter 11 'How Words Change Meaning' (270-98)

35 Ullmann (*Principles of Semantics* 117) approvingly quotes the following words of W.M. Urban: 'The fact that a sign can intend one thing without ceasing to intend another, that, indeed, the very condition of its being an *expressive* sign for the second is that it is also a sign for the first, is precisely what makes language an instrument of knowing. This "accumulated intension" of words is the fruitful source of ambiguity, but it is also the source of that analogous predication, through which alone the symbolic power of language comes into being' (*Language and Reality* 112). It will be noted that this cumulative character is described in the framework of descriptive semantics, in the section on polysemy.

36 *Principles of Semantics* 220 ff. *Précis* 270 ff.
37 On the signifier as acoustic image, see the *Course in General Linguistics* 12, 15, 66. On the signified as concept, see ibid. 12, 66, 103, 114.
38 W. Wundt *Völkerpsychologie*, 'die Sprache'
39 It is true that only the second sort of relation is called 'associative relation' by de Saussure (*Course in General Linguistics* 123 ff.). The syntagmatic relation is simply grafted on to the linear character of language, that is, the aspect of temporal succession; in no way is the syntagmatic solidarity called association by contiguity. Jakobson's interpretation thus constitutes an innovation: 'The constituents of a context are in a state of contiguity, while in a substitution set signs are linked by various degrees of similarity which fluctuate between the equivalence of synonyms and the common core of antonyms' ('Two Aspects of Language and Two Types of Aphasic Disorders' 243-4).
40 Léonce Roudet 'Sur la classification psychologique des changements sémantiques'
41 Z. Gombocz *Jelentéstan*
42 Henri Bergson 'L'effort intellectuel' in *L'Energie spirituelle, Œuvres* 930-59
43 G. Esnault *L'Imagination populaire: métaphores occidentales.* Cf. below, note 92.
44 Cf. above, Study 1, 33.
45 I have already alluded (Study 1, section 1) to Gérard Genette's denunciation of rhetoric restricted to two figures, or even to one alone, that being metaphor.
46 The quotation from Wordsworth should be noted (*Semantics* 213): 'The song would speak / Of that interminable building reared / By observation of affinities / In objects where no brotherhood exists / To passive minds.'
47 *Course in General Linguistics* 9, Robert Godel *Les Sources manuscrites* 42 ff.
48 Roman Jakobson 'Linguistics' 458
49 *Course in General Linguistics* 79 ff.
50 Ullmann takes this up: 'A purely synchronistic notion, polysemy bears important consequences of a diachronistic order: words can acquire new acceptations without losing their primitive meaning. The result of this faculty is an elasticity of semantic relations that is without parallel in the domain of sounds' (*Précis* 199).
51 Ullmann *Principles of Semantics* 40. This panchronistic perspective imposes itself equally on historical semantics (ibid. 231, 255-7).
52 Ullmann *Précis* 200-7
53 Ibid. 242: 'Vocabulary is not rigidly systematized, as are phonemes and grammatical forms: at any moment one can add to it an unlimited number of elements that are new in every case, comprising words as well as meanings.'
54 Ibid. 215-16
55 Ibid. 243
56 *Course in General Linguistics* 66
57 We have grafted this distinction between the signified and the denoted onto the fundamental dichotomy of the sign and the sentence, that is, in the terminology of Émile Benveniste, the opposition of the semiotic plane and the semantic plane; cf. above, Study 3, section 1.
58 On this equivocity in the word *meaning*, see my article 'Sens et signe.'
59 The distinction that Gottlob Frege makes between meaning (or sense) and denotation (*nominatum*, reference) is established first at the level of the proper name, then extended to the whole proposition: 'A proper name (word, sign, sign-compound, expression) expresses its sense, and designates or signifies its nominatum. We let a *sign express* its sense and *designate* its nominatum' ('On Sense and Reference' *Readings in Philosophical Analysis* 89).

60 Ullmann *Précis* 243
61 Groupe μ *Rhétorique générale* 97 ff.; see below, Study 5, section 4.
62 'It is in speech, the concrete realization of language, that changes present themselves' (*Précis* 237).
63 Study 7, section 4
64 Ullmann *Semantics* 195
65 Ibid. 248
66 *Course in General Linguistics* 126
67 Ullmann *Semantics* 195
68 Ibid. 193
69 'Linguistics'
70 This absence of grammatical autonomy reminds us that the word is the product of the analysis of a statement. Edward Sapir defines the word as 'one of the smallest, completely satisfying bits of isolated "meaning" into which the sentence resolves itself' (*Language: An Introduction into the Study of Speech* 35). Meillet's definition of the word, which incorporates grammatical use into the semantic function, was cited earlier (note 25). This is why the word has no semantic identity that can be separated from its syntactic role: it has meaning only when invested with a grammatical role corresponding to a type of employment in discourse.
71 Ullmann *Semantics* 55, 64-7
72 Wittgenstein *Philosophical Investigations* par. 43
73 Ibid. par. 11
74 Ibid. par. 31. For the same concept in de Saussure, see the *Course in General Linguistics* 22, 88, 110.
75 Gilbert Ryle 'Ordinary Language' 120-1
76 Wittgenstein *Philosophical Investigations* par. 7 ff.
77 Ullmann *Semantics* 67
78 Émile Benveniste 'La forme' 37
79 Wittgenstein *Tractatus Logico-Philosophicus* 2.01, 2.011, 2.02
80 Edmund Husserl *Ideas I* par. 94
81 Benveniste 'La forme et le sens'
82 Ibid. 38
83 Ibid.
84 Ibid.
85 Jakobson 'Linguistics' 422: 'The variability of meanings, particularly their manifold and far-reaching figurative shifts, and an incalculable aptitude for multiple paraphrases are just those properties of natural language which induce its creativity and endow not only poetic but even scientific activities with a continuously inventive sweep. Here, indefiniteness and creative power appear to be wholly interrelated.'
86 Ullmann *Semantics* 52
87 Strawson *Individuals* 20-1
88 Cited in Ullmann *Précis* 207
89 Study 5, section 3
90 Study 7, section 3
91 Esnault notes that metaphor appears to follow the order of things: 'It respects the pathways, the constant order of natural phenomena' (quoted in Ullmann *Précis* 285).

STUDY 5

1 One must add the important work by Michel Le Guern *Sémantique de la méta-phore et de la métonymie*, which also represents the most recent state of research in the French language. However, only brief references will be made to this work in the present Study, because of its strong ties with the theses of Roman Jakobson, which will be discussed only in Study 6, and because of the role given to 'the associated image,' a role that cannot be appreciated without the framework of the next Study.

2 L. Prieto and Ch. Muller *Statistique et Analyse linguistique*

3 A.-J. Greimas *Sémantique structurale, Recherche de méthode, Du sens: Essais sémiotiques*

4 G. Genette 'La Rhétorique restreinte'

5 G. Genette 'La rhétorique des figures.' See above, Study 2, 52.

6 Tzvetan Todorov *Littérature et Signification* appendix: 'Tropes et Figures'

7 See above, Study 3, 84.

8 Ibid. 90-9

9 It is enough to compare the two definitions: rhetoric is 'the knowledge of the different meanings with which a single word is used in a single language' (C. Dumarsais *Des tropes* v, quoted in Todorov *Littérature et Signification* 94); and on the other side, 'It is in the province of grammar to tell us the true sig-nification of words, and their meaning when used in discourse' (*Des tropes* 22)

10 G. Genette 'Figures' in *Figures I* 205-21

11 The following remark by Gérard Genette brings together all the traits discussed here (hiatus and consciousness of hiatus, virtuality of unmarked language, trans-latability in principle of figures): 'The spirit of rhetoric is wholly contained in this consciousness of a hiatus between real language (that of the poet) and a virtual language (the one that would have used the simple and common expres-sion) that needs only to be re-established in thought in order to delimit a space of figures' (*Figures I* 207). Again: 'The rhetorical fact begins at the point where I can compare the form of this word or of this sentence with that of another word or another sentence that could have been used in their place and in whose stead, one may speculate, they appear.' And again: 'Every figure is translatable, and carries its translation visible in transparency, like a filigree or a palimpsest, beneath its apparent text. Rhetoric is linked to this duplicity of language' (211). It is in this sense that Genette accepts the aphorism of Pascal inscribed as exergue to *Figures I*: 'Figure carries absence and presence.' This is also the source of the justification for Fontanier's opposition between catachresis, whose use is forced, and figure, which combines things freely.

12 Cf. above, Study 3, 95.

13 Jean Cohen *Structure* 22

14 The relative degree zero is attained by a series of successive approximations: (1) prose, (2) written prose, (3) written scientific prose. (1) 'We wish to compare poetry to prose, and by prose we provisionally understand usage, that is the assemblage of the statistically most prevalent forms in the language of a single linguistic community' (ibid. 21). (2) 'The principle of homogeneity demands that poetry that is written be compared to written prose' (ibid. 22). (3) 'Which among all the types of written prose is to be chosen as norm? From all the evi-dence, one must turn towards the writer who is least oriented to aesthetic goals, that is, towards the scientist' (ibid.).

15 Remarking that statistics is the general science of deviations and stylistics the science of linguistic deviations, Jean Cohen proposes 'to apply the results of the second to the first: the poetic fact then becomes measurable, and expresses itself as the average frequency of deviations presented by poetic language in relation to prose' (ibid. 15). Accordingly, the enterprise enters into an aesthetic-scientific project. Poetics must establish itself as a quantitative science: 'Poetic style will be the average deviation of the collection of poems, on the basis of which it would be theoretically possible to measure the "poetic degree" of a given poem' (ibid.).

16 Genette *Figures I* 211

17 Ibid

18 *Rhétorique générale* 30-44

19 Greimas *Sémantique structurale* 69 ff.

20 Cf. above, Study 1, 17-20.

21 Ibid. 34

22 Ibid. 31-2 and 37

23 P. Fontanier *Les Figures du discours* 63

24 Ibid. 64

25 Roman Jakobson 'Closing Statements: Linguistics and Poetics'

26 For his part, Jakobson assigns these two arrangements to the principle of similarity (choice among similar terms) and to the principle of contiguity (linear construction of the sequence). We will discuss this particular aspect of the Jakobson definition of metaphorical process in Study 6, which is devoted to the operation of resemblance.

27 Cf. Study 7, section 2

28 Todorov *Littérature et Signification* 102

29 The preceding section already quoted this text of Genette: 'The spirit of rhetoric is wholly contained in this consciousness of a hiatus between real language (that of the poet) and a virtual language (the one which would have used the simple and common expression) that needs only to be re-established in thought in order to delimit a space of figures' (*Figures I* 207).

30 Quoted in ibid. 220

31 'Espace et Langage' in ibid. 103

32 Northrop Frye *Anatomy of Criticism*

33 Todorov *Littérature et Signification* 99

34 Versification aims only at 'weakening the structuring of the message' (96), at 'jumbling the message' (99). 'The history of versification, followed through two centuries, exhibits the progressive increase of de-differentiation' (101).

35 Plato *Sophist* 251 d, 253 c

36 Noam Chomsky *Aspects of the Theory of Syntax*. On generative semantics, which has separated gradually from the generative and transformational grammar set out in this work by Chomsky, cf. Françoise Dubois-Charlier and Michel Galmiche 'La Sémantique générative.'

37 I leave aside the case of lack of determination (personal pronouns, proper names, demonstratives, adverbs of time and of place, tenses of verbs, which are without determination in context: 155-63), which poses another problem, that of the absence of contextual referent, and introduces another type of interpretation at the properly referential level. For this reason, this analysis is not exactly in the right place in a chapter on 'determination.' One does not determine the meaning of a link by determining the extension (of the chain involved); 'I' has no extension. Besides, these connectives are not in the position of epithets.

38 Cohen notes: 'If one extends the process on the diachronistic plane, one has the "metaphor in common use"; if one concentrates it into synchrony, one has the "newly-invented metaphor." This is the only one to be studied here; as we saw, by definition the metaphor in common use is not a poetic deviation' (*Structure* 114, note 1).

39 Perhaps Cohen over-extends the 'genus' a bit, by calling all figures metaphor, including rhyme and inversion. But, in order to speak of rhyme-metaphor, one would have had to demonstrate the phenomenon of reduction of deviation on the plane of versification, which was not done and which perhaps may be beyond doing. Indeed, in the final analysis it definitely seems that every reduction of deviation will be semantic.

40 Cf. above, Study 4, 131-2.

41 Le Guern's *Sémantique* and the *Rhétorique générale* have in common the hypothesis of componential analysis of the signified, taken over from Greimas, in virtue of which metaphor is to be treated as an alteration of the semic organization of a lexeme. But this thesis from structural semantics is transferred into the framework of an opposition borrowed from Jakobson, that of metaphorical and metonymic processes. For this reason I will postpone its examination until after discussion of Jakobson's thesis. Furthermore, the latter is reinterpreted so as to have the sense of an opposition between intralinguistic relation and extralinguistic or referential relation: 'In transferring this distinction from Jakobson's analysis, one must take care that the metaphorical process concerns the semic organization, while the metonymic process modifies only the referential relation' (Le Guern 14). As observed subsequently (15, note 17), a serious split results with the analyses of the *Rhétorique générale*. In fact, since the notion of semic organization is opposed to that of a switching of reference, it takes on a quite different meaning through the contrast. When the time comes, other important differences between Le Guern and the Groupe de Liège will be underlined. An analysis of the whole of Le Guern's work is to be found in Study 6, section 5.

42 Cf. Study 3, section 1; Study 4, sections 1 and 5.

43 The semantics of Le Guern and of the Groupe de Liège are entirely at one on the precise point of the definition of metaphor in terms of alteration of semic composition. Both of them confer the same primacy on the lexeme, that is, on the word ultimately and not on the sentence. Both of them suppose a semic composition prior to the lexeme, on the basis of which metaphor is explained 'through the suppression or more exactly by the bracketing of one portion of the constitutive semes of the lexeme used' (Le Guern *Sémantique* 15).

44 Greimas *Sémantique structurale* 42 ff.

45 Cf. below, Study 6, section 1.

46 Can the question of semantic segmentation be resolved without recourse to the structure of the referent? This is what Le Guern must presuppose, in order to reserve modifications of the referential relation for the operation of metonymy. The opposition between semantic reorganization and reference switching supposes that semic analysis and conceptual or objective analysis are entirely dissociated. In his chapter 'Towards Semic Analysis' (*Sémantique* 114 ff.), Le Guern reproaches most attempts at analysing the lexeme in terms of semes for sliding 'towards a structuring of the universe' (114), something that forces an encyclopaedic and therefore impossible responsibility on semic analysis (ibid.). This reproach is connected to the author's more general concern to dissociate semantics from logic, some important consequences of which – the role of the associated image, the difference between metaphor, symbol, similarity, comparison,

and so on – will be seen in the next Study. According to him, the metaphorical uses of a word mark precisely the difference between semic analysis and referential knowledge of the object. The difficulty with this criterion is that it involves only lexicalized metaphors, which, by the author's own admission, are but very few in number (82). Our constant theme, that the dictionary contains no living metaphors, says the same thing. Moreover, the argument runs the risk of circularity, if metaphor reveals semantics as such, an abstraction from metaphor, and if semic analysis is to explain metaphorical usage.

47 The authors use the name 'mode Σ' for the mode that breaks a class down into species, because the class is the sum (Σ) of its species; they call the mode of decomposition into disjunctive trees 'mode π,' because the object is the logical product (π) that results from the distributive decomposition.

48 The semantics of Le Guern resists this reduction of metaphor to a double synecdoche, not only in virtue of the polarity (borrowed from Jakobson) of metaphorical process and metonymic process, but for a reason derived from its own analysis of synecdoche (*Sémantique* 29-39). Synecdoche does not constitute a homogeneous category. One of its species – the synecdoche of the part and the whole – is similar to metonymy; like metonymy, it is defined as a switching of reference between two objects connected by an extra-linguistic relationship, and is explained by restitution of the entire reference that undergoes only an ellipsis in the figurative statement. Synecdoche of the part and the whole is just a somewhat special metonymy, in which switching of reference prevails over the ellipsis procedure. On the other hand, synecdoche of species and genus brings nothing into play but the procedure of abstraction which is at the base of all denomination. Here too, I would observe that the figure does not consist in the passage from species to genus, but in the misapprehension through which the one is designated in the terms of the other. But I agree completely that metonymy and synecdoche belong on the same side, in that they can be defined and explained as accidents of denomination.

49 Léon Cellier 'D'une rhétorique profonde: Baudelaire et l'oxymoron.' For the authors of the *Rhétorique générale*, the difference proposed by Cellier between antithesis and oxymoron ('contradiction tragically proclaimed for antithesis, paradisaically assumed for oxymoron') concerns only the *ethos* of figures, not their analysis on the formal level (120).

50 Jean Cohen 126

51 Jean Cohen writes: 'So we have the right to analyse "fox" as a "more cunning animal," the second trait alone being retained in metaphorical usage' (ibid. 127).

52 For this discussion, cf. Study 3, section 3.

53 Le Guern (*Sémantique* 39-65) offers a palpably different analysis of the family of language facts arising from the relation of similarity. We shall reserve its discussion for the next Study, section 5.

54 The negation of the referential function of metaphorical discourse by the new rhetoric will be examined in Study 7; let us here just underline the solidarity of this thesis with the postulates of the theory. Only the theory of the statement-metaphor, by reinserting figure into the framework of the theory of discourse, can reopen the problematic of meaning and reference that the reduction to the word closed off. The semantics of Le Guern poses an analogous problem, but for different reasons. The counterpart of the close link instituted between metonymy and reference is the exclusion of all problems of reference from the semic analysis of metaphor. Consequently, the denotative deficiency (in the sense of cognitive

information) can be made up only by an excess of connotation (in the sense of associated affective value); hence, an investigation of motivations (to teach, to please, to persuade) takes the place of an inquiry into the referential import of the metaphorical statement.

STUDY 6

1 The history of this reversal of priority between metaphor and simile after Aristotle is to be found in Marsh McCall *Ancient Rhetorical Theories of Simile and Comparison.*
2 *Course in General Linguistics* part 2, chapters 5 and 6
3 Roman Jakobson 'Results of the Conference of Anthropologists and Linguists' 567, 565
4 Nicolas Ruwet, the translator of 'Two Aspects of Language and Two Types of Aphasic Disturbances' into French, did not fail to expose the divergence between Jakobson's classification and that suggested by Freud in *The Interpretation of Dreams* (*Essais de linguistique générale* 66, note 1). Is it enough to claim, with Jakobson himself, 'the imprecision of the concept of condensation, which in Freud seems at the same time to cover cases of metaphor and cases of synecdoche'? Or must it rather be admitted that the phenomena that Freud placed under the general title of *Entstellung* escape language? My view on this topic can be found in *Freud and Philosophy: An Essay on Interpretation* 88 ff. and 134 ff.
5 The following table presents the succession of viewpoints under which the polarity of the two processes is effected:

process	operation	relationship	axis	domain	linguistic factor
metaphor	selection	similarity	substitution	semantics	code (signification in the code)
metonymy	combination	contiguity	concatenation	syntax	message (contextual signification)

6 'Two Aspects' 258
7 Pierre Fontanier *Les Figures du discours* 79
8 Jakobson 'Results of the Conference' 566
9 Michel Le Guern *Sémantique de la métaphore et de la métonymie*
10 A.J. Greimas *Sémantique structurale, Recherche de Méthode*
11 Le Guern speaks readily of the 'kinship,' the 'close connection' (24) of the two functions. These are, he states, two 'complementary aspects of the same mechanism' (*Sémantique* 28).
12 Cf. above, Study 5, section 4. We will return to the problem of reference in Study 7; but then reference will not be understood only as a correspondence at the level of denomination or naming, but as a capacity for describing reality that proceeds from the statement in its entirety. Cf. above also the discussion of metaphor *in praesentia* and of simile in the *Rhétorique générale* (Study 5, 166).

13 We will discuss this claim in Study 7, where the distinction between denotation and connotation will come under scrutiny again from the point of view of the referential function of the statement. The properly 'image-ing' function of metaphor will be discussed at the end of the present Study. What interests us here is the way in which denotation and connotation function together.

14 Le Guern's extremely rich and insightful work interests us on other counts as well. After outlining the facts of language under the jurisdiction of rhetoric and locating metaphor in relation to other expressions of analogy, the author introduces the analysis of motivations. This explanation is imposed within a theory that denies metaphor the referential thrust which it accords to metonymy, at least in the order of naming. It is established also by virtue of the relationship between denotation and connotation. Psychological connotation itself calls for an explication in terms of motifs. This will be taken up again in Study 7, where it will be asked whether the investigation of motivations must replace that of reference. But before that, reference must have been given another sense than the simple reference of naming, so that the reference of attribution might be considered. Finally, the valuable observations on the lexicalization of metaphor will be recalled when another debate takes place, on the role of 'dead' metaphor in philosophy (Study 8, section 3).

15 Paul Henle 'Metaphor' (this essay develops in modified form the 'Presidential Address' opening the *Proceedings of the Western Division of the American Philosophical Association*, 1953-4). The theory of M.B. Hester, which will be discussed later (section 6), belongs to the same network of problems.

16 Henle quotes the following statement of Kenneth Burke: 'Metaphor is a device for seeing something *in terms* of something else ... A metaphor tells us something about one character considered from the point of view of another character. And to consider A from the point of view of B is, of course, to use B as *a perspective* on A' (*Grammar* 503-4; 'Metaphor' 192).

17 Keats 'To Hope' in *Poems* (1807), quoted in Henle 'Metaphor' 176

18 In Study 7 I will propose an ontological, not just a psychological, interpretation of the 'transference of feeling' characteristic of the poetic function of metaphor.

19 On the relationship between metaphor and symbol (in the sense in which I have used this term since *The Symbolism of Evil*), see my article 'Parole et symbole.'

20 Cf. above, Study 3, section 2.

21 Max Black *Models and Metaphors* 43. Cf. above, Study 3, section 3.

22 Cf. above, Study 3, section 4.

23 The following references to Aristotle may be reinserted into the framework of the Aristotelian theory of metaphor set out in Study 1. In particular, see section 3 on simile,' and pages 34-5 on 'set before the eyes' and 'pronouncing the inanimate animate.'

24 Concerning 'making appear,' cf. Study 5, section 2 (on *figure*).

25 We are brought to the end of our discussion of Le Guern's *Sémantique* by this difficulty, namely, in what sense is the associated image a linguistic entity?

26 In an article in the *Nouvelle Révue Française* on 1 January 1935, Paul Valéry called figures 'these calculated errors' (*Œuvres* [La Pléiade] 1: 1289-90, quoted in Albert Henry *Métonymie et Métaphore* 8). The same author (to whom more space will be given in section 5) quotes this surprisingly apt observation from the poet Reverdy: 'The image is a pure creation of the spirit. It cannot be born from a comparison, but from the meeting of two distant realities. The more the relationships between the two proximate realities are remote and accurate, the stronger

will be the image – the more emotive power and poetic reality it will have' (ibid. 57). Claudel (*Journal* [La Pléiade] 1: 42) concurs: 'Metaphor, like reasoning, resembles, but from farther off' (quoted in ibid. 69, note 26).

27 This power of metaphor to reduce a 'distance' between logical genera comes up again in other contexts in Aristotle himself; in this vein the rapprochement of metaphor and enigma: 'For all metaphors imply an enigma; plainly, therefore, a metaphor (so borrowed) must be itself well converted' (*Rhetoric* 3, 1405 b 4-5); so too with the rapprochement of metaphor and antithesis, where antithesis and resemblance seek to be understood together (*ibid.*, 1410 b 35, 1411 b 2).

28 The theory of substitution overlooks this mechanism because its point of departure is metaphor *in absentia*, which is restricted formally to substituting the present term for an absent term that must be interpolated (thus Henle thought it necessary to interpolate a 'cloak' in Keats' verse that speaks of a soul 'enwrapped' in 'gloom'). But the dynamics of metaphor *in absentia* are revealed only by metaphor *in praesentia*, where it is the interaction among all the terms of the statement that instigates the substitution of a present term for an absent term.

29 Philip Wheelwright *Metaphor and Reality* 72 ff.

30 Gaston Esnault sees in metaphor 'a self-transferring intuition' [... *qui se transporte*]' (quoted in Henry *Métonymie* 55). It is 'direct intuition [... *en ligne droite*]'; thanks to it, 'the mind affirms an intuitive and concrete identity' (ibid. 57). We will use this affirmation in our own way, giving as the primary meaning of 'image' this same movement in its intuitive moment. Taking up the intuitionist tradition, Henry aptly says: 'Born of a sensible reaction, [metaphor] is a new intuition that departs from and attains imagination. The felicitous contemplation of the perceived brings about a rich moment in which a living synthesis, actualizing the interaction of two factors, is created' (ibid. 59).

31 Nelson Goodman *Languages of Art, An Approach to a Theory of Symbols* 69

32 On the Same and the Similar, see Aristotle *Metaphysics* Δ, chapter 9: 'Those things are called "like" which have the same attributes in every respect, and those which have more attributes the same than different, and those whose quality is one; and that which shares with another thing the greater number or the more important of the attributes (each of them one of two contraries) in respect of which things are capable of altering, is like that other thing' (1018 a 15-18). The second acceptation of the word *similar* or *like* would seem to be particularly appropriate to the case of metaphor.

33 Thus R. Herrschberger, in 'The Structure of Metaphor,' holds that metaphor 'refers to the likeness of otherwise unlike things' (434). The 'tension' consists in this, that the interpreter is invited by the poem to take account of the dissimilarities as well as the resemblances among its multiple referents: 'Perceiving the likeness between the multiple referents of a metaphor, a person thirsty for an aesthetic experience, and the poem permitting, *makes an effort* to include as many seeming-unlikenesses as possible' (ibid.). The reconciliation of opposites and the maintenance of their tension are equally necessary to the constitution of poetic experience. In the same sense, Douglas Berggren declares that metaphor 'constitutes the indispensable principle for integrating diverse phenomena and perspectives without sacrificing their diversity' ('The Use and Abuse of Metaphor' 237).

34 C.M. Turbayne *The Myth of Metaphor* 12

35 Gilbert Ryle *The Concept of Mind* 10

36 I concur entirely with Michel Le Guern on this point (*Sémantique* 52-65).

'Similitude' comparison rests on a logical usage of analogy; it is an implicit reasoning. Metaphor properly speaking rests on a purely semantic usage of analogy; it is a direct transference, expressed well by the unusual attribution in metaphor *in praesentia*. My only reservation concerns the use of the word *analogy* to cover these diverse uses. I prefer 'resemblance, similarity [*ressemblance*],' which is the substantive formed from 'similar [*semblable*].' The word *analogy* should be reserved either for Aristotelian analogy, i.e. proportional relationship of four terms (on which metaphor by analogy is constructed, a transference crossing over between the second and the fourth terms of the proportional relationship), or for the *analogia entis* of mediaeval metaphysics. (Analogy in this last acceptation will be discussed in section 2 of the last Study.)

37 Hans-Georg Gadamer *Wahrheit und Methode* part 3, 406 ff.

38 Stanislas Breton, reflecting on the work of Rubina Giorgi, works in a similar fashion with a view to ordering imagination, schema, and image. He subordinates these three terms to the symbol; and the symbol, itself issuing from the problem of the interval between 'limit' and the 'unlimited,' sets an interpretative activity in motion and opens a path. It is this path that is articulated in the triad named above: *imagination becomes image through the schema* (S. Breton, 'Symbole, schème, imagination: Essai sur l'œuvre de R. Giorgi'). Breton's reflections are not unrelated to my attempt at anchoring the image in semantic innovation. The notion of interval, however, presupposed by that of symbol, activates an inquiry into difference that exceeds the limits of this Study and relates more to the ontology articulated in Study 8.

39 Gaston Esnault *L'Imagination populaire, métaphores occidentales*

40 Bernard Pottier 'Vers une sémantique moderne' and *Présentation de la linguistique. Fondements d'une théorie*

41 A.J. Greimas *Sémantique structurale*

42 I am leaving aside the distinction between metonymy and synecdoche, which Henry connects to the quite subtle distinction between semic field and semantic or associative field (25-6): 'Metonymy and synecdoche are modalities of a single fundamental figure: a figure of focalization and of contiguity. They do not differ in their logic, but in their fields of application' (*Métonymie* 26).

43 This is how one might challenge the opinion of Charles Bally, who prefers to see nothing in figures but 'laziness of thought' and 'laziness of expression' (*Traité de Stylistique française* § 197).

44 The important stylistic developments established on this psycholinguistic foundation are bracketed here. I note only that the study of series (in Saint-John Perse, for example), the determination of dominant figures, and finally the interest shown in 'tonal adequacy' – that is, to appropriateness to context – enjoin consideration no longer of a word, nor even a sentence, but an entire *work* (49). We will encounter these problems again, raised by the link between style and work, in Study 7.

45 This is anticipated even more by Cl.-L. Estève than by Esnault: 'To metonymy or synecdoche, we see, metaphor always adds transference from one object to another, thanks to a feature that is common in some way to both of them' (*Études philosophiques sur l'expression littéraire* quoted in Henry *Métonymie* 65).

46 William Bedell Stanford *Greek Metaphor: Studies in Theory and Practice*

47 Deviation of language in Jean Cohen should rather be assimilated to change of denomination, which results, as Albert Henry and Hedwig Konrad have shown,

from perception of an identity between two foci with two semic fields superimposed on them.

48 Marcus B. Hester *The Meaning of Poetic Metaphor*

49 Susanne Langer *Philosophy in a New Key*

50 Northrop Frye *Anatomy of Criticism*

51 R. Wellek and A. Warren *Theory of Literature*

52 On sense and reference, see Study 3, 73-4, and Study 7.

53 John Hospers *Meaning and Truth in the Arts*

54 Hester *Poetic Metaphor* 160-9

55 Similarly, Michel Le Guern emphasizes that the 'associated image' is not a free
   connotation, but 'bound' (*Sémantique* 21).

56 Ludwig Wittgenstein *Philosophical Investigations* II, xi

57 Again we encounter Le Guern's distinction between logical comparison and
   semantic analogy.

58 Virgil C. Aldrich 'Image-Mongering and Image-Management,' and 'Pictorial
   Meaning, Picture-Thinking and Wittgenstein's Theory of Aspects' 75-6

59 Owen Barfield *Poetic Diction: A Study in Meaning* 81, quoted in Hester *Poetic
   Metaphor* 27

60 Gaston Bachelard *The Poetics of Space* introduction xi-xxxv; *The Poetics of
   Reverie* introduction 1-26

61 *The Poetics of Space* xix

62 Ibid. And further: 'The essential newness of the poetic image poses the problem
   of the speaking being's creativeness. Through this creativeness the imagining
   consciousness proves to be, very simply but very purely, an origin. In a study
   of the imagination, a phenomenology of the poetic imagination must concentrate on bringing out this quality of origin in various poetic images' (xx).

63 The term and theme are taken from Eugène Minkowski *Vers une Cosmologie*
   chapter 9.

64 Bachelard *Poetics of Reverie* 3-6

65 Ibid. 18

STUDY 7

1 Émile Benveniste 'La forme et le sens dans le langage' 35

2 Gottlob Frege 'On Sense and Reference'

3 Benveniste 'La forme et le sens' 37

4 P.F. Strawson *Individuals: An Essay in Descriptive Metaphysics*

5 Part 1, chapter 4, section 2, 'Axioms of Reference'

6 G.G. Granger *Essai d'une philosophie du style*

7 As an epigraph to his work the author uses this text, taken from the *Metaphysics*
   of Aristotle (A 981 a 15): 'Actions and productions are all concerned with the
   individual; for the physician does not cure *man*, except in an incidental way, but
   Callias or Socrates or some other called by some such individual name, who happens to be a man.'

8 Monroe C. Beardsley *Aesthetics* 134

9 Jakobson 'Closing Statements: Linguistics and Poetics' 353 ff.

10 Study 6, section 1

11 Suzanne Langer *Philosophy in a New Key*

12 W.K. Wimsatt *The Verbal Icon* 231

13 Marcus B. Hester *The Meaning of Poetic Metaphor*. Cf. above, Study 6, section 6

14 Suzanne Langer *Feeling and Form: A Theory of Art* 212, cited in Hester *Poetic Metaphor* 70

15 T. Todorov *Littérature et Signification* 102

16 Jean Cohen *Structure du langage poétique* 199-225

17 Mikel Dufrenne *The Phenomenology of Aesthetic Experience* 442

18 R. Ruyer 'L'expressivité'

19 *Rhétorique générale* 24

20 Michel Le Guern *Sémantique de la métaphore et de la métonymie* 20-1. See Study 6, section 1.

21 *Anatomy of Criticism* 80

22 Martin Heidegger *Being and Time* paragraph 29

23 *Languages of Art* 6, 3: 241-6

24 See the left side of the table opposite. The table does not originate with Goodman. Rather, I have drawn it up for myself as a guide through the distinctions and terminology of this difficult work, particularly its first two chapters.

25 *Languages of Art* 10-19

26 Ibid. 241-4

27 Ibid. 52-7

28 Ibid. 74-81

29 Ibid. 81-5

30 Ibid. 70

31 Ibid. 71-4

32 Ibid. 77

33 Max Black *Models and Metaphors* 37

34 Goodman *Languages of Art* 73, 80

35 Ibid. 85

36 Black *Models and Metaphors* 219-43

37 Mary B. Hesse 'The Explanatory Function of Metaphor'

38 Stephen Toulmin *The Philosophy of Science: An Introduction* 38-9 cited in Goodman *Languages of Art* 239

39 C.G. Hempel and P. Oppenheim 'The Logic of Explanation'

40 Stephen C. Pepper *World Hypotheses* 91-2 cited in Black *Models and Metaphors* 239-40

41 One can find in the work of Philip Wheelwright (*Metaphor and Reality*) an attempt to establish a hierarchy of metaphors according to their degree of stability, their 'comprehensiveness or breadth of appeal' (98 ff). For Wheelwright, metaphors endowed with integrative power are called symbols. At the lowest level he finds the dominant images of a particular poem; then the symbols that have 'personal' significance and permeate an entire work; next, the symbols shared by an entire cultural tradition; then those that link the members of a vast secular or religious community; and finally, at the fifth level, the archetypes that hold meaning for all of humanity, or at least a major part of it – for example, the symbolism of the moon and of shadows, or that of lordship. This idea of an organization into levels is taken up again by Berggren ('The Use and Abuse of Metaphor' 248-9). From a completely different point of view, that of stylistics, Albert Henry (*Métonymie et Métaphore* 116 ff.) shows that it is combinations of metaphors as second-level figures (which he details with extraordinary subtety) that integrate the rhetorical procedures of an entire work whose task it is to promote the poet's singular vision. When referring earlier to the analysis of Albert Henry (see above, 203), I empha-

METAPHORICAL
APPLICATION
OF A SYMBOL

	orientation of reference	category of symbols	logical extension	domain of application	
R E F E R	*to denote* ... (from symbol towards thing) →	verbal = description	multiple	objects and events	
		non-verbal = representation ≠ imitation	singular / null (painting of a] unicorn)		trans-ference → metaphysical denotation
R E N C E	*to exemplify* ... = to be denoted = to possess = relationship of a label ← sample	verbal = exemplified predicate			
		non-verbal = colour sample		feelings	'expression' → figurative possession or metaphorical exemplification (*sad* colours in a painting)

sized that reference to a world and return-reference to an author go hand in hand with this intertwining that raises discourse to the level of a work.

42 Study 1, section 5
43 Paul Ricoeur *Fallible Man* part 4 'Affective Fragility'
44 Berggren 'The Use and Abuse of Metaphor'
45 Ibid. 1: 249
46 Ibid. 1: 253
47 Ernst Cassirer *The Philosophy of Symbolic Forms* volume 1 *Language* chapter 5 'Language and the Expression of the Forms of Pure Relation: The Sphere of Judgment and the Concepts of Relation'
48 *Rhétorique générale* 114-15
49 Coleridge, appendix C to *The Statesman's Manual* quoted in I.A. Richards *The Philosophy of Rhetoric* 109
50 Owen Barfield *Poetic Diction: A Study in Meaning*
51 Wheelwright *Metaphor and Reality* 17
52 Philip Wheelwright *The Burning Fountain* 25-9, 55-9
53 Wheelwright *Metaphor and Reality* 38-9
54 Ibid. 19, 30, 130, and *passim*
55 Bacon *Novum Organum* 1: 44, quoted in Turbayne *Myth of Metaphor* 29
56 The expression belongs to William Bedell Stanford in *Greek Metaphor: Studies in Theory and Practice* 105. It has been taken up by numerous English-language writers.
57 *Closing Statements* 371

STUDY 8

1 É. Benveniste 'Catégories de pensée et catégories de langue' *Études philosophiques* (December 1958) 419-29, published also in *Problems in General Linguistics* 55-64
2 The first six categories refer to *nominal* forms: that is, the linguistic class of nouns; then, in the general class of adjectives, two types of adjectives designating quantity and quality; then the comparative, which is the 'relative' form by reason of its function; then the denominations of place and time. The next four are all *verbal* categories: the active voice and the passive voice; then the category of *mediative* verbs (as distinct from active verbs); then that of the *perfect* as 'being a certain state.' (It should be noted that Émile Benveniste's linguistic genius succeeds in interpreting these last two categories, which have embarrassed countless interpreters.) In this way, Aristotle 'thought he was defining the attributes of objects but he was really setting up linguistic entities' (60).
3 The second study bears the very direct title 'The System of Aristotle's *Categories* and its Logical and Metaphysical Signification' (44-125). I shall invert the order followed by Jules Vuillemin in his work because my purpose is different from his: Vuillemin wants to show that analogy comes from a pseudo-science which links up with theology. This is why he moves directly to a discussion of analogy and its logical deficiency in the first study of his book. Since I want to show the split between philosophical and poetic discourse at the point where they appear to be closest, I go directly to the point where the split is widest: this is the point where Jules Vuillemin does justice to the systematic construction of the Aristotelian treatise on the *Categories*.

4 Vuillemin *De la logique* 110

5 'In the same way, Aristotle assumes the theory of analogy in the *Categories*: being is said in different ways, but these different acceptations are ordered in that they all derive, more or less directly, from a fundamental acceptation that is the attribution of a secondary substance to a primary substance' (ibid. 226).

6 'For it must be either by an equivocation that we say [things] *are*, or by adding to and taking from the meaning of "are" (in the way in which that which is not known may be said to be known) – the truth being that we use the word neither ambiguously nor in the same sense, but just as we apply the word *medical* by virtue of a *reference* to one and the same thing, not *meaning* one and the same thing, nor yet speaking ambiguously; for a patient and an operation and an instrument are called medical neither by an ambiguity nor with a single meaning, but with reference to a common end' (*Metaphysics* Z 4, 1030 a 31 – b 4). In *L'Objet de la métaphysique selon Aristote*, Vianney Décarie exhibits the connection between book Z and the outline of the multiple meanings of being in book Δ; he underlines that 'the other categories derive their meaning from this primary being' (138). This pivotal semantic and ontological function of *ousia* is lost from sight somewhat in an aporetic interpretation of Aristotelian ontology.

7 Vuillemin *De la logique* 229. For Vuillemin, the 'pseudo-science' into which Western philosophy has strayed begins here. According to him, analogy was erased from modern philosophy only when, in Russell, Wittgenstein, and Carnap, a single, fundamental signification was attributed to the copula, namely, that an element belongs to a class. 'At that moment, the notion of analogy disappeared and Metaphysics as a science was made possible' (228). This, of course, assumes that the meaning of the word *to be* is exhausted in this logical reduction – precisely what we deny in the present work.

8 'It is indeed this ontological description, superimposed on logical description, that can properly be considered the guiding thread of the deduction' (ibid. 78). 'Philosophical analysis must continually correct grammatical appearances and reverse the order of subordination that grammar implies. At the same time, it makes the guiding thread of the deduction apparent' (ibid. 86).

9 This is what Jules Vuillemin does: 'So, if there is no quiddity, in the primordial sense, with respect to a composite such as *white man*, there will be quiddity in a derivative sense. There will be predications by analogy, not in a synonymous but in a paronymous fashion; the predication is thus "transcendental"' (ibid. 63).

10 Vuillemin restores the fundamental breakdown by subdividing each of the two classes of essential and accidental predication into primordial and derivative, then each of the four classes obtained in this way in terms of the difference between primary substance and secondary substance. The table of *a priori* possibilities of predication is found in ibid. 66-75.

11 Vuillemin recognizes this: 'The theory of analogy, implicit in the theory of paronyms, allows us to consider under the same principle – although, we might say, in a progressively diminishing relation – the signification of the copula, the relation of subordination between secondary substances, and the relations of subordination between abstract particulars and abstract generalities on the one hand and between abstract generalities on the other' (ibid. 111). We shall say nothing here regarding the fourth part of the *Categories* (paragraphs 10-15): Enumerating post-predicaments, Jules Vuillemin observes, allows the series of categories to be placed within Aristotle's metaphysics; by introducing the rudi-

ments of a theory of motion, the treatise sets out the distinction between three kinds of substance and the subordination of the universe to the third substance (God), and sketches 'the unity of logic, physics and theology' (ibid.).

12 'So, too, there are many senses in which a thing is said to be, but all refer to one starting-point: some things are said to be because they are substances, others because they are affections of substance, others because they are a process towards substance, or destructions or privations or qualities of substance, or productive or generative of substance, or of things which are relative to substance, or negations of one of these things or of substance itself' (*Metaphysics* Γ 2, 1003 b 6-10). On this point, we refer to V. Décarie's excellent commentary, which stresses again the 'common notion' role of *ousia*, thanks to which 'a single science is entrusted with studying all beings as beings' (*L'Objet de la métaphysique* 102).

13 Pierre Aubenque *Le problème de l'être chez Aristote: Essai sur la problématique aristotélicienne*

14 Aubenque goes so far as to see in Aristotle a tragic character comparable to that of Pascal, who upheld 'the impossibility of the necessary' (ibid. 219, note 2).

15 The text in question here is *Metaphysics* E 1, where Aristotle applies his notion of reference to a first term no longer to the sequence of meanings of being but to the very hierarchy of beings. Therefore, *ousia* is no longer the first of the categories; rather, divine *ousia* is supreme being. This reference to a first term, no longer on the level of meanings but on the level of beings, is supposed to serve as the basis for the very discourse on being. 'For one might raise the question,' Aristotle says, 'whether first philosophy is universal, or deals with one genus, i.e. some one kind of being; for not even the mathematical sciences are all alike in this respect – geometry and astronomy deal with a certain particular kind of thing, while universal mathematics applies alike to all. We answer that if there is no substance other than those which are formed by nature, natural science will be the first science; but if there is an immovable substance, the science of this must be prior and must be first philosophy, and universal in this way, because it is first' (*Metaphysics* E 1, 1026 a 23-30). V. Décarie's enquiry into 'the object of metaphysics according to Aristotle' attests to the continuity of the link between ontology and theology throughout the entire Aristotelian corpus (concerning this passage from the *Metaphysics*, see Décarie *L'Objet de la métaphysique* 111-24).

16 Aubenque readily grants this: 'The reality of *khôrismos* can be experienced less as an irremediable separation than as the invitation to overcome it. In short, between ontological investigation and contemplation of the divine, relations can and must exist that the word *separation* is not sufficient to express fully' (335).

17 Cf. Aubenque's analysis of theological appendices in various places in *Metaphysics* Γ and of the physical preparation in Λ 1-5 of the theological exposition in Λ 6-10 (*Le problème de l'être chez Aristote* 393 ff.)

18 'The impossible ideal of a world whose unity would be restored ... must remain, at the very heart of irremediable dispersion, the guiding principle of human investigation and action' (402). And a little further on: 'The unity of discourse could never be given in itself; nor could it ever be "sought," moreover, if discourse were not directed by the ideal of a subsisting unity' (403). Again: 'If the divine does not exhibit the unity ontology seeks, it nonetheless guides ontology in its search' (404). And finally: 'It is the necessity of motion that, through the mediation of philosophical discourse, divides being against itself according to a plurality of meanings, the unity of which is still indefinitely "sought after"' (438).

19 'Ousia,' Aubenque says, 'is one of the rare words that Aristotle employs to
    speak both of sub-lunary realities and of divine reality, without any indication
    that this common denomination is merely metaphorical or analogical' (Le Pro-
    blème de l'être chez Aristote 405). This remark should be followed by a more
    decisive recognition of the unitive function that falls to the category of ousia.
20 Aristotle 'can only have meant the following: human discourse must proceed
    as if the causes of essences were the causes of all things, as if the world were a
    well ordered whole and not a rhapsodic series, as if all things could be traced
    back to the first among them, that is to essences, and to the first of the essences,
    as to their Principle' (ibid. 407).
21 David Ross understands this in the following way: 'Except as regards the first
    cause, things in different genera have only analogically the same causes' (Aris-
    totle 175).
22 Jules Vuillemin De la logique 14. The author shows that the mathematical
    notion of analogy stems from the modification by Theaetetus of an earlier
    definition that applied only to rational numbers. It is through the operation of
    alternating diminution – which 'implies development ad infinitum' (ibid. 13) –
    that the idea of number could be extended to irrationals by Greek mathemati-
    cians.
23 '... (proportion being not a property only of the kind of number which consists
    of abstract units, but of number in general [holôs arithmou]). For proportion
    is equality of ratios, and involves four terms at least ...' (Nichomachean Ethics
    1131 a 30-2).
24 It is at this point in the continuous extension of mathematical analogy and in
    the weakening of its criteria that the relation of proportionality rejoins the
    theory of metaphor, or at least its most 'logical' aspect, proportional metaphor
    (cf. Study 1). But poetic discourse merely utilizes it, whereas philosophical dis-
    course sets out its theory, placing it on a trajectory of meaning somewhere
    between mathematical proportion and reference ad unum.
25 'The causes and the principles of different things are in a sense different, but
    in a sense, if one speaks universally and analogically, they are the same for all'
    (Metaphysics Λ 4, 1070 a 31-3). See also Λ 5, 1071 a 4 and 27, and, of course,
    the passage cited above (Λ 5, 1071 a 33-7).
26 Metaphysics Γ 2, 1003 a 34-b 4; Z 4, 1030 a 35-b 3
27 On this point, cf. Vuillemin De la logique 22.
28 Considering the terms of analogy themselves, he will observe that the common
    attribution of being to substance and to accident implicitly reduces judgments
    of relation to judgments of predication. Now, the true judgment of predication
    (if one puts aside essential definition) does not allow reciprocation. But above
    all, by placing substance at the head of metaphysics, philosophy designates a
    term for which no science exists, since substance is in every case a determined
    individual and science deals only with genera and species. For this reason, the
    order of things escapes the scientific order, which is abstract and does not
    treat substances in the primary sense. Considering in addition the relation of
    the other categories to substance, the logician can only repeat Aristotle's own
    admission: if science is generic and if the bond of being is not generic, then the
    analogical bond of being is not scientific. We must then recognize 'the lack of
    scientific communicability among the genera of being' (ibid. 41).
29 'In general, if we search for the elements of existing things without distinguishing
    the many senses in which things are said to exist, we cannot find them, especially

if the search for the elements of which things are made is conducted in this
manner. For it is surely impossible to discover what "acting" or "being acted
on," or the "straight" is made of, but if elements can be discovered at all, it is
only the elements of substances; therefore either to seek the elements of all existing things or to think one has them is incorrect' (*Metaphysics* Λ 9, 992 b 18-25).

30 Immanuel Kant *Critique of Pure Reason* book 2, chapter 3, section 7, A 632: 525.
Martin Heidegger *Was ist Metaphysik?* 19-20 (the English translation in Werner
Brock, ed. *Existence and Being* lacks this introduction).

31 Among the most recent works we must cite Bernard Montagnes *La Doctrine de
l'analogie de l'être d'après saint Thomas d'Aquin.* The author lays before us the
series of solutions attempted by Aquinas (65-114) in response to the excessive
role accorded by Cajetan to analogy of proportionality. According to G.P. Klubertanz in *St Thomas Aquinas on Analogy: A Textual Analysis and Systematic
Synthesis*, proportional analogy appeared at a particular point in Aquinas'
career and then disappeared. Book 4 of the *Commentaire au Livre I des Sentences*
and the *De Veritate* are held to provide evidence for this stage in the doctrine.

32 On the reasons for rejecting univocal attribution, see the *Commentaire au Livre I
des Sentences Dist.* xxxv, qu. 1, art. 3, ad. 5: 'Nothing is common to the eternal
and to the corruptible as both the commentator and the philosopher himself
assert. The science of God is eternal, ours is corruptible, a science we manage to
lose through forgetfulness and acquire through instruction or attention. Science,
therefore, is applied to God and to us in different ways.' And later (ibid. art. 4):
'His being (*esse*) is his nature, because of what certain philosophers say: namely,
that he is a being (*ens*) not in an essence (*essentia*) which he knows not by a
science, and so on, until we understand that his essence is nothing other than
his being (*esse*) and that it is the same for all other properties; as a result, nothing
can be said univocally of God and of creatures.' The *De Veritate* says in the same
sense that *esse* is proper to each being; that with respect to God, his nature is his
esse; and that the term *ens*, therefore, cannot be univocally held in common. The
De Potentia insists upon the diversity and the non-uniformity of being.

33 On the reasons for avoiding equivocal attribution Aquinas writes: 'Because if that
were so, it follows that from creatures nothing at all could be known or demonstrated about God; for the reasoning would always be exposed to the fallacy of
equivocation (*fallacia aequivocationis*). Such a view is against the Philosopher,
who proves many things about God, and also against what the Apostle says: "*The
invisible things of* GOD *are clearly seen being understood by the things that are
made*" (Rom. 1: 20)' (*Summa Theologiae* I a, qu. 13, art. 5 in *Basic Writings of
Saint Thomas Aquinas.*) The reconciling of St Paul and Aristotle is itself significant for its combination of two traditions and two cultures.

34 The division of predicates into univocal, equivocal, and analogous comes not
from Aristotle but from Arab Aristotelianism, which itself inherits the class of
ambiguous terms (*amphibola*) invented by Alexander of Aphrodisa in his commentary on Aristotle. Cf. H.A. Wolfson 'The Amphibolous Terms in Aristotle,
Arabic Philosophy and Maimonides.'

35 That Aristotle provided the basic thread of the solution by analogy is confirmed
by the several properly philosophical passages on analogy that do not deal with
divine names. Such is the case with the *De Principiis Naturae* and the *Commentary* to Γ 2 of Aristotle's *Metaphysics*. The *De Principiis* introduces the question
of analogy through that of the identity of principles (matter and form) within
the diversity of beings. Analogy is an identity distinct from generic identity; it

is based on a type of *attributio* (a term borrowed from Averroes' commentary on the *Metaphysics*), analogical *attributio*, which is based on *rationes* that are not totally different, as is the case in equivocal *attributio* (when a single *nomen* – dog – corresponds to different *rationes* – the animal and the constellation). *Attributio* in turn is ordered according to degrees of unity in beings. There follows the well known example of the predicate *sanum*, which is said analogously of the subject (man), of the sign (urine), and of the means (medicine), by reason of a fundamental signification, which in this case is the aim (health). But this basic meaning can refer to the efficient cause, as in the example of the predicate *medicus*, which is said first of the agent (doctor), then of the effects and of the means. It is therefore the unity in the order of the being that governs the unified diversity of the modes of attribution: being is said first (*per prius*) of the substance, then by derivation (*per posterius*) of the other situations. The analogical link among principles thus reflects that among beings. The agreement here is called *secumdum analogiam, sive secumdum proportionem*. Analogy is inserted between the identical and the heterogeneous. The commentary on Aristotle's *Metaphysics* (*In XII Libros Metaphysicorum expositio Liber IV*) follows the same line. The theme *ens* is said in various ways (*dicitur multipliciter*). But if the same notion (*ratio eadem*) does not govern the series of the acceptations of being, 'then it is said "to be predicated analogously," i.e., proportionally (*illud dicitur 'analogice praedicare,' idest proportionaliter*), according as each one by its own relationship is referred to that one same thing (*per respectum ad unum*).' Then the examples of *sanus* and *medicus* are brought up again. And St Thomas says: 'And just as the above-mentioned terms have many senses, so also does the term being (*ens*). Yet every being is called such in relation to one first thing (*per respectum ad unum primum*)' (*Commentary on the Metaphysics of Aristotle* John P. Rowan, trans., 218). The *Summa Theologiae* attests to the longevity (and the stability) of the properly transcendental theory stemming from Aristotle: 'In names predicated of many in an analogical sense, all are predicated through a relation to some one thing; and this one thing must be placed in the definition of them all. And since *the essence expressed by the name is the definition*, as the Philosopher says, such a name must be applied primarily to that which is put in the definition of the other things, and secondarily to these others according as they approach more or less to the first' (I a, qu. 13, art. 6).

36 See H. Lyttkens *The Analogy Between God and the World*. The first 150 pages of this work are devoted to the history of analogy from the pre-Socratics to Albert the Great; the author demonstrates the genuinely neo-Platonic ancestry of the theme of participation underlying the Aristotelian vocabulary of analogy by reference to a first term. More recently, C. Fabro in *Participation et causalité selon S. Thomas d'Aquin* shows that analogy constitutes only the semantics of participation, which, in conjunction with causality, concerns the very reality of being underlying the concepts by which being is represented. In the same way, Montagnes writes: 'The doctrine of analogy is composed of the synthesis of two themes: one of Aristotelian origin, that of unity by reference to a first term; the other of Platonic origin, that of participation' (*La Doctrine de l'analogie de l'être* 23).

37 The great work in this domain remains that of L.B. Geiger, *La Participation dans la philosophie de S. Thomas d'Aquin*: 'Analogy is the logic – more precisely, part of the logic – of participation' (78).

38 On analogy in Pseudo-Dionysius, cf. V. Lossky 'Le rôle des analogies chez Denys le Pseudo-Aréopagyte.' M.D. Chenu remarks: 'The slow maturation of the doctrine of the analogy of being can be taken as a criterion here. It is one of the points where the curious and fruitful meeting of Aristotle and Dionysius can be noted; this will be one of the first observations of the young Thomas Aquinas. Aristotle, so inexplicit concerning the exigencies of the transcendent, will soon supply the logical and metaphysical co-ordinates allowing the establishment of its conceptual status (potency and act); but it is Dionysius who will henceforth set out its being so strikingly' (*La Théologie au XIIe siècle* 313).

39 The scholasticism that comes down to us from John of St Thomas and Cajetan has identified the Thomist doctrine of analogy purely and simply with analogy of proportionality; cf., in particular, M.T.L. Penido *Le Rôle de l'analogie en théologie dogmatique*. In Montagnes' judgment, the chapter devoted to 'Preliminary Philosophical Questions' is merely 'an exposition of Cajetan's thought and not that of Saint Thomas' (*La Doctrine de l'analogie de l'être* 11, note 12).

40 This saying comes from Aristotle himself (text in Montagnes *La Doctrine de l'analogie de l'être* 84, note 34). Theology thereby recreates a certain incommensurability which could be compared to the situation the geometry of the Ancients had to confront. Like Greek *analogia*, the Scholastic *proportionalitas* turns terms that are not directly *proportionata* into *proportionabilia* (*De Veritate* qu. 23, art. 7 ad. 9; quoted in ibid. 85, note 36).

41 'But in the other type of analogy, no definite relation is involved between the things which have something in common analogously, so there is no reason why some name cannot be predicated analogously of God and creature in this manner' (*De Veritate* qu. 2, art. 11; in *Truth* 1: 113).

42 Cf. text in Montagnes *La Doctrine de l'analogie de l'être* 88-9

43 'By his creative presence, [God] is not distant but very close: *est in omnibus per essentiam, inquantum adest omnibus ut causa essendi* (I a, qu. 8, art. 3)' (ibid. 89).

44 L. de Raeymaeker ('L'Analogie de l'être dans la perspective d'une philosophie thomiste') stresses the subordination of the formal theory of analogy to the realist theory of causality and participation: 'It is through concrete participation and according to an individual mode that each particular being possesses its *esse* and takes part in the perfection of perfections. We must conclude from this that the principle of unity of the totality of concrete and individual beings cannot itself be anything but real as well. Located at the point where the lines of participation converge, it is the real source from which spring particular beings, and upon which, by virtue of their participation, these beings never cease to be entirely dependent' (105). No one has contributed more than Étienne Gilson to the recognition of the central position of the doctrine of being as act in the thought of St Thomas: see *The Christian Philosophy of St Thomas Aquinas*, and *Being and Some Philosophers* 74-107.

45 'Whatever is said of God and creatures is said according as there is some relation of the creature to God as to its principle and cause, wherein all the perfections of things pre-exist excellently. Now this mode of community is a mean between pure equivocation and simple univocation. For in analogy the idea is not, as it is in univocals, one and the same; yet it is not totally diverse as in equivocals; but the name which is thus used in a multiple sense signifies various proportions to some one thing ...' (*Summa Theologiae* I a, qu. 13, art. 5).

46 Vuillemin devotes a section of his first study on analogy to 'certain developments in the notion of analogy in St Thomas' (*De la logique* 22-33). He attempts to arrange within a single table distinctions that (according to the authors cited

above) were really substitutions for one another: namely, the distinction in the
Sentences between analogy according to *intentio* by itself, according to *esse*,
and according to *intentio et esse*; then the distinction in the *De Veritate*, where
analogy of proportionality is opposed to analogy of proportion; and finally the
distinction in the *Summa Contra Gentiles*, where the extrinsic relation of two
terms to a third is contrasted with the internal relation of subordination of one
term to another. The advantage of this systematization is that it accounts for all
the distinctions synchronically. Its major drawback is that it displaces analogy
of proportionality – which becomes just the 'element of rhetoric and of poetry'
(33), to the extent that it 'is in fact metaphor and equivocal' (32) – in order to
reserve for analogy of one term to another the domain of general metaphysics
and special metaphysics or theology (33). But this is to forget that analogy of
proportionality, besides its kinship with proportional metaphor, was called upon
in its time to occupy the same place and to play the same role as the intimate and
direct subordination of one term to another, when it functions between the finite
and the infinite.

47 On *agens univocum* and *agens aequivocum*, cf. *De Potentia* qu. 7, art. 6 ad. 7.
The *Summa Theologica* I a, qu. 13, art. 5 ad. 1, also proclaims the anteriority
of the equivocal agent in relation to the univocal agent: '... unde oportet primum
agens esse aequivocum.'

48 'Henceforth the structure of analogy and that of participation are strictly parallel
and correspond to one another as the conceptual aspect and the real aspect of the
unity of being' (Montagnes *La Doctrine de l'analogie de l'être* 114).

49 On the persistence of the solar metaphor and the heliotrope according to
J. Derrida, cf. the following section.

50 'Hence as regards what the name signifies, these names are applied primarily
to God rather than to creatures, because these perfections flow from God to
creatures; but as regards the imposition of the names, they are primarily applied
by us to creatures which we know first. Hence they have a mode of signification which belongs to creatures, as was said above' (I a, qu. 13, art 6, conclusion).

51 M.-D. Chenu *La Théologie comme science au XIIIe siècle*. The author shows
how the conflict of exegesis (the art of *lectio*) and theology (aspiring to the rank
of a science governed by the order of the *quaestiones*) is moderated by St Thomas
into a superior harmony without juxtaposition or confusion, but through
quasi-subalternation (67-92). The *Commentary on the Sentences* still leaves
the *modus symbolicus* of exegesis and the *modus argumentativus* of theology
unconnected. As Chenu notes, 'the method named by three synonyms – *meta-
phorica, symbolica, parabolica* – covers the very extensive content in Scripture
of non-conceptual forms of expression ... St Thomas founds such a method
upon the principle of the accommodation of the word of God to the rational
nature of man to whom this word was addressed: man knows intelligible truth
only through sensible realities' (43). Even when the understanding had by faith
and knowledge founded on principles are better integrated in 'theological reason' (8), forming an organic continuity, a split will remain between hermeneutics and theological science. The place of metaphor in hermeneutics attests to
this. Not only does metaphor belong to hermeneutics by reason of the place it
occupies in the theory of the four meanings of Scripture, but, along with parables and various figurative expressions, it is also part of the literal or historical
meaning, which is distinguished as a whole from the three-fold spiritual meaning
(7th *Quodlibet*, qu. 6, *Summa Theologiae* I a, qu. 10). The literal meaning per-

tains to things signified by the words employed, whereas in the spiritual meaning things signified on the initial level become in turn signs of other things (in this way, the Law of the Old Testament is the figure of that of the New). On this point cf. H. de Lubac *Exégèse médiévale* part 2, 2: 285-302. It is true that the literal meaning has a wide range, even multiple acceptations, as primary signification in contrast to a second signification and as the meaning intended by the author. For this reason, the expression *hand of God* still carries a literal meaning; but it attributes to God not bodily limbs but 'what is signified by bodily limbs, that is the operative quality' (1 a 2 ae, qu. 102, art. 2 ad 1; quoted in ibid. 277, note 7). De Lubac concedes, 'Ordinary language, however, even in the Church, has not always heeded the Angelic Doctor's suggestion, since today, quite to the contrary, we constantly speak of allegory in connection with what, in contrast to allegory, he termed parabolical or metaphorical meaning' (ibid. 278).

52 'Univocal predication is impossible between God and creatures. The reason of this is that every effect which is not a proportioned result of the power of the efficient cause receives the similitude of the agent not in its full degree, but in a measure that falls short; so that what is divided and multiplied in the effects resides in the agent simply, and in an unvaried manner. For example, the sun by the exercise of its one power produces manifold and various forms in these sublunary things. In the same way, as was said above, all perfections existing in creatures divided and multiplied pre-exist in God unitedly' (I a, qu. 13, art. 5, conclusion).

53 St Thomas ibid.

54 E. Husserl 'Author's Preface to the English Edition' *Ideas* 5-22

55 F. Nietzsche *Rhétorique et Langage* and S. Kofman *Nietzsche et la métaphore*

56 M. Heidegger *Der Satz vom Grund* 77-90

57 J. Greisch 'Les mots et les roses. La métaphore chez Martin Heidegger' 473

58 Heidegger *Der Satz vom Grund* 63-75

59 M. Heidegger *On the Way to Language*. For a general discussion of Heidegger's notion of metaphor, see below, section 5.

60 'And first of all we shall direct interest upon a certain wearing away of metaphorical force in philosophical intercourse. It will become clear that this wearing away is not a supervenient factor modifying a kind of trope-energy which would otherwise remain intact; on the contrary, it constitutes the very history and structure of philosophical metaphor' ('White Mythology' 6). 'It was also necessary to subject this notion of *wearing away* to scrutiny, for it seems to be systematically connected with the metaphorical perspective. It is to be found wherever the theme of metaphor has a special place' (13). And a bit later: 'This feature, the notion of wearing away, belongs without doubt not to a narrow historical and theoretical configuration, but more certainly to the notion of metaphor itself, and to the long metaphysical sequence which it determines, or which is determined by it' (14) (Moore's translation slightly altered).

61 Hegel *The Philosophy of Fine Arts* 2: 139-40 quoted in ibid. 24-5

62 Nietzsche 'On Truth and Falsity in their Ultramoral Sense (1873)' *Works* 2: 180 quoted in ibid. 15

63 Cf. above, Study 6, section 4.

64 Cf. Study 2, sections 4 and 5.

65 Michel Le Guern *Sémantique de la métaphore et de la métonymie* 44-5, 82-9

66 'By the ordinary (*kurion*) word I mean,' Aristotle writes, 'that in general use in a country' (*Poetics* 1457 b). As regards the 'proper' (*idion*) sense in Aristotle, we

have shown that it has nothing to do with some sort of primitive sense (*etumon*), cf. Study 1, note 24. See also the discussion of Derrida's interpretation of the Aristotelian theory of metaphor in Study 1, note 21.

67 On newly-invented and forced metaphor in Fontanier, cf. Study 2, section 6.

68 For example when the thing named by the proper sense is found much more rarely than that designated by the metaphorical sense (for instance, the latin *testa*); or when one of two terms for the same thing takes over the non-figurative acceptation (for instance, the French noun *aveuglement*, deprived by *cécité* of the non-figurative sense of 'blindness,' now usually means the state of being confounded or incapacitated as by a passion).

69 The theory of living metaphor governs the intentional genesis not only of the *wearing away*, which gives rise to dead metaphor, but also of *abuse* in the sense of Turbayne and Berggren (cf. Study 7, section 5).

70 A. Henry 'La reviviscence des métaphores' *Métonymie et Métaphore* 143-53

71 P. Fontanier *Les Figures du discours* 95

72 Jean Ladrière 'Discours théologique et symbole'

73 Ibid. 131

74 Edmund Husserl *Logical Investigations* volume 1: 348

75 Ibid. 299-300

76 Ibid. 342-3. H.H. Price's important work *Thinking and Experience* begins with a discussion of the fundamental choice implied in the problem of recognition: do things resemble one another because they are examples of the *same* which is universal, or do we find rather that they are 'the same again' because they evince a resemblance?

77 *Logical Investigations* 1: 309-11

78 Ibid. 1: 393-8. In this context, *Repräsentation* signifies to stand for, to take the place of, to be substitutable for (*vertreten*).

79 Ibid. 339

80 Husserl *Ideas I* §99 and §111. Despite the first two *Logical Investigations*, Husserl has written that 'the element which makes up the life of phenomenology, as of all the eidetic sciences, is fiction' (*Ideas* 184).

81 'By an aesthetic idea I mean that representation of the imagination which induces much thought (*viel zu denken*), yet without the possibility of any definite thought whatever, i.e. *concept*, being adequate to it, and which language, consequently, can never get quite on level terms with or render completely intelligible' (A 190; *Critique of the Faculty of Judgment* 175-6).

82 'If now, we attach to a concept a representation of imagination belonging to its presentation, but inducing solely on its own account such a wealth of thought as (*so viel ... als*) would never admit of comprehension in a definite concept, and, as a consequence, giving aesthetically an unbounded expansion to the concept itself, then the imagination here displays a creative activity, and it puts the faculty of critical ideas (reason) into motion – a motion, at the instance of a representation, towards an extension of thought, that, while germane, no doubt, to the concept of the object, exceeds (*mehr ... als*) what can be laid hold of in that representation or clearly expressed' (A 192, ibid. 177).

83 Like poetry and eloquence, which Kant will evoke a bit later, it 'gives the imagination an impetus (*Schwung*) to bring more thought into play in the matter, though in an undeveloped manner, than (*mehr ... als*) allows of being brought within the embrace of a concept, or, therefore, of being definitely formulated in language' (A 193, ibid. 178).

84 Frege states axiomatically that it is the search and the desire for truth that makes us pass from sense to denotation, in accordance with a 'design implied in speech and thought' (see above, Study 7, 218). Reality figures in Benveniste's semantics as a 'discourse situation,' as 'a series of circumstances unique in each case,' and finally as a 'particular object to which the word corresponds in concrete circumstances or in usage' ('La forme et le sens' 36-7). In the case of John Searle, it is the function of singularizing identification belonging to propositions that postulates the existence of something (above, Study 7, section 1, 219).

85 This thesis should not be confused with Whorf's interpretation: to say that language gives form simultaneously to the world, to the interchange between men and to man himself does not attribute this formative power to the lexical or grammatical structure of language; it says, rather, that man and the world are fashioned by the totality of the *things said* in a language, by poetry as well as by ordinary language and by science.

86 For Jakobson, the meta-linguistic function is one of the dimensions of the communicative relation, together with the other five – emotive, conative, phatic, referential poetic. The meta-linguistic function consists in the relation not to a referent, but to the codes immanent to the structure of a language; it is expressed, for example, in the definitions in the form of equations by which one element of a code is related to other elements of the same code (cf. above, Study 7, section 2).

87 Cf. above, Study 7, section 2.

88 Ibid., section 4

89 Cf. ibid., section 3.

90 Ibid., section 2

91 The Heideggerian tone of these remarks is undeniable; the opposition between truth-as-manifestation and truth-as-agreement, familiar to us since the exposition in *Sein und Zeit*, is easily recognized here. Nevertheless, I am postponing taking a firm position in regard to Heideggerian thought as a whole until such time as my own analysis has reached a more advanced critical state, namely, when it is no longer possible to evoke the 'early' Heidegger without forming an opinion in regard to 'late' Heidegger.

92 Concerning the word *being*, *Metaphysics* Δ 7 (1017 a 35-b 9) stresses that the distinction between potency and actuality holds throughout the series of categories (not only substance can be actually and potentially, but also quality, state, and so on). The distinction is thus a second-order ontological-transcendental distinction since it duplicates categorial analysis. In *Die Entelechie* 141-70 Uwe Arnold strongly emphasizes the very radical nature of the theory of entelechy as it relates to categorial analysis: 'The enunciative sense (*Aussagensinn*) of being, *ousia*, is implied in the determinations of possibility, energy, and entelechy, even before it is directly determined by the categories. Existence, possibility, energy, and entelechy are concepts that necessarily apply to everything that is categorially real, yet can add nothing at all to the empirical concept; they are transcendentally presupposed concepts; they mediate the actualizability of every natural potentiality, to the extent that they do not concern objects immediately, but, in a mediate fashion, concern the sense of immediateness that belongs to objects. It is this presuppositional meaning (*Voraussetzungssinn*) that forms the basis for the systematic character of Aristotelian philosophy' (142-3).

93 As quoted already from the *Poetics*, tragedy imitates life in that the tragedians 'present their personages as acting (*hôs prattontas*) and doing (*energountas*)' (*Poetics* 1448 a 28). In Aristotle, the transition between *praxis* and *energeia* is

made possible by a hinge-concept – *ergon* – with a dual function: in ethics, it designates the unique 'function' of man as such underlying the diversity of his acquired knowledge and abilities (*Nichomachean Ethics* 1: 6); in ontology, it is taken to be synonymous with entelechy. *Metaphysics* Θ 1 says: 'And since "being" is in one way divided into individual thing, quality and quantity, and is in another way distinguished in respect of potency and complete reality, and of function ...' (1045 b 33). And further on (Θ 8): 'For the action is the end, and the actuality is the action. And so even the *word* "actuality" is derived from "action" and points to the complete reality (*entelechy*)' (1050 a 22).

94 *Metaphysics* Δ 12 and Θ 1-5 define 'potency' in the strict sense of the word, that is as potency 'in relation to movement': it is a principle of change that is in something other than the thing changed or in that same thing *qua* other. But potency in the broad sense of being able to be (Θ 6-8) is simply a correlative: potency refers to actuality as the power to be refers to being; actuality is even said to be 'prior to potency' (Θ 8). What we think, then, is simply the difference between actuality and potency: 'Actuality, then, is the existence of a thing, not in the way which we express by "potentially" ... The thing that stands in contrast to each of these exists actually' (Θ 6, 1048 a 31-5).

95 The definition is inductive; it is based on particular examples ('We say that potentially, for example, a statue of Hermes is in the block of wood ...'). It is analogical; here we cannot define by genus and specific difference: 'But be content to grasp the analogy: that it is as that which is building is to that which is capable of building, and the waking to the sleeping, and that which is seeing to that which has its eyes shut but has sight' (Θ 6, 1048 a 37-b 3).

96 In the first section of *Metaphysics* Θ (§1-5), potency 'strictly speaking' is defined 'in relation to movement'; the question then has to do with how it becomes actual, according to whether it concerns an artificial, natural or rational being (Θ 2 and 5). In the second section (§6-7), potency is taken in a broader sense, corresponding to the scope of the concept of actuality which itself is defined, as we have seen, by induction and by analogy: 'And I mean by potency not only that definite kind which is said to be a principle of change in another thing or in the thing itself regarded as other, but in general every principle of movement or of rest' (1049 b 7-9). Actuality is the correlative of this sort of potency; it is in relation to this potency that actuality is prior with respect to definition, time, and substantiality (Θ 8). On this discussion, cf. V. Décarie *L'Objet de la métaphysique selon Aristote* 157-61.

97 In this sense movement is actuality – 'actuality of what is potentially' the *Physics* states; and the text quoted above from the *Rhetoric* (1412 a 10) calls this to mind. In *Metaphysics* Θ, movement and actuality are also related notions: 'for actuality in the strict sense is thought to be identical with movement' (Θ 3, 1047 a 32-3). The distinction between *praxis* and *poiêsis* tends, however, to separate them: immanent action (*praxis*) which has its own exercise for end, is alone truly actuality; transitive action (*poiêsis*), which reaches its end in the thing produced externally, is only movement (Θ 6).

98 In *Metaphysics* Δ 4, at the term *phusis*, we read: '"Nature" means: (1) the genesis of growing things ... (2) that immanent part of a growing thing, from which its growth first proceeds, (3) the source from which the primary movement in each natural object is present in it in virtue of its own essence ... From what has been said, then, it is plain that nature in the primary and strict sense is the essence of things which have in themselves, as such, a source of movement' (Δ 4, 1014 b 16-1015 a 15).

99 Heidegger *On the Way to Language* 99-100; cf. above, section 3.

100 O. Pöggeler *Der Denkweg Martin Heideggers*, O. Laffoucrière *Le Destin de la pensée et la 'mort de Dieu' selon Heidegger* 1-40, L.B. Puntel *Analogie und Geschichtlichkeit*

101 These expressions are taken from S. Breton *Du Principe* 137.

102 'Every thinker thinks one only thought ... The thinker needs one thought only. And for the thinker the difficulty is to hold fast to this one only thought as the one and only thing he must think; to think this One as the Same; and to tell of this Same in the fitting manner' (*What is Called Thinking?* 50). J. Greisch, who quotes this text, makes the following comment: 'To question Heidegger's thought in a thoughtful manner is to question oneself first in regard to this "Same" which keeps it going' ('Identité et différence dans la pensée de Martin Heidegger. Le chemin de l'*Ereignis*' 73).

103 Greisch 'Les mots et les roses': '*Ereignis* would be the ultimate recourse guaranteeing thought of metaphor in Heidegger, and consequently the survival of philosophical discourse itself' (449).

104 Heidegger 'The Thinker as Poet' in *Poetry, Language, Thought*. We shall pause at these aphorisms: 'The poetic character of thinking is still veiled over. – Where it shows itself, it is for a long time like the utopism of a half-poetic intellect. – But poetry that thinks is in truth the topology of Being. – This topology tells Being the whereabouts of its actual presence (*die Ortschaft seines Wesen*)' (12).

105 Heidegger *What is Called Thinking?* 71, *On the Way to Language* 192

106 Greisch 'Identité et différence' 83

107 The current tendency to include all of Western thought inside the great catch-all of 'representation' invites the same criticism. Those who do so forget that in philosophy the same words continually reappear with a new meaning formed by the constellation of other senses in a given context. On this point, I cannot agree with Jean Greisch when he sees in 'representative thought' 'the single look cast at being.' This is, he holds, 'the basic determination underlying all the historical realizations of this thought' (ibid. 84). Yet the same author writes: 'The *Ereignis* confronts us immediately with the perpetual torment of thought, which is the problem of its relation to being' (77). Does not Heidegger himself say with respect to *Ereignis* that, if it is what is Unheard in thought, it is also 'the oldest of the old in Western thought' (*On Time and Being* 24)?

108 G.W.H. Hegel *The Phenomenology of Mind* preface iv. Must we hold Hegel to task for having exalted the subject by writing 'truth is the subject'? This subject is not the pretentious and solitary self that Heidegger justly attacks. What applies to representation applies to the subject: there is no single philosophy of the subject, immobile and fixed behind us.

109 Martin Heidegger *What is Philosophy?* 95

110 The experience of belonging gives sustenance to modes of discourse other than poetic discourse. It precedes not only aesthetic consciousness and its judgment of taste, but historical consciousness and its critique of prejudices as well, along with all consciousness of language and its claim to master and manipulate signs. In this threefold division, we can see the three 'regions' of H.-G. Gadamer's hermeneutical philosophy in *Wahrheit und Methode*.

111 In 'The Task of Hermeneutics' and 'The Hermeneutical Function of Distanciation' I develop this dialectic of belonging and distanciation within the framework of German-language hermeneutics from Schleiermacher to Gadamer and in relation to the debate found in the latter, first with the abstract sciences and then

with the critical social sciences, mainly with ideology-critique. This last aspect is the central concern of my essay 'Herméneutique et critique des idéologies.'

112 In 'What is a Text?' I show in what way the notion of 'text' includes the multiple modes of distanciation associated not only with writing, but with the production of discourse as a work.

Works cited*

Aldrich, Virgil C. 'Pictorial Meaning, Picture-Thinking, and Wittgenstein's Theory of Aspects' *Mind* 67 (January 1958)
- 'Image-Mongering and Image-Management' *Philosophy and Phenomenological Research* 23 (September 1962)
Aristotle *The Basic Works of Aristotle* ed. and intro. Richard McKeon. New York, Random House 1941
- *The Rhetoric and the Poetics of Aristotle* intro. and notes Friedrich Solmsen. New York, Random House Modern Library 1954
- *Rhétorique* trans. J. Hardy. Paris, Editions des Belles Lettres 1932, 5th edition 1969
Arnold, Uwe *Die Entelechie* Vienna and Munich, Oldenbourg 1965
Aubenque, Pierre *Le Problème de l'être chez Aristote: Essai sur la problématique aristotélicienne* Paris, PUF 1962
Austin, John Langshaw *How to Do Things with Words* ed. J.O. Urmson. Oxford, Clarendon Press 1962
Bachelard, Gaston *The Poetics of Reverie* trans. Daniel Russell. New York, Orion 1969 (*La Poétique de la rêverie* Paris, PUF 1960)
- *The Poetics of Space* trans. Maria Jolas. Boston, Beacon 1969 (*La Poétique de l'espace* Paris, PUF 1957)
Bacon, Francis *Novum Organum* (1626) London, Routledge and Sons 1905
Bally, Charles *Traité de Stylistique française* Geneva-Paris, Georg et Klincksieck, 3rd edition 1951
- *Linguistique générale et linguistique française* Berne, A. Francke 1932, 4th edition 1965

---

* An extensive annotated bibliography of works on the subject of metaphor may be consulted in Warren A. Shibles *Metaphor: an Annotated Bibliography and History* Whitewater, Wisconsin, Language Press 1971

Barfield, Owen *Poetic Diction: A Study in Meaning* New York, McGraw-Hill 1928, 2nd edition 1964

Barthes, Roland 'L'ancienne rhétorique, aide-mémoire' *Communications* 16 (Paris, Éditions du Seuil 1970): 172-229

Beardsley, Monroe C. *Aesthetics* New York, Harcourt, Brace and World 1958

– 'Metaphor' in *Encyclopaedia of Philosophy* ed. Paul Edwards. New York, Macmillan 1967. 5: 284-9

– 'The Metaphorical Twist' *Philosophy and Phenomenological Research* 22 (March 1962): 293-307

Benveniste, Émile 'La forme et le sens dans le langage' *Le Langage: Actes du XIIIe congrès des sociétés de philosophie de langue française* Neuchâtel, La Baconnière 1967, 27-40

– *Problems in General Linguistics* trans. Mary Elizabeth Meek. Coral Gables, Florida, University of Miami Press 1971 (*Problèmes de linguistique générale* Paris, Gallimard 1966)

Berggren, Douglas 'The Use and Abuse of Metaphor' *Review of Metaphysics* 16 2 (December 1962): 237-58; 3 (March 1963): 450-72

Bergson, Henri *Œuvres* Édition du centenaire. Paris, PUF 1970, 930-59

Black, Max *Models and Metaphors* Ithaca, Cornell University Press 1962

Bloomfield, Leonard *Language* New York, Holt, Rinehart and Winston 1933, 2nd edition 1964

Bréal, Michel *Essai de sémantique: Science des significations* Paris, Hachette 1897, 5th edition 1911

– 'Les lois intellectuelles du langage' *Annuaire de l'Association pour l'encouragement des études grecques en France* 1883

Breton, Stanislas *Du Principe* Paris, Bibl. des Sc. Rel. 1971

– 'Symbole, schéme, imagination: Essai sur l'œuvre de R. Giorgi' *Revue philosophique de Louvain* February 1972

Brunschwig, Jacques Introduction in Aristotle *Topiques, livres I à IV* Paris, Éditions des Belles Lettres 1967

Bruneau, Charles and Ferdinand Brunot *Précis de grammaire historique de la langue française* Paris, Masson 1937

Bühler, Karl *Sprachtheorie: die Darstellungsfunktion der Sprache* Jena, Gustav Fischer 1934

Burke, Kenneth *A Grammar of Motives* New Jersey, Prentice Hall 1945

Cassirer, Ernst *The Philosophy of Symbolic Forms* trans. R. Mannheim. New Haven and London, Yale University Press 1953 (*Philosophie der Symbolischen Formen* 3 vols. Darmstadt, Wissenschaftliche Buchgesellschaft 1924)

Cellier, Léon 'D'une rhétorique profonde: Baudelaire et l'oxymoron' *Cahiers internationaux de symbolisme* no. 8, 1965: 3-14

Chaignet, Anthelme Édouard *La Rhétorique et son histoire* Paris,
    E. Bouillon et E. Vieweg 1888
Chenu, Marie-Dominique *La Théologie au XIIe siècle* Paris, Vrin 1957
– *La Théologie comme science au XIIIe siècle* Paris, Vrin 1957
Chomsky, Noam *Syntactic Structures* The Hague, Mouton 1957
– *Aspects of the Theory of Syntax* Cambridge, MIT Press 1965
Cohen, Jean *Structure du langage poétique* Paris, Flammarion 1966
Cope, Edward Meredith *An Introduction to Aristotle's Rhetoric*
    London and Cambridge, Macmillan 1867
Cope, Edward Meredith and John Edwin Sandys *The Rhetoric of
    Aristotle with a Commentary* 3 vols. Cambridge, Cambridge University
    Press 1877; Hildesheim and New York, Georg Olms Verlag 1970
Crane, Ronald Salmon, ed. *Critics and Criticism: Essays in Method by
    a Group of the Chicago Critics* Chicago, University of Chicago Press
    1952, 1970
Darmesteter, Arsène *La Vie des mots étudiés dans leurs significations*
    Paris, Delagrave 1887
Décarie, Vianney *L'Objet de la métaphysique selon Aristote* Montreal-
    Paris, Vrin 1961
De Lubac, Henri *Exégèse médiévale* Paris, Aubier 1964
De Raeymaeker, Louis 'L'analogie de l'être dans la perspective d'une
    philosophie thomiste' *L'Analogie, Revue internationale de philosophie*
    87 (1969) 1: 89-106
Derrida, Jacques 'White Mythology' trans. F.C.T. Moore *New Literary
    History* 6 (1974) 1: 5-74 ('La mythologie blanche' in *Rhétorique et
    philosophie, Poétique* 5. Paris, Éditions du Seuil 1971)
Dilthey, Wilhelm 'Die Enstehung der Hermeneutik' (1900) *Gesammelte
    Schriften* Leipzig-Berlin, Teubner 1921-58, vol. 5
Dobson, John Frederic *The Greek Orators* New York, Freeport 1919,
    1967
Dubois-Charlier, Françoise and Michel Galmiche 'La Sémantique
    générative' in *Langages* 27 (Paris, Didier-Larousse, September 1972)
Dufrenne, Mikel *The Phenomenology of Aesthetic Experience* trans.
    E.S. Carey *et al.* Evanston, Ill., Northwestern University Press 1973
    (*Phénoménologie de l'expérience esthétique* Paris, PUF 1953)
Dumarsais, César *Des tropes ou des differents sens dans lesquels on
    peut prendre un même mot dans une même langue* Paris, Dabo-
    Butschert 1730, 1825
Düring, Ingemar *Aristoteles, Darstellung und Interpretation seines
    Denkens* Heidelberg, Carl Winter 1966
Durkheim, Émil and M. Mauss *Primitive Classification* trans. R. Needham.
    London, Cohen and West 1963 ('De quelques formes primitives de la

classification: Contribution à l'étude des representations collectives' in *Année sociologique* Paris 1901-2)

Eberle, Rolf 'Models, Metaphors, and Formal Interpretations' appendix to Colin M. Turbayne *The Myth of Metaphor* University of South Carolina Press 1970

Else, Gerald F. *Aristotle's Poetics: The Argument* Cambridge, Mass., Harvard University Press 1963

Esnault, Gaston *L'Imagination populaire: métaphores occidentales* Paris, PUF 1925

Estève, Cl.-L. *Études philosophiques sur l'expression littéraire* Paris, Vrin 1938

Fabro, Cornelio *Participation et causalité selon S. Thomas d'Aquin* Louvain, Publications universitaires de Louvain 1961

Firth, John Rupert 'The Technique of Semantics' *Papers in Linguistics* (1934-51). Oxford University Press 1957 (originally in *Transactions of the Philological Society* 1935)

Fontanier, Pierre *Les Figures du discours* (1830) Paris, Flammarion 1968 (introduction by Gérard Genette 'La rhétorique des figures')

Frazer, Sir James *The Golden Bough* New York, Macmillan 1923

Frege, Gottlob 'On Sense and Reference' in *Philosophical Writings of Gottlob Frege* trans. Max Black and Peter Geach. Oxford, Blackwell 1952; also in *Readings in Philosophical Analysis* ed. H. Feigl and W. Sellars. New York, Appleton-Century-Crofts 1949 ('Über Sinn und Bedeutung' *Zeitschrift für Philosophie und philosophische Kritik* 100, 1892)

Freud, Sigmund *The Interpretation of Dreams* trans. James Strachey *Standard Edition* London, 1953 forward: vol. 4 and 5 (*Die Traumdeutung. Gesammelte Werke* Frankfurt, S. Fischer 1961, vol. 2 and 3)

Frye, Northrop *Anatomy of Criticism* Princeton University Press 1957

Gadamer, Hans-Georg *Truth and Method* translation ed. Garrett Barden and John Cumming. New York, Seabury Press 1975 (*Wahrheit und Methode* Tübingen, J.C.B. Mohr 1960, 3rd edition 1973)

Geach, Peter *Mental Acts* London, Routledge and Kegan Paul 1957
– *Logic Matters* Berkeley, University of California Press 1972

Geiger, Louis-Bertrand *La Participation dans la philosophie de S. Thomas d'Aquin* Paris, Vrin 1942, 2nd edition 1953

Genette, Gérard *Figures I* Paris, Éditions du Seuil 1966
– 'La rhétorique des figures' introduction to Pierre Fontanier *Les Figures du discours* Paris, Flammarion 1968
– 'La rhétorique restreinte' *Communications* 16. Paris, Éditions du Seuil 1970

Gilson, Étienne *The Christian Philosophy of St. Thomas Aquinas* trans.

L.K. Shook, CSB. New York, Random House 1956 (*Le Thomisme* Paris, Vrin, 6th edition 1965)
- *Being and Some Philosophers* Toronto, Pontifical Institute of Medieval Studies 1952 (*L'Être et l'Essence* Paris, Vrin 1948)
Godel, Robert *Les Sources manuscrites du Cours de linguistique générale de Ferdinand de Saussure* Geneva, Droz; Paris, Minard 1957
Golden, Leon 'Catharsis' *Transactions of the American Philosophical · Association* 42 (1962): 51-60
Golden, Leon and O.B. Hardison *Aristotle's Poetics, a Translation and Commentary for Students of Literature* Englewood Cliffs, Prentice-Hall 1958
Gombocz, Zoltàn *Jelentéstan* Pécs 1926
Goodman, Nelson *Languages of Art, An Approach to a Theory of Symbols* Indianapolis, Bobbs-Merrill 1968
Granger, Gilles-Gaston *Essai d'une philosophie du style* Paris, A. Colin 1968
Greimas, Algirdas Julien *Sémantique structurale, Recherche de méthode* Paris, Larousse 1966
- *Du Sens. Essais sémiotiques* Paris, Éditions du Seuil 1970
Greisch, Jean 'Identité et différence dans la pensée de Martin Heidegger. Le chemin de l'*Ereignis*' in *Revue des sciences philosophiques et théologiques* 57: 1 (Paris, Vrin, January 1973): 71-111
- 'Les mots et les roses. La métaphore chez Martin Heidegger' in *Revue des sciences philosophiques et théologiques* 57: 3 (Paris, Vrin, July 1973): 443-56
Grice, Paul 'Meaning' *Philosophical Review* 1957
- 'Utterer's Meaning, Sentence-Meaning, and Word-Meaning' *Foundations of Language* August 1968
- 'Utterer's Meaning and Intentions' *Philosophical Review* 1969
Groupe μ (J. Dubois, F. Edeline, J.M. Klinkenberg, P. Minguet, F. Pire, H. Trinon, Centre d'études poétiques, Université de Liège) *Rhétorique générale* Paris, Larousse 1970
Gueroult, Martial 'Logique, argumentation et histoire de la philosophie chez Aristote' in *La Théorie de l'argumentation. Perspectives et applications* (essays in honour of Ch. Perelman) Louvain-Paris, Nauwelaerts 1963
Hardison, O.B. *See* Leon Golden
Hardy, J. notes in Aristotle *Rhetoric* trans. J. Hardy. Paris, Éditions des Belles Lettres 1932, 5th edition 1969
Harris, Zellig Sabbettai *Methods in Structural Linguistics* Chicago, University of Chicago Press 1951
Hegel, Georg Wilhelm Friedrich *The Phenomenology of Mind* trans. J.B. Baillie. New York, Macmillan, 2nd edition 1931

Heidegger, Martin *What is Philosophy?* trans. W. Kluback and J.T. Wilde. New Haven, College and University Press 1956 (*Was ist das – die Philosophie?* Pfullingen, Neske 1956, 3rd edition 1963)
– *Der Satz vom Grund* Pfullingen, Neske 1957
– *Being and Time* trans. John Macquarrie and Edward Robinson. New York and Evanston, Harper and Row 1962 (*Sein und Zeit* Tübingen, Niemeyer 1927, 10th edition 1963)
– *Was ist Metaphysik?* with 1949 introduction. Frankfurt, Klostermann, 9th edition 1965
– *What is Called Thinking?* trans. F.D. Wieck and J.G. Grey. New York, Harper and Row 1968 (*Was heisst Denken?* Tübingen, Niemeyer 1954, 3rd edition 1971)
– *On the Way to Language* trans. Peter D. Hertz. New York, Harper and Row 1971 (*Unterwegs zur Sprache* Pfullingen, Neske 1959)
– *Poetry, Language, Thought* trans. Albert Hofstader. New York, Harper and Row 1971 (*Aus der Erfahrung des Denkens* Pfullingen, Neske 1954)
– *On Time and Being* trans. Joan Stambaugh. New York, Harper and Row 1972 (*Zur Sache des Denkens* Tübingen, Niemeyer 1969)
Hempel, C.G. and P. Oppenheim 'The Logic of Explanation' in *Readings in the Philosophy of Science* ed. H. Feigl and M. Brodbeck. New York, Appleton-Century-Crofts 1953
Henle, Paul 'Metaphor' in *Language, Thought, and Culture* ed. Paul Henle. Ann Arbor, University of Michigan Press 1958
Henry, Albert *Métonymie et Métaphore* Paris, Klincksieck 1971
Herschberger, Ruth 'The Structure of Metaphor' *Kenyon Review* 5 (1943)
Hesse, Mary B. 'The Explanatory Function of Metaphor' appendix to *Models and Analogies in Science* University of Notre Dame Press 1966, 1970; originally in *Logic, Methodology and Philosophy of Science* ed. Y. Bar-Hillel. Amsterdam, North-Holland 1965
Hester, Marcus B. *The Meaning of Poetic Metaphor* The Hague, Mouton 1967
Hirsch, Eric Donald *Validity in Interpretation* New Haven and London, Yale University Press 1967, 1969
Hjelmslev, Louis *Prolegomena to a Theory of Language* 1943; English trans. University of Wisconsin Press 1961
– *Essais linguistiques* (*Travaux du Cercle linguistique de Copenhague, XII*) Copenhagen, Nordisk Sprog-og Kulturforlag 1959
Hospers, John *Meaning and Truth in the Arts* Chapel Hill, University of North Carolina Press 1948
Humboldt, Wilhelm von *Über die Verschiedenheit des menschlichen Sprachbaues und ihren Einfluss auf die geistige Entwicklung des Menschengeschlechts* 1836. Bonn. Dümmler 1960

Husserl, Edmund *Ideas I* trans. W.R. Boyce Gibson. London, Collier-Macmillan 1962 (*Ideen I* in *Husserliana III* The Hague, Nijhoff 1950, 'Nachwort zu den *Ideen I*' in *Husserliana V* 1952)
– *Logical Investigations* trans. J.N. Findlay. London, Routledge and Kegan Paul 1970 (*Logische Untersuchungen* Halle, Niemeyer 1913)
Jakobson, Roman 'Results of the Conference of Anthropologists and Linguists' in *Selected Writings. II: Word and Language* Paris-The Hague, Mouton 1971; originally in *Supplement to International Journal of American Linguists* 19/2 (1953)
– 'Closing Statements: Linguistics and Poetics' in *Style in Language* ed. T.A. Sebeok. Cambridge, MIT Press 1960
– 'Linguistics' in *Main Trends of Research in the Social and Human Sciences. I: The Social Sciences* The Hague-Paris, Mouton-UNESCO 1970
– 'Two Aspects of Language and Two Types of Aphasic Disorders' in *Selected Writings. II: Word and Language*. Paris-The Hague, Mouton 1971; originally in Jakobson and M. Halle *The Fundamentals of Language* The Hague, Mouton 1956
Kant, Immanuel *Critique of the Faculty of Judgment* trans. James Creed Meredith. Oxford, Clarendon Press 1952
– *Critique of Pure Reason* trans. Norman Kemp Smith. New York, St Martin's 1965
Kennedy, George Alexander *The Art of Persuasion in Greece* Princeton University Press 1963
Klubertanz, George Peter *St Thomas Aquinas on Analogy: A Textual Analysis and Systematic Synthesis* Chicago, Loyola University Press 1960
Kofman, Sarah *Nietzsche et la métaphore* Paris, Payot 1972
Konrad, Hedwig *Etude sur la métaphore* Paris, Lavergne 1939; Vrin 1959
Ladrière, Jean 'Discours théologique et symbole' *Revue des sciences religieuses* 49, 1-2 (Strasbourg 1975): 116-41
Laffoucrière, Odette *Le Destin de la pensée et la 'Mort de Dieu' selon Heidegger* The Hague, Nijhoff 1967
Langer, Susanne K. *Philosophy in a New Key* New York, New American Library 1951
– *Feeling and Form: A Theory of Art* New York, Scribner's 1953
Le Guern, Michel *Sémantique de la métaphore et de la métonymie* Paris, Larousse 1973
Linsky, Leonard *Referring* London, Routledge and Kegan Paul 1967
Lossky, Vladimir 'Le rôle des analogies chez Denys le pseudo-Aréopagite' *Archives d'histoire doctrinale et littéraire du Moyen-Age* 1930, 279-309
Lucas, Donald William *Aristotle's Poetics* Greek text, introduction, commentary and appendices. Oxford, Clarendon Press 1968
Lyttkens, H. *The Analogy between God and the World. An Investigation*

of its Background and Interpretation of its Use by Thomas of Aquino
Uppsala, Almqvist and Wiksells 1952

Martinet, André *Éléments de linguistique générale* Paris, A. Colin 1961

– *A Functional View of Language* Oxford, Clarendon Press 1962

– 'Le mot' *Diogène* 51, Paris, Gallimard 1965

Marty, Anton *Untersuchungen zur Grundlegung der allgemeinen Grammatik und Sprachphilosophie* Halle, Niemeyer 1908

Matoré, Georges *La Méthode en lexicologie. Domaine française* Paris, Didier 1953

– *Le Vocabulaire et la société sous Louis-Philippe* 2nd ed. Geneva, Slatkine Reprints 1967

McCall, Marsh *Ancient Rhetorical Theories of Simile and Comparison* Cambridge, Mass., Harvard University Press 1969

McKeon, Richard 'Literary Criticism and the Concept of Imitation in Antiquity' *Modern Philology* August 1936; reprinted in *Critics and Criticism* (*see* R.S. Crane)

– 'Imitation and Poetry' in *Thought, Action and Passion* Chicago, University of Chicago Press 1954, 1968

Meillet, Antoine 'Comment les mots changent de sens' *Année Sociologique* 1905-1906; reprinted in *Linguistique historique et Linguistique générale* 2 vols. Paris, Champion 1921 and 1938

Minkowski, Eugène *Vers une cosmologie: Fragments philosophiques.* Paris, Aubier 1936

Montagnes, Bernard *La Doctrine de l'analogie de l'être d'après St Thomas d'Aquin* Louvain-Paris, Nauwelaerts 1963

Morier, Henri *Dictionnaire de poétique et de rhétorique* Paris, PUF 1961

Navarre, Octave *Essai sur la rhétorique grecque avant Aristote* Paris, Hachette 1900

Nietzsche, Friedrich 'Rhétorique et Langage' texts translated, edited and annotated by P. Lacoue-Labarthe and J.-L. Nancy *Poétique* 5, Éditions du Seuil 1971, 99-142

Nyrop, Kristoffer *Grammaire historique de la langue française* vol. 4: *Sémantique* Copenhagen, E. Bojeson 1913

Ogden, Charles Kay and Ivor Armstrong Richards *The Meaning of Meaning* London, Routledge and Kegan Paul 1923, 8th edition 1946

Osgood, Charles Egerton 'The Nature and Measurement of Meaning' *Psycholinguistic Bulletin* 49 (1952): 197-237

Osgood, Charles Egerton and Thomas A. Sebeok *Psycholinguistics: A Survey of Theory and Research Problems* Bloomington, Indiana University Press 1965

Peirce, Charles Sanders *Collected Papers* Cambridge, Mass., Harvard University Press 1931-58, vol. 2: *Elements of Logic*

Penido, M.T.L. *Le Rôle de l'analogie en théologie dogmatique* Paris, Vrin 1931

Pepper, Stephen C. *World Hypotheses* Berkeley, University of California Press 1942

Perelman, Ch. and L. Olbrechts-Tyteca *The New Rhetoric: A Treatise on Argumentation* trans. J. Wilkinson and P. Weaver. University of Notre Dame Press 1969 (*La Nouvelle Rhétorique: Traité de l'Argumentation* 2 vols. Paris, PUF 1958)

Plato *Collected Dialogues* ed. Edith Hamilton and Huntington Cairns. New York, Pantheon Books 1961

Pöggeler, Otto *Der Denkweg Martin Heideggers* Pfullingen, Neske 1963

Pottier, Bernard 'Vers une sémantique moderne' in *Travaux de linguistique et de littérature* Strasbourg, Centre de Philologie et de Littératures romanes de l'Université de Strasbourg 1964, 2, 1

– *Présentation de la linguistique: Fondements d'une théorie* Paris, Klincksieck 1967

Price, Henry Habberly *Thinking and Experience* London-New York, Hutchinson's University Library 1953, 2nd edition 1969

Prieto, L. and Ch. Muller *Statistique et Analyse linguistique* Strasbourg, Faculté des lettres et sciences humaines de Strasbourg 1966

Puntel, L.B. *Analogie und Geschichtlichkeit* vol. 1. Freiburg i. B., Herder 1969

Quintilian *De Institutione Oratoria Libri Duodecim* Leipzig 1798-1834

Richards, Ivor Armstrong *Principles of Literary Criticism* New York, Harcourt, Brace 1925

– *Coleridge on Imagination* London, Routledge and Kegan Paul 1934, 3rd edition 1962

– *The Philosophy of Rhetoric* Oxford University Press 1936, 1971

Ricoeur, Paul *Fallible Man* trans. Charles Kelbley. Chicago, Henry Regnery 1965 (*L'Homme faillible* Paris, Aubier 1960)

– 'Sens et signe' in *Encyclopaedia Universalis* Paris 1968

– *Freud and Philosophy: An Essay on Interpretation* trans. Denis Savage. New Haven and London, Yale University Press 1970 (*De L'interprétation: Essai sur Freud* Paris, Éditions du Seuil 1965)

– 'What is a Text? Explanation and Interpretation' in David Rasmussen *Mythic-Symbolic Language and Philosophical Anthropology* The Hague, Nijhoff 1971 ('Qu'est-ce qu'un texte?' in *Hermeneutik und Dialektik*, *Festschrift* in honour of H.-G. Gadamer. Tübingen, Mohr 1970, vol. 2, 181-200)

– 'Discours et Communication' in *La Communication, Actes du XVème Congrès des Sociétés de philosophie de langue française* Montreal, Éditions Montmorency 1973

- 'Herméneutique et critique des idéologies' in *Démythologisation et Idéologie* ed. Castelli. Paris, Aubier 1973
- 'The Task of Hermeneutics' and 'The Hermeneutical Function of Distanciation' trans. David Pellauer *Philosophy Today* 17 2/4 (1973): 112-41
- 'Parole et symbole' *Revue des sciences religieuses* 49, 1-2 (Strasbourg 1975): 142-61

Ross, William David *Aristotle* London, Methuen 1923, 1949

Roudet, Léonce 'Sur la classification psychologique des changements sémantiques' *Journal de psychologie* 18 (1921)

Russell, Bertrand 'On Denoting' (1905) in *Logic and Knowledge: Essays (1901-1950)* London, Allen and Unwin 1956

Ruwet, Nicolas 'Préface' to Roman Jakobson *Essais de linguistique générale* Paris, Éditions de Minuit 1963

Ruyer, Raymond 'L'expressivité' *Revue de métaphysique et de morale* 1954

Ryle, Gilbert *The Concept of Mind* London, Hutchinson 1949; Harmondsworth, Penguin 1963
- 'Ordinary Language' *The Philosophical Review* 62 (1953) also in *Philosophy and Ordinary Language* ed. C. Caton. Urbana, Ill., University of Illinois Press 1963

Sapir, Edward *Language: An Introduction into the Study of Speech* London 1921

Saussure, Ferdinand de *Course in General Linguistics* trans. Wade Baskin. New York Philosophical Library 1959; New York, McGraw-Hill 1966 (*Cours de linguistique générale* critical edition ed. Tullio de Mauro. Paris, Payot 1972)

Searle, John *Speech Acts* Cambridge University Press 1969

Shelley, Percy Bysshe 'Defence of Poetry' *The Complete Works of Percy B. Shelley* 10 vols. New York, Gordian Press 1965, vol. 7

Shibles, Warren A. *An Analysis of Metaphor* The Hague, Mouton 1971
- *Metaphor: an Annotated Bibliography and History* Whitewater, Wisconsin Language Press 1971

Stanford, William Bedell *Greek Metaphor: Studies in Theory and Practice* Oxford, Blackwell 1936

Stern, Gustaf *Meaning and Change of Meaning, with Special Reference to the English Language* Göteborgs Högskolas Årsskrift 1931, Indiana University Press 1968

Stevens, Wallace *The Collected Poems of Wallace Stevens* New York, Knopf 1955

Strawson, Peter Frederick 'On Referring' *Mind* 59 (1950)
- *Individuals: An Essay in Descriptive Metaphysics* London, Methuen 1959

- 'Intention and Convention in Speech Acts' *The Philosophical Review* 63 (1964)

Thomas Aquinas (Saint) *Commentaire au Livre des Sentences* Rome, Piana 1570

- *Summa Theologiae* in *Basic Writings of Saint Thomas Aquinas* ed. Anton C. Pegis, revised trans. New York, Random House 1945 (*Summa theologica* Rome Léonine

- *Lexicon of Saint Thomas Aquinas* R.J. Deferrari and McGuiness. Washington, Catholic University of America Press 1948

- *De Potentia (Quaestiones disputatae)* Turin, Pession 1949

- *De Principiis Naturae* Fribourg, Pauson 1950

- *Truth* trans. R.W. Mulligan, SJ. Chicago, Henry Regnery 1952 (*De Veritate* [*Quaestiones disputatae*] Turin, Spiazzi 1949)

- *Commentary on the Metaphysics of Aristotle* trans. John P. Rowan. Chicago, Henry Regnery 1961 (*In XII Libros Metaphysicorum expositio Liber IV* Turin, Cathala-Spiazzi 1950)

Todorov, Tzvetan *Littérature et Signification* Paris, Larousse 1967

Toulmin, Stephen Edelston *The Philosophy of Science: An Introduction* London-New York, Hutchinson's University Library 1953

Trier, Joseph *Der deutsche Wortschatz im Sinnbezirk des Verstandes: Die Geschichte eines sprachlichen Feldes, I: Von den Anfängen bis zum Beginn des 13 Jh.* Heidelberg 1931

- 'Deutsche Bedeutungsforschung' *Germanische Philologie: Ergebnisse und Aufgaben: Festschrift für O. Behaghel* Heidelberg 1934

- 'Das sprachliche Feld. Eine Auseinandersetzung' *Neue Jahrbücher für Wissenschaft und Jugendbildung* 10 (1934)

Turbayne, Colin Murray *The Myth of Metaphor* Yale University Press 1962; revised edition with appendix by R. Eberle, 'Models, Metaphors, and Formal Interpretations,' University of South Carolina Press 1970

Ullmann, Stephen *The Principles of Semantics* Glasgow, University Publications; Oxford, Blackwell 1951

- *Précis de Sémantique française* Berne, A. Francke 1952, 3rd edition 1965

- *Semantics: An Introduction to the Science of Meaning* Oxford, Blackwell 1962, 1967

Urban, Wilbur Marshall *Language and Reality* London, Allen and Unwin, New York, Macmillan 1931, 3rd edition 1961

Vinsauf, Geoffroy de *Poetria Nova* ed. E. Faral in *Les Arts poétiques des XIIe et XIIIe siècles* Paris, Champion 1958

Vuillemin, Jules *De la logique à la théologie: Cinq études sur Aristote* Paris, Flammarion 1967

Wellek, René and Austin Warren *Theory of Literature* New York, Harcourt, Brace and World 1949, 3rd edition 1956

Wheelwright, Philip *The Burning Fountain* revised edition Indiana University Press 1968
- *Metaphor and Reality* Indiana University Press 1962, 1968
Whorf, Benjamin Lee *Collected Papers on Metalinguistics* Washington, Foreign Service Institute, Dept. of State 1952
Wimsatt, W.K. with M. Beardsley *The Verbal Icon* University of Kentucky Press 1954
Wittgenstein, Ludwig *Philosophical Investigations* trans. G.E.M. Anscombe. Oxford, Blackwell 1953, 3rd edition 1968 (*Philosophische Untersuchungen* Oxford, Blackwell 1953, 3rd edition 1968)
- *The Blue and Brown Books* New York, Harper 1958
- *Tractatus Logico-Philosophicus* trans. D.F. Pears and B.F. McGuiness. London, Routledge and Kegan Paul 1961 (*Logisch-philosophische Abhandlung* 1922)
Wolfson, Harry Austryn 'The Amphibolous Terms in Aristotle, Arabic Philosophy and Maimonides' *Harvard Theological Review* 31 (1938): 151-73
Wundt, Wilhelm *Völkerpsychologie: Eine Untersuchung der Entwickelungsgesetze von Sprache, Mythos und Sitte* 2 vols. Leipzig 1922

Index of authors

Val McDermid is a top ten bestseller, translated into more than thirty languages, with over two million copies sold in the UK and over ten million worldwide.

She has won many awards internationally, including the CWA Gold Dagger for best crime novel of the year and the the Stonewall Writer of the Year Award. In 2011, Val was the recipient of the Pioneer Award at the 23rd Annual Lambda Literary Awards.

In 2010, she was awarded the prestigious CWA Cartier Diamond Dagger. This followed her induction into the Hall of Fame at the ITV3 Crime Thriller Awards in 2009, the same year in which she was elected to an Honorary Fellowship at St Hilda's College, Oxford.

CROSS
AND BURN

VAL McDERMID

Little, Brown

LITTLE, BROWN

First published in Great Britain in 2013 by Little, Brown
Reprinted 2013

A CIP catalogue record for this book
is available from the British Library.

Hardback ISBN 978-1-4087-0456-1
Trade Paperback ISBN 978-1-4087-0455-4

Typeset in Meridien by M Rules
Printed and bound in Great Britain by
Clays Ltd, St Ives plc

Papers used by Little, Brown are from well-managed forests
and other responsible sources.

MIX
Paper from
responsible sources
FSC® C104740

Little, Brown
An imprint of
Little, Brown Book Group
100 Victoria Embankment
London EC4Y 0DY

An Hachette UK Company
www.hachette.co.uk

www.littlebrown.co.uk

For my friends by the sea – thank you for
taking me in and bringing me home.

Acknowledgements

Somewhere in my youth or childhood, I must have done something good. I can't think of any other reason why I am so lucky in the support systems that enable me to put this book in your hands. Some of them are experts who give up their time and expertise; some of them are my own backroom team; others go above and beyond the call of professional duty.

So I'd like to say thanks to Professor Dave Barclay for his DNA expertise; to Catherine Tweedy for her fascinating exposition of fingermarks; to Professor Sue Black for her unerring ability to astonish me; and to those who prefer to remain anonymous. Thanks to Marie Mather whose generous donation to the Million for a Morgue campaign is the reason why she appears in these pages.

The character of DCI Alex Fielding was first created by Patrick Harbinson for *Wire in the Blood*, the TV series based on the Tony Hill and Carol Jordan novels. I have appropriated her for my own purposes with the kind permission of Coastal Productions.

Unstinting gratitude to Kiri, who organises my life; to Carolyn, who makes it beautiful; to Tony, who keeps me on the fiscal straight and narrow; and most of all, to Kelly, Cameron, the cousins and their mums, who save me from myself. Not to mention the dog.

Finally, a big shout out to the professionals: Jane and the team at Gregory & Co, David Shelley and his crew at Little, Brown, my copy editor Anne O'Brien, Amy Hundley and her colleagues at Grove Atlantic, and all the booksellers, librarians and bloggers who have helped my books find their readers.

Lucky me.

The hardest thing in life is to know which bridge to cross and which to burn.

David Russell

But you're not here, now, to lead me back
To bed. None of you are. Look at the snow,
I said, to whoever might be near, I'm cold,
Would you hold me. Hold me. Let me go.

'Hammersmith Winter'
Robin Robertson

1

Day one

He woke every morning with a prickle of excitement. Would today be the day? Would he finally meet her, his perfect wife? He knew who she was, of course. He'd been watching her for a couple of weeks now, growing used to her habits, getting to know who her friends were, learning her little ways. How she pushed her hair behind her ears when she settled into the driver's seat of her car. How she turned all the lights on as soon as she came home to her lonely flat.

How she never ever seemed to check in her rear-view mirror.

He reached for the remote controls and raised the blinds on the high skylight windows. Rain fell in a constant drizzle from an unbroken wall of featureless grey cloud. No wind to drive the rain, though. Just a steady downpour. The sort of weather where people hid under umbrellas, heads down, paying no attention to their surroundings, faces invisible to CCTV.

First box ticked.

And it was a Saturday. So she'd have no appointments booked, no meetings arranged. Nobody to notice an unplanned absence. Nobody to raise an alarm.

Second box ticked.

Saturday also meant the chances were much higher that her plans would take her somewhere suitable for their meeting. Somewhere he could follow the first steps of the carefully worked-out plan to make her his perfect wife. Whether she wanted that or not. But then, what she wanted was irrelevant.

Third box ticked.

He took a long slow shower, savouring the sensual delight of the warm water on his skin. If she played her cards right, she'd get to share it with him, to make a pleasant experience even more rewarding for him. What could be better than starting the day with a blow job in the shower? That was the sort of thing that a perfect wife would be thrilled to perform for her man. It had never occurred to him before, and he happily added it to his list. It had never occurred to the first one either, which was typical of her many failures to meet his high standards.

New tick box added to the mental list. It was important to be organised.

He believed in organisation, in preparation and in taking precautions. An outsider, looking at how much time had passed since that bitch had thwarted him, might have thought he'd given up on his quest. How wrong that outsider would have been. First, he'd had to deal with the mess she'd made. That had taken a ridiculous amount of time and he begrudged her every second of it. Then he'd had to be clear about his objectives.

He'd considered trying to buy what he wanted, like his father had done. But pliable though the Asian women were, it sent the wrong message to turn up with one of them on your arm. It screamed inadequacy, perversion, failure. The same went for mail-order brides from the former Soviet empire. Those harsh accents, the chemical blonde hair, the criminal tendencies ingrained like grime – that wasn't for him. You couldn't parade one of them in front of your work-mates and expect respect.

Then he'd looked at the possibilities of internet dating. The trouble with that was you were buying a pig in a poke. And he didn't want to poke a pig. He sniggered to himself at his cleverness, his skill with language. People admired that about him, he knew. But the even bigger trouble with inter-net dating was that there were so few options if things went wrong. Because you'd left a trail a mile wide. It took effort, skill and resources to be truly anonymous online. The risk of exposure with one split second of inattention or error was too high for him to take. And that meant if it all went wrong, he had no way to make her pay the proper price for her failure. She'd simply retreat to her old life as if nothing had happened. She'd win.

He couldn't allow that. There had to be another way. And so he'd conceived his plan. And that was why it had taken so long to reach this point. He'd had to develop a strategy, then examine it from every possible angle, then do his research. And only now was he ready to roll.

He dressed anonymously in black chain-store jeans and polo shirt, carefully lacing up the black work boots with their steel toecaps. Just in case. Downstairs, he made himself a cup of green tea and munched an apple. Then he went through to the garage to check again that everything was in order. The freezer was turned off, the lid open, ready to receive its cargo. Pre-cut strips of tape were lined up along the edge of a shelf. On a card table, handcuffs, a taser, pic-ture cord and a roll of duct tape sat in a row. He put on his waxed jacket and stowed the items in his pockets. Finally, he picked up a metal case and headed back to the kitchen.

Fourth and fifth boxes ticked.

He gave the garage one final look, saw he'd trailed in some leaf debris last time he'd been in there. With a sigh, he put down the case and fetched a brush and dustpan. Women's work, he thought impatiently. But if everything went right today, soon there would be a woman to do it.

2

Day twenty-four

Dr Tony Hill shifted in his seat and tried to avoid looking at the wreckage of her face. 'When you think of Carol Jordan, what comes into your mind?'

Chris Devine, still formally a detective sergeant with Bradfield Metropolitan Police, cocked her head towards him, as if to compensate for a degree of deafness. 'When you think of Carol Jordan, what comes into *your* mind?' Her voice had a deliberate teasing quality. He recognised it as a bid to deflect him from his line.

'I try not to think about Carol.' In spite of his best efforts, the sadness seeped to the surface.

'Maybe you should. Maybe you need to go there more than I do.'

The room had grown dim as they'd talked. The day was dying outside but the light seemed to be leaching out of the room at a faster rate. Because she couldn't see him, it was safe for once to let his face betray him. His expression was the opposite of the lightness of his tone. 'You're not my therapist, you know.'

'And you're not mine. Unless you're here as my mate, I'm not interested. I've told them I'm not wasting my time with a counsellor. But then, you know that, don't you? They'll have told you the score. You're still their go-to guy. The rabbit they pull out of the hat when all the other magic tricks have fallen flat on their arse.'

It was amazing she didn't sound more bitter, he thought. In her shoes, he'd be raging. Lashing out at anyone who sat still long enough. 'It's true, I do know you've refused to cooperate with the therapy team. But that's not why I've come. I'm not here to try and counsel you by the back door. I'm here because we've known each other for a long time.'

'That doesn't make us friends.' Her voice was dull, all animation stripped from the words.

'No. I don't really do friendship.' It surprised him how easy it was to be candid with someone who couldn't see his face or his body language. He'd read about the phenomenon but he'd never experienced it at first hand. Maybe he should try wearing dark glasses and feigning blindness with his more intransigent patients.

She gave a dry little laugh. 'You do a decent facsimile when it suits you.'

'Kind of you to say so. A long time ago, someone called it "passing for human". I liked the sound of that. I've been using it ever since.'

'That's pitching it a bit high, mate. What does the length of time we've known each other have to do with the price of fish?'

'We're what's left, I suppose.' He shifted in his chair, uncomfortable at the way the conversation was going. He'd come because he wanted to reach out, to help her. But the longer he sat here, the more he felt like he was the one who needed help. 'After the dust has settled.'

'I think you're here because you hoped that talking to me

would help you understand whatever it is you're feeling,' she pointed out with a note of sharpness. 'Because I took the hit for her, didn't I? That's a closer bond than we ever had in all those years of working together.'

'I thought I was the psychologist here.' It was a weak response, barely a parry to her thrust.

'Doesn't mean you can figure out what's going on in your own head. Your own heart, come to that. It's complicated, right, Doc? I mean, if it was only guilt, it would be easy, right? That'd make sense. But it's more than that, isn't it? Because there's a dark side to guilt. The rage. The feeling that it's just not fair, that you're the one left carrying the weight. The outrage because you're left with a sense of responsibility. That sense of injustice, it's like heartburn, like acid burning into you.' She stopped abruptly, shocked by her own figure of speech.

'I'm sorry.'

Her hand moved towards her face, stopping millimetres from the shiny red skin left by the acid booby trap that had been targeted at someone else. 'So, what does come into your mind when you think about Carol Jordan?' she persisted, her voice harsh now.

Tony shook his head. 'I can't say.' Not because he didn't know the answer. But because he did.

3

Even from behind, Paula McIntyre recognised the boy. She was a detective, after all. It was the kind of thing she was supposed to be capable of. All the more so when the person in question was out of context. That was where civilians fell down. Without context, they generally failed. But detectives were meant to make the most of their natural talents and hone their skills to the point where people were once seen, never forgotten. *Yeah, right,* she thought. Another one of those myths perpetuated by the double-takes of TV cops confronted by the familiar in unexpected circumstances.

But still, she did recognise the boy, even from the quarter-profile of her angle of approach. If she'd entered the station via the tradesmen's entrance – the back door from the car park – she'd have missed him. But this was her first day at Skenfrith Street and she didn't know the door codes. So she'd taken the easy way out and parked in the multi-storey opposite and walked in the front door, coming up behind the teenager shifting from foot to foot before the front counter. There was something about the set of his shoulders and the angle of his head that suggested defensiveness and tension. But not guilt.

She paused and tried to get the measure of what was going on. 'I understand what you're saying. I'm not stupid.' The boy's voice was miserable rather than aggressive. 'But I'm asking you to understand that this is different.' He lifted his shoulders in a small shrug. 'Not everybody's the same, man. You can't just go with one size fits all.' His accent was local but, in spite of his best attempts, unmistakably middle-class.

The civilian staffing the counter muttered something she couldn't make out. The boy started bouncing on the balls of his feet, all wound up and nowhere to go. He wasn't the sort of lad who would kick off, she thought she knew that. But that was no reason not to try and placate him. Keeping a lid on things wasn't the only point of getting to the bottom of what was bothering the punters.

Paula stepped forward and put a hand on the boy's arm. 'It's Torin, isn't it?'

He swivelled round, his face startled and anxious. A thick mop of dark hair framed the pale skin of a teenage boy-cave dweller. Wide blue eyes with dark smudges beneath, a prominent wedge of nose, a narrow mouth with incongruous rosebud lips under the faintest shadow of what might one day become a moustache. Paula cross-checked the mental catalogue against her memory and ticked all the boxes. No mistake here.

The tightness round his eyes relaxed a little. 'I know you. You've been to our house. With the doctor.' He frowned, struggling for a memory. 'Elinor. From casualty.'

Paula nodded. 'That's right. We came round for dinner. Your mum and Elinor are mates from work. I'm Paula.' She smiled at the small grey man behind the counter as she produced her ID from her jacket pocket. 'Detective Sergeant McIntyre, CID – DCI Fielding's team.'

The man nodded. 'I'm telling this lad, there's nothing we can do for him till his mum's been missing for twenty-four hours.'

'Missing?' Paula's question was drowned by Torin McAndrew's frustrated riposte.

'And I'm telling this . . . ' He breathed heavily through his nose. ' . . . this man that you can't treat every case the same because everybody's different and my mum doesn't stay out all night.'

Paula didn't know Bev McAndrew well, but she'd heard plenty about the chief pharmacist from Elinor Blessing, her partner and the senior registrar in A&E at Bradfield Cross Hospital. And nothing she'd heard tended to contradict Bev's son's adamantine certainty. None of which would cut any ice with the civilian behind the counter.

'I'm going to have a chat with Torin here,' she said firmly. 'Have you got an interview room?' The man nodded towards a door on the other side of the barren waiting area. 'Thanks. Please call up to CID and let DCI Fielding know I'm on the premises and I'll be up shortly.'

He didn't look thrilled, but he did pick up the phone. Paula gestured with her thumb towards the interview room. 'Let's have a sit-down and you can tell me what's going on,' she said, leading the way.

''Kay.' Torin followed her, shuffling his oversized trainers across the floor in the typical slouch of an adolescent who's still not quite accustomed to the margins of his body.

Paula opened the door on a tiny boxroom with barely enough space for a table and three steel-framed chairs upholstered in a zingy blue-and-black pattern. *Seen worse*, she thought, ushering Torin to a seat. She sat opposite him, pulling from her shoulder bag a spiral notebook with a pen rammed down its metal spine.

'Right then, Torin. Why don't you start at the beginning?'

Being stalled at the rank of Detective Constable had been the price Paula had willingly paid for membership of DCI Carol Jordan's Major Incident Team. So when that squad had been wound up, she'd applied for the first three-stripe job that had come up with Bradfield Metropolitan Police. It had been so long since she'd passed her sergeant's exams, she was afraid they'd make her resit.

This wasn't how she'd imagined her initiation into the rank of Detective Sergeant. She'd thought doing preliminary interviews would be someone else's scut work now. But then, that was the thing about being a cop. Not much ever turned out the way you imagined.

4

The blackout blinds did exactly what they were supposed to. And that was good, because pitch-black meant you didn't get shadow tricks setting your imagination on fire. The one thing Carol Jordan didn't need was anything to stimulate her imagination. She could manage quite enough on her own without any extra provocation.

It wasn't as if she was a stranger to bloody crime scenes. Most of her adult life had been punctuated by images of sudden violent death. She'd been confronted with victims of torture; banal domestic violence gone overboard; sexual sadism that was nothing to do with middle-aged, middle-class fantasy; pick your brutality of choice and Carol had seen its end result. Sometimes they'd kept sleep at bay, driven her to the vodka bottle to blur the outlines. But never for more than a few nights. Her need for justice had always stepped in, transforming horror into a spur to action. Those images became the engine that drove her investigations, the motivation for bringing killers to face the consequences of their crimes.

This time was different, though. This time, nothing diminished the power of what she'd seen. Not time, not drink, not distance. These days, there seemed to be a film running on a perpetual loop in her head. It wasn't a long film, but its impact wasn't dulled by repetition. The weird thing was that it wasn't simply a rerun of what she'd seen. Because she was in the film. It was as if someone had been right behind her with a hand-held camera, making a jerky home movie of the worst moment of her life, the colours slightly off, the angles somehow wrong.

It began with her walking into the barn, the view over her shoulder the familiar interior with its inglenook fireplace, exposed stone walls and hammer beams. Sofas she'd once lounged on; tables where she'd discarded newspapers, eaten meals, set wine glasses down; hand-stitched wall hangings she'd marvelled at; and a sweater she'd seen her brother wear a dozen times, casually thrown over the back of a chair. There was a crumpled T-shirt on the floor near the dining table, where the remains of lunch still sat. And at the foot of the gallery stairs, two uniformed bobbies in their high-vis jackets, one looking appalled, the other embarrassed. Between them, a concertina of fabric that might have been a skirt. Disconcerting, but not terrifying. Because film couldn't convey the stink of spilt blood.

But as Carol approached the wooden stairs, the camera panned back to reveal the ceiling above the sleeping gallery. It was like a Jackson Pollock painting whose sole palette was red. Blood; sprayed, slashed and streaked across the stark white plaster. She'd known then that it was going to be very, very bad.

The camera followed her up the steps, recording every stumbling step. The first thing she saw was their legs and feet, marbled with blood, drips and smears on the bed and the floor. She climbed higher and saw Michael and Lucy's bloodless bodies marooned like pale islands in a sea of scarlet.

That was where the film froze, locked on that single terrible frame. But her brain didn't stop running just because the film had. The blame circled and rattled in her head like a hamster on a wheel. If she'd been a better cop. If she'd taken matters into her own hands instead of relying on Tony to come up with answers. If she'd forewarned Michael that a man on the loose had his own twisted reasons to wreak vengeance on her. If, if, if.

But none of those things had happened. And so her brother and the woman he loved had been butchered in the barn they'd restored with their own labour. A place with walls three feet thick, where they had every right to feel safe. And nothing in her life was untainted by that single terrible event.

She'd always found much of her self-definition in her work. It was, she had thought, the best of her. A clear channel for her intelligence, it offered a place where her dogged determination was valued. Her ability to recall verbatim anything she'd heard had a practical application. And she'd discovered she had the knack of inspiring loyalty in the officers she worked with. Carol had taken pride in being a cop. And now she had cut herself adrift from all that.

She'd already handed in her notice with Bradfield Metropolitan Police when Michael and Lucy had been murdered. She'd been about to take up a new post as a Detective Chief Inspector with West Mercia. She'd burned her bridges there and she didn't care. She'd also been planning to take a deep breath and share the sprawling Edwardian house in Worcester that Tony had unexpectedly inherited. But that dream was over too, her personal life as much a victim of a brutal killer as her professional life.

Homeless and jobless, Carol had returned to her parents'

house. Home, according to popular mythology, was where they were supposed to take you in when all else failed. It seemed her judgement had missed the mark there too. Her parents hadn't turned her away, that much was true. Nor had they openly blamed her brother's death on her choices. But her father's silent misery and her mother's sharpness had been perpetual reproaches. She'd stuck it out for a couple of weeks, then she'd repacked her bags and left.

All she'd left behind was her beloved cat Nelson. Tony had once joked that her relationship with the black cat was the only functional one in her life. The trouble was, that was too close to the bone to be funny. But Nelson was old now. Too old to be stuffed in a cat carrier and traipsed round the country from pillar to post. And her mother was better able to be kind to the cat than she was to Carol. So Nelson stayed and she went.

She still owned a flat in London but it had been so long since she'd lived there, it no longer felt like home. Besides, the difference between her mortgage payments and the rent from her long-term tenant was all she had to live on until the lawyers were done picking over the remnants of Michael's life. Which left her with a single option.

According to Michael's will, in the absence of Lucy, Carol inherited his estate. The barn was in his sole name; their house in France had belonged to Lucy. So once probate had been granted, the barn would be hers, blood and ghosts and all. Most people would have hired industrial cleaners, redecorated what couldn't be cleaned, and sold the place to some off-comer ignorant of the barn's recent history.

Carol Jordan wasn't most people. Fractured and fragile as she was, she held fast to the determination that had dragged her through disasters before. And so she'd made a plan. This was her attempt at carrying it out.

She would remove every trace of what had happened

here and refashion the barn into a place where she could live. A kind of reconciliation, that's what she was aiming for. Deep down, she didn't think it was a likely outcome. But she couldn't come up with anything else to aim for and it was a project that would keep her occupied. Hard physical work during the days to make her sleep at night. And if that didn't work, there was always the vodka bottle.

Some days, she felt like the writer in residence at the DIY warehouse, her shopping list a liturgy of items newly discovered, laid out on the page like a sequence of haikus. But she made sense of the dense poetry of home improvement and mastered unfamiliar tools and new techniques. Slowly but inevitably, she was erasing the physical history of the place. She didn't know whether that would bring her soul any ease. Once upon a time she would have been able to ask Tony Hill's opinion. But that wasn't an option now. She'd just have to learn to be her own therapist.

Carol snapped on the bedside lamp and pulled on her new working uniform – ripped and filthy jeans, steel-toed work boots over thick socks, a fresh T-shirt and a heavy plaid shirt. 'Construction Barbie', according to one of the middle-aged men who frequented the trade counter at the DIY warehouse. It had made her smile, if only because nothing could have been less appropriate.

While she was waiting for the coffee machine to produce a brew, she headed through the main body of the barn and stepped out into the morning, seeing the promise of rain in the low cloud that shrouded the distant hills. The colour was leaching out of the coarse moorland grass now autumn was creeping up on winter. The copse of trees on the shoulder of the hill was changing colour, its palette shifting from green to brown. A couple of tiny patches of sky were visible through the branches for the first time since spring. Soon there would be nothing but a tracery of naked branches, stripping the only cover from the hillside. Carol leaned on the wall and stared up at the trees. She breathed deeply, trying for serenity.

Once upon a time, the highly evolved sixth sense that keeps talented cops out of trouble would have raised the hairs on the back of her neck. It was a measure of how far she'd come from the old Carol Jordan that she was completely oblivious to the patient eyes watching her every move.

5

R ob Morrison glanced at his watch again, then pulled out
his phone to double-check the time. 6:58. The new boss
was cutting it fine if she wanted to make a good impression
on her first day. But before he could settle into his smugness,
the clatter of heels on floor tiles alerted him to an arrival
from the street door rather than the underground car park.
He swung round and there she was, mac shimmering with
raindrops, shoes splashed with dirt. Marie Mather, his new
opposite number. Director of Marketing to his Director of
Operations.

'Morning, Rob.' She shifted her laptop bag to join her
handbag over her shoulder so she could free up a hand to
shake his. 'Thanks for taking the time to get me settled in.'

'Might as well start off on the right foot.' He squeezed out
a half-smile that took the sourness from his face. 'Since we'll
be yoked together like horses in the traces, pulling the mighty
chariot that is Tellit Communications.' He enjoyed the flash
of surprise as the extravagance of his sardonic comment sank

in. He liked to upset people's general assumption that a man who ran the operations side of a mobile phone company must be a stranger to culture. 'You didn't drive in?'

She shook the sparkle of rain from her thick blonde bob and gestured with her head towards the street outside. 'We're only five minutes' walk from the tram terminus so I always get a seat. It's a better start to the day than fighting the rush-hour traffic.' When she smiled, her nose wrinkled, as if she'd smelled something delicious. In terms of aesthetics, Rob reckoned she was a distinct improvement on Jared Kamal, her predecessor. 'So. What's the drill?'

'We'll sort you out with security passes. Then I'll take you up to the main floor and give you the guided tour.' As he spoke, Rob steered her over to the security desk, a hand on her elbow, aware of a spicy floral aroma that clung to her in spite of the tram and the Bradfield rain. If she was as good at her job as she was at brightening the place up, Rob's working life was set to improve exponentially.

Minutes later, they emerged from the lift straight on to the main sales floor. At this time of day, the lighting was dim. 'Staff operate the lighting levels at their own pods. It gives them the illusion of control and it gives us a quick and easy way to spot who's actually working.' Rob led the way across the room.

'Somebody's early.' Marie nodded towards a pool of light in the far corner.

Rob rubbed his hand over his chin. 'That's Gareth Taylor.' He arranged his features in a standard expression of sorrow. 'Lost his family recently.' Personally, he was over Gareth's grief. Time to move on, get a life. But Rob knew he was in the minority on that one so he kept quiet around the water cooler, content to grunt supportively when colleagues went into one of their 'Poor Gareth' spasms.

Marie's expression softened. 'Poor bloke. What happened?'

'Car crash. Wife and two kids, died at the scene.' Rob forged onwards, not a backward glance at his bereaved colleague.

Marie broke stride momentarily then caught up. 'And he's in here at this time of the morning?'

Rob shrugged. 'He says he'd rather be here than staring at the walls at home. Fine by me. I mean, it's been three or four months now.' He turned and gave her a dark smile. 'We're fucked if he starts claiming his TOIL though.'

Marie made a noncommittal noise and followed him into a generous cubicle at the end of the room. A desk, two chairs. A couple of whiteboards and a paper recycling bin. Rob gave a cynical little bow. 'Home sweet home.'

'It's a decent size, at least.' Marie put her laptop on the desk, tucked her bag in a drawer and hung her coat on a hook on the back of the door. 'Now, first things first. Where's the coffee and what's the system?'

Rob smiled. 'Follow me.' He led her back into the main office. 'You buy tokens from Charyn on the front desk. Five for a pound.' As they grew closer to his workspace, the light from Gareth Taylor's pod revealed a door tucked away in a nearby alcove. It led to a small room furnished with a pair of coffee machines. Rob gestured at a series of bins that contained little plastic pods. 'You choose your poison, slot the pod in the machine and pay for it with a token.' He rummaged in the pocket of his chinos and produced a red disc. 'Have your first one on me.' He handed it over as if conferring a great honour. 'I'll let you get settled in.' He glanced at his watch. 'One or two things I need to deal with before the hordes arrive. I've arranged a meeting with key personnel at half eight in the small conference room. Ask anybody, they'll direct you.'

And that was it. He was gone, leaving Marie with an array

of beverage choices. She opted for a cappuccino and was pleasantly surprised by the result. She stepped back into the main office, where there were now three or four illuminated work stations. She decided to start getting to know her staff and moved towards Gareth Taylor, consciously applying a warm smile.

He glanced up as she approached, his expression startled. His fingers flew over the keyboard and as she rounded the corner of his partition, she had the impression of a computer screen quickly refreshing. It looked like Tellit resembled everywhere Marie had worked, with employees who liked to feel they were scoring points by doing their own thing in company time with company resources. Human nature, the same all over. It was a tendency that didn't bother Marie, so long as productivity was acceptable and nobody took the piss.

'Hi. I'm Marie Mather. The new marketing director.' She held out a hand.

Gareth accepted the handshake with no enthusiasm. His hand was cool and dry, the pressure firm but not aggressive. 'I figured that's who you must be. I'm Gareth Taylor, one of the screen and phone grunts.'

'I prefer to think of you as frontline staff.'

Gareth raised his eyebrows. 'Doesn't change the reality.'

'You're in early.'

He shook his head, sighing. 'Look, I know Rob will have given you the bullet points. Coming to work is the only consistent thing in my life right now. I don't want sympathy. I'm not like him with his "pity me, my wife left me" shtick. I just want to be left alone to get on with things, all right?' His voice was tight with frustration. She could only imagine how hard it was to deal with other people's well-meaning interference on top of such a devastating loss.

Marie leaned forward and peered at his screen. 'Message received and understood. So what are you working on?'

21

She'd hoped he might at least smile. Instead, he scowled. 'It won't mean anything to you till you've got your feet under the table. I'm implementing a strategy to switch silver surfer customers to long-term contracts. And I think we're doing it wrong, so maybe you might want to come back and talk to me about it when you're up to speed.'

There were two ways of taking Gareth's brusque response. For now, Marie elected to avoid confrontation. 'I'll look forward to that.' She sipped her cappuccino. 'I'm always happy to hear from my team.'

Tonight, when she relaxed with a glass of white wine while Marco cooked dinner, she'd enjoy telling him about this encounter. As they often did, they'd set up some light-hearted wagers about how it would go with her new colleagues. Would she win Gareth over or would he be determined to remain alienated? Would Rob's obvious desire to flirt cross the line to the point where she'd have to bring HR into the picture? She and Marco loved to play their little game of speculation, sometimes even using their fantasy workplace lives to spice up their own bedroom games.

It was harmless fun, Marie thought. Completely harmless.

6

Torin's adolescent inability to disguise his anxiety was immediately obvious to Paula. Luckily for her, maintaining a cool façade under pressure took more skill and effort than he had at his command. Normally she'd have offered him a drink to settle him down, but Skenfrith Street was alien territory for her and she didn't know how long it would take her to rustle something up. The last thing she wanted was to keep her new boss waiting any longer than absolutely necessary.

Technically, she should probably have sorted out a so-called appropriate adult before she questioned Torin. But she reckoned she was more than appropriate enough. And it wasn't as if he was being interviewed about a crime. Paula gave Torin an expectant look. 'When did you start to worry there might be something wrong?'

'I don't know exactly.' He frowned.

'What time does she usually get in from work?'

He raised one shoulder in a shrug. 'About half past five,

but sometimes she'll do the shopping on the way home, so then it's more like quarter to seven.'

'So it's fair to say that by seven, you were beginning to worry?'

'Not worry, exactly. More like, wonder. It's not like she's not got a life. Sometimes she goes out with one of her mates for a pizza or a movie or whatever. But if she's doing that, she usually tells me in advance, in the morning. Or she texts me if it's more, like, spontaneous.'

Paula wasn't surprised. Bev McAndrew had struck her as a sensible woman. 'So did you text her?'

Torin nodded, chewing the corner of his lower lip. 'Yeah. Just, you know, what's for my tea, will you be back soon, kind of thing.'

Standard teenage-boy stuff. 'And she didn't respond?'

'No.' He fidgeted in his chair, then leaned forward, his forearms on the table, his hands clenched together. 'I didn't know what to do. I wasn't really worried, more, like, pissed off.' He gave her a quick up-and-under glance, checking whether he was going to get away with a mild swear word in front of a copper.

Paula smiled. 'Pissed off and hungry, I'm guessing.'

Torin's shoulders relaxed a degree or two. 'Yeah. That too. So I looked in the fridge and there was leftover cottage pie from the night before, so I nuked it and ate it. And still nothing from my mum.'

'Did you call any of her friends?'

His head reared back slightly in a gesture of incomprehension. 'How would I do that? I don't know their numbers. They're all in her phone, not written down anywhere. I mostly don't even know their names.' He waved a hand in the air. 'And there's no way to look up, like, "Dawn from work", or "Megan from the gym", or "Laura that I was at school with".' He had a point, she realised. It used to be when someone went missing, you checked their address book, their diary, the list of numbers by the phone. Now everybody carried their whole lives around with them and when they disappeared, so did the means of tracking them.

'No relatives you could call?'

Torin shook his head. 'My gran lives in Bristol with my auntie Rachel. Mum hasn't spoken to my dad this year, and anyway, he's doing a tour of duty in Afghanistan. He's an army medic.' A note of pride, Paula thought.

'What about work? Did you think of ringing there?'

He glowered. 'They only answer the outside line during regular opening hours. In the evening, the pharmacy's just for hospital emergency prescriptions. So even if I'd rung, nobody would have picked up.'

Paula cast her mind back to her own early teens and wondered how unnerved she'd have felt if her staid and respectable parents had gone inexplicably AWOL. In the circumstances, she thought Torin was doing pretty well not to lose control in the face of what probably felt like pointless questions that only served to slow down the process of finding his mother. It was that understanding of other people's points of view that had helped Paula develop her skills as an interviewer. Now she needed to keep Torin on side, make him feel someone cared about his plight so she could extract enough information to do something useful.

'So what did you do?'

Torin blinked fast and furious. Ashamed or upset, Paula wasn't sure which. 'I went on my Xbox and played Minecraft till I was tired enough to go to sleep. I didn't know what else to do.'

'You did well. A lot of people your age would have panicked. So what happened this morning?'

'I woke before my alarm went off. At first I thought it was Mum moving around that had woken me, but it wasn't. I went through to her room, and the bed was still made.' He chewed his lip again, dark eyes troubled. 'She hadn't come home. And she just doesn't do shit like that. One of my mates, his mum sometimes stops out all night without telling him. And that geezer on the front counter there, you could tell he was thinking, "Poor mutt, his mum's a slapper and he's the last to know it."' He was on a roll now, words tumbling into one another. 'But I'm telling you, my mum's not like that. She's really not. Totally. Not. Plus it's, like, a house rule. We always text each other if we're going to be late. Like, if I've missed the bus or somebody's parent's late picking us up. Or she's been held up at work. Whatever.' He ran out of steam abruptly.

'And so you came down here.'

His shoulders slumped. 'I couldn't think of anything else to do. But you lot don't care, do you?'

'If that was true, I wouldn't be sitting here with you, Torin. Usually, we wait twenty-four hours to start a missing person inquiry, it's true.' *Unless there's a vulnerable individual in the picture.* 'But not when it's someone like your mum, someone who has responsibility for a child or an old person, for example. What I need to do now is take down some details about you and your mum so I can set the ball rolling.'

A tap at the door interrupted Paula's flow. Before she could say anything, the front-counter officer stuck his head round the door. 'DCI Fielding wants to know how long you're going to be.' He didn't do any kind of job of hiding his self-satisfaction.

Paula dismissed him with a pitying look. 'I'm interviewing a witness. It's what I'm trained to do. Please tell the DCI I'll be with her as soon as I've finished here.'

'I'll pass the message on.'

Torin gave him a look of contempt as the door closed. 'You in the shit now? For talking to me?'

26

'I'm doing my job, Torin. That's what matters. Now, I'm going to need some background information.'

It didn't take long. Torin, fourteen. Pupil at Kenton Vale School. Bev, thirty-seven, chief pharmacist at Bradfield Cross Hospital, divorced eight years ago from Tom, currently serving at Camp Bastian. Torin and Bev shared a semi-detached house at 17 Grecian Rise, Kenton, Bradfield. No known reason why Bev wasn't where she should be. No history of mental illness or depression. No known financial pressures, other than the ones everyone in the public sector lived with these days.

Paula jotted down mobile numbers for mother and son then put her pen down. 'Have you got a picture of your mum?'

Torin fiddled with his phone, then turned it to face her. Paula recognised Bev from the picture, which wasn't always a given with smartphone snaps. It was a head shot, apparently taken on a sunny beach. Thick blonde hair, mid-blue eyes, oval face with regular features. Pretty but not drop-dead gorgeous, a face animated by a cheery smile complete with laughter lines. Seeing the picture reminded Paula that she'd found Bev attractive. Not that she'd exactly lusted after their dinner host. More of a private acknowledgement that Bev was her type. In the same way that Carol Jordan was. A particular configuration of features and colouring that always caught her attention. Not, interestingly, a match for Dr Elinor Blessing. Paula knew her partner was beautiful; her heart always rose at the sight of her fine black hair with its threads of silver, and the laughter in her grey eyes. But it hadn't been Elinor's looks that had tweaked Paula's attention when they first met. It had been her kindness, which trumped blonde every time. So yes, there had been a moment when she'd appreciated Bev's appeal. And if she'd noticed it, chances were that she wasn't the only one.

'Can you email that to me?' She flipped to a fresh page in her notebook and wrote down her mobile number and email address, tore it out and passed it to Torin. 'Has she got any scars, or birthmarks, or tattoos? It makes it easier for us to check with the local hospitals in case she's had an accident and been brought in without her handbag.'

He glanced at the scrap of paper Paula had given him then met her eyes again. 'She has a tattoo of a bluebird on her left shoulder. And she's got a scar on her right ankle where she broke it and they had to put a pin in.'

Paula made a quick note. 'That's very helpful.'

'What are you going to do about my mum?'

'I'll make some phone calls. Talk to her colleagues.'

'What about me?'

It was a good question. Torin was a minor and she knew she should phone the social services department and get a case worker assigned to him. But Bev might prove Paula's professional unease unfounded. She might still turn up, embarrassed and awkward after an unpredicted night on the tiles. Then unpicking the process set in train by the social workers would be a nightmare for mother and son. She'd be stigmatised as an unfit mother and he'd be classified 'at risk'. It might even have an impact on her job. Paula didn't want that on her conscience. 'Why don't you just go to school?'

'Like normal?'

She nodded. 'Text me when you get out of school and we'll take it from there. Hopefully, she'll have turned up at work and that'll be the end of it.' She tried to reassure him with a smile that matched her voice.

He looked dubious. 'You think?'

No. But, 'Chances are,' was what she said as she stood up and eased him out the door. She watched him as far as the front entrance, his shoulders hunched, his head down. She wanted to believe Bev McAndrew was fit and well and on her way home. But convincing herself would have required a triumph of hope over experience, and Paula didn't have it in her.

She turned away, momentarily nostalgic for her old team. They would have understood exactly why she was bothering with Torin and his barely missing mum. But that was then. Instead she had DCI Fielding to face. She'd heard good things about Fielding's conviction rates and this was definitely a team she wanted to hitch her wagon to. But already she'd kept her new boss waiting. It was far from the perfect start she'd hoped for. Hopefully, it wasn't too late to redeem herself. She'd simply have to try that little bit harder.

7

The tram rattled across the high Victorian viaduct, sleek modern lines a contrast to the soot-stained redbrick arches. It was, Tony thought, a powerful metaphor for the whole area surrounding the Minster Canal Basin. Opposite the viaduct was the ruined apse of the medieval minster itself, its stained limestone tracery all that had been left standing when a stick of Luftwaffe bombs had reduced the rest of the building to rubble. A dozen years ago, the viaduct and the minster had bookended a higgledy-piggledy scrum of random buildings, half of them empty and decaying, their window frames rotten and their rooflines sagging. The canal district had been the least lovely and least loved of inner-city Bradfield's precincts.

Then a bright spark on the city council had discovered an EU fund aimed at reinvigorating depressed and deprived inner-city environments. These days, the canal basin was the hub of a lively area. Craft workshops, indie publishers and software developers worked cheek by jowl, flats and studio apartments occupied the upper floors and a sprinkling of bars and bistros provided somewhere for locals and visitors to mingle. One of Bradfield Victoria's premier league stars had even lent his name to a Spanish tapas bar that he occasionally deigned to grace with his presence.

The basin itself had become a mix of permanent residential moorings and short-stay marina slots for the narrowboats that provided holidays and day trips where once they'd shifted cargoes round the country.

Attractive though it now was, it had never previously crossed Tony's mind as a possible home. He'd sat outside one of the waterside pubs with Carol Jordan once, when they'd been pretending to be normal people who could have a drink and a conversation that didn't involve the interior life of fucked-up individuals. Another time, he'd shared a clutter of tapas with a couple of American colleagues who'd come to look round the secure mental hospital where he worked. More than once, he'd walked the canal from one side of the city to the other while he mulled over a complex case. There was something about walking that freed up his mental processes to consider options other than the obvious.

So, he was familiar with the basin. Yet he'd never wondered what it would be like to live on the water in the heart of the city until it was all that was left to him. His former house in Bradfield was gone, sold to strangers when he thought he'd finally found a place he could with conviction call home. And now that was gone too, a burned-out shell that was an uncomfortable metaphor for what had happened to the life he'd imagined he could lead there. Everywhere he looked, bloody metaphors galore.

Tony crossed the cobbled area that separated the tapas bar from the houseboat moorings and swung aboard a pretty narrowboat whose name, *Steeler*, unfurled on a painted gold-and-black ribbon across the stern. He unfastened the heavy padlocks that held the hatch closed and clattered down the steep steps to the cabin below. As he passed, he threw the switches that activated the boat's electricity supply, generated by an array of solar panels. Even gloomy Bradfield skies provided enough energy for one person whose power needs were far from extravagant.

He'd been surprised by how readily he'd adapted to living in so confined a space. Life with a place for everything and everything in its place had proved unexpectedly soothing. There was no room for anything inessential; living like this had stripped his material life down to the bone, forcing him to reconsider the worth of stuff that had cluttered his life for years. OK, he didn't love the practical necessities like emptying the toilet tank and topping up the water reservoir. Nor was he entirely at ease with the camaraderie of the water, a connectivity that seemed to draw together the most unlikely combinations of people. And he still hadn't mastered the heating system. Now the nights were getting colder, he was growing fed up with waking in a freezing cabin. He was going to have to settle for the action of last resort – sitting down with the manual and actually reading the instructions. But in spite of all the inconveniences, he had grown comfortable in this calm, contained world.

He dumped his bag on the buttoned leather banquette that ran along the saloon bulkhead and put the kettle on for a cafètiere of coffee. While he waited for the water to boil, he booted up his laptop and checked his email. The only new message was from a cop for whom he'd profiled a serial rapist a few years before. Half-hoping it was an invitation to work with him again, he opened it.

Hi Tony. How are you doing? I heard about the business with Jacko Vance. Terrible thing, but without your input it could have been so much worse.

32

The reason I'm writing is because we're
organising a conference to promote the use of
offender profiling in high-visibility cases. Not just
murders, but other serious offences too. It's getting
harder to persuade top brass and police authorities
that it's cost-effective in these times of austerity
all round. We're trying to make the case that it's a
front-end expense that saves a lot of back-end
costs. I thought Carol Jordan would be the perfect
keynote speaker, given how closely she's worked
with you over the years. But I'm having some
difficulty tracking her down. BMP tell me she's no
longer on their books. They informed me she was
transferring to West Mercia. But they say she's not
on their strength. I tried the email address I had
for her, but it bounced back at me. And the mobile
number I had for her isn't working any more. I
wondered if maybe she was deep undercover, but
either way I reckoned you'd know where I can get
in touch with her.

Can you give me some contact details? Or if
that's not practical, can you at least ask her to get
in touch with me?

Thanks in advance,

Rollo Harris,

Detective Chief Superintendent,

Devon & Cornwall Police

Tony stared at the screen, the words blurring. Rollo Harris
wasn't the only one who didn't know where Carol Jordan
was, or how to get in touch with her. Most people who
knew them both would have struggled to believe it, but
Tony hadn't spoken to Carol for the best part of three
months. And he wouldn't have known where to find her if

he'd felt able to break that silence. The last thing she'd said to him after the hunt for Vance was done was, 'It's not all that's over, Tony.' And it appeared she'd meant it. She'd cut herself loose from his life.

At first, he'd managed to keep track of her. Although her final weeks at Bradfield Metropolitan Police had been classified as compassionate leave, she was obliged to let her employers know where she was. And because Paula McIntyre knew better than most how close the bond between Carol and Tony had been, she'd kept him in the loop. Carol had rented a service apartment in Bradfield for a month, then she'd moved into her parents' house.

Then she stopped being a DCI with BMP and, according to Paula, within days she was no longer under her parents' roof. 'I called her mobile and it wasn't working. So I rang her parents' number and spoke to her dad. He wasn't very forthcoming but he did admit she wasn't living there any more. He either didn't know or he wouldn't say where she is,' Paula had told him. Given the quality of Paula's interrogation skills, Tony reckoned David Jordan probably didn't know where his daughter was living.

He couldn't help wondering how that had happened. Going home to her parents, in the circumstances, wouldn't have been his professional advice. Her brother was dead, murdered by a killer he and Carol had failed to catch soon enough. And grief generally imposed a need to distribute blame. Was it Carol's guilt or her parents' pain that had driven a wedge between them?

However it had played out, it hadn't ended well. Tony would have put money on that. And since Carol needed to hold him responsible for Michael and Lucy's death because he had been too slow to realise what Vance had planned, then it followed that she would blame him for the rift with her parents. Insult to injury.

Tony rubbed his eyes with a knuckle. Wherever Carol Jordan was hiding, he would be the last to know. Sooner or later he was going to have to man up and either do something about that or let it go for ever.

8

Gartonside was a district nobody had ever chosen to live in. Even when the narrow streets of basic brick terraces had been built back at the tail end of the nineteenth century, their original residents knew they were destined to be slums before the decade was out. Thin walls meant cold and damp were perennial problems. Cheap materials diminished privacy. Outside toilets and no bathrooms did nothing for the hygiene or health of the factory workers who filled the two-bedroom houses to bursting point. Gartonside became the cheerless port of call of the feckless, the hopeless and the city's newest arrivals. Only the immigrants ever escaped its dead-end streets.

Finally, in one of the last hurrahs of the twentieth century, Bradfield city council had decreed that Gartonside was to be bulldozed and replaced with a planned housing estate of more spacious houses with parking spaces at the front and tiny gardens at the rear. A decade later, the first phase – the emptying of existing residents and the demolition of their former homes – was not yet complete. There were still a handful of streets in the shadow of Bradfield Victoria's vast stadium where residents lingered on. And beyond them, a huddle of houses were boarded up, waiting for the wrecking crews to reduce them to rubble.

Paula's satnav still believed in the streets of Gartonside, which made her even later to the crime scene. By the time she reached Rossiter Street, the perimeter was well established with festoons of crime-scene tape and stony-faced uniforms in high-vis jackets. She added her car to the impromptu parking lot at the end of the street and logged into the scene. 'Where's DCI Fielding?'

The constable with the clipboard nodded towards a mobile incident room parked further down the street. 'In the van, getting suited and booted for the scene.'

That was a relief. Not quite as late as she feared. When she'd finally said goodbye to Torin and found her way to the CID squad room, Paula had been taken aback by the absence of bodies. Instead of the usual buzz of chat and phone conversations there was a preternatural quiet broken only by the mutter of laptop keys struck by a couple of heavy-fingered operatives.

The one nearest the door looked up and raised his unruly eyebrows. 'You must be the new skip, right? McIntyre, yeah?'

Paula was tempted to slap him down with a quick *Sergeant McIntyre to you*, but she didn't know the lay of the land yet so she settled for, 'And you are?'

He pushed a thick fringe of black hair back from his shiny forehead. 'Detective Constable Pat Cody.' He gave an expansive sweep of his arm. 'And this is Skenfrith Street CID. Only, most of the firm are on a shout. A murder, down Gartonside.'

So much for hopes of a quiet day. 'Is that where DCI Fielding is?'

Cody gave a twisted little smile. 'Got it in one. And she's not very happy that her new bag man isn't with her.' The caterpillar eyebrows rose again. He was enjoying himself.

Paula wasn't about to explain herself to him. 'You got an address for me?'

'Rossiter Street, Gartonside.'

'Do we have a number?'

He smirked. 'The numbers fell off those doors years ago. The houses are boarded up, waiting for the council budget to afford bulldozers. You'll recognise the crime scene from the activity.'

And so she had. Paula dodged the puddles and potholes and climbed the metal steps into the mobile incident room. As she entered, a tiny woman wrestling her body into a white protective suit paused to look her up and down. 'McIntyre?'

Clearly the standard form of address in this firm. 'That's right. DCI Fielding?'

'That's me. Nice of you to join us. Get suited up, quick as you like.' There was something bird-like about Fielding. It wasn't simply her size or her fine-boned appearance. Her eyes darted around, even as she climbed into her suit, and there was a quick jerkiness to her movements that made Paula think of a blackbird raiding the earth for worms.

'I was taking a witness statement. Misper.' Paula checked the pile of J-suits. Fielding had snaffled the only small. She settled for a medium and began the inconvenient process of getting into it.

'That's a bit beneath your pay grade.' Fielding's Scottish accent was the honey-seductive rather than the half-brick aggressive sort.

'I happened to recognise the teenager who was reporting.

I've actually met his mother. I thought it would save time if I dealt with it since the front counter was sticking to the letter of twenty-four hours.'

Fielding paused with the zip halfway over her small bosom. She frowned, olive skin crinkling into a relief map of shallow furrows and ridges. 'That's because he's been trained to follow protocols. Protocols that are put in place so detectives like us don't waste our time on folk having a spur-of-the-moment night out.'

Paula shoved a second leg into the suit, annoyed by her trouser leg rucking up around the knee. 'I've always understood that when there's a child or a vulnerable adult left at risk by a disappearance, we take action straight away.' According to the grapevine, Fielding was a mother. She should get it.

Fielding grunted. 'Been a while since you've been at the sharp end, McIntyre. Major Incident Team's spoiled you.' She pulled a face. 'In an ideal world, you'd be right. But we're not in an ideal world. Cuts and redundancies have fucked us all up.' She frowned again, brown eyes glaring at Paula. 'We haven't got the bodies to jump in early on mispers. We leave that to uniforms. I need you here. Not fucking about on the tail of somebody who's probably chosen not to be where they're expected to be.' She held up a hand to shut Paula up before she could speak. 'I know. The reasons for those choices are usually fucking horrible. But we're not social workers.'

'Ma'am.' Angered but not chastened, Paula turned away and finished zipping herself into the suit. OK, Fielding had a point, but that didn't mean Paula had to hang up her humanity at the door. She'd check Bev's movements on her own time. Somehow. Still facing away from Fielding, who had the kind of physical presence that filled more space than seemed possible, she dragged the conversation away from her supposed transgression. 'So what are we looking at here?'

'Junkie squatters have been using one of the houses on and off for a few months now. They were at some music festival near Sheffield at the weekend. They got back a couple of hours ago and found the body of a woman in the middle of the living room.' Her voice muffled as she bent to pull on the blue plastic shoe covers. 'I suppose we should be grateful they phoned us instead of doing a runner.'

'Did they recognise her?'

'They say not.'

Paula raised the hood to cover her hair and pulled on the chilly blue nitrile gloves. 'Given that they phoned it in and didn't leg it, they're probably telling the truth. If they'd known her, they'd have been less likely to report it. People who live outside the mainstream tend not to trust us to do an unbiased job.'

Fielding cocked her head to acknowledge the comment. 'Good point. OK, let's do it.' She didn't mess around holding the door open for Paula, who caught it seconds before the spring slammed it shut. As they headed for the house, Fielding looked over her shoulder. 'I'd have liked a quieter start, so we could be clear about how it's going to work between us. I am aware this is your first assignment as a sergeant.'

'I worked as DCI Jordan's bagman on MIT, ma'am.' Paula was quick to stand up for herself. Fielding needed to understand she wasn't someone who could be pushed around. She needed to know she could count on Paula. 'I understand about having your back.'

Fielding's expression shifted, cold assessment giving way to acceptance. 'I'm proud of my team. We might not have the specialists you had at MIT, but we get more than our share of results. I've heard good things about you. Don't prove your friends wrong.'

It wasn't the most welcoming speech Paula had ever heard. But it was a start. And given how much she wanted her career to have a future, she'd make the most of it.

Just as soon as she'd found out what had happened to Bev McAndrew.

9

The carefully chosen furniture was gone now, carried off by the man and a van she'd picked from the small ads in the local paper. Actually, it had been two men and a van, and it had taken two trips to strip the barn of Michael and Lucy's possessions. Everything personal, Carol had packed in plastic crates from the DIY warehouse and stacked in the garage. All the rest was a memory, doubtless gracing the house of some lucky punter who was blissfully ignorant of its history.

The one part of the barn she'd left intact was the separate room that Michael had created at one end of the building. It was a studio-sized spare bedroom with its own toilet and shower, completely cut off from the remainder of the space by a new wall as thick as the traditional stone that protected the interior from the bitter weather. The reason for the sound insulation was that the room had doubled as Michael's office. Here, he wrote code and developed software for games and apps. Along one wall was a long table where an array of computers and games consoles still sat. As far as Carol was aware, this room was untainted by the presence of her brother's killer. When she came in here and closed the door, she could still feel as close to Michael as she had been when he was alive.

Back when she'd first come to Bradfield, they'd shared a loft conversion in the centre of the city. Outside their tall windows the city had hummed and throbbed, sparked and glittered. But inside, it had been a space where Michael had worked and they'd both lived. She remembered how she'd often opened the door to the rattle of gunfire or the electronica of a futuristic soundtrack. Once he realised she was home, Michael would always put headphones on, but he preferred to work with the sound effects blasting at him from all sides.

These days Carol had got into the habit of drinking her coffee and eating a bowl of cereal with tinned fruit in the room where she slept, music pouring out of the tall speakers that bookended the work table. Every morning, it was Michael's final playlist, the last music he'd been listening to while he worked. A mixture of Michael Nyman, Ludovico Einaudi and Brad Mehldau. Nothing she would ever have chosen. But she was growing comfortable with it.

She ate quickly, eager to return to the hard physical work that made introspection impossible. When she walked back into the barn, she was astonished to see a black-and-white Border collie crouching on the floor a couple of yards inside the door, pink tongue lolling between strong white teeth. Her heart leapt in her chest, a cascade of reproaches and terrors flooding her head. *How could you be so stupid? Leaving the door open, are you mad? This is how people die. This is how people have died. Dog means human, human means stranger, stranger means danger. Have you learned nothing, you stupid bitch?*

For a moment, she was frozen, incapable of figuring out

what to do. Then the old Carol Jordan kicked in. Slowly she stooped and put her bowl and mug on the floor. She knew where her tools were; she'd always had good recall. She retreated a little and moved sideways. Neither she nor the dog took their eyes off each other. Her left hand strayed outwards till her fingertips brushed the handle of the sledgehammer. As she gripped it, the dog's ears pricked up.

Carol swung the hammer up and held the shaft of the hammer across her body, hands apart. Then she launched herself towards the dog, roaring wordlessly at the top of her voice. Startled, the dog jumped up, backed off, then turned tail.

She followed it through the door, still raging at the blameless animal who was now, she saw, sitting at the heels of a strange man, peering round his legs with ears flat to its head. She skidded to a halt, not sure whether to feel foolish or frightened. He didn't look very frightening. She fell into her old habit of mentally creating an APB description in her head. A shade under six feet tall, medium build. Flat tweed cap over dark hair, silvering at the temples. Full beard, neatly trimmed. Narrow lips, fleshy nose, dark eyes nested with outdoor wrinkles. He wore a waxed jacket, open to reveal a brown suede waistcoat over a heavy cream cotton shirt with, God help her, a cravat at the neck. Toffee-coloured corduroys tucked into green wellies. He looked as if he should have a shotgun broken on his arm. A smile twitched at the corner of his mouth. 'You seem to have terrified my dog.' *Public school accent. The yap of the posh boys who don't know the price of milk.*

'I don't like trespassers.' Carol let the heavy hammer swing down till the head was resting on the ground.

'I do apologise. She's too curious for her own good.' This time, the smile was full on.

'The dog has an excuse, then. What's yours?' She didn't

44

care that she was being rude. After what had happened here, any local would cut her slack, confronted with a stranger on her own ground.

'I thought it was about time I came to introduce myself. I'm George Nicholas. I live in the house over the brow of the hill.' He turned and pointed behind him to his right.

'Would that be the bloody big house over the brow of the hill?'

He chuckled. 'I suppose you might call it that.'

'So you're the guy who owns all the land I can see apart from my own patch here?'

'Not quite all of it. But yes, most of it. And this is my dog, Jess.' He rumpled the fur on the dog's head. 'Say hello, Jess.' The dog sidled out from behind him and sat in front of Carol, raising a paw.

It was, she had to admit, a good routine. Completely dis-arming, if you were the sort of woman who allowed herself to be disarmed. Carol shook the dog's paw then crouched down to stroke its thick fur. 'You're a lovely girl, aren't you?' Then she stood up. 'I'm Carol Jordan,' she said, firmly avoiding a handshake by sticking her free hand in her trouser pocket.

'I know. I was at the funeral.' He looked pained. 'No reason why you would know that. I . . . I was very fond of Michael and Lucy.'

'They never mentioned you.' It was a harsh response, but she didn't care. It was a lie too. Lucy had talked about going to dinner at the big house and Michael had teased her about abandoning her socialist principles.

'And why should they have,' he said easily. 'I gathered you didn't live in each other's pockets. But we were neigh-bours and we socialised from time to time and, for what it's worth, I liked them both very much. Like everyone around here, I was appalled by what happened to them.'

Carol cleared her throat. 'Yes. Well. It was appalling.'

Nicholas looked at his feet. 'I lost my wife three years ago. Drunk driver rammed her car on the motorway slip road.' He drew in a long breath and tilted his head back to stare at the sky. 'Obviously nothing like the scale of what happened here, but I do have some understanding of losing people one loves to sudden violent death.'

Carol tried to care, but she knew she didn't. Not really. She couldn't be bothered with people who tried to convince her they knew what she was going through. She was done with empathy. She'd watched Tony Hill being Mr Empathy for years and look where that had got her. Fuck empathy. Still. The obligations of good manners remained. 'I'm sorry,' she said.

'So am I.' He met her eyes again. This time, the smile was sorrowful. 'Anyway, I wanted to say hello. And to invite you to supper. Next week, perhaps? I've got a couple of friends from the village coming over on Tuesday, if you'd like to join us?'

Carol shook her head. 'I don't think so. I'm not very good company right now.'

He nodded, brisk in his understanding. 'Of course. Another time, perhaps.' There was an uncomfortable silence, then he glanced at the barn door. 'How are you getting on with ...' His voice tailed off.

'I'm gutting it. Come and have a look.' Seeing his hesitation, she gave him a grim smile. 'It's all right, there's nothing left to see.'

He followed her inside to the hollow shell of the barn. Seeing it through his eyes, she understood the extent of what she'd done. Only the kitchen area remained unscathed. Everything else was stripped to the bare bones. The last job was the demolition of the gallery floor where Michael and Lucy had been murdered on their bed. She'd already ripped out the staircase. Today's task was to break down the supporting beam that held up the floor so she could set about the final stage of destroying it. She pointed to the sturdy timber. 'That's my next job.'

'You're not taking the whole beam out, are you?' He craned his head to follow the beam up to the A-frame joist that ran the width of the barn.

'If I take that out, the floor will start to collapse. It'll be much easier to break it down.'

Nicholas stared at her as if she was mad. 'If you take that out, your whole roof will collapse. That's a major structural beam. It's been there since the barn was built.'

'Are you sure?'

'I'm sure. I'm not an engineer, but I've been around old buildings all my life.' Suspicious, Carol followed his pointing finger as he outlined the structure of the hammer beam truss. 'If you don't believe me, get a structural engineer in to have a look. But please, don't get rid of it until you've taken advice.' He looked so distressed that she surrendered her instinctive mistrust of anyone trying to tell her what to do.

'OK,' she said. 'I'll work around it.' She crouched down again and ruffled the dog's fur. 'Looks like you did me a favour, Jess.'

'We're always happy to help,' Nicholas said. 'I'll be off now. No doubt I'll see you around?'

Carol made a noncommittal sound and followed him to the door. She stood and watched him leave her land and strike out across the rough pasture towards his home. It occurred to her that she'd been more friendly to the dog than to its owner. There was a time when that would have embarrassed her.

Not any more.

10

There was a terrible moment when Paula misunderstood what she was looking at. The shaggy blonde hair, the square shoulders, the legs that had always brought Anne Bancroft to mind; all markers for Carol Jordan. She'd never seen her naked except in fantasy, but her imagination was enough to blur the reality in front of her for a split second. Then she understood that the dead woman sprawled on the floor was not Carol Jordan. She was the wrong body shape. Too heavy in the hips and thighs, too squat in the torso. But it had been a head-swimming moment.

Fielding had caught it too, which wasn't going to help her respect for Paula. 'You all right, McIntyre? I'd have thought you'd be used to this by now.'

Paula coughed into her paper mask. 'With respect, ma'am, I never want to be used to it.'

Fielding turned away with a shrug. 'Fair enough.' She took a couple of steps towards the body, stooping for a closer look. 'He didn't want us to recognise her, that's for sure.

Look at that.' She pointed to the mash of flesh and bone that had been the woman's face. The naked body was a mass of bruises and abrasions. Paula had seen plenty of victims of violence, but she couldn't remember a body that had taken such a comprehensive beating.

Then another possibility flashed across her mind. She'd been slow to make the connection. But a description of this bludgeoned woman would also fit Bev McAndrew. Her breakfast coffee burned at the back of her throat and she side-stepped a CSI photographer for a better view. For the second time, relief made her weak in the knees. This wasn't Bev. Torin's mother was taller and slimmer, with bigger breasts. Whoever this woman was, she wasn't the missing pharmacist.

Paula looked around the room. It was a dismal place to die. The walls were stained with damp and mould and the floor-boards were filthy with ground-in dirt. A sagging sofa faced a scarred coffee table whose missing leg had been replaced with a pile of crumbling bricks. Beer cans were piled at either end of the sofa and three ashtrays overflowed with cigarette butts and roaches. Empty blister packs of over-the-counter painkillers were scattered around among crushed boxes that had once held pizzas and burgers. The stench was a grue-some mixture of all the things she wished she'd never smelled.

Paula turned back to stare bleakly at the murdered woman. She longed for Tony Hill's facility for reading a crime scene and understanding something of the mind that had created it. But her skills were for interrogating the living, not the dead. She'd go through the motions at the crime scene, but she knew she'd always have to rely on other specialists for what it could reveal.

And right on cue, one of those specialists walked in on them. 'DCI Fielding. You have something for me, I've been told?' Paula recognised the warm Canadian drawl of Dr

Grisha Shatalov, the Home Office pathologist who generally worked Bradfield's homicides. He clapped Paula's shoulder softly as he passed her. 'Paula. Good to see you.'

Fielding stepped aside with what looked like relief on the little Paula could see of her face. 'She's all yours, Doc. Brutal, this one.'

'Taking someone's life? That's always brutal in my book.' Grisha hunkered down by the body. 'Even when it looks gentle.' He moved his hands over her body, gradually applying pressure and pausing to gauge temperature and rigor.

'Did she die here?' Fielding's question was brusque. It sounded to Paula as though her reputation for impatience was well-founded. There was clearly no place here for the exchange of pleasantries she'd always seen between Carol and Grisha. Straight to business and no messing around, that seemed to be Fielding's style. Like a lot of women in senior positions, she set out her stall to out-tough the men.

Grisha glanced over his shoulder. 'I'd say so. You've got blood spatter from the head wound, you've got lividity that looks to me like she hasn't been moved post-mortem. Chances are high she was still alive when he brought her here.' He looked up at the photographer. 'Are you done here? Can I move her?'

'She's all yours, mate.' The cameraman stepped away and left them to it.

Grisha carefully tilted the victim's head to one side. 'Look, here. You see this?' He pointed to a depression in the skull, blonde hair turned dark and matted with a mixture of blood and brain matter. 'A blow to the head with something long, rounded and heavy. A baseball bat or a metal pipe. I'll have a better idea once I get her to the lab. If nothing else had happened to her, chances are that would have killed her. But he made sure by giving her a good kicking.' He gestured at the bruises on her torso. 'Large, irregular rounded shapes, it's a classic bruise from a kick. And the colour, red shading towards purple. That tells us she was still alive when he gave kicking her to death his best shot.' He sat on his heels and considered. 'Either he's smart or he got lucky.' He paused expectantly.

'I've not got time for twenty questions,' Fielding groused. 'What do you mean?'

'He kicked her. He kept on kicking her. He didn't stamp on her. It would have been better for you if he had. You might have got a sole pattern from his boots.'

'Bastard.' Fielding sounded disgusted. 'Boots, not shoes?' Her face gave nothing away, but she folded her arms across her chest as if to defend herself from the violence.

'Given the extent of the damage – her face is wrecked, Fielding, look at it – my best guess would be steel toecaps. And that tends to boots rather than shoes.' Grisha pointed to her left ankle. 'Check out those abrasions. Looks like a restraint tell-tale to me. A shackle of some description. But one with a straight edge. Maybe designed for pipework rather than humans. That's why it's torn the skin the way it has. I'll check her wrists when I get her on the table.'

Before Fielding could say more, they were interrupted by another white suit. 'Guv, I thought you'd want to know. It looks like we've found her clothes and her bag. Stuffed behind the bath.'

'Good work, Hussain. Bag the clothes and get them straight to the lab. Paula, you go and have a look at the contents when we're done here. You're a woman, you'll have a better sense of what's what than these hairy-arsed lads.'

Paula bit her tongue. Only because she was glad to have first crack at the victim's possessions. But if Fielding thought she could defuse her by putting her in the little woman box, she was going to have another think coming. 'Ma'am,' she said.

'What about time of death?' Fielding was already on to the next thing.

Grisha took hold of the woman and gently rolled her on to her stomach. 'Let's see what she has to tell us.' He opened the plastic satchel he always brought to crime scenes and took out a thermometer. He parted her legs slightly so he could take a rectal temperature reading. Then Paula heard his breath hiss over his teeth. 'Jesus Christ,' he said. Grisha seldom showed any emotion, but the disgust was obvious in his tone.

'What is it?' Fielding demanded.

Grisha bent forward and stared intently between the woman's legs. He reached out gingerly with one finger. 'I thought I'd seen everything.' His voice was so quiet Paula could barely hear him.

'What is it, Grisha?' she asked, laying a hand on his shoulder.

He shook his head. 'It looks like he's superglued her labia together.'

11

By late morning, Marie had a list of questions for Rob Morrison. In her experience, there was no point in holding back out of a misplaced sense of politeness. She needed answers so she could make a start on the strategic developments she'd been hired to initiate and see through. Worrying whether Rob would take her enquiries as subtle criticisms wasn't helpful. If his finer feelings were going to stand in the way of progress, he'd better develop a thicker skin, she thought. And quickly.

So she double-checked the handwritten list she'd made – always better to write down a list of questions; they had a tendency to stick in the mind that way and they were less likely to fall through the cracks during the discussion – and bustled across the open-plan area to Rob's office.

Marie scanned the room as she went, taking note of who had their head down, talking on the phone or frowning at their screen, and who was staring into space or leaning back in their chair chatting to the person in the next carrel. She wasn't about to start anything as crude as a time-and-motion study any time soon, but it was never too soon to begin gathering impressions of the staff. Gareth, for example. He might well be one of the most productive employees, but right now he was paying no attention to work. He was half-turned away from his screen, chatting to a smug-looking bloke in a pink shirt and khaki chinos, hair immaculately groomed. Even from across the room she could make out the Ralph Lauren Polo logo. She'd have put money on him reeking of aftershave or cologne. She hadn't noticed him earlier when she'd been introduced to the floor, and she thought she would have if he'd been there. She knew his type and she didn't like it.

Dismissing him from her mind, she walked through Rob's open door to find him at his computer, mouse clicking as furiously as if he was in the throes of some annoying computer game. 'Have you got a minute?' she asked.

He immediately stopped what he was doing and before she could possibly have seen his screen, he closed the window he was working in. 'Sure. Is there a problem?'

'I need to go through some of our procedures,' Marie said, drawing a chair up at right angles to his desk. 'I want to be clear how we're doing things at present so I can work out where we can make strategic improvements.'

He nodded enthusiastically, rubbing his chin then tugging his earlobe. He was, she realised, one of those people who can't stop touching their face. It made her want to avoid touching anything he'd touched. He smoothed one eyebrow and scratched the side of his nose. 'Makes perfect sense,' he said.

They had barely made a start when Ralph Lauren Man swaggered into the room. He let his eyes slide over Marie, lingering on her breasts and her legs before turning his attention to Rob. 'Are you up for tonight?' he said, his tone almost accusatory rather than inviting.

Rob gave him what appeared to be a warning frown. 'Nige, I'd like you to meet Marie Mather, our new Director of Marketing. Marie, this is Nigel Dean. He's one of the boffins from upstairs. Software development for our data-gathering systems.'

Nigel inclined his head towards her. 'We're Big Brother,' he said. 'The one that is watching you, that is, not the one that you watch on your telly. We manage data for every-thing from your local supermarket to speed cameras to mobile phone networks. I could track you from your front door to the office without your knowing.'

Rob laughed nervously. 'Pay no attention to him, he likes to wind us all up, does Nige.'

Creep, she thought. 'I'll bear that in mind,' she said mildly, not making it clear which one she was responding to.

'I was just making sure Rob's coming along tonight. A bunch of us are going out to celebrate landing a tasty new contract. We're going to Honeypots, do you know it?'

You didn't have to be a lad about town to be aware of Honeypots, Bradfield's biggest and brashest lap-dancing club. Marie would rather have nailed her hand to the wall than spend an evening there. Not for the first time, she counted her blessings and was grateful for her Marco. 'I never go out on a school night,' she said.

Nigel raised one side of his mouth in a sneer. 'You ladies and your beauty sleep. Another time, maybe. On a Friday?'

Marie gave her sweetest smile. 'I'll bring my husband. He likes a good laugh.' She gathered her papers and stood up. 'Rob, perhaps we could finish this when you're free?'

Twat, she thought as she marched back to her office. It didn't seem to matter where you worked, you couldn't escape them. *More's the pity.*

12

The mobile incident room was bedlam with the volume turned down. A constant stream of police officers, CSIs and civilian support staff tramped in and out, covering all the bases from grim and grumpy to crass and chirpy. One look told Paula it was the worst possible place to examine evidence that might end up as a key plank in a court case. Clearing it first with Fielding, she left the crime scene and headed back to Skenfrith Street to find a quiet corner. And if she was honest, she wanted to put some distance between herself and the dead woman.

During her years with Carol Jordan's Major Incident Team, Paula had confronted a wide range of the hideous things human beings could do to one another. The things she'd seen had disturbed her nights and her days, but she'd always managed to put them in a box in her head where they couldn't contaminate the rest of her life. She'd known what it was to be at risk herself, and she'd lost colleagues to the job. It was only by chance that she'd escaped the act of violence that had destroyed Chris Devine's future during the hunt for Jacko Vance.

All of this horror she'd got through. Maybe a few extra drinks on the bad nights, a spike in her cigarette consumption on the bad days. Still, she'd absorbed the pain, dealt with the anger. Deep down, she'd learned to live with it. But today's victim had messed with her head. There was no escaping that. The brutal beating on its own would have been hard to stomach, but she'd have got past that without too much trouble. The other thing – she could hardly bear to articulate the act, even in her head – was somehow infinitely worse. It was as if her killer wanted to deny her everything that made her who she was. Wrecked face, ruined body, not even any use for sex. He'd rendered her utterly worthless. It spoke of a contempt that chilled Paula's heart. This, she suspected, was a murderer who wasn't going to stop at one.

The rest of the team would be gossiping and speculating about it. She knew what cops were like. And for a little while she wanted not to be part of that. Putting together a profile of the victim based on the contents of her bag would be a good enough excuse.

In the unfamiliar territory of her new base, she managed to find the canteen and set herself up with coffee and the comfort of Jaffa Cakes. And because the canteen staff always knew what was what, she acquired directions to a small meeting room on the fourth floor where nothing was scheduled for the rest of the day.

Gloved and masked, her coffee and biscuits on a separate table, she finally addressed the dead woman's life. The bag was businesslike – black leather, worn in but not scuffed, decent quality and capacious. It looked a bit like a scaled-down briefcase, with its neat compartments and pockets. Methodically, Paula emptied the contents on to the table, not pausing to study anything till she was sure the bag was completely empty. She was impressed with the relative absence of crap and made a mental note to clear her own bag of the accumulated detritus of everyday living.

She went with the obviously female stuff first. Lipstick, mascara, blusher, all own-brand from a chain chemist. Plastic folding comb with a narrow mirror in the handle. So, someone who cared about how she looked but didn't make a fetish of it.

Pack of tissues, only a couple left. A small tin that had once held sweets but now contained four compact tampons. A couple of condoms in a plastic pouch. Blister pack of birth control pills, three remaining. So, almost certainly straight, probably single. If you were in a relationship, you generally left those things at home, in the bathroom or the bedside-table drawer. You weren't going to spend the night in another bed on the spur of the moment.

Blister pack of strong painkillers. Paula frowned. She didn't think you could get these off prescription. When she'd torn a muscle in her calf a few months before and she'd been in excruciating pain for a couple of days, Elinor had sneaked her a couple from the hospital, swearing her to secrecy. Paula had teased her about it. 'Is one of your post-op patients on paracetamol tonight, then?' Elinor had confessed that they were samples from a pharmaceutical rep.

'All doctors have a drawer stuffed with freebies,' she said. 'You'd think we'd know better, but we self-medicate like mad.'

Was the victim a doctor? Or someone who had a problem with pain? Paula filed the question away for now and returned to the bag's contents. Three pens; one from a hotel, one from a stationery supply chain, one from an animal charity. A bunch of keys – a Fiat car key, two Yales, two mortises. House, car, office? House, car, somebody else's house? No way of telling yet. A couple of crumpled receipts from a Freshco Express in Harriestown revealed a taste for pepperoni pizza, chicken tikka pies and low-fat strawberry yoghurt.

The iPhone would be the treasure trove. Paula woke it from its slumber. The screen saver was a fluffy tortoiseshell cat lying on its back. When she tried to open the screen, it demanded a password. That meant the phone would have to go off to the technical team, where one of the geeks would unlock its mysteries eventually. Not like on MIT, where their own IT specialist Stacey Chen was always on tap. Stacey would have coaxed every last morsel of data from the phone in record time, speeding the investigation on its way. But here in her brave new world, Paula's evidence would have to join the queue. No rush jobs here; the budget wouldn't take the strain. Frustrated, she wrote a label for the phone and bagged it separately.

All that remained was a slim metal case and a fat wallet. She flicked open the case to reveal a short stack of business cards. Nadia Wilkowa was apparently the North West Area Representative for Bartis Health. There was a web address as well as a mobile number and email address for Nadia. Paula took out her phone and rang the number. The bagged iPhone did a jittering shimmy across the table before the voicemail cut in. 'Hi, this is Nadia Wilkowa.' There was a faint East European accent, but it had been almost completely painted over by polite Bradfield. 'I'm sorry I can't talk to you right now, but please leave a message and I'll return your call as soon as I can.' A welcome confirmation.

Paula flipped open the wallet. Three credit cards in the name of Nadzieja Wilkowa; loyalty cards for Freshco, the Co-op and a fashion store group; a book of first-class stamps with two remaining; a tight bundle of receipts and forty pounds in cash. No photographs, no convenient address. She took a quick pass through the receipts. Car parking, petrol, sandwich shops, fast-food outlets and a couple of restaurant bills. She'd pass them on to the officer in charge of doling out assignments to the team. Someone else could go through them in more detail, preferably after they'd got her diary off her phone.

And that was it. It was all very well to live an orderly life, but it didn't help detectives like Paula when you ended up dead. What they really needed was a home address. She opened the internet browser on her phone and navigated to Bartis Health's home page. Their offices were located in a town in Leicestershire she'd never heard of. Their business model appeared to be based on producing cheap generic versions of drugs whose patents had expired. Plenty of uptake but tight margins, Paula suspected.

She called the number on the contact page. The woman who answered the phone was rightly suspicious of her request for information but agreed to call back and ask to be connected to the extension perched on a corner table. Paula had little confidence in the capabilities of the system, but she was happy to be proved wrong less than five minutes later. 'Why are you asking about Nadia? Has something happened? Surely she's not in any kind of trouble,' the woman asked as soon as they were connected.

'Do you know Nadia well?' Paula was careful with her tense.

'I wouldn't say well. I've met her a few times. She's a very friendly, open sort of person. And they think very highly of her here. But what's happened? Has she been in an accident back home?'

'Back home?'

'In Poland. She emailed . . . let me see, it must be three weeks ago? Anyway, she said her mother had been diagnosed with stage three breast cancer and she asked if she could have compassionate leave to go home and be with her mother for the surgery. Because her mother's on her own now, with her dad being dead and her sister in America. It was inconvenient, but you don't want to lose somebody that's as good at her job as Nadia, so the boss said yes, she could have a month.' The woman stopped for breath.

Baffled, Paula said, 'You're sure about that?'

'I opened the email myself,' the woman said. 'And I had to email her only last week with a query about a customer's repeat order. She answered me the same day. She said her mum was making a slow recovery but she'd be back next week.'

It made no sense. Had Nadia made an unscheduled early return? Or had her killer sent the emails, pretending to be her, covering up the fact that she'd never left Bradfield? Was it an elaborate sham, a scam to cover Nadia's disappearance? But the woman was talking again, cutting through Paula's racing thoughts. 'So has something happened to Nadia? Is that why you're calling?'

Paula closed her eyes and wished she'd asked someone else to make this call. 'I'm very sorry to have to tell you that Nadia has died in suspicious circumstances.' It was true without being anywhere near the whole truth.

A moment's silence. 'In Poland?'

'No. Here in Bradfield.'

'I don't understand.'

'We're still making inquiries,' Paula said, stalling.

'That's terrible,' the woman said, her voice faint. 'I can't believe it. Nadia? What happened?'

'I'm afraid I can't go into details. But we need help. We don't have any addresses for her. Home or work. Or a next of kin. I was hoping you might have access to that information?'

'Let me get Nadia's personnel file on the screen,' the

woman said. 'She worked from home, so there's no office as such.' One less place to take apart looking for answers to the questions raised by Nadia's death.

Ten minutes later, Paula had every scrap of information Bartis Health knew about Nadia. There wasn't much, but it was a start. She had an address in the Harriestown district. She also knew that Nadzieja Wilkowa was twenty-six years old and had worked for Bartis for eighteen months. She had a degree in pharmacology from the university in Poznan and spoke excellent English. She visited head office every two or three months. Her territory covered the North of England and she had been one of the company's most successful sales reps. The next of kin she'd given was her mother, with an address in Leszno. A place Paula had never heard of, let alone been able to point to it on a map. She wasn't sure of the process involved in informing overseas next of kin, but she knew there would be one. At least that was one death knock she wouldn't have to deal with herself. Or the interview to ascertain whether Nadia had been in Poland recently.

Paula checked her watch. What she should do now was pass on Nadia's phone to the techies, scoop up a couple of junior detectives and turn over her flat in a bid to find how her life intersected with her killer. But she was conscious of the promise she'd made to Torin McAndrew and that she'd done nothing to fulfil it. She had a few hours before the boy would be texting her. Nadia was dead, and Torin was very much alive.

In one sense, it was no contest. But Paula had been drilled by Carol Jordan that her duty was to speak for the dead. And as well as speaking for the dead, she also had a responsibility to the living. A killer was walking free and it was her job to find him before he killed someone else. What could be more important than that?

13

Bev felt as if she was swimming upwards through something thick and heavy. Not heavy like mud. More like
milkshake or emulsion paint. Her limbs felt weighted down,
the world impenetrably black. It slowly dawned on her that
her eyes were closed. But when she opened them, nothing
changed. Her head throbbed when she moved it, but she
forced herself to turn it back and forth, yet still there was
absolutely nothing to be seen. The thought drifted through
her muzzy brain that this must be what a black hole was
like. Black, black and more black beyond that.

Slowly the wooziness lifted, enough for her to understand
that this darkness was something to fear, not simply wonder
at. As the fog of unconsciousness dispersed Bev tried to
make sense of where she was and what had happened to
her. Her head hurt and there was a sickly sweet taste at the
back of her throat. The last thing she remembered was
opening the boot of her hatchback to stow a couple of bags
of groceries she'd picked up on the way home. After that,
nothing. A blank. A terrifying blank.

She had no way of knowing how long she'd been unconscious. Minutes? No, surely more than minutes. Wherever she was, it wasn't the car park at Freshco. Hours, then? How many hours? What was Torin thinking? Was he afraid? Was he angry with her? Did he think she'd abandoned him and gone off to have fun without letting him know? What would he do without her? Would he raise the alarm or would he be too scared of what might happen to him without her? The thoughts scampered in her head like a hamster on a wheel. Christ, she had to get a grip.

'OK. Don't think about Torin. Put it behind you and move on.' She said the words aloud then wished she hadn't. Wherever she was, the acoustic was dead, her voice flat and muffled. Still determined to keep her fear at arm's length, Bev decided it would make sense to discover the limits of her location. She was sitting down, on a smooth surface. That realisation led to another. She wasn't wearing her trousers, socks or shoes any more. Her hand crept down her body. She was wearing her own bra, but the lower underwear definitely wasn't hers. Skimpy lacy panties were not her style. Lace made her itch, and she liked loose-fitting cotton against her skin. She refused to think about what that meant.

It was just flesh, when you got right down to it. She'd had no knowledge, no emotional engagement with anything that had happened while she was unconscious. In a sense, she told herself, it was no more a violation than any surgical procedure carried out under general anaesthetic. Most people would freak out if they had to witness what was done to their bodies on the operating table. Ignorance wasn't only bliss, it was what allowed them to be grateful for the surgeon's knife. Bev could manage ignorance, she was pretty sure of that.

She explored the surface she was sitting on. Smooth, cool

but not cold. When she moved her leg, it was warm from where her flesh had been resting. She extended her arms slowly, but couldn't straighten them. Then she slid down till her feet hit the far end of her prison. She moved one foot around and realised there was a sort of step there. Finally, she returned to a sitting position. There were a few inches between her head and the immovable top of what she had to admit to herself was a box. A metre wide, a metre and a half long and a little over a metre high. Plastic lined. A softer plastic seam round the top that made it light-tight, and presumably airtight too. With what felt like a step at one end. The only thing she could think of that fitted the description was a chest freezer.

She was locked inside a chest freezer.

Bev wasn't someone who panicked easily, but realising where she was set her heart pounding in terror. If the person who had put her here wanted to kill her, all they had to do was flick a switch and let hypothermia do the job for them.

Or just wait till the air ran out.

14

The middle of the afternoon wasn't the best time to get the undivided attention of anyone in the pharmacy at Bradfield Cross Hospital. Especially on a day when they were short a member of staff. But then, from what Paula had gathered from Dr Elinor Blessing and from Bev herself, there wasn't a spell during the working day when the pharmacists and their assistants weren't run off their feet. The accurate filling of hospital prescriptions was a process that never let up. Sometimes Paula thought the advancement of human learning came down to nothing except more sophisticated ways not to feel the pain.

Bev's deputy, Dan Birchall, looked like a member of a minor boy band run to seed. The lineaments of a handsome young man lurked beneath the slack fleshiness of his face, the neatly trimmed beard unable to disguise the jowls forming along his jawline. He still moved with a certain grace, almost dancing between the shelves and cabinets. But it was a dance whose tempo was starting to slip and whose steps looked a little more desperate with every passing year. 'You're Dr Blessing's lady, aren't you?' was his response when Paula introduced herself. It wasn't a line that endeared him to her.

'I'm looking into the whereabouts of your chief pharmacist, Ms McAndrew.' Paula smiled. There was no mileage in anything other than working the witness for whatever he might know. 'Her son has reported her missing.'

Dan rolled his eyes. 'Right,' he said, stretching the word as far as it would go. 'Well, suddenly, something makes sense. We've been at sixes and sevens all day, wondering what was up with Bev. Because Bev would never just not show. Totally not her style.'

Paula pulled up a lab stool and sat down, indicating he should do the same. But he remained on his feet, leaning against the counter with ankles crossed and arms folded. It made her wonder what he had to hide. If she'd been Tony Hill, no doubt she'd have worked it out already. But her gift was for interrogation; she was accustomed to taking the long way round. 'So you've had no communication from her?'

He shook his head. 'Not a word. Not a text, not an email, not a message. At first, I assumed she'd been caught up in traffic. Except Bev somehow always manages not to get caught up in traffic.' He rolled his eyes again. 'That's Bev. So organised she listens to the travel news with breakfast. But once it got to half past nine, I thought there was no way Bev would be an hour late without calling in. So I tried her home number and her mobile. I got the answering machine and the voicemail.' He spread his hands. 'What else could I do?'

'Did it occur to you to go round and check she was OK?'

He gave her a peevish look. 'Why would I do that? It's not like she lives alone. If anything had happened to her, Torin the Wonder Boy could have called for help. Besides—' He waved impatiently at the bustle in the dispensary. 'Look at this place. We were already one down. I couldn't walk away from the rest of the team. We only took half an hour each for lunch as it was.' He seemed more irritated than worried. Paula hoped that whatever had happened to Bev wasn't the kind of thing that would make his annoyance come back to haunt him.

'I appreciate that. You've got patients to consider.'

Dan pounced on the get-out. 'Exactly. People rely on us.'

'So, when did you last see Bev?'

'Yesterday. A bit after half past five. She was through in the office.' He pointed to a cubicle tucked away in the far corner. 'I was going for a birthday drink with Bob Symes, one of the porters. I asked her if she fancied joining us, but she said she had some paperwork to wrap up and then she had to go to Freshco on the way home. So I left her to it.'

'Was there anybody else still working?'

'Well, the duty pharmacist, obviously. She comes in at five and she's on till half past midnight. The night-duty dispenser does midnight till eight thirty.' He flapped a hand dismissively. 'But you won't be interested in the hell that is our staffing roster.'

Paula made a note on her pad. 'I'll need the details of the duty pharmacist.'

Dan nodded. 'No problem. Vahni Bhat, that's her name. I'll give you her numbers when we're done. She'll be in tonight, if you want to see her.'

'Thanks.' She looked around. Two young women and an older man were focused on what they were doing, paying no attention to her and Dan. Paula didn't often find herself in a workplace where the staff were so overwhelmed with their own tasks that they ignored a police inquiry in their midst. 'Was Bev particularly close to anyone here at work?'

Dan scratched his beard and frowned, his eyes sliding

away from hers. 'I wouldn't have said so. Don't get me wrong, we're good enough mates here. And heaven knows, I've worked with Bev for a million years. But we don't live in each other's pockets.' Still he wasn't meeting her eyes, using the pretext of keeping an eye on his colleagues to avoid her. 'Come the end of the working day, we all do our own thing. Bev was very family orientated. Torin came first with her.' A little edge there, she noted. Had Dan wanted Bev to be more interested in him? Or had there once been something more than friendship between them? It was hard to tell. Paula thought she might run that one past Elinor and see whether there had been any gossip.

'You called him Torin the Wonder Boy. What's that about, Dan?' Paula kept her tone light, almost teasing.

One corner of his mouth twisted downwards in a rueful grimace. 'I tease her because she's always going on about how great he is. I've got a kid of my own, Becky, but I don't make out she's the smartest, the prettiest, the most talented. The way Bev speaks about Torin, you'd think nobody ever had a kid before. That's all.' He shrugged and smiled, sharing a look of complicity with her. 'No big deal.'

'He knew enough to report her missing.' Paula looked around the room. 'So as far as you're aware, Bev had no plans for yesterday evening?'

'What she said to me was, Freshco and then home.'

'Would she have said if she'd had plans?'

Another shrug. 'She'd sometimes say if she was going to a movie or the football with Torin or something like that. Or if there was something on the telly she was looking forward to. But it wasn't like she'd routinely tell me what she was planning on doing. To be perfectly honest, it's always full on in here. You have to concentrate. It's not like being on a factory production line, where you can chat about all sorts while you work. Here, if we screw up, people get more sick.

Sometimes they can die. So we don't go in for much casual chit-chat.'

'Do you know if she was seeing anybody?'

'If she was, none of us knew anything about it. Look, you live with Dr Blessing. You must know what it's like. A hospital is a rumour factory. And this place is gossip central.'

'I thought you didn't have time for chit-chat?' Paula took the sting out of the barb with a teasing tone and a knowing smile.

'Not when we're dispensing. But at the counter, when they drop off and pick up, that's where all the info passes back and forth. And I haven't heard a whisper about Bev seeing anyone. After the divorce, she went out with a couple of blokes, but both times she felt like it was going nowhere so she knocked it on the head. She's been on her own for a couple of years now, as far as anybody here knows.' All at once it seemed he was protesting too much.

'And you? You went for a drink with Bob the porter? Did you see Bev later?'

Dan became very interested in the contents of the shelves next to him. 'Actually, in the end I didn't go. I wasn't in the mood. I went for a drink on my own on the way home.'

'Do you remember where?'

'The Bertie.'

'You mean the Prince Albert?' Paula knew the place. It was a busy barn of a pub on the edge of the city centre, always packed because of its cheap beer.

He nodded. 'That's the one.'

'Not exactly a place for a quiet drink.'

He made a face. 'Nobody bothers you, it's too rammed for people to strike up casual conversations. I like it when I want to be alone in a crowd.'

And nobody remembers whether you were there or not. Another avenue closed off. 'Had Bev fallen out with anybody that you know of? Any colleagues? Other staff? Patients? Some-body outside of work.'

Dan looked blank. 'She never said anything. I mean, we all get into a bit of a ruck at the counter from time to time. The punters aren't always sweet reason on a stick. But Bev's generally pretty good at calming things down. She doesn't provoke people.' He gave a wry smile. 'Not like me. I'm not good at taking their crap. Sometimes I just walk away, and that's when Bev steps up to the plate and pours oil on the troubled waters.'

'So, no boyfriend, no enemies. Did she seem at all uneasy lately? Rattled, frightened?'

Again he scratched his beard. 'Not her style. Bev's not a scaredy cat. I'd say the only thing she'd be scared of would be something happening to Torin. And nothing's happened to him, has it? Not from what you were saying.'

Apart from mislaying his mother. 'If I'd said to you last night that Bev would go missing, is there any part of you that would have thought, "Yeah, that makes sense".'

Without hesitation, Dan shook his head. 'No. Bev's totally reliable, totally organised. If she was going to do a runner, she'd do it in such a way that nobody would notice it was a runner until she was history.'

Paula could think of nothing more to ask Dan. Though she had a feeling there might be more later. She stood up and fished her card out of her pocket. 'Text me Vahni Bhat's number, would you? And let me know if anything occurs to you. Anything unusual, or anything Bev said. We're treating this seriously, Dan.'

'OK. Tell Torin we're thinking of him.'

That would be the easy part, Paula thought, checking her watch. She'd sent a pair of DCs to Nadia Wilkowa's flat, promising to join them there. Unless Nadia had lived in a monastic cell with no possessions, they'd still be there,

71

poking through her underwear drawer and kitchen cupboards. Which gave her a small window of opportunity to
conclude some more unorthodox arrangements.

She sent a quick text to Elinor, asking for five minutes in
the fifth-floor coffee shop that she knew was near the wards
where her partner would be dealing with post-op patients
from the morning. Paula was halfway through a mug of hot
chocolate when Elinor appeared, businesslike in white coat
and stethoscope. Time had done nothing to diminish the
physical jolt of pleasure Paula still felt whenever they were
reunited. Even if only a few hours had passed. It was crazy,
it was adolescent, but she didn't care. When she'd met
Elinor, her life hadn't held much joy. Now, the reason for
getting up in the morning overwhelmed any argument on
that score.

Elinor made straight for Paula's table, missing out a visit to
the coffee counter. She leaned over and kissed her on the
lips as she sat down. 'Not that it isn't always a delight to see
you, but I genuinely only have five minutes,' she said.

Paula held up both hands in a gesture of apology. 'Sorry.
I'm tight for time too. But it's important.'

'Give me the ten second version.' Elinor reached for the
mug and took a swig, shivering with pleasure. 'Sugar rush,
I love it.'

'Torin McAndrew reported his mother missing this morning. She's not in work, nobody's heard from her and—'

'Bev's missing?' Elinor interrupted.

'Apparently.'

'But she wouldn't leave Torin. Paula, something serious
must have happened. Have you checked the hospitals?'

'First thing I did. And the custody records. She's not been
in an accident and she's not been arrested. Believe me, I'm
taking an interest.'

Elinor clapped her hand over her mouth. She knew only

too well the sort of cases Paula generally ended up dealing with. Anyone would be horrified at the thought of a friend ending up at the heart of one of those. 'What can I do?'

'Who's her best mate?'

'Probably Dan.' Elinor answered without hesitation. 'He's straight, but he's so camp he might as well be a gay man. There was a moment a couple of years ago where it nearly spilled over into more than just good friends. But they both backed off. She didn't want to risk his marriage and really, neither did he.'

'Was it mutual, the backing off?'

Elinor paused, thinking. 'To the best of my recollection. I've been in their company a few times since and I didn't sense any awkwardness between them.' She gave Paula a sceptical look. 'You're not thinking Dan's got anything to do with Bev going missing, are you?'

'I'm not going to apologise for covering all the bases, Elinor. But there's something a lot more pressing than what kind of guy Dan is. Here's the thing. I can't leave Torin home alone. I know he stayed there last night without Bev, but he didn't really believe she'd be out all night. He doesn't have any family near at hand. And I don't want social services taking him into emergency care.'

'You want him to come and stay at ours?'

Paula couldn't help smiling. 'This is why I love you,' she said. 'You have such a generous heart.'

'Obviously. I chose you.' Elinor tapped Paula's hand with a finger. 'How do we do this?'

'He's going to text me after school. Can I send him over here? Can you find him a quiet corner where he can do his homework till you're ready to leave? I don't want him going to a friend's house and letting slip that his mum's disappeared and he's staying with a couple of big old lezzas he hardly knows.'

Elinor thought for a moment. 'Sure, I'll come up with something. And you? What about you? When will you be home?'

Paula sighed and shook her head. 'I'm not sure. We caught a murder this morning. We've barely got started.'

'Just as well I'm an easy-going soul,' Elinor said.

'I know. Sometimes I think I behave like the worst of my male colleagues. I'm sorry.'

'The difference is, you know you're doing it. And I get to stake out the moral high ground.' Elinor grinned. 'It's OK, Paula. We both pay the price of caring about what we do. I'd love you less if you took your job less seriously. What's the new boss like?'

'Too soon to know. But she's not Carol Jordan, that's for sure.'

'That's not exactly informative.'

Paula picked up her bag. 'Later. You have patients, I have my back to cover.' She stood up, put a hand on Elinor's shoulder and kissed the top of her head. 'I'll send Torin over. See you when I see you.'

15

The rain had sloped out of a steel sky all day, relentless and depressing. He'd noticed it only intermittently, there being no window in his eyeline at work. Rain would have been a nuisance when he'd been waiting for the last two. There hadn't been anywhere unobtrusive to shelter. But this time, there was no problem. On the other side of the street from Tellit Communications HQ was a row of fast-food outlets. Subway, McDonald's, an indie café that promised the best roast in Bradfield. As if. He'd started off in McDonald's with a cheeseburger and made it last half an hour. Next, he stretched a chocolate chip cookie and a Diet Coke to forty minutes. Where the hell was the woman? Didn't she have a home to go to?

The irony of that last thought forced him to stifle a giggle. The home he was planning for her was very different from the one she'd be going back to tonight. If she played her cards right, if she made him happy, she could have a new life as well as a new home. If not, she could pay someone else's debt and join the others. His first one and the one before that, the one who should have been his one and only. Of course, he knew he might not need this latest one. But chance had dropped her in his path and he wasn't a man who failed to answer when opportunity knocked. He had a feeling the one he had now wasn't going to measure up and it was as well to be prepared for that eventuality.

He crumpled his napkin into a ball and stood up, about to move on to the café when he spotted her, tripping down the hallway from the bank of lifts. She crossed the foyer with an unexpected spring in her step. Most people dragged themselves wearily out of the office after a long day, but this one had a bounce to her. That was what had caught his eye in the first place, before he even registered she was a perfect fit. She looked like someone who was heading towards something worth waiting for. He made a point of storing that lustrous image away in his memory. That was what she'd have to replicate for him, if she was going to have any chance of survival.

She paused on the threshold, opening a folding umbrella. He pushed through the customers to the door, eyes fixed on his target, heedless of the complaints of the ones who'd been in his way. They were irrelevant. All that mattered was keeping her in view. By the time he made it on to the street, she was halfway to the corner. He moved a little faster, closing the gap, but careful not to get too close. He pulled his beanie hat further down over his forehead, tucked his chin into his scarf and checked the glasses with their clear lenses were still in place. It was amazing how much difference small things made to a man's appearance. People noticed the externals, not the essentials. Not that he was planning on doing anything that would get him noticed. But there were closed-circuit cameras everywhere in the city centre. He wasn't taking any chances.

She turned left at the end of the street, into the early evening bustle of Bellwether Square. Again, he speeded up, not wanting to lose her in the crowd. She wasn't tall and he worried that he might lose sight of her. It wouldn't wreck his plans, not in the long term. But it would be an inconvenience and he hated inconvenience. He needed to find out where she lived and he didn't want to waste another evening on something so basic.

She veered off to where the tramlines formed one side of the square and walked up the ramp to a tram stop, closing her umbrella as she gained the shelter of the canopy. He hung back until she'd chosen her spot on the platform, then daringly walked right up behind her. She didn't even glance at him as he approached, head down against the weather. It amazed him how these women walked in the world with no understanding of the threats that were everywhere. Sometimes he felt he radiated power as tangible as the heat rising from a log fire. How could they be oblivious to him? Dogs bared their teeth at him, cats hissed when he held out his fingers towards them. But women were so out of tune with their environment, they just didn't pay attention.

She'd pay attention to him soon enough, he promised himself that.

Now he was so close he could distinguish each blonde hair on her head. Sufficiently close to tell that she was a natural. No tell-tale roots here, which was as it should be. If he'd been betrayed by the thinnest line of brown, he'd have walked away. Because he was only interested in perfect matches. He wasn't some kind of inadequate who would settle for second best. He'd been deprived of what was rightfully his, but that didn't mean anything would do.

The tram glided into sight, the rain making its blue-and-claret livery gleam under the street lights and restaurant neon of the square. She'd chosen her spot perfectly, right opposite one of the opening doors. He stepped in behind her. She turned left, he turned right and slipped on to a jump seat where he could see her but she couldn't see him unless she turned her head. He sighed in satisfaction. Soon he'd know everything he needed to.

She didn't have a clue.

Marie Mather congratulated herself on getting a seat on the tram. She'd spent just over eleven hours inside Tellit Communications. For a first day, she reckoned that showed more than willing. It would probably be gone seven by the time she got in. But unlike most working women, she wouldn't be dashing home to put dinner on the table. Marie was lucky enough to be married to a man whose Italian mother had compensated for her lack of daughters by teaching Marco everything she knew about cooking. He mostly worked from home these days, designing furniture for an online retailer, so Marie came home to freshly prepared dinners that made her feel cherished every time.

It would be something special tonight, she was certain of that. Perhaps Marco would have splashed out on a leg of lamb or a steak. Or maybe even a truffle to grate over a risotto or a pasta dish. Her mouth was watering at the thought.

She spent the twenty-minute tram ride turning over the day's encounters in her mind. All in all, not a bad start to a new job. She knew she was there to shake things up and already she could see possibilities for change. But Marie had no plans to rush into anything. She'd feel her way in gently, get under the skin of the organisation and then start a quiet revolution that would leave them reeling. Oh yes, she had plans for Tellit.

The tram drew into the terminus, its electric motor making a sound like a soft moan of contentment. There were only a handful of travellers left on the tram, bunching together by the doors till the tram came to a smooth halt. And then she was off down the platform, heels clattering on the concrete. The rain had finally stopped, she realised as she reached street level. The air still felt thick with damp, but there was no need for an umbrella now.

Marie hurried down the street, her mind on her job, her sense of self-preservation entirely asleep. Then, struck by a sudden desire to finish the evening with a box of chocolates in front of the TV as she passed the newsagent on the corner, she wheeled round to return and almost cannoned into a man who was only a few feet behind her, his head down and shoulders hunched against the cold. Her heart leapt in shock. She'd had no notion anyone was that close.

He barged past her without a word and she was surprised by her relief when she entered the shop. *Silly woman*, she chided herself as she left a few minutes later, reassured by the empty street and the box of Ferrero Rocher tucked into her bag. Nothing more than a typical bad-mannered city encounter; what could be more normal than that?

She rounded the corner into the street where she and Marco lived, completely unaware that the man she'd almost bumped into was standing in the shadow of the house on the opposite corner, taking very careful note of Marie's destination and wondering how many more times she'd be walking through her own front door.

16

Of course there wasn't a legal parking space in the Minster Canal Basin. Cursing, Paula slotted the car into a disabled slot and propped a sign saying 'police' on the dashboard. It went against the grain, but then so did getting soaked to the skin on semi-official business. She consoled herself with the thought that not many disabled people would fancy negotiating the cobbles of the canal basin in monsoon conditions.

As she headed for Tony's floating home, she wondered fleetingly whether she should have phoned ahead. He didn't exactly have a vibrant social life, but it wasn't unusual for him to take long walks through the city. They were, he'd told her, a cross between sociological observation and thinking time. 'Watch and learn, that's what psychologists need to do,' he'd said in an uncharacteristically frank exchange about the way he approached his work. 'And then you have to apply what you've learned to what you observe.'

'You're better at it than most,' Paula had commented.

'It's not rocket science. It's mostly common sense mixed up with a bit of compassion and empathy. You could do it, you know.'

She'd laughed. But he'd continued, absolutely serious. 'You're already doing it. I've watched you interviewing witnesses and suspects. You might not know the theory, but your practice stands comparison with most of the clinical psychologists I've seen in action. Maybe you should think about applying to the national faculty and training to be a police profiler.'

'No way,' she'd said. 'I get my buzz from being on the front line. I don't want to be a backroom person like you.'

He'd shrugged. 'Your choice. But when you do get to the point where you've had enough of the grind of procedure and the pettiness of the top brass, it's an option.'

What Tony had suffered in the course of his work cast a bitter light on the conversation now. Paula had seen the destruction at first hand, and she was grateful that she had routine and procedure to cling on to among the wreckage. She wasn't sure if she was doing the right thing by coming here, but her instincts, both professional and personal, had led her inevitably to his door. Or hatchway, she supposed you'd have to call it. At least it wasn't a late call. Shortly before seven, Fielding had sent the team home. 'There's no budget for overtime and until we've got something back from the lab and the CCTV, you're all just spinning your wheels.' Paula had been stunned. Overtime had never been an issue on her old squad. They got on and did what had to be done when they were in the thick of it. The theory was that they'd take it easier in the quiet spells. Only there never had been any quiet spells.

She stood on the quayside, momentarily flummoxed by the etiquette. When she'd been here before, they'd arrived together and she'd simply followed Tony aboard. But it felt somehow intrusive to climb aboard and knock on the hatch. Logically, it was no different to walking up someone's path to knock on the door. Yet it felt wrong.

'Get a grip, woman,' she muttered, stepping aboard the steel-hulled narrowboat, not quite prepared for the definite movement of the deck beneath her feet. She almost stumbled, caught herself and rapped on the hatch. The top section swung open almost at once and Tony's startled face appeared below.

'Paula. I thought you were a drunk.'

Her smile was grim. 'Not quite. Not yet. You get a lot of drunks dropping by?'

He busied himself with opening up to let her in. 'Sometimes. Usually later than this. They think it's amusing to jump on and off boats. It can be disconcerting.' He spread the doors wide and beckoned her in with a grin. 'And I wasn't expecting you.' His face clouded in a frown. 'Was I?'

Paula squeezed past him down the galley and into the saloon. The TV screen was frozen in a scene apparently set in a deep mine. A games console lay discarded on the table. 'No. It was a spur of the moment decision.' She took off her damp coat and hung it on a hook on the bulkhead then sat down on the buttoned leather banquette that surrounded three sides of the table.

'Well, it's always good to see you.' He sat down opposite her, then stood up almost immediately, remembering the social conventions of dealing with a visitor. 'Do you want a drink? I've got coffee and tea. Orange juice. Some of that Indian lager, goes well with takeaways.' He gave a wry smile. 'And white wine and vodka. Though there's not been much call for those lately.'

Carol Jordan's drinks of choice. 'I wouldn't mind a lager.'

Two steps and he was by the fridge. Tony pulled out two

bottles, reached up for two glasses and was back at the table in a matter of seconds. The bottle opener was in a shallow drawer under the table. It was convenient, no denying that. 'So, what brings you here?' he said, pouring a beer for his guest.

'I've had a strange day.' Paula raised her glass. 'Cheers. And I wanted to talk about it with somebody who understands what I'm talking about. Because I've started on a new team and—'

'And your new boss isn't Carol Jordan and you don't have Chris and Stacey and Sam and Kevin to bounce things off.'

'All of that, yes. And I know you're not on the payroll any more and I know you don't owe BMP anything. But I suppose I've got used to using you as a sounding board—'

'Even when the boss says no.' That wry twist to his mouth again. They both remembered only too well the times they'd sneaked behind Carol Jordan's back for what they saw as the right reasons.

Paula scowled. 'OK, I don't have her scruples about exploiting you. I think if you want to help, we should let you. And if you don't, all you have to do is say no.'

'I know. I wasn't having a go at you, Paula. I've got skills and I prefer to use them rather than keeping them nicely polished on a shelf.' This time his smile was uncomplicated but sad. 'Besides, you're the nearest thing I've got to a friend. If I can't help my friend, what's the point of me?'

Paula shook herself like a dog emerging from a river. 'Oh, for fuck's sake. Listen to us. What a pathetic pair.'

'We are, aren't we? Best get some work done and stop auditioning for *Oprah*. So, what's been strange about the day? Apart from it being the first day on your new firm.'

And so she told him about Torin. About the unaccountable absence of Bev McAndrew and her rescue of the boy from the uncertain clutches of social services. 'I spoke to the duty pharmacist who did the handover with her last night. Bev said nothing about any plans for the evening other than picking up some shopping on the way home. I've tracked down a couple of her female friends. Neither of them have heard from her.' She ran her finger round the rim of her glass. 'I'll be honest, Tony, I don't like it.'

He leaned back and studied the low roof of the cabin. 'Let's consider the possibilities. Not an accident or an incident involving the emergency services.'

'I told you. I checked.'

'I know you did, I'm just running through the options. Amnesia? Hard to believe she could have gone twenty-four hours without attracting the attention of somebody who would do the responsible thing. And besides, real amnesia is incredibly rare. Usually memory loss is connected to a head injury which would have landed her in hospital. And you've ruled that out.'

'She's dead, isn't she?'

He held up a hand, palm towards her. 'You jump to that conclusion because it's what you know. In your world, murder is something that happens on a weekly basis. But that's not how it is for most of us. Even if you consider six degrees of separation, most of us get closer to Kevin Bacon than we do to a murder victim. We need to look at more likely scenarios first.'

'Like what?' Paula's jaw had a stubborn set. She knew what was coming and she'd already dismissed the other options.

'A boyfriend – or a girlfriend – she's gone off with spontaneously.'

'She's straight. But everybody I spoke to says she hasn't been seeing anyone in the last couple of years.'

Tony leaned forward. 'How likely does that seem to you? You described her as bright, funny, attractive. I'm assuming she's late thirties, early forties. A bit young to be going for the life of a nun, I'd have thought.'

Tell that to Carol Jordan. How many years have you two been avoiding getting your act together? Paula kept her face straight and said, 'What is it the straight women say? By the time you get to thirty-five, all the best blokes are taken or gay.'

'And by the time you get to forty, the divorces kick in and they're looking for a second bite of the cherry. I can imagine plenty of reasons why Bev might not be shouting from the rooftops about a new man. Maybe it's someone at work. Maybe it's someone who's married. Maybe it's one of Torin's teachers.'

Someone at work? Dan who protested too much? 'She'd tell her best mate. Women do.' *Unless it was her best mate . . .*

'Have you never had a secret love?'

Paula laughed, embarrassed. 'Of course I have. I'm a lesbian. Half my life I've felt like Doris Day. But I always told my best mate.' Then she caught herself, hand to her mouth. 'Except when it was her girlfriend. Oops, I'd forgotten that.'

'See?'

'Yeah, but I didn't have a kid. You're forgetting about Torin.'

'I'm not. I wanted to remind you that assumptions always have exceptions. You once had a good reason for a secret. So might Bev. But even allowing for a secret, you're right. It doesn't on its own account for her disappearing without a word. She wouldn't abandon Torin without a word. Some mothers would, there's no getting away from that. But what you know of Bev personally, from her colleagues and from Torin himself, doesn't make that a credible proposition?'

'She'd never leave him high and dry,' Paula confirmed. 'I'd say that, in some respects, he's quite a young fourteen.'

'But if she is seeing someone, that someone might have

their own agenda here. And he might have prevented her from contacting anyone.'

Paula took a deep breath. 'What you're really saying is that whether it's a boyfriend gone rogue or a stranger stalker, Bev isn't on the missing list from choice.'

Tony pinched the bridge of his nose between finger and thumb. It was a gesture she'd seen many times before. 'I think it's inescapable, Paula. I think she's been taken. What's the official status of the inquiry?'

'I processed Torin's statement this morning. If they do things at Skenfrith Street like we used to do them, it'll be actioned in the morning. I'll brief Fielding on what I've done so far – she'll kick my arse for going off on my own, but at least the formal stuff will get started. Like tracking her mobile.'

'Everybody knows about mobiles these days. If it's switched on, it'll be nowhere near where Bev is.'

'Have you got any bright ideas?'

He shook his head. 'You're always looking for the point of intersection. Where did Bev cross paths with the person who took her? Was it a stranger who plucked her off the street? Or was it a sexual scenario that went somewhere she didn't want to go? Let's face it, Paula, after *Fifty Shades of Grey*, women are a lot less wary of being tied up by men they don't necessarily know that well. If you had Stacey, you could get her to go through Bev's home computer. That would be a good place to start. Can you get Stacey?'

Paula looked disgusted at the thought of what had happened to Stacey Chen, the terrifyingly effective analyst she'd worked alongside in Carol Jordan's Major Incident Team. 'They've got her working on computer fraud. She says it's like sending a Lear jet on the school run. All the forensic computer work in CID gets farmed out to private companies now.'

'She should quit the force and set up in competition to them.'

'Don't think she hasn't thought about it. But running a company would interfere too much with the programming she does in her spare time. That's where the real money comes from in Stacey world. Besides, if she wasn't a cop any more, she wouldn't have the licence to go poking around in other people's hard drives.'

'Could you ask for a copy of the hard drive before it goes off to the specialists? Would that work for Stacey?'

'Good idea. I'll ask her. And if it was a stranger?'

'You don't need me for this bit, Paula. This is nothing but old-fashioned coppering with new-fashioned methods. Interrogating the CCTV, looking for her car on the number-plate-recognition software records, examining her Facebook page and her Twitter feed, seeing who she's connected to on LinkedIn, checking her phone records. A profiler's no use to you at this stage. I need data, and that's what you haven't got. All I've done is confirm your worst fears.'

'I need a smoke,' Paula said, standing up abruptly.

'Just go out the back.'

'Come with me, would you? I want to take you through the rest of my day.'

'Will I need my coat and my keys?'

Paula's smile promised dark mischief. 'Only if you fancy a bit of transgression.'

Tony grabbed the waxed jacket that was hanging next to Paula's coat. 'For a lesbian, your knowledge of the way to a man's heart is remarkable.

17

Carol had never really grasped the concept of survivor guilt. She'd always believed that being a survivor was a good thing, something to be proud about, not ashamed of. Her past was dotted with struggles to get past bad things that had happened to her; if she'd been pushed, she'd have said she was gratified not to have caved under their weight. That was something else that had changed.

Now she understood the guilt and shame of being the one left behind. Loss had removed the old underpinnings of her beliefs and changed how she viewed the world. She would happily stop dead in her tracks if it meant Michael and Lucy could have their lives back. After all, they had been making a better job of living well than she was. They'd put something back into the world, restoring the barn. And the work they did. Well, the work that Michael did. Lucy's commitment to criminal defence work had always baffled Carol. She'd spent too many days sitting in court, disgusted at the barristers who exploited legal technicalities and twisted the words of witnesses, all in the service of getting nasty little shits off the hook of their own criminality. She'd tried not to argue with Lucy over the dinner table, but sometimes she couldn't restrain herself. 'How can you defend people you know are guilty? How can you feel satisfaction when they walk free from court, leaving their victims without any sense of justice?'

The answer was always the same. 'I don't know that they're guilty. Even when the evidence seems overwhelming, it may be misleading. Everyone's entitled to a defence. If you people did your job thoroughly, they wouldn't be walking free from court, would they?'

It was an argument whose speciousness left Carol almost speechless with rage. A desire for justice was what drove her, what made it possible for her to tolerate the horrors of her job at the sharpest of sharp ends. To see it constantly thwarted by hair-splitting lawyers who generated doubt where none should exist was the ultimate insult to the broken lives and broken bodies that occupied her memory. She'd always been with Dick the Butcher on that one. 'The first thing we do, let's kill all the lawyers.'

Except, of course, she hadn't been. Not really. Not when it came to the woman her brother loved. The woman who had transformed him from a single-minded geek to a relatively civilised human being. A transformation Carol had never managed for herself. Would never have to manage now.

It would have been bad enough if it had been some chance event that had cut their lives so brutally short. But there had been nothing chance about it. They'd been deliberately slaughtered with one aim in mind. To make Carol suffer. The man who had come to the barn with murder on his agenda didn't care about Michael and Lucy. The corrosive hatred in his heart was directed at Carol and he understood only too well that the best way to destroy her was to kill them in her stead. They were murdered because they were connected so intimately to her. No other reason.

And it should never have happened. They should have figured out – no, Tony Hill, forensic psychologist and offender profiler, *he* should have figured out what might happen. She had the resources at her command to have protected them. But she never had the chance to put those resources in place. It had never occurred to her that anyone could be so twisted. It should have occurred to Tony, though. Most of his professional career had been intertwined with people who were seriously twisted. She hoped he felt as gutted by their deaths as she did.

Two deaths on her hands would have been grounds enough for crippling guilt. But for Carol, there was more. One of her team had been maimed and blinded in a hideous booby trap that had been set for Carol and sprung by Chris Devine. Chris, a former sergeant in the Met, who had moved to Bradfield because she believed in what Carol was trying to do with her Major Incident Team, a raggle-taggle band of specialists who didn't quite fit in for one reason or another but who had learned to work together and grown into a formidable outfit. And Chris at the heart of it, the most unlikely of mother figures holding them all together. Chris, whose career was now at an end and whose life had been wrecked beyond mending because of a simple act of helpfulness.

When Carol thought about Chris, she felt ashamed. She'd been so wrapped up in her own pain, she hadn't paid the debt to friendship. Others had sat with Chris through her pain, talking to her, reading to her, playing music to her. Others had taken their turn supporting her through the first difficult steps towards regaining some of what she'd lost. Others had been there for her while Carol had busied herself elsewhere.

No doubt Tony would have some clever explanation for her inability to face Chris. But it wasn't complicated. It was guilt, pure and simple. Chris's fate was what had lain in store for Carol. She'd dodged the bullet. And as with Michael and Lucy, someone else had paid the price for her determination to see justice done.

Carol swung the sledgehammer through the gallery floorboards in a steady rhythm to accompany her thoughts. She'd paid heed to George Nicholas's suggestion about the beam and she'd set a ladder against the gallery and attacked it from above. Strictly speaking, scaffolding would have been a better option, but that exceeded her DIY skills and she was determined to see this through herself, no matter how long it took. She was done with getting a man in to solve her problems for her. She paused for breath, chest heaving with the effort, sweat running down her back.

Her encounter with George Nicholas kept cutting into her familiar mantra of guilt and shame. It had reminded her that there was a world beyond her self-regard. A world she used to inhabit. A world where people sat round tables and talked together, drank together, laughed together. She'd had a place in that world and she suspected walking away from it was not entirely healthy. She'd deliberately set herself apart so she could begin the process of healing. But how would she know if she was getting any stronger if she lived like a hermit? Reluctantly, she reminded herself she'd tried that once before and it hadn't been the answer. What had brought her back to life had been engaging with the world.

Maybe it was time to start again.

The closest Carol had ever previously come to a police convalescent home was sticking a twenty in the collection box at social events. She had no idea what to expect. When she'd called Chris's Police Federation rep to check her whereabouts, she'd half-expected her to be back home. 'She's at the convalescent home in Ripon,' the helpful rep had told her. 'She's working with the physios there on her range of movements. Scar management, that sort of thing. They wanted to keep her in hospital longer, but because we were able to provide specialist care, she's been able to start living a more normal life.'

Carol cringed inwardly at the words, unable to imagine how anyone would begin to cope. 'Has there been any improvement in her sight, do you know?'

'I believe not. They're talking about lining her up with a guide dog. But that'll be a bit down the road.'

Carol thanked her and ended the call, wondering whether she had the strength for this. But building a bridge between her and Chris was the first step to regaining her humanity. She'd called ahead to ask about visiting times and been told that visitors were expected to leave by nine o'clock. So she'd finished work in the late afternoon, showered the sweat and dirt away and put on one of her business suits for the first time in months. She stretched the process out as long as she could, taking time out for a large glass of cold pinot grigio. Then another. But finally there was nothing for it but to set off across the rolling green landscape to the tiny cathedral city.

The convalescent home was on the edge of town, not far from the ruined grandeur of Fountains Abbey. It was hidden at the end of a twisting drive, obscured from sight by a shrubbery that looked mature enough to have been planted by the original owners of the sprawling Victorian villa that formed its heart. There were modern two-storey wings on either side of the main house and small chalets dotted the fringes of the wide lawns, all linked by well-groomed paths. Lights burned in several windows, but the curtains were already drawn in the downstairs rooms. If she hadn't known what she was coming to, Carol would have been hard pressed to identify its purpose from outside.

A heavy Gothic door stood open into a substantial porch. The doors leading inside were modern, however, and slid open as they detected her presence. Inside was more like a hotel foyer than a hospital facility. A way, Carol thought, of communicating to people that this was a step on the road to something approaching normal life. It even smelled like a hotel rather than a hospital, a vague floral scent like supermarket pot pourri hanging in the air.

In keeping with this image, the young woman behind the curved reception desk wore a cheap business suit that was slightly too tight across the bust. She smiled in greeting. 'Good evening. How can I help you?'

For a moment, Carol was nonplussed. She'd been introducing herself by rank for so long she'd almost forgotten the art of plain announcement. 'I'm here to see Chris Devine,' she said. 'Sergeant Devine.'

'Is Sergeant Devine expecting you?'

Carol shook her head. 'I'm her commanding officer,' she said, slipping uneasily into the persona she'd abandoned months ago. 'DCI Jordan.' She took a slim leather wallet from her pocket. She wasn't sure whether BMP had forgotten to tell her to return her ID or nobody had had the nerve to ask for it. Either way, she'd hung on to it. She wasn't a sentimental woman. She could only suppose that at some level, she'd kept it because it might come in handy. She didn't want to think about what that might mean. Right now, she was happy just to milk it. She flipped the wallet open and let the receptionist take it in.

The woman tugged her jacket down, as if attempting a parade-ground attention. 'Have you visited us before?'

'This is my first time. Can you direct me to Chris's room?'

The directions were straightforward. Carol smiled her gratitude and set off towards one of the modern wings. Her normal brisk pace slowed as she neared her destination. By the end she was dawdling, pausing to look at the vibrant abstract paintings that hung on the corridor walls. Outside Chris's door, she ran a hand through her hair and wished she'd had a large vodka. She clenched the fist of her left hand so tight she could feel her short fingernails digging into her palm. And gently rapped on the door.

A voice that didn't sound like Chris said, 'Come in.'

Carol opened the door and stepped across the threshold. She'd barely registered that the figure in one chair was Chris when the woman in the other chair jumped to her feet, a look of welcoming enquiry switching in an instant to one of hostility. 'I'm sorry, I think you've got the wrong room,' Sinead Burton said, her voice warm and polite, her face the diametric opposite. She held a finger to her lips. 'Can I show you the way?' She crossed the room, practically pushing Carol out through the door. 'I'll be back in a minute, love,' she called over her shoulder to Chris, who had turned her head towards them, her face a twisted pink and purple mask. Carol had tried to prepare for it, but still it shook her.

Sinead closed the door firmly behind her and shooed Carol down the hall with her hands. As soon as they were far enough from the door not to be overheard, she started on Carol, her voice tight with suppressed anger. 'What the hell are you doing here? I thought you had the good sense to stay away. What the hell are you playing at?'

Carol backed away. Her previous encounters with Chris's partner hadn't prepared her for this. 'I wanted to say sorry,' she stuttered.

'You wanted to say sorry?' Sinead's Irish accent grew more pronounced as her anger rose. 'You don't think it might be a wee bit late for that? My wife nearly dies instead

94

of you and it takes you all these weeks and months to get round to saying sorry? Talk about a day late and a dollar short. Jesus.'

Carol felt tears closing her throat. But she knew she had to hold it together. It was obvious that tears would cut no ice with Sinead. 'I know. Believe me, I know. But I couldn't handle it.'

Sinead cut straight across her. 'You couldn't handle it? What the hell do you think it's been like for her? The excruciating pain. The loss of her sight. The loss of her face, for God's sake. Couldn't handle it? You should have crawled on your hands and knees the day after and begged for her to forgive you.'

'I'd just lost my brother and sister-in-law,' Carol said.

'It's not a bloody fucking *competition*.' Sinead's voice was cold and hard as stone. 'You should have been here right from the start.'

Carol swallowed. 'I know that, Sinead. Nobody could feel more guilty and ashamed than I do.'

'As you should. Well, you're not welcome here. You haven't earned the right to be here. I don't care how hard it's been on you, it's been a hundred times harder on her. Other people have been here for her, you know. Paula and Kevin, they come a lot. Sam stops in, and even Stacey the geek. And you know who comes regular as clockwork? Tony. He's been coming right from the start. And believe me, he's a man who wears his guilt on his sleeve. But the one person she wanted to hear from, the woman she respected more than any other officer she ever worked under, the person she ended up sacrificing herself for – you couldn't be bothered to show your face. Well, fuck you, Carol Jordan. You don't get to stroll in now Tony's done the hard stuff for you. So are you going to walk right out of here or am I going to get security on to you?'

Carol wanted to slump to the floor and sob till her throat was raw. Instead, she simply nodded. 'I'm sorry.' She turned and walked back the way she'd come, desperate to make it to her car before she fell apart.

Sinead's last words hit like a handful of hail in her face. 'And don't fucking come again.'

18

Tony paused in the cramped hallway that smelled faintly of smoked paprika. 'Are we going to get in trouble?'

'Only if you grass me up. I did log the keys out officially. I told Fielding I wanted another look. I'm not mad – I'm not going totally off the reservation.'

'Fair enough. You said you had a set of the crime-scene photos,' he reminded Paula. 'Can I see them before we go in?'

'This isn't where she was killed,' Paula said, opening her bag to get the folder of photos she'd printed off before leaving the CID office. 'There's nothing to suggest the killer was ever here.'

'I realise that. But until we know how and where he acquired Nadia, I don't want to rule out any possible connections.'

'I hate that word.' Paula pulled out the folder.

'Connections?' Tony sounded confused.

'"Acquired" – it's so cold. So clinical.'

'I am a clinician. This is supposed to be scientific, not emotional.' He shrugged, doing his 'helpless' face. 'But you're right, it is cold. Would you prefer me to talk about "intersections"? That always sounds like a traffic report to me.' He took the proffered photographs and slipped them out of the folder. In the dim light of the hallway, he flipped through them quickly, taking a first impression of the body and its surroundings. Then he tugged a pair of owlish black-rimmed specs from his inside pocket and put them on. 'I'm getting old,' he said. 'I can't see detail without my glasses.' Taking his time, he studied each photograph from different angles. 'I once had a tutor, quite a young bloke, who thought wearing glasses made people take him more seriously. One day, I was sitting behind him when he took them off to polish them and I realised they were plain glass. Whether it was vanity or insecurity that drove him to it, it cost him my respect. And because I was young and smart-arsed, I told my fellow students what I'd spotted. So the trick he'd used to earn gravitas ended up making him look a fool.'

'And there endeth the sermon for today,' Paula said. 'What about my crime scene?'

Tony sighed. 'I'm wasted here. All that hard-won wisdom, and where does it get me?' He selected a full-length shot of Nadia's body. 'What did Grisha say about the damage to her body?'

'He said he'd given her a good kicking. Probably with steel-toecapped boots.'

'What about stamp marks? Did he say anything about that?'

'He made a point of saying the killer got lucky because he couldn't see any stamp marks.'

'And that's the dog that didn't bark in the night,' Tony said. 'He didn't stamp on her, which is the natural thing to do when you're frenziedly attacking someone and they fall on the ground. You kick and you stamp. So right there, you've got a contradiction. Battering her face to a bloody pulp, to the point where she's unrecognisable, that looks like frenzy. As if the killer is out of control. But the fact that he very carefully doesn't stamp on her suggests his actions are deliberate. He's thought this through. He doesn't want to leave forensic traces. He doesn't want to get caught.'

'So why the overkill on the face?'

'I'm not sure yet. The textbook answer is, to deperson-alise her. To objectify her. To make her less than human so what he's doing isn't really murder, because she's a thing not a person. But that doesn't feel right here somehow. Because the other business, the sealing up of the labia, that's very personal. That's making a statement of posses-sion. "I'm done with you but nobody else can have you." That's what that says to me. It's not a generalised statement of misogyny, it's specific, it's aimed directly at her. And that runs directly counter to the notion of smashing her face to depersonalise her.' He frowned at the photograph, turning it this way and that. 'I don't know, I'm going to have to think about this.'

'Good. I like what happens when you think about things. Now, are you done with the pics? Because I'm getting claustrophobia here. Any chance we could move into a room-sized space?' She handed him a pair of nitrile gloves.

Three doors led off the lobby. Tony opened the nearest one and revealed a poky, windowless bathroom with a shower cubicle, a toilet and a tiny sink. The lingering smell of toiletries couldn't quite hide the fetor of damp. 'Later,' he muttered and hastily pulled the door to.

The next door led to a room that comprised living room, dining corner and kitchen. The separate components could have made for a comfortable, welcoming space if they hadn't been crammed into half the area they actually required. Instead, it felt crowded and confined. 'Deceptively poky. Isn't that what the estate agents never say?' Tony looked around, taking in the pockets of clutter that had infiltrated the few available spaces. Piles of magazines, stacks of DVDs, cardboard boxes half-full of drug samples and promotional giveaways – pens, mouse mats, coasters. He squatted beside the DVDs and scanned the titles. 'No sign of anybody else's taste here. *Bridesmaids, How to Lose a Guy in 10 Days, The Wedding Singer, Eight Women, Juno, Notting Hill, There's Something about Mary, Amelie, My Best Friend's Wedding.* The fairytale reimagined for the twenty-first century.'

'Fairytales for straight girls. Nothing in Polish?'

Tony stood up and grunted as his knees cracked. 'No. She was probably trying to improve her English. Given her job.' He crossed to the dining table, where there was a laptop-shaped space between a stack of papers, an all-in-one printer, scanner and copier, and an A4 pad with a few lines of scribbled notes. 'Did forensics take the laptop?'

Paula nodded. 'They did. I'll ask them for a copy of the hard drive in the morning. If I'm going to talk Stacey into looking at Bev's hard drive, I might as well get her to see what she can find on Nadia's computer as well.'

But Tony wasn't listening. Now he had advanced into the kitchen area, he'd spotted a corkboard on a short section of wall that jutted into the room. The board had been obscured from sight when he'd been in the main part of the room. He made straight for it and stared at it, frowning as if he was cataloguing the contents for the crime-scene equivalent of Kim's Game. 'This is more like it,' he said.

Three takeaway menus – Indian, Chinese and catch-all pizza, kebab and burger. He turned and glanced round the kitchen area. 'She cooked. You can smell it, you can see it from the pans and the knives and stuff. And there's vegetables in the rack. Onions, potatoes, carrots, garlic. OK, the onions and potatoes are sprouting and the carrots are as wrinkled as a Shar Pei's scrotum . . .'

'That's probably because, one way or another, she left here three weeks ago,' Paula interrupted.

He nodded. 'She worked hard, she worked late. She didn't always have time to cook.'

'Maybe she couldn't be bothered.'

'Take a look in the cupboards,' he said, anticipating open packets of ingredients, jars of herbs and spices, tins he'd have no idea what to do with.

Paula revealed exactly what he'd expected. 'You win. She cooked.' She picked an open cardboard box off the shelf and peered inside. 'Now I know the Polish word for lentils.' While she was on this theme, she opened the fridge. It smelled of over-ripe cheese and bad fruit and the plastic bottle in the door shelf was solid with spoiled milk. 'Well, that's one question answered. I don't believe she ever went to Poland. She'd never have left all this food to go off in the fridge. She certainly didn't come home at the weekend just in time to be abducted. At the very least she'd have binned this rotten stuff.'

Tony turned his attention back to the corkboard. A postcard from Ibiza. He unpinned it. 'Sun shining, booze cheap, plenty guys!!! You should have come. Ashley xxx' He replaced it. Business cards from a computer repair shop, a Polish deli in Harriestown, a dressmaker specialising in alterations and a taxi firm. The police would check them all, he knew. Chances were high that they would lead nowhere. Although Ashley might be able to colour in some of the background to Nadia's life.

There were a couple of flyers for upcoming pub gigs by local bands, a bus timetable for the 183 from Harriestown to

Bellwether Square and a cartoon about Polish builders. Finally, he turned his attention to the photographs. A dog-eared and faded colour snap of a wedding party – bride and groom and two presumed sets of parents. 'Her mum and dad?'

'No reason to think otherwise.'

Next, three women, arms around each other, in a night-club or a fun pub, all mugging drunkenly at the camera. The kind of photograph half the women in Britain under thirty had on display, commemorating some celebratory night out with the girls. Tony was about to pass on, but something nagged at him. He took the photo off the board and studied it more closely. 'The one in the middle,' he said. 'She looks familiar. I can't place her. She's not someone I know. But I've met her somewhere.' He looked up at Paula, whose expression was unreadable. 'Do we know who she is?'

'Oh yeah, Tony. We know exactly who she is. She's the victim.'

His confusion was obvious. 'That's Nadia Wilkowa?'

19

Bev had no way of measuring how long she'd been conscious inside the freezer. She'd started trying to count the minutes, going from one elephant to sixty then back again, but she couldn't keep track. Her mind was too busy skittering from one awful possibility to another. And beneath them all, the constant thrum of anxiety about Torin. How would he be coping without her? How would he cope if she never got back to him? Would he go to the police? Would they find her in time? She tried to push the worst of her imaginings away from her, but there was no escaping it. This wasn't the kind of predicament that generally had a positive ending.

As well as losing all sense of time, Bev had also given up on dignity. She'd grown uncomfortably conscious of her full bladder but she'd held it in for as long as she could. Then she'd asked herself why she was bothering. She was locked in a chest freezer wearing nothing but a pair of pants that didn't belong to her. There was nothing dignified in any of that. How could it be worse to be sitting in a puddle of her own piss? If it – literally – pissed off the person who'd put her in here, then score one to her.

When the light came it was a physical shock. Without warning, the lid of the freezer suddenly lifted and a blaze of brilliant white light stunned her optic nerve. All she had time for was to cross her forearms across her face in a timeless gesture of self-defence and supplication before excruciating pain shot through her body and reduced her muscles to jelly. Completely disorientated, Bev felt herself lifted through the air then dumped face down on the floor. As her senses gradually returned, she was aware of rough cement against her skin. There was some kind of cold cuff round her left ankle and she felt her hands being secured behind her. She opened her mouth to scream but before she could make a sound, a terrible blow to the ribs knocked the air out of her. Strong hands turned her on her back and punched her in the side of the head. Colours flashed behind her eyes and thick pain throbbed through her head. 'Shut the fuck up, bitch,' a man's voice said. It was all the more terrifying for being matter-of-fact.

And then there was some kind of wide sticky tape smacked into place across her mouth. Bev had no choice but to shut up. She looked up at the man who was doing this to her. Blue overalls, scuffed black work boots. Quite tall, brown hair, blue eyes, bulbous nose, long straight mouth, square chin. Her first thought was to memorise these unremarkable features. But in a split second her determination gave way to dismay. She'd watched enough crime series on TV to know that if they let you see their face, it was because they were planning to kill you. A wordless moan came from behind her gag and this time he slapped her hard. 'If you did what you were told, I wouldn't have to hit you, would I?' His tone was reasonable, as if he were explaining to a child why they shouldn't stick their hand in the fire.

He grabbed her shoulders and pushed her into a sitting position. Then he gripped her upper arms and yanked her to her feet. She heard a metallic rattle as she struggled upright and looked down. A shiny metal cuff was secured to her ankle with a heavy padlock. A sturdy-looking chain trailed backwards from the padlock. He forced her forward and the chain came too, a heavy drag on her ankle.

From somewhere, Bev dredged up a shred of determination. What about all those cases where girls and women had been taken captive and ended up escaping? She could be one of those. She wasn't a quitter, she was a survivor. Whatever it took, she could find it in herself. Without making it obvious, Bev checked out the room she was being marched across. Cement floor, workbench, blank walls covered with hooks that held tools and garden equipment. A garage, then. He was pushing her towards a door that stood ajar in a side wall. He shoved her hard through the door, making her stumble and fall. Polished stone tiles, wooden cupboards, a fridge. A kitchen, then. Bev tried to get to her feet, but with her hands fastened behind her, it was impossible. She heard the rattle of the chain then slid across the floor as he pulled on it. The skin round the cuff tore, giving her a new centre of pain.

When she came to a standstill, he kicked her thigh, so hard she felt the muscle numb. 'You're mine now,' he said. 'Do you understand? You're my wife. If you do what you're told and you behave like a good wife should, everything will be fine. But if you give me any grounds for complaint, I will hurt you. Is that clear?' He spoke with an educated Northern accent, at odds with his working man's outfit. She couldn't pin his origin down precisely. Never mind. It was something else to store away for the future. Bev didn't know how, but it might be useful.

He picked up the slack in the chain and waved it at her. 'You see this? The other end is chained to the wall. There.' He pointed to a solid metal eye screwed into the door frame. 'Don't even think about it. Four screws, each one three inches long. You've got free range for the length of your chain. There's no knives within reach. Nothing you can hurt me with. And I've got this.' He took a slim black object from his trouser pocket. 'It's a taser. That's what I used on you when I took you out of your kennel. Remember how that felt? Well, that was just a taster. A taster of the taser.' He smiled at his own cleverness. 'I can disable you from twenty feet away.'

All at once, her hands were free. He stepped smartly clear of her. Bev looked round to see him dangling a pair of pink furry handcuffs, the novelty kind sold in sex shops. His lips were turned up in a parody of a smile. 'Don't be under any illusion, Bev. I don't want to hurt you, but if you make me, I will.' He backed away from her, putting some distance and a breakfast bar between them. He pulled out one of the high stools and set it against the far wall. She wasn't good at estimating distances, but even she knew they were less than twenty feet apart.

Bev looked around her, trying to work out whether she had any options. A dining kitchen in a modern house. The rear wall had been opened out to lead into a conservatory. All the blinds were drawn and they were effective. She couldn't even tell if it was day or night. She couldn't see out and nobody could see in.

She was shackled at the far end of the room, nearest to the garage door. She could reach the appliances – cooker, hob, dishwasher, fridge. But she wouldn't make it past the island in the middle of the cooking area. All the doors of the ground-level cupboards had childproof fasteners. There might be potential weapons inside but they would take too long to get at, she reckoned. By the time she'd unfastened the locks, he'd be on her, taser knocking her over, boots flying.

The worktops were clear of appliances and there was no sign of chef's knives or utensils that had anything approaching an edge. On a thick wooden chopping board sat a fillet steak, half a dozen chopped mushrooms, a sliced onion, a plastic bottle of olive oil and three new potatoes. On the stove was a heavy frying pan and a small saucepan. A wooden spoon rested against the frying pan. She couldn't quite take it in. Did he want her to cook his dinner? Had he gone to all this trouble to have her wait on him? She'd seen plenty of crazy people at her hospital counter but this was madness of an order she had never previously encountered.

'So get on with it.' He sat on the stool, looking perfectly normal and relaxed, apart from the little black box that rested casually on his thigh. She wasn't fooled, though. She knew he was alert for the slightest reason to hurt her again. She shrugged and spread her hands wide, as if to indicate she wasn't sure what he wanted.

'Cook the fucking dinner,' he shouted, exploding into sudden loud anger. 'I can't make it any more clear, can I?'

Bev lowered her eyes. *Avoid confrontation.* She picked up the saucepan and crossed to the sink. There was just enough play in the chain to allow her an awkward reach to the taps. She half-filled the pan with water and returned to the stove. It was a gas hob, similar to the one she had at home, but she pretended to struggle with the ignition. Maybe he'd grow impatient and come over to light the gas himself then she could deck him with the frying pan.

'What's the problem?' A mocking drawl from the other side of the room. 'Are you too stupid to light the gas? Do I have to beat the instructions into you?' The sarcasm darkened to threat as he tapped the taser against the breakfast bar.

Scrap that idea. Bev lit the gas under the pan and dropped the potatoes in. She poured a little oil into the frying pan and put it on a medium heat. Fear and incredulity were taking turns in her head. Why would anyone pick her if they were looking for the perfect wife? She hadn't been that good a wife when she'd had a husband, and Tom at least had professed to like his women with a mind of their own. If her kidnapper had bothered to find out anything about her, he'd have learned pretty quickly she was never going to make housewife of the year. Well, if she was going to stay alive, she'd better start working at it. She stared at the bleeding meat, trying not to think how it got that way. Thank goodness she was a half-decent cook, according to her ex, her son and her friends.

When the potatoes came to the boil, she added the onions to the hot oil and stirred them around with the spoon. At least the frying onions killed the smell of piss that hung around her. But how in the name of God was she supposed to know how he liked his steak? There was a world of difference between blue and well done. She picked up the steak and turned to face him, shrugging a question at him.

He laughed, sounding genuinely delighted. 'Medium rare,' he said. 'Good girl. The last one didn't even ask. She turned my steak into shoe leather. Useless cow.'

The last one. Bev blinked back tears as she turned her attention to the stove, trying not to show a reaction to those distressing words. She remembered a poem she'd learned at school that had the same murderous chill. What was it? 'That's my last Duchess painted on the wall, Looking as if she were alive.' Scary then, scarier now. Blindly, she tossed the mushrooms in the pan, mixed them with the translucent onions and cleared a space for the steak. She slapped it into the pan and started counting in her head. When she got to a hundred and eighty, she flipped it over and began the count again. She lifted a potato and tested it by squeezing. Almost there.

Bev was startled by the sound of a plate hitting the granite top of the island behind her. She whirled round. He was on the far side of the island, just feet from her, pushing a dinner plate towards her. For a mad moment, she thought about grabbing the pan and swinging for his head, but common sense prevailed. She wasn't fast enough, he wasn't close enough. If she was going to make it home to Torin, she needed to choose her ground well.

Instead, she picked up the plate and turned back to the stove. She switched off the heat under the pans, drained the potatoes as best she could at full stretch, then served up the meal. She placed it on the island then stepped away, lowering her eyes, determined to offer him no excuse to criticise. Bev tried not to hate herself for becoming so cowed so quickly. It was a strategy, she told herself. A strategy for staying alive.

He took the plate to the breakfast bar and started eating. After a couple of mouthfuls of steak and vegetables, he glared at her. 'You cooked the steak properly.' He ate another chunk of meat, frowning. Then he cut into a potato and his face cleared. 'You stupid bitch,' he snarled. 'How can you not know how to cook a potato? Fucking children in primary schools know how to cook a potato. These are like bullets.' He picked up a potato, took aim and hurled it at her. Bev tried to dodge it, but it caught her on the shoulder, surprisingly painful, then skittered across the floor.

'Pick it up, you lazy slut,' he yelled. She tried but it was beyond the limit of her chain. 'You can reach it if you lie down, you thick cow,' he said, turning back to his steak.

Bev did as she was told. She had to stretch full length, straining with her fingertips to reach the potato, driven on by his sadistic grin. But she finally managed to tease it within reach. She picked it up and pushed herself to her feet. She held the potato up, raising her eyebrows in a question.

'Shove it up your arse for all I care,' he said, finishing off his steak and pushing the plate away from him. 'Now, what does a good wife do to please her husband after dinner?' As he rounded the breakfast bar, she could see his erection tenting the front of his overalls.

Oh Christ. It was going to get a lot worse before there was any chance of it getting better.

20

Paula watched Tony cross the cobbles and climb aboard *Steeler*. She waited till he was safely below and the hatch was closed. Not because she feared for his safety but because she wanted a few moments to gather herself before she headed home.

When he'd recognised Nadia Wilkowa in the photograph from the corkboard, Paula had assumed that he'd made the same mistake she had. That he'd been tricked by the superficial resemblance to Carol Jordan into thinking that he knew a woman who was in fact a stranger. When she'd said, 'We know exactly who she is. She's the victim,' she'd thought she was kicking a misapprehension into the long grass.

He'd looked confused. 'That's Nadia Wilkowa? Then I must have encountered her at some point.'

'You don't think it's your mind playing tricks?'

'What do you mean, my mind playing tricks?'

'Tony, she looks like Carol.'

He'd taken a step back, as if she'd poked him in the chest. 'You think so?' He looked again. 'No, you're wrong. The haircut's the same, but that's all. Look.' He thrust the photo at Paula. 'Her face is a different shape. Cheekbones, totally different angles.'

'The jawline's similar, so are the eyes.'

Tony shook his head stubbornly. 'She's . . . I don't know, ordinary. You wouldn't look twice at her in a crowd.'

Paula turned away. 'For a moment, for a split second when I first saw the body . . . I thought it was her, Tony. The hair, the legs, the line of the shoulders. Then I realised the body shape was wrong.'

'But her face was wrecked, Paula. If you'd seen her in life, you wouldn't have taken her for Carol. You're overlaying your first impressions on this picture. And she doesn't look like Carol.' His voice changed, bitterness creeping in. 'Believe me, Paula. I am the man who sees Carol Jordan everywhere. And I don't see her in this woman's face.'

Paula turned in time to catch the shadow of grief cross his face. She put a hand on his arm. 'I'm sorry.'

He gave a harsh little cough of laughter. 'I don't even know where she's living. All those years when I knew where she was sleeping every night, even when she was undercover. Even when she went to ground after Germany. And now, I don't even know what bloody country she's in.' He hung his head and sighed. 'The one time I needed to be good at my job, and I failed her.'

'You couldn't have known what was in Vance's mind. Nobody could.'

He raised his head, his eyes wide and angry. 'My job is to work with probabilities, Carol. That doesn't mean discounting the improbabilities. And I didn't even give them house room during that investigation. I was blinkered because I was convinced I knew Jacko Vance so well.'

The silence between them was like the air before a thunderstorm. 'You just called me Carol,' Paula said.

He looked thunderstruck. 'God help you, then, Paula.' His voice was husky with emotion.

'I miss her too, Tony.'

Hesitantly, he reached out and put an arm round her shoulders. They seldom touched, he and Paula. Never hugged as a greeting or as a farewell. This was a moment that mattered to them both. 'She's got no bone to pick with you, Paula. She'll be back in your life one of these days.'

She leaned her head on his shoulder and tried not to cry. After a while, she cleared her throat and stepped away. 'You really think you know her? Nadia?'

Tony pinched the bridge of his nose. 'I think so. It's not coming, though. I'm going to have to tuck it away and make my subconscious do the work when I'm asleep. What we do know about her, looking at this picture, is that she liked to go out and have fun, and she had mates to do that with.'

'How do you know it's not just a one-off and she's been stuck with Brittney and Bubble from Accounts for somebody's camera-phone shot at the company Christmas party?' Although her tone was teasing, deliberately trying to shift the mood, Paula genuinely wanted to know.

'None of them is self-conscious or awkward with each other.' He swung round and flicked through the menus. Tucked away behind the rest was another shot, on ordinary printer paper. 'And look, there's another one of the three of them. Different night, different outfits, very relaxed on a banquette.' He was right. She'd missed that on her first cursory look at the board. 'You need to find these women and speak to them. But you don't need me to tell you that.' He wheeled away and headed for the hallway. 'I don't know what I'm doing here, pointing out the obvious to you, Paula. Is this the investigative equivalent of the pity fuck? "Poor Tony, I should give him something to think about."'

Her first reaction had been to feel insulted. 'Of course it isn't. It's not about you. I want to crack this case and I don't have anybody to bounce ideas off, OK? It's about me, feeling lost without my old team. I'm sorry if you think I'm wasting your time. I wanted another pair of eyes that I could trust, that's all.'

'I'm sorry.' He sighed again. 'I'm not at my best right now. Let's take a look at the bedroom and see if there's anything there that rings my bell.'

But there hadn't been. The room was neat, no piles of laundry on the floor, no half-worn outfits thrown over the single chair. The duvet cover, a bright abstract, was the only splash of colour in the room. It had been straightened up, the pillows plumped. There was nothing in the wardrobe that didn't fall into the category of work, casual or night-on-the-town. No fetish outfits, no fantasy props, no sex toys. On one bedside table sat a paperback with a Polish title. It looked more chick lit than Booker Prize. Beside it, a half-empty sports bottle of water and a pair of glasses. Three pairs of understated earrings nestled in a tiny wooden tray beside a small gold crucifix on a fine chain. 'The kind of girl every mother wants her son to meet,' Paula muttered.

Tony snorted. 'Maybe not mine.' He opened the dressing-table drawer. A box of tissues. A tub of peach-flavoured lip balm. A scatter of condoms and a half-squeezed tube of lubricant. 'Sexually active.' He picked up the lube and tested the cap. 'But maybe not recently. See, it's hardened round the cap.'

'Or maybe she'd been having the kind of sex that doesn't need lube,' Paula said drily. 'It happens.'

'So I'm told.' He turned to the small chest of drawers in the corner. The top drawer contained a wide selection of inexpensive make-up. Second drawer, practical but pretty lingerie. Third drawer, T-shirts. Bottom drawer, a couple of thick sweaters. 'I think Nadia might have been on the inter-section of nice and dull. Which is interesting, because that's a combination that reduces her risk factors significantly. Most victims have chaotic elements in their lives. That's usu-ally how their killers cross their paths. But Nadia seems the opposite of chaotic. Which makes your job that bit harder.'

And that had been the sum total of Tony's insights. She'd tried not to feel disappointed, but she couldn't escape the realisation that she'd hoped for more. She'd wanted some-thing to drive the investigation in a new direction, something that would show her new boss that she was someone worth watching.

Paula straightened up in her seat and started the engine. She'd stop off at Skenfrith Street on her way home and put a rocket up the uniforms. Get them to take Bev's disappear-ance seriously, not just stick it on the back burner and hope it would simmer away to nothing.

'It's like the bloody Marie Celeste in here,' she said aloud as she tried to find someone to direct her to the duty inspec-tor's office. She ended up descending to the custody suite in the basement in the hope of finding signs of life. A radio was playing softly, a low mutter that sounded like sport com-mentary. The custody sergeant, a craggy-faced tough in his thirties, looked up from his paperwork and raised his eye-brows.

'Have you lost your way?' He stood up, wary but not unfriendly. 'We've not met, have we?'

'DS Paula McIntyre. I'm the new face on DCI Fielding's firm. I was looking for the duty inspector, but there doesn't seem to be anybody about upstairs.'

He gave a snort of laughter. 'Are you not from round here?'

'I've lived in Bradfield all my adult life. Why? What's so special about Skenfrith Street? Don't you do crime outside school hours?' Paula kept her tone light, but she wished Sergeant Banter would cut to the chase.

'Bradfield Victoria are playing Manchester United at home. Every warm body is at the game, in case of any crowd trouble. Including the duty inspector.'

'Are they expecting crowd trouble?'

This time, he laughed properly. 'Nay, lass. But they're expecting a bloody good game of football. Now, is there owt I can help you with?'

Paula shook her head. Whatever the uniform branch were doing about Bev Andrews' disappearance, they clearly weren't doing it tonight. 'I'll speak to them in the morning. I hope you have a quiet night,' she added on her way out.

'Fat chance. There'll be drunks galore later, whatever the scoreline is.'

There was nothing for it but to go home empty-handed and see how Elinor was getting on with Torin. Maybe the boy would have thought of something that might open up a more promising line of inquiry. Something that would command attention more than a bloody good game of football.

21

There must be an algorithm that described the twist in the space-time continuum that occurred when a teenage boy was in the room, Paula thought, pausing on the threshold of her living room. Adolescent lads seemed to occupy a space out of all proportion to their actual size. The room usually seemed spacious when it was only occupied by herself and Elinor. It didn't even feel crowded when they had friends round. But with Torin sprawled on the sofa, legs stretched across the rug, shirt untucked and tie at half mast, it seemed to have shrunk. She'd have to find a *Doctor Who* geek and ask.

Elinor was in her favourite armchair, legs curled under her, knitting in her lap. The pair of them were watching *Shaun of the Dead*. Paula wasn't sure it was the best viewing for a boy whose mother was missing, but presumably Torin and Elinor had chosen it between them.

As she entered, Torin straightened up, his face stripped of teen anomie, naked anxiety exposed for anyone to see. 'Has my mum turned up?'

'I'm sorry. I've got no more news.' Seeing the crestfallen look on his face, Paula wished she had something else to offer. She perched on the arm of the sofa. 'I know you're going to want to shout at me for even asking, but are you totally sure she didn't say anything to you about any plans to meet someone?'

He glared at her. 'I told you. No. And even if she had and I missed it, she'd still have texted me to remind me. She always does. She says I never listen, so she always does a back-up.' His lower lip trembled and he looked away, covering his mouth with his hand. 'But she's wrong anyway. I do listen.'

'I'm sure you do, Torin,' Elinor said. She paused the DVD.

'So what are your lot doing to find her?' Torin demanded, belligerence a cover for his fear. His shoulders hunched defensively inside his thin shirt.

'The information I took from you this morning will have been put on the computer and circulated nationally. Tomorrow, they'll get started on the painstaking stuff of tracking down friends, checking out any activity on her bank accounts and credit cards.'

'Why are they waiting so long? Why aren't they doing it right now?' His voice was a howl of outrage.

Because it's not a priority. Because they'd rather be at the football. Because nobody else is worried about her the way you are. 'Because these things are all easier to do during normal working hours,' Paula said. Elinor's raised eyebrows told her what her partner thought of that pale excuse. Guilt-tripped, Paula said, 'I'll tell you what I'll do, if you like. I'll go round to your house tonight and put together all the stuff they'll need so they can get started right away in the morning. How does that sound?'

He chewed the skin on the side of his thumb. 'OK, I suppose.'

'Where does she keep stuff like bank statements and her passport? Do you know?'

'There's, like, a boxroom between her bedroom and the bathroom. It's a cupboard really, but my dad fitted it out like an office. Built a desk in and everything. All our official stuff's in the bottom drawer.'

'Thanks. I'll need to pick up some clothes for you too, if you're going to stay with us. Is it OK for me to go into your room?'

He looked mutinous but he nodded. 'OK, I suppose.'

'Do you want to stay here with us, Torin? It's up to you. If you've got a mate you'd rather stay with, or another friend of your mum's? You can say what you want, you know.'

'Do you not want me here, then?'

Paula could have wept for him. 'You can stay as long as you need to. As long as it's what you want.'

'It's OK here.' He jerked his head towards Elinor. 'She doesn't make a fuss. And if I'm under your feet, you'll crack on, get some answers so you get your space back, right?'

'Fair enough.' She tried to hide her surprise at his insight. 'Can I have your keys?'

'Not so fast,' Elinor said. 'You haven't eaten, have you? We saved some pizza for you. So before you go over to Bev and Torin's, you're going to sit down and have some dinner.'

Paula didn't even bother trying to protest. And if she was honest, as she headed back out into the night, she was glad she'd taken the time to eat. Not just because it recharged her physical batteries but because it gave a face to the task ahead. That was something she'd learned from Carol Jordan. Until then, she'd listened to the colleagues who said you couldn't afford emotional involvement with cases because it would burn you out. Working with Carol, she'd come to understand that you deliver a better quality of justice when you care. Yes, the price was high. But why do the job if you didn't care about the outcome?

It felt strange, letting herself into a house where she'd been a guest. Usually when she was searching premises or interrogating in someone's space, as she had been with Tony earlier, she was coming to it fresh. Here, she'd have to put aside the embarrassment of raking through the life of someone she knew and liked. For Bev's sake, she couldn't put personal squeamishness ahead of scouring the house for anything useful.

Of course, the house should have been searched already by whoever had been given her original notes. Paula suspected that Bev had been identified as low risk, the lowest rung on the ladder of missing persons. A by-the-book classification – 'no apparent threat of danger to either the subject or the public' – that would allow the officer concerned to put Bev on the bottom of the pile for someone else to pick up on the morning shift. They might not search the house at all at this stage. If Paula had been in charge, she'd have opted for an assessment of medium risk and not simply because Bev was a mate. The manual said, 'The risk posed is likely to place the subject in danger,' and she thought Bev slotted right into that category. Women like Bev did not go missing voluntarily. She tried not to dwell on the single sentence capitalised and highlighted in its own box near the start of the missing person protocol – 'If in doubt, think murder.'

There was a corner of her professional mind that had already been thinking precisely that.

She made a note of the time in her pocket book and stepped inside. The first phase was the Open Door search. Her former colleague Kevin Matthews used to call it the 'Don't-discount-the-bleeding-obvious search'. They all remembered unnerving cases where missing kids had turned up hidden in obscure corners of houses and flats, sometimes off their own bat. But more often at the hands of others. So Paula made her way through the house, checking every room and cupboard, every cubbyhole and boxed-in space big enough to accommodate a woman of Bev's dimensions. And as anticipated, she drew a blank.

She expected the next phase to be more productive. Now she would sweep the house in a quest for anything that would give her the inside track on Bev's life. Notes, diaries, phones, photos, computers. Torin had his own tablet with him; he'd said Bev never used it and he never touched her laptop, not now they'd got a wireless printer he could command from his own machine. She'd already spotted the laptop on the desk in the cubbyhole office Torin had described, but she didn't want to fuck that up for the techies. Time to call in a favour.

Paula took out her phone and checked the time before she keyed in the call. Half past nine wasn't too late to call a woman who spent her spare time communing with the digital world. To her surprise, it took four rings before Stacey answered. 'Paula, hello, what's going on?'

If Paula hadn't known her better, she would have said Stacey sounded flustered. But that wasn't her style. She'd never seen the former MIT's computer analyst anything less than cool under pressure. And Paula didn't think a call from her qualified as pressure. 'This and that. Started today in my new firm at Skenfrith Street. And you?'

'Don't ask. I'm doing stuff that a GCSE student could manage. It's not a productive use of my skills.'

'I thought as much. That's why I was wondering if you might be interested in doing a favour for me?'

Stacey gave a prim little laugh. 'It did cross my mind that might be why you're calling. What do you need?'

'I've got a misper. It's a bit complicated. I know the

woman concerned so I'm doing the prelims myself. I'll have to hand the laptop over to the CSIs. And they'll take for ever and they won't fillet it the way you will.' Paula let her voice tail off.

'And you want me to come over and make a shadow hard drive and analyse it, all without leaving a trace for the CSIs to find?' Stacey was back to her usual calm deadpan.

'Pretty much, yeah.' And then Paula heard what sounded like a male voice in the background. 'Have you got company? Is this a bad time?' Then it hit her. 'Oh my God, it's not Sam, is it?'

'It's OK,' Stacey said briskly. 'I'll pick up an external hard drive and meet you there. Text me the address. I'll see you soon.' And she ended the call. With anyone else, it would have been rude. But with her, it was just Stacey.

While she was waiting, Paula scouted out the kitchen and living room. A calendar fixed to the side of the fridge revealed the routines of normal life. Football practice, chess club, a school in-service day, a couple of sleepovers for Torin. A dental appointment for Bev. A trip to the movies, a gig for Torin, some friends for dinner. She flicked back a couple of months; it was much the same. A wood-framed blackboard fixed to the wall acted as a memo board. 'Spaghetti, bacon, milk, nutmeg' to one side, 'School trip deposit, tickets for Leeds fest, dry cleaning' on the other. Drawers and cupboards revealed nothing she wouldn't expect to find in a kitchen. The living room was no more productive. There wasn't even a notepad beside the phone. Nobody wrote down messages any more. They texted each other instead.

Paula was on the point of heading back upstairs when Stacey arrived. The daughter of Hong Kong Chinese parents, Stacey had proved to be a computer prodigy, seeming to grasp the finer elements of programming as readily as if they were a child's building blocks. She'd set up her own software company while she was still at university, coming up with a couple of boilerplate programs that had made her enough money never to have to work again. Then she confounded everyone by joining the police. She'd never explained her motives but over the years Paula had learned enough about her colleague to suspect that what Stacey loved was the licence to poke around in other people's data without fear of being arrested for it. She was also convinced that Stacey was firmly ensconced somewhere on the autism spectrum, so socially awkward was she. But towards the end of the MIT, it had dawned on Paula that Stacey was carrying a torch for another colleague, Sam Evans.

Sam's naked ambition and lack of team spirit had been obstacles to friendship as far as Paula was concerned. She didn't trust him to have her back when the shit came down, and that was a problem in a close team. Nevertheless, she'd nudged Stacey in the direction of making her feelings known. Life was too short not to go for the things that mattered. Of course, Stacey had said nothing since. They'd gone out for a meal a couple of times since the MIT disbanded, but Stacey had stolidly avoided talking about Sam. However, she had changed her hairstyle to something much more flattering and her clothes had definitely become more interesting than her standard uniform of beautifully tailored business suits. She was wearing more make-up too, emphasising the dark brown of her almond-shaped eyes and giving a palette of colour to unlined skin that looked surprisingly healthy considering how little daylight it ever absorbed. For the first time since Paula had known her, Stacey looked like a woman who thought she deserved to be loved.

Now, as they climbed the stairs, Paula said again, 'Did I interrupt something? Was that Sam's voice I heard in the background?'

123

Behind her, Stacey sighed. 'He was at my place for dinner. OK? That's all. Same way you'd come to my place for dinner.'

Paula smiled triumphantly, knowing Stacey couldn't see her face. 'Stacey, I've known you, how many years? And how many times have I been to your place for dinner? That would be a big fat zero. We always eat out, remember?'

'You could have come if you'd wanted to.'

At the top of the stairs Paula turned and pulled a face at Stacey. 'You are such a liar. Look, I'm actually glad you're seeing him.'

'Dinner. I didn't even cook,' Stacey said firmly. 'I had it catered.'

'It's a start.'

Stacey looked around the landing, her lips pursed, hands on her hips. 'So where is this computer? And who is this woman?'

Paula pointed to the cubbyhole door and gave Stacey the key points. She was done by the time Stacey was settled in front of the laptop. Stacey swung round in the chair and stared at Paula, frowning. 'You've taken in a teenage boy? You?'

'What? You mean, as in "the lesbians"?'

'No,' she said impatiently. 'You know I'm not like that. I mean you, as in, never shown any interest in parenting.'

Paula rubbed her tired eyes. Just what she needed. A discussion on her maternal instincts, or lack thereof. 'I'm not parenting, for fuck's sake. I'm taking in a stray. For the time being. Besides, Elinor's the one doing the hands-on. Look at me. Here I am. Not on a sofa with Torin. OK?'

Stacey turned back to the screen and pressed the power button. 'Fine. So long as you remember the prime directive of mispers. If in doubt . . . '

'Think murder. I know. We'll cross that bridge when we

come to it. Now, can you shove over enough to let me at that bottom drawer? Apparently that's where all the paperwork is.'

Stacey obliged but there was still barely room for Paula to crouch beside her. She opened the drawer and found it almost filled to the brim with folders, envelopes and loose papers. 'You'd be better taking the whole thing out and sitting down on the landing with it,' Stacey muttered, her head already in what she was doing. 'It never ceases to amaze me – how can you not password your computer? Especially when you share your home with a teenage boy? Are you listening, Paula?'

'No, I'm not.' Paula finally wrestled the drawer free of its runners and backed out of the room. She took it through to Bev's bedroom and sat on the edge of the rumpled duvet. Unlike Nadia Wilkowa, Bev wasn't a neat freak, which made Paula feel a little better about her own untidiness. She'd seen enough of the mess left by lives cut unexpectedly short to have learned the lesson of what's left behind but it still hadn't been enough to make her change her ways.

But at least Bev was careful with the paperwork. The top folder contained birth certificates for her and Torin, plus her marriage certificate and the divorce decree. The next envelope held National Insurance numbers, National Health Service numbers, a note of blood groups and Torin's red record book from babyhood. A folder of bank statements and another of credit card bills. Bev was one of those people who paid off her balance dutifully every month.

Then came the passports. Wherever Bev was, it wasn't abroad. At least, not by conventional means. There was a will leaving everything to Torin and granting guardianship to her ex-husband; an exchange of lawyers' letters arranging the terms of Tom's contact with his son; a bundle of Christmas and birthday cards to Bev from Torin; a folder of

Torin's school reports; and finally, right at the bottom, a battered old address book.

Stacey appeared in the doorway, waving a small silvery box in the air. 'A copy of Bev's hard drive. And nobody will ever know I was in there. I'll take a quick look tonight and forward her emails on to you. The rest I'll let you have as soon as I can.' She glanced at a slim gold watch that Paula reckoned must have cost a few months' salary. 'If I shoot off now, I'll still have time for dessert.'

'Good luck with that.' Paula shovelled everything back into the drawer except the address book. 'Thanks for this, Stacey. It's looking darker and darker.'

'I'm sorry, for your friend's sake. I'll be in touch.' She half-turned to go then paused. 'Have you heard from the DCI, by the way?'

Paula shook her head. 'Not a word. I don't even know where she is or what she's doing.'

'I expected her to come home to BMP once the dust had settled.'

'Ha. You have to be joking. The brass don't want her. She makes the bureaucrats look like a bunch of useless wankers. No, they were thrilled when she handed in her notice so she could move to West Mercia. But she never turned up. She resigned before she even started.'

'I know. That's why I thought she'd come back. For the sake of familiarity. And Tony, of course. He's still at Bradfield Moor, isn't he?'

'Oh yes. They were over the moon when he said he wasn't leaving after all. He's living on a narrowboat down at the Minster basin. But he hasn't heard from her either.'

Stacey slipped the hard drive into her pocket. 'Maybe she's the one you should be treating as a misper.'

22

Day twenty-five

Fielding definitely had presence, Paula decided. She appeared different in almost every respect from Carol Jordan, but the one thing they had in common was the ability to hold the attention of a room full of hard-arsed coppers. Nobody was whispering to their neighbour or texting their girlfriend while Fielding was running a briefing. She might be petite and pretty, but when she started talking you forgot those fleeting fantasies and focused on what she was saying. It reinforced Paula's desire to make the right mark on this firm.

It was a kind of performance. DCI Fielding did her briefing on PowerPoint. She had one of those soft Scottish accents that took the harshness out of her words and made her audience want them not to stop. 'The body of Nadzieja Wilkowa, known as Nadia, was found yesterday morning in a squat in Rossiter Street, Gartonside.' A picture of the exterior of the house. 'She had been beaten to death.' A shot of the body in situ. Fielding clearly didn't believe in sparing the squeamish or the hung-over. 'A blow to the head from a pipe or a baseball bat, then battered and kicked. We think she was killed here, judging by the blood spatter. Our killer's finishing touch was to superglue her labia together.' An explicit photograph that made Paula feel angry and nauseous. 'As we can see, her genital area had been shaved. When we find a boyfriend, I want to know if the shaving was her usual practice or if it's something our killer likes to do.'

The next shot showed the bathroom. Fielding used the laser pointer as she went through the key information. 'The victim's clothes and bag were stuffed down here. Not really hidden, just out of the way. It's possible he may have made her wash in the bath. Or washed her himself. The water to the property has been cut off, but the squatters have rigged up a rainwater catchment system that provides a limited water supply. There was a puddle of water in the bath.'

Back to the exterior shot of the house. 'Gartonside is no-man's-land. So there are no cameras on the approach to Rossiter Street or the surrounding area. I'm thinking the killer knew that. He seems too careful an offender simply to have got lucky. One of the many interesting questions is how he knew that the squatters would be gone for the weekend. Black, Hussain, I want you to talk to them. Find out exactly who knew they were going to be away. And who knows they live there.' She flashed a smile at the two detectives, the kind of smile that Paula reckoned made you feel the love.

'Nadia was a sales rep for a pharmaceutical company. Not one of those multinationals that are always coming up with new miracle cures that make you constipated or increase your risk of breast cancer. A small British company that does generic versions of common drugs. The kind of stuff your GP puts you on when she's trying to save the NHS a bob or two. She'd been working for them for eighteen months. No complaints, she was a good worker. A bright girl. Did well.' A photo of Nadia in life, her shaggy blonde hair tousled and her smile reaching her eyes. 'Although she was Polish she spoke exceptionally good English, her employers say. But still.' She scanned the room. 'Stachniewski, you've got the right kind of name. Talk to the Polish community, put some feelers out, see whether she was known in the pubs and clubs and grocery stores.' A lanky ginger-haired officer nodded gloomily. 'Oh, and Stach? Give the Polish cops a call and see if you can find out whether Mrs Wilkowa has cancer. Because, three weeks ago, an email was sent from Nadia's account to her employers, stating that her mother had been diagnosed with cancer. She asked for a month's compassionate leave. The company didn't want to lose her because they thought she was a good worker so they agreed. Last week, they emailed her with a query about a client account. They got a reply, answering the query and also indicating that she would be back next week, as originally planned. Now, we don't know at this point whether she ever went to Poland, though DS McIntyre reckons she wouldn't have left her fridge full of perishables if she had. Black, check with Immigration and the Borders Agency to see whether there's any record of her leaving and returning. And talk to the airlines that fly to Poland out of Manchester and Leeds/Bradford, see if she's on any of their passenger lists. It's probably a waste of time, but we have to cover the ground. We don't want some defence counsel ambushing us down the line over things we left undone.' Everyone nodded sagely, like a roomful of car parcel-shelf ornaments.

'What's really interesting is that her killer managed to extort from her enough information to make the emails possible and plausible. As far as we can tell, she made no attempt to turn those messages into a cry for help.' Fielding paused, her professional demeanour slipping for a moment into an expression of pity. 'Her phone is passworded, which is a nuisance, but the techies tell me they'll have her call records today and hopefully we'll get into the phone for texts and messages very soon. We got luckier with the computer. Apparently the password was her birthday, so easy peasy for the CSIs to crack. Inspector Gardner is co-ordinating the actions, so he'll be setting a bunch of you on to the tedious but important job of working your way through the emails and the tweets and the Facebook contacts. I know it's boring . . . ' She paused, giving them her best sympathetic smile. 'But it's also potentially crucial. Nadia crossed her killer's path somewhere and we have to find out precisely where and when. The answer could be buried in one of those emails. I'm counting on you not to let anything significant disappear in the slipstream of boredom.'

Bloody hell, she's talking like a poet now. Slipstream of boredom, for fuck's sake. Paula kept her face straight. She didn't want to draw attention to herself in case she got lumbered with the emails. 'Another group will be backtracking on all her recent appointments. I want anything you can squeeze out of them. And I would like alibis, please. I know this is a nightmare assignment because of the number of contacts involved, but we have to lift up every stone and expose the white bellies and the creepy crawlies beneath them.

'And finally. The CSI working on the computer has also identified two women who seem to be her closest pals. DS McIntyre, you and I will take them. I'll be doing a press conference later this afternoon. Till then, the ID is still under wraps.' She turned off the screen. 'That's it for now, everybody. I'm counting on you. And so is Nadia. Let's do it for her and her family.' Fielding finished with a dazzling smile. She knew how to use her charm, that much was obvious from her performance, Paula decided. But judging by her failure to turn it on for Grisha at the crime scene, she used it only when it was going to earn her clear advantage. Making her team love her was a priority; getting the pathologist to go the extra mile hadn't been.

Paula made her way through the bustle of officers discussing the briefing to Fielding's side. 'Morning, McIntyre,' Fielding said absently, flicking through a bundle of papers. 'Give me ten minutes to deal with this lot and we'll head out.'

'I need to talk to the duty inspector in uniform first, ma'am.' Paula was at her most conciliatory. 'The misper I caught on my way in yesterday. I have to brief them, make sure they're taking it seriously.'

Fielding's perfectly groomed eyebrows rose. 'Any reason why they wouldn't take it seriously?'

Paula knew she had to tread carefully. She was the new girl here; she had no idea where the political lines were drawn in this nick. 'No reason. But I know the misper, ma'am. Her son gave me the key to their house. I wanted to pass it on personally. Just so they know I've got an interest. And so I can give them a backgrounder.'

'Have you been poking your nose in where you shouldn't, McIntyre? You're not with the MIT any more. We respect each other's boundaries in this nick. Have you not got enough on your plate with a murder that you have to do uniform's job for them?' Fielding didn't bother to lower her voice. The officers nearest them pretended not to notice, but Paula knew it was all sinking in. She could feel her ears burning.

'Like I said. I know the misper. Her son is staying with us for the time being.'

Fielding froze in the middle of turning a page. 'Are we talking minor here?'

'He's fourteen.'

Fielding stared at her as if she was mad. 'What were you thinking? You should have called social services. Or a relative. Last time I looked, you weren't on the list of appropriate adults.'

Righteous indignation was in danger of trumping good sense. 'His nearest relatives are in Bristol. His dad's in the army, in Afghanistan. I considered he was less at risk in my spare room than in an emergency placement.' She paused. 'Ma'am.' She couldn't make Fielding out. Where was her compassion? This woman was a mother. If anyone should understand Paula's reasoning, it was someone who had a kid of their own.

Fielding gave an exasperated sigh. 'Go and brief the duty inspector, then. And make it quick. We've got a murder here and that takes precedence over everything else.' She waved a hand at Paula in a gesture of impatient dismissal. Paula was halfway to the door when Fielding called after her. 'And if you plan on carrying on with the child-minding, for Christ's sake get consent from the relatives. I don't want to have to arrest you and your girlfriend for unlawful imprisonment.'

Someone guffawed, another sniggered. Welcome to Skenfrith Street, Paula thought bitterly. The home of modern policing.

Dean Hume, the duty inspector, had the mangled ears, thick neck and asymmetric nose of a rugby player who had never shirked in the scrum. His scalp had a five o'clock shadow that revealed his male pattern baldness and his eyes nestled in tired grey folds of skin. He inhabited a tiny glassed-in cubicle in a corner of the main squad room. His computer monitor was the size of a bedside cabinet and it was surrounded by stacks of file folders. His white shirt was already wilting under the pressure of work. When Paula explained why she was there and what she had discovered at Bev's house, he looked as thrilled as Fielding had. 'You used to be on the MIT team, right?'

Paula was starting to get tired of this. 'That's right, sir. DCI Jordan's firm.'

'You were a bit of a law unto yourselves there.' To her surprise, Hume smiled. 'Got some good results, though.'

'We did, sir. We thought we were bloody good value for money.'

He grunted. 'Shame the brass didn't agree. The thing is, Sarge, we're a bit more by the book here. DCI Fielding runs a tight ship. And she gets results too. So if you're going to go off piste, you'll need to be discreet about it.' It was a warning, but in the friendliest of terms.

For the first time since she'd arrived at Skenfrith Street, Paula felt part of a team. Shame it was the wrong team. 'Thanks, sir. I'll bear that in mind. As far as Bev Andrews is concerned, I typed up a full report of my actions and the information I gathered. It should give your officers a head start. Who should I email it to?'

He gave her the details of his sergeant. 'From what you tell me, it's not looking too clever,' he said. 'I'll have a word with media liaison and see if we can get something in the *Sentinel Times* tonight. And we'll have to talk to the lad again.'

'I doubt he's got anything else to give.'

Hume nodded. 'I'm sure you're right. I heard you're the whizz kid when it comes to interviews. But we've got to cover all the bases. You can sit in as the appropriate adult if you like?'

Paula's smile was grim. 'I don't think DCI Fielding's going to cut me any slack on that score. My partner is probably your best bet.' She scribbled down Elinor's details and handed them to Hume. 'She's a doctor at Bradfield Cross.'

'Thanks. Any developments, I'll let you know.'

Paula stood up to leave. But Hume hadn't quite finished. 'And, Sergeant – leave this to us now. None of your maverick MIT tricks, please? Nobody's got your back here. Where DCI Fielding's concerned, you're on your own.'

23

Bev's first return to consciousness inside the freezer had been bewildering; the second was excruciating. Every time she took a breath, her ribs hurt, sharp pain like a handful of daggers stabbing her in the chest. Gradually, as she grew more aware, she understood that if she kept her breathing shallow and moved as little as possible, the pain ceased to be all-consuming. But that left room in her nervous system for the other agonies to make themselves felt. There was a dull ache in her lower back. Kidneys, she thought. Her head throbbed and when she moved her jaw, lightning shot from the point of her chin to the top of her skull. A fire burned between her legs, spreading up into her groin. The pinkie on her left hand was hot and swollen. Probably broken. The least of her worries.

She'd been determined to do whatever it took to survive, to make it home to Torin. But it had quickly dawned on her that her captor was as determined to find fault as she was to obey his every whim. She'd fallen into the hands of a man whose only satisfaction came from causing pain. It wasn't enough just to rape her. He had to make the excuse of her inadequacy to hurt her. He'd subjected her to humiliating sexual acts, all the while maintaining the sick pretence that she was a failing wife. God help any genuine wife who had fallen prey to this monster, Bev thought, shuddering involuntarily, a groan of pain seeping from her bruised lips.

He'd ripped the tape from her mouth while he'd been fucking her in the kitchen. He said he wanted to hear her appreciate his sexual prowess. But if she made any other kind of noise, she'd be sorry. Tasering would be the least of her worries.

Then he unchained her and dragged her upstairs. He fastened her to another metal eye in a room furnished with nothing but a bed covered with a rubber sheet. He punched her hard in the face and forced her on to the bed, tying her by her wrists and ankles so she was spread-eagled across it. He'd left her alone briefly, then returned with a can of shaving foam, a pair of scissors and a plastic razor. 'If you move, I'll cut you to ribbons,' he said, as matter of fact as if he'd been asking for sugar in his tea. Then his hands had been on her, snipping away at her pubic hair, carefully trimming it to the skin. Her flesh crawled at his touch, but she bit her lip and forced herself not to flinch. Next came the shaving foam, then the rasp of the razor against her most tender skin. Bev had never shaved herself; being blonde, she hadn't even needed a bikini wax for sunshine holidays. The feeling of air against her bare skin was strange. But at least he was careful and he didn't hurt her. She wondered why, when his sole aim till then had been to punish her.

The respite didn't last long. This time, he made her beg. Hating herself, she did as she was told, though not convincingly enough to avoid another beating. When he'd finally reached the point where he couldn't raise an erection, that had been her fault too. Bev refused to remember what had come next. Some things didn't bear thinking about. She thought she'd passed out in the end.

Now she was back in her box. Her kennel, he'd called it. As if she was an animal. Bev had seen plenty of anger in her life. But she'd never come across such a sustained level of aggression directed at a stranger. Not even rape victims. From what she'd seen in the hospitals where she'd worked, women were only beaten this badly, this systematically, by their partners. This was domestic violence gone rogue.

And she was caught at the heart of it.

Tears seeped from her swollen eyes. She'd tried to hold on to the promise of seeing her son again. But Bev was no fool. She knew she couldn't withstand another night like that. She'd seen his face. She could identify his home.

She wasn't going to make it out of here alive.

24

Tony had always liked the room where he visited Dr Jacob Gold. Nothing in it reminded him of anywhere he'd spent any significant amount of time; it was emotionally neutral. The walls were lemon yellow, broken up by four large paintings of beaches, seascapes and tidal estuaries. Two armchairs at an angle to each other sat on either side of a gas fire, separated by a striped rug in muted colours. In the shallow bay window sat a chaise longue with another armchair close to its head. A low table sat in the centre of the floor displaying an exotic collection of polished sea-shells.

It was the kind of calm space that was perfectly suited to the supervision sessions most psychologists saw as a key part of their professional lives. The relationship was all about helping them to develop skills and become better practitioners, which was something Tony took seriously. The problem he had with supervision was that he didn't have a whole lot of respect for most of the supervisors he'd encountered. He was well aware that his was an unconventional mind. It wasn't arrogance to acknowledge he was also smarter than most of the people doing his job. Then he'd heard Dr Gold speak about damaged lives at a symposium. This, he thought, was the man for him. He'd approached him afterwards, but Dr Gold had refused. 'I don't do supervisions,' he'd said in a tone that left no space for discussion.

That had never stopped Tony. 'I know why,' he said. 'Compared with your patients, practitioners are boring. Well, I'm not. I'm the one passing for human.'

Dr Gold frowned, turning his attention properly to the little guy in the ill-assorted clothes and the bad haircut. That had been back in the days before Carol had made some subtle changes that Tony had barely noticed happening. 'Who *are* you?'

'You remember that serial killer in Bradfield last year? Young male victims?'

Something shifted in Dr Gold's expression. 'You're the profiler.' Tony nodded. There was nothing more to be said. Either Jacob Gold would bite or he wouldn't. They stood, eyeing each other up, heedless of the conference bustle around them. 'Come and talk to me next week. I'm based in Leeds. You can contact me via the university.'

And so it had begun. After that first session, Tony knew he'd found someone who could help him live with himself and his work, his achievements and his mistakes. Luckily for him, Jacob Gold had also discovered someone worth breaking his own rules for.

Tony had always conceived of the role of supervisor as analogous to that of the priest in confessional. As he understood it, the theory of Catholic confession was that you went when you had sins to confess; that the priest helped you to see the error of your ways; that you underwent a penance to remind you of the way, the truth and the light; that you departed, ostensibly to sin no more; and that whatever you brought into the box stayed between you and the priest. And presumably, God. Though He never seemed to intrude much on the practical proceedings of the Church.

Tony made an appointment with Dr Gold once or twice a year, when some aspect of his clinical practice was troubling him, when he felt he wasn't dealing well with some element of his professional life, or, more rarely, when his personal life was throwing him conundrums he couldn't readily solve. A fifty-minute hour under Jacob's gentle probing usually suggested a solution to whatever he'd brought to the session. At the very least, it brought Tony a degree of clarity. The equivalent of Catholic penance was the process of digging away at the roots of the issue during their session. And of course, he would leave with the firm intention of making the changes that would resolve his difficulty.

And often he would fail.

But that was part of the process too.

Tony knew he should have talked sooner to Jacob after the debacle with Jacko Vance. He was conscious that he'd been avoiding it. Jacob, who wore his supervision lightly, had clearly been well aware of the media coverage and had left a message of support. Which, in the terms of their relationship, had been the equivalent of shouting, 'Oi, get your arse down here, pronto.'

But he was here now, and that was what mattered. Today, he'd chosen the armchair rather than the chaise longue. Jacob sat across from him, long legs crossed, an elegant notebook open on his lap, Mont Blanc pen lying in the crack between the thick cream pages. 'How are you?' It was the question that always began their sessions. Unless Jacob had been living on a desert island with no access to the electronic media, he had to have a pretty good idea, given the coverage of the recent events in his life.

'Well, let me see.' Tony steepled his fingers in front of his chest. 'BMP decided they no longer need my services, my new home was burned to the ground, people died because I wasn't good enough at my job and Carol walked out of my life because she needs someone to blame for her brother's murder and in her head, I'm that someone. By the same argument, another colleague would have grounds for blaming me for the fact that she's been blinded and disfigured for life from acid burns, but she's forgiven me and I'm not sure, but that almost feels worse. I'm living on a boat with my books in storage, but on the positive side, one of my former police colleagues came round last night looking for my insights. Apart from that, Mrs Lincoln, how did you enjoy the play?' His tone was light but he knew that wouldn't fool Jacob. Hell, it wouldn't fool a block of wood.

'And which item in this catalogue of disaster is the one that costs you most peace of mind, would you say?'

The trick with these sessions, Tony had found, was to try to answer without pausing for thought. His discomfort generally came from thinking too much. Trying something different was one of the reasons for supervision. So he replied at once. 'Carol. I failed her. And she's out of my life. I don't even know where she's living. What she's doing to get through the days. And I miss her. Every single day, I miss her.'

'What makes you think you failed her?'

'I'm supposed to be able to work out what's going on inside the heads of people with aberrant minds. But on this case, I was thinking in straight lines. It's as if I forgot I was dealing with someone whose defining characteristic was wrong-footing everyone around him. I didn't explore the possibilities properly. I had half my mind on other things and I didn't drill down deep enough. And people died. Among them Carol's brother and his partner.' Tony hung his head, the sense of failure as vivid as it had been at the time. 'If I'd been rigorous, they would have been warned. And the chances are, they'd be alive today.'

'You know this is magical thinking, don't you? You're claiming control over circumstances you can't control.'

'Don't, Jacob. Don't try and get me to let myself off the hook. I know I didn't do my job well enough. I'm not looking for excuses. I'm looking for a way to move forward from the consequences.'

Jacob picked up his pen and made a short note. Just a few words. 'To move forward, you have to accept the truth of a situation. Not persist in myth-making. Wouldn't you say?'

'It's not myth-making. It's acknowledging failure.'

Jacob's considering expression didn't alter. 'He was a clever man, your opponent?'

'Yes. An exemplar of Narcissistic Personality Disorder. An arch-manipulator.'

'So, a man perfectly capable of second-guessing whatever tactics you might have chosen to employ against him?'

Tony gripped the arms of his chair. 'Maybe. You're saying he would have found a way to circumvent whatever defences I'd constructed?'

'He had the advantage. He was working in the shadows. In the interstices. It's impossible to guard against someone like that if they are clever enough and determined enough. He was determined to have his revenge. Or so it seems to me. Does it seem so to you?'

It was an invitation to a shift of perspective. Tony wanted to grasp it, but that very desire made him suspicious. 'I think I should have stopped him.'

'You don't think you might be taking responsibility for the actions of another?'

'I know I didn't kill Michael and Lucy. I know I have no direct responsibility for what happened. But I can't escape the indirect responsibility. It's what Carol believes too.'

'If Carol didn't hold you responsible, do you think you would feel this level of guilt? This is not the first time that victims have died in the course of an investigation you've been party to. I've sat in this room and listened to your grief on that score. But all I have heard from you in terms of responsibility is a wish that you could have done better or done differently. Not this scourging guilt.'

And this time, Tony had no instant reply. At last, he said, 'Adler would have had a field day with this, right?'

'How might he have characterised this, do you think? How would you characterise it if a patient presented with this shift in their belief system?'

'I'd think it was hubris. I had a friend once. She knew me when I was a teenager. She was kind to me, but she thought I needed toughening up. She used to say, "You're like a man with a big nose who thinks everybody's talking about him. Well, they're not, and the sooner you thicken that skin of yours, the happier you'll be."'

'Was she right, do you think?'

Tony gave a rueful chuckle. 'I don't think I ever learned the lesson. I've always thought that was why I had such powerful empathy.'

Jacob nodded, so slight a movement that Tony wondered whether he'd imagined it. 'And still you haven't answered the question. If Carol didn't hold you responsible, do you think you would feel this level of guilt?'

'Probably not.' The honesty was hard but there was no point in being here if he didn't try.

'And if this source of feeling bad about yourself was reduced or removed, do you think the other things that are causing you difficulties would be made easier?'

'That's one of those questions that provokes only one answer,' Tony said, an edge of annoyance in his voice.

'And that may well be why you need to ask it.' Jacob sighed. He closed his notebook and put it on the floor next to him, pen aligned with the end. 'Tony, I've been your supervisor for many years. I like to think I have formed a good idea of how you function. I know you have made an accommodation with aspects of your personality that many people would find problematic. I also know you want to move forward in your practice and in your personal life. For a long time, Carol Jordan has been the centre of your emotional life. At times, she has appeared to be the only component of your emotional life. Would that be a fair assessment?'

Tony's shoulders were tightening involuntarily. He had an uneasy sensation in his stomach. Jacob had never spoken to him in these terms. He'd probably never actually said so much in the whole of a session before. 'I do have other friendships,' he said, hearing his own defensiveness. And who were those other friends, when the chips were down? Paula? Alvin Ambrose? Cops who had been colleagues and had grown into more than that. But not the kind of friends most people had. Nobody he went to the football with. Nobody he was on a pub quiz team with. Nobody he'd kept up with from his student days. Nobody he went hillwalking with. Not even anybody he regularly gamed with online.

'The only one you've been bringing into this room for years is Carol.'

'You think it's going nowhere, don't you? You think it's holding me back? Trapping me in the same place?'

Jacob breathed heavily and pushed his gold-rimmed glasses up to the bridge of his nose in a rare moment of fidgeting. 'It's not what I think that matters. But we both know there is significance in you even asking those questions in those terms.'

Tony's expression was bleak, his eyes blank. 'In so far as I've ever loved anyone, I love Carol.' Even to say it was a wrench, like something twisting in his gut.

'What would happen if you let that feeling go?'

He shook his head. 'You don't just let feelings go.'

'You can allow time to release you from them. Grief and mourning are part of the process, but there is a process. When you clear out the attic, it's amazing what you make room for.' Jacob sighed again. 'It's not my job as a supervisor or as a therapist to tell you what to do. But I will say this: living with so much pain is neither healthy nor necessary. You need to look at your life and decide what really serves you. And what you should let go.'

'You've helped me understand one thing today. If it had been anyone else's brother, I would feel bad about it. But I wouldn't be taking all the weight. I need to think about what that means for me.'

'You don't have to carry this alone. You can always bring it here. And as you reminded me, you have friends. You will find comfort.' Abruptly, he stood up. 'Would you wait a moment?'

Jacob left the room without a backward glance. Baffled, Tony stared at the closed door. Jacob had never walked out of a session before, no matter how challenging it had become. What was going on? Had his supervisor heard something outside the room that he'd missed? He fretted over what had happened, finding that easier than returning to his own problems.

And then Jacob was back, carrying a slim hardback book with an olive-green and cream jacket. He handed it to Tony. *Rings on a Tree* by Norman MacCaig. 'I don't know how you feel about poetry. But I find it helpful as a way of interrogating myself and my own process. There is a poem in this collection, "Truth for Comfort". I think it would be a good place for you to start.'

'You want me to cure myself with *poetry*?' He couldn't help his incredulity showing. Jacob, that rigorous psychologist, suggesting poetry was like Elinor Blessing suggesting crystal healing as a cancer treatment.

Jacob smiled, settled into his chair. 'There is no cure for what ails us, Tony. But I think we can manage something better than palliative care, don't you? And so, how is work?'

That was one of the things Tony liked about working with Jacob. He didn't linger once the patient had understood his next step. 'I'm on a part-time contract at Bradfield Moor again,' he said. 'They seem happy to have me back. And I like the work.' He outlined the bare bones of his clinical practice, explaining his thinking in a couple of interesting cases.

'And the profiling?'

'Bradfield don't want me any more. They say it's about economy, but I think it might have something to do with the fact that I haven't hit it off with their new Chief Constable. James Blake and I, we're chalk and cheese.' Before Jacob could say anything, Tony held up one finger. 'Which I am not blaming myself for. It's one of those things. I'm doing bits and pieces with other forces, but there really are cuts that are affecting outside experts like me. They see us as a luxury they can't afford. And with them training up their own so-called experts . . . ' He puffed out his cheeks and blew the air out. 'I miss the work. I like it and I'm good at it.'

'You are.' Jacob took off his glasses and polished them. It was weird to see him shifting around so much. 'And I have been thinking about that too. A man who has found his calling should be able to practise it, wouldn't you say?'

Tony grinned. 'Some might say it's better to have no call for someone with my particular skills.'

'There is, I think, nobody with your expertise and experience in the field. It's time you shared that, Tony.'

He held his hands up, defensive. 'Oh no. No more teaching. I'm not doing dog-and-pony shows again.'

'I'm not talking about the academic life. I'm talking about writing a book. Taking the reader through your custom and practice. Showing and telling how you profile, how you resolve cases. How you work with the police, how you make your arguments. There is nothing comparable out there, Tony. You could create a future generation of profilers in your image. If the police are going to train their own, don't you think they should be informed by best practice?'

Tony shook his head, almost laughing. 'I'm not a writer. That's not my skill set.'

'You're a communicator, though. And publishers have editors to make your prose pretty. Don't make a decision now. Go away and think about it. It may provide you with a double satisfaction. Working through those old cases might help you work through your other process. Cleansing, not wallowing.' Jacob looked at his watch. 'Our time is up.' He stood up and pointed to the book of poetry. 'Think about what we've talked about. Remember what they say about bridges. The hard thing is to know which ones to cross and which ones to burn. Make some changes, Tony.'

Tony gave a wry smile and scrambled to his feet. 'Physician, heal thyself?' But even as he spoke, he knew he was trying to make light of what might be the most difficult choice of his adult life. Was it really time to cut Carol Jordan out of his heart for good?

25

A quick pass through Nadia Wilkowa's Facebook page had indentified the two friends in her memo-board photos as Ashley Marr and Anya Burba. Anya was a teaching assistant in a primary school in Todmorden, a twenty-minute drive from Bradfield. Ashley was closer, a receptionist in a GP-run health centre in Harriestown, a ten-minute walk from Nadia's flat. Fielding decided Ashley would be their first target. The head receptionist wasn't thrilled when they asked to interview her, but Fielding made it clear she wasn't going to argue the toss. With a great deal of emphatic breathing, the receptionist showed them into a tiny room with four chairs and a table. 'It looks more suited to a poker school than anything medical,' Paula muttered as the woman left them alone so she could fetch Ashley.

'Let's hope Ms Marr doesn't have a poker face,' Fielding said. 'Right then, McIntyre, let's see what you're made of. You lead off on the interview.'

Paula was gratified at Fielding's confidence in her. But

there was no opportunity for her to say so. Ashley Marr stuck her head round the door, looking more confused than worried. 'Are you the police? Are you sure you've got the right person?'

There was no mistaking the woman in the photo. Ashley looked in her mid-twenties. She had a round, cheerful face framed with a mop of auburn hair. Her large green eyes were widely spaced and coupled with a neat little nose and a small mouth, they gave her the look of a happy kitten. Her black jeans and pink jumper were both tight, as if she'd put on a few pounds since she'd bought them. Paula gave her a welcoming smile. Best to keep things relaxed and informal till they got the young woman settled, then hit her with the bad news. 'Come in, Ashley. I'm Paula McIntyre and this is Alex Fielding. We're police detectives here in Bradfield. Have a seat, please.' Paula waved her to the chair furthest from the door and sat down at right angles to her.

Ashley perched on the edge of the chair. 'I don't understand. I haven't done anything. What's all this about? Do I need a lawyer? They always ask for a lawyer on the telly.'

Paula inwardly cursed the ubiquitous inaccuracies of TV drama. 'You really don't need a lawyer. It's nothing you've done, Ashley. We need to talk to you about one of your friends.' From her bag, she produced a copy of one of the photos from Nadia's kitchen. She pointed to Nadia. 'Do you recognise this person?'

Ashley looked scared. 'It's Nad. My mate, Nad. Nadia. What's happened to her? Why are you here?'

'I'm afraid I've got some very sad news, Ashley.' Paula reached across the angle of the table and put a hand over hers. 'Nadia's dead.'

The colour drained from Ashley's cheeks, making her pale freckles distinct as a rash. Her hands flew to the sides of her head and she looked stunned. 'I don't believe it. Not Nad. You must have made a mistake. It's her mum that's got cancer, not her.'

'There's no mistake, Ashley. I'm very sorry. I know this is a terrible time for you, but we really need your help.'

'Can we get you a cup of tea or a drink of water?' Fielding leaned forward and for a moment, Paula could see that she'd be the kind of mother you could rely on.

Ashley shook her head. 'What happened? How can she be dead? She's in Poland, she texted me only the other day, saying the weather was crap where she was and how she was looking forward to coming home.' Her hand flew to her mouth. 'She never texted me on Monday, is that when she died?' Paula felt Fielding's quick glance at her. The squatters had returned on Tuesday morning to find Nadia's body in their living room. It looked as if the killer saw no need to pretend Nadia was alive after he'd murdered her. He simply wanted to prevent anyone raising the alarm while she was still with him.

'We think someone took Nadia,' Paula said. 'He kept her prisoner. And then he killed her.'

'In Poland?'

'We think she never left Bradfield,' Paula said.

'But she texted me. She said she had to go home at short notice because her mum had cancer and she thought she was going to die. I said to Skype me when she got there but she said she couldn't because her mum didn't have internet access. So we texted.' She pulled her phone out. 'Look, I'll show you.'

'That's really helpful, Ashley. And we'll need a copy of those text exchanges between you. Did anything strike you as odd about anything she said in her texts? Or the way she said it?'

Ashley frowned. 'Everything was just normal. That's why

none of this makes any sense. Are you sure you've got the right person?'

Paula's heart went out to her. 'I know this is a terrible thing for you to hear, but we're sure. And we need all the help we can get. The sooner we get it, the more chance there is that we'll catch whoever did this to your friend. So we'd like to ask you some questions. Do you mind?' It was heartless, to demand such a thing when the woman was still in shock. But necessary.

Ashley's eyes brimmed with tears and she started to shake. Paula put an arm round her shoulders and let her sob. Her eyes met Fielding's. Any suggestion of sympathy had disappeared. Her boss made a rolling gesture with her hand; hurry it up. *Fuck that.* Paula let Ashley cry, finding a packet of tissues in her pocket to wipe her eyes and blow her nose when the first storm had passed. 'I'm s-s-sorry,' Ashley hiccuped, smudged mascara giving her racoon eyes.

'Don't be. She was your friend. It's right to feel upset.' Paula sat back but kept a hand on Ashley's arm. 'So, tell me when you last saw Nadia.'

Ashley gulped and swallowed, then managed to speak. 'It was a Saturday.' She counted back, her lips moving silently. 'Three weeks ago. We went down Manchester to go shopping at the Trafford Centre. They've got, like, a load of cool shops there. We met up with Anya – that's our other mate, Anya Burba. She's Polish, like Nad. Anyhow, we met up at Burger King at noon and had a burger then we went round the shops.' She stopped, smitten by memory, her bottom lip quivering.

'Did you buy anything?' Paula sounded chatty, interested in the shopping rather than the sinister.

'I got some purple jeggings and a sequinned top to match. Nad got two blouses for work. A yellow one and a blue one. They had, like, a white pinstripe. They were really pretty, she looked lush in them. Anya, she got some stuff out of Body Shop. Bath stuff. She'd live in the bath, give her half a chance. Then we went to the food court and had chips and Cokes. Then Anya gave me a lift home. 'Cause Nad decided she wanted to see this movie that me and Anya didn't fancy.'

There was always a moment in an interview when the witness said something whose significance wasn't obvious to them. The trick was not to show that it mattered. Paula had to struggle to keep her hand from gripping Ashley's hand tightly, as if she could squeeze information from her. 'What film was that?'

Ashley shrugged. 'Dunno, really. It was something French. Nad, she speaks French as well as English. It had subtitles, like, but I'd rather watch the telly or go down the pub. If I wanted to read all night, I'd buy, like, a magazine.'

'So Nadia was planning to go to the cinema alone?'

'Yeah. She did that sometimes. She was into films, way more than me and Anya.'

It made sense. Paula remembered a couple of French films in the stack of DVDs in Nadia's flat. 'And she was happy to go by herself?'

'Yeah, why not?'

'And you're sure she hadn't made plans to meet anyone there?'

Ashley shook her head. 'It was a spur of the moment thing. We went and had a look at what was on, to see if there was something we all fancied. And when Nad spotted that French film she was made up.' Her face crumpled. 'That might have been the last thing she ever did before he got her, right?' Tears dribbled down her cheeks again.

'We don't know, Ashley. Now, here's how you can help us even more. I want you to cast your mind back to that Saturday. Were you aware of anyone following you? Was there anybody you kept catching sight of?'

Ashley frowned, concentrating on recall. 'Nothing springs to mind. We were just out having a laugh and a shop, we weren't paying attention to anybody else.'

'And you didn't get into a ruck with anybody? Nobody hit on you?'

She shook her head. 'Nothing like that. Like I said, we weren't interested in anybody else.'

'You didn't see any guys you fancied, then?'

Ashley gave her a shrewd look. 'Not that we did anything about. We were looking, like. When we were sitting down eating, we were checking out the talent. But not in any serious way. Just, like, "he's hench", or, like, "he's got a nice bum". We never spoke to any of them and they never spoke to us. It was totally, like, normal.'

'What about boyfriends? Was Nadia seeing anybody?'

Ashley looked down at the table. 'Not any more.'

Paula caught Fielding's eye. They were both like pointers who had caught a whiff of prey. 'She'd been seeing someone?'

'Yeah, but it's been over and done for months.' She looked up and cottoned on to Paula's interest. 'It's not what you're thinking. She was going out with this Polish bloke, Pawel. She started seeing him soon after she moved over here. When it was all done and dusted, she said she thought she'd fallen for him because she was feeling homesick and he made her feel safe. She was going out with him when I first met her. He was a nice bloke, he was working as a hotel receptionist. Anyway, one night they were out in Leeds and they ran into this other Polish woman who totally freaked out. She called Nad a slapper. Well, she said it in Polish, but that was the gist of it. She said Pawel had a wife and two kids in Gdansk and Nad was a dirty whore. All at top volume in the middle of a bar. Well, Pawel tried to make out it was a case of mistaken identity, but the woman wasn't having it.

She whipped out her phone and took a photo of the two of them and said if he didn't get his sleazy arse home to Gdansk, she would send it to his wife so she'd know what a bastard she'd married. And that was that, pretty much.'

'She dumped him?'

Ashley shrugged. 'One of those things where you're not sure who got the shaft in first. She dumped him or he dumped her on his way to the airport. He went back to Poland and she said she was taking a break from men.'

'And did she? Take a break?'

Ashley looked mildly shifty. 'Pretty much. She had a one-night stand with one of the doctors at Bradfield Moor after a Christmas party, but they were both off their chops. No hard feelings the next morning, but neither of them was interested in taking it further.'

'There's a set of keys on Nadia's keyring that don't fit her flat. Do you know whose keys they are, Ashley?'

She nodded, her face bleak. 'They're Anya's house keys. She's, like, totally dozy, always locking herself out. So she gave a set to Nad because Nad's dead organised and that way Anya wouldn't be screwed the next time she left her keys sitting on the breakfast bar.'

It made sense. Paula pulled the photo of the three women towards her. 'Looks like you three like to party. Did you ever get anybody bothering you? Taking an unhealthy interest in Nad?'

Ashley chewed the skin at the edge of her pinkie nail. 'We like a night out,' she said eventually. 'We have a few drinks, but we're not like some of those mad bitches that get so off their faces they don't know their own names by the end of the night. We're not silly little girls, Detective. We have a laugh but we don't take stupid risks. That's why I can't believe Nad's gone.'

'What about drugs? Did Nad ever do drugs?'

Ashley sighed and rolled her eyes. 'Everybody over thirty thinks our generation's permanently off our tits. Look, I did E when I was a teenager. A few times, when I was out club-bing. I did coke half a dozen times when I was twenty. But I don't do that shit now. I've got a good job, my own flat, my own car. I'm not going to flush all that down the toilet. And Nad was the same. She came over here to make enough money to go back to Poland and have a good life. She wasn't going to risk all that for one daft night. No way.' She gave a twisted little smile. 'We're the good girls, Detective.' Then the bravado crumbled and tears spilled again. 'Shit like this, it's not supposed to happen to girls like us.'

Except that this time it had.

26

Fielding was already on the phone as the door of the
health centre swung shut behind them. She talked as she
walked, moving surprisingly fast for such a small woman.
Paula almost had to break into a trot to keep up.

'Get a car round here now,' Fielding said briskly, heading
for the car. 'Yes, Harriestown Road Health Centre. Pick up
Ashley Marr and take her to the Trafford Centre. She can
identify where Nadia parked her car on arrival that
Saturday ... Yes, that's right, three weeks ago. Nadia said she
was going to watch some French film at the multiscreen that
same evening. I need another team down there, finding out
when the film ended and checking out the CCTV for routes
from the multiscreen to where the car was parked ... I
appreciate that ... Pull them off the diary contacts, this is the
strongest lead right now.'

Fielding ended the call as she got into the passenger seat.
'What's Ashley not telling us?'

Paula eased into a space in the steady flow of traffic. 'You
think she's holding on to something?'

Fielding popped a piece of nicotine gum into her mouth. 'There's always more. They don't always know it, but there's always more.' She rubbed one eye with a knuckle and stifled a yawn, skin stretching taut over her fine bones. Paula realised she wasn't the only one who'd been up late the night before. 'Another thing,' Fielding added. 'Why is he going to all this trouble to cover up the fact that he's taken her? All the texts and the emails?'

'I wondered that too. The only thing I could think of was that most private security cameras recycle their recordings, whether it's tape or digital. They only keep them for a certain length of time. Maybe he was worried about the CCTV at the Trafford Centre and reckoned a month of blue water between the abduction and the alert would keep him in the clear.'

Fielding brightened up for a moment, her brown eyes alert and shining. Then she scowled. 'So why kill her after three weeks if you've bought yourself some extra time?'

'I don't know,' Paula admitted. 'Maybe he didn't mean to kill her when he did. Maybe she did something to make him lose his temper. And then once she was dead, he just wanted rid.'

Fielding gave a little snort of cynical laughter. 'Aye, right enough. You wouldn't want a corpse lying around making the place look untidy.'

'They are a nuisance,' Paula said. 'It's always easier to deal with them sooner rather than later, before they start decomposing and leaking all over your car boot.'

'Yeuch. But you're right, McIntyre.'

'Thank you. Todmorden, then? Anya Burba?'

'Sure.' There was a moment's silence, then Fielding said, 'I had respect for Carol Jordan. I imagine you learned a lot, working for her.'

It was a statement, not a question. In Paula's head, she'd worked *with* Carol Jordan, not *for* her. Not that there had

157

been any doubt who was in charge. It was more that Carol had always acknowledged the different skills in her squad and had made sure they all understood that MIT was greater than the sum of its parts only when they played as a team. A team of mavericks, admittedly, but a group of people who saw the personal advantage of being part of a successful unit. Paula didn't sense that same collegial spirit in Fielding. She was very clearly the boss and apparently everything went through her. Paula knew which style she preferred. But her preference was irrelevant. She had to work with what she had. Not to mention that Fielding's methods also seemed to get results. 'We all came out of MIT better cops than when we went in,' she said, trying not to make it sound like a challenge.

'I'm glad to hear it. You're my bagman from choice, not necessity. But on this firm, we don't go off on our own, McIntyre. We do things through the proper channels. We clear on that?'

Paula kept her eyes on the traffic and her face expressionless. 'Yes, ma'am.'

'Is that what you called Jordan? "Ma'am"?' It wasn't quite a straight question.

Paula wasn't comfortable with where this was going, but she wasn't willing to start lying over something so apparently trivial. 'No. I called her "chief". She wasn't very keen on "ma'am".'

'No more am I. Ma'am's what you call the queen. It's fine in formal situations, fine from the grunts in uniform to remind them who's in charge. But it makes me feel a bit of a twat coming from my own officers. My lads call me "boss", but "chief" would be fine.'

So, it was a power play. *Call me 'chief' or I'll assume you rate me lower than Carol Jordan.* Paula had never had a conversation like this with a senior officer before. Was that because men just assumed they'd be treated appropriately according to their rank but women had to fight for that right? Whatever. She'd try to avoid calling Fielding anything. If she had no choice, she'd go with boss. If it was good enough for the lads, it was good enough for her. She was saved from answering by the beeping of Fielding's phone.

'Text from the pathologist,' she said, bringing it up on her screen.

'What's Grisha got to say?'

'He's finished the post-mortem. I need to call him.' She plugged her phone into the car jack so she could make the call on speaker and keyed in the number.

'Shatalov speaking,' came from the tinny speakers.

'DCI Fielding. I got your message. What have you got for me?'

'I completed the post-mortem on Nadzieja Wilkowa. Cause of death was internal bleeding from multiple blunt trauma injuries.'

'Not the head injury?'

'The blow to the head was probably sustained first, given the bleeding around the site, but it's doubtful whether that would have been enough to kill her on its own. I'd say she was beaten with a tapering cylindrical object such as a baseball bat. And she was kicked repeatedly. So much so that the skin was torn and bleeding. That's not all. There was a considerable amount of old bruising at various sites all over her body, consistent with regular assaults over a period of up to two weeks.'

'Not longer than that?'

'Bruises generally fade completely after two weeks. So any predating that will have disappeared.'

There wasn't much to say to that, Paula thought. But Fielding found something. 'On the scale of beatings you've seen, where would this figure? Top five? Top ten?'

A moment's silence then, his voice flat, Grisha said, 'I have only ever seen one body more severely beaten than this. And that was the victim of a biker-gang punishment beating.'

'Thank you. What about sexual assault? I mean, before the superglue, obviously.'

'I treated the superglue with solvent so I could examine the genital area. I would say she had recently had violent sexual intercourse, vaginally and anally. There are internal tears that would suggest a pretty brutal rape scenario. Again, there's old bruising in the genital area, and some internal tearing that is partially healed.' He let out a heavy sigh. In all the years she'd known him Paula had never known Grisha to be blasé. Being confronted with the terrible things humans did to each other still caused him distress. 'No semen. Either he used condoms or a foreign object.'

'A foreign object?' Fielding's question was clinical.

'A dildo. Maybe even the baseball bat he used on her head. It's impossible to say.'

'Then theoretically it could be a woman?'

Grisha gave a hollow laugh. 'Theoretically it could be a woman, yes. She'd have to be pretty strong, to move your victim around. But yes, it could be a woman.' Silence, while they all thought about that one. 'One other thing,' Grisha said. 'It was hard to pick up at first because of the bruising and the damage to the skin. But I found three instances of two puncture wounds close together. One on her right shoulder, one on her left thigh and one on her stomach, by the navel. The one on her shoulder was almost totally healed. All that's left are the purple-pink marks of scar tissue.'

'Knife wounds?'

'No. Much smaller and shallower. There are some tears to the skin in four of the cases. I can't be sure but I think they might be damage inflicted by taser probes.'

'You think he's tasered her?' Fielding sounded intrigued.

'I can't be certain, I don't have much experience in this area. I'll need to do some research. But yes, that would be my cautious opinion at this point.'

'That would explain how he acquired her without any report of a struggle somewhere public ... ' Fielding's voice tailed off as she thought through what she'd just heard.

Paula took her chance. 'Hi, Grisha. It's Paula here.'

'Hi, Sergeant Paula. How're you enjoying your promotion?'

'I can't remember when I last had this much fun without laughing. Grisha, what have we got on time of death?' Fielding gave her a dirty look, as if she'd been caught speaking out of turn.

'I'd say between nine in the evening and four in the morning. Can't do better than that, sorry. Stomach contents are no help because there are none. The small intestine's also empty, so it looks like it was at least twelve hours between her last meal and the time of death.'

'No question that he kept her before he killed her, then?'

'Looks that way. And that he beat her regularly while he had her.'

'That fits with our thinking,' Fielding snapped. 'Thank you, Doctor. I appreciate your help. When will we have your full report?'

'My secretary will email it to you as soon as she's finished the transcript. Good luck with your investigation. This is a bad one, Inspector.' And he closed the connection.

'Nothing there we couldn't have predicted,' Fielding said, her tone suggesting that Grisha had failed them.

'Apart from the possible taser wounds.'

'Well, he had to have some way of subduing her and that's one of the more straightforward methods.' Fielding wasn't giving any ground.

'Three separate times, though. And only one of them in a place where the taser would get you from behind. That's interesting. And what Grisha said? It does support our theory that she never went to Poland.'

Fielding grunted and started typing texts into her phone. There was none of the batting around of ideas and possibilities that Paula had grown used to in the MIT. All of her colleagues had thrived on speculation, trying out theories and testing them against the evidence. Whatever was going on in Fielding's head, she was keeping it to herself.

Anya Burba was stashed behind the closed door of the head teacher's office. Her sharp features were swollen with tears, her make-up streaked and ugly. 'Ashley texted me,' she said as soon as the head left them alone with her. 'I couldn't believe what she says. How can Nadia be dead? How is this possible? You must have made a mistake.'

'Sorry, Anya. There's no mistake. I'm very sorry for your loss.' Fielding's sympathy was underscored with briskness. 'We need your help so we can find the person who did this.'

They sat at a round table in a corner of the office. It was strewn with children's artwork. Anya cleared it impatiently to one side with a sweep of her arm. 'Stupid art competition,' she said, her voice shaky. 'How did she die?'

'We can't go into details, I'm afraid,' Fielding said.

'Was it quick? Tell me she didn't suffer.'

Paula reached out and touched her shoulder. 'There's a lot we don't know, Anya. But Nadia was your friend and we need you to share what you know about her so we can stop this happening to somebody else.'

She shivered and wrapped her thin arms round her body, pushing her small breasts upwards. 'Please God, not that.'

And so Paula worked her way through the final Saturday

again. Anya confirmed what Ashley had told them, and had
nothing to add. But when she turned to the subject of
Nadia's ex-boyfriend, Anya turned slightly in her seat, away
from Paula, and abruptly became noncommittal.

Whatever was making her uncomfortable, Paula was
determined to get to the heart of it. 'There's something
more, isn't there, Anya? Something you don't want to tell
us?' Her voice was gentle. 'Nothing you say can hurt Nadia
now, Anya. But I think she'd want you to tell us anything
that could help bring her killer to justice.'

Anya shook her head. 'It's nothing. It's not connected to
her death. It's just . . . nothing.'

'Anya, I'm trained to make connections that nobody else
can see. But if you don't give me something to work with, I
can't make anything. Please, tell me what you know.'

Anya blew her nose noisily. 'Pawel – he has no wife and
children.'

If she'd been intent on stopping them in their tracks,
she'd succeeded. Even Paula, the consummate interviewer,
faltered. 'What? What do you mean, no wife and children?'

Anya looked embarrassed. 'The row, in the nightclub? The
woman? I was at the bar, getting drinks. I was on my way
back when it happened, the woman shouting and accusing
Pawel and taking their photo. I think if I had been with
them, it wouldn't have happened. Well, it wouldn't have
happened then.'

This was making no sense. 'I don't understand,' Paula
said.

'I know this woman. Maria is her name, I don't know her
family name. She isn't even from Gdansk. She worked in a
bar in Lvov, where I used to live. I couldn't figure out what
was going on. I didn't say anything at the time, because I
wanted to get the truth. So next evening, I went to the
coffee shop where she works now. It's out at the university,

we never go there normally. And I told her, I know you're lying about Pawel. Tell me what's going on or I bring Anya here and make you tell her.' She fiddled endlessly with the cheap silver rings on her fingers.

'And what was it she told you?'

Anya looked haunted and hunted. 'I want to go outside, I need to smoke.' She jumped to her feet and headed for the door. The detectives followed her as she ran down the hallway and out the front door. They rounded the corner of the building and saw her slip behind a steel container. By the time they caught up, she had a cigarette at her lips, her fingers shaking uncontrollably. Paula took her lighter from her pocket and held the flame to Anya's cigarette, taking the opportunity to have one of her own in spite of Fielding's frown. 'What was it, Anya?'

'She knows Pawel. She used to be a waitress at the hotel where he works. He paid her money to make a scene in the club so he could break up with Nadia.'

Paula was completely baffled now. Fifty ways to leave your lover, and still people were coming up with new ones. 'I don't get it. Why couldn't he just tell her it was over?'

'He has a new job in Cornwall. A promotion. He thought if he told her, she'd want to come with him. And he didn't want to be tied to her. So he thought the best way was to make her hate him.' She exhaled a stream of smoke and gave a twisted smile. 'Worked perfectly. And poor Nadia had no idea.'

'You didn't tell her?'

Anya gave her an incredulous look. 'Why would I tell her? I love Nadia. She already knew he was shit. She didn't need to know precisely what kind of shit. It would only have made her feel bad about herself, like she was some piece-of-crap person he couldn't wait to get rid of. No, I didn't tell her. I didn't tell anybody. Not even Ashley.' Her chin came up, defiant and defensive. 'So you see? Is nothing to do with somebody killing her. Pawel, he is in Cornwall, being the big shot assistant manager. He didn't have to kill her to get rid of her, just pay someone to tell his lies for him.'

She had a point, Paula thought. 'And you're sure Nadia had no suspicions?'

Anya shook her head. 'She trusts people, Nadia. She always thinks the best of people. I think that's why she is good at her job. She treats people like she expects the good from them, and that makes us better, I think.'

There was nothing wrong with Anya's psychology, Paula thought. Carol Jordan worked in a similar way. Expect extraordinary things from your people and they'll go flat out to give you what you hope for. Paula was beginning to think she'd have liked Nadia Wilkowa. 'Ashley told us that Nadia carried a set of your keys. Is that right?'

She nodded. 'Always. On her own keyring so they were always with her.' She kicked at the ground with the pointed toe of her shoe. 'I am hopeless. Always forgetting my keys and locking myself out like an idiot.' Her face crumpled again. 'Now who will I trust to take care of me?'

They talked to Anya for as long as it took her to smoke another two cigarettes, but by then she was shivering with cold and even Paula thought there was nothing more to be had from her. They said goodbye in the car park, Paula double-checking she had the correct details for the woman Pawel had paid to lie for him.

'We'll have to check out this Maria,' Fielding said. 'We've only got Anya's version of events.'

'Even so, it's hard to think of any twist on the circumstances that gives Pawel or Maria a motive. Or would provoke the kind of fury that drove this killer. If anybody's got a possible motive in this scenario, it's Nadia.'

'But as we know, McIntyre, motive is the least important

piece of the jigsaw. Give me means and opportunity and the complete absence of a decent alibi and I don't give a toss about motive.'

'Juries like motive,' Paula said. 'People want to know why.'

'As my mother always used to say to me, want doesn't get. Facts, McIntyre. Facts.'

'I take it you're not an advocate of psychological profiling, then?'

Fielding frowned. 'There's no budget for anything you can't reach out and touch any more. What I believe is neither here nor there. Solid evidence, that's what we need to focus on. So we'll get someone to talk to this Maria and we'll get Devon and Cornwall to pay a visit to Pawel the Shit to see what he's been up to lately. Because, frankly, we've got bugger all else happening for us. Drop me at Skenfrith Street, then swing by the lab and see what the CSIs have got for us. Seeing a human face sometimes acts like a kick up the arse.' She sighed. 'Remember the good old days when we were in charge? When we wanted a quick turnaround, all we had to do was tell them to get their fingers out? Now, they're their own bosses, they claim to rank equal to detective constables in the pecking order and if you want them to move faster than techtonic plates, it costs you about as much as a small family car. Bastards.'

It was hard to disagree. Privatising the Forensic Science Service had turned lead investigators into accountants, sitting down with a calculator to work out which tests their budget could run to. Juries weaned on *CSI* knew all about forensics, and when the prosecution didn't reel out all those juicy test results, they assumed it was because the tests didn't support the case. Not that the tests had never been done because there wasn't enough money in the kitty and the tests they *had* done should have been enough to satisfy those sitting in judgement. When you weighed that in the balance, it was hard to argue that Tony Hill was a luxury they should afford.

'I'll see what I can chase up,' Paula said.

'Good. Because I'm not holding out too much hope for the CCTV footage after all this time. This guy's smart. We need to be smarter, McIntyre. We need to be smarter.'

27

It had been a bloody awful day. Paradoxically, Carol found that easier to endure than the other kind. It was what she felt she deserved. But so far this one had been particularly grim. After her abortive visit to Chris the night before, she'd driven home and blitzed the vodka bottle. She'd woken in the small hours with a raging thirst and a banging head. The pint of water she'd glugged down came straight up, along with the paracetamol she'd swallowed. She tried again, this time sipping the water, and managed to keep the painkillers down.

She'd gone back to bed, tossing and turning, sweating and cursing. Eventually accepting there would be no more sleep, she dressed in her work clothes, added a padded jacket and went outside, hoping the chill would make her feel better. A smudge of paler sky in the east took enough of an edge off the darkness for her to walk by and she set off up the field behind the barn to the skyline trees on the hill-top.

It was hard going, tufts of grass and uneven footing threatening to trip her every other step. But Carol struggled on, chest heaving, making herself suffer all the way to the top of the hill. Instead of being rewarded with a sunrise, all that dawn brought was a chilly rain and a lightening of the grey sky. By the time she got down the hill, her hair was plastered to her head and her cheeks were numb with the cold and wet.

She brewed coffee, but it only made her stomach burn and her heart race. Work was no help either. The day's tasks were dull and repetitive, offering nothing to distract her from revisiting her disastrous encounter with Sinead. A slip of a chisel gouged a slice in the ball of her thumb, which bled madly till she packed it with medicated lint and slapped a dressing on it. After that, it just hurt like a bastard. Somehow, she dragged herself through the morning without resorting to the vodka bottle, but it was never far from her mind.

At last, she finished clearing the first section of the gallery flooring and its underpinnings. She'd created a substantial pile of timber to haul outside and add to the heap she was stacking ready for the next bonfire. She was halfway to the door with the first armful when the unexpected thump of a knock made her drop the lot with a loud clatter.

Swearing under her breath, Carol hauled the door open. George Nicholas stood on the threshold, a sheepish smile on his face. 'I seem to have the knack of arriving at the wrong moment,' he said, looking past her at the scatter of timber on the floor.

'There aren't many right moments,' Carol muttered. She was annoyed at his presence. It made her aware of her vodka breath, her unwashed hair, the stale alcohol reek of her sweat. She was aware and ashamed of her disintegration. But not enough to do something about it, she thought defiantly.

'Might I come in?' He gave a plaintive glance upwards at the heavy drizzle that was still falling. She opened the door wider and stepped aside, waving her arm in a gesture of invitation. 'And the dog?' He pointed to the black-and-white collie at his heels.

'Hello, Jess,' Carol said. 'Always happy to see you.'

Nicholas stepped inside. He snapped his fingers and the dog followed, then lay down, head between its paws, eyes on Carol. 'Actually, this isn't Jess.'

'That shows you what I know about dogs.' Carol closed the door on the weather.

'An easy enough mistake. This is Flash. Jess is her mother.' George took off his tweed cap and shook the rain from it. 'I don't suppose there's any chance of a hot drink?'

Carol felt her smile had been forced from her. 'You're a brave man, Mr Nicholas. Not many people who know me would be so bold.'

'Not brave. Cold. And please, it's George.' Confident, but not arrogant.

'Tea or coffee? The coffee is good, the tea is basic.'

'In that case, I'll take the coffee.'

Carol headed for her living quarters to brew up. She'd barely got the kettle on when she heard the clank and clatter of wood striking wood. She stuck her head round the door to see Nicholas shifting the splay of fallen wood into a neat pile by the door. 'You don't have to earn your coffee,' she said.

He gave her an amused glance. 'I'm here to ask a favour. I need all the capital I can get.'

Her heart sank. She didn't want to do anyone a favour. She didn't want him to owe her anything in return. Besides, she couldn't imagine any favour she'd be inclined to grant George Nicholas.

By the time the coffee was brewed and poured into a pair

of mugs, most of the wood had been stacked by the door. 'Thanks,' she said ungraciously.

'You're very welcome.' He looked around, as if expecting a chair to have materialised while his attention had been elsewhere. Failing that, he sat on the floor with a pleasing disregard for its lack of cleanliness. Carol leaned against the wall. The dog stayed put, her eyes shifting from one to the other.

'So what's this favour, then?' She pushed her sweaty hair from her face with the back of a dirty, bloodstained hand.

Nicholas pointed to the dog. 'I kept a couple of Jess's pups from her last litter. We've expanded our holding of sheep and we need more working dogs. Jess is a terrific sheepdog, but she can't be everywhere. The idea was that we'd train up the pups so they would fill the gap.'

Carol took a cautious sip. This time, it tasted good. Finally she had the hangover on the run. 'Makes sense. I don't see where I come in, though. You may not have noticed, but I don't actually have a flock of sheep out there.'

'That's entirely the point.' Nicholas looked pained. 'This is an embarrassing thing to have to confess, but Flash is afraid of sheep.'

Carol snorted with laughter. 'You're making that up.'

'No, honestly. As soon as they bleat, she runs away. If it wasn't so pitiful, it would be funny. I'd heard this sometimes happens, but I never believed it either.'

'A sheepdog that's afraid of sheep? That's hysterical.'

Nicholas looked at the dog, shaking his head and smiling sadly. 'But once you get past funny, it's bad news for the dog. The options for a working dog who can't work are pretty limited. Keeping her as a pet alongside a working mother and brother is a bad idea, or so my shepherd says.' His face grew serious, his eyes downcast. 'And so it comes down to rehoming her or having her put down.'

171

'And you thought of me?' Carol made no attempt to keep the incredulity from her voice. 'I've never had a dog. I'm a cat person. The only reason my cat isn't here is that he's too old to adapt to this life.'

'It's never too late to become a dog lover,' Nicholas said. 'Come, Flash.' The dog got to her feet then settled beside him, head on his thighs. He buried his fingers in her fur, massaging the base of her skull. 'She's a lovely dog. Ten months old, fully house-trained. She does come, heel, sit, down and stay. And, as you saw, you snap your fingers and she comes to you and lies down. She's a perfect dog for a beginner. If she was a pure-bred collie, I wouldn't dream of offering her to you. Far too skittish, demanding and neurotic.' He gave a rueful smile. 'We thought we were breeding from another collie, but Jess must have sneaked out when we weren't looking. What we've ended up with is a collie crossed with a black Labrador. And that's a much more biddable option. Intelligent but soft as butter.'

'I don't want a dog.'

He grinned, taking years off. 'You just don't know you want a dog,' he said. 'They're great company. And better than a burglar alarm. Nobody burgles a house where there's a dog barking inside.' The unspoken history of what had happened here underpinned what he said. He had more sense than to refer to it directly.

'Won't she need a lot of exercise?'

'I can't deny that,' he said, scratching the dog's head. 'But so do we. Problem is, we don't take it. Here's the thing, though, Carol. Collies love to run. And you've got miles of moorland on your doorstep here. You can let this dog run in absolute security because you know for sure the one thing she's not going to be doing is worrying sheep.' He smiled up at her. 'Why don't you give her a try? Give it a week. See how you both take to each other? No obligation. If it doesn't work out, I'll take her back without a word of recrimination.'

'Back to be put down?'

Nicholas rubbed the dog's flank. 'Hopefully, it won't come to that. Look, Carol, I'm absolutely not going to guilt-trip you into taking a dog you don't want. That would be even more unfair to Flash than having her humanely put to sleep.'

'I don't know anything about dogs. What they eat, what they need.' She heard the whiny weakness in her response and despised herself for it. 'I'm not the person you're looking for.'

'They don't need much. I've brought her bed down in the Land Rover, along with a bag of dog food and a leash. She can sleep in there with you—' He waved towards the closed door. 'Or out here. Though she does prefer company. Human, if canine isn't available. Feed her twice a day, three-quarters of a bowl. You can add table scraps to her bowl if you want to, but don't feed her from your hand or you'll make a beggar of her. She needs at least one good run a day, preferably two. How hard is that to accommodate?'

'I won't be doing this restoration for ever.' It was a rear-guard action, and she knew it.

'You'll be doing it for a good while yet. Look, you can cross that bridge when you come to it. But I think a dog in your life would be nothing but positive right now.'

'How do I know she'll do what I tell her?'

'Try it. Call her. You might as well, Carol. What have you got to lose?'

28

M arie Mather was pleased with how the new job was going. She'd split the team into groups of half a dozen and she was working her way through short but intense briefing sessions, group by group. She encouraged frankness in the people who worked for her. That meant the first step was making them feel secure in their dealings with her. They had to believe there was common ground they all occupied, and a common enemy in their business rivals. Once they'd reached that point, they could be manipulated into all sorts of work practices and agreements. Having everyone facing in the same direction – that was how to make progress.

Rob had sat in on the first two group sessions. He claimed he wanted to see how she worked so he could make sure his tactics fitted in with her overall strategies. Marie suspected it was more to do with him wanting to stare at her legs, given that his eyes never left them and he didn't take a single note. It didn't matter; whether she won him over with the shapeliness of her calves or the competent way she wrangled her staff, he would be firmly on her side in no time at all.

So far, the staff seemed eager to impress her. That was the joy of an economy in the doldrums. Anyone who was in work was desperate to stay that way. Even people whose natural inclination was to be cross-grained whatever the situation generally knew enough to turn on a smiley face when it came to impressing the new boss. They all wanted to make sure that if the new broom was going to sweep clean they wouldn't be the ones in the dustpan.

Of course, there were always the exceptions. Gareth, for example, had made no contribution in his group session. He'd sat with folded arms, head cocked to one side, an expression of bored superiority on his face. She had tried to get him to tell the group what he had hinted at when they'd spoken the day before, but he'd only grunted and said, 'Best if I run it past you first. No point in getting this lot excited about something that isn't going to happen, is there?'

Maria had looked at Gareth's performance indicators and understood that he was one of their most productive workers. It was clear he knew that too. But she wasn't prepared to let him trade on it, to take his quarterly bonus as a given. If she didn't turn the screws a little to show him who was boss, he could easily become a thorn in her flesh, stirring up unease at the way she was going about things. So she'd smiled sweetly and said, 'I always think the more the merrier when it comes to thrashing out new ideas. We'll be having short group meetings every fortnight from now on. Gareth, I'd like you to write a proposal for the next meeting that outlines your ideas and the reasoning behind them. I'm sure we can find better ways to achieve our goals, and nobody understands that better than you. I'm counting on all of you to come up with constructive suggestions.

Gareth, I'm delighted you're going to lead the way on this one.'

He'd scowled at her, clearly baffled at being outflanked. But he'd said no more. And he hadn't had the chance to foment dissent round the water cooler because, like Rob and half a dozen others, he was using his accumulated time owing to take the afternoon off. Bradfield Victoria were due to play Newcastle United in the FA Cup, and their loyal fans were leaving work early to travel up to the North East for the game.

When lunchtime rolled around, Marie followed the football fans out. She wanted half an hour outside the office, looking at faces that weren't her responsibility, stimulating her mind with images of beauty rather than office cubicles. The city art gallery was a brisk three-minute walk from the office, and she particularly liked their collection of Scottish Colourists on the second floor. Twenty minutes of staring at the paintings of J. D. Fergusson and William McTaggart and she would be refreshed and renewed, ready to face the next bunch of employees who needed to be energised and inspired.

Marie sat on a leather-covered bench in front of a large canvas showing the impressionistic figures of two small children in white smocks kneeling among sea grass and pinks, behind them the tousled blues and whites of the sea, above them a sky filled with plump cumulus clouds. She took from her bag the carrot and home-made piccalilli salad she'd made that morning and munched her way through it, eyes fixed on the painting, drinking in the complicated build-up of brushstrokes that came together to create certainty in the mind of the spectator. She'd loved these paintings ever since she'd first encountered them in a small Scottish town where she'd been seconded to a branch of her previous employer. She'd escaped to the art gallery during the lunch hour and she'd been astounded by the effect they had on her. She'd hardly been able to credit that there was a whole collection of them in the very city where she lived. 'We're philistines,' she'd said to Marco, insisting he visit the gallery with her. 'Imagine not knowing this was right here on our doorstep.'

She knew that Marco didn't share her enthusiasm for the paintings. But he liked to come with her, to share her excitement. And somehow, it gave her a sense of security to know he was sitting on one of the benches, playing Angry Birds on his phone while she moved among the paintings.

But it wasn't Marco who was watching her that day. Marie ate her lunch, oblivious to the fact that she was being studied. On a similar bench in the next gallery, a man was apparently enjoying a pair of L. S. Lowry seascapes, a surprising contrast to the artist's usual subject of working-class life. However, the target of his attention was quite different. He was intent on Marie, fixated on every move she made. She was a neat eater, he thought. You wouldn't want just anyone eating their lunch in the midst of expensive artworks. But Marie was someone who could be trusted not to splash or drip or even leave a trail of crumbs behind her. He liked that about her. A woman who took care about how she ate in public would probably be fastidious in other ways. Not one of those sluts who couldn't look after a man properly.

The world seemed to be full of women who were rubbish at being a woman. It took a man like him to see clearly that something needed to be done about that. The trouble was his foolish optimism. Three times now he'd been mistaken. He'd had such high hopes of the latest one, but it was already obvious she wasn't capable of meeting his criteria. He'd been willing to deal with the consequences of his mistakes, but deep down, all he really wanted was a woman who would fulfil his dreams of womanhood. It wasn't as if he asked too much. The failure was theirs. Every time. And it was his right to set things straight. He was doing the world a favour by weeding out the ones who would never be fit for purpose.

He looked across at Marie and smiled. This time, he'd chosen well. She was smart, well turned-out and she knew how to behave in public. If she showed the same ability in private, he'd be very happy.

Otherwise, he'd keep on searching. It wasn't like it was a hardship.

29

The last time she'd been out to the Kenton Vale industrial estate, Paula was pretty sure the building that housed the private forensic lab had been a CD-pressing plant for the indie music business. But the world moved on. People downloaded music directly to their devices and criminal investigation was outsourced.

Gaining access would probably have been easier when it had been churning out CDs. In order to get inside, Paula had to display her ID to a camera, wait while it was checked against who knew what database, then press her right index finger against a small glass screen. By the time she had crossed the foyer to the reception desk, a laminated ID was waiting with her photo, her fingerprint and a QR code.

'Nice to see you again,' the woman behind the counter said with a friendly smile. 'I see you've been promoted. Congratulations.'

Given that the company had occupied completely different premises and that her last visit had been months ago, the welcome made Paula deeply uncomfortable. It tripped over the border of what she considered normal behaviour and landed somewhere in the intersection of *1984* and *Blade Runner*. It occurred to Paula that even her choice of references dated her. There was no longer any possibility of her passing for young or cool. Not that she'd be mourning that any time soon.

She managed an uneasy smile and said, 'I'm here to see Dr Myers.'

'He's expecting you.' She gestured to a door behind her with a waist-high pillar beside it. 'Hold your visitor ID against the glass panel and the door will open for you. There's a cubicle on the right where you can suit up. Don't forget the shoe covers. Dr Myers' lab is the second on the left. But don't worry if you forget.' She pointed to the ID. 'That's the only door your ID will open.'

Paula found Dr Dave Myers in a white suit and gloves, filling tiny test tubes from a large syringe, his big brown hands moving with surprising delicacy. He glanced up when she walked in and nodded. 'Gimme a minute, Paula, while I get this lot started.' He finished what he was doing and slotted the tray of samples into a tall fridge. While she waited, Paula looked round the lab. She realised she had no idea what most of the equipment was for these days, nor which reagents and stabilisers did what. It was a relief to spot a microscope in the middle of a bench. It felt like Neanderthal technology alongside the other analytical tools.

Amidst the lab equipment were bagged and labelled evidence bags sitting in plastic boxes to avoid any possibility of cross-contamination. Paula recognised Nadia Wilkowa's clothes from the crime scene; she was pleased to see they'd made it that far up Dave Myers' priority list.

He closed the fridge and gestured to a lab stool. Paula sat down and he perched next to her, pulling his protective mask down. 'New facial hair,' she said, nodding towards a geometrically precise soul patch beneath his lower lip.

He pulled a face at her. 'Male pogonotrophy is often culturally associated with virility and strength.'

'But in your case, we'll make an exception.'

'You're not growing more charming with age, Paula,' he said, clutching at his heart in a mockery of pain.

They'd known each other for years. When Paula had first joined CID, Dave had worked in the police lab, analysing the assorted traces humans left behind them at crime scenes. DNA analysis was in its infancy; Dave and his colleagues were on the cusp of a series of biological breakthroughs that would transform what they could glean from criminal carelessness. It would spawn TV shows whose relationship to reality would be, as always when it came to anything to do with criminal investigation, tenuous at best. It would create unrealistic expectations in both prosecutors and the victims of crime. But it would also produce the kind of evidence that was impossible to argue against. It would take criminals off the streets and put them behind bars. Most importantly, it would promote a conviction among the population that justice was being better served.

All of which came at a price. And when budgets were squeezed to the point of strangulation, bean counters made ruthless decisions about which categories of crime merited forensic intervention. Within those categories, there were very clear guidelines governing how much a Senior Investigating Officer could spend. If those guidelines were exceeded – and Paula had been involved in MIT cases where they had been smashed to smithereens in the interests of saving lives and nailing killers – the money had to be found elsewhere. So now a key part of any serious criminal investigation was weighing up how little they could get away with in terms of forensic expenditure. It was hardly satisfactory, in Paula's opinion. But nobody in the budget team much cared what the troops on the front line thought.

So, for officers like Paula, who had learned her priorities from Carol Jordan, cultivating relationships with individual forensic scientists and crime-scene investigators had become as essential as developing what the acronym-obsessed hierarchy termed CHIS – Covert Human Intelligence Sources. What used to be called 'snouts'. A CSI who was your friend could be persuaded to go the extra mile for you, to cut bureaucratic corners in processing crime-scene material, even to suggest what might be fruitful lines of inquiry and evidence-gathering. When you actually liked them, it was a bonus.

And Paula liked Dave Myers. They'd discovered early on that they shared the same tastes in music and comedy. Dave, ever the scientist, used to prepare monthly spreadsheets of upcoming gigs and email them to Paula. They'd spend half a dozen evenings a month in scuzzy pubs and crummy music venues sampling whatever took their fancy, occasionally branching out into bigger auditoriums when their favourites hit the big time. They'd kept up the habit for years, until eventually Dave married Becky and became a dad. Then Paula had teamed up with Elinor. Now they met up as a foursome every couple of months at a comedy club or a more salubrious music venue than in the old days. Dave no longer did the spreadsheets, but he still had the knack of picking good nights out.

'King Creosote,' he said now, crossing his lanky legs and leaning one elbow on the upper knee.

'Definitely. Email me the date.'

'It's at the Methodist Central Hall, so you'll have to smuggle in your own drink.'

'Not a problem. OK, Nadia Wilkowa. Where are we up to?'

'Crime scene's a mess of prints so we haven't even bothered processing the DNA. It's a waste of your money at this point, unless any of the prints throw up a person of interest. Obviously, if you hit a brick wall down the line, we'll revisit that decision with your guv'nor. Based on past experience, DCI Fielding doesn't like spending unless she's pretty damn sure it's going to move the case forward.' He made an apologetic face. 'She's keen on clear-up but she likes to keep the top brass happy too.'

'No bad thing these days.' Paula pointed towards the evidence bags. 'What about the clothes? Have you had a chance to examine them? We're looking at an underlying sexual assault.' She shrugged. 'Might be something there?'

'Harley went through them and I had a quick eyeball earlier, but I'm not hopeful. You know yourself how it goes when the killer's abducted his victim. He's usually careful and he usually gets her stripped as soon as possible. It's not like a street assault, where you've got DNA all over everything.'

'All the same ... May I?' She nodded towards the bags.

'As long as you're gloved and masked,' Dave said. While Paula pulled a mask on, he brought over the bagged-up clothes, then turned back to his bench and started checking some bar charts on his computer.

Item by pathetic item, Paula went through the clothes. It looked as if Dave's assessment was correct. There was no obvious sign of disturbance or of unexpected staining. The last item out of its bag was a fitted dark navy jacket with a line of small buttons up the front. It was clearly not new, but Paula recognised the signs of someone who took care of her clothes. There were no obvious stains on the front of the jacket and the buttons were all firmly attached. The inside of the collar was worn but clean, the lining intact though sagging a little along the seams. Finally, she went to check the cuffs for stains. What she found startled her. 'Did you notice this, Dave?'

He looked up sharply, his brown eyes narrowing in a frown. 'Did I notice what?'

'There's a button missing on the left jacket cuff. Look, there's six on the right sleeve, but only five on the left.'

'I never counted,' he said, peering at the two sleeves where she'd laid them side by side on the bench. 'Harley did the preliminary pass, I only took a very quick look.' He took a magnifying glass from a drawer in the bench and studied the fabric. Then he turned the sleeve inside out and examined it. 'There's still some threads left, pulled through to the inside. That suggests a recent event, if she wore this jacket regularly.'

'She didn't have many clothes. Even if she rotated them regularly, she'll have worn this once or twice a week. So maybe this button came off when she was taken? Either in a struggle, or just the process of him getting her into his vehicle? What do you think?'

'It's possible.' As he spoke, Dave was reaching for a box of cotton swabs. 'And if there was a struggle . . . '

Paula finished the thought. 'Then maybe there's some blood.'

'Exactly.' He scanned the shelf above his work station and took down three bottles.

'What are you going to do?'

'A Kastle-Meyer test. To see if we've got any latent blood-stains. It's very accurate and you only need a trace for it to work.' He opened one bottle and dipped the swab in the liquid. 'Ethanol first. Pure alcohol, Paula. But not for the Methodist Central Hall. We use it to break down the cell walls and release the stain. Makes the test more sensitive.' He rubbed the swab over the threads on the inside sleeve and then took a second swab and applied it to the material on the outside.

The second bottle had a rubber bulb and dropper built into the cap. Dave added a globule of the contents to each swab. 'Phenolphthalein reagent,' he said. 'And finally, a single drop of what the laydeez use to bleach their moustaches. Hydrogen peroxide.'

'Don't be mean, you – holy shit, it's turned pink. That means blood, doesn't it?'

Dave nodded, a rueful smile on his face. 'It does. And how crap does that make me look, that it takes a plod to come into my lab and spot what my highly paid crew has missed?' Dave tried to sound as if he was taking it lightly, but Paula could tell he was genuinely pissed off.

'Like you said, Dave, you'd only given it a preliminary once-over. Someone would have picked it up down the line. All I've done is speed things up a bit.'

'Which DCI Fielding will be pleased about. We'll get on this straight away, Paula. You'll have a full sample and a database search tomorrow morning.'

'Thanks, Dave. Oh, and I meant to say, Grisha thinks the killer might have used a taser on her. Could you check for any bloodstains on her clothes on the right shoulder, the left thigh and the stomach in the navel area?'

He rolled his eyes. 'Now she tells me. I'll get somebody on it and see what we can come up with. Go on, get out of here before you end up busting the budget.'

Paula grinned. 'It'll be worth it when we catch the bastard.'

'Save it for Fielding,' Dave said. 'Times like these, I bet you miss Carol Jordan.'

Paula's good humour vanished, banished by his words. 'Every day. Every bloody day.'

The hours had passed in a blur of pain and discomfort. Sometimes Bev had drifted off into a kind of sleep, only to jerk into consciousness when the centre of hurt shifted and sent a new bolt of agony shooting through her nervous system. At one point, the pain in her head had been so intense it had morphed into nausea and she'd retched and coughed bile over her legs. Normally so fastidious, she had reached a stage beyond disgust and she didn't even try to shift away from the puddles of vomit.

When the light came back, it was just another source of distress, stabbing her eyes and making them water. The taser was almost a relief because it was so all-encompassing a sensation. She really didn't care when he grabbed her by the hair and dragged her out of her white coffin.

The shock of the freezing spray from the hosepipe smacked her back into consciousness as nothing else had done. All at once, Bev was herself again, her fight and determination reawakened by the sharp cold needles of water. She struggled on to hands and knees, squinting in a vain attempt to see past the deluge to the figure behind it. She screamed in rage, struggling to get to her feet.

He kicked her in the head so hard she felt her jaw separate from her skull, a tearing crack that made her recoil into a whimpering heap. Before she knew what was happening, he had rolled her in polythene sheeting, fastened it tight with packing tape and dumped her in the boot of her own car.

Hardly able to breathe, terrified and driven mad with pain, Bev McAndrew made her last journey. This time, when the light came back, she didn't even notice. And that was the closest she came to mercy.

30

The session with Jacob Gold had left Tony profoundly unsettled. He'd seen two patients at Bradfield Moor Secure Hospital that afternoon and he could barely remember any of the ground they'd covered. When his own mental state interfered with the quality of treatment he was delivering, it was clearly time to take seriously the uncomfortable conclusion he'd been irresistibly drawn towards.

After work he'd gone home to the narrowboat, determined for the first time to see it not as a poor fallback position but as a symbol of change and possibility. That he had adapted to living in a place and style he'd never previously contemplated was a positive thing, he told himself, summoning up an image of himself wagging a finger in his own face. And when he stopped to think about it, he had to admit how much he liked the compact nature of life on board. The only drawback was the lack of space for his books. But surely there had to be a way round that? Lateral thinking, that was what he needed. Maybe he could rent a nearby storage unit and use that as a book room, somehow? It wasn't as if he'd mind the walk. He gave a hollow chuckle. 'Chances are, I'd have worked out whatever it was I needed the book for by the time I got there,' he said aloud.

'It's not books you need right now,' he continued, opening the fridge and the storage cupboard next to it. 'It's food. What use is pasta sauce without pasta? Or milk without breakfast cereal? Or butter without bread?' Time for an emergency shopping trip. He grabbed one of the sturdy reusable carrier bags that Carol – *ouch, no, let her go, you can't get sentimental over a bloody carrier bag* – had made him buy when they'd ended up late-night grocery shopping in the middle of a case. There was a convenience store branch of a supermarket chain a couple of streets away; he'd be back inside half an hour.

But back to what? Unresolved thoughts chasing round his brain like a ball in a pinball arcade, empty chairs reminding him of his empty life, case notes for patients who frankly felt more stable than he did right now. He needed to fill the hours before sleep with something more constructive than brooding.

Tony put on his coat and set off into the evening, determined to walk Carol Jordan out of his system. What he needed was to occupy his mind with something else, something more challenging. He let his mind drift backwards, waiting for it to find a baited hook to snag on.

And there it was, as he rounded the corner of the tapas bar. Paula's missing woman. He fished his phone out and called her. As soon as she answered, he dived straight in. 'Paula, is your missing woman still missing?'

'And hello to you too, Tony. Yes, as far as I know. I haven't been directly involved today, but I would have heard if there had been any developments.'

'So the last anyone knows is that she was going to stop at Freshco on the way home? She left work as usual and nobody saw her after that?'

'I haven't heard anything to the contrary. Here's something else that might interest you. You know the murder I'm on? Nadia Wilkowa? We think he used a taser on her.'

'That narrows things down, doesn't it? I mean, it's not like spiking a drink in a crowded bar and waiting for it to kick in. It's up close and personal. And he's acquired her somewhere relatively private. You can't taser someone in front of an audience. Not unless you're a cop. Plus, you've got to have your getaway lined up, because a taser, that's not like knocking somebody out. Your victim gets their body back in pretty short order, isn't that right? So you've got to have a plan, it can't be a spur-of-the-moment thing.'

'Are you done?' Paula's tone was mild, amused.

'Just thinking aloud, sorry.'

'No, it's fascinating, listening to your mind work. If I hear anything more about Bev, I'll keep you posted. But I thought you weren't that interested?'

He turned up his collar against the chill wind that hit him as he emerged from the shelter of the buildings around the basin. 'I'm trying to take my mind for a walk.'

'OK. Have you got it on a leash?'

'Very funny. I don't suppose you know which Freshco she used?'

'Not for sure, but the logical route from the hospital to home would take her past the big Freshco on Kenton Vale Road. You know the one I mean?'

'On the right as you're coming from town? Before the roundabout?'

'That's the one. Why?'

'I need some groceries.' And, having nothing further to say, he ended the call. As he replaced his phone in his pocket, he wondered whether his tendency only to use the phone for what was absolutely necessary was a hangover from his youth, when landline phone calls were comparatively expensive. His grandmother, who had done most of the hands-on work of raising him, had regarded the phone as a means of parting fools and their money and only permitted its use in what she considered emergencies. He remembered she'd lived in terror of losing her low-user rebate. And then when mobile phones had first been introduced, they'd been prohibitively expensive to call and to make calls from, reinforcing his grandmother's message of frugality. It couldn't just be a generational thing, though; he knew plenty of his contemporaries who chatted away on the phone with casual disregard for what it might cost. No, it had to be one of his own personal quirks. A notion that was borne out by the reaction of most of his friends and colleagues to his own reticence during their phone conversations. Carol had always – No. He wasn't going to allow his memories of Carol to take up space in his mind.

Kenton Vale Road was about two miles away. There wasn't a direct route; he'd have to zigzag across the outskirts of the city centre, but the map he carried in his head was up to the task. He could manage this more or less on automatic pilot while he did some real thinking.

What exactly would it mean, to cut Carol Jordan out of his life for good? Take it step by step. In practical terms, compared to how things used to be between them, she was already out of his life. For the past few years, they'd lived in the same building. His house had occupied the top two floors, her basement flat a staircase and a locked door away from him. They hadn't lived in each other's pockets, but he'd always had a general awareness of her presence and absence. He was like the Lord in the Psalms, preserving her going out and coming in.

Then he'd inherited the house in Worcester. For the first time in his life, he had somewhere to live that felt like home. The moment he'd stepped inside the big Edwardian house by the park, he'd finally understood what people meant when they said they belonged. Edmund Arthur Blythe's house could have been built around Tony, so perfectly did it match. And it was a homecoming that seemed to have room in it for Carol. Living together under the same roof; a tentative step closer that might lead further still.

Everything had always been tentative between them. Two wary people whose life choices had inflicted emotional scars and psychological damage. Neither of them the sort of person you'd choose to love. But they had grown to understand that what bound them together was a kind of love. Not the conventional sort that quickly morphed into sweaty bodies in tangled sheets. It was never going to end up there, not with Tony's inability to perform.

Instead, they'd fashioned a different sort of relationship that accommodated their professional and personal lives. They trusted each other in a way that neither trusted any-one else. Although they had never lived together, there was a connection in the dailyness of their lives that had made her absence very hard to bear.

But absent was what she had become. In her grief, instead of turning to him, she'd lashed out with all the pent-up vio-lence in her heart. She'd made no bones about blaming him and the night she'd walked away from him had been the hardest he'd ever known. He'd tried to convince himself she would be back, but he'd been right to fail. She'd walked away from all of them without a backward glance. It was as if she had died, but in some shameful way that prevented people coming together to celebrate what she'd meant to them. The mourning was real, though.

Yet he had managed that first step beyond the rawness of

grief. He was living somewhere that had no associations with her. She'd been on the boat only once, when it had been moored in another city, and it wasn't a visit that had left a trail of happy memories. He wasn't beset by images of her everywhere he looked; this was his domain, and that made getting along without her a little easier.

The second step was accepting that it was over. Whatever name you wanted to give what had existed between them, it was done. There might have been a way back to their easy companionship and affection if she'd returned after a short break and been willing to draw a line under what had happened. Hard though that would have been, it would have at least privileged the living over the dead. Something he always advocated with his patients. Now he had to practise what he preached.

Tony trudged on, paying no attention to his surroundings except to look up at road junctions so he could check his directions. When he walked like this, it acted like the release of a brake on thoughts and emotions. He could brace himself and be stern, tell himself he had to stop hankering for what he'd lost and accept that it was gone. There was no point in wistful yearning. It wasn't going to happen.

He wasn't there yet, he knew. But wanting to get there was half the battle. Then he could take the final step and, as the sort of therapist he despised would say, move on. Accept that chapter of his life was closed and give it a new shape. Believe that there were people out there who could fill the spaces in his life and in his heart.

Yeah, right.

It was going to take a few more sessions with Jacob before he could convince himself that life after Carol Jordan was somehow going to be magically better than it had been before the slow build of their relationship. The truth was, she was the only woman he'd ever dropped his defences for.

She knew his dark places. She'd even survived his mother. How likely was it that he'd find another like her?

'Stop it.' His voice was as loud as a parade-ground command. It startled two teenagers minding their own business in a bus shelter, but he was oblivious to them. Luckily, he'd reached the main road in time to break his chain of thought. The supermarket was only a couple of hundred yards away and he began to rehearse his shopping list. 'Pasta, cereal, nice bread. Maybe some ham or salami. Tomatoes, that would be good.'

Rather than use the pedestrian entrance, he walked into the car park by the route Bev would have taken. In the early evening, the supermarket was busy, the car park a constant juggling of traffic. Nearest the store, cars jockeyed for position, looking for parking slots that meant they had only a short distance to walk. 'If you were in a hurry,' Tony mused as he walked, 'you'd be quicker to park in an outlying space and walk that bit further. Maybe that's what you did, Bev. You didn't want to deal with the hassle, just a quick in and out then home to your boy.' He stopped and looked around him. The car park was pretty well lit, but he wondered how good Freshco's CCTV coverage was. Out on the edges, it seemed the cameras were few and far between.

Tony continued into the supermarket, wondering about Bev McAndrew and Nadia Wilkowa. Two apparently blameless women gone missing, one dead already. No obvious source of conflict in their lives. He hoped he wasn't the only one considering whether to put two and two together.

By the time he got to the checkout, he had managed to fill his basket to the brim. Coffee, a couple of pizzas, apples, grapes, eggs, bacon and cans of beans had mysteriously joined his existing list. Dismayed, he realised he'd never fit all this in one bag. Worse, he'd have to lug it across town. There was no time for revision, not unless he wanted to be lynched by the people behind him in the queue, so he shelled out for another bag-for-life and walked back to the car park while he considered his options.

He didn't want to walk home. He'd done his thinking, it was starting to rain and his knee hurt, reminding him he was supposed to make an appointment with the consultant to talk about surgery. The very thought of what Mrs Chakrabarti had in mind made Tony sweat. He was on the point of calling a taxi when a double-decker bus lumbered through the car park and pulled into a bay only yards away from him.

According to the destination board, it was bound for Preston Street bus station. A mere five-minute walk from his mooring. It was a no-brainer. He waited while a handful of shoppers boarded ahead of him. He knew he didn't have the correct change; boarding the bus would involve sighs and moans from the driver, and not in a good way.

As he expected, the driver tutted and muttered all the way through the process of issuing a ticket and changing a twenty-pound note. Tony raised his eyes to the heavens, seeking patience.

What he found was something quite unexpected. Mounted above the driver's seat was the familiar CCTV monitor. Tony had never studied it before; if he'd ever given it any thought, he would have assumed it would show only the interior of the bus. But the reality was very different. The screen was split into nine sections, showing upper and lower decks, the entrance and exit doors and the rear of the bus, to make it easier for reversing, he presumed. What he hadn't expected was how much of the outside of the bus was under surveillance. A wide-angle lens revealed the whole width of the pavement, extending as far as the plate-glass windows of the store; another showed the roadway on the far side of the bus. Tony imagined that if it was blown up on a single monitor it would be possible to read number plates. Maybe even identify drivers.

'How often does this service run?' he asked the driver, who was dropping pound coins one by one into his waiting hand.

The driver gave a weary sigh. 'Every twenty minutes from seven in the morning till ten at night.'

'Is this the only bus service that runs into the super-market?'

'Do I look like Google? Go and sit down so I can get moving.'

'Can I stand here and watch the monitor?'

The driver pointed to a sign on the Perspex screen that protected him from his passengers. 'Can you not read? No passengers beyond this point while vehicle is in motion. That means sit down and leave me alone. You can do that, or you can get off.'

Tony perched on the edge of a double seat already occu-pied by a large elderly woman with two bulging bags that seemed to contain only potatoes and biscuits. 'Miserable git,' she said. Seeing his startled face, she giggled. 'Him, not you. There's two other buses stop at Freshco, love. The thirty-seven runs down through Kenton to Kenton Vale then back round to Colliery End. Every half-hour, I think. And there's a little ring-and-ride coach that serves the estate. It doesn't have a timetable, as such.'

'Thanks. That's very helpful.'

She looked at him curiously. 'It's a funny question, though. Why are you so interested in the buses?'

'It's a long story,' he said. 'And I can't really explain it. But it's all about different ways of looking at things. And how you don't always think about the things you think you know about.' He smiled. 'A lot of what I say doesn't make sense. But don't worry, I'm perfectly safe.'

She gave him an appraising look. 'Are you sure about that?'

He shook his head, rueful. 'Probably not.'

31

There was an air of excitement in the incident room when Paula got back to Skenfrith Street. 'What's up?' she asked one of the DCs on her way to Fielding's office.

'They keep their CCTV for a month at the Trafford Centre. Pat Cody's picked up the vic on it. And it looks like they've captured the killer on camera too.'

'That's great news. Is he emailing it across?'

He shook his head. 'He's got it on a memory stick. He's on his way over with it now.' He offered a tentative high-five and Paula returned it. Even if high-fives were childish American nonsense, building bridges was the key to settling into a new nick. Make friends with your underlings, build a bulwark till you've figured out how to make the DCI happy.

DC Black had something else to add. 'Devon and Cornwall got their arse in gear too. They've interviewed Pawel the Shit and the bad news is he's alibied rock solid for that Saturday and for Friday through to Tuesday morning this weekend. He was either at work or shagging the arse off one of the chambermaids. No way he had enough time between shifts to get up here and dump Nadia's body.' The news didn't come as a blow to Paula. She'd never had any conviction that Pawel had the heft for this kind of crime.

She found Fielding at her desk, intent on her computer screen. The DCI barely looked up when Paula walked through the open door after a token knock. 'Any news from the lab?' Fielding asked, fingers rattling over the keyboard with the fluency of a touch-typist. Her hair had lost some of its glossy perfection; she almost resembled a mere human who struggled with the hours and the demands of the job.

'Would you settle for a bloodstain on her jacket?'

Fielding stopped typing and gave Paula her full attention. 'Tell me more.'

'I noticed there were six buttons on one cuff but only five on the other.' Paula wasn't in the habit of playing up her own role in investigations, but she reckoned she still had a long way to go when it came to making Fielding understand how good she was.

'Have you been at the Sherlock Holmes again?' Fielding's tone was severe, but for the first time, she treated Paula to a sardonic smile.

Paula shrugged. 'I'm such a girl. Anyway, Dave Myers took a closer look and he reckons the button came off recently.'

'So it could have happened when she was taken.'

'Exactly. There was nothing to be seen, but the test for blood came up positive. We might have some of the killer's DNA.'

'That's a good start. Fingers crossed that we get the DNA.'

'And double-crossed that he's on the database.'

'How soon will Dr Myers have a result for us?'

'In the morning. I also mentioned Grisha's theory about the taser, so Dave's going to check whether there's any of Nadia's blood in the relevant places.'

'Good, that helps us build up a narrative for the jury. He stalks her, he walks up on her, he tasers her and boom! It's over. Juries always resist abduction unless there's a good struggle. But the taser ticks that box for us.' Fielding's laptop chirruped and she glanced at the screen. 'Is that all?' she asked absently.

'You know about the CCTV at the Trafford Centre?'

Fielding nodded impatiently. 'Yes. Give me a shout as soon as Cody's in the house. Well done, McIntyre. Go and get yourself a coffee before we look at the CCTV, it could be a long night.'

Never mind the coffee. Now she had a minute to herself, Paula wanted to catch up with whoever was dealing with Bev Andrews. It took her a few phone calls to establish who had been put on the case then track him down. She found PC John Okeke in the canteen, working his way through a double all-day breakfast. He was a big lad who looked like he needed the fuel. If she'd been his boss, she'd have been more inclined to assign him to crowd control than investigating a missing person, on the basis of his unnerving size alone.

She bought a couple of coffees and parked herself opposite him. He looked surprised, then she saw the wheels go round and gain traction. He chewed and swallowed then said, 'Are you DS McIntyre?'

'I am. And you've taken on Bev McAndrew's disappearance, is that right?'

He nodded. 'Not that you left me much to do. Thanks for the report. And for doing the search. You saved me a lot of time.'

'So where are we up to?' She half-expected him to find a polite way to tell her it wasn't her case and she should butt right out. But he was surprisingly willing to share.

'In terms of results, not much further forward. I went to the Freshco you said she usually shopped at and looked at their CCTV for the hour after she left work. She shows up on the cameras in store. She picks up some milk and bread and sausages. She comes out of the store and that's where we lose her. She walks into the car park and out of their coverage.'

'Don't they have the whole car park covered?'

'No. The area in front of the shop is well covered, but as soon as you get away from there, it's pretty sketchy. They cover the trolley return points, but once you're outside that ring of coverage, we're screwed. Sorry.'

Paula sighed. 'Bugger. Good thinking, though.'

He dipped his head in acknowledgement and bit into his toast. Chewed, carried on speaking. 'I talked to her colleagues again. She didn't show at work today, no messages, out of character for a very responsible boss, no worries or hassles that anybody knew about.'

Paula interrupted. 'What did you think of Dan the man?'

Okeke's eyes took on wariness. 'I thought he was straight up. Worried, a bit upset, but nothing that set my bells ringing. Did you think different?'

Paula pulled a face. 'Not really, no. I just felt he was a tad evasive.'

Okeke swallowed half a tomato. 'You have to factor in the way people get around cops. And around the opposite sex. I thought there might be more between him and Bev McAndrew than he was letting on, but he seemed more concerned than guilty to me.' He speared a mushroom. 'I know what you're thinking. "That's what people said about Ian Huntley during the Soham murder hunt." And it might have been what the punters and the hacks said, but I bet it's not what the cops said behind closed doors. We get a smell off the bad guys, don't we?'

'Not always,' Paula said, recalling the killer who had come so close to ending her life. 'But this time, I think you're right.'

He nodded, satisfied. 'I also did a formal interview with your nephew—'

'My nephew?' Paula squeaked.

Okeke looked surprised. 'I thought with you and his auntie being civil partners, you'd think of Torin as your nephew too. Did I get that wrong?'

Her first thought was that Torin was a cheeky little bugger, telling lies to keep out of the hands of social services. Then it dawned on her that he was alone and afraid and clinging to her and Elinor because he didn't really have anyone else. Hastily, she backtracked. 'No, no, you're fine. I never think of myself as an auntie, that's all. More like a big sister.' Her smile felt false. Okeke was trying to keep his face stern, but one corner of his mouth kept twitching in a half smile.

'Anyway, I spoke to Torin but he didn't have anything of substance to add to your report. To tell you the truth, I'm worried.' It didn't stop him shovelling another forkful of food in his mouth.

'We all are.' Paula sipped her coffee. 'What's your guv'nor saying?'

'If she's not turned up by tomorrow morning, he thinks we should do a media appeal. Not with Torin, obviously. Just a release with a photo and a request for sightings.'

Paula nodded. It was what she'd been going to suggest. 'What's your gut feeling?'

He wouldn't meet her eyes, concentrating instead on cutting up a sausage. 'Not good. Woman her age, no history of depression or abusive relationships, decent job, decent home, no significant debt that we can pinpoint. And a kid.' He took a swig of coffee. 'Women like that don't generally take off. And they definitely don't take off without their passport or their driving licence.'

'I didn't find the driving licence,' Paula said.

'It was in her desk drawer at work.'

'You think something bad has happened.'

Now he looked her square in the face. 'Don't you?'

Paula stared into her coffee. 'Yeah.'

'I'm sorry. But there's no point in pretending.'

Paula pushed her chair back and stood up. She wasn't a small woman but she was barely taller than Okeke sitting. 'Keep me in the loop, would you?'

He dabbed his lips delicately with a napkin and nodded. 'Likewise. If Torin remembers anything . . .'

Paula stood outside the back door in the lee of the building, huddled with the other smokers. She'd checked upstairs and Cody hadn't returned yet. One short encounter with Cody and she'd already have put money on him taking a detour via one of the outlets in the shopping-mall food hall. Out here by the car park, she'd see him when he finally showed up. She lit up and called Elinor's mobile, half-expecting it to go to voicemail. But she was in luck. 'It's your wife,' she said. 'Torin's auntie.'

'Ah,' Elinor said. 'It was his idea. He's desperate to avoid being taken into care. Even if it's only for a night or two. And your very charming colleague seemed willing to accept me as the half-sister of his absent father. He told me his family is also complicated.'

'And you call him charming. Sounds like you had PC Okeke eating out of your hand.'

'Police officers and their weak spots. I'm an expert. I'm presuming since you didn't begin this call in a burst of enthusiasm that there's no news?'

Paula tried not to sound as glum as she felt. 'In my job, no news is good news.'

'That's tough. Listen, I'm perfectly happy to keep Torin with us, but I think we've reached the point where we need to talk to his dad, to put this on an official footing. Not to mention his grandmother and his real auntie. Torin says there's a facility called ArmyNET that lets him communicate with his dad in real time, so we'll use that. Are you happy to let me take care of it?'

Again, Paula remembered why she loved Elinor. What was it Tony had once said to her? 'There's nothing clever about being clever. In the MIT, everybody's clever. What's really clever is being kind.' And nobody did kind better than Elinor. 'I would be in your debt. As usual.'

'I'll do it when I get home. Torin's going to a friend's house for tea and homework. He's going to text me so I can pick him up. How different their lives are from what ours were . . . ' There was a tickle of laughter in her voice.

'I'll catch you later. I might be late. I love you.'

'Love you too. Take care out there.'

Paula ended the call and, right on cue, her cigarette. She contemplated one more cigarette. She'd been good all day, not wanting to push her luck with Fielding. And she'd already been warned it might be a long night. 'Sod it,' she said, fishing out another and sparking up her lighter.

She'd barely taken her first drag when her phone rang. The *X Files* ringtone she reserved exclusively for Tony. 'Tony,' she said. 'How's things?'

'Has Bev McAndrew turned up?'

No small talk, as ever. 'No. Not a trace of her since she walked out of work.'

'I went shopping this evening. I thought I'd go over to the Freshco on Kenton Vale Road. You know how it is.'

She knew how it was. He liked to look at the scene, to think himself into the head of the victim and the perpetrator, to walk a mile in their shoes in a physical exercise of empathy. 'And what did you learn?'

'I learned a very interesting thing about buses,' he said.

'That doesn't sound very likely,' Paula said.

'Round the fringes of the Freshco car park, the CCTV footage is pretty poor. But that's exactly where the buses go.'

'You think someone on a bus might have seen Bev?'

'Of course they might have, but what matters is the buses themselves. They're festooned with cameras. And they show what's going on outside the bus as well as inside. Not close-up, really quite a distance from the bus. I thought maybe you'd get lucky and find some footage with Bev on it if she's not parked close to the store.' He stopped.

'That's brilliant. I knew they had cameras on the buses but I had no idea they filmed the outside.'

'Me neither. It's because you never go on buses.'

'You think we should be actively looking for Bev?'

'It's not my call. But according to you, you've already got one murdered woman with nothing apparently problem-atic in her life. Now you've got a second one missing. Have you found the intersection between Nadia and her killer yet?'

'Nothing definite. We think he may have picked her up in the Trafford Centre and taken her in the car park. But I haven't seen the footage yet.'

'And you've got another missing woman who might have been abducted in a car park. Plus they look kind of like each other, Paula.'

'You think? There's about twelve years' difference in age, their body types aren't that similar.'

'You don't want to see it because you're scared for your friend, Paula. But they're both blonde, medium height, med-ium build. They dress like professional women, not bimbos. They've driven themselves to the shops. One's dead and the other's missing. I know your precious Chief Constable once accused me of seeing serial killers round every corner, but sometimes I'm right, Paula. Sometimes I'm right.'

'More often than not, unfortunately. I'll pass this on to

the uniform who's looking into Bev's disappearance. And I'll talk to Fielding, OK?'

'I think you should. I'll back you up, if it helps.'

Paula choked on her cigarette smoke. 'Are you out of your mind? Have you forgotten how pissed off Carol got when I fed you confidential case info behind her back? Multiply that by ten and you've got DCI Alex Fielding.' She sighed. 'I miss Carol.'

'I'm trying not to.'

And he was gone, the phone a dead lump of plastic in her hand. Across the car park, she saw Pat Cody and another bloke get out of a car and hustle towards the building. 'Showtime,' she muttered, tossing her cigarette into a puddle and heading indoors.

'What have we got, Cody?' she asked, falling into step beside him.

He tapped the side of his nose. 'That's for me to know and you to find out.'

A flash of anger lit her up. If she let this go, it would shape how Cody and his mates treated her. 'Constable, you need to remember who the sergeant is around here,' she snapped. 'I'm in your line of command and when I ask you a question relating to an ongoing case, I expect an answer.'

Cody flushed. It wasn't an improvement. 'No disrespect intended, Sarge.' His heavy eyebrows lowered in a frown.

'He's always making daft jokes,' his mate chipped in, trying to defuse the atmosphere.

'And you are?'

'DC Carpenter, Sarge.'

'I love jokes, me,' Paula said conversationally. They climbed the stairs in a tight knot. 'Only thing is, they need to be funny. Bear that in mind, Cody, and we won't fall out. Now, tell me what we've got. Save the full briefing for the boss. Just give me the bullet points.'

He grunted, but told her what she wanted to hear. 'Nadia comes out of the cinema and walks out to the car park. Her car's a way off because she parked up earlier when the place was hopping. A bloke tails her across the car park. He's carrying a metal box, like a camera case. She opens her boot to put her shopping in the car. He comes up behind her. You can't really see what goes on but he tips her in the boot, puts the case in the boot, leans over her for a minute or so. Then he gets in her car and drives off.'

'We've asked the DCI to put a request in to the National ANPR Data Centre to track the car,' Carpenter chipped in, sounding more excited than anyone should at the thought of data mining. 'All the roads round the Trafford Centre are well covered. We should be able to track him without any problem.'

They walked into the incident room together, greeted by a few whoops of delight. Fielding came out of her office and gave a couple of handclaps. 'We're all set up, Cody. Get that memory stick plugged in and let's see what we've got.'

Everyone settled down to watch the interactive whiteboard and someone turned off most of the lights. 'Here we go,' Cody said. It was as he had said. Nadia emerged from the cinema and walked through to the car park a level below. As she stepped outside, she put her bags down to fasten her jacket against the cold. The line of small buttons took a few moments to close. Paula recognised the jacket from the lab. Pity there was no prospect of counting the cuff buttons at this level of definition. Nadia walked forward out of shot. Next out was a couple, the man with his arm round the woman's shoulders. They were laughing and talking, paying no attention to their surroundings, unaware that a third figure was walking close behind them, head lowered, hard to see. He stayed tucked in behind them till they moved out of shot.

'The next camera picks Nadia up on the diagonal. Here she comes. Bottom right,' Cody explained. Head down against the wind, Nadia was cutting across the almost empty car park at an angle. *How often have I done that without a second thought?* Paula felt a frisson of fear as the figure following Nadia entered the frame.

Fielding took centre stage now. 'Look at this guy. Study everything about him. Look at that case he's carrying. Commit him to memory.'

Which sounded great except that there wasn't much to commit to memory. It was dark, the lighting was designed to help people find their cars, not to allow CCTV operatives to make like Martin Scorsese. All you could definitively say about the stalker was that he was medium height, medium build, wore glasses with thick frames and owned a jacket whose hood, pulled forwards, almost completely obscured his face. He kept his head down; he was clearly well aware of the risks of being captured on pixels. The rectangular case in his hand seemed quite heavy, though that fact offered no clue to its contents. Nadia disappeared from the top left of the screen, followed by the man. Even the gender was a presumption, Paula thought.

The third camera was the one that had picked up the action. Nadia's car was close to the limit of its field of view, so again, there wasn't much detail to be seen. She unlocked the car as she walked, taking the keys from her handbag. As she opened the boot, the man suddenly speeded up. 'He takes something from his pocket,' Cody said, his voice rising with excitement.

'We think it's a taser,' Fielding said, watching Nadia put her shopping in the hatchback boot.

'Where's the confetti?' Hussain asked.

'Not all taser cartridges contain confetti,' Paula said. 'Usually it's only law enforcement who use it, so there's a record.'

'And she kind of crumples forward as he comes up from behind,' Cody continued.

It was over in next to no time. The kidnapper scooped up Nadia's legs and shoved them in the boot. He straightened up and took something out of his other pocket then leaned into the boot. 'What's he doing?' one of the others asked.

'Hard to say,' Cody said. 'We watched it a few times and couldn't make it out.'

'Packing tape,' Paula said. 'He's restraining her.'

Cody flashed a quick look at her. She couldn't tell whether he was impressed or pissed off.

'Could be,' Fielding said. 'We'll take another look after we've seen the rest of it.'

There wasn't much more of it. He finished whatever he was doing, closed the boot, walked round to the driver's door, got in and shortly after, drove out of shot. All of it without letting the camera have even a fleeting glimpse of his features. It was as if he knew exactly where he was being surveyed from, so effectively did he avoid the lens, Paula thought.

'Let's have it again,' Fielding said. This time, Cody slowed it down after the man tipped Nadia into the boot. It still wasn't clear what was happening; the man's body obscured what he was taking from his pocket. But Fielding conceded Paula was probably right. With a marker pen, she wrote what they knew about the man on the board. 'Anything else?'

A hand went up in the far corner of the room. A woman who looked like she wanted to disappear into the woodwork. 'Boss? I think he's got a limp.'

'A limp? How do you work that out, Butterworth?' Fielding was already moving away from the whiteboard.

'You can't see it in the diagonal shot because of the angle. And then he's running. But when he walks round to the driver's seat, it looks like he's limping.'

Fielding frowned. 'Play it again, Cody. Just the last bit. And slow it down.'

Cody did as he was told. And as they watched, it was clear that DC Butterworth had spotted something the rest of them had missed. The man was limping. Whether it was temporary or permanent, they had no way of knowing. But that Saturday night in the car park of the Trafford Centre, the man who had abducted Nadia Wilkowa had something wrong with his left leg.

32

Day twenty-six

The sun was a thin brilliant line across the top of the moors. For the first time in more than a week, the morning sky was clear, dark blue fading into eggshell as dawn broke. The light crept down the side of the hill, bringing the colours to life. White Edge Beck sparkled as the broken water caught the light and the rocks glistened. Early morning dog walking didn't get any better than this, Paul Eadis thought as he drove up the twisting single-track road to the National Trust car park. His two lurchers, caged in the rear section of his estate car, were restless, as if they too could sense a change in the weather.

He rounded the last bend. As usual at this time of the morning, the White Edge car park was empty, the only break in the skyline the stone rubbish bin and the hollow cairn where motorists were supposed to deposit a pound whenever they parked. Paul had never paid to park here; that was for tourists, and he considered himself a local. For five years now, he'd been running George Nicholas's dairy operation. He'd done more for the local economy in that time than most folk around here managed in a lifetime.

He turned off the road and parked in a random slot. Paul liked to pretend to himself that he was an enemy of habit; the truth was he fetishised variety in small things so he could kid himself he wasn't hidebound in the things that mattered. It was one of the things that made him such an effective herd manager.

Humming under his breath, he got out of the car and released the lurchers from their captivity. They took off with their usual enthusiasm. But in the business of closing the tailgate and locking up, Paul missed the sudden arrest of their headlong plunge for the moors. When he turned, expecting to see the dogs a distant blur of movement, he was astonished to see they'd stopped behind the bin, nosing at something on the ground. 'Bloody dead sheep,' he muttered, pulling leashes from his pocket and heading for the dogs.

But it wasn't a sheep.

Startled awake by an unfamiliar sound, Carol was out of bed and halfway to the door before she registered what she was actually hearing. A scratch at the door, followed by a soft whimper. Then a more insistent scratch. The bloody dog, that's what it was. She let out the breath she'd been holding and felt her muscles loosen as the adrenalin fled. 'OK, Flash, I'm coming,' she called through the door, hastily pulling on jeans, T-shirt and fleece. She opened the door into the main body of the barn and a bundle of black and white threw itself at her, threading a figure of eight round her legs, barking with delight at being reunited with the new human.

Carol staggered under the onslaught, laughing in spite of her grumpiness at being wakened on a schedule other than her own. She ruffled the dog's fur, then said, 'Sit,' in her most commanding voice. Flash obeyed, but looked over her shoulder at the door to the outside world, another soft whimper escaping from her mouth. 'You need to go out,' Carol said. She crossed the room barefoot, looking out for wood splinters and stone chips, then opened the door on a glorious clear morning, the chill in the air invigorating and inviting. Flash ran out into the yard, heading for the rough grass at the edge of the cobbled parking apron. Carol watched while she peed, concerned in case the dog made a run for her old home over the hill. But Flash simply trotted back to the barn after she'd finished, rubbing herself against Carol as she re-entered.

'Good dog,' Carol said. She headed into her room to put on socks and boots so they could go for a walk. 'Listen to me,' she grumbled. 'Already I'm talking to you as if you're going to answer.' The dog thumped her tail on the floor. 'It was at least a month before I started talking to my cat like that, you know. I'm turning into a weird old hermit.'

She grabbed her waxed jacket and the leash Nicholas had left her and headed for the hill. The dog stayed at heel until they climbed the stile into the rough pasture, then she ranged back and forth, scenting the air and the ground, but always checking to see where the human was. Carol was amazed at how quickly the dog appeared to have bonded with her. Flash had watched Nicholas leave with apparent indifference. No crying, no casting around as if wondering where he might have gone, nothing that remotely resembled pining. Instead, she'd followed Carol round, lying down with her head between her paws near where she was working. They'd gone for a walk along the lane in the afternoon, Flash docile on the leash, apart from a couple of tugs towards open ground.

In the evening, Flash had sat politely by while Carol cooked and ate, then she'd lain at her feet while she drank wine and browsed the news on her iPad. Come bedtime, though, Carol had shooed her into the main barn, pointing to the dog's bed and blankets, set next to the door behind which her new mistress would be sleeping. She drew the line at sharing her bed – or even her bedroom – with a dog. Nelson had been a relatively unobtrusive bed-sharer. She suspected Flash didn't know what unobtrusive meant.

She'd been mildly surprised that there had been no protest from Flash. According to Nicholas, Flash had been accustomed to sleeping in the utility room with her mother and litter mates. Carol had worried that the dog might be lonely. But she seemed perfectly content with her lot, and she showed no signs of wanting to escape from her new life.

'Didn't take me long to fall for you, did it?' she said, scrambling up the hill behind the happy dog, feeling notice-ably more cheerful than she had the previous day. Maybe it was the weather. But maybe the dog's *joie de vivre* was irre-sistible. 'What exactly did Michael tell George Nicholas about me that made him think I needed a dog? Because, damn it, he might be right.'

They covered the ground to the trees at the top of the hill in good time. The dog seemed as fresh as when they'd left and Carol recalled Nicholas's injunction about exercise. 'Come on then, we'll go through the trees and along the ridge,' she said, striking off at an angle through the mix of birch and alder that struggled against the prevailing wind on the shoulder of the hill.

Ten minutes brought Carol to the far side of the woodland and a breathtaking vista of the moors and the valley below. But this morning, the view she'd grown accustomed to had an added element. A familiar element, but one seen from a very different angle.

Over to the east, perhaps quarter of a mile away, spotlit by the newly risen sun, the roadside past White Edge car park was occupied by a string of vehicles though the car park itself was empty. She identified half a dozen police cars and Land Rovers, the ID numbers emblazoned on their roofs revealing them to be from the West Yorkshire force. One displayed the solid circle of a Dog Unit but the others were standard response units. There were also four unmarked cars and an ambulance. She could see what looked like crime-scene tape fluttering round the perimeter, and several figures were milling around something she couldn't identify. Something waist high, stone-built, possibly.

It was a crime scene. And a serious one at that. The only crimes that would merit this sort of police presence so early in the day were murder, attempted murder or serious sexual assault involving a high level of violence. The kind of crimes that had been her bread and butter, her meat and drink, and the icing on her cake for years. The kind of crimes she'd built a career on. The kind of crimes that both answered and thwarted her fundamental craving for justice.

It felt strange to be a distant spectator at the first stages of an investigation. For so long, she had been the person controlling the scene. Taking the decisions. Deploying the personnel. Driving everyone to do their best for the dead and the living. And now, she was just another rubbernecker.

'Flash, come,' she said, snapping her fingers for the dog, who was quartering the hillside a hundred yards away. Low to the ground, Flash moved swiftly to her side and dropped down beside her, tongue lolling out of her mouth. Carol crouched down and buried her hand in the thick mane at the back of the dog's neck. She didn't want to leave yet; her history wouldn't let her go. But she didn't want to be obvious to anyone scanning the landscape from below.

While she watched, another car came hammering up the road. And instead of West Yorkshire's 13 on the roof, this one carried the 51 that signified Bradfield Metropolitan

Police. What had brought BMP officers to a West Yorkshire crime scene? She knew from her own experience that there was little love lost between the detectives of the two forces. There would have to be a very good reason for BMP cops to be here this early in an investigation.

The BMP car pulled up by the entrance, double parking to let two people out. Even from that distance she could see they were women. Carol couldn't rely on the evidence of her eyes to identify them. But common sense told her the small, dark figure who had been in the front seat could only be DCI Alex Fielding. Her equal in rank, but her opposite in so many other aspects. Fielding was authoritarian and formal where Carol was more relaxed and inclined towards teamwork. Fielding was all about hard facts and never mind the story behind them; Carol loved working with Tony because he helped her to understand why. Fielding was married with a son, a hinterland of emotional connection that Carol had failed to establish. And now it appeared Fielding had a new bagman. Her former sergeant had been a lanky raw-boned Ulsterman who always talked about going home. Wherever he'd gone, the person filling his shoes looked very familiar. Carol couldn't have sworn to it, but she'd have put serious money on Fielding's new bagman being Paula McIntyre.

The realisation provoked a confusion of feelings in Carol. Outrage at Paula's skills being put at the service of so unimaginative a boss; a stab of regret that it wasn't her down there; an acceptance that that life was behind her; and a benediction to Paula, who could still manage to do what she would not.

Carol stood up, backing into the trees. This was no place for her. She'd turned away from all that was going on down there, and she was slowly growing better for it. Hard physical work, all those books and movies she'd missed out on

214

over the years, a dog for company. Somewhere in the middle of that, she'd finally manage to forgive herself.

Let other people speak for the dead.

When she turned to go, a spasm of shock flashed across her chest, stopping her breath and making her heart clench. A few feet away, a man stood watching her. How could he have come so close without her realising? And why was the dog not reacting? Carol was on the point of making a run for it when her brain clocked on and she understood what she was seeing. The reason for Flash's passivity was that the man standing in the shelter of the trees was George Nicholas. At his heels, Jess, cheerfully licking her pup's head.

He held up his hands in a placatory gesture. 'Sorry. I didn't mean to startle you. You were so intent on that lot down there—' He nodded towards the cars and cops in the valley below.

'What are you doing up here?' Carol didn't care how rude she sounded. She was rattled but not so much so that she could let go of instincts honed by years of policing serious crime.

'Same as you. Walking my dog. Nothing more sinister than that, I promise you.'

He looked innocuous enough in his waxed jacket and tweed cap, recently shaven face pink with the cold autumn air. But she knew only too well the viciousness and treachery that could lie behind so harmless an appearance. 'I thought she was a working dog? Doesn't that give her the exercise she needs?'

Nicholas smiled. 'What she needs and what she wants are two different things. Jess loves to run more than anything else. Answering her whims keeps me fit. If I didn't do this, I'd sit around getting fat. Usually we don't see anyone else up here. This morning, it's a bit like Bellwether Square. What are they doing down there, do you know?'

Carol shook her head. 'Something serious. A murder or a serious sexual assault, given the number of warm bodies and the presence of two forces.'

'Two forces? How can you tell?'

She pointed to the vehicles below. 'Different transport codes. West Yorkshire and Bradfield Met.'

'Your former colleagues. That must feel strange.'

Carol deliberately walked past him, not wanting to give anything away. 'It's exactly the sort of case I would have been called out to when I was still a serving officer,' she said. 'Being a spectator is ... unexpected.'

'Nowhere's immune these days,' Nicholas said. 'My wife. Your brother and Lucy. And now this. The world has become smaller, Carol. And that means the unpleasantness infects places like this, places that used to be immune from the worst excesses of human behaviour.'

'You're wrong. This isn't some communicable disease that's spread out from the city. It's always been here. Lurking under the beauty. Wherever you are, somebody's inflicting horror on another human being. It's just that there are some environments where it's easier to get away with it. You can pretend all you like, but underneath your country idyll, the bad stuff is simmering and seeping in all directions.'

Nicholas tilted his head back and laughed. 'Christ, Carol, you make it sound like *The Wicker Man*. Look, why don't you come down and have breakfast with me? So I can show you that the big house isn't a dark, brooding presence on the far side of the hill? Come on. There will be fresh eggs and—' He pulled a paper bag out of one of his big side pockets and dangled it at her. 'Fresh field mushrooms. I picked them on the way up. And sourdough bread from Bentley's in the village.' He looked eager and open-faced. And if there was anything sinister about his presence on the hilltop, either because of her presence or that of the police, she would have the chance to ferret it out at close quarters.

'All right,' she said, making it sound as if it was as appealing as a colonoscopy. Nicholas lit up like a birthday boy. 'Come on, Flash.' The dog didn't need telling twice. Carol almost wished she could find so uncomplicated a response in her own heart. But those days were long gone. With one last look over her shoulder, she set off down the hill.

Let other people speak for the dead.

33

The call had roused Paula from the glorious depths of sleep. They'd gone to bed before midnight, but Elinor had wanted to revisit her conversation with Bev's sister Rachel. 'But after I IM'd with Torin's dad and he gave us his blessing, I'm still not sure I was right to encourage her to come up,' she'd said for what Paula reckoned was the eighth or ninth time.

'Torin's in limbo,' Paula said. For only the third time, she thought. 'He needs the stability he'll get from his family. He hardly knows us, love.'

'According to Torin, he hardly knows his aunt either. Be honest with me, Paula. Do you think Bev's coming home alive?'

Paula sat up and punched her pillow into shape. 'I honestly don't know. I think someone took her, but I have no way of knowing if she's being kept prisoner or ... We're in the dark here. I can't help thinking that Auntie Rachel arriving like the cavalry is going to feel like a worst-case scenario to Torin. In his shoes, I'd start giving up hope.'

'Maybe that's the best thing for him.' Elinor snuggled into Paula's side. 'Facing up to what's most likely to be the reality. And having his aunt here might help him with that.'

Paula yawned and patted Elinor's hand. 'It won't hurt for them to get to know each other better, that's for sure. If Bev doesn't come home, he's going to end up living with her. Or his gran. At least until his dad gets a home posting.'

Elinor gave a noncommittal grunt and kissed Paula's shoulder. 'Let's see what tomorrow brings.'

That was the last thing Paula was aware of until her phone began ringing. She looked at the time as she answered. Twenty-seven minutes past six. 'DS McIntyre,' she moaned.

'DCI Fielding here. West Yorkshire have got a body. The ID says it's Beverley McAndrew, your misper. I've got a squad car coming, I'll pick you up in twenty minutes. Be ready.'

'OK,' Paula said. But she was talking to no one. Still half asleep, she sat up and ran a hand through her dark blonde hair. She wanted to believe the phone call was a bad dream, but she knew it wasn't. Bev was dead.

Elinor turned over and murmured sleepily, 'Did your phone just ring?'

'It was Fielding. She's picking me up in twenty.' This wasn't the time to tell Elinor. It wasn't fair to expect her to go through breakfast with Torin hugging that terrible knowledge to herself. And it wasn't right to tell Torin anything until his mother's ID was confirmed.

'What's happened?' Elinor was alert now. She knew the ways of her lover's job too well.

'I think it's a break in the Nadia Wilkowa case.' Which was sort of true. Paula stood up, then bent to kiss Elinor. 'See you later.'

She barely made it out the front door in time, but she'd managed to be waiting for Fielding. To her surprise, her boss had handed her a cardboard cup of coffee when she climbed into the car. 'The body's up on the moors. I don't suppose there will be catering,' Fielding said drily.

'What have we got?' It was easier to listen than to talk ahead of her first coffee. And Fielding definitely seemed to be a morning person.

She leaned through the gap between the front seats so she could more easily talk to Paula in the rear. 'If I had a fiver for every dog walker who finds a body, I'd be sunning myself on a yacht in the Caribbean. Local farm manager out with his lurchers didn't make it past the car park. The body was stashed behind a stone rubbish container. West Yorkshire didn't specify whether it's a primary scene or a body dump. She's a match for Nadia Wilkowa. Battered unrecognisable, badly beaten, genitals glued shut.' She paused to take a swig from a water bottle. 'But that's not why they called us.'

'Why did they call us?'

'Her clothes and bag were dumped at the site, same as Nadia. In this case, they were stuffed in the rubbish bin. When they ran her ID through the computer, the misper alert came up. They rang John Okeke – he's down as the point of contact. Soon as he heard the details, he told their SIO to call me. So here we are.'

'But Nadia was kept for three weeks before he killed her. Bev's not even been gone three days. That's a hell of a difference.'

'The key elements of the MO are the same, McIntyre. There's more that links them than distinguishes them.'

'Her son's only fourteen,' Paula said.

'It's going to be rough on him,' Fielding acknowledged, then moved right along. Her face gave no clue whether she couldn't bear the thought or simply didn't much care. 'What was she like, Beverley McAndrew?'

'Bev,' Paula corrected her automatically. 'I didn't know

her that well – my partner, Elinor, knew her better than me. They both work at Bradfield Cross.'

'Yes, Bev was the chief pharmacist. Okeke sent me the file, I've skimmed the details. What I want is the human stuff. What was she like?'

'She was smart. Opinionated, but not pushy. Good company. Her and Elinor, they were very funny when they got talking about their colleagues. You'd be amazed how much pomposity goes on inside a hospital.'

'I doubt it. I've been a cop for twenty years. We've got plenty of pompous arseholes of our own. So, was she on your team?'

'You mean, was she a lesbian?'

Fielding pursed her lips and gave Paula a pissed-off look. 'Unless there's another team you're not telling me about.'

'As far as I'm aware, she was straight. Her marriage to Torin's dad didn't break up because she ran off with another woman.'

'Why did it break up?'

'She said Iraq changed him. He began drinking heavily and she felt scared all the time when he was around. He was never actually physically violent towards her or Torin, but he shouted a lot, he was always angry. She felt they were living on a knife edge. Ironically, once they got divorced, they got on better. He had a good relationship with Torin. Bev reckoned having to take responsibility for being a family man was one stress too many, given what he was dealing with on the front line.'

Fielding nodded. 'That's squaddies for you. The Army acts like their parents and that's an easier family to belong to than real live ones, with all their demands and issues. So have we checked that the husband is where we think he is?'

'I haven't. I expect PC Okeke made inquiries.'

'Check it with him. So what kind of social life did Bev

have post-divorce? Was she a party animal? Did she have boyfriends?'

'She'd been out with a couple of guys since the divorce, but nothing recent, according to her colleagues. From my observations, I'd have said she was someone who took her job and her role as a mother seriously, which didn't leave a lot of room for much else.'

'But you admitted you didn't know her that well. What about internet dating? Do you think she might have been into that?'

Paula shrugged. 'I wouldn't have thought she was the type. But what do I know? What is the type? Presumably forensics will be able to tell when they have a crack at her computer.'

'Though God knows when that will be.' Fielding looked gloomy. 'Remember when they told us computers would make everything quick and easy? So how come it takes for ever for the geeks to get them to spill their guts?'

'We never had that problem in the MIT,' Paula said. 'We had Stacey Chen.'

'Yeah, well, lucky you. The rest of us have to live in the real world. So who gets the kid? With the dad in Afghanistan and mum dead? Where is he now? With relatives? Or social services. You sorted that out, right?'

Fuck, fuck, fuck. Truth or lies? 'He's with friends,' Paula said, setting for the half-truth and moving swiftly on. 'He's got a maternal grandmother and an aunt in Bristol. I believe the aunt is coming up to Bradfield today.'

'Good timing. We need to go through Nadia Wilkowa's life again, see if there are any intersects with Bev McAndrew. That might bring us closer to finding how he acquired her. Pharmaceutical rep, pharmacist – not such an outrageous thought.' Fielding turned away and stared out at the moorland landscape. 'Christ, it's bloody bleak. Why the hell would you want to live out here at the arse end of nowhere? What do people *do* all day? There's nothing as far as the eye can see. Even the bloody sheep have given up.'

Paula had never had much faith in her sense of direction, but she was beginning to wonder about where they were heading. She took out her phone and opened the map app. A flashing icon marked their movement along the road. In the 'search' box, she typed in an address she recalled from the Jacko Vance investigation. The app took a moment to load, then it informed her that the barn where Vance had killed Michael Jordan was a mere seven miles away by road. Looking at the map, it was a lot less than that as the crow might fly if it had any interest in making the trip.

She had no idea whether Carol Jordan had visited her late brother's home since his death, but if she was going to be out this way again, it might be worth taking a swing by to see if there were any locals who could help to pinpoint Carol's location. Because she really didn't want to lose contact with the boss she had come to count as a friend.

Moments later, they were slowing down, driving alongside other parked police vehicles. They emerged into the bright morning, eyes narrowing against the sunlight, and identified themselves to the PC who was controlling and noting access to the crime scene. 'Where's the SIO?' Fielding asked.

The PC pointed. 'DCI Franklin's over by the body.'

'Which one is he?'

Paula's heart sank as she followed the PC's finger. 'The tall one who looks like a Neanderthal undertaker,' she said under her breath, barely loud enough for Fielding to hear. Her boss gave her a quick, raised-eyebrow look. 'I know DCI Franklin,' she said more loudly for the PC's benefit.

They set off on the short demarcated route leading to the cluster of men round the stone box, stepping with care on the metal trays laid down to protect the ground and any clues it might ultimately yield. 'Good description,' Fielding said, nodding towards the craggy man with the pronounced eyebrow ridge and distinctive beak of a nose. 'I take it there's some history there?'

Paula nodded. 'Mutual antipathy, it would be fair to say. We thought he was a patronising obtuse bastard. He probably thought we were a bunch of smartarses.'

'Some validity on both sides, I suspect.' Fielding forged ahead and called out, 'DCI Franklin? I'm DCI Fielding from Bradfield.'

He swung round, his scowl lifting as he took in Fielding's trim figure and groomed appearance. Then he saw Paula and his face clouded again. 'DC McIntyre,' he said, ignoring Fielding. 'They split you up, then, you and DCI Jordan?' He delivered each word in a Yorkshire accent heavy as a paving slab. The other officers around him stopped what they were doing to catch the cabaret.

'It's DS McIntyre,' Fielding said, to Paula's surprise. 'And you don't have to bother your pretty little head about the threat from DCI Jordan any more. I'm the person you have to deal with now.'

Franklin smirked. 'Is that right?' He stepped back and made a sweeping bow. 'Well, be my guest.'

As he moved aside, they were confronted with what remained of Bev McAndrew. It was as if Nadia Wilkowa had been transplanted from Gartonside to the high moorland of West Yorkshire. Only when she got past first impressions could Paula discern the differences. Bev's body type was different – she was an apple to Nadia's pear – and her shoulders were broader, the muscles more defined. But as far as identifying her from her features was concerned, it was a non-starter. Again, the victim's face was a mash of bloody tissue, the white of bone showing through on cheeks and jaw. Determined though she was to reveal no weakness in front of Franklin, Paula couldn't help biting her lip.

'She's the twin of the one we caught on Monday,' Fielding said, her voice blank of any emotion. 'I think that makes her ours.'

'Not to mention that this looks more like a body dump than a crime scene,' Paula added. If this was going to turn into a turf war, better to get all the cards on the table as soon as possible.

But the response from Franklin was not what she expected. He dug his hands into the pockets of his trench coat. 'And according to her ID, she's come from your patch. Be my guest, ladies. You want us to process the scene or do you not trust us?'

'It's not a question of trust. It's a question of chain of responsibility.' Fielding looked around the car park. 'I'd appreciate the loan of some uniforms to secure the scene till my team gets here.'

'Where's her possessions?' Paula asked. 'The stuff you ID'd her from?'

'Bagged up,' Franklin said. 'We're not fucking turnips. We do know how to handle evidence.' He looked over his shoulder. 'Grimshaw?'

A chubby detective in a white suit that clung to the contours of his body approached. 'Sir?'

'The victim's clothes and bag. You need to hand them over to the nice ladies from Bradfield.' Grimshaw grinned and rolled off towards the line of vehicles. 'Anything else I can help you with?'

'Cameras,' Fielding said. 'Where's the nearest coverage?'

Franklin slowly made a 360-degree scan of the surrounding area. 'There's nothing on this road. It's four miles north to a junction with a main road, five miles south-west, where you came from. There's a couple of speed cameras on each of those, but I doubt there's anything much in terms of number recognition till you get to the outskirts of Todmorden, Hebden or Colne. Sorry.' He turned and walked away, a jerk of his head telling his team to follow.

Paula watched them cross the car park and reconvene round the nearest car. 'Nice to see DCI Franklin staying true to himself.'

'Whatever you lot did to piss him off, it worked.' Fielding sounded less than thrilled.

'His bark is worse than his bite. He won't obstruct us.'

'He bloody better not.' Fielding took out her phone and made a call. 'I need a full homicide forensic team up here . . . PC Okeke has the directions . . . There's no doors, so I won't need a door-to-door team, just some uniforms to secure the scene. What I need is for you to plot this locus on a map then figure out which are the nearest roads with ANPR. Get the data and work out which vehicles disappear between cameras where there's a turn-off on to this road . . . Soon as.'

Grimshaw returned with a couple of sealed blue polythene evidence sacks and a sheet of paper at risk of being snatched by the bitter wind. 'You'll need to sign for this,' he said, sounding as if he was already arguing with a refusal.

Paula dug in her bag for a pen and scribbled a signature on the damp paper. 'Thank you,' she said politely, holding out her hand for the sacks. Grimshaw dropped them at her feet and headed back to his boss. She liked to think she'd never been that petty to anyone her boss despised. She couldn't be certain, however.

She picked up the sack containing Bev's handbag and its contents. Staring at her, tinted blue by the plastic, Bev smiled out from her hospital ID. Her throat tightened, and she blinked away tears. How was she going to tell Elinor her friend was dead? Worse, how was she going to face that moment when she had to tell Torin his mother was never coming home? The death of hope was always the hardest part of any investigation. Knowing the victim, feeling so personal a loss intensified Paula's sense of failure. But it was also a potent spur to action.

Paula examined the contents of the bag as well as she could through the plastic. A moorland car park wasn't the place to take them out of their protective covering. There was nothing that she didn't expect. But the mobile phone did give her a moment's pause. She pointed it out to Fielding, who was studying the body intently.

'What about it?'

'Nadia's phone was among her things too,' Paula said. 'That suggests her killer knew there was no threat to him from the phone. He knew we weren't going to find his name or his number on their phones. Doesn't that suggest a stranger or a stalker rather than somebody they knew?'

'Either that or he used a false name and a pay-as-you-go phone so it wouldn't matter.'

She had a point, Paula thought. 'But it would still be taking a risk. If we found messages from untraceable numbers on both victim's phones, we'd know we might be looking for someone in their lives. Surely to be on the safe side, he'd take the phones?'

Fielding shrugged. 'On balance, you're probably right. Unfortunately it doesn't take us any further forward.'

A little encouragement would go a long way, Paula thought. It almost made her not bother offering her other idea. But she couldn't let pettiness interfere with the hunt for Bev's killer. 'Another thing struck me,' she said.

Fielding looked up. 'What?'

'The lack of cameras. Here and around the crime scene in Gartonside. When you think how much of our road system is covered by ANPR or speed cameras, it's a bit of a coincidence that he dumped both his victims in places he could approach without any concerns about being recorded.'

'You don't think that's a stretch?'

'I think it's worth bearing in mind. We should ask Traffic how you could find out where the camera blind spots are and how somebody could find that out.'

Fielding nodded. 'Not a bad idea. But it feels a bit like clutching at straws. Let's see what the forensics give us on both victims and, if we're no further forward, you can talk to Traffic. I tell you what I'm more concerned about right now . . . '

'What's that?'

'Franklin was a pushover about handing the case over to us. I'm wondering whether he knows something we don't.'

34

By the time their forensics team arrived with the uniformed officers who would see to it no unauthorised feet trampled the car park, Paula was chilled and bad-tempered. There was nothing useful for her to do at the crime scene, but she and Fielding had to stay put to make sure there were no gaps in the preservation of the scene that a defence counsel could later exploit. Fielding had retreated to the car and her mobile, but Paula had chosen to remain with the body. She knew it was pointless, but she felt the need for some sort of gesture. Keeping vigil was the least she could do.

The first of the support vehicles had no sooner appeared in the distance than her phone rang. 'DS McIntyre.'

'Hello, Sarge. It's PC Okeke here.'

'Hi, John. What can I do for you?'

'Well, I know the misper's turned into a murder investigation and your team will be handling things from now on. Just a couple of things. The dad is definitely with his unit in Afghanistan. And after our talk yesterday evening, I got the

229

bus company to release their CCTV footage. I hadn't finished going through it when I spoke to DCI Fielding this morning, so I thought I might as well complete the job.'

'Good thinking. That's one less action for our squad. Appreciate it. Any joy?'

'A little bit. I ran it through a few times, to make sure I wasn't imagining what I wanted to see, you know what I mean?'

'I know exactly what you mean.' She didn't want to hurry him but she wished he'd get to the point. 'So what did you see?'

'I think Ms McAndrew must have parked a row over from the outside of the car park. It looks to me like her car is just out of shot. As the bus drives by, I saw her walking up the space between the rows of cars, then she moves off to the side and out of shot. I'd say she's walking quite fast. She's got her head down because it's raining. Next thing is, a few seconds later, another figure comes up the same way. I'd guess it's a man, but it's hard to be sure. He's wearing a waterproof jacket with the hood up. You can't see his face at all, except a bit of light glinting off glasses. He was carrying a case. Looked like it was made of aluminium, like photographers have. About the size of a pilot's case. And he carried it like it was quite heavy. Anyway, he goes the same way as Ms McAndrew, only he speeds up as he gets closer. Almost running. You'd have to say he was following her. And then he disappears out of shot, right where she did. It's not a lot of video. Only about fifteen seconds.'

'You did well to get that, John. Now, how would you describe this figure? Was he tall, short? Build?'

'Not tall. Medium height, I'd say. Not more than five feet ten. He was slim to medium build. It was difficult to tell. I couldn't be sure how thick his jacket was. And like I said, he's got his hood obscuring his face. The only distinctive thing is I think he might have a bit of a limp. It's hard to be sure. The quality isn't great and the weather doesn't help.'

It was a tiny shred of corroboration, but Paula's heart leapt at Okeke's words. 'That's very interesting, John. Can you say which leg he's limping with?'

He paused for a moment. She could hear him breathing. 'I'd want to look again, to be certain. But I think the weakness was in his left leg.'

Bingo. Not that it was exactly a break in the case. But it would help if it came to issuing an appeal for witnesses. Unless the killer was smart enough to fake a limp to throw them off. They already knew he was forensically careful. If he suspected there was any chance of being picked up on camera, he may have deliberately chosen to create a false image. 'I'm going to need you to make a formal report of this, John. File it with the incident room team, but send a copy directly to me and to DCI Fielding. I don't want this to get lost in the white noise.'

'Will do. You'll have it within the hour.'

Smart lad, she thought, readying herself to brief the forensic team. Once they were here, they could move the body. The way Bev was lying, it was impossible to see either the scar on her ankle or the tattoo on her shoulder. Those identifying marks would enable them to formally identify the body without having to wait for DNA. And then it would be time to break the news to Torin. Paula thought her chances of dodging that bullet were nil.

She walked across to the roadway and lit a cigarette while she waited for the specialists to suit up. Fielding got out of the car and Paula took the opportunity to bring her up to speed on what Okeke had discovered. 'There's no doubt about it,' Fielding said. 'We've got a single perp and two victims that we know of. Chances are he's got a record for violent offences, which means as soon as we do get some forensic evidence, he should show up on one of the data-bases.'

'Let's hope so.'

'Once we get her turned and we confirm the tattoo and the scar, I want you to talk to the son. You know him, it'll be better coming from you than a stranger. Presumably you know where he goes to school?'

Paula nodded. 'Kenton Vale. You don't want to wait till the end of the school day? Or until his aunt gets here?'

Fielding looked at her as if she was mad. 'Paula, this is the twenty-first century. There's no such thing as a hermetically sealed investigation any more. I don't want this kid finding out his mother's dead from Twitter or Facebook. As soon as we know for sure, we need to move on it. Line up an appro-priate adult. What about the friend he's staying with? Presumably there's a parent in the picture?'

Now she was in the shit. 'Actually, the friends he's staying with are me and Elinor. My partner.'

Fielding surprised her again, given her child-minding jibe the day before. 'Why didn't you say so? It's no big deal, as long as the family's happy with that.' She sounded more exasperated than angry. 'Frankly, I'd rather he was safe under your roof than camping with some mate we know nothing about. Can you get your girlfriend to come and hold his hand?'

'It depends on her schedule. She's a registrar at Bradfield Cross; if she's got a clinic or ward rounds, she can't just walk away from it.'

'When does the aunt arrive?'

'Not until this afternoon.'

'I don't want you tied up till then. See what you can do.' She glanced at the white-suited CSIs, lugging their boxes of kit across the bleak car park. 'Looks like we're getting some action.'

She set off in their wake, but Paula's phone rang and she hung back to answer it. The screen told her it was Dave Myers. 'Hi, Dave. I hope you're ringing me with some good news,' she said. 'We've got another body and it's looking like the same killer. So any help would be really welcome right now.'

'I'm sure it would,' he said, sounding unusually down-beat. 'Can you swing by the lab? There's something I want to show you.'

'That sounds intriguing. You want to give me a clue?'

'Not on a mobile.'

Paula wasn't used to Dave in worried, cagey mode. 'Will it take long? I've got to drive into Bradfield soon, but I won't have much time to spare.'

'It won't take long. What might take longer is figuring out what to do about it.'

Forty-five minutes later, Paula was climbing into a white paper suit at the forensics lab once more. Once they'd confirmed it was Bev's body that had been abandoned in the moorland car park, Fielding had despatched Paula back to the city. On the way, she'd managed to get hold of Elinor and arranged to swing by for her after she'd seen Dave. The police car had dropped her at home so she could pick up her Toyota; she was running on her own clock again.

When she walked in, Dave was in front of his laptop, pecking at the keys with two fingers. She placed the two polythene bags on the counter beside him. 'A gift from West Yorkshire police. If there's any issues of contamination, blame them.'

Dave stood up and lifted the bags one by one, peering into them. 'They've been out all night?'

'We don't know when they were dumped. The clothes

and the handbag were shoved in a rubbish bin so they've been pretty well protected from the elements.'

'But who can say what they've picked up from the contents of the bin.' He sighed, prodding the clothes bag with a finger.

'The victim is Beverley McAndrew. She was a friend of Elinor's.'

'I'm sorry to hear that. Tell her I'll do everything I can.'

'You always do, Dave. So, what's this mysterious thing you want to show me that you can't talk about on the phone?' Paula said, perching on a stool.

'The blood sample I recovered from Nadzieja Wilkowa's jacket. I extracted DNA from it without any difficulty. And I ran it through the NDNAD. There was no hit. This sample belongs to someone who isn't on the national database. But I didn't stop there. I decided to run a familial DNA search. You know what that is?'

'It tells you if there's someone on the database who's a close relative to the person whose sample you're testing, right?'

'Right. There have been some spectacular results since we started using it. Cold cases being solved. They've even caught serial killers with it in America. Some people bleat about human rights and privacy, but personally I think it's my human right to live in a world where murderous bastards don't get to roam unmolested in my community.'

'Here endeth the sermon.'

Dave conceded with a rueful smile. 'Yes, but here beginneth the lesson. So, I ran a check for familial DNA. Basically, the computer analyses the alleles and comes up with a list of people who have a degree of commonality. So, number one on the list has most alleles in common, and so on, right down to number one thousand, three hundred and forty-nine, in this case. Now, experience shows that if you're going to get a familial match, it's going to be in the top thirty.

We've got a little formula that incorporates the genetic match, the ages of the people concerned and their geographical location, and that gives us a likelihood of a particular relationship. But even before I had to use the formula I spotted someone in my top three who lives within a dozen miles of where your sample was taken. When I looked more closely, what do you know? I got what I consider a definite hit.' He neither looked nor sounded happy about it. 'The family member is a woman. It's my opinion, based on the DNA analysis, that this woman is a close relative of the man – and it is a man, by the way – whose blood was deposited on Nadzieja Wilkowa's jacket.' He leaned across the desk and clicked a tab on his screen. Up popped a pair of the familiar DNA profiles, one above the other, with their jagged peaks at irregular intervals. 'See for yourself. Where the alleles align, that's the key factor. So, how close is this genetic relationship? Now, we all have around five alleles in common with any given person. But the direct relationship of mother to offspring means there would be at least ten alleles from the crime stain which must have come via the mum.' Dave tapped each of the allele peaks with the tip of his pen. 'Eleven, you see?'

'I believe you, Dave. And so will a court. You seem really anxious about this. I don't know why. It's not like it's ground-breaking science.'

'The integrity of the science is not what's bothering me. Well, it is, but not for the reasons you're thinking.'

Paula shook her head. 'I'm a simple copper, Dave. I can't do cryptic crosswords. Just tell me straight. What's the issue?'

He looked pained. 'The identity of the person on the database. It's a woman called Vanessa Hill.'

Paula gawped at him, her mouth open. She couldn't quite credit what she'd heard. 'Did you say "Vanessa Hill"?'

Dave nodded, his expression miserable. 'I did.'

'What's her DNA doing on the database?' Paula clutched at what she knew was a broken straw.

'She was arrested and charged over the stabbing, remember? Even though the charges were dropped pretty much overnight, the DNA stays on the record.'

Paula shook her head, disbelieving. 'Could it have been transferred by someone else? Planted, even?'

'It's very doubtful. The way it's soaked into the threads and the cloth around the button – it would be hard to replicate that unless you had a liquid sample. And if you were trying to fit him up, wouldn't you leave the bloodstain somewhere more obvious? We could have missed that, even on a detailed second pass. If you hadn't been counting buttons, it could easily have gone unnoticed.'

'There must be a mistake. You've got to run the test again.'

'I will, of course. But I'm confident the answer will be the same. And I'll also run a mitochondrial DNA test. That's the DNA that comes direct from the mother to the child. If that's a match, there's no room for doubt.'

'What if she had another child? A sibling he doesn't know about?'

'You're reaching, Paula. That hypothesis breaks down as soon as we test his DNA, unless it's his secret identical twin. Which starts to sound like *The Man in the Iron Mask*.'

Paula stared at the screen, willing it to metamorphose into something different. 'Can we keep this to ourselves?' She saw the look of horror on Dave's face. 'Not completely, obviously. But at least till you've double-checked that there hasn't been a cock-up with the test. Or with the database. And you've checked the mitochondrial DNA. And' – she pointed to the evidence bags she'd delivered – 'you expedite the evidence from this latest murder and see whether that gives us a more viable suspect.'

He sighed. 'I'm not happy with this, Paula. This is important evidence in a murder inquiry.'

'Evidence that we both know makes no sense.'

He rubbed his soul patch between finger and thumb. 'The science doesn't lie, Paula. The blood on that jacket – you can't get away from it. That blood came from Tony Hill.'

35

Marie was on her way back from the bathroom when she heard the raised voices. If she needed any help in working out where they were coming from, she'd only have had to follow the eyes of everyone who worked within earshot of Rob Morrison's office. Even with their headsets on, they could clearly still pick up the sound of aggravation.

As she got closer, she recognised Ralph Lauren Man's arrogant tones. 'And I'm telling you, we'll fall flat on our arses if we put this out to Gareth and his merry men in marketing now. It's going to take at least another six weeks before we're ready to roll it out to civilian punters.'

'That's not what you promised me two months ago,' Gareth protested. 'You said it was only a matter of tweaking the front end. Making the user interface more idiot-proof, you said.'

'And that's what will happen. It's taking a bit longer than anticipated, that's all. How many times do I have to put that in words of one syllable?'

'"Anticipated" is five syllables,' Rob muttered.

'What's all the bloody rush about anyway?' Nigel demanded as she pushed the door wider. He had his back to the door but even so, he should have registered the consternation on Rob's face and the amusement on Gareth's. 'Is it the new boss? You're crapping yourself over a woman? Do you think she'll even understand what we've put together here? Give me a break, she's only a bloody skirt.'

'A bloody skirt who outranks you, Nigel,' Marie said sweetly. 'And who fully intends to get to the bottom of why your department can't deliver its promises on time.' He spun round, fury on his face.

'What are you doing, sneaking up on us?' His right hand curled into a fist.

Marie shut the door behind her. 'I never sneak. I don't have to. Next time you decide to throw your toys out of the pram, do it behind closed doors, please. There's a room full of workers out there absolutely agog. Generating water-cooler gossip doesn't help any of us to achieve our goals. We're all after the same thing. Success is what makes the world go round. We'll get there much quicker if we help each other.' Her smile was as warm as she could make it. Even Nigel seemed to settle down, shifting across the room to lean against a filing cabinet with his hands in his pockets.

'Boys will be boys,' Gareth said.

'Speak for yourself,' Nigel sneered.

'I'd like to get to the bottom of this, but not while you're all wound up. Why don't you each write me a memo explaining what all the fuss is about? In words of one syllable, obviously.' She pulled the door open again and walked briskly to her office, feeling quite pleased with herself. There was nothing like finding out where the fault lines were in an office community. And then you could exploit them to the full.

Marie smiled. She had to admit, she enjoyed the exercise of power.

36

Carol was at the top of a ladder, prising a reluctant chunk of mortar from the stonework, when the dog started barking. She looked down to see Flash hunkering before the door, front paws splayed in front of her, haunches bunched and ready to spring, head jerking back and forth in a frenzy of noise. 'Shut up, Flash,' Carol yelled, only now realising that she didn't have a command for quieting the dog.

She climbed down as quickly as caution permitted and hurried to the door, clicking her fingers at the dog, who obediently stopped barking and fell in at her side. Whoever was on the other side of the door, she'd bet it wasn't George Nicholas. But apart from the postie, he was the only person who had visited since she'd moved in. Cautiously, keeping one foot firmly behind the door, she cracked it open.

If she hadn't recognised the looming presence on her doorstep, his size alone would likely have provoked her into setting the dog on him. Whatever command that was. But it only took seconds for her to make the connection. After all, this had been the place where she'd last seen DCI John Franklin.

The corners of his mouth lifted in a smile without warmth. 'DCI Jordan,' he said, dipping his head in a curt nod.

'Not any more,' she said.

'No, I know. I was . . .' He tailed off, and this time, the smile had a twist of sardonic humour in it. 'I was using it as an honorific,' he said. 'Like when officers retire from the regular army and march around in their Barbour jackets and tweed caps calling themselves "captain". Cops like us, we never really think of ourselves as civilians, do we?'

'I don't think of myself as a cop, DCI Franklin. So what brings you to my door? And how did you know it was my door?'

Franklin ostentatiously turned his collar up against the wind. 'Are you not going to invite me in? This is Yorkshire, we believe in hospitality. Come in, sit down, have a cup of tea.'

'I don't remember that aspect of my relationship with West Yorkshire Police.' What she remembered was blood and death and nobody ever listening to a word she or Tony said. What she remembered was bloody-mindedness and prickliness and men who used words like bludgeons. What she didn't remember was cosy cups of tea and slices of parkin. The dog picked up on her mood, grumbling gently at her side.

Franklin's shoulders rose and fell in a huge sigh. 'Look, Carol – OK if I call you Carol?' She nodded. Better that than a title she didn't hold and didn't want. 'We got off on the wrong foot and I reckon we're a pair of stubborn bastards who don't like to back down. How's about we call a truce? We're practically neighbours.' He spread his hands in a generous gesture.

'Come in,' she said, sullen rather than welcoming. 'There's nowhere to sit.' The dog followed her as she walked to the middle of the room.

He proved her wrong by perching on a sawhorse. He looked around and she could see him calculating where he was in relation to what had happened here. She couldn't complain. If anyone had the right to curiosity about what she was doing to the place, it was the cop who had had to confront the bloodbath up on the gallery, where the blood of her brother and his partner had turned the walls and ceiling into a grotesque abstract painting. But he said nothing about the past or the present state of the place. 'I suppose a cup of tea's out of the question?'

'Only when you tell me how you knew I was living here.'

He gave a dry guffaw of laughter that took all the threat out of his heavy brows and sardonic mouth. 'This is my patch, Carol. And what happened here is notorious for miles around. I knew the day you arrived. There's not a soul living round here that doesn't know you're living in your brother's office and gutting the place. What they're all gagging to know is what you're going to do with it once you've stripped it to the bare bones.'

Carol folded her arms and gave him her best hundred-yard stare. 'What I plan to do here is nobody's business but mine.'

'Fair enough. But I answered your question. Now do I get a cup of tea?'

'My coffee's better.' It was a grudging concession.

'Happen. But I don't like coffee.' He thrust his hands in his coat pockets. 'Oh, go on, Carol, it'll not kill you.'

She turned on her heel and marched through to her private quarters, Flash at her heels. She didn't like anyone inside the barn, least of all a man like John Franklin. Behind that bluster and bullshit, there was a tenacious terrier toughness in play. Whatever his reasons for being here, it wasn't an act of good neighbourliness. Carol hastily made a mug of tea, and brewed some fresh coffee for herself.

When she returned, he was prowling round the perimeter, studying the exposed stonework and the original beams as if he knew what he was looking at. He'd lost weight since she'd seen him last. His suit hung loose on his big frame, his shirt billowing out above his belt. The lines round his eyes were more deeply etched, his cheeks hollow. 'Ta,' he said, taking the tea. 'You've pretty much rubbed out all your brother and his missus did here.'

'Apart from the far end. Where Michael worked. It's a kind of guest suite. Or granny flat or whatever. It's self-contained.'

'And Vance was never in there.'

Carol's mouth tightened. She said nothing.

Franklin looked as if he was about to say something then stopped himself. He changed tack, crossing to the sawhorse. 'You'll make summat of it, I expect.'

Carol leaned against the wall, one hand on the dog's head. 'Why are you here? Is it because of the body over the hill?'

She caught a momentary flash of surprise in his eyes. 'Still a copper at heart, Carol. How did you find out about that? You don't talk to anybody round here except George Nicholas, and he's not on the bush telegraph.'

She toyed with the notion of refusing to tell him. She didn't owe him anything. 'I was walking the dog up on the shoulder of the hill. I know what a crime scene looks like, even at that distance.'

He sighed in satisfaction, and not at the tea. 'Mr Nicholas picked the right day to give you the dog.'

'Depends on how you look at it. I've got no interest in dead bodies or crime scenes any more.'

'How do you know it was a body?'

'Too much activity for anything less. A body or a serious sexual assault, I thought. But there's other places on the way up there if you're after a bit of lay-by sex. So I assumed a body.'

Franklin drummed the fingers of his left hand on the sawhorse. 'Here's the funny thing,' he said. 'Well, two funny things. First is, she's from Bradfield. A misper, but according to DCI Fielding, she's a match for another body they caught earlier in the week. Looks like the same killer, so I've graciously handed it over to her.'

'Very generous of you. I don't remember you being so open-handed with that murdered teenager a while back. I had to fight you tooth and nail for that one. Or maybe you prefer brunettes. Blokes always seemed to be suckers for Alex Fielding's charms, as I recall.'

He shrugged. 'Never noticed she had any. I was too busy getting into Detective *Sergeant* McIntyre's ribs.'

Sergeant. She hadn't known that. It was hardly a surprise. Carol would have promoted Paula in a heartbeat if she'd had the budget for another sergeant. 'Still,' she said. 'You handed it over without a fight.'

'This one's Bradfield through and through. The crime scene we've got, that's a body dump if ever I saw one. There's no blood to speak of, no weapon, no nothing except her clothes and her bag with her ID. Just as well that was there, because there wasn't much left of her face. I can't recall seeing a body so badly battered.'

'Why are you telling me this? It's got nothing to do with me.'

He put the mug on the floor and stuffed his hands in his pockets again. 'See, that's the other thing. To my mind, it's got everything to do with you. Because she looks like you.'

For a moment, it was too bizarre to be frightening. 'A

woman with no face looks like me? Do you have any idea how mad that sounds?'

'Not as mad as you think. She's got the same hairstyle as you.' He took a second look and corrected himself. 'Well, the same hairstyle you had when a proper hairdresser used to cut it. And she's about the same height and build as you. I tell you, Carol, when I first clapped eyes on her, for a few seconds I thought it was you. The resemblance, plus the fact I knew you were living here, right over the hill? Well, it was an understandable mistake, let me put it that way.'

'Are you trying to scare me, DCI Franklin?'

He shook his head vigorously. 'Of course not. I'm trying to warn you there's a killer out there who likes women who look a lot like you. You live in a building that's already notorious for murder. A stone-cold killer's out there, looking for victims who fit his type. One that lives in a place with these associations could be irresistible.' To her surprise, he looked away, staring up to where the bedroom gallery used to be. 'One crime scene here was enough, thank you very much.'

Carol didn't know what to say to that. She turned and crossed to one of the lancet windows cut into the thick stone walls. She could see all the way up the moor to the trees on the skyline where she'd walked the dog earlier. 'I'll be on my guard.'

'That would be good,' Franklin said. 'Happen it's nowt to do with you, this body turning up on your doorstep. But if it's some evil bastard leaving a calling card, you need to take care.' He stood up and left his mug on the sawhorse. 'I'm glad you've got the dog.'

'She does appear to be a good guard dog.'

Franklin walked to the door. 'Aye. She won't let anybody creep up on you.'

Except George Nicholas. Carol squashed the thought as ridiculous and unworthy. 'Thanks for keeping me in the loop.'

He gave another harsh bark of laughter. 'I'm not in the bloody loop myself. DCI Fielding made that crystal clear. But if I hear anything you should know about, I'll let you know.' He opened the door and scowled at the sleety rain that had come out of nowhere, as it so often did up on the moors. 'You might want to give Sergeant McIntyre a bell. She's the one with her finger on the pulse.'

Carol watched him leave. She didn't believe there was a killer out there who was trying to put the fear of death into her by killing women who looked a bit like her. And until she did, there was no reason to put in a call to her old life. No reason at all.

37

'I wish we could have waited until his auntie Rachel was here,' Elinor said, buckling herself into her seat belt.

'Me too. But Fielding's got a point. It's not like the olden days where information was safe till the next edition of the newspapers hit the street. Now, all it takes is one inadvertent slip or one idiot from West Yorkshire keen to make a bob or two by slipping something to the papers and suddenly it's all over Twitter. Can you imagine what it would be like to find out your mother was a murder victim from your Twitter feed?' Paula eased out of the hospital ambulance bay and into the stream of traffic.

Elinor shuddered. 'I take your point.' She laid a hand on Paula's thigh in a companionable gesture. 'It must have been a horrible shock for you, being confronted with Bev like that.'

Paula sighed. 'To be honest, Elinor, it was almost a relief. Not seeing her like that, obviously, but for the uncertainty to be over. I've been pretty sure she was dead for the last twenty-four hours. She wouldn't have walked away from her life. She loved her son. No matter how bad things had been for her – and we've found no evidence of anything amiss in her life – she would never have abandoned Torin without a word. She had to have been taken. And stranger abductions never end well.'

'I couldn't help hoping that she was being kept somewhere. That you'd somehow manage to find her alive. You read about these cases, where people have been kept captive for years and then they're rescued. And Nadia was held prisoner for three weeks, according to this morning's paper.' She bit her lip. 'I really wanted to believe.'

Paula wished she had Elinor's optimism. In spite of years of watching patients fail to recover, she still approached every case as if a good outcome were possible. 'Those cases, though, they all involve very young women or young girls. They're at an age where they're compliant and impressionable. They can be bullied and manipulated. They haven't learned how to stand up for themselves against an adult. It doesn't work that way with women of our age. We're too bloody stroppy.'

'I suppose. What's it like, working a major case with a new team?'

Paula turned on to the main road that would take them to Kenton Vale School. It was clogged with traffic, cars and vans all doggedly trying to get from one side of the city centre to the other. Times like this, she wished she had a blue light to clamp on top of her anonymous little car. Put the fear of god in White Van Man and carve a path through traffic. 'It doesn't feel like a team yet. Fielding is keeping me close. I've not had the chance to bond with the rest of the squad. Plus there's the baggage of coming from the MIT. That's a red rag to a bull for some people. It's a no-win. If you do something smart, it's "Ooh, get you, who do you think you are?" and if you fall over your own feet, it's "Not as clever as you think you are, are you?" I'm only trying to keep my head down and do my job. And that's not easy in this case.'

'Why not?'

'Partly because everybody knows I knew Bev, so they assume it's going to be personal. And partly because . . . ' She momentarily lifted her hands from the wheel in a gesture of frustration. 'I can't really tell you. Just, something that's . . . problematic about the evidence.'

'Can you tell me how it's problematic?'

Paula blew out a puff of breath. 'It's a matter of interpretation. And I want to be clear about it before I lay it out for Fielding. It would have been a lot more straightforward with Carol. I could have counted on her and the rest of the team not to leap to the wrong conclusion. I don't know that I can do that with Fielding. And it's not the kind of thing I can keep to myself. Plus the only explanation for it is impossible. So I have to figure out a way through it.'

'You will.' Elinor's confidence wasn't rubbing off on her partner and she could tell. 'If you take the next left, you can escape the traffic and circle round the industrial estate and come at the school from the other direction.'

Paula gave her a quick glance. 'How do you know that? Have you been moonlighting as a cabbie?'

'When I first moved to Bradfield, I had a horrible little bedsit down by the canal. That was the quickest way to get there in the rush-hour traffic.'

'I never knew that.'

'My feminine mystique. I have to keep you on your toes somehow.'

They drove in silence for a couple of minutes. Paula was dreading what lay ahead. Breaking the worst possible news was something she'd done more times than she cared to remember; it never got any easier. As if she read her mind, Elinor said, 'No matter how many times I give people bad news, I still feel inadequate to the task.'

'I've never had to tell someone I know.' Paula turned in at the school gates.

'Sometimes I've grown to know a patient quite well. At least you have a sense then of how to approach it. Take Torin. Like you, he's already expecting the worst. There's no leading up to it gently. Direct but kind is the best way for him, I'd say.'

Not for the first time, Paula thought her partner was Blessing by name and a blessing by nature. She'd cut straight to the heart of what was troubling Paula and she'd resolved it. If only the inconvenient issue of Tony's DNA could be so readily settled.

The news barely caused a ripple with the head teacher, a man who clearly believed that emotional crises needed practical responses. Paula warmed to him straight away. He installed them in a cosy room with soft armchairs and a low table. 'Our main guidance suite,' he explained. 'I'll send someone for Torin's form teacher and have her bring him here. What about tea, coffee?'

'Just water. And a box of tissues if possible,' Elinor said, matching brisk with brisk. His secretary swiftly brought what they'd asked for and left them to wait. It felt like a long time, but it was only minutes before the door opened and a large-bosomed woman in her forties ushered Torin into the room.

One look at the pair of them and his face crumpled. All his efforts at toughing out Bev's absence crumbled away, leaving him lost. 'She's dead, isn't she?' It was a roar of anguish. His knees couldn't hold him and he crouched low on the floor leaning into the side of a chair, his arms over his head, racking sobs tearing through him.

Elinor was first to his side, kneeling on the floor next to him, pulling him close and folding her arms round him. She didn't speak. She just held him and let the wave of grief suck him under and drag him with it.

Slowly, the sobbing subsided. Between them, Elinor and Paula helped him into a seat while the teacher watched helplessly. 'We're not supposed to touch them,' she muttered to Paula, who managed to restrain herself. Elinor sat on the arm of the chair, a hand on Torin's shoulder.

He looked up at Paula, eyes swollen, cheeks wet with tears, lips trembling. 'What happened?'

She chose her words carefully. 'Someone took her against her will, Torin. And then he killed her. I'm so very sorry.'

'Did he hurt her? Was it over quick? Did she suffer?'

The first thing they always wanted to know. With murder, you couldn't lie because the details would eventually come out in court and they wouldn't thank you for misguided attempts to spare them. 'I won't lie to you, Torin. He did hurt her. But I don't think she was in pain for long.'

His face twisted with the struggle not to crack up again. 'Thank you,' he stammered. 'For being honest. Did he— Did he interfere with her?'

The other thing they always wanted to know. This was, for some reason, the place where you had to let them down easy, without actually lying. 'We don't know at this point,' Paula said.

Torin started shivering, like a dog left out in winter rain. 'I d-d-d-don't know what to do,' he moaned through chattering teeth. 'What about the funeral? Who sorts all that out?'

'Come home to ours,' Elinor said. 'Your auntie Rachel will be here this afternoon.'

'Perhaps your form teacher could collect your bag and your coat?' Paula said firmly. The teacher looked dubious but left the room anyway. Paula followed her out into the hallway. 'He's been staying with us,' she said. 'Elinor's a doctor. She worked with his mum at Bradfield Cross. We'll take care of him.'

'Shouldn't you contact social services? He's only fourteen.'

'You think he'd be better off in emergency care?' Paula shook her head in bewilderment. 'Listen, in my line of work, I see too many vulnerable kids screwed up by the so-called care system. Let's see what happens when his aunt gets here. Nobody'll get on your case for leaving him in the hands of a cop and a doctor, for heaven's sake.'

'There's no need to be like that,' the woman said huffily. 'We have a duty of care here.'

'I understand that. But let's not get into a ruck. Torin's just lost his mum. He knows us and he trusts us. There'll be a family member with him this afternoon. This is the best course of action. If you stand in my way, there's a simple solution. I can take him in to the police station for questioning and there's nothing you can do to stop me. That's not the option I want to take, but I will if I have to.' Paula heard the words coming from her mouth with a sense of shock. She hadn't known she was going to take so adamant a line in respect of a teenage boy she hardly knew. *Bloody hell*. What was happening here?

The woman pursed her lips and put her hands on her hips as if she was squaring up for a fight. 'Right,' she said. 'I'll get his stuff then.'

38

It was all in the planning. He'd always been good at planning. Flow charts, fault tree analysis, cause-consequence diagrammatics – he'd been using all of those before he even knew the correct terminology. The first lesson his father had taught him was that actions have consequences. B follows A as surely as night follows day.

He remembered little of his mother. She'd been a timid woman, unassertive and bland, always scurrying to meet her husband's requirements. But she'd been a poor excuse for a wife and mother, forcing his father to constant complaint. When words didn't work, he'd had to resort to slaps, then punches and kicks. That was the way the world worked. When you failed, you had to take your punishment.

Then one April afternoon, when he was only seven years old, he'd come home from school to find the house locked and empty. He'd banged on the door but there had been no reply. Even at seven, he knew better than to make a fuss.

He'd slipped down the side of the house to the back garden and settled down to wait on the doorstep. By the time his father came home from work a little after six, he was chilled to the bone but he didn't complain.

His father explained that he'd thrown his mother out. Just like a piece of rubbish, the boy had thought at the time. If people didn't live up to the appropriate standards, they had to face the consequences. His mother had let them both down, so there was no place for her in their family any more.

He missed his mother's cooking and holding her warm hand on the way to school in the morning. But not for long. His father explained the need to be tough and self-reliant, and he absorbed the lesson. There was no alternative.

Not long after he turned eleven, he was sent off for two weeks of the summer holidays to an outdoor activity camp in the Lake District. A trio of ex-Army fitness instructors ran it like boot camp. Most of the boys spent the first few days in a state of shell-shock. They'd never been yelled at so much, never been expected to take responsibility for themselves and others, never had to face tests of physical endurance like it. For him, it had been business as usual. He wondered what all the fuss was about.

When he returned home, he discovered he had a new mother. While he'd been gone, his father had travelled to Thailand and returned with what the boy later discovered was a mail-order bride. This time, his father had chosen a wife who came much closer to his idea of perfection. Sirikit was subservient, polite, hard-working and eager to please. She never answered back, she cleaned house like a dervish and she never complained, even when his father criticised her for minor infringements of his regime. And she was a great cook.

By the time he hit fourteen he realised something else

about Sirikit. Practically every move she made had the capacity to arouse him. Every meal became a kind of torture, his penis straining against the tight underpants he'd taken to wearing in a bid to control his rebellious body. Luckily, his father paid him almost no attention unless he'd broken the house protocols, which he hardly ever did these days.

As he lay in bed one night, engaged in his nightly ritual of wanking to mental images of Sirikit spreadeagled over the kitchen table, smiling flirtatiously over her shoulder at him, it dawned on him that this didn't have to stop with fantasy.

The next afternoon when he came home from school, he found her in the kitchen preparing dinner. He approached from behind, reaching round to grab her small taut breasts. He pushed himself against her, as hard as he'd ever been. She squealed and squirmed, trying to break free. But he was strong and held her tight. 'I'll tell your father,' she screamed at him. 'And he will kill you.'

'No, you won't,' he'd growled into her neck. 'Because if you do, I'll tell him you're making it all up to cover the fact that you tried to seduce me because you're tired of an old man and you want young flesh.'

She hissed at him. 'He won't believe you. I am his wife.'

'And I'm his flesh and blood. He bought you. The bottom line is you're a whore and I'm his son. And he'd love the excuse to beat the crap out of you.'

The fight had gone out of her then. She knew her husband too well. And so Sirikit became his. Until he left home to go to university. His father had made it clear to him that he was on his own now. He'd sold up and taken Sirikit to live in Thailand, where she couldn't be further tainted by independent Western women. He never sent his son so much as a birthday card. Clearly, he was done with parenting.

Really, he should have learned from his father's choices and found himself a younger version of Sirikit. But he'd grown beyond his father and his crappy job working for the council. He was a graduate, a man with possibilities his father had never known. He was better than his father. He'd find a perfect wife without having to buy one. He'd find one who wasn't a whore.

For a while, he thought he'd done just that. She'd come for a job interview at the office where he used to work. On paper, she was well qualified as a market analyst but she was so shy she could barely answer the questions he and his boss put to her. She was demure and deferential and she couldn't believe it when he asked her on a date as he showed her out after her failed interview. Even on that first date, her eagerness to please was obvious. He used every technique at his disposal to undermine her, and within weeks she was cowed and controlled. Her parents lived sixty miles away in York and the first measure of his success was to turn her from a devoted daughter to one who never called. In spite of her parents' unease, they were married six months after that first meeting. By the end of the year, he had separated her from all her previous connections. He deliberately kept in touch with the only one of her cousins who lived in Bradfield because he didn't want to be blindsided. Information was power.

As far as he was concerned, he'd achieved exactly what he set out to do. Digital technology provided so many more opportunities for power and control. She didn't have to go out shopping; everything could be delivered from the internet, from groceries to sex toys. She didn't even need a bank account. He okayed or vetoed all the online spending, paying with credit cards she had no access to. He gave her small sums of money to pay for things like bus fares when she had to take one of the kids to the clinic, but he made her account for every penny. And whenever she fell short of the perfection he demanded, he made sure she understood the magnitude of her failure. He instructed her in ways she would never forget; it encouraged her not to repeat her errors. And it was effective.

Until it wasn't. He didn't know how or why, but she started to stand up to him. In small, almost imperceptible ways at first. But then she'd outright contradict him when he was commenting on the TV news or something in the *Daily Mail*. He confronted her with her betrayal of their love, but even though he punished her, she persisted. He reached the point where he knew he would have to put a stop to her behaviour once and for all.

That was when she paid him the ultimate insult. She deprived him of what was his right.

And now he had to replace her. And if those replacements didn't come up to scratch, then he'd have to make sure they didn't dodge what she should have had.

39

By the time Paula made it to Skenfrith Street, Fielding was in the middle of briefing the squad on Bev's murder. Paula expected a bollocking for being gone so long, but when they eventually convened in her boss's office, Fielding simply asked whether Torin had remembered anything useful.

'I don't think there's anything useful to be remembered,' Paula said. 'There's no reason to believe the killer knew Bev ahead of the abduction.'

'You think it's random? He chooses women who look similar, who both work in the pharmaceutical business, both in car parks? You don't think he's maybe been planning this a while? Maybe stalking them?' There was a sarcastic edge in Fielding's voice that pissed Paula off. She wondered whether that was intentional, designed to spur her on to greater efforts.

'Even if that's the case, everything we know about this killer is that he's careful. I can't see him behaving in a way that would catch the attention of your typical self-absorbed teenager.'

'Don't assume, McIntyre. It makes an ass out of you and me.'

Paula couldn't believe Fielding had actually uttered such a dismal cliché. 'I'll talk to him again. See if he noticed anybody hanging around.'

Fielding nodded her approval. 'Any strange cars parked near the house. We've got a line in to the boy through you. We might as well make the most of it.' She moved papers across her desk then looked up. 'What about the lab? What did Dr Myers have to say for himself?'

'He wanted to run more tests. I dropped off the evidence bags from this morning's crime scene and he's got a team working on them as a priority.' Well, it was almost true. She was getting good at finding a path between truth and lies with her new boss.

Fielding reached for her phone. 'I'm going to call him, remind him the DNA is our number one priority. Because we don't want to lose sight of Nadia Wilkowa in all this. I need you to review her appointment diary and see if she had any connections at Bradfield Cross. I know most of her contacts were GPs, but anything that links her to Bev McAndrew's workplace gives us a link. And look at her Facebook page too, see if she's got any friends listed who work there.'

Paula was on her way out of the door when Fielding spoke again. 'Torin. What kind of name is that? It's not Polish, is it?'

'It's Scottish, I think. Bev's dad was from Scotland.'

'Oh. OK. Just thought I'd check there's not a Polish connection we're missing. Wood, trees, that kind of thing.'

Paula went to her desk and started working through Nadia's data. She'd barely begun when her phone beeped.

The text was from Dave and read simply, Summoned by AF. Sorry . . .

No point in feeling too glum, Paula thought. The DNA analysis would have to come out eventually. She'd been hoping she could figure out an explanation before it did. As if it was ever going to be that straightforward.

Twenty minutes later, Dave Myers walked in. He sketched a wave in Paula's direction but headed straight for Fielding's office. Under cover of checking Nadia's records, Paula kept a discreet eye on their meeting. The DCI's face gave nothing away at first. Then slowly, she moved back in her seat, shock and incredulity chasing each other across her face. And then a slight flush on her cheeks. Her lips parted and the tip of her tongue moved quickly from one side to the other. *Fuck, she's actually loving this.*

Now Fielding was leaning over the desk, clearly making Dave go through all the data, point by point. Finally, she stood up and opened her door, patting Dave on the shoulder as she passed. 'McIntyre,' she called. 'My office, now.'

Feeling numb, Paula did as she was bid. Fielding pointed to the chair next to Dave. 'Dr Myers has brought us some extraordinary evidence. Doctor, can you tell Sergeant McIntyre what you told me?'

She had to sit and listen to it all again. But she didn't have to feign her astonishment. Hearing it a second time didn't make it any more credible. 'And there's no doubt about any of this?' she asked when he'd finished.

'No. We double-checked. I know it's hard to believe, but I'd stake my reputation on the accuracy of these results. The DNA from the bloodstain on Nadia Wilkowa's jacket belongs to the child of Vanessa Hill.'

'Dr Tony Hill.' Fielding stood up. 'Thanks for coming in with this, Dr Myers. And now that we've got a viable suspect, you know what we're looking for from the Bev McAndrew evidence, right?'

Dave looked outraged. 'You'll get what's there. Nothing more, nothing less.'

'That's all I want. But where there's room for doubt, I expect your team to drop on the right side of the fence, Dr Myers. In times of financial constraints, we have to be sure we're getting the best value in our forensic services, after all.'

Dave looked murderous as he gathered his papers together. 'I'll email you a full report.' He gave Paula a pained look as he turned for the door.

Paula waited till she heard the snick of the catch close behind him. 'There's got to be a mistake,' she said. 'Nobody who knows Tony could imagine for a moment he could kill. And certainly not like this.'

'Are you sure about that? Don't they say the best profilers are the other side of the coin from the people they hunt?'

'Only people who like to come up with lazy sound bites.' Angry now, Paula didn't much care whether she pissed off her boss. Getting her to see sense about Tony was more important. 'Tony Hill has dedicated his working life to preventing this kind of crime. He's about redemption and rehabilitation, not killing women.'

'McIntyre, sit down.' Fielding's voice was firm but not hostile. Paula hadn't even realised she was standing. 'Put your personal feelings to one side and look at the evidence. His blood is on Nadia Wilkowa's jacket. He limps with his left leg. He knows how to leave a body forensically clean. And the victims, Sergeant. The victims. They both look like DCI Jordan. Who, if I'm not mistaken, has shaken the dust of Tony Hill from her shoes along with the rest of us.'

What Fielding said only made sense if you looked at the world reflected in a distorting mirror. But Paula could see how seductive that picture would be to senior officers keen for a quick arrest that the media would love. The wolf in sheep's clothing, the gamekeeper turned poacher, the healer undone by his love for the woman who'd abandoned him. 'And what if someone's framing him somehow? What then? I don't believe it.'

Fielding rested her elbows on the desk and her chin on her fists. She appeared to be on the verge of asking a purely philosophical question. 'I'd expected more from you than grasping at straws. But you're entitled to that view, McIntyre, paranoid though it might seem to some. The question is, can you put it to one side and do your job?'

Paula felt the hot flush of annoyance burn her cheeks. 'It's my job to bring the guilty to account. I've never let personal feelings stand in the way of that.'

'You see, Sergeant, this is where you have to nail your colours to the mast. Can you concede that Dr Hill might be guilty? Can you commit to pursuing this investigation without your friendship getting in the way? Can you arrest and interrogate this man? If you can't say yes to those questions, say yes and mean it, there's no place for you on this case. There's plenty of other crimes need a talented investigator. Plenty of other SIOs who could use a smart sergeant. But I can't use somebody who's a secret squirrel for the other side.'

Even through her suppressed fury, Paula found a moment to wonder where this woman got her vocabulary from. *Secret squirrel?* What was that about? 'I'll do what's necessary,' she said, her voice thick with anger. 'I'll go where the evidence takes me. I'm not afraid of the truth.'

Fielding gave her a long hard look, head cocked to one side, considering. 'I think I believe you, McIntyre.' She looked at her watch. 'I want to do this quietly. No big media ruckus. Presumably you have Dr Hill's phone number?' Paula nodded. 'What would bring him in here?'

'A request for help.'

'Perfect. There's no way that can be construed as entrapment. Text him now. Tell him you need his help, ask him to come here.'

Paula stared at her phone screen for a long moment then typed in, Need your help. Can you stop by Skenfrith Street later? She showed the screen to Fielding, who nodded. Paula sent the text. *This is how Judas felt.* She stood up. 'I'll get to work on Nadia's diary. I'll let you know as soon as he gets back to me.'

She sat at the computer, the screen blurred and meaningless. Her stomach churned and her hands felt cold and clammy. She felt disloyal and disgusted, but the treachery she'd chosen at least had the virtue of keeping her on the front line. From this position, she was best placed to help her friend. Maybe even to save him. She only hoped he'd see it like that.

40

Rachel McAndrew bore little resemblance to her sister. The dark business suit over a kingfisher-blue polo-neck jumper that she'd chosen to travel in was formal, in opposition to Bev's more casual outfits. Where Bev was blonde and smiling, Rachel was brunette and reserved. Elinor didn't want to rush to judgement – the woman had just lost her sister, after all – but she sensed in Rachel a more complicated and closed-off personality. Torin had insisted on meeting his aunt at the station and breaking the news himself. Elinor hadn't tried hard to dissuade him. She reckoned he had the right to make some decisions. She'd be there to support him, and his aunt if need be.

Rachel had leaked tears at the news, but she'd composed herself quickly. 'I feared as much,' she said, her Northern accent still noticeable after years in Bristol. 'I lay awake last night, trying not to give in, but I couldn't convince myself. She wouldn't walk away from her responsibilities, not our Bev.' She'd tucked her arm proprietorially through Torin's.

'Come on then, Torin, let's get back to yours and see what needs to be settled.'

Torin stood still, a stubborn cast to his jaw. 'I don't want to go home,' he said. 'Not yet. I'd rather be at Elinor's.'

'Torin, Dr Blessing's done enough. I'm here now, I can take you off her hands.' Rachel tried to draw him along with her, but he refused to move.

'You're both very welcome to come home with me,' Elinor said.

'That's what I want,' Torin said, stepping towards Elinor.

The atmosphere on the drive was awkward. Torin crouched in the back seat in silence while Rachel alternated between dripping tears into a tissue and turning to tell him how dreadful he must be feeling. Elinor had seldom felt more uncomfortable.

She left them in the living room while she made tea and opened a fresh packet of biscuits. It was the last one in the cupboard. Grief had done nothing to diminish Torin's ado-lescent appetite. Either that or he'd taken to comfort eating like a terrier to rabbits. She carried a tray through and found them sitting on opposite sides of the room.

Rachel dived in straight away. 'When can I see her?'

'I don't think that's a good idea,' Elinor said, aware of how little detail they'd given Torin.

'Someone has to identify her, surely?'

'You need to talk to my partner, Paula, about the details.'

'She's one of the people in charge,' Torin said. 'Paula's determined to find out who killed my mum.'

'She'll be home later,' Elinor added.

'Will she be able to tell us how soon we can make the funeral arrangements? We need to get all that settled.' Rachel took a box of sweeteners from her handbag and dropped one into her tea. She sat back in the chair, her legs tight together at knees and ankles.

'When someone dies like this, you can't have the funeral right away,' Elinor said, trying to find a sensitive way to explain the situation.

'Why not?'

'It's a question of evidence,' she said. 'After someone's arrested, they've got the right to have their defence team examine the body.'

'But that's terrible. That could be months. How can you do that to people?' Her voice rose in outrage. Displacement, Elinor thought.

'I think some families hold memorial services. To mark the passing of someone they love.'

'That's not what's important,' Torin said angrily. 'She's dead, that's what matters. Not what they do to her body. It's just dead meat now.'

Rachel's hand flew to her mouth, revealing perfectly manicured plum-coloured nails. 'Don't say that, Torin. That's your mum we're talking about.'

'It's not my mum. My mum's gone. What they've got at the morgue, it's nothing but a bag of flesh and bones. It doesn't matter. This is where she is now.' He clapped a hand to his heart, his face screwed up in his determination not to cry.

'Of course she's still in our hearts.' Elinor passed the biscuits to Torin. 'About your mother,' she said to Rachel. 'Will you phone her and break the news? Or is there a neighbour . . . ?'

'I'll phone her later. I told her I'd speak to her this evening, once I knew what was what. So, if we can't have a funeral, there's no real reason why we have to stay up in Bradfield, is there?' It was as if she couldn't wait to get away.

'Well, you'll have to register the death. And deal with the estate,' Elinor said.

'Because the sooner we get Torin down to Bristol and

settled in there, the better,' she continued, as if Elinor hadn't spoken.

Her words galvanised Torin, who straightened out of his slump and shifted to the edge of his seat. 'Bristol? I'm not going to Bristol.'

'Of course you are, don't be silly. We're your family, we're all you've got left now, with your dad off wherever he is. You'll come to Bristol and live with me. Or your gran, whichever you prefer. We've both got room.' She sounded matter of fact, as if it was open and shut.

'Why would I want to go to Bristol? All me mates are here. I go to school here. I sing in a band here. Tell her, Elinor. I belong here, in Bradfield. It's bad enough losing my mum without you making me lose everything else as well.' Now he was on the verge of tears again. He rubbed his nose vigorously with his fist. 'I'm stopping here.'

'You can't stop here. You're only fifteen—'

'Actually, he's fourteen,' Elinor said.

Rachel looked momentarily cross, but she quickly reversed into sympathy. 'Torin, you can't live by yourself. You have to see sense. A clean break's best all round. You can make a fresh start.'

Now tears were spilling down his face. 'I don't want a fresh start. I want to be where I belong, where the places I go remind me of her and me and our life. I don't want any kind of break. My dad said I could stop in Bradfield. If you make me go to Bristol, I'll run away, I swear.' He banged his mug down so hard that tea slopped over the table.

'I understand why you're so upset. I am too. I'm tearing up just sitting here. She was my sister, and my heart's broken.' Rachel delicately wiped a tear away with a tissue. 'I want you with us because you're part of her.'

'What do you care? You don't know me. You hardly see us from one year's end to the next. You came for exactly one weekend last year, you and my gran. If Mum hadn't dragged me down to bloody Bristol for half-term, that would have been it. So don't pretend we're close, because we're not. You don't know anything about me.'

'We'll learn,' Rachel said softly. 'We should have spent more time together, you're right. But you always think there'll be time, down the line. You never think it'll be too late, just like that. You never think. I can't make it up to Bev, but I can make it up to you.'

'I don't want you to,' Torin said plaintively. 'I need to be here. This is all I've got left.'

'But you're too young to be on your own, Torin.'

Elinor knew it was coming before he turned to her. 'You'd let me stay, wouldn't you, Elinor? I could rent out our house and pay you the rent. It wouldn't cost you owt.'

'You know you're welcome here, Torin. But your aunt has a point. Your family can give you support we can't. When you need to talk about your mum, about her past, about what she was like when she was your age, we don't know the answers to those questions.' Being so generous was surprisingly hard. To her amazement, Elinor felt an ache inside at the thought of Torin leaving them. She wanted him to stay. It was unfathomable. She'd never wanted children. But this boy had touched her in a way she hadn't imagined possible.

'We can phone. I can go there for my holidays. But please, Elinor, let me stay. I want to be here.' He buried his face in his hands and wept. Elinor waited for Rachel to make a move, but she didn't. So Elinor got up and perched on the arm of his chair and hugged him close. She'd be damned if she was handing the boy over to a woman who didn't have the instinct to comfort him in his distress. When he eventually got himself under control, he stood up and said, 'I'm going up to my room.'

'I'm sure this isn't what Bev had in mind,' Rachel said as he closed the door behind him.

'I think it will be up to Torin and his father to decide what's going to happen in the long run,' Elinor said. 'Either way, this isn't the time or the place. You're both in a very emotional state. I suggest Torin stays here for now. We've spoken to Tom and he's sanctioned Torin living here with us for the time being. You'd be welcome too. There's a sofa bed in the study.'

'I don't think so,' Rachel said. 'I've got keys for Bev's. I'd rather feel her all around me than be in a strange place with strangers.'

'Of course. The police have already searched it – my partner, Paula, did it as soon as we realised Bev was missing. It's been hard for her, being so closely involved in the case. But if you like, I can call her and check that the police have finished with it?'

Rachel shook her head. 'I'll take my chances. If there's a problem, I'll go to a hotel. I just want to get things sorted out. I was pretty sure I was coming to bury my sister. All I wanted was to organise a nice funeral and take Torin home with me. It looks like I won't be doing either of those things.'

'I'm sorry,' Elinor said. And she was, because, as Paula regularly pointed out, Elinor was the nice one. But part of her felt a deep satisfaction that Torin wanted to stay.

41

The first thing Paula said when she came to meet him in the waiting area at Skenfrith Street was, 'I'm sorry.'

Tony was puzzled. 'Sorry for what? It's not like I was doing anything else.'

Uncharacteristically, Paula made no quip about him being a sad bastard. Instead, she briskly ushered him through into the main part of the station and down a hallway lined with doors. The signs said 'Interview Room' followed by a number. 'I misled you. I had to. It's the only way I could stay on the inside.'

'I don't understand.'

Paula stopped in front of a closed door, number four. 'You will.' She opened the door and gestured for him to enter.

The claustrophobic room was painted battleship grey with a low ceiling covered with acoustic tiles. There was no two-way mirror, just bare walls and a video camera mounted in one corner. DCI Fielding was already sitting in one of the grey plastic bucket chairs arrayed on either side of the grey table with the recording equipment. She didn't even raise her head from the file in front of her when they walked in. All she did was wave a hand at the chairs opposite her.

Tony had been in plenty of police interview rooms, but always on the questioner's side of the table. Unsure of what was going on, he sat down facing Fielding and was even more disconcerted when Paula took the seat next to her. Paula took out a notepad and pen and arranged them in front of her. He could see there was a list, presumably of questions, but he couldn't read her handwriting upside down.

'What's going on, Paula?'

Fielding looked up. 'Let's get the tape running, McIntyre.'

Paula gave him an apologetic look but she pressed the buttons on the recording equipment. After the long beep sounded, she said, 'Interview commenced at six twelve p.m. Present are DCI Alex Fielding, Detective Sergeant Paula McIntyre and Dr Tony Hill. Dr Hill, it's our intention to interview you under caution in connection with the murders of Nadzieja Wilkowa, known as Nadia, and Beverley McAndrew, known as Bev.'

'Are you arresting me?' There would be no mistaking his incredulity on the recording.

'Not at this point, no. We simply wish to ask you some questions. You're entitled to have a lawyer present. Would you like to have a lawyer?'

The role reversal was so startling that Tony couldn't quite process it at first. 'What do I need to be lawyered up for? I haven't done anything. Apart from a couple of unpaid parking tickets. On you go, Paula. Ask anything you want.'

'You do not have to say anything. But it may harm your defence if you do not mention when questioned something which you later rely on in court. Anything you do say may be given in evidence. Do you understand?'

'What defence? I thought you weren't arresting me?'

'It's a form of words, Dr Hill. As you well know. This isn't the time or the place for levity. Two women are dead.' Fielding's eyes held no promise of warmth. He'd heard she didn't hold much of a brief for his dark arts; he hadn't realised how deep her dislike for his work was. And of course, she was ambitious, which could be a hard thing for a female cop to negotiate. Solving these crimes quickly and nailing them on a high-profile offender would do her nothing but good in the eyes of those to whom those things mattered. Was he about to become a scapegoat? It was an unnerving thought. The only option was to pretend he had no idea what was going on.

'Of course. I apologise. Please, I'm happy to answer your questions. Is this to do with the bus? Only, that was just by chance that occurred to me. I bought more shopping than I intended and I had to get the bus.'

Now it was Fielding's turn to look baffled.

'Tony,' Paula said. 'All in good time. The first thing I have to ask you is to cast your mind back three Saturdays ago. Can you tell us where you were that Saturday afternoon and evening.'

'Saturday three weeks ago?' Theoretically, it should be easy. A day when he had no appointments. A day when he could please himself. But with nothing to differentiate one Saturday from another, how could he say what he had actually done?

'Bradfield Victoria were playing Chelsea at Stamford Bridge, if that helps.' Knowing his love for the Vics, Paula had checked the fixture list ahead of the interview.

His face cleared and he smiled. 'Of course. Ashley Cole conceded a penalty and looked like he was going to cry. I thought about watching it live at the pub, but I didn't fancy fighting for a seat and all that relentless camaraderie. So I watched the game at home. I had a couple of beers. Then I walked up to the chip shop on Mistle Row and bought cod and chips for my dinner.'

'Will they remember you?'

'Three weeks on? I shouldn't imagine so for a moment. It was busy after the game, I didn't talk to anyone.' He gave a hapless little shrug. 'I didn't know I was going to need an alibi.'

'And afterwards?'

'I went back to the boat.' He smiled at Fielding. 'I live on a narrowboat on Minster Basin. I spent the evening alone. I'm finally catching up with Scandinavian *noir*, so I probably watched a couple of episodes of *The Bridge* or *The Killing* then chances are I played Arkham City or Skyrim on my Xbox.'

'Do you enjoy violent computer games?' Fielding butted in.

'I enjoy computer games,' Tony said. 'Nobody gets hurt. It's fake, DCI Fielding. Whatever the *Daily Mail* likes to think, the jury's still out on any direct correlation between gaming and IRL violence.'

'For the tape, what's IRL?' Paula asked.

Tony rolled his eyes. 'In real life.'

'Did you make any phone calls?'

'I shouldn't think so. You have my permission to check my records with my mobile provider though.'

'Did anyone phone you?'

He locked his fingers behind his head and leaned back, making it obvious that he was thinking. At last he said, 'I think that's the Saturday when the Clinical Director of Bradfield Moor Secure Hospital phoned me but I didn't pick up the call. I was in the middle of my game and I didn't want to be interrupted by work on a Saturday evening.'

'It might have been an emergency relating to one of your patients.'

Tony inclined his head. 'Not very likely, but yes, it might have been. But I'm not the only clinical psychologist on the staff. I'm learning not to be indispensable.'

'You're sure that's what you did that Saturday? You didn't go shopping?'

'I don't do shopping, not in the sense of a leisure activity. I buy most of what I need online, and I buy my food at the supermarket. And I don't go there any Saturday. I go weekdays when it's quiet. Sometimes in the middle of the night, if I can't sleep. I went there yesterday evening. As you know, Paula, because I phoned you up afterwards to tell you to look at the bus CCTV to see whether you could spot Bev McAndrew.' He smiled at her, to remind her he was on her side.

'Like I said, we'll come to that. You didn't go to see a movie that Saturday, did you?'

He shook his head. 'No. I definitely didn't do that. I can't remember the last time I went to a cinema to see a movie. Either I stream them or I watch them on DVD. I hate the smell of cinemas. Popcorn and hot dogs.' His face echoed his disgust.

And so it crawled onwards. On Monday evening, when Bev had been abducted, he'd been at home, working on a parole report on his laptop. 'You can get some techie geek to check the time stamps on my computer.'

'Time stamps can be faked,' Fielding said dismissively.

The previous night, when Bev had been killed and dumped, he'd explained that he'd walked across town to Freshco and come home on the bus.

'Why did you go all the way to that Freshco? There are plenty of places you could have shopped closer to home,' Fielding asked.

Tony frowned, his eyes flicking back and forth between the two women. 'Because that's where Bev was most likely to have gone shopping after work. It was a reasonable hypothesis that her abductor might have acquired her there.'

'And how did you know all that?'

'Because Paula told me.' The 'duh' was unspoken, but Paula heard it loud and clear.

Fielding gave Paula a look of angry perplexity. Tony realised he might have dropped Paula in it even more than himself. Was this what all this was about? Was Fielding using him to destroy Paula?

'DS McIntyre?' Her expression was certainly severe enough for his theory to be on the money.

Paula wasn't conceding ground, however. She spoke clearly and confidently. 'I talked to Dr Hill after Bev went missing. I wanted to see if he had any suggestions that might help me trace her. I spoke as a friend of the family. Not as a police officer. It was barely a police case at that point.'

Fielding's grim expression indicated that Paula hadn't heard the last of this. 'So you decided to mount your own investigation, Dr Hill?'

'Not really. I needed a walk, I needed some shopping. Bev was at the back of my mind, that's all that was going on.' He leaned forward, his expression pained. 'Am I a suspect here?'

'At this point, we're just trying to resolve some issues,' Fielding said.

Tony wondered again what those issues were. Surely there were easier ways to bump Paula off the case, if that was what Fielding wanted? Perhaps he needed to be a little more proactive. With his skills, he should be able to control this interview. He tried his best conciliatory smile. 'Only, if I'm a suspect, why would I call Paula and suggest looking at the bus CCTV? Why would I help your investigation?'

Fielding sat back. 'If you figured it was going to come out

anyway – which it would have, once we had a full-scale murder investigation under way – you'd be diverting suspicion by pointing us in the right direction.' She let a tiny smile escape. 'Plus, aren't you profilers always telling us that killers like to inject themselves into the investigation? Seems to me that's one interpretation of what you did with DS McIntyre.'

Tony gave a self-mocking groan. 'Hoist by my own petard, eh?' He paused, frowning. 'What is a petard anyway? I've often wondered.'

'It's a bomb,' Fielding said. 'Stop trying to derail this interview, Dr Hill.'

'Busted,' he said, offering Paula a rueful look.

Fielding passed a couple of sheets of paper to Paula, who laid them on the table facing Tony. She tapped one. 'That's Nadia Wilkowa.' And the second. 'That's Bev McAndrew. Have you met either of these women?'

He had to admit, Paula was good. She'd asked the question in such a way that he could answer honestly without dropping her further in the shit. It was in nobody's interest right now for him to reveal she'd taken him to Nadia's flat. It would simply muddy the waters. He'd worn gloves so there would be no prints and he hadn't done anything to shed significant DNA there. Really, they should be in the clear. For now, at least.

'I'm not sure,' he said. He pulled Nadia's picture closer. 'She looks familiar. Actually, they both do. But I can't place either of them. I'm sorry.' He looked up, giving his best little-boy-lost. 'Bev worked at Bradfield Cross, right? They call me in for a psych consult from time to time. And occasionally I have meetings there. I might have run into her there. But I can't be certain.'

Fielding took another two pieces of paper from her folder and looked at them. 'You're an only child, is that right?'

'Why is that relevant?'

'Just answer, please.'

'Yes. I am an only child as far as I'm aware.'

'As far as you're aware?'

He shrugged. 'None of us can ever be certain of that. But I was brought up as an only child and I've no reason to think otherwise. Why do you care?'

Fielding set the two sheets of paper in front of Tony. The names had been blanked out with Post-it notes. 'Do you know what these are?'

He glanced down at the graphs with their jagged peaks. 'They look like DNA profiles.'

'This one came from the National DNA Database. And this one came from a bloodstain on Nadia Wilkowa's jacket. Even as a layperson, you can see the similarities,' Fielding said. 'Would you agree?'

'I've no expertise in this area,' Tony said cautiously. It was dawning on him that something more serious than fucking up Paula was going on here.

'The reason for the similarities is that there's a genetic relationship between these two people. What we call a familial relationship. A is the mother of B. Would you like to guess who A is?'

He met Fielding's level, triumphant gaze. 'No.'

'It's Vanessa Hill. Your mother. And this is presumably you. Can you explain how your blood came to be on the cuff of Nadzieja Wilkowa's jacket?'

It was as if someone had punched him hard in the chest. For a moment he couldn't breathe. Then the adrenalin rush of fear surged through him, switching his senses on full alert. His brain raced frantically, synapses firing crazily, rifling through his store of memories to find this woman. He knew he was innocent, so he knew the answer had to be in there somewhere.

He had no idea how long had passed before Paula said gently, 'Tony? Can you answer the question, please? Can you explain how your blood came to be—'

His expression was stricken. 'I've no idea,' he said, his voice dry and tight.

Fielding shook her head. 'I'd have thought you could do better than that.' She turned back to her folder.

Before she could ask another question, Paula's phone beeped. She glanced at the screen then showed it to Fielding, who nodded and got to her feet. 'Interview suspended.' Ushering Paula ahead of her, she left the room. Tony watched them go, feeling genuine fear for the first time since he'd arrived at Skenfrith Street.

'Fuck,' Fielding said as she closed the door behind her. 'He's got nothing. No rebuttal, no excuse, nothing. Now, let's see what your pal Dr Myers has for us.' The text from Dave Myers had simply said, Buy me a coffee. Seven minutes later Paula pulled in by the coffee stall that crouched under the North Stand of Bradfield Victoria's premier league stadium. Dave liked meeting here; it reminded him of American cop shows, glossing their dull lives with a spurious glamour. Seeing her car, he stepped away from the counter carrying two coffees in a cardboard tray. He looked worryingly glum. His face fell further when Fielding climbed out of the passenger seat.

He gave a wry smile and passed a coffee to each of the women. Paula leaned on the open driver's door and peeled away a section of the lid and enjoyed the aroma of the spicy dark roast the Italian owner preferred. She had a feeling there wasn't going to be much else to enjoy at this encounter.

'Nice of you to offer my sergeant a coffee, Dr Myers.'

'We go back a long way,' Paula said.

'So what do you have for us?'

'That evidence bag you left us this morning – there was a phone in there, right?'

'Yes. Presumably Bev's,' Paula said.

'It is hers. We checked.' He tugged at his soul patch. 'There's a partial thumbprint on the back of the phone.' He took a folded sheet of paper from his jacket pocket and handed it to Fielding. It was an enlarged photocopy of a fingermark, smudged down one side and slightly distorted where the thumb that made it had shifted slightly. 'Because I know you're in a hurry on this one, I gave it to my best fingerprint tech as a matter of urgency. She ran it through the AFIS database. Nothing came back from criminal records. But in Bradfield, we keep our own database of prints for elimination purposes. Serving police officers, CSIs, pathologists. And anybody else who regularly attends crime scenes or has contact with evidence.'

Fielding looked visibly brighter. 'I hope this is going where I think it is.'

Paula's response was markedly different. She snatched her emergency cigarette packet from the door pocket of the car and lit up.

Dave grimaced as the smoke blew across his face. He half-turned away from Paula towards Fielding. 'Her preliminary opinion is that the thumbprint on Bev's phone could have come from Tony Hill.'

'Could have?' Fielding was clearly disappointed. 'You can't do better than that?'

'It was a rush job. Obviously she'll be looking at it again.'

Paula's chest was tight with fear. These days, there was always room for doubt with fingerprints. No CPS lawyer would give the thumbs-up to a case that rested solely on fingermarks. But as a consolation, it was still rock-solid where juries were concerned. And would a jury be so wrong?

It was unimaginable to her, but what else but guilt could explain DNA *and* fingerprint evidence?

Tony had spent the half-hour of Paula and Fielding's absence racking his brains for an explanation as to how his blood had ended up on Nadia Wilkowa's cuff and he'd drawn a blank. It didn't help that he was feeling anxious. Stress was an enemy of recollection. Tranquillity, that was how you got the memories to flow. Not being wound up to a pitch.

When they finally returned, he practically jumped to his feet. 'This is crazy,' he said. 'Paula, we've known each other for years. You know I didn't kill anyone.'

'Sit down, Dr Hill,' Fielding said. 'This isn't about how well any of us knows you. It's about following the evidence where it leads us. And right now, it's only leading us in one direction.' She plonked her folder down on the table and drew a piece of paper out of it. 'Let's see what you make of this, shall we? You know what that is?'

'It's a fingerprint. Kind of smudged, but it's a fingerprint.'

'Actually, it's a thumbprint. The right thumb, to be exact. And so is this.' She proffered a printout of an official print card. 'Identical, I think you'd have to agree?'

This was starting to feel very uncomfortable. 'I have no expertise,' Tony said, his lips tight.

'You don't need expertise, you only need eyes. The print on the official record card was freely given by you just over three years ago. The other one was lifted from the back of Bev McAndrew's phone earlier today.'

There was a long silence. Tony could hear his blood pounding in his ears. The wheels were going round but they were gaining no traction. 'When did she go missing?' he asked, trying to buy time.

'She left work on Monday at the usual time. Shortly after half past five,' Paula said.

He ran a hand through his hair. 'I think I was at a meeting in Bradfield Cross on Monday afternoon ... I need to check my diary.'

'I'm not impressed with the absent-minded professor act,' Fielding said. 'Monday. This week. Where were you?'

Now it was time to find some steel. 'I already said. I need to check my diary.' He pushed the chair back. 'Are we about done here?'

'Not quite.' When she smiled, Fielding could look almost gentle. Nobody would have guessed, looking at her granite face then. 'Dr Hill, when did you last see ex-DCI Carol Jordan?'

Now he'd really had enough. He wasn't going to talk to this idiot any longer. He stood up. 'This interview is terminated. I'm done with answering your short-sighted questions. I've spent years trying to instil some understanding into police officers. And this is where it ends up.' He shook his head in disgust. 'Find somebody else to monster, DCI Fielding. I'm not playing any more.' He made for the door, but Fielding was ahead of him.

'Anthony Valentine Hill, I am arresting you on suspicion of murder. You do not have to say anything. But it may harm your defence if you do not mention when questioned something which you later rely on in court. Anything you do say may be given in evidence.'

He took a step back, turning to Paula, his face a mask of shock. 'Is she serious?'

'She's serious, Tony.'

He walked away from Fielding and sat down heavily in one of the chairs. 'Then, no comment.' Tony folded his arms across his chest and stared straight ahead. Inside, he was in turmoil. But on the outside, he would give nothing away.

Not until he'd figured out how to dig himself out of this hole.

42

Paula watched the duty sergeant walk Tony down to his cell. She'd processed him herself, making sure he was clear what he was entitled to. And that the duty sergeant knew she was looking out for her prisoner. 'You should call a lawyer,' she said.

'You can make the call from here,' the sergeant added, pointing to a payphone.

'I'll sleep on it,' Tony said. His face was drawn and tired and he seemed to have shrunk since he'd arrived at the station.

'I'm sorry,' Paula said.

He nodded. 'I know. It's OK. We're good.'

She desperately wanted to say more, but couldn't risk it. This was Fielding's nick, not hers, and she didn't know who to trust yet. Weary and unsure of what to do for the best, she headed upstairs, pausing for a cigarette break before facing Fielding and the murder squad. Cody was leaning against the wall by the door, blowing a stream of smoke upwards. 'Nice work,' he said.

'You think?'

'It's always good to get a collar early on. Gets the brass off your back and the media out of your face.'

'Even if it's the wrong collar?'

'Oh, I forgot. He's a mate of yours, isn't he? He's always been an oddball, from what the lads are saying.'

'It's a long way from oddball to sexual homicide. And I don't think he's capable of it.'

'Word is he lost the plot after the Jacko Vance business. That's why Jordan walked away from him. She knew he'd turned.'

All at once, Paula's moment of doubt became history. She stepped right into Cody's personal space and jabbed a finger into his chest. 'Where are you getting this crap from, Cody? Or are you making it up as you go along to wind me up? Jesus Christ,' she exploded. 'You sound like one of those tabloid reptiles who go in for trial by headline. Carol Jordan lost her brother. That's why she walked back from all of us. It's called grief, you twat.' She stepped back and turned away from him. 'It's got fuck all to do with this.'

'Take it easy, Sarge,' Cody said, his voice sarcastic. 'People'll think you've cracked an' all.'

'If I hear you or anyone else talking this kind of shit, I'll go straight to Fielding with it. That's a promise.'

Cody gave a soft, dark chuckle. 'What makes you think it's not coming from Fielding, Sarge?' Paula whirled round and crushed out her cigarette against the wall millimetres from his ear. He yelped as hot ash hit the sensitive skin. 'You mad bitch,' he yelled.

'You mad bitch, *Sergeant*. I'd advise you not to forget either part of that sentence, Cody.' She turned on her heel and stomped back inside, glad anger had replaced the fear and depression that had been building up all evening.

She found Fielding in her office, packing files into her

laptop bag. 'You should have told me you'd spoken to him about Bev McAndrew going missing.'

'I know. I'm sorry.' Paula waited for the bollocking. But to her surprise, Fielding walked away from it.

'I understand how it happened,' she said, sounding almost as weary as Paula felt. 'You're used to him being inside the tent, it was a natural thing to do.'

'What do you want me to do now?'

'Go home. Eat something. Sleep. We'll go back on the attack in the morning. Hopefully, the fingerprint techs will give us a definite yes rather than "could be". And we'll conduct a full search of his home and his office. Do you know if he has a storage unit or a lock-up or something as well as his boat?'

'No idea.'

'We'll check it tomorrow. I've got the grunts looking at the CCTV footage to see if we can pick him up anywhere relevant.'

Paula rolled her shoulders to loosen up the tightness that had been building there. 'Do you really think he did it?'

'I'm following the evidence, McIntyre. And that's where it's leading me. You're letting your emotions cloud your judgement.'

'Am I? I don't think it's my emotions. It's my knowledge and experience. I've worked with Tony Hill for years. He *saves* lives, he doesn't take them.'

'And I think you could be totally wrong. But it's good that you're digging your heels in. It gives me something to push against. It means we'll test our case properly and not get ambushed in court by the defence. Right now, though, we're just at the start. Away home now and come back in the morning refreshed and ready to go.'

'What about the media? Have we told them we've made an arrest?'

Fielding shook her head. 'I've told the squad to say nothing. Which probably means it'll be all over the internet by bedtime. But I'm saying nothing officially.' She fastened her case and shooed Paula out of the office. 'See you in the morning. With a bit of luck, we'll see his happy little face on the Trafford Centre cameras.'

And she was gone, leaving Paula all wound up with nowhere to go.

Home had never been like this. It was like walking into the middle of an intense TV drama. Torin was on his laptop at the dining table, a strange woman Paula presumed to be Rachel McAndrew was in an armchair with an iPad and a glass of wine and Elinor was ironing a white shirt. Ironing a shirt? Paula hadn't realised Elinor knew where the ironing board lived. But death – particularly sudden, violent death – always left people unsure of how to fill their time. The look of relief on Elinor's face told Paula all she needed to know for now.

'Hey, Torin,' Paula said. 'Hello, love,' to Elinor. And, 'You must be Rachel. I'm Paula. I can't tell you how sorry I am about Bev. We were very fond of her.'

Rachel put down her wine and stood up, extending a slim hand adorned with a couple of diamond rings. 'It's such a shock,' she said, her voice tremulous. 'And Elinor says we can't even bury her.'

Paula flashed a quick look at Torin, whose head lowered even closer to his screen, hair hiding his eyes. 'I've arranged for a Family Liaison Officer to come over tomorrow morning to take you through what's happening and explain how to go about the official side of things. He'll be here at half past nine.'

'Rachel's planning to stay at Bev's tonight, if that's OK with the police,' Elinor said. 'But Torin would rather stay here.'

Paula smiled. 'No problem, mate. I don't think I'd want to go back there just yet if I was you. There's no rush.' Torin's head bobbed in acknowledgement. 'I do have some news about the investigation which I wanted to share with you.' The atmosphere in the room quickened. Torin looked up, his eyes beseeching her. Rachel froze, her hand halfway to her wine. And Elinor gave her a tiny nod of encouragement.

'This evening we made an arrest in connection with Bev's death. And that of Nadia Wilkowa, another woman whose body was found earlier this week.' Paula held her hands up, palms out, urging caution. 'I don't want you to overreact to this. It's very early in the investigation and I'll be honest with you. I have serious reservations about the guilt of the person in custody. This happens sometimes in serious crime investigations. We arrest a suspect early on, with minimal amounts of evidence. That doesn't mean the investigation is over. In this case, the investigation's barely begun. But this arrest will be all over the media tomorrow and you should be prepared for that. It would be best if you don't speak to the media, but obviously that's up to you.'

'Who is it?' Torin demanded. 'Who did this to my mum?'

'The man we've arrested is called Dr Tony Hill. He's a psychologist who works at Bradfield Moor Secure Hospital and for years now he's also been working with us at BMP, drawing up profiles of serious offenders.'

'This man *worked* with you? And you had no idea he was a killer?' Rachel's outrage was obvious. It would only get worse, Paula suspected. Grief had to find an outlet somewhere.

'We don't know that he's a killer. Personally, I don't believe it. It goes against everything I know about the man.' But she had to be honest. She owed that to Bev's family. 'There is some evidence that points towards him though. We have to test that evidence and see whether we can actually build a case against him.' She looked to Elinor for support, but her partner was speechless, her face aghast.

'I don't understand,' Torin said. 'Did this guy know my mum from work? Why did he pick her?'

'We don't know, Torin. Right now, we have a lot more questions than we have answers. All I can say is that we're doing our job. None of this helps you to deal with your mum's death, I know. But I'm doing my best for her.'

'Great speech, Detective,' Rachel said. 'I think it's time I went over to Bev's.' To Elinor, 'Have you got a taxi number?'

'I could drive you over,' Elinor said. 'It's no trouble.'

'Thanks, but you've done more than enough for us,' Rachel said. It was a line that could have been taken either way and Elinor clearly got that.

Elinor called their usual taxi firm and Paula escaped to the kitchen. She was staring gloomily into the fridge when Elinor joined her. 'Taxi's on its way, thank goodness. She's hard work, Rachel. I made sandwiches for us all earlier. I'm afraid I used all the ham and cheese and salad.'

Talk of food was a displacement activity that displaced nothing for either of them. Paula closed the fridge. 'I'm not actually hungry. This has been one of the worst days of my working life. Not quite up there with the Temple Fields ordeal, but pretty damn close.'

'I can't believe it. Has Fielding lost her mind? Tony? If I had to compile a list of everyone I know in order of how likely they were to commit murder, I'd put him very near the bottom.'

'Same here. But she doesn't know him like we do. To Fielding, he's just another prospect in a sea of possibilities. But he is the scalp that will make her name. Can you imagine the headlines?' She shuddered. 'It's so ironic. One of the reasons she's convinced he's the one is that the victims look a bit like Carol Jordan. According to her armchair psychology, he's killing surrogates because he can't have her. But the truth is, the only person Tony would kill *for* is Carol.' Paula sighed and opened the fridge again. This time, she took out a pot of yoghurt. She stared at it for a long moment then put it back and closed the door again.

Elinor put her arms around her from behind and kissed the soft skin behind her ear. 'What are you going to do about it?'

'I don't know. I think Fielding's testing me. Am I good enough to be her bagman? If I put a foot wrong, she'll have my stripes, maybe even my job. So I have to be very careful not to be seen to be helping Tony. But I can't just stand by and let this happen to him. I understand exactly how the momentum builds behind an arrest.'

'The juggernaut of justice.'

'Exactly. People focus on anything that supports the arrest and dismiss any faint indications of other directions.' She leaned her forehead on the cool fridge door. 'I've never missed the MIT more.'

'Carol would know what to do.'

'Carol would never have arrested Tony in the first place. She'd have viewed the evidence against him as some kind of pointer towards the real killer. Or something.'

'You need her now. She'd be ferocious as a lioness protecting her cub.'

Paula gave a sad little laugh. 'Once upon a time, maybe. Now I'm not so sure. Whatever the glue was that held those two together seems to have come unstuck. And besides, she's not a cop any more.'

'All the better, surely? Paula, I know you. You need to do something or you're going to be awake all night, smoking too much and drinking too much coffee and twitching. And taking years off your life, which makes me very unhappy because I need you to be around for a very long time. Go and find Carol. Let her do the heavy lifting.'

Paula shook with silent laughter. 'You're crazy. You say "go and find her" like it was straightforward. She's gone off the radar. Even Stacey doesn't know where she is.'

'Stacey only knows machines. You know people.'

Elinor's words triggered something inside Paula's head. Not quite fully formed, but the teasing start of something. It was interrupted by the doorbell. 'That'll be the taxi,' Elinor said. 'I'll see Rachel off the premises. Don't move, I'll be right back.'

Preoccupied, Paula opened the fridge for a third time and took out a plastic container of leftover chilli. She flipped the edge of the lid open and stuck it in the microwave. By the time Elinor returned, she was forking it into her mouth, frowning into the middle distance.

'She's gone,' Elinor said. She sighed. 'It hasn't been an easy afternoon. She wants to take Torin to Bristol with her.'

'That's good, surely?'

'Except that Torin doesn't want to go. His arguments are very reasonable – his friends are here, his school, his band—'

'He's in a band?'

'Apparently he sings. Who knew? Also, he wants to be somewhere that holds memories of his mum. Not ripped out of the ground and transplanted to a strange city to live with people he barely knows.'

'Like you say, reasonable.' Paula was focusing on Elinor now, realising there was more going on than was being said. 'And?'

'It's a "but" really, not an "and". But he has no family here. And he's only fourteen.' She took a deep breath. 'He wants to stay with us, Paula. At least until his dad deploys back to the UK.'

Paula's eyes widened. 'Here? Living with us?'

Elinor pushed a stray strand of hair from her face. 'I don't know how I can say no.'

Paula's smile was wry and knowing. 'Even if you wanted to. Fuck, Elinor, this wasn't in my life plan. Somebody else's teenage kid.'

'Right now, he's a good kid, Paula. What happens to him next will determine if he carries on being a good kid. You know that. You see the results of fucked-up young men every working day. So do I. A&E is full of them. I think we should say yes.'

'What does Auntie Rachel say?'

'She's not happy. But then, I have a sense that Auntie Rachel isn't happy about much in her life. Ultimately, it's his father who has to make the decision. He might think the worst thing that could happen to his son is to be left to the tender mercies of a pair of big old dykes. But until that happens, I think we need to hang on to Torin. It's what he wants, and I think you in particular might be what he needs.'

Paula gobbled some more chilli, suddenly starving. 'I don't seem to have much say in this.' It was, they both recognised, an objection for form's sake only. More a gentle demurral than a righteous protest.

'Like you're going to start walking away from doing the right thing. Now finish up that chilli and get on the trail of Carol Jordan.'

Paula smiled. 'I had an idea about that.'

43

The cuisine that Marco Mather had learned from his mother was one of the healthiest in the world. At its heart, the Southern Italian food was the diet of peasants, too poor for obscure or luxurious items. It was based on a handful of easily grown vegetables and herbs, olives and their oil, cheeses made from the milk of hardy goats and sheep, and small amounts of game and poultry. But like so many other aspects of modern life, it had become corrupted by money.

That frugal but delicious diet had spread like a spare tyre to embrace all manner of richness. Estate-bottled olive oil used as a dip for enriched breads; cream and butter liberally added to sauces and ragus which contained more meat than their original creators would have eaten in a month; full-fat cheeses from grass-fed dairy cows; and an endless supply of tasty processed pig products. Italian food at its worst had become an invitation to obesity and furred-up arteries.

It was an invitation that Marco had embraced. The food

he created for their daily dinners was loaded with calories and cholesterol. Marie loved it, but she fought its effects by skipping breakfast and sticking strictly to so-called healthy options at lunchtime. Marco, working from home at his desk, had only his willpower to keep him from food during the day, and it generally let him down at least once between breakfast and bedtime. For a long time, his natural metabolism had kept his weight more or less under control. But as middle age crept closer, so the pounds were creeping on. His trousers were tighter and his thighs had begun to rub together as he walked.

And so he'd decided to lose some weight. He'd read several articles online and watched a documentary on TV about a new regime of exercise that involved short bursts of intensive aerobic exercise. The results were little short of miraculous. For less than two hours a week, his heart would be healthier, his weight would reduce and he'd live longer. He'd always resisted exercise in the past because it bored him. But surely he could manage a few minutes a day without losing his mind? It would be worth it, if it allowed him to continue cooking and eating the food he loved.

Marco had told Marie his plan, and she'd been delighted. She loved her husband and she hadn't wanted to make him feel bad about himself, she said. But she wouldn't mind if he lost a few pounds. So he'd ordered a state-of-the-art exercise bike and had it installed in the garage that morning. Now he was going to go for the burn. He hadn't done any exercise since he'd given up squash a dozen years before but he was confident he'd nail this.

He stripped to his boxer shorts, pulled on a pair of trainers and climbed aboard. He understood the importance of going flat out. He had to push himself to the very limit and go as fast as his legs could pump. He set the timer and started out, driving his legs up and down like pistons, pedalling as fast as he was able. In no time at all, his heart was hammering, sweat was bursting out in beads on his forehead and his breathing was ragged and painful. But he kept going. Surely to god he could exercise for five minutes?

Marco drove himself on, pushing forward, convinced he would break through the pain barrier to some zen-like state. But his distress just kept increasing till a spasm of pure agony seized his chest and rippled through his upper body. His arms were on fire, his chest gripped by an iron band.

He toppled from the bike, in the grip of a massive heart attack. Even if Marie had been there to summon the paramedics, it's doubtful whether they could have saved him.

And so, when a killer stole Marie Mather on the very street where she lived, there was nobody to notice she hadn't come home. Nobody to report her missing. Nobody to add her name to the list of victims.

Nobody to exonerate the man in custody.

44

Paula was glad it was dark as she drove out across the Yorkshire moors. It hid the interminable bleakness that always filled her heart with gloom. Other people saw splendour in the scenery, she knew that. But thanks to years of exposure to the worst of human behaviour, she saw it as a place where terrible things could go unwitnessed. A potential body dump. The landfill of loss.

Franklin had been reluctant to confirm what she'd guessed. 'Why would I know where your old DCI is hiding?' he'd said on the phone, sounding more amused than truculent. 'It's not like we were pals.'

'I had you down as somebody who knows when a mouse farts on his patch,' Paula said. 'So if you don't know where she is, I'd have to conclude she's not in West Yorkshire. And focus my attentions elsewhere.'

As she'd expected, the challenge to his capability did the trick. 'I never said I didn't know,' he replied.

'Any reason why you wouldn't tell me?'

'Is this a police inquiry, Sergeant? Or a personal one?'

'Does it make a difference, sir?'

'We're all entitled to our privacy and our family life, according to the human rights lawyers. If Jordan doesn't want to play nice with you lot any more, that's her choice. And it wouldn't be my place to deprive her of those rights.'

'And if it was an official inquiry?'

'I'd expect it to come through official channels.'

'I'm a detective sergeant, sir. How official do you need it to be?' There was a long pause. She could hear the rasp of him scratching stubble.

'Ah, fuck it,' he said. 'Why are we playing stupid games with each other? She's living at the barn. Her brother's barn. She's stripping it to the bare bones. There's nothing left to show what happened.'

'Thank you. I owe you a pint, sir.'

'You do. But I'll pass. I don't like you Bradfield bastards. That goes for Jordan just as much as the rest of you. So there's enough pleasure for me in grassing her up. Drive safe, Sergeant, we're not keen on dangerous drivers over here.'

He was gone before she could say more. And now it was after nine o'clock and the only thing between her and despair was the satnav. Every road looked the same, bordered by the wild grasses of the moorland or drystone walls that looked drunk but always seemed to stay upright. Occasional lights glimmered in the dark and now and again she'd pass a huddle of buildings claiming to be a village. Finally, a large building loomed on her right and her bossy navigator said, 'You have reached your destination.' Paula pulled into the parking area and turned off the engine. She felt sick.

Still, she forced herself out of the car and set off across the flags towards the barn. Security lights flooded the area, making her blink against her blindness. The stillness of the night was split open by a volley of barking that was barely diminished by the thick stone walls of the barn. A dog? Carol Jordan, the ultimate cat woman, had a dog? Had Franklin told her the truth? For a moment, Paula considered turning tail. But she'd come all this way. She might as well knock on the door.

As she raised her hand to the black iron knocker, the door opened far enough to reveal a familiar face. Carol Jordan did not look pleased to see her, and the dog whose muzzle was pushing against her knee didn't seem any more welcoming. A low grumble in the back of its throat would keep most sensible people at bay.

Paula tried a smile. 'Any chance of a cup of coffee? There isn't a Costa for miles.'

'Is that your best door-opener? Don't, for Christ's sake, abandon the job for a career in sales.' The door didn't budge. 'Give me one good reason why I should open the door?'

Paula reminded herself that Carol wasn't her boss any more. 'Because it's a bloody long drive and it's bloody cold out here. That's the smart-arsed answer. If you want the sincere one – you should open the bloody door out of friendship.'

Carol's eyebrows rose. 'You think we're friends?'

'You think we're not? We had each other's backs for years. I always thought we liked each other. Respected each other. I never even considered a future you weren't part of.' Paula flushed, wondering whether she'd gone too far. Carol's reserve in personal matters was as much part of her as her devotion to taking criminals off the streets.

Carol lowered her eyes. 'I'm not sure friendship is one of my strengths.'

'You'll never find out if you carry on running away from everybody who cares about you. Now, are you going to let me in before I freeze my tits off?'

Almost a smile. Carol opened the door and stepped back. She clicked her fingers and the dog lay down at her feet. 'Come in.'

The space Paula entered was a building site, a work in progress. A couple of industrial lamps in their metal cages lay on the floor, casting light and shadow in a complicated chiaroscuro, making it difficult to get a clear picture of what was going on. She clocked the sawhorses, a workbench, bare stonework and bundles of cable and wire sticking out at odd angles. 'Funny,' she said. 'I never had you down as a DIY queen. Or are you just getting in touch with your inner butch?'

'It's therapeutic. I'm undoing the past and making a future.'

She sounded like a cut-price version of Tony. 'Is there anywhere to sit?'

Carol gestured with her head for Paula to follow her. They went through a door and into another world. For a start, it was warm. The room resembled a small loft apartment. Bed, workspace, cooking area. No living area. Just a couple of office chairs in front of three computer monitors and a flat-screen TV.

The light was brighter here too. Paula could see Carol clearly, and as she'd never seen her before. Her hair was thicker and cut more bluntly than previously. There was silver among the blonde, glinting as it caught the light. Either she'd given up dyeing her hair or the years had finally caught up with her. She wore no make-up and her hands were scarred and scabbed from the snags and scratches of physical labour. Even under the thick sweater and jeans that she wore, it was obvious her upper body was more solid, her thighs stronger. In spite of it all, Carol looked healthier than she had for years. And Paula couldn't help remembering that she'd carried a torch for her former boss. Until Elinor

297

had come along and reality had consigned fantasy to the dustbin.

'What's with the dog?' Paula held out a hand to Flash, who sniffed it disdainfully then turned away and followed his mistress as she filled the kettle and set it to boil. Carol readied a cafètiere with ground coffee. 'And where's Nelson?'

'I left him with my parents. He's too old for all this. The dog is a misfit who's here for the time being. We're both on trial, I think.' She turned to face Paula and leaned against the worktop. She pushed up her sleeves, revealing muscular forearms which she folded across her chest. 'So have you come to warn me too?'

'Warn you?'

Carol shook her head, disappointment on her face. 'Don't try to kid a kidder, Paula. John Franklin told me you were Fielding's bagman. Come to that, I saw you myself this morning at the crime scene. So let's start again. Have you come to warn me too?'

'Carol, I really don't know what you're talking about. Has Franklin been here? Today?' This wasn't making any sense to Paula.

'He stopped by this morning after Fielding handbagged him and took the case away.'

'Pissed off, was he?'

'Oddly enough, no.' The kettle boiled and she poured hot water on the grounds. The smell was tantalising. One thing Carol and Tony still had in common; you always got a better than decent cup of coffee. 'He said he was here to warn me.'

'What? To keep your nose out?'

'Warn me, not warn me off,' Carol said impatiently. 'He told me there's a killer on the loose who seems to have a thing for women who look like me.'

Paula was taken aback. 'Well, women who look like you

used to look. I'll be honest, you don't look like anybody's potential victim these days. Not that you ever did,' she added hastily, seeing the danger signs in Carol's expression. 'So, was that a surprise, Franklin showing up?'

'Completely out of the blue.' Carol smiled. 'I was gobsmacked. I'd always thought if there was any chance of me being murdered, Franklin would be out there selling tickets.'

'Only if it was happening well away from his patch.'

'True. So if you're not here to warn me to lock my doors and avoid the lonely graveyard at midnight, why are you here? I'm not naïve enough to think it's because you missed me.'

'But I do miss you. And not just because DCI Fielding is most emphatically not you.' Paula accepted a cup of coffee and blew gently to cool it. 'You made it clear you were done with Bradfield, done with the lot of us. And we all respected that. I respected that. Even though what I wanted was to be your friend. To take you out and get drunk with you. To listen to your pain. To bring you home and let Elinor cook you chicken pie and mash.' To her annoyance, Paula could feel her throat constrict with all the tears she hadn't shed with Carol.

'I understand that. What I did was the only thing I knew how to do. The last time I thought I'd lost everything, I ran away. And it worked. I was able to heal myself enough to come back into the world. That's what I'm trying to do this time.' She opened a cupboard and took out a bottle of brandy and poured a slug into her coffee.

'You drank too much last time too,' Paula said, feeling the crack of thin ice under her.

Carol's lip curled. 'Tony always did over-share with you.'

Paula shook her head. 'Tony never said a word out of place about you. I know you drank too much because you were still drinking too much when you set up the MIT. You

299

think we didn't know about the miniatures of vodka in your handbag and the quarter bottles in the desk drawer?'

Carol started as if she'd been slapped. 'And you never said anything? You knew I was drinking on the job and you never said anything?'

'Of course we didn't. Even Sam the Snitch had more sense. Besides, why would we? It's not like you were falling over drunk. It never interfered with the way you ran the team.'

'Christ, I never realised you all knew. Call myself a detective?' She turned away, embarrassed. 'So, why are you here? Really? Because if you'd come here with the olive branch of friendship, Elinor would have sent a Tupperware box of home baking with you.'

The time for bridge-building banter was over. Now it was time to cut to the chase. 'I'm here because DCI Fielding has arrested Tony for the murder of two women.'

Carol stared, open-mouthed, the cup halfway to her lips, disbelief growing on her face as the words sank in. She craned her head forwards as if she was straining to hear. 'Come again?' she said, full of obvious scepticism.

'We interviewed him under caution this evening and then she decided to charge him. And it's mad. I know it's mad, you know it's mad. But there's evidence. And Fielding can't see past that to the man. He needs your help.'

Carol put her coffee down and held her hands up. 'Whoa. Back up there. I'm not a cop any more, Paula.'

'You think I don't understand that? That's exactly why he needs you and not me. I'm on a knife edge here. I shouldn't be telling you this stuff. If Fielding finds out, it'll be all over for me. I'll have a dazzling career in Traffic.'

Carol frowned. 'So why are you here?'

'I told you. Tony needs your help. He's hopeless. Carol, you know better than anybody else what he's like. He thinks just because he's innocent that nothing bad will happen to him. And we both know how naïve that is.'

'I couldn't agree more,' Carol said, her voice the epitome of chilly reasonableness. 'But why would you think I'd leap to his defence?'

Now it was Paula's turn to be shocked. 'Because ...' She couldn't bring herself to use the l-word. 'Because he's your friend?'

Carol's face had grown bitter. Now her tone matched it. 'Look around you, Paula. I know you didn't see what happened here, but imagine the scene. Now imagine two people you love at the heart of that scene. That's what I went through because Tony failed them. He failed me. He didn't do his job and we paid the price. Me and my parents and my brother and the woman he loved.'

Paula shook her head in dismay. 'You can't blame Tony. He's a psychologist, not a psychic. How can you expect him to know the details of what Vance had planned? What Vance did was off the scale of vengeance. None of us, not one of us imagined for a moment that the people we loved were at risk. Carol, I know you're hurting. And I know how grief messes with our heads. Believe me, I know. But it was Vance who did this to you. Not Tony.'

Carol's mouth had a stubborn set to it. 'It's his job to think of the things that don't occur to the rest of us. And everybody else paid the price, not him. Michael and Lucy, Chris, that stable lad, my parents, me. Even Vanessa suffered more than he did.'

'And you think that doesn't torture him every day? You think he's not torn apart with guilt? I've watched him suffer his own sense of failure. Believe me, Carol, you can't load more blame on him than he does on himself. How long is this going to go on? His shame and your blame? Are you going to let this define the rest of your lives? Because from where I'm standing, frankly, it's a colossal waste of two people's lives.' It was out before Paula knew she was going to say it. Challenging Carol wasn't something she'd been able to do in the past; the obligations of rank had always been the final stumbling block.

'It's none of your business, Paula.' Carol walked out of the room, through to the barn. The dog gave Paula a baleful look then went after Carol into the chill.

Paula hung her head and sighed. 'Blew that one,' she said under her breath. She waited to see whether Carol was coming back, but she was out of luck. So she returned the way she'd come. Carol was standing by a window, staring out at the dark. Paula could see her face in the glass. Her expression was as hard as the reflective surface.

'This is so unfair,' Paula said. 'Fielding's got everything on her side. Me included. And he's got nothing and nobody. He hasn't even got a lawyer.'

'I don't do pity, remember?'

Paula kicked out at a sawhorse in her frustration then shouted at Carol for the first time in her life. 'It's not about pity, for fuck's sake. It's about justice. The woman I used to know cared about justice.' The slam of the door behind her as she left was the only satisfying moment of the whole encounter.

45

Tony sat on the edge of the narrow ledge that passed for a bed in the Skenfrith Street custody suite, his elbows on his knees, his hands clasped. He'd been in police cells before, but only in the course of business. Talking to the damaged, the deranged and the demonised had brought him to places like this, but always with the door open. He'd often tried to put himself in the shoes of the captive, imagining how it must feel when that door slammed shut and they were alone. But he'd always started from a place of empathy – what it would be like for them. As opposed to how he would feel himself.

Mostly what he felt was uncomfortable. Being on his own in a small space didn't bother him. For a man who had learned to live on a narrowboat, it was no big deal. The noises-off didn't bother him either. Working in a secure mental hospital was an inoculation against unexpected and inexplicable human clamour. He wasn't hungry or thirsty yet, so that wasn't an issue. But there was no getting away from the discomfort. The bed was hard. There was a thin wafer of foam which he assumed was meant to be a pillow. It was lumpy and peculiarly distorted. Using it was like putting his head on a bag of liquorice allsorts. The physical discomfort made thinking much harder. And thinking was what he needed to do.

When the custody sergeant had closed the door behind him, Tony had almost expected him to throw it open and shout, 'Surprise!' That was how hard it was for him to credit what had happened. All through that bizarre interview with Paula and Alex Fielding, part of him had refused to take it seriously. He couldn't escape the notion that it was either a wind-up or a terrible mistake that he'd be able to put right in no time. Then it had dawned on him that Fielding was serious. Serious as only someone who didn't know him could be. Serious as only a detective driven by ambition could be.

Paula knew. Paula understood that whatever the physical evidence said, it was impossible to envisage him as a killer. But Paula wasn't the one making the decisions in that interview room. Paula was on trial too, her loyalty to the new boss under fire. Would she follow blindly where the evidence appeared to lead? Or would her fidelity to the old regime undermine Fielding's determination to get a quick and spectacular resolution to the case? On the walk down to the cells, she'd indicated she was on his side. But she had to be careful. For both their sakes, it was vital that she didn't get moved off the investigation. And there was only so much good that she could do by stealth.

Fielding scared him. That rush to judgement, that adamantine certainty that the evidence was king, that unwillingness to twist the Rubik's cube and look at things from a different angle – they all unsettled him, because there was no room for discussion. It wouldn't be enough for him to provide an explanation for the physical evidence against him. He'd have to find a reason to direct her hunter-killer instincts towards the real murderer.

Tony shifted awkwardly from one buttock to the other. If he hadn't let Carol down so badly, he'd never have found himself in this position. She simply wouldn't have allowed it to happen. No matter what cards might have been stacked against him, she would have taken his part, because she understood the limits of his capabilities.

He permitted himself a wry smile. Nobody knew his limits better than Carol. He'd always thought she could do better than him, that there must be other men out there who could give her more of what she needed than he had. But either she wasn't looking or she wasn't meeting the right men. Until her brother's death, she'd been happy to settle for their incomplete and inconclusive relationship. And then they'd found something that divided them so deeply nothing could bridge the gap. Not a shared history, not a mutual understanding. Not even love.

Impatient with himself, Tony jumped to his feet. If sitting or lying was torture, then he would pace. Six strides one way, ninety-degree turn then eight strides the other way. Six, eight. Six, eight. Stop brooding about Carol. She was gone. She wouldn't be there to pull him out of this particular pile of shit. It was over. He was on his own. Perhaps with a little help from his friend. Six, eight.

So. He had to explain the bloodstain. Others could find the verification of his story once he'd reached deep inside and accessed the truth. The thumbprint, too. That wasn't ringing any bells. 'I know I live in my head half the time, but you'd think I'd remember picking up somebody else's phone,' he shouted in exasperation.

Tony stopped pacing and leaned his forehead on the cool cement wall. He closed his eyes and dropped his shoulders. He deliberately relaxed his muscles from his scalp through his neck and arms. 'Think about blood. Your blood. About bleeding. Bleeding enough to stain somebody else,' he said out loud. There was the knee. The time when a crazed patient had gone on the rampage with a fire axe and had taken a swipe at Tony when he tried to talk him down. But that had been years ago, long before Nadia Wilkowa had ever come to Bradfield. A couple of times, he'd cut himself in the galley, unaccustomed to the occasional sudden movement of the boat. But there had never been anybody else there and besides, there hadn't been much blood. It had to be something that happened at work. In Bradfield Moor. He summoned up the hospital, as if he was offering someone a guided tour. The reception area. The locked doors, the faceless corridors. His office, the therapy rooms.

And then he remembered. Suddenly, it was all there, in crystal clear Technicolor detail. He threw his arms in the air. 'Halle-fucking-lujah!' The explanation of the thumbprint could wait. The DNA was the killer piece of evidence and now he knew how it had got there.

Tony grinned. Paula would be pleased. Now he just had to think of something that would lead them to the person who was actually killing women who looked like Carol Jordan.

46

While Tony was dredging his memory, another conversation went like this: 'Bronwen Scott here.'

'This is Carol Jordan.'

A pause. 'As in, DCI Carol Jordan?' Cautious, very cautious.

'As in ex-DCI Carol Jordan. I'm not a cop any more. But you, I presume, are still the best criminal defence lawyer in Bradfield?'

'That's quite an accolade, Ms Jordan. And I always thought you hated me.'

'I don't have to like you to appreciate your professional qualities.'

'So, to what do I owe this call? I'm assuming you didn't phone me at this time of night just to bolster my self-confidence. Don't tell me someone's had the temerity to arrest you?'

'I have a job for you. A client for you to represent. And a proposition in relation to that.'

'Sounds fascinating.' A long-drawn breath. 'But it's late. Won't it wait till morning?'

'I don't think so, no. Can you meet me in the car park opposite Skenfrith Street police station in half an hour?'

'Very Deep Throat. Why should I do this, Ms Jordan? What's in it for me?'

'A high-profile case. And the chance to fuck up BMP. I imagine no day is wasted for you if you get to fuck up an SIO.'

A throaty chuckle. 'You know which buttons to push, Ms Jordan.'

'I had an excellent teacher. Do we have an appointment?'

'It had better be good. It had better be very good.'

Carol smiled. 'I don't think you'll be disappointed.' She ended the call and changed down to third gear to negotiate a series of bends that climbed over the moor top before the descent into Bradfield. It hadn't been easy to maintain her composure during the phone call to the toughest criminal defence lawyer she'd ever jousted against. To say her feelings about the course of action she'd settled on were mixed was like saying the government had racked up a few debts. Her gut was churning and her hands were clammy on the wheel. Part of her wished she'd managed to ignore Paula altogether.

But she hadn't. When Paula had stormed out, Carol had barely paused before she gave chase. She caught up with her before she was halfway to her car. It didn't take much to persuade Paula back inside, where she gave Carol the kind of briefing that had been second nature when they worked together. The more she heard, the more Carol had been inflamed by the absurdity of what had happened to Tony. 'Not all evidence is created equal,' she'd protested. 'More often than not, it's coloured by its connections. You look at someone like Tony and your starting point is, this man

308

didn't kill two women. So how is it that the evidence seems to point towards him? You don't just go, "Here's a bit of evidence, it must be you." That's not how you get justice.'

And so of course she had to wade in. It wasn't quite that simple, though. She couldn't entirely escape the notion that she'd been played by Paula. She suspected the detective had motives that went beyond unpicking Fielding's over-hasty decision. But if Paula thought she had set Carol on the road to reconciliation with Tony, she was in for a disappointment. This was about justice, pure and simple. The only sense in which it was about her and Tony was that their past history meant she knew him well enough to understand he wasn't a killer. On a personal level, she wasn't averse to the idea of him rotting in jail for something he didn't do, since the law had no way to punish him for what he had done. But that would leave a killer at large, and that was unacceptable. She might not be a cop any longer but Carol understood what justice was about.

That was more than she could say for Bronwen Scott. Having to get into bed with Scott was almost as hard as having to stand up for Tony. For years, Scott had been a thorn in her side, exploiting every weakness in the law to help the guilty. In theory, Carol held fast to the idea that everyone deserved a defence, no matter what their crime. But its manifestation in practice made her want to weep. She hated Scott for the maxim the lawyer regularly delivered with an air of injured innocence – 'Do your job, Detective. Then there would be no technicalities for me to exploit.' She despised Scott's cavalier ability to defend clients who were manifestly guilty. Most of all, she hated the way she felt when criminals walked free because Scott had played on sentiment and emotion in the teeth of evidence.

But now she no longer had the power of the job on her side, she'd have to exploit Scott's skills if she wanted to see justice done. Crucially, there was no doubt in Carol's mind that someone had to speak for the two dead women. Fielding wasn't doing that and because she wasn't, Paula couldn't. Somebody had to fill the breach. Getting Tony off the hook was merely the first step on a journey to the truth.

All these high-flown ideals were a perfect distraction. The more Carol wrapped herself in the flag of justice, the less she had to consider her feelings for Tony. The notion that she was reaching for a way to bridge the distance between them was one she would have dismissed with contempt if she'd allowed herself even to admit it as a possibility. It wasn't about forgiveness. It was simply that she didn't want him in her life.

Driving into Bradfield was a strange sensation. It had been months since she'd travelled city streets and although she could still easily navigate routes that used to be second nature she felt like a tourist following a map she'd learned by heart. This had been her home for years but she had cut her ties and already there were changes to the traffic flow. Nothing major; the odd lane change at junctions, an alteration of priorities at traffic lights. Enough to make her a stranger.

She pulled into the multi-storey car park in Skenfrith Street five minutes early. The sixties brutalist structure was stark in the fluorescent lights. It was past eleven and there were few cars left on the ground level. Carol parked her Land Rover Defender in the middle of a strip of empty slots and got out. Her footsteps echoed on the stained concrete like a clichéd movie soundtrack. She leaned against the front of the Landie, feeling a faint flutter of nervousness. She was a woman alone in a deserted late-night city-centre car park. When she'd been a cop, the simple fact of that status had acted as a protection. Now, although it made no sense, she felt distinctly more vulnerable. Even her choice of clothes contributed to that element of risk. She'd grown accustomed to the aura of strength and competence that came from her new work clothes. Donning her former work uniform of suit and blouse and low heels made her much more of a target for passing predators. She hoped Bronwen Scott wasn't going to be late.

Right on schedule, a set of tyres screamed as an Audi TT took the car park entrance a little too fast. It reversed into the space opposite Carol, like a pair of gunslingers facing off. Bronwen Scott's legs appeared first, gleaming in the light, black patent spike heels leading the way. Carol's eyes were drawn upwards to a pencil skirt topped with a tailored jacket over a camisole. Over it all, a loose, flowing camel coat. Her hair was dyed a hundred shades of dark blonde, shoulder length and glossy, and her immaculately made-up face showed no trace of the same years that had carved lines into Carol's. Although much of her practice was state-funded legal aid, the fancy clothes and the expensive car came from representing people who had not come by their wealth honestly, and every cop in the city knew it. The pursuit of justice was pushing Carol into the arms of strange bedfellows.

Scott stopped a couple of feet from Carol. 'Who'd have thought it?'

'That might possibly work in our favour,' Carol said.

'So what's all this cloak and dagger in aid of?' Scott swept her hair from her face in a practised gesture. Carol wondered what it must be like to devote so much attention to your appearance. She wasn't stupid; she'd seen the way men looked at her and she was aware that she was attractive. But it had never been how she defined herself, so when her looks began to lose the gloss of youth, she took it in her stride. But women like Bronwen Scott seemed to see ageing as a challenge, a war to be fought every day, taking advantage of every possible weapon, be it surgical or pharmaceutical. Carol had never seen the point of battles you couldn't win.

'There's a prisoner in the cells in Skenfrith Street who needs a good lawyer.'

'What's the charge?'

'Murder, times two.'

'Who's the arresting officer?'

'DCI Alex Fielding.'

'And what's your interest?'

Carol tilted her head back and studied the fluorescent tubes. 'Easily misconstrued.' She sighed and met Scott's curious stare. 'My interest is in seeing justice done. The man under arrest didn't do it. So there's a killer out there on the street who's going to kill again while Fielding's busy playing games with an innocent man.'

'I still don't see why you're bothered. I spend half my life clearing up the mess made by stupid cops who can't get past the first idea in their heads. What's special about this case? Apart from the fact that the accused man apparently can't pick up a phone himself?' Scott was beginning to sound irritated. That wasn't the goal. Time to get to the point.

'Tony Hill.'

Scott frowned. 'What about him? He's been keeping a very low profile since Jacko Vance.'

'He's under arrest. He's across the street in the cells. He thinks he doesn't need a lawyer because he's not done anything wrong.'

Scott cackled. 'One born every minute. You'd think he'd know better. Did you teach him nothing, all those years?'

'I think he needs you. Because there's some very tasty evidence stacked up against him.'

'Can he afford me?'

'Inheritance. Insurance. He can afford you.'

'Go on.' Scott was on the hook. Now Carol just had to reel her in.

'His blood on the cuff of the jacket of the first victim. His

312

alleged thumbprint on the mobile phone of the second victim. And the key evidence, as far as Fielding is concerned, is that both of the victims look a bit like me.'

The tip of Scott's tongue slipped between her lips then she bit her lower lip. It was almost sexual. 'Interesting,' she said. 'And where is this coming from?'

'Do you remember Paula McIntyre?'

Scott made a sardonic face. 'Killer interviewer. Yes, I remember Paula very well.'

'She's Fielding's bagman now. She's always had something of an alliance with Tony. She doesn't like what's happening, but she can't put her head above the parapet or Fielding will shoot it off.'

'Makes sense.' Scott shivered and pulled her coat closer. 'So what do you want me to do about it?'

'I want you to go over the street and demand to see your client and do what needs to be done before Fielding gets her claws into him in the morning. They did an interview under caution and they plan to reinterview him and search his home and his office, according to Paula.'

'Will he do what he's told?'

Carol shrugged. 'That's debatable. I imagine it will depend on what you tell him.'

Scott shook her head, resigned. 'They never know what's best for them. Not even the smart ones. I suppose I should thank you for dropping this in my lap. So, thank you, Carol.' She laid a hand on Carol's arm, the dramatic scarlet nails drawing attention from her hand's betrayal of the attrition of age.

Carol looked down at the false gesture of intimacy and Scott withdrew it, though not hastily. 'I'm not done,' Carol said.

Scott cocked her head to one side. 'Of course you're not. I presume you want to be briefed?'

'More than that. I want to come in with you.'

Scott laughed, the sound echoing spookily round them. 'You know better than that, Carol,' she said merrily, as if it was the funniest thing she'd heard all day.

'Why not? I'm not a police officer. And you're the kind of superstar lawyer who's always got interns running after you, carrying your files and sharpening your pencils. What could be more natural than an ex-cop considering a career in the law?'

Scott was still grinning. 'Gamekeeper turned poacher with a vengeance. What's in it for me? How does it help my client?'

'I have the inside track. Paula's never going to trust you with confidential information. But spilling the beans to me? That's second nature to her. Plus you get all the benefits of a shit-hot investigator on your side at no extra charge.'

Scott shook her head, still unconvinced. 'It stretches the limits of credibility.'

'That's never stopped you before. Come on, you know you want to. If only for the look on Fielding's face. Think of it, Bronwen – you'll be dining out on that one for months. Especially when she's forced to release Tony without charge.'

'It's appealing, I'll admit. But we'd never get it past the custody sergeant.'

'I thought you liked a challenge?' Carol's smile dared Scott.

'Oh, fuck it.' Again the flip of the hair. 'Why not? I've not had a ruck with a custody sergeant for weeks. I'm getting rusty. Let me get my briefcase and we'll go and give them hell.'

They crossed the street side by side like a latter-day Cagney and Lacey. As they were about to walk into the police station, Carol paused and said, 'There is one thing you should know.'

Scott looked almost relieved, as if this was the dropping shoe she'd been waiting for. 'What?'

'Tony and I haven't actually spoken to each other since the Jacko Vance investigation. I said some pretty harsh things to him. It's possible he might not be too thrilled to see me.'

Scott smiled like a gratified cat. 'This just gets better and better.'

47

He stood in the garage doorway and stared at the freezer. He had high hopes of this one. She was, he reckoned, the right raw material for his project. He'd been too hasty, and that had led him into error. He'd been impatient to find the right replacement; he'd forgotten what it took to break a woman in from scratch. Like horses and dogs, it was always easier to work with one that had been taught some of the basics already.

That was where he'd gone wrong. That Polish bitch didn't even have a live-in boyfriend. She had no idea of what it took to be a perfect wife. How could she? She couldn't even speak English properly, for starters. He hated her stupid accent. If he'd realised she was a foreigner, he wouldn't have chosen her. Her looks had confused him, tricked him into thinking she was the one. That had always been what let Sirikit down. Her English was good, but she still had a bit of an accent, which grated on him. But more than that, she was dark. He wanted a blonde. He'd always wanted a blonde.

Ever since he'd seen Lauren Hutton in *American Gigolo* when he was barely a teenager, that was what he'd wanted. That was what he'd married, and the replacement would have to be blonde too.

It was naïve to think that a woman who didn't already know how to take care of a man could be broken in easily. The Polish bitch had fought him every inch of the way. He'd made it plain to her that, just like in *Star Trek*, resistance was futile. He'd tried every trick in the book, every technique he could think of before he finally had to concede you couldn't alter their fundamental nature. This one wouldn't give in and she wouldn't give up. In the end, the only satisfaction for him had been the final beating. He'd stripped everything from her that defined her and in the process he had made it clear what she really was – a lump of faceless, useless meat. No use even for sex. He'd washed her clean of any trace of him, made sure nobody else could get any use out of her then kicked her to death.

At least it had confirmed that there was, as he had suspected, genuine satisfaction to be had from finishing with the ones who let him down. He'd planned it for the very first one but he'd been thwarted. He'd fantasised about doing it, but the reality had outstripped the fantasy. That heady, drunken moment of absolute power when life finally leaked away was the best feeling he'd ever known.

But still. He was an optimist. He wanted to believe there could be as much delight in the perfect wife as there was in the perfect dealing out of death. And so he'd tried again. But the next one had been no better. He should have known. He'd hoped that the reason she was divorced was that her husband had been a poor excuse for a man, giving her no opportunity to demonstrate what she was capable of.

It didn't take long for him to realise she was probably divorced because she was a crap wife. He'd been hopeful when he'd tasted the steak she'd cooked. But the potatoes had been unforgivable. If she'd reached that age without being able to boil a potato properly, there was no hope for her. After that, the sex had been a formality. Even if she'd been the most exciting shag on the planet, it was too late for redemption. Perfection was always going to be out of her reach. All she was good for by that point was killing.

In spite of that, he was still hopeful. Sirikit had shown him that it was possible to find a woman who could be what he demanded. This latest one was married, that was a start. Just so long as she hadn't fallen into irreversible bad habits thanks to a weak and indulgent husband. He blamed other men for letting women get away with too much. It was like what they said about dogs. There was no such thing as a bad dog, only a bad master. Well, he was the good master. And this new one would be best in show, he felt it in his heart.

For now, she had to learn the first lesson. He was master. This time, he'd leave her locked away in the freezer for longer. Then she'd be properly grateful when he eventually let her out. Gratitude went a long way, in his experience. It was the same at work. You gave a little, and because people had such low expectations, you got a lot. It was one of the secrets of his success. Now all he had to do was teach it to the woman in the freezer.

48

The reception area of the custody suite was without comfort. It smelled, bizarrely, of stale sausage rolls and rotting fruit. Behind the scarred and untidy counter was a middle-aged man with a tonsure of chestnut stubble and a white shirt that strained over a barrel chest. The custody sergeant had a face like a rumpled Boxer, all creases and jowls. Carol almost expected him to slobber as he looked Bronwen Scott up and down. 'You're a bit late tonight, Ms Scott,' he growled. 'Will it not wait till morning?'

'The clock's running, as you well know, Sergeant Fowler. My client's facing very serious charges and we need to make a start at clearing his name.'

'Funny, he never mentioned having a solicitor. And he never made a phone call after he was brought down here. You developing telepathy as one of your skills?'

Scott leaned on the counter and produced a menacing smile. 'I don't think my means of communicating with my clients is any of your business. Now, I want to see my client.

And in an interview room, not some nasty little cell that smells of piss and vomit.' It was an impressive performance, Carol thought, remembering all the times Bronwen Scott's production numbers had driven her to distraction. Being on the same side was a lot more fun.

Sergeant Fowler made great play of consulting his watch and comparing it to the clock on the wall behind him. 'Let me see. DCI Fielding will be wanting to interview at nine, and your client is entitled to eight hours' rest, and it's half past eleven already. So I reckon that gives you an hour with your client, tops.'

'I'll take as long with my client as I need. If that means DCI Fielding has to rearrange her plans for the morning, that's the way the cookie crumbles, Sergeant Fowler. Now, are you going to produce Dr Hill?'

'One moment,' he said ponderously, his forehead corrugating. He scratched his armpit then pointed at Carol, who had been hanging back in the doorway. 'Is she with you?'

Scott gave a nonchalant glance over her shoulder. 'My intern? Of course.'

'Do you think I'm daft? Your intern?' He leaned forward, his mouth moving as if he was chewing a wad of tobacco. 'It's DCI Jordan, as was, right?'

'With the emphasis on "as was", Sergeant Fowler. I don't think our paths actually crossed while I was still working.' She stepped forward and produced her most winning smile.

'What am I supposed to call you, anyway?' he asked Carol.

'Ms Jordan will do nicely, Sergeant. It's my name. I don't have a rank any more.'

He scratched the band of stubble that ran round his head, frowning. 'Well, Ms Jordan. I can't let you sit in on an interview between a prisoner and his solicitor. You're just a civilian, you've no cause to be there.'

'I'm shadowing Ms Scott. I'm planning on a career in the law, Sergeant Fowler. It's a shame to waste all that hands-on experience. My role here is purely as an observer.'

'But you know him. You used to work with him.' He threw his hands in the air, a gesture that threatened his shirt buttons. He was clearly struggling for a valid reason why Carol shouldn't be involved. 'It's not . . . appropriate.'

'Oh, behave, Sergeant. Anybody would think you were still wet behind the ears,' Scott said. 'I'm always dealing with people I've encountered before. Defence witness one week, accused the next. And who do you think defends bent coppers? Criminal lawyers like me. So get down off your high horse and give Ms Jordan some credit for choosing an exciting new career path.'

'It's not as if I can leak confidential information to the defence, is it?' Carol wondered whether she was laying it on too thick, but Sergeant Fowler looked relieved at the thought.

'So can you fetch Dr Hill for us? The sooner we get started, the quicker we'll be done and the happier DCI Fielding will be in the morning,' Scott said in the kind of tone it was hard to argue against.

Fowler hauled himself to his feet and emerged from behind the counter. 'You can use the interview room at the end of the cell corridor. Follow me, ladies.'

He set off past the steel doors. Scott turned to Carol and winked. 'Overture and beginners,' she said under her breath. 'Let's do it, Carol.'

No turning back. She'd spent months literally working Tony Hill out of her system. And now she was about to discover whether she'd succeeded.

49

Tony had taken off his jacket and folded it under him to make the bed a more comfortable seat. Though it left a lot to be desired, at least he could sit cross-legged with his back to the wall in a relatively relaxed posture, eyes closed and hands loose in his lap. He didn't know whether he could sleep sitting up, but he was absolutely certain he couldn't do it lying down on that pallet. Still, buoyed up by his realisation of how his DNA had ended up on Nadia Wilkowa's jacket, he could finally chill a little.

The window in his cell door opened with a sharp metallic clang, startling him with a jolt. It clanged shut again before he had composed himself enough to work out what was happening. Then the door opened and the sergeant who had checked him into the cell stood in the doorway, hands on hips to make himself look bigger, eyebrows lowered to add to his threat level. All textbook stuff. 'Wakey wakey, Hill. Your lawyer's here for a conference.'

He understood the words but they made no sense. 'I've got a lawyer?'

'Don't you bloody start. I've had enough from her end. If you didn't have a lawyer, she wouldn't be in the interview room asking me to produce you, would she?'

Paula. She must have ignored him and decided to sort him out with a lawyer regardless. It wouldn't hurt to sit down in a more comfortable room and tell them that he really didn't need legal representation now he'd worked out how to explain the key evidence against him. Still, it would pass some time. So he unfolded his legs and stood up. He picked up his jacket and tried to put it on both arms at once, like Martin Sheen always did in *The West Wing*. As usual, he got into a tangle. It needed more practice, that was all. He caught the eye of the custody sergeant, who was struggling not to laugh. 'A man needs a hobby,' Tony said, stepping gratefully out of the cell into the corridor. He was about to head for the counter where he'd emptied his pockets earlier, but the sergeant blocked his path, directing him towards a door that stood ajar at the end of the corridor.

Feeling surprisingly jaunty, Tony pushed the door open. At first his brain denied what he was seeing. Bronwen Scott, he accepted that. She was the sort of person he'd expected to see. But the blonde head facing away from the door – it couldn't be. He was hallucinating. Or delusional. Then she turned her head and something inside him lurched and twisted. The ground beneath his feet seemed to tilt and he stumbled. 'Carol?' His voice held a mixture of wonder and doubt. So much for cutting her out of his heart. Apparently his heart hadn't got the message.

'You've got an hour,' Sergeant Fowler grunted as he closed the door firmly behind him.

Bronwen Scott got to her feet and greeted him with a wide smile. 'Dr Hill. I didn't expect to encounter you in circumstances like this, but we'll have this sorted out in no time at all.'

He ignored her and walked round to the far side of the table like a sleepwalker. 'Carol?' He grabbed the back of the chair for support and subsided into it. He wanted to reach out and touch her, to confirm that he wasn't lost in some psychotic break.

Carol pushed her hair off her forehead, her eyes flinty, her face forbidding. 'I'm not here for you. I'm here because Paula knows how stupid you can be. You need Bronwen to get you out of this mess. Otherwise more women will die. If you'd thought about something other than yourself for five minutes, you would have understood that. So don't fool yourself that you're the big draw tonight. I'm here for Paula and for justice and for the women whose names we don't even know.'

Right then, he didn't care why she was there. All that mattered was that they were sitting in the same room again. The edifice he'd built to protect himself from his feelings for her was already a crumbling ruin. How could he have considered for a moment the possibility of excising her from his life? It was like rediscovering a limb he'd been managing without. A limb he'd thought amputated for ever. He couldn't keep the grin from his face, even in the teeth of her unflinching glare.

He was aware that Bronwen Scott was speaking but he had nothing to spare for her. He drank in every detail, checking it against the mental checklist he hadn't even known he'd been keeping. Her hair was styled differently – the lines more blunt, the shagginess thinned out more. The lines around her eyes were deeper, the new traces in her face from sorrow rather than laughter. Her shoulders seemed broader, the seams of her jacket straining slightly where before there had been ample room for a shrug. She'd always been self-contained; now she was like a door slammed in his face.

'Dr Hill?' Scott had raised her voice and finally penetrated. 'We don't have long. I need your version of events so we can set about getting you out of here.'

'And finding out who killed those two women,' Carol said.

'That's not my job,' Scott said briskly. 'And actually, Carol, it's not your job any more either.'

Tony found his voice. 'Maybe not, but I'd put my money on Carol without resources ahead of Alex Fielding and her murder squad.'

Carol rolled her eyes. A familiar gesture but denuded of the tolerant affection he'd grown used to. 'I couldn't be less interested in flattery. Like I said, I'm here for Paula.'

Her disdain was hard to take. It made something inside him clench in pain. But it was still better than not having her in the room at all. 'What do you want to know?'

'Do you know why DCI Fielding has arrested you?' Scott thrust herself back into the driving seat.

He nodded. 'Because she's one of those cops who can't see past the evidence. You remember Alan Coren, the humorist? He once told his son, "Don't write the first thing that comes into your head – the dim kids will have had that idea. Don't write the second either – the clever boys will probably have thought of that one. Write the third idea – that will be yours alone." Well, Alex Fielding's never bothered to give the third idea house room.'

'Very entertaining, Dr Hill.' Now it was Scott's turn to roll her eyes.

'Tony, please.' He knew he was showing off but he might never get another chance to remind Carol of what he could be.

'I appreciate you see the world through the prism of the psyche, but could we focus on the evidential reasons why Fielding arrested you? Tony?'

When he'd sat in the observation room and watched Bronwen Scott in action, Tony had often wondered how different she was with her clients than when she was an opponent. Tougher than he'd expected, was the first answer. She wasn't falling for his practised skills and she wasn't indulging him. Time to return her moves in the same style. 'The bodies of two murdered women have been found this week. For the record, I didn't kill either of them. They were both brutally beaten, to the point where their faces were unrecognisable. Their labia were shaved and glued together. There's no obvious connection between the two of them, although there might be a professional link. Nadzieja Wilkowa was single and Polish, she worked as a rep for a pharmaceutical company. Bev McAndrew was divorced, mother of a teenage son, and she was the pharmacist in charge at Bradfield Cross Hospital.' He stopped. 'You're not taking notes.'

'I'll get all this in disclosure from Fielding. At this point, it's interesting to have the background but I want to know where you come into the picture. And your version of events, of course.'

Carol raised a finger, indicating she wanted to speak. Scott nodded briskly. 'How much of this did you know before Fielding questioned you?'

She hadn't lost a yard of her pace, he thought, impressed with the question. 'I knew quite a bit about Nadia Wilkowa. And I knew Bev was missing. She's a friend of Paula's and she asked my advice about her disappearance. I wasn't much help. But in the course of that conversation, we talked about Nadia.' He gave Carol a pained smile. 'Actually, she took me to Nadia's flat.'

'Oh, Christ,' Scott said. 'So your prints and DNA are going to be all over the victim's flat?'

'I was gloved up,' Tony said. 'I'm not entirely hopeless.

There shouldn't be any obvious DNA traces. But DNA is one of the issues. There's a bloodstain on Nadia's jacket that has tested positive for my DNA.' Carol nodded wearily, but Scott merely looked resigned. 'When they interviewed me, I had no idea how that happened. But I've had time to think, and I can explain it.'

'I'm pleased to hear that. So how did it come about?' Scott leaned forward, fixing him with her attention.

'As I think you both know, I do most of my work at Bradfield Moor Secure Hospital. I deal with a wide range of patients who come to us because they are either a danger to themselves or a danger to society. Their lives are often car crashes and they're left stranded in the wreckage. When they first come in, they're often frightened and angry and violent. About a year ago, I was called out to assess a young man who had run amok with a machete in his school staff-room. Luckily, he'd been tackled by a very brave teacher before anyone had been seriously injured.'

Tony clasped his hands in front of him, running his thumbs over each other again and again. 'He'd been sedated before he came to us, but what I didn't realise was that he'd been growing increasingly agitated before I went in to talk to him. He seemed calm on the surface but as soon as I started asking him to talk about what had happened, he managed to free one arm from its restraints and he punched me in the face. My nose was bleeding copiously and I left the room to get it stopped and cleaned up.'

Carol gave the barest of nods. 'I remember you telling me about it.'

He looked straight at her. 'You know how clumsy I am, Carol. I stumbled out into the corridor and through a set of swing doors, not really looking where I was going, paper towels up to my face. And I crashed into a woman coming the other way. She put her arm up to protect herself.' He closed his eyes, replaying the scene. 'I'm pretty sure it was her left arm. I apologised. She said, no harm done and went on her way.' He opened his eyes. 'She was a pharmaceutical rep, right? That's what it said in the paper. So she had a reason to be there.' It sounded thin. Artificial. Even to his ears. But that was often the way with the truth.

'You bumped into a woman a year ago when you were having a nosebleed? And she still has your DNA on her sleeve?' Scott sounded almost amused, as if this was the most outrageous attempt at exoneration she'd ever heard.

'I'm just telling you what happened.'

'You think she went a year without having her work clothes cleaned? Without realising she had your blood on her jacket?'

'All I know is what happened. Now I've had my memory jogged, it's quite clear.'

Carol's investigative instincts cut in. 'Was the incident logged in the Bradfield Moor accident book?'

'It will have been,' Tony said. 'Because I needed an ice pack from the nursing team.'

'We need to check that date and then we need to cross-check it with Nadia Wilkowa's work diary,' Carol said, tapping a note into her phone. 'I'll chase that up with Paula.' He loved watching her doing what she'd always done best.

'It's a pity there's no way of telling how old the DNA sample is. That would have resolved it on the spot,' Scott added.

'Even more of a pity that the blood ended up on something that gets dry-cleaned rather than shoved in the washing machine. If it had been through the hot wash a dozen times, it would be so degraded it would be obvious that it wasn't made this week,' Carol pointed out, not to be outdone in the DNA knowledge stakes.

'Next time, I'll aim for the blouse. So you think we can

demolish the DNA evidence if we can prove the nosebleed incident?'

'It gives reasonable doubt a helluva knock, that's for sure,' Scott said. 'Was that it, then? Was that all she had?'

Tony shook his head sorrowfully. 'Then there's the thumbprint.'

Carol closed her eyes momentarily as if in pain. 'What thumbprint, Tony? I thought you said you wore gloves at her flat?'

'No, not on Nadia's stuff. My thumbprint is on Bev's phone.' He tried the pitiful puppy smile again. This time, both women scowled at him. 'I was completely baffled when they interviewed me about it earlier. Clueless. I've no recollection of ever clapping eyes on Bev in the flesh, never mind touching her phone.'

'Was it a clear print?' Scott asked.

Tony shook his head. 'It was a bit smudged on one side and a bit distorted by the shape of the phone. But when Fielding showed it to me, I could see the points of similarity.'

'Can you remember how many points of comparison were highlighted?'

'I think it was six.'

Scott smiled. 'I'm not worried about a fingerprint ID like that. I can put up half a dozen experts who'll discredit it. These days, unless you get a crystal-clear fingermark on a flat surface, you can knock the feet from under any prosecution expert witness. Fingerprint comparison is so subjective it's not even regarded as a science any more. All you have to say in court these days is "Shirley McKie" then watch the prosecution shrivel and die.'

'I don't understand,' Tony said. 'Who's Shirley McKie?'

'She was a Scottish police officer. Her fingerprint was wrongly identified inside a murder scene where she swore she'd never been. The Scottish forensic experts stuck to their guns and she was charged with perjury,' Carol explained. 'And then it all fell apart. Turns out that while it's true all fingerprints are unique, identifying them is riddled with human error.'

'So we can kick their fingerprint evidence right into the long grass,' Scott said. 'It's history.'

'That's good,' Tony said. 'Because as it turns out, I was in Bradfield Cross on Monday afternoon. When Bev went missing.'

Carol groaned. 'Why am I not surprised? Are you going to share it with us? Or shall we just play twenty questions?' She shook her head. 'Nothing changes.'

'Actually, Carol, you might be surprised on that score. But this isn't the time or the place for that conversation.'

'There is no time and place for that conversation. Monday?'

Slapped down again. Tony took a deep breath and picked himself up. 'I was at a meeting in Bradfield Cross Hospital late Monday afternoon. I tend not to agree with the consultant there, Will Newton. The man's a moron. I think he got his qualifications by saving up Coco Pops box tops. By the end of the meeting, I was furious. I stomped out of the meeting room. All I wanted was to get out of there before I said something that would only make every-thing worse.'

'Did you go anywhere near the pharmacy?' As usual, Scott was straight to the point.

'I don't think so. I was pissed off and I wanted to vent my energy so I walked home. I wasn't really paying attention to my surroundings. I don't think I passed the pharmacy but I don't know whether I passed Bev.'

Scott sat back in her chair and contemplated him. 'Please tell me that's all?'

'Well, the other things are circumstantial.' He spread his

hands. 'Nothing I've done. The sort of thing that could happen to anyone.'

'But only do happen to you,' Carol pointed out. 'You said, "things". Plural. What are we talking about here?'

'I was trying to be helpful,' he said. 'After Paula told me about Bev, but before we knew she was dead, I thought I'd take a look at the supermarket where she'd supposedly been shopping. I needed some bits and pieces and I fancied the walk, so I went over to Freshco at Kenton Vale.'

'It says on the custody record you live on a boat in Minster Basin. So you walked from the basin to Kenton Vale Road to pick up a few bits and pieces at the supermarket? That must be, what? Two miles?' Bronwen's deadpan delivery did nothing to hide her scepticism.

'He likes to walk. It helps him think.'

'She's right. I do. And it does. And what it made me think is that this is a careful killer. Because the CCTV in the car park at Freshco isn't great. There's plenty of holes in the coverage. According to Paula, the body dump for Nadia was in Gartonside, where it's scheduled for demolition and there are no cameras. And from what I can gather, Bev was found up on the moors in the middle of nowhere. So again, no cameras.'

'And? There has to be an "and", right? There generally is with you,' Carol said, bitterness still evident in her voice. She wasn't loosening up, he thought. He'd hoped they'd slip into old rhythms without realising it, but she was too watchful of herself for that. Time appeared not to have done much healing of her hurt.

'There is. I bought more shopping than I'd intended *and* I got the bus home. And that's when I realised buses have CCTV that films outside the bus as well as inside. Bradfield buses have fourteen cameras on each double-decker bus, did you know that? So I suggested to Paula that they take a look at the footage. Which they did.'

'Was it helpful?' Scott asked.

'Oh yes. They got a bit of Bev on one camera. And they caught a few seconds of the bloke who was following her. It wasn't much use for ID. Medium height, medium build, though he could have been a slim guy wearing bulky clothing. He was wearing a hoodie and he kept his head down. You can see he's wearing glasses, but that's about all. They told me they had footage of the man who abducted Nadia, and it was pretty much the same. There's only one distinguishing feature.' Tony looked down at the table. He hated this piece of information. In his head, it was the one that made him look guilty. 'He's got a noticeable limp. He limps with his left leg.'

'Oh, fuck,' Carol said. With feeling.

'You have a limp?'

Sometimes it was tempting to go for the crass one-liner. This probably wasn't one of those times. 'I had major knee surgery a couple of years ago. A patient attacked me with a fire axe. Someone else's patient, I always like to point out.'

'And you were supposed to have a second surgery to deal with the limp,' Carol said. 'I take it you're still dodging Mrs Chakrabarti?' She half-turned to Bronwen. 'He does have a limp. It's worse when he's tired. Such as, when he's tramped two miles across town to shop in a non-local branch of Freshco.'

Scott gave him a sharp, assessing look. 'I don't like the limp,' she said. 'That's the sort of circumstantial that the CPS gets very hot and horny over.'

'Lots of people have a limp,' Tony protested.

'No, actually, they don't,' Carol said. 'And if you'd done what you were supposed to, neither would you. Doing nothing just gets you into trouble, Tony. And not for the first time.'

332

She'd never held back. He'd always admired that in her. But it was hard to take when he was the target of her sharpest assaults. 'I'm sorry,' he said.

'Can we put the thrust and parry on the back burner for now, please?' Scott sounded almost as pissed off as Carol. 'What's the other circumstantial?'

Tony looked at Carol and gave a wry smile. 'Before I say this, in the interests of not getting my face slapped, I want to be clear that this is DCI Fielding's journey into absurdity. Not mine.'

'Fielding thinks the victims both look like me,' Carol said heavily. 'She's got a bee in her bonnet about it. She thinks Tony's killing women who look like me because I walked away from him.'

There was a long sticky pause. Then Scott said chattily, 'And are you, Tony?'

50

Patience was a virtue he'd learned young. His father had never tolerated tantrums or whining, so he'd understood at an early age that keeping his mouth shut and learning to wait was the key to minimising the pain of his existence. Therefore it was no hardship to him to extend the time she would spend in the freezer before he let her out to play.

But that didn't mean he had to sit around twiddling his thumbs. By now, her husband must be starting to panic. It was almost midnight – five hours later than she should have been home, given when she'd left work. At first, the husband would have assumed a hold-up in the transport system – a delay on the tram. An accident throwing the city centre into gridlock. Something relatively benign. But as the minutes ticked by and no text or phone call arrived, he'd have started to feel anxious.

What would he have done then, this Marco Mather, this man whose annoyingly handsome face smiled out of the photo in her purse? He'd have tried to phone her, of course.

But by then, her phone was not only turned off, it had its battery and SIM card removed. He'd put them back later, when it didn't matter if she was traced or not. But for now, he was taking every available precaution.

So, Marco would get a dead phone. What would his next step be? He'd probably call her friends to see whether she was them or if she'd confided any plans to them. He'd draw a blank, of course. He wouldn't be able to phone anyone from work because she'd only just started her new job and she wouldn't have built up a social network yet. He wouldn't even know the names of her colleagues, never mind their phone numbers.

So he'd have to go to the Tellit Communications building, where the night security guard would explain there was nobody left in the office. If Marco Mather kicked off, the guard might even show him the computer record from when she'd swiped herself off the grid and into the lift.

He might think about the police then. But that would get him nowhere at all. Five hours late wouldn't earn a mention in the incident log. Not even in the light of two female murder victims in the same week. Because there was nothing to connect Marco Mather's wife to a Polish pharmaceutical sales rep or Bradfield Cross's chief pharmacist. There couldn't be because apart from the fact that they looked right, they were random selections. People said you couldn't judge a book by its cover, and unfortunately that was true. But he'd had to go by the cover. They were replacements, not substitutes. So they had to look right. They had to fit the fantasy in his head, the dream that had grown from those images of Lauren Hutton up on the screen. It was an exhausting process, but eventually he would find the right one. The one to replace the one who had cheated him out of serving up her just deserts.

But he was wandering off the point. Which was, what

would Marco Mather do? He was so tempted to go and see for himself. There would be a delicious pleasure in glimpsing him through a window, wringing his hands or crying on the phone.

Why not give in to temptation? There was no virtue in denying himself that pleasure, was there? So he pulled on a pair of latex gloves and picked up her keys. Just in case Marco had gone out to drown his sorrows and he got the chance to pick over their pitiful married life.

Less than quarter of an hour later, he'd found a parking space in the next street and, sticking to the shadows, he walked briskly round the corner. In spite of the limp one of his father's beatings had left him with, he could still move faster than most. At this time of night, the majority of the houses were in darkness, occasional slivers of light creeping through bedroom curtains, a few hall lights dimly seen through glass panels in front doors. This wasn't the sort of area where people stayed up late and had fun, he thought. Solid suburbia to the core; either they had to get up for work in the morning or else they'd retired and acquired the old persons' habit of early to bed and early to rise. Like they had something to get up for, he thought, imagining those unsatisfied lives where they'd settled for less than perfection. Not like him.

He wasn't entirely surprised to see plenty of lights on at the Mather house. The front room curtains weren't closed, and light leaked in from the bright hallway. He checked to make sure he was unobserved, then cut into their tiny front garden, slinking past the front door and peering in through the window. No sign of life. A couple of deserted sofas, a TV, shelves that seemed to contain DVDs and a few books. No clutter whatsoever. There were paintings, or prints, he supposed, all over the walls. He couldn't make them out in the dim light, but they looked colourful.

He slipped past the front door and down the side of the garage. A small window cast a parallelogram of light on the ground, and he ducked low to avoid being seen. Then he turned and edged his head forward so he could look inside. The usual crap-filled garage, he thought. Lawnmower, gardening tools. A tall freezer. Shelves crammed with tins of paint, household chemicals, assorted car products. He inched forward to improve his field of vision and saw something completely unexpected.

The top of a man's head, motionless on the floor.

Startled, he jerked back. When his heart stopped racing, he crept forward again, this time bolder than before. He could see the rest of the man's head from behind. Unsurprisingly, it was attached to a body. A body that was sprawled on the floor beside an exercise bike, one leg still trailing over the frame.

Marco Mather wasn't pacing the floor, panicking over his wife's absence. Marco Mather was dead.

Either that or he was going to be dead very soon.

51

Bronwen Scott enjoyed the moment then pushed her chair back. 'I need a quick word with the custody sergeant,' she said. 'Five minutes, Carol, any more and he'll start to get antsy.'

Tony and Carol stared at each other, stony-faced, waiting for her to leave. The door closed and they were alone for the first time in months. A scenario both had imagined but neither had expected. Tony cleared his throat. 'How have you been?'

'That's really none of your business.' The severity of her expression didn't diminish. He'd seen her look at colleagues she despaired of and criminals she despised in the same way.

'I think it is. You blamed me for what happened to Michael and Lucy.' Most people would have missed the infinitesimal flinch in her eyes at the mention of their names, but he didn't. Undeterred, he carried on. 'You probably still do. That gives me a burden of responsibility and I think our history runs so deep that you owe me the chance to discharge it.'

She shook her head. 'Even if I could translate that out of Tony-speak into something a normal person would understand, I suspect it would still be bollocks. I owe you nothing. No amount of twisted logic can change that.'

'So why are you here?'

She made a dismissive gesture with her hand. 'I told you. Paula feels the need to save you and she can't do it the straight way.'

He let himself consider whether she might be speaking the truth. He wanted not to believe her, but he had to concede it made more sense to accept what she was saying. 'But you agree with her, that I'm innocent?'

'I can imagine situations where you might kill. But I don't believe you're this kind of killer. And I think if you were pissed off enough with me to want to kill me, you'd get on with it. Not fuck about with surrogates.' There was a grim twist to her mouth that might almost have been a smile.

'You think somebody's really killing women who look like you?' Tony was genuinely curious. He thought he knew her well enough to predict the answer but he wanted to hear what she had to say.

She shrugged one shoulder. 'Other people seem to. Senior detectives with years of experience, some of them.'

'But you,' he persisted. 'What do *you* think?'

'I don't think they look that much like me.'

'There's a generic similarity. Same blonde hair, blue eyes. Same haircut. Similar build. Professional women who go to work suited up. Has it occurred to you that it's not them that look like you – it's you that looks like them?'

Carol frowned. This was how it had always played out between them. He said something impenetrable that she couldn't resist and she was hooked. It had been like that since the very first case they'd worked together, all those years ago. And here he was, doing it to her again. She wanted to get to her feet and walk out, but more than that she needed to understand what he was driving at. 'What do you mean – it's me that looks like them?'

'That's not quite right.' He spoke absently, as if thinking aloud. 'It's more that you all look like her.'

'Like who?' She almost howled in frustration.

'The one he wanted to kill.'

'Don't you mean "wants" to kill?'

Tony ran a hand through his hair. 'No. He's clever, he's organised and he's resourceful. If she was available to be killed, he'd have killed her and that would be an end to it.' He spread his arms wide as if trying to draw her in to embrace the idea. 'I think she's already dead. I think he was planning to kill her, working up to it. But somehow she thwarted him.'

'She killed herself?' Carol was intrigued now in spite of herself. She leaned forward, forearms on the table. He noticed the changes in her hands – scars, bruises, broken nails. What on earth had she been doing, this woman who he remembered barely being able to manage flat-pack furniture?

'Either that or she just died,' he said, distracted by his more private speculation.

'And this helps us how?'

'Find her, and you find him.' He shrugged. 'Obviously you're going to have to find her.'

Before Carol could respond, the door opened and Scott stuck her head into the room. 'Time to go, Carol. We'll see you in the morning, Tony. Chin up. She's never going to charge you.'

'So what happens now?' Carol asked Scott as soon as they were clear of Skenfrith Street police station.

'I'm going home to catch some zeds before I have to get up and go head to head with DCI Fielding,' the lawyer said. 'I recommend that you not show up for that conversation. It'll only get messy. Besides, you have plenty of other things to be getting on with. It'll be bloody ages before Fielding gives us disclosure on Nadia Wilkowa's work diaries. You're going to need to pull your strings and find out when this alleged incident happened at Bradfield Moor and whether Nadia was in the building that day to bump into Captain Clumsy.'

'You want me to go back to Paula?'

Scott broke her stride to give Carol an incredulous look. 'Well, duh. I want you to do whatever it takes to get the information that will clear my client. You always had the knack of coming up with the goods when you were working the other side of the fence.'

Carol gave a snort of bitter laughter. 'I did have one or two resources at my disposal.'

'You still do. Human resources. You've got friends. So has he. Use them.'

Carol suppressed a sigh. After the reaction she'd had from Sinead, she wasn't so sure how much reliance she could place on her old networks. How bitter would it be to have to rely on Tony's name to open doors? Tony, who was even more crap at intimacy than she was. 'I'll see what I can do,' she said wearily.

'And I'll line up someone to demolish her thumbprint evidence. We're going to leave her without a leg to stand on.'

They entered the dank car park and headed for their cars. Before they separated, Scott put a hand on Carol's arm. 'Did he say anything useful after I left you alone with him?'

Carol didn't know where to begin to explain the way Tony's mind worked to an outsider. 'No,' she said. 'It was private.' The words were out before she had time to think.

She walked to her car, thinking how hard it was to break the habit of mistrust.

She climbed into the Land Rover and took out her phone, keeping one eye on Scott, whose engine purred into life as soon as she'd settled herself into her seat. Carol waited till the solicitor had driven out of the car park, considering her options. It was late and she was tired, but the clock was ticking for Tony. There were strict limits on how long the police could hold him after arrest. If the defence couldn't blow apart the evidence against him, Fielding would charge Tony when the time ran out – or before that, if she could build a stronger case – and everything would become much harder. The police would stop looking for an alternative suspect. Mud would stick, even if Tony was subsequently cleared.

It dawned on Carol that she minded the idea of his name being blackened. She tried to convince herself that it was simply because it offended her sense of justice. She wasn't ready to accept that her history with Tony might mean there was a possible future for them. She was merely reacting as she would to the idea of any innocent person being unjustly imprisoned ahead of a trial for a crime they could never have committed. That was all it was. But that was enough to sanction any amount of unreasonable behaviour. Wasn't it?

52

The journey back in the car from the Mather house to his place wasn't long enough. He needed to savour what had happened, to replay it in his head and set it in stone so it would be the bedrock for what came next. This was so beautiful, you couldn't make it up. It was the perfect scene-setter for turning Marie Mather into the perfect wife. And the joy of it was that he hadn't had to do a thing himself.

He'd forced himself to stand at the garage window for a full five minutes, to be certain that Marco Mather wasn't moving. Five motionless minutes meant death or, at the very least, a deep unconsciousness he could take advantage of.

He'd debated whether to try the back door or to brazen it out at the front. There were a pair of mortise keys on her ring, but only one Yale. He guessed that, like most people, there would be a Yale and a mortise on the front door and a mortise on the rear. So, only one unfamiliar lock to fumble with at the back, and out of sight at that. On the downside, his limp made him less than stealthy, and gardens were notoriously cluttered with plant containers and hoses and bags of compost. Better to risk the front door than clatter around the pitch-black patio and rouse the neighbours.

Treading carefully, he returned to the front of the house and slipped the Yale into the keyhole, gambling that it would be the only lock engaged while Marco Mather was at home expecting his wife to return from work. It turned and the door swung silently open. He stepped inside confidently, for the benefit of anyone glancing out of their window on the way to bed. And he breathed in the smell of her home, nosing it like a wine connoisseur, relishing the faint scents of cooking herbs and the heady notes from the vase of lilies on a recessed windowsill. Yes, she had the basics of good taste, even if the lilies were a little florid for his liking.

Down the hall and into the generous dining kitchen. It was clearly the heart of the house, the sort of kitchen where cooking was observed like a religious ritual. A well-used *batterie de cuisine* was on parade and ready for use, a small array of battered cookbooks on the windowsill alongside pots of thyme, basil and oregano. His heart lifted. She was going to be the one. She'd cook like an angel and fuck like a whore.

The door to the garage was closed. He moseyed across the kitchen, helping himself to a baby tomato from a bowl sitting on a butcher's block. He popped it into his mouth and burst it with his teeth, enjoying the sudden explosion of flavour, sharp and sweet. Oh yes, this was going to be special.

There were no surprises on the other side of the door. Marco Mather was lying in exactly the same position. Only now he could see Marco's face. There was no doubt about it. The guy was definitely dead. And from the looks of him, there had been nothing peaceful about it. Heart attack, at a guess. Fat bastard on an exercise bike, what did he expect? Greedy twat couldn't resist her excellent cooking and look where it had got him.

The beauty of it was that there would be no worried husband reporting his woman missing. No chance of some smart-arsed copper eager to make a name for himself connecting this to any other crime. Nobody would be looking for a woman who wasn't missing. He could phone her office in the morning. Pretend to be Marco. Claim she was sick. That would buy him plenty of time.

And he could use this to help bring her to heel. Once she saw Marco was dead, she'd know there was nothing to go back to. She'd have to make the most of what she had. It was bound to make her even more eager to please, to offer him the perfection he deserved. He was her future. He was her only future. She was a smart woman. She would understand.

To ram home the point to her, he took out his phone and took half a dozen photos from various angles. He thumbed through them, making sure they left no room for doubt. Then he left, turning off all the lights behind him. Nothing suspicious to alert friends or neighbours.

When he arrived home, he poured himself a Jack Daniel's and Coke and sat down at the breakfast bar, scrolling through the pictures of Marco Mather. He slowly savoured both his drink and the photographs, deciding how best to play the upcoming scene. He uploaded the photographs to his tablet. 'All the better to see you with,' he said.

At last, he rinsed his glass, dried it and put it away. Then he went through to the garage, snapping on the harsh white fluorescent tubes that bled life and colour from the scene. He unlocked the lid of the chest freezer and threw it open with a flourish.

The woman's face was a caricature of surprise and terror. Her hands jerked up to cover her eyes from the shock of the light. He could see her eyelids fluttering through the lattice of her fingers. Normally he liked to go on the attack right away, to catch them on the back foot. But for once, he was happy to wait, to enjoy the anticipation of her reaction.

Gradually, she grew accustomed to the light. One hand slipped down from her face to conceal her breasts. She peeked fearfully at him through the fingers of her other hand. 'You?' Incredulity made her voice tiny and tremulous.

'Here's the deal. If you scream, I hurt you. And I tape your mouth up so you can never scream again. Is that clear?'

Eyes wide, she bit her lip and nodded.

'I am the husband. And you are the wife.'

Tears brimmed and spilled from her eyes. 'I have a husband.' It was barely a whisper.

He shook his head, smiling indulgently. 'You used to have a different husband. Now you have me. There's no going back.'

53

Talking to Carol had left Paula too jazzed to go home. She hated to inflict her edginess on Elinor, especially when she was carrying particularly heavy burdens of her own. Like a bereaved teenage boy in the living room. So she'd headed into Temple Fields, where the gay village rubbed shoulders with the hookers and the lap-dancing bars. A lot of her colleagues thought of Temple Fields as Bradfield's badlands, but Paula had always felt at home here. She was old enough to remember when being gay meant you were an outlaw, not the darlings of a coalition government desperately trying to make itself relevant to anyone under forty. In those olden days, Temple Fields had been one of the few places it was possible to be openly gay, and she still relished the bustle and buzz of its streets in spite of some of the more recent memories her job had overlaid on those streets.

She headed for Darlings and pushed her way through the press of bodies to the bar. Armed with a bottle of Belgian beer, she pushed back through to the tiny patio at the rear of the pub. In the old days, it had been the yard where the empties were stacked. Now, it boasted outdoor space heaters and tall cocktail tables where the smokers could hang out even in the dead of winter. She spotted a couple of women she recognised and joined them, lighting up as soon as she'd put her beer down.

They swapped gossip, took the piss out of a new lesbian sitcom and diplomatically refrained from talking about their jobs. Two cigarettes later, Paula drained her bottle of beer, made her apologies and left, feeling like she'd turned the stress dial down to manageable levels.

The house was dark and silent when Paula let herself in. She dumped her bag and keys on the hall table then went through to the kitchen for another beer before bed. She took one from the fridge then crossed to the patio doors so she could go outside and smoke. Suddenly the shadows beyond the breakfast bar shifted and she almost dropped her beer in shock. 'Jesus,' she exclaimed, taking a step back, eyes wide with apprehension.

'It's only me,' Torin said as the darkness resolved itself into his shape.

Paula reached for the switches and turned on the low-level lighting under the cabinets. In the soft light, she could see he was wearing what passed for pyjamas these days – baggy plaid trousers and a grey V-necked T-shirt. 'You nearly gave me a heart attack,' she complained, reaching for the patio door and hauling it open.

'I'm sorry.' He looked as if he was about to burst into tears. 'I couldn't sleep.' He gestured at the half-empty glass of milk on the breakfast bar. 'My mum always said that milk helped you sleep. Something about the calcium. It's not working too well, though.' He hitched himself on to a tall chair.

Paula stepped outside with her beer, lit a cigarette and grimaced at the acrid taste that filled her mouth. Why was it that you only ever knew you'd reached the limit of daily cigarette pleasure when you went one too far? And what the hell was she supposed to say to this kid that wasn't some desperate cliché? 'You're going to have a lot of broken nights,' she tried. 'The only advice I can give you is not to fret over it. It's natural. Part of grieving.'

'What's going to happen to me, Paula?' His voice shook.

A lot of bad stuff. 'I'm not going to lie to you. You're going to have a shit time for a while. You're going to feel raw, like somebody scraped your insides with a spoon. You're going to feel like the tears are never more than somebody else's careless comment away. You're going to feel like nothing will ever be right in your life again. But I promise you, all of that passes. It's not that you stop missing your mum or loving her. Somehow it becomes bearable.'

'I don't know. It's like that would be letting her down.'

She remembered that feeling only too well. When her colleague Don Merrick had died, it had felt like every day on the job was part of a long process of failing his memory. 'What would be letting her down would be to not live your life as fully as you possibly can. You've got a helluva touchstone there, Torin. When you're confronted with hard choices, you can always ask yourself what would have made your mum proud.' Paula took a last drag and crushed out the half-smoked cigarette in the ashtray Elinor reluctantly allowed on her precious deck. She came back inside and sat in the chair next to him.

'I want to kill the man who did this to her,' he said, staring bleakly at his milk.

'I know.'

'But what's worse is knowing that, even if he was standing in front of me, I wouldn't be able to. I'm just a kid,

349

Paula. And there's nothing I can do to make him feel the misery he's made for everybody that knew her.' He banged his fist on the table. 'I feel pathetic.'

'We're doing everything we can to bring him to justice. It won't be the kind of wild justice that we all crave when we're hurting, but it will deprive him of everything that makes life worth living for most people.' She put her hand over his. 'And you're already in a better place than him because you've got people all round you who care about you. When we catch him, his friends will melt into the darkness. His family will disown him. He'll have nothing. You'll always have more than him.'

Torin didn't look convinced. 'I wish my dad was home.' He gave a jerky laugh. 'Listen to me. Fourteen years old and I want my daddy, like I was a little kid.'

'Of course you want your dad. It doesn't matter what age you are when you lose a parent, you want somebody you love to take care of you. I'm sorry your dad can't be here, but we're going to do our best for you, Torin. Don't bottle up how you're feeling. Don't worry about what we think of you, because what we think is that you're a great lad.'

All at once, his shoulders were shaking with sobs, huge gulping moans that filled the room with his anguish. Not knowing what else to do, Paula got up and gathered him in her arms. It was like hugging an alien; the feel of his body, the faint boy-smell of his skin, the vibration of his grief in her own chest were all foreign to her. She'd thought the best thing she could do for Torin was to nail his mother's killer. Now she understood this was a case that was going to make far greater demands on her than that.

And then her phone rang.

54

Sleep was a distant stranger for Tony. Simply being in the same room as Carol had sparked his engines back to life. He had imagined so many scenarios where the weight of grief and loss had driven Carol to destruction, and now he'd seen her apparently intact the relief made him feel buoyant in spite of being locked in a smelly cell with no prospect of walking free just yet.

He ran an inventory of what he'd clocked. She'd always cheated time, looking younger than her years, but now her history had caught up with her. In his eyes, she was as attractive as ever, but the bloom had started to fade into something that told a darker story. She did look as if she was sleeping well though. The dark bruises under her eyes that had been a regular feature when she'd been up half the night trying to find a resolution to serious crimes had faded out, but her blue-grey eyes still had a weariness to them.

Carol had never been vain, but the one aspect of her appearance she'd always taken trouble with was her hair.

Naturally thick and blonde, it was always styled to look informally shaggy, but she'd once explained to Tony that it took a lot of skill to make it appear so casual. Now, whoever was cutting it lacked the necessary proficiency and it looked untidy. And the silver she'd kept at bay with clever colouring had asserted itself, changing the shade from honey to ash. The alteration he saw in her spoke volumes to Tony. Carol had lost her pride in herself. She no longer saw value in who she was and what she did.

And what exactly *was* she doing? Her body shape had undergone some subtle changes too. Her shoulders were broader and she wasn't carrying any spare weight round her midriff. She'd abandoned the silver twelve-piece Turkish puzzle ring she used to wear and her hands carried the marks of physical labour, yet she'd always been the first to insist on getting someone in when there were any problems with the house. As far as he was aware, she barely knew what a screwdriver was for. Whatever displacement activity she had chosen as her form of therapy, she had moved well outside her previous comfort zone.

And here he was, well outside his own comfort zone, completely reassured by the arrival of a woman who was adamant in her desire not to give a damn about him. Her very presence gave him hope. And now that he had genuine hope, it was possible to examine honestly the hopeless position he'd been in previously. He wondered what he represented to Alex Fielding to make her so swift and sure in her condemnation of him. Was it simply that she sensed a sensational scalp? A headline-grabbing arrest and conviction? It seemed a giant leap to believe him capable of such crimes. After all, BMP had consulted him for years. He'd been trusted to maintain confidentiality and to produce profiles that could be relied on by its officers. He was aware that a significant number of powerful officers thought he was odd, to say the least, but as far as he knew, they didn't consider him potentially lethal. But for Fielding to have gone on the attack like this, she must have been confident of support from the top brass.

And, realistically, that meant no matter what Paula believed, she couldn't rescue him from behind the barrier of her official position. If she hadn't already broken the rules for him, he'd have been lost. Fielding would almost certainly have charged him in the morning and the magistrates almost never granted bail on a murder charge. Definitely not on a double murder charge, regardless of who the accused was. Oscar Pistorius would have had no chance of making bail in a British magistrates' court.

Without Carol, he had been lost. With Carol, he stood a chance. And the best thing he could do to help her set him free was to focus not on her and how she'd changed and what was going on inside her head, but on the man who was killing a subset of women that she fitted into.

He got to his feet and started pacing. Profiling, that's what he was supposed to be good at. He needed to think about this killer in those terms. He'd written the introduction to his profiles so many times he knew it by heart. As he paced, he recited it aloud like a mantra to put his head in the right place. 'The following offender profile is for guidance only and shouldn't be regarded as an identikit portrait. The offender is unlikely to match the profile in every detail, though I would expect there to be a high degree of congruence between the characteristics outlined below and the reality. All of the statements in the profile express probabilities and possibilities, not hard facts.

'A serial killer produces signals and indicators in the commission of his crimes. Everything he does is intended, consciously or not, as part of a pattern. Discovering the underlying pattern reveals the killer's logic. It may not appear logical to us, but to him it is crucial. Because his logic is so idiosyncratic, straightforward traps will not capture him. As he is unique, so must be the means of catching him, interviewing him and reconstructing his acts.'

He stopped and rested both palms flat on the chilly wall. He wished he had a set of the crime-scene photos in front of him; his memory, like his eyesight, was not quite as sharp as it used to be, and a lot had happened since he'd flicked through the photos Paula had shown him. Some things were still vivid, however. The smashed face of the victim. The primitive markings of the bruises that covered her torso. The shaving of her genital area and the sealing of her labia.

'Mixed messages,' he said. 'The destruction of her face looks frenzied. The bruising on her body is organised. You didn't stamp on her at all, which you almost certainly would have done if you'd been in a frenzy. So, as with the facial destruction, in spite of appearances to the contrary, there's a reason. Here, it's because you are careful not to leave forensic traces. You're determined not to be caught and you're smart enough to have developed a strategy to deliver that result. You knew about the limitations of the CCTV coverage but still you took care to make sure you couldn't be identified. The things we think we know about your appearance we may not know at all. You're wearing glasses but they might have plain lenses. You've got a limp but you might be faking it. You look reasonably strapping but you could just be wearing bulky clothes on your upper torso. The only thing we will be able to say for sure, once some techie has done the biometrics, is how tall you are, give or take an inch.'

He pushed off from the wall and began pacing again. 'So how do we use these contradictions to provide investigative value?' He started numbering points on his fingers. Pinkie. 'First, the victims resemble each other. Similar height and

build, blonde, blue eyes, professional women, not in a relationship. As far as we know. You're going for a type that
means something to you. You want them to fit a specific
niche in your picture of the universe. And when they don't,
you destroy their faces.' Six, eight. Six, eight, brow furrowed
in thought.

'You destroy their faces because it turns out they don't
live up to the template. They look right but they don't act
right. So they don't have the right to belong in that cohort
any more. They've forfeited the right to be on the team. Let
there be no mistake about it. They're worthless. They're history.'

Ring finger. 'So it's not a frenzied attack at all. It's more in
sorrow than in anger. And now the other stuff makes sense.
You kick them to death to teach them a lesson. How dare
they fail you? How dare they trick you into thinking they
were the one and then not be the one? You're sending a
message, only there's nobody there to read it. If only she
knew it, you're sending a message to the next one. "This is
what will happen to you if you don't pass muster."' He
paused, frowning. 'It's savage, it's lethal, but you never lose
control, do you?'

Middle finger. 'And that's the thing with the washing and
the shaving and the superglue. It's not just about removing
forensic traces. It's another message. It's like stamping the
carcase "not fit for human consumption". You're warning
the rest of us, don't get taken in, this one isn't even worth
shagging. You're protecting other men from the mistakes
you made. You're the good guy, you're providing a service,
making sure nobody else wastes time on them.'

Tony scratched his head with both hands, as if creatures
were crawling over his scalp.

'So what is it that you're looking for? It's more than auditioning a girlfriend. I think you're looking for a replacement.

You had your perfect woman and something went wrong. And before you could make her pay the price for her fall from grace, she got away. And you can't find peace without her so you need a replacement.'

He threw himself down on the bed, forgetting it was so hard. He yelped and sat up again. 'I didn't think it through when I told Carol to find a dead woman who looks like her. But that's it. She's either dead or on the missing list. Because if she was around to be killed, he wouldn't need to bother with anybody else. And he didn't kill her then, so although he kids himself he's looking for a replacement, what he's actually looking for is an excuse to kill them. He kept Nadia alive for three weeks. He believed he could mould her but then he had to kill her when she couldn't make the grade. But killing her was such a kick he's convinced himself that it's a waste of time trying to get them to toe the line. He's run out of patience when it comes to training them because, whether he'd admit it or not, he'd rather kill them than keep them.' Index finger. 'He's not looking for a replacement now, he's looking for satisfaction, and unless he gets a perfect replica more or less straight away, he's going to be just like Mick Jagger. Trying and trying.'

All of which was interesting but not helpful when it came to catching a killer. What Carol – and Paula – needed was something a bit more concrete. 'You're not young,' he said thoughtfully. 'Bev was in her late thirties and you thought she was a possibility. Which probably puts you between thirty-five and fifty. You're authoritarian and arrogant, contemptuous of others. You let people know when they don't come up to scratch, which has probably hurt your career. And that makes you even more resentful. You're practical. You turn up with a taser and whatever is in that case.' He paused for a moment then smacked himself in the forehead. 'Of course. It's a portable anaesthetic kit. Like paramedics use. You're putting them under so they don't make a noise in the boot of the car. That's what you're doing.' He patted his pockets for his phone out of habit. Then it dawned on him he couldn't call Carol or even text her to share his revelation. Disappointment rippled through him, leaving him frustrated and annoyed.

'Focus, you moron,' he chided himself. 'Just make sure you remember it in the morning. And as for you, you clever bastard – you're probably in a white-collar job, though not a highly qualified professional. Not a doctor or a lawyer. Maybe a middle-manager of some sort. But you think you're better than that. That's why you're leaving them where they'll be found. You want us to pay attention, to take you seriously.'

Tony stood up again and walked the perimeter of the room, trailing his fingers along the wall as he went. 'You're local. Both your victims are from Bradfield. I think you're picking them at random. You see them on the street or on the bus and they look right and you stalk them to see whether they'll do. You acquired and killed Bev very soon after Nadia, which makes me wonder whether you've got a little list of possibles.

'You've probably got a house with a garage or a private area for parking cars. You're taking their cars somewhere, then going back for your own later. Then you dump theirs. We need to find out where those cars end up. Burned out? Left with fake plates in long-term parking? What are you doing with them?

'The other thing is, you need to be able to contain them. Keep them captive without being overlooked or overheard. No nosy neighbours wondering what the screaming is all about.'

It was thin, he had to admit. But with the limited resources at his disposal, he'd made a start. He was beginning to have a sense of what kind of man this killer was. And if he was right about the portable anaesthetic machine, Paula might be able to develop that into a viable lead.

He sat down on the edge of the bed, feeling the adrenalin finally ebb away, leaving him weary and depleted. But the despair was gone. Carol might not know it yet, but her arrival at Skenfrith Street signalled the installation of the caissons. Now the real work could begin on rebuilding the piers that would hold up the bridge that needed to be built between them.

For the first time in months, he actually believed it might be possible.

55

Marco would save her. Marie kept repeating the words like a sacred invocation. Marco would save her. She whimpered and shifted her position. It didn't matter how often she rearranged herself, some part of her body complained. How could anyone do what he'd done to someone they knew? She wasn't some stranger he'd dragged off the street. She was a person with a name and a place in his world. It made no sense in Marie's universe, where life was comfortable and people behaved in predictable, conventional ways. She wasn't stupid. She knew there were lots of people who lived in chaotic, illogical, even violent ways. But until today, she thought people like that were safely contained outside the neat borders of her life.

After this, nothing would ever be the same for her again. She'd look at the world in a different way once Marco had saved her from this hell. Right now, he'd be talking to the police. They'd be looking for her. They had all sorts of ways of tracking people down these days. There was CCTV everywhere. They'd be talking to people from work, people who got on the same tram as her morning and evening. The newsagent. Someone must have seen something. Or else he'd crack, this madman. He'd give something away without even realising it. And then they'd be on to him.

She wasn't going to think about what he'd done to her. The way he'd slapped her and dragged her across the concrete floor, ripping her skin in a painful graze from hip to knee. The kicks and punches he'd aimed at her when she'd tried to explain in as placatory a way as she could that she had no idea how to cook a steak because Marco was the cook in their house. He'd laughed incredulously then he'd gone mad with his fists and his feet.

But she wasn't going to dwell on that. She was going to hold fast to her hopes. Marco would save her. He wouldn't rest till she was home. And there would be no need to tell him about what had happened after the beating. He wouldn't press her for details. She'd never have to relive that horror. The pain, the humiliation, the things Marco had never dreamed of asking her to do – she would make herself forget them. She would be strong, because that's who she was. She wasn't whatever this beast wanted to make of her. She was Marie Mather, wife of Marco. Who would save her.

A moan escaped from her bruised lips. She had to be strong. She couldn't give in. She had to be the woman Marco loved. She had to be worthy of him. Because Marco would save her.

Then the lid was thrown open and her resolve wavered at the sight of him looming over her again. 'What was it you said earlier? Something about your useless wanker of a husband coming to save you?'

Although she was so scared she thought she might throw up, Marie managed to choke out, 'He will.'

He leaned forward and laughed viciously in her face. He

produced a tablet computer and turned it to face her. At first, she couldn't make sense of what she was seeing. And then it dawned on her that this was Marco. Sprawled over their garage floor. It made no sense. The beast leaned into the freezer and held it closer so Marie could see it more clearly.

Her mouth dropped open in horror. 'No,' she said, disbelief raising the volume.

He dragged his finger across the screen to bring up the next photo. 'Oh yes. Like I said, you used to have a different husband. But now he's dead.' As he spoke, he eased the taser out of his pocket. If he was going to need it, now was probably the time.

'You killed him? You killed my Marco?'

'I didn't have to. His cooking killed him. Your demands killed him. I'm not going to let you do that to me.'

She was oblivious to his words, completely focused on the image on the screen in front of her. 'No,' she said, this time more loudly still. 'No.' It was a shout now, suddenly deadened as the freezer lid slammed back down and plunged her into darkness.

Marco wasn't going to save her after all.

56

It was almost like old times, Carol thought. Sitting round a table at midnight with Paula and Stacey, drinking coffee and going over a live case, trying to come up with a line of inquiry that would do the business for them. Except it wasn't. She was kidding herself. Old times had never included Tony in jail, Chris in various kinds of therapy, a teenage kid upstairs and Elinor Blessing in the kitchen making the coffee. Kevin and Sam, the other members of the MIT, had moved onwards and upwards too; she had no idea where they were or what they were doing. This, she had to accept, was a new chapter with scant connection to the past.

'Thanks for joining us,' she said to Stacey.

Stacey flipped open a slender laptop. 'Paula explained about Tony. I wanted to help.'

I deserved that. 'Of course. He was always ready to put himself out for us.'

Elinor came through with a tray of steaming mugs.

'Coffee all round. I'd worry about it keeping you awake, except that you're all cops and it has as much effect on you as on doctors.' She handed out the drinks and put a plate of chocolate digestives on the table. 'Lucky for you I got fresh supplies of biscuits in. Torin seems to inhale them.'

'How is he doing?' Carol stirred milk into her coffee and reached for a biscuit.

'I don't know him well enough to be certain,' Elinor said. 'He's obviously deeply upset but I think he doesn't really know how he's supposed to react. He's got no experience of grief to draw on. It's like he's not sure what he's feeling.'

'Still in shock,' Paula said, keeping his secrets. 'I don't think it's begun to sink in yet.'

'Poor boy,' Stacey said.

Carol tried not to show her surprise at Stacey displaying empathy with a carbon-based life form. Then she remembered Paula's revelation that their former computer guru had been seeing Sam Evans socially. Maybe even romantically. Yet another reminder that this was not old times. 'Arresting the wrong person's not going to help,' she said.

'I've already said I'm sorry about that. I did try to persuade Fielding to wait, but I think she's got one eye on the brass. Trying to make an impression.' Paula shook her head. 'And Tony doesn't help himself.'

'I never thought I'd be grateful for Bronwen Scott,' Carol said. 'All we have to do now is demolish your case, Paula.' She held up a hand as Paula opened her mouth to protest. 'I'm not blaming you, I know it's DCI Fielding who drove this. I just said "you" because you're the only one here officially involved.'

'Exactly,' Stacey said. 'I'm not actually here.'

'And I'm not either,' Elinor said. 'Someone has to do the sleeping.' She kissed Paula on the cheek. 'I'm going to leave you to it. Don't stay up too late, ladies.' She patted Carol on the shoulder as she passed. A day ago Carol would have flinched at the contact. Now, it felt good.

They all waited politely till Elinor left the room, then Carol said, 'I take it as a given that none of us believes Tony could be responsible?' Paula looked outraged, Stacey rolled her eyes. 'OK, I had to ask. So I'm tasked with undermining the case against him enough to make Fielding back away from charging him.'

'And you don't have much time. She's going to want to reinterview him first thing and my guess is that unless Bronwen Scott gives her a very good reason not to, she's going to charge him at the end of that interview.'

'Would demolishing your DNA evidence be a good enough reason?' Carol asked sweetly.

Paula sat up straight. 'What do you mean?'

'He's remembered how it got there.' Carol revealed what Tony had told her earlier, leaving them both shaking their heads in disbelief. 'Stacey, Paula told me you've found your way into Nadia Wilkowa's data. Is that right?'

Stacey nodded. 'It wasn't hard.' She tapped a couple of keys and angled the screen so they could both see a diary page. 'I merged the data on her laptop and her phone so we have as full a picture as possible of her day to day life. So . . . ' She clicked on something and the display changed. 'On any given day I can tell you what her business appointments were, whether she had any personal appointments, what texts she sent and received and her emails.'

'Did I ever tell you how much you scare me?' Carol gave Stacey a thumbs-up.

'Just make sure you stay on her good side,' Paula muttered.

'So can you pull up dates she had appointments at Bradfield Moor?'

Stacey reclaimed the laptop. They waited while the keyboard whispered under her fingers, then she turned it to face them. 'Five times since she started the job. She had meetings with Joanna Moore, the Medical Director.'

'Can you email me those dates? I need to compare them with the incident log at Bradfield Moor. One of those dates should correspond to an occasion when Tony was punched in the face by a patient and had a nosebleed.'

Stacey snorted. 'Nothing changes, does it?'

'The thing is, I do actually remember that incident,' Carol said. 'His nose was swollen like a strawberry for a few days. It was last year some time. I can't be more precise than that.'

'I swear to God, you couldn't make him up,' Stacey muttered.

'Will they let you see the log?' Paula asked.

'If I have authorisation from Tony, I don't think they can refuse. I'll get on to that first thing tomorrow. On the downside, he was at a meeting with Will Newton in Bradfield Cross on Monday. He stomped out at the end because he was so pissed off. He walked home to work off his bad mood, so he's not got any kind of alibi for when Bev went missing.'

Paula groaned. She gave Carol a direct look. 'The "no alibi" isn't exactly a surprise. He misses the life he had when the MIT was still running. He doesn't really have much social contact without us.'

Carol knew the true opinion lurking behind Paula's words but she wasn't willing to engage with it. 'See what you can do.'

Paula dipped her head, acknowledging her failure to get Carol to open up with a wry twist of her mouth. 'You want me to get one of my firm to check the hospital CCTV and the street cameras?'

Carol nodded. 'You'll get a better response if you do it officially than I will if I try to get anything out of hospital bureaucrats. Meanwhile we'll be finding expert witnesses to knock down your fingermark evidence. Because obviously, it's not Tony's.'

'This isn't enough,' Stacey said, twirling a strand of her sleek black hair round her finger. 'Explaining the blood and the thumbprint would probably convince a jury there was reasonable doubt, but it's not going to hold Fielding back from charging him.'

Paula's expression was grim. 'I've barely got my feet under the table, but I'd say you're right. If we're going to get Tony off the hook before she charges him, we're going to have to find a stronger suspect.'

Carol leaned forward, hands flat on the table, intense and focused. 'Tony has a theory based on the way the killer treats his victims.' She looked at Paula. 'You know how Fielding has this mad idea that Tony's killing women who look like me because I walked away? Well, Tony suggested that he's not killing women because they look like me. It's that we all – me and the two victims – we all look like the woman he actually wants to kill.'

'So what's stopping him killing the woman he really wants to kill?' Stacey drummed the pads of her fingers softly against the laptop casing, alert and interested now there was some fresh meat on the table.

'Tony thinks she cheated him out of it. Suicide, accident, whatever. But she might be dead already. And quite recently. He thinks if we can find her, we find the killer.'

Paula stood up abruptly and lit a scented candle that immediately filled the air with the festive scent of cinnamon and cranberries. Then she flipped open her cigarette packet and sparked up a cigarette from the candle flame. 'Bloody hell,' she said at the top of the in breath. 'And how does he propose we do that?'

Carol pulled a face. 'He didn't get that far.'

'Surprise, surprise.'

Stacey frowned. 'That's an interesting challenge. It's not like you can google "dead blonde Bradfield" and expect anything useful.'

'A few tasteless blonde jokes maybe,' Paula sighed. 'But that doesn't help us any.'

'I thought I might trawl through the *Sentinel Times* archives. The hard copies, not the online version,' Carol said. 'I think they still keep them on file at the central library.'

'If that hasn't gone in the local government cuts,' Paula said gloomily.

'It's not exactly exhaustive,' Stacey pointed out.

'Maybe not, but funeral directors recommend a death notice as part of the package and the overwhelming majority of people still go for it,' Carol said. 'It's the best we can do.'

'And I'll try and persuade Fielding not to charge Tony in the morning.' Paula cracked a yawn and rolled her shoulders. 'I'm sorry, girls, but I'm going to have to go to bed.'

Carol stood up. 'Lucky you. I've got the best part of a forty-minute drive before I get to sleep.'

'There's a sofa bed here,' Paula said. 'We seem to be the unofficial home for waifs and strays.'

Carol smiled and shook her head. 'Thanks, but I've got to get home for the dog. I'm new to this game. I don't know how long you can leave them alone without them freaking out.'

'Where did you leave her?' Paula looked worried.

'In the main barn. There's nothing to chew except sawhorses and scrap wood.'

'Probably just as well.'

'I'll bring her with me tomorrow. She can sleep in the Land Rover and I can take her for a walk at lunchtime.'

'Are you sure that's legal?' Stacey asked, looking concerned.

'I don't see why not. The weather's not exactly warm and I'll obviously leave a window open. And I'll walk her whenever I can.'

Paula pushed herself to her feet. 'It'll be fine. I'm glad you came, Carol. Tony needs you on his side.'

All the relaxed bonhomie drained from Carol's face and her shoulders tightened. 'I'm not on his side. I'm on the side of justice being done. That's all. And when it's done, I'm going straight back to my own life. I'm done with him, Paula. I'm done with Tony.'

57

Day twenty-seven

It was infuriating. Why were women so stupid? You didn't have to be Einstein to work out that, if your husband was dead, you'd better make a good impression on the man who was willing to take his place. But that didn't seem to have penetrated her thick skull. He'd left her in peace all night so she could get Marco out of her system and get used to her new reality, but he might as well not have bothered.

He'd set his alarm especially early so he could provide her with her first lesson before he set about the business of the day. But when he opened the lid of the freezer, she barely reacted. No panic, no terror, no offer of obedience. She remained huddled at one end of the freezer, knees against her chest, arms wrapped around her head. He shouted at her but she didn't flinch. It didn't seem to register at all. He'd heard about catatonic states, but he couldn't believe he was seeing one for real. He was convinced she was putting on an act, so he slapped her a couple of times to snap her out of it.

But all he achieved was to sting the palm of his hand. She made no attempt to protect herself or to fight back.

He tried tasering her and throwing her on the floor of the garage but she remained where he dropped her, sprawled in an ungainly way across the concrete. He shouted at her to get up, but she stayed where she was. He booted her in the midriff; she rose and fell like a sack of meat. She made no protest, not even a whimper.

He didn't have time for this. Not now. So he tasered her again and threw her into the freezer. 'You need to buck up your ideas,' he said. 'You could have a great life with me. Or you could end up in the mortuary like the other ones. It's your choice. When I get home tonight, I expect you to have had an attitude readjustment. Marco's dead. Get used to it. You can join him or you can join me. I'd say it's a no-brainer. But people make shitty choices all the time. Still, you're supposed to be a clever bitch. Show me how smart you really are. Choose life, bitch. Or pay the price.'

Then he'd slammed the freezer shut. Rage burned like acid in his throat. Who the *fuck* did she think she was? Failure was one thing, but defiance was another. That's where the first one, the original, had gone wrong. When things came to a head between them and he made it clear her behaviour was unacceptable, she'd flouted his instructions to improve herself. She'd thought she could go against him. Take his children and walk out the door. She'd thought she was escaping.

Instead she'd driven so bloody badly that she'd ended up in a pile-up on the M62. That she was dead was fine with him, even though there would have been more satisfaction in dealing out death himself. But she'd destroyed his kids with her treachery. His kids. His son and his daughter, still in the process of being moulded into a pair of children anyone would be proud of. And she'd taken herself beyond revenge at the same time. He'd cheerfully have killed her again and again and again for the affront of leaving him. The outrage of taking his children from him was worse; for that, he'd have tortured her slowly, grimly, gruesomely for as long as he could possibly make it last.

Well, this one would discover the price of defiance soon enough. First, though, he had to go to work.

58

The dog had greeted her so rapturously on her return that Carol felt obliged to take her for a walk. She hadn't fancied stumbling over the rough pasture in the dark, so she'd stuck to the margin of the field where the ground was relatively even. Flash didn't seem to mind. She raced off in random directions before returning at regular intervals to make sure Carol hadn't lost her way. 'A bit like my brain,' Carol said once she'd recognised the pattern.

Even when she'd finally gone to bed, her mind was still racing, running over the same problems in the hope of finding a solution. In the end, she'd pummelled the pillows one last time and managed to drift off to the sound of the World Service. When the alarm roused her a few hours later, the same thoughts were still rattling round her head.

There was no time to take the dog for a run; she had to meet Bronwen Scott at eight so they could go over things once more with Tony before Fielding arrived to interrogate him again. Scott had redoubled her suggestion that Carol avoid the interview itself. 'I'm sure Fielding will know by then that you're on the team, but I don't want to feel she's got something to prove because you're in the room.' It was a good point. It was also a way of protecting Paula.

Carol might not have known much about dogs, but even before Stacey had weighed in, she had realised it wasn't acceptable to leave the dog alone for long periods of time. They were supposed to keep each other company, after all. So she opened the rear door of the Land Rover and spread a couple of blankets on the floor. Flash jumped aboard as if it was routine. Carol added a litre-bottle of water and a plastic bowl to her dog-walking kit of leash, training treats and plastic bags, and they were ready to roll. One way or another, she'd find time to walk the dog.

She beat Scott to Skenfrith Street by five minutes but she didn't go inside, thinking it more sensible to wait at the car-park entrance. Scott was perfectly groomed as ever, immaculate in a fitted charcoal-grey suit over a sharply tailored blue-and-white pinstriped shirt. The narrow skirt, coupled with teetering heels, showed off her legs to distracting advantage. Carol felt like a frump in her best black trouser suit and flatties, both from the Hobbs' sale a couple of years ago. This time, they were shown to an interview room away from the custody suite, fitted with recording equipment and a long narrow wall mirror. It had the familiar grey walls and the mingled smell of stale bodies and cleaning chemicals. Without thinking, Carol headed straight for the chairs that weren't bolted to the floor. Scott laughed. 'Old habits die hard, Carol. You're on the wrong side of the table.' As Carol made to stand up, Scott waved her back down. 'It's OK, it's only us here. Stay where you are for the time being.'

Scott sat down and put on a pair of rectangular glasses with thin black frames. They made her look like a sexily strict headmistress. She opened a file and studied the contents page by page. When Tony was shown in a few minutes later, she closed the file and stood up. As he approached the table, she moved towards him and put a hand on his arm. 'How was your night?'

He looked across at Carol, who had not moved. 'It passed,' he said, moving past Scott to sit down opposite Carol. 'I don't know how long we've got here, but there are a few things I need to say. I think he's local. Given that men tend to go for women younger than them and he chose Bev as a possible surrogate, I'd say he's at least thirty-five. One thing that bothered me was that the women don't seem to have tried to escape or draw attention to themselves after he loads them in the car. I'd have thought if there had been any reports of pedestrians hearing someone kicking or shouting in the boot of a car Paula would have said something about it. So I wondered if what he's got in that metal case is a portable anaesthetic kit. Like paramedics carry. That would explain both why he's carrying the case and the women's apparent passivity. It's because they're unconscious. So maybe it's worth checking if any of the local hospitals have lost one?'

'Given the professions of the victims, he might even be a paramedic,' Carol said.

Tony ran a hand through his hair. 'I don't think so. I'd put him in a white-collar job. But you could be right,' he added hastily.

Trying to suck up. Pathetic. Carol made a note. One for Paula to suggest to Fielding, maybe. To make it look like she was on her boss's side. She looked across at Scott. 'Could I have a sheet of paper?' Scott tore a blank page out of her legal pad. 'I need you to write me a letter of authority to Bradfield Moor, asking them to give me access to any entries in the incident log involving you. We've got the dates when Nadia

Wilkowa had appointments there and if we can match them up, we can undermine Fielding's case.'

Even before she'd finished speaking, he was writing. 'If we can do that, they'll have to let me go, right?'

'Not necessarily,' Scott said. 'Especially since somebody's bound to leak to the internet or the local media that they've arrested someone as high profile as you.'

'High profile? Me?'

'In crime terms, you're the bee's knees. A profiler gone rogue? It doesn't get any better than that.'

He looked shaken. 'They're going to put me all over the papers, right? Like that poor bloke in Bristol who got demonised for nothing more than having a weird hair-style.'

Scott sighed. 'Probably. So far, I've not had any calls. But Fielding kept this very quiet and the overnight custody ser-geant is notorious for hating the media. That won't last once the dayshift briefing happens. You're almost certainly going to get screwed over. All the Jacko Vance stuff will be raked up again.' She nodded towards Carol. 'They might come after you too.'

'I'll enjoy that,' she said grimly.

Tony signed the letter and passed it across to Carol. 'Ask for Maggie Spence, the Assistant Director. She likes me, she'll be helpful.'

'Unlike your boss,' Carol said drily. She knew the history between them. Power never forgives those who know its dirty little secrets.

A wry smile. 'Hard to believe how much pleasure this will give him.' He swept his arm to encompass the depressing room.

'They'll have a search warrant by now,' Scott said, impa-tient to get on with the serious business of the morning. 'They'll be going through your home and your office. If there's anything you don't want them to find, now's the time to tell us.' She cocked an eyebrow at him.

Tony shrugged, spreading his hands in a gesture of openness. 'Good luck to them. If they find the data CD for Tomb Raider 3, I'd be eternally grateful.' He gave a strained smile. 'I really don't have any dark secrets. Hidden shallows, that's me.'

Carol had had enough. She pushed her chair back and folded Tony's letter away in her bag. 'Unless there's anything else you think I need to know, I'm going now. I've got inquiries to make and the clock's ticking. And my dog needs walking.'

'Dog?' Tony looked bemused.

'I'll fill you in later,' Scott said to her retreating figure.

Tony's spirits sank as Carol walked out of the interview room. Bronwen Scott made him feel nervous and inadequate; a woman for whom he could never have enough right answers. He watched the door close then said, 'She's got a dog?'

Scott looked baffled, but in an amused sort of way. 'I have no idea what Carol's domestic arrangements are.'

Tony pulled a face. 'Neither do I, apparently. So, what's going to happen now?'

'Fielding will interview you again. Unless she's got something new we don't know about she'll just try to rerun yesterday's questions and you're going to go "no comment" to everything she puts to you. She'll try to unsettle you, to provoke you. But you mustn't let her get to you.'

'I'll pretend she's a patient. They generally try to divert attention from what's ailing them by asking me questions. I'm quite good at avoiding the answers.' He stared down at the table. 'I know I shouldn't take this personally, but it's hard not to feel hurt by how quick off the mark Fielding has been to arrest me. Call me sentimental, but I'd have expected her to cut me a bit of slack. I mean, I've been at the heart of so many investigations, I'd have thought they'd think twice before they jumped to the conclusion that I'm a serial killer.' He met her eyes, his expression pained.

'Fielding's showing the brass her independence. And maybe trying to take some of the gloss off Carol's achievements at the same time. That's why she's so keen on having Paula on the team. Fielding wants to be seen as the rehab unit for officers contaminated by the maverick tendency.'

Tony managed a tired smile. 'And I thought I was the psychologist. So, do you think they're going to charge me?'

'I think she's going to keep you hanging on till the last possible minute. She'll get another DCI to authorise an extra twelve hours' detention, which will take us up to tomorrow morning. Then she'll either charge you or let you go, or, if she thinks she's got enough with the DNA and the thumbprint, she'll go to the magistrates for an extension. At which point we'll wheel out all the undermining evidence that Carol will have assembled plus something from the fingerprint expert my office is lining up, and they'll order your release. Probably on police bail. If we hang on and do it that way, your exoneration is more public.'

'That sounds good.'

Scott held one hand out flat and swivelled it at the wrist. 'Yes and no. The exoneration is more public, but the downside is that the media and the twittersphere will have had a full twenty-four-hour news cycle to rip you to shreds.'

'They're going to rip me to shreds anyway by the sounds of it, so the more publicly I'm taken off the hook, the better, surely? Or are you thinking the mags won't let me go?'

Scott twisted her mouth in an expression of uncertainty. 'I'd be very surprised if they backed Fielding on this one once her so-called evidence is thoroughly undermined.'

Before Tony could respond, the door slammed open. Fielding stood in the doorway, a tiny ball of barely contained fury. Her mouth was tight, her eyes narrowed and her hands curled into fists. 'A word, Ms Scott,' she said. It wasn't a request.

Scott took her time, pausing to give Tony's shoulder a quick squeeze. 'I'll be right back, Tony.'

She'd barely closed the door behind her when Fielding stepped into her personal space and hissed, 'What the hell do you think you're playing at?' Today, Fielding's accent had abandoned charm in favour of blunt threat. It would have made nobody want to visit Scotland.

Scott smiled sweetly and looked over Fielding's shoulder to where Paula stood, frowning with worry, trying to melt into the wall. Scott nodded a greeting to Paula then made a deliberate show of looking down at Fielding. 'You're going to have to give me more of a clue, DCI Fielding.'

'You know exactly what I mean, lady. Bringing Carol Jordan in here to meet your client under the pretence of being your intern. Do you think my head buttons up the back?'

Scott's expression was of amused condescension. 'I don't understand why you're so upset. Carol isn't a serving officer. She's entitled to explore new career options. She approached me asking for the opportunity to shadow me to decide whether a career in the law might be for her. I was willing to take that at face value and not assume she was trying to infiltrate my office on your behalf.'

'On *my* behalf?' Fielding sounded like a gasket about to blow.

'It wouldn't be the first time your colleagues have tried to undermine my attempts to provide my clients with the best possible defence.'

'That's a disgraceful allegation,' Fielding spluttered.

'No worse than your imputation of inappropriate motives to me and Carol.'

'So why was she here, if not to try and compromise my operation?'

'How could she do that? Are you suggesting your officers are going to sneak around behind your back and leak things you should be disclosing to the defence anyway? All out of some misplaced loyalty to a retired colleague? It must be depressing to have such little faith in your team, DCI Fielding.' Scott turned away, her fingers on the door handle.

'I trust my team,' Fielding spat, her words like sharp little darts aimed at Scott's heart.

'Good. Then shall we get on with our "no comment" interview? And perhaps I could have disclosure of the fingermark evidence?' The last word and the last smile to the defence, Scott thought as she sailed back to her client's side.

59

Bradfield Moor Secure Hospital perched on the side of a hill on the north-western side of the city at the point where cultivated greenery gave way to the untamed hodge-podge of moorland vegetation. The buildings were angled so they faced down the hill at trees and roofs and lawns and shrubberies and flowerbeds rather than the weatherbeaten grasses and stunted shrubs of the peat bogs above. Tony had once described it to Carol as a Victorian metaphor directed at the patients within. 'They're supposed to turn their backs on the jungle of madness and become part of the ordered consensus below,' he'd said. Typical Tony, she thought, then felt irritated with herself for enjoying the richness of his take on the world. Now he was the one implicitly accused of madness and she was the one with the task of restoring him to the mainstream.

The hospital had extensive grounds and once she had cleared the security gates and parked well away from the buildings, Carol clipped the leash on Flash and let her out of the Land Rover. The sky was grey and heavy with the promise of rain, but it was still only a promise. She walked down the driveway in the teeth of a stiff breeze and when she was sure there was nobody around, she let the dog run free. As she'd done the night before, Flash ranged across the terrain but kept returning to her mistress without being summoned, before taking off on another zigzag run. Carol let the dog run for quarter of an hour, then put her back in the Landie with a bowl of water and a handful of treats.

By the time she reached the main entrance, she could feel a few drops of rain. 'Not a moment too soon,' she muttered, pushing the door open. The reception area was the usual institutional beige and grey, but someone had taken a little effort and imagination to make it more appealing. There were attractive photographs of tranquil mountain scenery around the walls and a pair of large blue glazed pots containing an assortment of house plants. Too heavy to be lifted and thrown, of course, Carol recognised. Off to one side was a doorway without a door leading to a seating area where visitors could wait before being processed and allowed in to see inmates. Behind the glassed-in reception desk, one woman was on the phone, another at a computer.

Carol stood patiently waiting for one of them to pause in their vital tasks to deal with her. It took a couple of minutes, but the woman on the phone eventually finished her conversation and slid open a panel in the glass. 'Visiting hours don't begin till noon,' she said, not unkindly. 'They should have told you that at the main gate.'

'I'm not a visitor.' Carol produced the old warrant card that had got her on to the premises and flashed it at the women. 'I'd like to see Maggie Spence.'

'Have you got an appointment?'

'No.'

'Can you tell me what it's in connection with?'

381

'It's confidential.'

The woman at the computer glanced up at the word, like a dog picking up a scent. She frowned momentarily, then her face cleared. 'I've seen you with Dr Hill,' she said, smiling. 'Molly, this lady works with Dr Hill when he's doing his profiling.'

Molly squeezed a smile out. 'I'll see if Mrs Spence is available.' She slid the panel shut and returned to the phone. A brief conversation, glancing at Carol a couple of times, then she replaced the phone and reopened the panel. 'She's coming through.' She produced a clipboard and handed Carol a pen. 'If you wouldn't mind signing in?'

Carol completed the formalities and was pinning a visitor pass to her jacket when a heavy door to one side of the desk clicked open and a woman emerged. Somewhere in her mid to late fifties, Maggie Spence looked like a woman for whom comfort was the headline priority. She wore loose khaki chinos topped by a baggy blue T-shirt and a hand-knitted multicoloured cardigan. A pair of scarlet-rimmed glasses perched on the end of a nose that wouldn't have looked out of place on Santa Claus. Her plump face was lined with the tell-tale tracks of smiles rather than frowns. Seeing Carol, she gave an automatic grin. 'Hi, I'm Maggie Spence. I gather you wanted to talk to me?' She extended a hand and Carol found her fingers enveloped in a warm grip.

'I'm Carol Jordan,' she said. 'Thanks for seeing me. Is there somewhere we can talk?'

Maggie glanced at the visitors' waiting area. 'Molly said it was confidential, right?' Carol nodded. 'This is too public, then. Come with me and we'll use my office.'

Carol followed as Maggie used a swipe card to lead her through a series of locked doors and short hallways to a neat little room with a view across the grounds to the distant moors. Apparently the staff were allowed to enjoy the wild grandeur of nature. Maggie's office was crammed with books, files and paper, but unlike Tony's, everything was organised in neat piles. The only wall space not fitted with shelves was covered by a colourful patchwork hanging that appeared to be an impressionistic image of a mountain landscape. Maggie waved Carol to a chair and settled herself behind the tidy desk. 'So, what's all this about?'

Carol took Tony's letter out of her bag. 'I'm here under false colours, I'm afraid. I'm not a police officer any longer. I'm working with Bronwen Scott, who is a criminal defence lawyer.'

Maggie leaned forward and opened her mouth to speak. But Carol held up a hand. 'Please. Hear me out?' Maggie subsided, but the smile was gone.

Carol cut to the chase. 'Tony Hill was arrested last night on suspicion of committing two murders. You know Tony. You know how absurd that is. But there is some circumstantial evidence and a cop who has decided this is how she's going to make her name. I'm working with his lawyer to establish his innocence.' She pushed the letter across to Maggie. 'He's asking for your help.'

Maggie looked stunned. 'Tony? Arrested? Are you sure?'

'I've just come from Skenfrith Street police station. I know it's hard to believe—'

'Hard to believe? It's surreal. I've never met a man with more compassion. The idea that he could intentionally kill anyone is ridiculous.'

'Unfortunately, not everyone knows him like we do. And he doesn't come across like most blokes.'

Maggie gave a little snort of laughter. 'No kidding. All the same. Working in here, you think you've heard everything. And then you walk in and tell me Tony Hill's suspected of murder. Incredible. Poor Tony.' She picked up the letter and pushed her glasses up her nose. She read it carefully then put it down on the desk. 'All right. We have some data protection issues here. I can't let you have access to our incident log because of our duty of confidentiality to staff and patients. But because I have Tony's permission, I believe I can give you copies of entries in that log that relate to him, provided that I redact the names of the patients involved. Will that give you what you need?'

Carol nodded. 'I don't need much in the way of detail. All I'm interested in are the dates and the nature of the incidents.'

Maggie nodded. She pulled her keyboard towards her and started hammering the keys with the energy of someone who had learned her skills on an old manual typewriter. Every now and again she paused and massaged her forehead with her fingertips. 'Luckily everything's online these days,' she muttered. 'And searchable.'

After a few minutes, she said, 'I'm going to cut and paste all the incidents involving Tony into a separate document then I can redact any identifying features relating to patients and I can print it out for you. That fine?'

Carol nodded. 'Perfect.'

The tip of Maggie's tongue slipped out between her lips as she concentrated on what she was doing. Finally, she looked across at Carol and smiled. 'That's it. Four incidents. I expect you already knew about the knee?'

A swirl of recalled emotion caught Carol unawares. She had a vivid recollection of the axe attack that had left Tony lying in a hospital bed and its aftermath. No need for redaction there. Lloyd Allen's name was carved on her memory. 'I was around at the time,' she said calmly, hiding what was going on beneath the surface.

Just then the door swung open behind her. Carol turned in time to catch the arrival of Aidan Hart, Clinical Director of Bradfield Moor. It had been at least a year since she'd seen him last and time was definitely not on his side. He didn't look as if he'd gained weight, but somehow, his face had grown pasty and jowly. Although he'd barely turned forty, there were deep lines between his eyebrows, and the whites of his eyes looked liverish. She'd never considered him attractive – particularly given what she knew about him – but now he was becoming positively repulsive. 'What the hell is going on here?' he demanded. For a psychologist, his interrogatory techniques seemed somewhat lacking.

Maggie was clearly inured to his belligerence. 'I'm just sorting out something Dr Hill asked for,' she said calmly.

'On whose authority?' Hart moved further into the room, using his height and bulk to dominate the women.

Maggie was undominated. She picked up Tony's letter and waved it at him. 'On Dr Hill's authority. He has the right to access his own records.'

Hart looked around him theatrically. 'I don't see Dr Hill here.'

'His letter authorises Ms Jordan here to access the information on his behalf.'

'He can't do that. It's a data protection issue.'

Maggie shook her head. 'I've redacted everything that could identify patients or other staff.'

'I'm not prepared to release any of our records to a third party, however redacted they are. She's not a police officer any more, you know. She's here under false pretences.'

'No, she's not, she told me that.'

Hart's crocodile smile crept across his face. 'She didn't tell the gatehouse staff or reception. She used police ID to bypass our security.'

Carol shrugged. 'I needed photo ID. That was all I had. I never said I was a serving police officer.'

Two stripes of scarlet appeared on his cheeks, as if a child had drawn on his face with lipstick. 'Don't split hairs with me, Miss Jordan. I'd like you to leave now.' He was wholly focused on her, but beyond him, Carol could see Maggie's fingers move stealthily on the keyboard.

'Not without what I came for. It's completely uncontroversial. We could easily get a court order.' Carol wasn't going to give up without a fight.

'Get one, then.' He threw the door open. 'Maggie, show Miss Jordan out, would you?'

'No point in making a fuss,' Maggie said, taking Carol's elbow and steering her to the door. Hart watched them leave, then, as Maggie opened the first locked door, he turned and marched off in the opposite direction. Maggie looked after him and smirked. 'I figured something as menial as seeing you off the premises would be beneath him. He is the absolute antithesis of a class act. I don't know how Tony puts up with him. I don't know how *I* do, come to that.'

As she talked, she led the way towards reception. But just before they emerged into the foyer, she turned abruptly into another office. A young man in a nurse's tunic sat at a desk, working on a spreadsheet. He looked up when they walked in and grinned. 'You owe me a drink.' He leaned across the desk and picked up a few sheets of paper from the printer tray.

'Thanks, Stephen.' Maggie accepted the papers and handed them to Carol. 'There you are. Tuck them away so the snitches on reception can't see them. Now it really is time to go, Carol.'

'Thanks. Nice move,' Carol said as she followed Maggie into the corridor. 'I have the impression you've done that before.'

'We look after each other here,' Maggie said. 'Aidan only looks after number one. Tell Tony, chin up.'

On her way out, Carol made a point of glaring at the

receptionists. Anything else would have looked suspicious. She didn't so much as glance at the papers until she was out of sight of the security guards on the front gate. Then she pulled in to the first woodland track she came to for a read. It wasn't easy to make sense of the redacted reports, but when she compared them with the dates Nadia Wilkowa had been in Bradfield Moor, one thing rapidly became clear.

Tony had been treated for a nosebleed following an incident with a patient on a day when Nadia Wilkowa had been there. 'You fucking beauty,' Carol said, kissing the sheet of paper. The first piece of evidence against Tony had been perfectly undermined.

60

The absence of their bosses didn't let the workers at Tellit Communications off the hook. They knew their computers recorded every detail of their working lives. Their keystrokes were counted, their phone calls timed, their absences from either form of communication logged and monitored. The workers were so wrapped up in what they were paid to do that they barely looked around them. So Rob Morrison had been in his office for a good twenty minutes before Gareth Taylor appeared in his doorway.

'Marie Mather's husband phoned earlier,' he said. 'I was the only one in, so I picked up the call. Apparently she's been taken to hospital with a suspected burst appendix.'

Rob winced. 'That sounds painful. Did he say how long she'd be off?'

Gareth shook his head. 'He said he'd phone again when he had a better idea of the prognosis, but not to expect her in for the rest of the week. He sounded fucking terrified,' he added with a sneer.

'That's not a great start to a new job,' Rob said.

'I don't suppose she planned it.' Gareth pushed off from the door jamb and turned back to the busy room. Unobserved, Rob gave a sly smile. Marie Mather's big ideas had definitely been put on ice and he wasn't in the least sorry about that.

Paula had felt her phone vibrate against her thigh while they'd been conducting their miserable 'no comment' interview with Tony Hill but she'd known better than to take it out in front of Fielding. The DCI was obviously right on the edge of losing her temper and Paula definitely didn't want to be her target.

The interview had run into the sand when Fielding had started repeating questions. Bronwen Scott had leaned back in her chair and smiled with the weary charm of one who has seen it all before. 'Charge my client or release him,' she'd said.

Fielding had thrown her pen on the table. 'We're continuing our inquiries. We have search warrants for Dr Hill's home and his office, and officers are conducting those searches right now. So we won't be releasing your client just yet.' She'd pushed her chair back and stabbed a finger at the recording equipment. 'This interview terminated at 11.17 a.m.' Then she'd stalked out of the room, leaving Paula to make an apologetic face and follow. She took the chance to glance at her phone and see a message from Carol Jordan. 'Think the metal case might be portable anaesthetic unit? Check any missing? Check paramedics?'

Chiding herself for not having thought of that, Paula hurried to catch Fielding. 'Bloody woman,' Fielding snarled, climbing the stairs with the energy of fury. 'And bloody Carol Jordan.' She stopped in her tracks and turned on Paula and lowered her voice to a growl. 'Don't even think about leaking to Jordan.'

'I'm not stupid,' Paula said. 'But I did have a thought while you were asking Dr Hill about hospitals. That metal case the killer is carrying in the CCTV footage? What if it's portable anaesthetic apparatus? When he tips them into the car boots, he puts the box in and leans over them. We can't see what he's doing. What if he's putting them under so they can't escape or give the alarm?'

Fielding's face lit up. 'That's a bloody great idea, McIntyre.' She clapped her on the shoulder. 'Hill could easily have figured out how to get his hands on one of them. Head upstairs to the incident room and get that actioned right away. I want a check on hospitals that Nadia Wilkowa visited, see if they've had any portable anaesthesia units stolen. Paying particular attention to Bradfield Moor and Bradfield Cross. Although Tony Hill's credentials could get him in anywhere.' She looked almost gleeful. 'Bloody brilliant! Well done, McIntyre.' She bounded off up the stairs leaving Paula in her wake, feeling stricken. The suggestion was meant to shake Fielding's certainties. Instead, it seemed merely to have re-inforced them.

'Bloody hell,' Paula muttered, heading up to the incident room. If they uncovered any stolen anaesthetic sets, that would give fresh life to the investigation. At least she could set the guys on to checking out paramedics rather than solely focusing on Tony. She wondered whether the search teams were suitably baffled by Tony's life – psychology text-books, computer games, superhero comic books, case notes and cryptic memos to himself. She couldn't imagine they'd find anything to link him to the victims or the crimes. Wasting police time, that's what this was.

Somehow, she didn't think anybody would be charging Fielding.

61

Buoyed up by her success at Bradfield Moor, Carol was eager to get to the Central Library so she could pursue the next stage in her investigation. But her life wasn't quite as simple as it had been a few days before. She couldn't just drive straight to the library and immerse herself in bound copies of the newspaper for as long as it took; she had Flash to consider.

She texted Bronwen to fill her in on the outcome of her inquiries at the hospital then let Flash run free again while she walked several hundred yards up the track and back again. As before, the dog ranged far and wide but always returned at intervals to make sure Carol was still there and, presumably, in one piece. After this second run, Carol considered the dog could be left in the Landie for a while. Later, she could take the dog down to the canal and let her have a walk along the towpath, safe from the city traffic.

Carol left the Land Rover in a multi-storey near the library, cracking the window open to give the dog air. She'd always been a little intimidated by the massive Victorian building. Its highly polished marble columns, staircase and wall panels came in colours she associated with the sort of old-fashioned butcher's shop where the meat had lost its first bloom. There were no books in the grand entrance hall to absorb sound, and every noise seemed magnified by the hard surfaces, echoing in a swirl of footsteps and snatches of speech.

She hurried up the stairs to the octagonal gallery where the local collections were kept. Bookshelves lined the walls from floor to ceiling, starting with ancient leather spines at one end and travelling through a chronological catalogue of book bindings to privately published memoirs bound with adhesive cloth tape.

At the far end stood a line of angled wooden tables, designed so that a person could sit and browse the large bound volumes of the newspaper collection. Here, this year's copies of the *Bradfield Evening Sentinel Times* were fastened together week by week, clamped in place between long thin wooden batons. Carol found an empty chair and logged in with her tablet to the library's wifi. Then she settled down with the previous week's papers, working backwards from the day before Nadia Wilkowa's disappearance.

She pored over the news pages, checking even the shortest snippet of news. Then she moved on to Births, Marriages and Deaths. She'd settled on fifty as a sensible upper-age limit for her target. Whenever she found a woman in the right age group, she turned to her tablet and went to the online edition for the day in question. A few months before, the *BEST* had started offering those who placed notices in the BMD section of the paper the opportunity to post a digital photograph in the online edition. It was a clever marketing ploy – it cost the paper nothing, but it generated a huge amount of goodwill. Now, when people died, their families and friends chose their favourite photo and up-loaded it to the BMD pages online. So Carol was able to ascertain quickly whether the dead women were blondes.

It was a slow, painstaking process. By lunchtime, she only had two potential candidates. One had died, aged forty-four, 'after a long battle with cancer. Beloved wife of Trevor, mum to Greta, Gwyneth and Gordon, gran to Adele. Much missed by her dear friends from the Fleece darts team.' Her blonde looked as if it had come from a bottle. Somehow Carol didn't think a killer with the control-freak tendencies Tony had outlined would allow his wife to join a pub darts team.

The other was, on the face of it, more promising. The woman was thirty-five and she'd died with her two small children in a motorway pile-up on the M62. Carol reckoned from her colouring that she was a natural blonde. There was no BMD announcement, just a news story about the accident. A lorry driver had been critically injured and two other motorists hurt in the late-night collision. An eye-witness said the lorry had appeared to swerve without warning across the outside lane before smashing into the crash barrier. The photograph of the woman showed her holding a baby on her lap with a toddler cuddled into her side. To Carol's eye, she didn't look very relaxed. But people often didn't in posed photos.

According to a short follow-up in the following day's paper, the woman had been taking the children to visit their grandparents in York. Ironically, she'd set off late in the evening to avoid the traffic. So said a police spokesman who gave the standard spiel about the dangers of driving while overtired.

Carol couldn't find the news stories in the online edition, so she took photocopies. She decided to walk the dog then return and do another month. That would make three in total. She reckoned that was far enough back.

It was a relief to be out in the fresh air and Flash showed her pleasure at Carol's return with extravagant tail wagging and a long pink tongue aimed at her owner's face. Carol avoided it with an exclamation of disgust and let the dog jump free. Ten minutes' brisk walking brought them to the Minster Basin. Carol tied Flash to a table outside one of the pubs and went inside to get a glass of wine, a bowl of water and a bag of crisps. She gave the dog some water and shared her crisps. She let her gaze wander idly across the boats in the marina, stopping short when she spotted a stern she recognised. There couldn't be two boats with that name, not painted in the same design. How in the name of God had Tony managed to get the narrowboat from Worcester to Bradfield? A man who could barely navigate from his own front door to work?

Even as she stared, a stocky man with a shaved head and a tight suit made from an unfortunate shiny grey material backed out of the main hatchway. He was carrying a laptop, its connection cable trailing behind him. He stumbled ashore and put the computer in the boot of a Toyota saloon. Then he returned to the boat. Either Tony was being burgled or this was Fielding's search team. She didn't mind which, but it might be fun to freak them out.

She untied the dog and the pair of them crossed the cobbles to the boat. The dog was reluctant at first, but with Carol's encouragement she jumped aboard, followed by her owner. 'Hello?' Carol called.

Almost immediately, the bald head reappeared, a frown on his pink face. 'Who the—' And then recognition dawned. He looked over his shoulder. 'Harry?'

'What are you doing on my friend's boat?' Carol demanded. Flash obligingly gave a couple of brusque barks.

'We're—' This time his shout was more frantic. 'Harry?'

'What?' The voice came from below.

Baldy's face creased with the effort of working out what to say. 'It's DCI Jordan,' he finally settled on.

'Ex-DCI Jordan,' Carol gently reminded him. 'You still haven't explained who you are and what you're doing on Dr Hill's boat.'

'We've got a warrant,' a nasal Scouse voice said.

'Might I see it?' Carol said sweetly. 'And your ID?'

Baldy turned away from her and held a brief muttered exchange with his colleague. He swung back to face her and presented two sets of ID and a search warrant. Carol gave them a quick once-over and handed them back. 'Thanks. You can't be too careful these days. Shame you've had a wasted journey,' she added.

'What do you mean, a wasted journey?' Baldy was wary.

Carol smiled. 'She'll have to release him. Her case is falling to bits around her ears.' She shook her head. 'They should never have disbanded the MIT.' Then she turned away and leapt ashore, dog at her heels. Pathetic, really, but she'd enjoyed herself. A pleasant interlude before heading back to the library.

By half past three, she had added one more possible to the pile. Another natural-looking blonde who'd died from cancer aged thirty-three. Unmarried but with a partner, according to the death notice. Three sisters and two brothers, a slew of nieces and nephews. Carol checked she'd copied the page to her laptop then packed up.

The question now was what to do with the results of her inquiries. There wasn't any point in sharing them with Bronwen or even Paula; this was something for Tony to ponder. She wondered whether the custody sergeant at Skenfrith Street would allow her to speak to Tony, in her assumed role as assistant to his lawyer.

There was only one way to find out.

62

Stradbrook Tower had been the city council's final mistake of the sixties. Paula reckoned they must have been the last local authority in the country to commission a tower block for council tenants. It had been the destination of last resort for residents for over ten years, but in the early eighties the council gave up trying to force their tenants into the damp-ridden condensation-plagued flats. The block had stood empty for a few years, then a bright spark in the housing department had realised it was relatively close to the mushrooming campus of Bradfield University. A deal was done, six months of remedial work was carried out and now the flats were home to hundreds of students.

It was still a sore point with the locals, who felt, not unreasonably, that the flats could have been made habitable for them rather than the privileged scions of the middle class. Or spoilt rich bastards, as they preferred to think of them. And so the area around the tower block had become the perennial site for the ceremonial burning of stolen cars. From where she was standing, Paula could see three burnt-out wrecks. The one nearest to her had belonged to Bev McAndrew.

The ANPR system had picked it up a little after two in the afternoon, careering out of the car park at Bradfield Central station. By the time they'd alerted BMP, it had traversed the city centre, heading out past the university towards Strad-brook Tower. Control had scrambled the nearest Traffic car, which had arrived in time to see two lads, heads covered by hoodies, jump out of the car and toss lighted petrol bombs inside as they fled.

Flames filled the car, and before the traffic cops could even release their small fire extinguisher from its clips, it exploded with a low boom. It was such a regular occurrence that nobody so much as ventured out on to their balconies to watch.

'There goes our trace evidence,' Fielding said. 'Wee fuds.'

'But not at Tony Hill's hand,' Paula pointed out.

'We don't know that.' Fielding scowled. 'We don't know what he told Carol Jordan to set in motion.'

Paula fought to hide her scorn. 'Carol would never destroy evidence,' she said. 'That would be a betrayal of everything she believes in.'

'Isn't that what working with Bronwen Scott is? You lie down with dogs, you get up with fleas.' Fielding turned on her heel and walked over to the sheepish traffic cops. 'Find out who those wee thugs were,' she said. 'I want to know how they knew to steal that car.'

Carol still wasn't accustomed to wearing a visitor's pass in a police station. It felt wrong to sign in when she arrived at Skenfrith Street, to have to wait till someone came to escort her past the front counter, to be confined to the places where she was led. At least she'd had the good sense to phone Bronwen Scott's office and have them pave the way for her solo prisoner visit. It had, she suspected, saved her a degree of humiliation.

While she was waiting in the tiny airless room they'd been in the previous night, Carol powered up her laptop and opened the details of the women in the death notices. She took out the photocopies of the news stories and set them down beside the laptop. Then she softly drummed the pads of her fingers on the blank metal flanking the mousepad. Realising what she was doing she stopped abruptly, cross with herself. There was no need, no reason, no point in nervousness. Whatever their history, there was no future for her and Tony. She was doing this simply to save Paula from being caught up in a career-wrecking miscarriage of justice. This wasn't about Tony. Businesslike efficiency, that was what she needed now. Not twitching like a teenager.

The door opened and Tony walked in. As with all prisoners held in police cells, his appearance had started the downward slide away from respectability. His hair was unruly and unkempt. He had a day's growth of stubble, an oddly pathetic patchwork of dark and silver. He wasn't young any more, she thought with a stab of sadness. Because that meant she wasn't either. His clothes were crumpled and creased and he'd begun to look more criminal than the average citizen.

His face lit up when he saw Carol on her own. 'It's good to see you,' he said. 'I've never had a problem with my own company, but time passes slowly when you've nothing to read.'

'And no computer games to play.' There was no lightness in her tone, no room to interpret her remark as friendly. 'I looked through the newspaper archive. Obviously, it's not definitive . . .'

'But almost every family still puts a death notice in the paper. Undertakers steer them in that direction, and it's a shortcut to let friends and workmates know the funeral details.'

'And the *Sentinel Times* publishes photos in its online edition.'

He grinned. 'Of course. I wondered how you were going to weed out the blondes. I'd forgotten about that. Imagine what a miserable job that would have been until recently – calling up the recently bereaved and going, "Was your wife blonde? And was it natural?"'

She couldn't help a wry smile. She'd taken part in some crass inquiries over the years, because sometimes that was the only way to secure the information they needed. She wasn't sorry about this particular forward march of technology. 'So, there are two death notices and one news item that seem to me to fit the bill.' She turned the laptop to face him and slid the photocopies across.

He read everything through once, then repeated the process more slowly. He rubbed his chin, the rasp of his hand across the stubble clearly audible. Then he pushed the photocopies back towards Carol. 'No death notice that corresponds to this?'

She shook her head. 'Not that I could find. Her parents live in York, though. So maybe it was in the local paper there.'

Tony looked grim. 'If it was, it will have been put there by her parents. Not by the husband.'

'What makes you say that?'

'I think this might be the one.'

'Why?'

He shifted the laptop so they could both see the screen. 'This one first. She had enough freedom to be out there playing darts in a pub. If I'm right, this guy is a control freak. He's never going to let her out of the house with a bunch of other women to have a social encounter that doesn't include him.'

'That's what I thought too. And the other death notice?'

'Look at her family group. Five siblings and a football team of nieces and nephews. Obviously a close sibling group. A man as controlling as this wants his victim to be isolated, not at the heart of an intimate family group.'

'We don't know that they're close,' Carol objected.

'We don't, that's true. It's a reasonable assumption, though. But even if they weren't, the killer I have in mind wouldn't acknowledge their existence. He wouldn't include them in the death notice at all. No, Carol –' he stabbed the photo-copies with a finger – 'check this out. No death notice. No quote from the grieving widower.'

'Maybe he was too grief-stricken.'

Tony shrugged. 'It's possible. But look at this photo. She's strung as tight as a bow string.'

'Some people don't like having their photographs taken.'

'She's posing with her kids. Most women are so con-cerned about how the kids are coming across and whether they're behaving that they lose their own self-consciousness. I think she's anxious. I'd go so far as to say scared. That's the kind of expression you see on the faces of victims of abuse. Terrified of putting a foot wrong, of provoking the rage that's always just round the corner.'

'I think you're reading a lot into a photograph.' Without even thinking about it, Carol had fallen back into her old patterns with Tony. She was the test-bed for his ideas. He threw them at her and she poked them and prodded them and pronounced them fit for purpose. Or not.

'It's one small part of a bigger picture, Carol. Who sets off after eleven at night with two small children to drive to York? To visit parents who are definitely past the first flush of youth and probably like to be tucked up in bed by then?'

'It says there. She wanted to miss the traffic.'

'If you want to miss the traffic, you leave at eight, not eleven,' Tony scoffed. 'You set off at eleven in the car with the kids because you're in fear for your life.'

There was a pause while Carol considered his words. Finally, she said, 'It's a long shot.'

His shoulders slumped. 'It's always a bloody long shot. But it's paid off more often than I have any right to expect. Carol, I'm penned up in this bloody awful place. I'm accused of two murders that I didn't commit. If long shots are all I have, I'll take them.'

'I understand that. But it's probably whistling in the dark.'

The mask slipped and she caught a glimpse of his despair. 'Carol, I need you to help me. For whatever reason, Fielding sincerely wants to nail me. And I don't know anyone who has a better chance of getting me out of this mess than you. I know you still blame me for Michael and Lucy, but I didn't hold the knife. Yes, I made a mistake. I set my focus too narrowly. And believe me, nobody could give me a harder time for that than I give myself. But I don't think any reasonable person could have figured out what Vance's agenda was at that point. I don't believe there's another profiler around who would have worked it out. I did my best and it turned out crap. Don't think I don't know that.' His eyes were glistening with tears, his voice cracking with emotion. 'Carol, you've been the most important person in my life since I first got to know you. I would take a bullet for you. I'd have taken a bullet for Michael, for your sake.' He gave a wry smile. 'Maybe not for Lucy, mind.'

His words twisted in her gut like a knife. The dark gallows humour struck a chord in spite of her determination not to give him an inch. 'Don't be a smartarse,' she said, surprised to find her own voice catching in her throat.

'We all make mistakes, Carol. Sometimes they're more expensive than others. But I don't deserve to lose you,' he said, spreading his hands in appeal.

Abruptly she slammed the laptop shut and grabbed it. 'I'll check it out,' she said gruffly, stumbling to her feet and heading for the door. She wasn't willing to let him back into her life. Not now, not ever. No matter what he said. No matter how well he manipulated her emotions. And that was all that was going on here. It wasn't real. Just Tony playing her for his own benefit. It didn't change anything. Michael and Lucy were still dead. Well, she'd show him she was a better person than him. She'd do the right thing because it was the right thing. Not for his sake. For its own sake.

Carol had no recollection of leaving the police station. The blur resolved itself as she reached the Land Rover. She climbed inside and leaned her forearms on the steering wheel, staring straight ahead, trying to recover herself. After a couple of minutes, she composed herself enough to take out her phone and send a message to Stacey:

Everything you can give me on Gareth Taylor from Banham village. ASAP.

Now it was simply a question of waiting.

A moment's inspiration was never enough in police work. Generally, it had to be followed up by the painstaking slog of asking questions and making checks. And then sometimes it paid off. Paula might have scored the credit for inserting the idea of a portable anaesthetic machine into the investigation, but it had taken a hardworking detective constable bashing the phones all day to come up with the strongest lead.

He bounced up to Paula's desk with all the abandon of a small boy who's won a treasure hunt. 'I've got a stolen portable anaesthetic machine for you,' he said, waving a piece of paper at her.

She couldn't help feeling a lift in her spirits. Sometimes the slightest forward motion in an investigation felt like a giant stride. 'Good work. Where was it nicked?'

'There was an emergency services conference five weeks ago at Manchester University. They had an exhibition hall full of stands for equipment manufacturers. Everything from ambulances to satellite radios. And a company that makes portable anaesthetic units had one that went a bit too portable, if you get my meaning?' He grinned at her as he handed her the details of the exhibition. 'It went missing overnight from their stand. They'd been using it to demo how it works on site.'

'Did they report it to us?'

He shook his head. 'The organisers persuaded them there was no point. They refunded their exhibitors' fee, so the company weren't out of pocket and the organisers didn't have to deal with the embarrassment of having cops crawling all over their exhibition. That's why it didn't show up on our records.'

'Fantastic. Well done. So, does anybody have any idea who might have nicked it?' Even as she spoke, Paula knew it was too much to hope for.

Now he looked crestfallen. 'If they have any suspicions, they're not letting on.'

'Have you got a map of the layout of the exhibition?'

His eyebrows rose in surprise. 'Of course. No, I haven't. I didn't think of that. I'll track it down.'

'And a list of accredited attendees. One other thing – what about the gases that the machine uses? Did the thief get those as well?'

He nodded. 'Apparently the machine was loaded up with the real thing. Bloody stupid, if you ask me.'

Paula sighed. 'If you don't expect to be a victim of crime, you don't always take the sensible precautions. Still, nice work. Let me have a look when you've got that exhibition map. Plus a list of delegates and exhibitors.'

He took off, bounce restored at the prospect of having something useful to do. Once the PC had done his job, she'd have to persuade Fielding to check whether it was possible that Tony could have attended the conference or the exhibition. Paula couldn't help hoping he'd have a cast-iron alibi for the days in question. It was a pity she couldn't reveal the ultimate source of this latest development to her boss. Demonstrating Tony's usefulness to the investigation might remind Fielding of his value to BMP but it probably wasn't the best way to improve Paula's career prospects.

63

Stacey's speed had always been a thing of beauty. Working at less than full stretch thankfully hadn't blunted her skills. Within half an hour of Carol sending her text, Stacey had replied with a hyperlink to a cloud-based application. Tapping the link took Carol to the fruits of Stacey's searches.

Under Gareth Taylor's name was a list: date of birth, National Insurance number, driving licence details, passport number, address, vehicle registration number, bank details and current account balance, and the name of his employer, Tellit Communications. He had no criminal record and a first-class degree in computer science. Photographs from his passport application and his driving licence were next. Then came a separate list of details for his late wife. A note from Stacey read, Can't find a UK bank account. No employment history after marriage. NHS records for both coming later. At the bottom of the report, there was another note from Stacey.

Tellit are more than just a mobile phone company.
They deal in a wide range of electronic
communication. Among their contracts are the
comms system used by the ANPR cameras and also
one of the main systems used by fire and
ambulance services. Working for Tellit could give
GT access to a vast range of data. His actual job
seems quite low level for his skills. But sometimes
the side benefits of data access outweigh that!

Carol read the note with an increasing surge of excitement. A viable suspect. She didn't know much about Gareth Taylor, but already she had more belief in him as a potential killer than in Tony. She forwarded the link to Paula, adding a note: Check with ANPR for any sightings of Taylor's vehicle near body dumps, or homes and workplaces of victims. Am going to stake out Tellit office/Taylor's house.

The address Stacey had supplied for Gareth Taylor's workplace was on the other side of the city centre, so Carol decided to change car parks. But before she did, she called Stacey. 'Brilliant job,' she said as soon as Stacey answered. 'Does Tellit have a staff car park?'

'I'll get right back to you.'

Five minutes ticked past to the sound of Carol beating time on her steering wheel. Then her phone beeped. The text from Stacey read, No dedicated car park. But discount parking in Ramshorn Street multi-storey.

Ten minutes later, Carol was cruising the car park, looking for Gareth Taylor's red BMW. She found it on the third floor but she couldn't find another slot with a view of his car. She sat for a moment with her engine idling, wondering what to do next. Now she knew where his wheels were, she could always leave the car park and set up outside. But she'd have to be careful where she chose. Leaving the multi-storey, drivers could turn left or right. If she parked facing the wrong way, she could be stranded, given the appalling turning circle of the Land Rover. Or she could circle round inside the car park, taking temporary station in areas that weren't, strictly speaking, parking spaces.

In the end, she settled for a side road a little further down the street. She could emerge quickly enough on his tail from there, she reckoned. The Land Rover was about as far from an ideal surveillance vehicle as it was possible to get, especially in the city centre, but the one advantage it possessed was its height. She could stay several cars behind Taylor and still remain in touch with his car. At this time of day, nothing moved faster than a crawl in town anyway, so it wasn't like she was going to lose him at the lights.

All the same, Carol knew she would have to find another solution if the surveillance ended up lasting any length of time. Wrong vehicle, not to mention that she was sitting on a double yellow line. She daren't leave the Landie in case she got ticketed, clamped or towed. Now she was beginning to realise how much she'd taken for granted when she had still been a copper. How in hell did private eyes manage any kind of effective stake-out?

Luckily for her nerves, she didn't have long to wait. Barely twenty minutes had passed when the scarlet nose of Taylor's BMW stopped at the exit barrier. He turned right, and Carol fell in behind him with three cars between them.

Their progress across town was slow, the rush-hour stream of buses, cars, vans and trams clogging the tight mesh of streets that had been built for horses and carts two centuries before. But as they left the city centre and moved into the outer suburbs, the traffic thinned and Carol had to work a bit harder at staying in touch but unobtrusive. From the route Taylor had taken, it looked as if he was heading home.

Carol couldn't help wondering where he was in his murderous cycle. Did he have another victim lined up? Was there already another woman in captivity? It was clear that he kept them before he killed him. Might he be headed back to an imprisoned victim right now?

The short-term answer to her question came just before the ring road, when he pulled off into an out-of-town development packed with the traditional selection of carpet warehouse, fast-food outlet, discount sofa store, white goods and computer emporia and a sprawling DIY megastore. For a brief uncomfortable moment she was right behind the BMW. She hung back while he parked in a distant area of the car park then watched as he jinked through the lines of parked cars to arrive at the DIY store entrance. He paused to retie his shoelace, and as he set off again, she could see he had a slight but noticeable limp. Just like Tony.

'Yes,' Carol hissed triumphantly. She left the Landie in the first available slot and ran after him. By the time she made it through the door, he'd vanished from sight. She hurried up to the aisle that bisected the shelves at the midway point and walked briskly along, scanning in both directions as she went.

She spotted him in the locks and home security section, checking padlocks and chains. It was a terrible cliché, but she supposed clichés only reached that status because there was truth in them. She turned down the next aisle, then came up behind him, pretending an interest in brass and chrome door furniture. He didn't turn his head. He selected a heavy padlock and started walking towards the rear of the store. Carol followed, keeping her distance and constantly ready to turn aside and examine whatever was on the shelves.

He was making for the trade counter, she quickly realised. Even though this was a different chain from the store she used for her own building requirements, they all had a similar layout. Taylor clearly knew his way around, making straight for the doorway that led to the timber-cutting area. He must be ordering or collecting made-to-measure wood, she thought. She found a vantage point where she could keep an eye on the doorway without looking suspicious, and stared unseeing at a catalogue of bathroom fittings.

Time trickled past, but Taylor didn't reappear. At first, Carol wasn't concerned. She knew from experience that it could take a while to straighten out a customer's requirements, especially if several different pieces were being ordered. But after ten minutes, she began to feel uneasy. This wasn't right.

At last, after twelve minutes had passed, she walked into the timber-cutting area. Behind the counter, a man in company livery was going through a sheaf of paperwork, comparing it to a computer screen. Another assistant leaned against a rack of different woods, deep in conversation with Gareth Taylor. *Fuck.* Carol crossed to a bin of scrap wood and rummaged through it, as if she were looking for something in particular. She pulled out a piece of plywood, pretended to check something on her phone, tutted and replaced it, then walked out. *Fuck.*

She returned to the bathroom fittings, cursing herself for her lack of patience. All she'd had to do was wait, but she couldn't even do that. Tony's words echoed in her head. 'We all make mistakes, Carol. Sometimes they're more expensive than others.' She pushed him to one side in her head, hoping this wasn't going to be one of the truly expensive ones.

Another fifteen minutes crawled by. And then the man from behind the counter appeared in the doorway, reaching above his head to grasp a metal shutter. Galvanised, Carol hurried over as he hunkered down to padlock it shut. 'Are you closed?'

He looked up at her. 'Aye. We close at half five. If you want some timber cutting, you'll have to come back in the morning.'

'Damn,' she said. 'I wondered – is there a loading entrance here, so I don't have to trail my wood through the store?'

The man straightened up. 'Not officially, like,' he said. 'But we've got a roller shutter at the rear for deliveries – we let people drive round and load up.'

She turned away, hollow with anger and disappointment. Not only had she made Taylor suspicious, she'd lost him. He'd clocked that she was taking an interest and he'd shaken her off. He could be anywhere now, doing anything. And she had nothing on him except a limp and Tony's theory based on a dead wife. Even Bronwen Scott would struggle to make something out of that.

Carol trudged to the exit, all her earlier exhilaration gone. Maybe she should call Paula and the pair of them could work out what to do next. But the way things were going, if justice was going to be served, Carol wasn't going to be the waitress.

At least driving a Land Rover Defender meant you never mislaid your vehicle in a car park. The high Landie stuck out even among the pick-up trucks and fat clumsy 4x4s. Head down, thinking hard, she set off. Given how full the car park was and how busy the store had been, it was surprising how few people were in sight. A cluster round the burger van, but mostly it was deserted. Unsurprisingly, Gareth Taylor's red BMW was no longer parked where it had been. She'd obviously lost him.

As she approached the Landie, Carol raised her arm over her head and pressed the door release button. It was always a bugger, this remote. You had to be right next to the driver's door before it conceded and the locks clicked open. She decided to let the dog out for a quick pee before they set off for wherever they were going next, so she turned away from the driver's door to walk round the back.

That was the only reason she saw Gareth Taylor coming at her with the taser.

64

Carol's message had given Paula a dilemma. Tracking Gareth Taylor's car using the ANPR system wasn't a problem in itself. But in the byzantine world of contemporary police administration, every search had to be justified. And somewhere down the line, she'd have to explain why she'd asked for this particular search at this particular time. An alert defence lawyer might well pick up on the fact that she had actioned a search at a point when Gareth Taylor's name had never appeared in the official investigation. 'Woman's intuition' wouldn't cut it, she knew that much.

As usual, when faced with intractable problems, Paula sought refuge in nicotine. She sneaked out of the incident room and huddled in a quiet corner of the car park, inhaling and thinking. She couldn't see any point in coming clean to Fielding. Her DCI was so committed to the idea of Tony Hill that she would reject any lead emanating from him as automatically tainted. But if Paula left her own paper trail in her notebook, pointing the finger at the defence as the source of a tip-off, she might just get away with it. It would have to be a paper trail, though, since there were no texts from Bronwen Scott in her phone and she wasn't about to give Carol up as her source.

Satisfied that she'd come up with something that would cover her back, Paula returned to the incident room and sanctioned the ANPR request. Because she was Fielding's bagman, nobody questioned her authority and the data wheels started turning. She was about to go in search of her boss when DC Pat Cody called her over. 'Got a funny one here, skip,' he said, tapping his screen with a chewed ball-point.

'What's that?'

'We put out a routine request for any female misper reports. A bloke phoned in this afternoon. Control passed the details on to us. I don't know if it's owt to do with us, but it's a funiosity, as my gran used to say. His name's Rob Morrison and he's Director of Operations at Tellit Communications' Bradfield office.'

'Tellit?' Gareth Taylor's workplace. Anything unusual connected to Tellit set the alarms flashing on Paula's radar.

'You know, the mobile phone and data network company? Apparently they started a new Director of Marketing this week, a woman called Marie Mather. She didn't turn in for work this morning but one of the staff took a call from her husband saying she'd been rushed to hospital with a suspected burst appendix. This Morrison guy decided to send flowers, so he rang Bradfield Cross to find out what ward she was on. And they've never heard of her. He tried the cottage hospital and they said the same. Her mobile's turned off, there's no answer to her home phone and the number he has for her husband goes straight to voicemail.' Cody scratched his head with the end of his pen then stuck it in his mouth like a cigar.

412

'She might be skiving off. Having a fun day out with her old man,' Paula said, not believing it for a moment.

'She might, except that she's just started this important new job. "Strategic", your man Morrison called it. And here's the thing. She's thirty-one, blonde, blue eyes, medium height and build and a professional woman. She fits our victim profile to a T.'

Paula felt a buzz of adrenalin surging through her. 'Which would mean that the suspect we have in custody isn't the killer.' She couldn't help smiling at that realisation.

Cody made a face. 'Not necessarily. I called this Morrison bloke. She left work about an hour before Hill checked in here. If he's keeping them before he kills them, he could have stashed her before he walked in here.' His turn to smile. 'That's the kind of brass neck a proper serial killer would have, isn't it?'

'Only in a film,' Paula said repressively. 'Have you told Fielding about this yet?'

He shook his head. 'It's not long in.'

'OK. Send a couple of uniforms over to her home address to see whether Mr and Mrs Mather are having a duvet day. Meanwhile, check with Bradfield Cross admissions. Maybe Mather is her own name and she was admitted under her married name. See whether anyone was brought in with a suspected burst appendix. Let's get our ducks in a row before we bother the DCI with this.' She didn't quite know what to make of this latest information. But if there was any chance at all that it might exonerate Tony, she'd strip Marie Mather's life to the bone.

Years of frontline policing kicked in and, faced with danger, Carol acted instinctively. She gave a banshee yell and lunged towards Taylor, aiming to knock him off balance. But he was equally quick off the mark and fired the taser before she

413

covered the few feet between them. Her cry was cut off abruptly but her momentum carried her forward and he held out his arms to catch her before she hit the ground. He staggered under the impact but managed to keep his footing, thudding into the side of the Land Rover.

Taylor quickly looked around, but nobody seemed to be paying them any attention. He half-dragged, half-carried Carol round to the rear of the Landie, his brain efficiently processing the options. As soon as he'd got the big back door open, he'd be secure from prying eyes. He could chuck her in the back and improvise. If there was nothing to tie her up with, he could bang her head on the floor and knock her out for long enough to get her back to his place. That would show the bitch the kind of man she was dealing with. Who the fuck did she think she was, tracking him across the city like he was a common criminal? Well, he had her now. He'd soon show her who was boss. Finding out who she was and what she thought she was doing would be an unexpected pleasure.

He reached up and pushed the door handle upwards. It was stiff, and he grunted with the effort. As he struggled with the catch, Carol regained control of her limbs. She blinked repeatedly for a few seconds as he tried to get the taser aligned in his hand. The she snapped back into full consciousness. The arm that had been hanging loose at her side swept up in a long looping punch that connected with Taylor's ear.

He yelped, instinctively clapping his hand to the side of his head and letting the taser fall to the ground. Carol saw it fall, but he still had one arm gripping her close and she had no chance of reaching it. She pulled her arm back for a second punch but he saw this one coming and grabbed her wrist.

But Carol didn't mind fighting dirty. She ducked her head

and clamped her teeth round his wrist, clenching her jaw as hard as she could. Simultaneously, she brought her knee up sharply between his legs, making satisfying contact with his balls. *Bastard, bastard, bastard.* Taylor's breath shot out in a long squeal and he let her go. But as he let her go, he rammed his fist hard into her gut, forcing the air out of her lungs in a searing rush. Reflexively, she released her bite and gasped for air. They reeled around each other like a pair of late-night drunks.

Carol lunged to the ground, aiming for the taser. But he wasn't giving up. As her hand closed around the black plastic, he stamped hard on her wrist, numbing everything below it. He leaned over her and grabbed the taser. 'You fucking bitch,' he gasped as he pressed the trigger. Her body jerked and twitched then lay still.

This time he'd get the Land Rover door open before he lifted her up. He strained at the handle again, pushing it upwards. But as soon as the catch released, the heavy metal door catapulted towards Taylor, the edge catching him in the middle of the forehead. He clutched his head and staggered, tripping over Carol's prone body and crashing to the ground. A flying bundle of black-and-white fur flew through the air and struck him in the chest, taking him down. Taylor heard the deep terrifying growl of a hostile dog as he hit the tarmac. He took his hand away from the bump on his forehead and saw gleaming white teeth bared inches from his face. He screamed.

Groggy but almost in control of her limbs, Carol pushed herself upright and shouted 'Help!' at the top of her lungs. What the fuck was she supposed to do now? She had no handcuffs, no authority. Taylor was squirming at her feet, screaming at Flash, who had him pinned down, front paws on his chest, slavering mouth dripping on his face. A couple of blokes had peeled away from the hot-dog van and were

415

running towards them. Carol reached inside the Land Rover and pulled out the lovely new tack hammer she'd bought only a few days before. It wasn't heavy, but she knew she could do some serious damage with it if she had to. With her free hand, she pulled out her phone and called Paula. She had a funny feeling it was going to be a long night.

65

Day twenty-eight

When she got Carol's call, Paula wasted no time on explanations. She yelled for Cody and ran for her car, gunning the engine till he piled in next to her. She tore out of the car park with a screech of tyres. Unlike TV cop shows, she didn't let the crisis go on playing itself out till she personally made it to the scene. She called up the control room on her radio and had them send the nearest patrol car to the DIY store car park.

The patrol car arrived to find a terrified man cradling a bleeding wrist sitting on the ground beside a Land Rover. An angry-looking blonde toting a hammer that looked more like a toy was standing over him, a taser sticking out of her jacket pocket. A black-and-white dog stood at her side, lip curled in a snarl. Around them stood a horseshoe of blokes in puffa jackets and football shirts, some of them munching on burgers.

'Fucking twatted her with a taser, didn't he,' one of them volunteered as the two uniformed officers rolled up, hands at the ready on their utility belts.

The woman half-turned and the driver, a grizzled veteran of the traffic division, drew his breath in sharply. 'DCI Jordan,' he said. 'Ma'am.'

'Not any more,' Carol said. 'This is Gareth Taylor. I think DS McIntyre wants to interview him in connection with two murders.'

'This is grotesque,' Taylor yelled. 'She attacked me, not the other way around. Who's got the taser, for God's sake?'

Everyone ignored him apart from the dog, who growled. Carol continued, unruffled. 'But he's just committed an assault and an attempted abduction, so I suggest you cuff him and stick him in the back of your car until DS McIntyre gets here.' She smiled sweetly. 'Not that I'm telling you how to do your job, officer.'

The traffic officer's smile mirrored hers. 'Couldn't have put it better myself, ma'am.' He went to drag Taylor to his feet, but the man protested his innocence loudly, struggling against the cop. 'Do you want me to add resisting arrest to the charge sheet?' the officer snarled, hoicking him up by his arms, not caring about the shout of pain from Taylor. He snapped a pair of cuffs on him, not bothering to avoid the bleeding bite-mark on one wrist. Then he frogmarched him to the traffic car and stowed him in the rear seat, effortlessly ignoring Taylor's litany of complaint. Carol sat down on the tailgate of the Landie, looking relieved. The dog jumped up beside her and licked her ear, as if in consolation.

The officers moved among the men, taking down names and addresses and bare-bones preliminary statements. And that was when Paula rolled up with Cody. She practically ran to Carol's side. 'Are you OK?'

Carol nodded. 'I'm fine. Look at those guys. It's gradually dawning on them that they've just been involved in something that's going to earn them pints in the pub for years to come. I can hear them now: "Did I ever tell you how I took on a serial killer?" Though the real hero is the dog. Flash saved me.' She rumpled the dog's mane. 'You've got him on assault and attempted abduction at the very least.'

'Well done,' Paula said. 'That's all we need to get warrants for his house and his car and his workplace.'

'Even someone as single-minded as Fielding can't ignore this,' Carol said.

Paula shook her head. 'Unless she thinks they were in it together, him and Tony.'

'I think that would be a bridge too far, even for her.'

'I wouldn't bank on it.'

'Are you going to take him in and interview him?'

'I'll get Cody to take him in. I want to be with the team that does the house search—' Her phone rang and she reached for it. As she listened, her face grew grave. 'I understand. You need to notify DCI Fielding directly, I'm pursuing another line of inquiry right now. And make sure CSI are on standby.' Paula ended the call and closed her eyes, taking a deep breath.

'Trouble?'

'This case gets uglier all the time. We thought we might have a third missing woman so I sent a patrol car to her home address. They've just radioed in to say they've spotted what appears to be the dead body of a white male through the garage window. Sounds like Marie Mather's husband got in the way of what that bastard wanted.' She jerked a thumb over her shoulder towards the patrol car. 'Nailing him is going to be a pleasure.'

In one sense, Banham village was the last place people would expect to find a serial killer. It straddled the Yorkshire–Lancashire border, changing its allegiance with every local government reorganisation since the War of the Roses. Grey stone cottages formed a tight triangle round the village green, a Norman church at the apex. Beyond the village centre were clusters of houses that had accreted like cankers over the past three hundred years, a mishmash of styles that had evolved its own distinctive character over the centuries. It had avoided being swallowed up by the urban sprawl of Bradfield thanks to the deep cleft of a valley that separated it from the main thrust of urbanisation. Banham wasn't the easiest commute in the area, but it was definitely one of the most desirable.

On the other hand, if you wanted to keep a woman prisoner undisturbed, it was a much better option than any-where in the city. For Banham was only a fake village. It had none of the sense of community that knit together real villages. Here, nobody looked out for each other. Nobody knew each other's business. Nobody knew when their neigh-bours went on holiday or where they were going. There was no epicentre – no pub to run quizzes, no village hall, no WI or Autumn Club or Brownie pack. The detached cot-tages and houses were separate and inviolate. It was the sort of place people lived when they wanted to impress. It was also the sort of place where nobody lived for more than a few years.

Driving into the village, Paula reckoned that once upon a time living somewhere so anonymous might have appealed to her. Nobody knowing she was a cop, nobody questioning the women who occasionally drove up to her house at weekends and stayed over. But that was when she allowed anxiety to circumscribe her life. She hadn't felt like that for a very long time. And part of that was because of Carol Jordan and her MIT.

Taylor's house wasn't hard to spot. It was stone-built, like most of the houses in Banham. Even though it was probably only about thirty years old it was solid and well-proportioned. Unless he had another source of income, it must have stretched Gareth Taylor to afford it. The white CSI van sat in the driveway and a liveried BMW was parked on the roadway outside. A huddle of people in white Tyvek suits milled around in the drive, waiting for her as she'd instructed them to do. She wanted to be here every step of the way. All they had on Taylor so far was circumstantial. A car repeatedly showing up on the ANPR records was suggestive. But it wasn't proof. Going armed with a taser and using it on Carol Jordan was suggestive but it wasn't proof, particularly since, by her own admission, she'd been following him. Working in the same office as Marie Mather was suggestive but it wasn't proof. Having a limp was suggestive but it wasn't proof. If she was honest and impartial, there was still more solid evidence against Tony than there was against Taylor right now. If she was Fielding, she probably wouldn't be releasing Tony just yet.

Paula suited up, put on shoe covers, then nodded to the officer carrying the door ram. In one smooth sweep, he delivered a massive blow to the heavy front door. The wood splintered and gave up its lock, which clattered down hard enough to leave a dent in the parquet. Softwood tarted up to look like hardwood, Paula thought. *How very Banham.*

There was nothing untoward about the hallway. An attractive Afghan-style runner sat precisely in the middle of the floor. A console table held a bowl with keys and a vase of authentic-looking silk sweet peas. Photographs of glittering waves and frolicking dolphins lined one wall. Paula advanced cautiously. A door on the right opened on to a living room that looked as if it had been styled for a magazine feature. Some might say uncluttered; Paula thought sterile. On the face of it, nothing to interest them. But they would come back to it. No stone unturned. Just that some stones were definitely more promising than others.

Next off the hall, a dining room. Again, not much in the

way of homely touches. The only personal item in the room was a large studio portrait of Taylor and two children hanging opposite the door. Neither child looked particularly happy to have Daddy's hands heavy on their shoulders. Paula told herself off for projecting. Really, there wasn't much you could tell from a photo.

At the end of the hallway an archway led into the kitchen. Paula caught her breath. At her shoulder, the lead CSI swore softly. 'Arrogant twat clearly never expected to get nabbed,' he said. 'Look at this. There's forensic traces bloody everywhere. Blood, fingerprints . . . There's a clump of hair on the floor over there by the bin. And look at those metal eyes screwed into the door frame and the wall. First time I've ever seen a kitchen that looked more like a dungeon.'

Paula hung back while the CSIs placed metal trays across the floor to create a walkway that would preserve any evidence. This was the kind of result that was like a double-edged sword. As an investigator, it hit the jackpot. As a human being, it made her heart heavy. Now she could imagine what her friend had endured and it was a horrible thought. While she waited, she directed the other CID officers upstairs. 'Take a quick look around,' she said. 'Just an Open Door search to make sure Marie Mather isn't on the premises.

'Does that door lead to the garage?' she asked, pointing to the frame where the metal eye was fastened.

The CSI glanced out of the window, orientating himself. 'Looks like it. You want to take a look?'

'We've still got a missing woman, so yes. Soon as you like.'

The final chequered plates were laid down, providing a route to the door. The lead CSI opened it with a flourish and Paula crossed the threshold. At first glance, it was a regular suburban garage. Tools and garden equipment, all hung up

422

neatly in their allotted spaces. A workbench and a stack of folding garden chairs. A chest freezer.

And then you looked more closely and saw the pre-torn strips of duct tape hanging from a shelf. And the trails of blood and what looked like skin snagged on the rough concrete floor. And the metal eyes screwed in strategically in three places. 'Oh, fuck, the freezer,' Paula said softly and started across the garage.

'Wait,' the CSI shouted. 'You're fucking up the evidence.'

'There's a woman in that freezer!' Paula shouted over her shoulder, breaking into a run, blood and adrenalin pounding in her head. She pulled the lid up. The rubber seal released loud as thunder in her ears. And there was Marie, curled in the foetal position, in a pool of blood and piss. Blonde and bruised and battered. Still as death. Paula reached in and felt warm flesh, the flutter of a pulse under her jaw. 'Get her the fuck out of there, she's still alive.'

'We need photos,' the CSI shouted at her.

'I'm right here,' the videographer said. 'Step away a second, Paula.'

All her instincts screaming against it, Paula did as she was asked. But only for as long as it took her to count to five. Then she was yelling at them all to help her, to call an ambulance, to get Marie Mather out of what was intended to be her coffin and back into life.

Back at Skenfrith Street, Fielding was steadfastly ignoring the fact that she still had Tony Hill in custody even though the compass needle was swinging round to point unwaveringly elsewhere. This was supposed to be her big day, the press conference where she got to announce the arrest of a high-profile double murderer. In her head, it was the point where she put down a marker that she was destined for the top.

Instead, she'd had to listen to Bronwen Scott's pitiful attempt to explain away the evidence against Tony Hill with an improbable story of nosebleeds and a collision in a corridor. It was obviously a fabrication that would fall to pieces under scrutiny, but checking it out would waste time while the clock was ticking. It was clearly a ruse to postpone charging him, so she'd have to let him go on police bail. And that would give that bitch Scott time to line up her so-called experts to cast doubt on the fingermark.

And now McIntyre was off on a tangent of her own. Some nonsense based on nothing that Fielding could put her finger on. A bagman was supposed to be unquestioningly loyal, but Fielding was beginning to think McIntyre had loyalties that were nothing to do with her. How else had Carol Jordan turned up with Bronwen Scott in the middle of the night when Hill hadn't even made a phone call? When this was all over, McIntyre was going to be shipped out to another firm and Fielding was going to find a bagman who understood what a privilege it was to be so close to the heart of an investigation.

And then McIntyre herself hustled into the squad room. Fielding opened her office door in time to hear her sergeant say, 'Hussain, Wood – we've got more data in from ANPR. See if we can put Taylor anywhere near the acquisition sites or the body dumps. And one of you check with the local lads and see if they've given anyone a tug yet for joyriding Bev McAndrew's car. I want to know where it was nicked from.'

Fielding took a deep breath. 'McIntyre? In here.'

Paula closed the door behind her. 'We found Marie Mather.'

Fielding looked stunned. 'Why did nobody tell me?'

'I've just come from the hospital,' Paula said. 'I imagine the team assumed I would tell you. Which I'm doing now.' Her tone bordered on the insolent.

'You should have called me right away.'

'I was more concerned with getting Marie Mather to hospital. She's still alive. Barely, but at least she's in with a chance now. And if she makes it, she makes our case for us.'

'Which team?' Fielding clutched at the last available straw. There were search teams going through Tony Hill's home and office. As well as the one McIntyre had called out to Gareth Taylor's house.

'Didn't I say? We found Marie in a chest freezer in Gareth Taylor's garage.'

There was a long silence. *Wrong, wrong, wrong.* The word echoed in Fielding's head like a bell tolling.

Paula had her hand on the door, getting ready to leave. 'I think you should release Dr Hill now,' she said gently.

'You do it,' Fielding said brusquely. 'You're such good pals. And you've worked so hard to get him off the hook.'

Anger finally flared in Paula's eyes. 'Just as well someone did, since he's innocent.'

'We followed the evidence, McIntyre. I'd have been irresponsible if I'd released him earlier.'

'We followed it down the wrong road, ma'am. And I'm busy right now. I have to interview the victim of a serious assault who will only talk to me. So I suggest you do it yourself.'

66

Carol had been confined in an interview room for hours. First, in spite of her protestations that she was absolutely fine, they'd had to wait for a doctor to confirm that she was well enough to be questioned. Then there had been a certain amount of discussion about the dog. Carol had refused to leave Flash locked in the Land Rover indefinitely and the dog team had pointed out it was nothing to do with them. Eventually, before she'd disappeared upstairs, an exasperated Fielding had said Carol could keep the bloody dog with her and claim it was a guide dog if anybody complained.

Then Carol had refused to be interviewed by anyone except Paula, which meant she had to wait till she was free.

When Paula finally sat down with Carol, it was almost midnight. Paula set down two tall cardboard cups. 'Not cop-shop crap, proper coffee-shop coffee from the all-night stand by Central Station.' She dug a paper bag out of her pocket. 'And a couple of muffins. Slightly squashed, I'm afraid.'

'Caffeine and sugar. That should do the trick,' Carol said.

She broke off a chunk of her muffin and dropped it at her feet, where Flash wolfed it before it hit the ground. 'Has Fielding released Tony yet?'

'I think she's doing it now. Me, I'd have done that the minute we arrested Taylor, but she wasn't taking any chances. Or so she said.'

'I hardly know the woman, but I'd say she's not someone who takes it well when she's proven wrong.'

Paula gave a grim little smile. 'I've a funny feeling I'm not going to be her bagman after tonight.'

'I'm sorry.'

'I'm not. I don't want to spend my time running around with a brush and dustpan after someone who can't keep an open mind.' She shrugged. 'There's other firms. I'm good at my job, people know that. Now, we have to figure out a way to spin this that doesn't drop anyone in the shit.'

Carol grinned. 'Just like old times.'

Paula shook her head. 'No way. Old times was me and Tony figuring out how to avoid you going ballistic at one or both of us for bending the rules.'

Carol's smile disappeared. 'I suppose so. Well, one thing we all know for sure. That won't be happening again.'

In another part of the building Bradfield's Chief Constable was wondering why he'd been so keen to take on this job. He believed he'd put together an efficient and effective team, but he'd just had to listen to the woman he thought his best DCI explain how she'd let a bee in her bonnet drive her over the edge of professionalism into a kind of stubborn madness. In the old days, he could have rammed a lid on her fuck-up with a fair degree of certainty that it would never leak out to the public. But these days, with a twenty-four-hour rolling news cycle and a ravenous social media, the chances of keeping things quiet were nil. You could only

427

cling to the hope that something else would make a louder noise to distract the twitterati.

James Blake exhaled heavily and pushed himself to his feet. He opened a cupboard and stared longingly at a bottle of cognac. What he wouldn't give for a large drink right now. But he still had a truly horrible encounter to deal with, and he daren't go into it smelling of drink. He closed the door and pulled himself up to his full height. He knew he could be imposing in a certain way, and God knew he needed that now. He slipped into his executive bathroom and checked himself in the mirror. There was something old-fashioned about his looks, he knew that. His wife said he had the air of a man who should be astride a horse leading a pack of hounds in pursuit of a fox. And although his background was relentlessly lower middle class, he played up to that image. He'd cultivated an accent several degrees above his natural station, he tended to wear country tweeds with double-vented jackets over Tattersall checked shirts, his pink cheeks were always freshly shaven, his hair treated with some expensive unguent from Floris. He'd moved to Bradfield from Devon, where he'd fitted in better, but had felt constrained by the lack of serious crime.

Well, this was where serious crime got you. Standing in your office in the middle of the bloody night waiting to be eviscerated by a woman who could stand as the dictionary definition of 'bitch'. James Blake tightened his stomach muscles and stalked back into his office. He crossed to the door, opened it and gestured to the waiting pair. 'Do come in.'

Paula walked Carol down to the Skenfrith Street car park and her Land Rover. She watched her tail lights disappear then lit a cigarette, shivering in the damp night air. She'd barely smoked half of it when her phone rang. When she saw it was Elinor, she was tempted to send it straight to

428

voicemail. She imagined the arrest was on the news and she couldn't talk about it yet with Elinor or Torin. But loyalty won over expediency and she took the call. 'DS McIntyre,' she said, using their standard code to make it clear they were in work mode.

'This is only a quickie. I saw the news and I know you must be up to your eyes. But I thought you'd want to know.'

'Know what?'

'We've spoken to Torin's dad again. Actually, Torin did most of the speaking. They've had a really good chat. He talked about how he feels about his mum. He really opened up. And then I was able to talk to Tom. The upshot is that Tom would be very grateful if we'd have Torin to stay until he's finished his tour of duty in Afghanistan.'

Paula could hear the genuine pleasure in Elinor's voice. She wasn't entirely sure how much of that delight she shared, but she was willing to go along for the ride. She'd never dreamed of a quiet life. Which was probably just as well. She stubbed out her smoke and walked into the warm fug of the station. 'I'm glad,' she said. 'I think Bradfield's the best place for him right now.'

'I love you, DS McIntyre. I'll see you later.'

Paula grunted. 'I doubt it, the way things are going.' She walked back into the squad room. And the moment's respite was over.

Because then an eager detective constable with an unruly mane of ginger curls raised a hand, as if she was in a GCSE maths class. 'Sergeant, you know how we were wondering how he knew it was safe to dump Nadia's body in that squat?'

'Yeah?'

'Well, I've been taking another look at the reports. Taylor's wife's maiden name was Waddington. And one of the lads who live in the squat is called Waddington. It's not that common a name. What's the betting they were related?'

'Good work. Check it out,' Paula said. She glanced across to Fielding's office. Empty. No surprise there. Hussain and Wood were communing with their computer screens and Cody was on the phone, his expression grave. He put the phone down and smacked his fist on the desk. Startled, everyone looked up.

'She didn't make it,' he said angrily. 'Marie Mather. She was bleeding internally. They couldn't stabilise her. Fuck.'

Paula stood in the middle of the room, feeling like a failure. All the things that had gone wrong with this case felt like a personal rebuke. She should have resisted Fielding more forcefully. She should have confronted Gareth Taylor as soon as Carol came up with his name. Certainly as soon as there was any suggestion that Marie might be missing. Like all cops, Paula carried the burden of what she might have done differently. Marie Mather's death had just added major weight to that burden.

Tony's first thought after release had been a fierce longing for his own bed. But Bronwen Scott had been waiting for him. She'd whisked him off to a quiet corner and given him a brief rundown on what had happened in the previous few hours. 'Carol did the business, and Paula picked up the pieces,' Scott had said, a feline smile of contentment on her face.

'What about Fielding?'

Scott's smile widened. 'Fucked. I see a great future for her in Traffic.'

'I'm glad they've stopped him.'

Scott appeared to have lost interest. 'Yes, yes. That's always good.'

'So, can I go home now?' He tried not to sound like an overtired plaintive child, but he suspected he'd failed. Twenty-eight hours in custody could do that to a man.

Scott laughed. He'd always wondered what writers meant

when they described a laugh as a tinkle. Now he knew. A brittle, musical sound. 'Sorry, Tony, but there's still work to be done. We're going to see Blake.'

'The Chief? Why?'

'Because you're going to be suing BMP for a very large sum of money for wrongful arrest, false imprisonment and damage to your personal and professional reputation.'

'I am?'

'You are.'

'I don't believe in suing public institutions. It's a waste of taxpayers' money that could be better spent doing other things.'

She looked at him as if he were mad. 'Fielding fucked you over. They've damaged your reputation, and that's what you live by. You deserve to be compensated.'

He shrugged. 'I don't think there was malice involved. Fielding just got a crazy idea in her head and dug herself in too deep.'

'Nevertheless. This is payback time. BMP owe you.'

'I don't want—' He'd been about to say 'their money', but then a better idea occurred to him. 'OK,' he said. 'Let's go and see Blake.'

So here they were, walking into Blake's office, a sanctum like a gentlemen's club. Tony wondered if you could buy a room spray that smelled of leather and cologne and cigars, because he'd have sworn that's what it smelled like.

'Come in, sit down,' Blake said, waving expansively at a group of leather tub chairs set around a low table. 'I do hope this hasn't been too traumatic an experience, Dr Hill. But of course, our officers do have to follow the evidence,' he said before they were even settled.

'That's what they're supposed to do,' Scott said, ice in her tone. 'But not at the price of making preposterous decisions. Every fragment of circumstantial evidence against Dr Hill was readily demolished by my team within a handful of hours. Arresting him and holding him in custody was completely unnecessary.' Blake tried to speak but she held a hand up. 'Dr Hill is a Home Office-accredited police consultant. He's devoted his professional career to helping police solve cases like this, for heaven's sake. You know where he lives and works. Even if there had been solid evidence to link him to these crimes, he was never any kind of flight risk. This has been preposterous from start to finish.' She exhaled sharply through her nose.

Blake shifted in his chair, crossing his legs at the ankles. 'However, matters have been resolved very quickly. I hope we can put it all behind us.' He steepled his fingers and gave an avuncular smile. 'Then it will all die down and reputations won't be unduly damaged.'

'I don't think you understand,' Scott said. 'We're looking for substantial compensation here. Wrongful arrest, false imprisonment and damage to Dr Hill's professional reputation. This is a major lawsuit, Mr Blake.'

Blake made a strangled mumbling sound. 'There hasn't been any significant publicity,' he pointed out.

'We haven't given our side of the story yet,' Scott said sweetly. 'We have an extraordinary tale to tell. A man of spotless reputation is thrown in the cells on the scantest of evidence. The police are so incompetent that I have to turn to a retired officer for help. And within twenty-four hours, we civilians not only destroy the case against Dr Hill but also expose the identity of the real killer. I imagine this one will run and run across the traditional and the digital media.'

Tony sat up straight, galvanised by this unexpected turn of events. To judge by the expression of shock that had crossed Blake's face, he hadn't expected that line of attack either. He looked like a man staring down the barrel of the end of his career. 'That's a shocking distortion of the facts,' he blustered.

'In what respect?'

Tony could tell Blake was on the point of closing the meeting, which wasn't what he wanted. He had an agenda of his own, and now was the time to pursue it. He cleared his throat and said, 'There is one way to avoid a costly and embarrassing lawsuit.'

They both swung round in their seats to stare at him. 'I don't think this is a good idea,' Scott said.

'Of course you don't,' Tony said. 'You're a lawyer. Conflict's your bread and butter. James, there's no denying that this has not been BMP's finest hour. I believe this whole debacle would never have happened if the MIT had still been up and running. When Carol Jordan's brother was killed, you shouldn't have let her go. You should have clasped her to your bosom and helped her through it, not cut her loose.'

'DCI Jordan had handed in her resignation before that happened. Which you very well know, Dr Hill.' Blake was like a dog with its hackles up.

'It doesn't matter. You should have taken care of her. But it's not too late. It's obvious from what's happened here that she's still got what it takes to make a difference. Here's the deal. You go to Carol Jordan and you offer her whatever it takes to get her back on board. I'm not saying you have to eat dirt and publicly reinstate the MIT. But you bring Carol back and find a way to put that team back together, and you'll hear no more about this.' He smiled at them both. Scott looked ready to thump him.

Blake, however, had the air of a man reprieved. 'What if she says no?'

Tony gave an apparently guileless smile. 'You need to make sure she doesn't.'

67

Day twenty-nine

When she finally got home and read Paula's message about Marie Mather, Carol's first instinct had been to pour herself a drink. But instead of knocking back the very large vodka in a oner, she sat staring at the glass for a long time. She took off her jacket and slung it over a hanger, then gave the glass her full attention. Stepping back into the world had given her pause. There was nothing wrong with what she was doing here in the barn. But she'd let that become an end in itself and the past few days had shown her that wasn't enough.

She'd only been on the periphery of the investigation but that had been enough to remind her that she had a talent for justice. Not to exercise that talent was wrong. Not just because of the end result; the lives that would be changed because she wasn't there to do what she was best at. But because it was bad for her to ignore the things she was good at, the things she could be proud of.

If she carried on like this, Jacko Vance would have scored

the ultimate victory. He'd set out on his campaign of vengeance with the aim of making her life not worth living. She hadn't been able to see past her grief to understand how well he'd succeeded. But the last few days had helped her to comprehend what had happened to her.

If she carried on like this, Jacko Vance would have won.

It wasn't only her professional life that had been poisoned by his actions. He'd managed to estrange her and Tony. Vance was the worst kind of clever psychopath; he'd understood how things would play out downstream of his actions. He'd worked out how to cause them maximum pain. And she'd walked right into the trap. She'd blamed Tony when really, the only person to blame was Vance himself.

Carol raised the glass to eye level and stared long and hard at the drink. It was time for her to make some changes. Her life wasn't over yet.

Slowly and steadily, Carol stood up and poured the vodka down the sink.

Dawn broke in a sky that seemed almost as watery as the canal basin. Grey, pearl and eggshell ran into each other in an uncertain muddle of sky and cloud. Tony sat on the roof of his boat up by the bows. His hands were folded round a cup of instant soup that had stopped steaming a while ago. His face was drawn and tired, his eyes gritty with lack of sleep. He'd returned to the boat shortly after one in the morning, so tired his very bones hurt. But as soon as he'd climbed into bed, sleep had slipped from him, leaving him restless and weary. He'd tried to fight the wakefulness, but he'd eventually given up and come outside to watch the orange glow of street lights lose their hold on the sky.

He'd had the sort of experience he could learn from, no doubt about that. He would better understand some of his patients as a result. Still, it was something he could have done without. Except that it had brought Carol back into his life, however briefly. He took her words at face value – that she wasn't there for him but for the sake of justice. It had always been what drove her. He wasn't arrogant enough to think that was a smokescreen for her true feelings. He knew her true feelings. She blamed him and she couldn't bear his presence. And yet, if he could be certain she'd be there every day, he'd have settled for a life sentence.

He'd felt on the verge of tears ever since he'd returned to the boat. He knew it was partly because he was tired but it was also because he'd lost her again.

Even as that thought crossed his mind, the boat rose and fell with the familiar sudden lurch that came from someone boarding. He almost didn't want to turn round because he couldn't bear the disappointment of seeing Paula at the other end of the hull. But he did turn, because he wanted to think of himself as someone who could be strong.

And there she was, standing at the stern, dressed for business in the same suit she'd been wearing the day before. Different shirt, though. Her hair was rumpled and her eyes were bleary with tiredness. But she was there and that was all that mattered to him.

He scrambled to his feet and couldn't think of a single thing to say that wasn't banal.

Carol spoke first. 'Do you know anywhere we can get a decent cup of coffee this time of the morning?'

He gestured to the open hatch. 'I have coffee.'

She shook her head. 'Neutral territory.'

He glanced at his watch. 'The only place I know is the all-night coffee stand at Central Station.'

She nodded. 'I'll see you there in ten minutes.' And she jumped ashore, a black-and-white dog at her heels as she strode across the cobbles with more energy than he could have managed.

Tony scrambled along the boat and locked the hatch, leaving his mug on the roof. He stumbled ashore and ran across to where his car was parked by the tapas bar. He reached Central Station with three minutes to spare and bought coffee for them both. He stood by the coffee stand, a cardboard beaker in each hand, waiting.

The dog still by her side, Carol rounded the corner and gestured with her head to a bench opposite the station entrance. He joined her there, silently handing over her drink. He still didn't know what to say. 'I heard you'd got a dog.' Hell of an ice-breaker.

'Always the master of the irrelevant.'

'It's not irrelevant. It means something.'

She sighed. 'And what does it mean in Tony world?'

'It means you've decided to let yourself form an emotional attachment. And that's a good thing.'

'If you say so.' She sipped her coffee. 'You blackmailed Blake,' she said.

'I did.'

'Why did you do that?'

'Because I'd rather someone like you was investigating serious violent death in this city than the Alex Fieldings of this world. And because everyone should practise the craft that they're best at.'

'You're still a psychologist, then?' There was an incredulous edge to her voice that cut him.

He sighed. 'It's the only thing I'm equipped for.'

'Scary thought.'

Sitting side by side, he couldn't see her face. There were no clues in her tone. Time was, she would have said things like that ironically, as a joke. 'Did you say yes?'

'I told him I'd think about it.'

'You should say yes. You got me out of jail.'

Now she sighed. 'I'm used to having the full weight of a

437

professional team behind me. I made mistakes in the last twenty-four hours that might have got me killed. Marie Mather might still be alive if I'd done things differently.' She buried her free hand in the dog's luxuriant coat. 'It forced me to realise that I'd been blaming you for not being flawless. And none of us is flawless.' Another sigh. 'I was so angry with myself for what happened to Michael and Lucy that I had to turn my anger somewhere else and you were the easiest target.'

He tried to speak and found he couldn't. He took a swig of coffee and tried again. 'I knew that. And I also knew the only way back for us was if you worked it out for yourself.'

'You think there is a way back for us?' A train rumbled over the bridge and disappeared into the station.

He shifted round so he could look at her. 'You're here, aren't you?'

**Now turn the page for
your free Val McDermid short story!**

Keeping on the Right Side of the Law

Just imagine trying to get a straight job when you've been a villain all your life. Even supposing I could bullshit my way round an application form, how the fuck do I blag my way through an interview, when the only experience I've got of interviews, I've had a brief sitting next to me reminding the thick dickheads on the other side of the table that I'm not obliged to answer? I mean, it's not a technique that's going to score points with the personnel manager, is it?

You can imagine it, can't you? 'Mr Finnieston, your application form was a little vague as to dates. Can you give us a more accurate picture of your career structure?'

Well, yeah. I started out with burglary when I was eight. My two older brothers figured I was little enough to get in toilet windows, so they taught me how to hold the glass firm with rubber suckers then cut round the edge with a glass cutter. I'd take out the window and pass it down to them, slide in through the gap and open the back door for them. Then they'd clean out the telly, the video and the stereo while I kept watch out the back.

All good things have to come to an end, though, and by

the time I was eleven, I'd got too big for those toilet windows, and besides, I wanted a bigger cut than those greedy thieving bastards would give me. That's when I started doing cars. They called me Sparky on account of I'd go out with a spark plug tied on a piece of cord. You whirl the plug around like a cowboy with a lasso, and when it's going fast enough, you just flick the wrist and bingo, the driver's window shatters like one of them fake windows they use in the films. Hardly makes a sound.

Inside a minute and I'd have the stereo out. I sold them round the pubs for a fiver a time. In a good night, I could earn a fifty, just like that, no hassle.

But I've always been ambitious, and that was my downfall. One of my mates showed me how to hotwire the ignition so I could have it away on my toes with the car as well as the sounds. By then, one of my brothers was doing a bit of work for a bloke who had a secondhand car pitch down Strangeways and a quiet little backstreet garage where his team ringed stolen cars and turned them out with a whole new identity to sell on to mug punters who knew no better.

Only he wasn't as clever as he thought he was, and one night I rolled up with a Ford Escort and drove right into the middle of a raid. It was wall-to-wall Old Bill that night, and I ended up in a different part of Strangeways, behind bars. Of course I was too young to do proper time, and my brief got me out of there and into a juvenile detention centre faster than you could say 'of previous good character'.

It's true, what they say about the nick. You do learn how to be a better criminal, just as long as you do what it tells you in all them American self-help books in the prison library. You want to be successful, then hang out with successful people and do what they do. Only, of course, anybody who's banged up is, by definition, not half as fucking successful as they should be.

Anyway, I watched and listened and learned and I made some good mates that first time inside. And when I came out, I was ready for bigger and better things. Back then, banks and post offices were still a nice little earner. They hadn't learned about shatterproof glass and grilles and all that bollocks. You just ran in, waved a shooter around, jumped the counter and cleaned the place out. You could be in and out in five minutes, with enough in your sports bag to see you clear for the next few months.

I loved it.

It was a clean way to earn a living. Well, mostly it was. Ok, a couple of times we ran into one of them have-a-go heroes. You'd think it was their money, honest to God you would. Now, I've always believed you should be able to do a job, in and out, and nobody gets hurt. But if some dickhead is standing between me and the out, and it's me or him, I'm not going to stand there and ask him to move politely aside, am I? No, fuck it, you've got to show him who's in charge. One shot into the ceiling, and if he's still standing there, well, it's his own fault, isn't it? You've got to be professional, haven't you? You've got to show you mean business.

And I must have been good at it, because I only ever got a tug the once, and they couldn't pin a thing on me. Yeah, OK, I did end up doing a three stretch around about then, but that was for what you might call extracurricular activities. When I found out Johnny the Hat was giving one to my brother's wife, well, I had to make an example of him, didn't I? I mean, family's family. She might be a slag, but anybody that thinks they can fuck with my family is going to find out different. You'd think Johnny would have had the sense not to tell the Dibble who put him in hospital, but some people haven't got the brains they were born with. They had him in witness protection before the trial, but of course all that ended after I went down. And when I was getting through my three with visits from the family, I had the satisfaction of knowing that Johnny's family were visiting his grave. Like I say, families have got to stick together.

By the time I got out, things had changed. The banks and building societies had wised up and sharpened up their act and the only people trying to rob them were amateurs and fucking eejits.

Luckily, I'd met Tommy inside. Honest to God, it was like it was written in the fucking stars. I knew all about robbing and burgling, and Tommy knew all there was to know about antiques. What he also knew was that half the museums and the stately homes of England – not to mention our neighbours in Europe – had alarm systems that were an embarrassment.

I put together a dream team. And Tommy set up the fencing operation, and we were in business. The MO was simple. We'd spend the summer on research trips. We'd case each place once. Then we'd go back three weeks later to case it again, leaving enough time for the security vids to be wiped of our previous visit. We'd figure out the weak points and draw up the plans. Then we'd wait till the winter, when most of them were closed for the season, with nothing more than a skeleton staff.

We'd pick a cold, wet, miserable night, preferably with a bit of wind. That way, any noise we made got swallowed up in the weather. Then we'd go in, seven-pound sledges straight through the vulnerable door or window, straight to the cabinets that held the stuff we'd identified as worth nicking. Here's a tip, by the way. Even if they've got toughened glass in the cases, chances are it's still only got a wooden frame. Smack that on the corner with a three-pound club hammer and the whole thing falls to bits and you're in.

Mostly, we were off the estate and miles away before the

local bizzies even turned up. Nobody ever got hurt, except in the pocket.

They were the best years of my life. Better than sex, that moment when you're in, you do what you do and you're out again. The rush is purer than you'll ever get from any drug. Not that I know about that from personal experience, because I've never done drugs and I never will. I hate drug dealers more than I hate coppers. I've removed my fair share of them from my patch over the years. Now they know not to come peddling their shit on my streets. But a couple of the guys I work with, they like their Charlie or whizz when they're not working, and they swear that they've never had a high like they get when they're doing the business.

We did some crackers. A museum in France where they'd spent two million quid on their state-of-the-art security system. They had a grand opening do where they were shouting their mouths off about how their museum was burglar-proof. We did it that very night. We rigged up pulleys from the building across the street, wound ourselves across like we were in the SAS and went straight in through the skylight. They said we got away with stuff worth half a million quid. Not that we made anything like that off it. I think I cleared fifteen K that night, after expenses. Still, who dares wins, eh?

We only ever took stuff we already knew we had a market for. Well, mostly. One time, I fell in love with this Rembrandt. I just loved that picture. It was a self-portrait, and just looking at it, you knew the geezer like he was one of your mates. It was hanging on this Duke's wall, right next to the cases of silver we'd earmarked. On the night, on the spur of the moment, I lifted the Rembrandt an' all.

Tommy went fucking ape. He said we'd never shift that, that we'd never find a buyer. I told him I didn't give a shit, it wasn't for sale anyway. He thought I'd completely lost the plot when I said I was taking it home.

I had it on the bedroom wall for six months. But it wasn't right. A council house in Wythenshawe just doesn't go with a Rembrandt. So one night, I wrapped it up in a tarpaulin and left it in a field next to the Duke's gaff. I rang the local radio station from a call box and told them where they could find the picture. I hated giving it up, mind you, and I wouldn't have done if I'd had a nicer house.

But that's not the sort of tale you can tell a personnel manager, is it?

'And why are you seeking a change of employment, Mr Finnieston?'

Well, it's down to Kim, innit?

I've known Kimmy since we were at school together. She was a looker then, and time hasn't taken that away from her. I always fancied her, but never got round to asking her out. By the time I was back in circulation after my first stretch, she'd taken up with Danny McGann, and before I worked up the bottle to make a move, bingo, they were married.

I ran into her again about a year ago. She was on a girls' night out in Rothwell's, a gaggle of daft women acting like they were still teenagers. Just seeing her made me feel like a teenager an' all. I sent a bottle of champagne over to their table, and of course Kimmy came over to thank me for it. She always had good manners.

Any road, it turned out her and Danny weren't exactly happy families any more. He was working away a lot, leaving her with the two girls, which wasn't exactly a piece of cake. Mind you, she's done well for herself. She's got a really good job, managing a travel agency. A lot of responsibility and a lot of respect from her bosses. We started seeing each other, and I felt like I'd come up on the lottery.

The only drawback is that after a few months, she tells me she can't be doing with the villainy. She's got a proposition for me. If I go straight, she'll kick Danny into touch and move in with me.

So that's why I'm trying to figure out a way to make an honest living. You can see that convincing a bunch of suits that they should give me a job would be difficult. 'Thank you very much, Mr Finnieston, but I'm afraid you don't quite fit our present regulations.'

The only way anybody's ever going to give me a job is if I monster them into it, and somehow I don't think the straight world works like that. You can't go around person-nel offices saying, 'I know where you live. So gizza job or the Labrador gets it.'

This is where I'm up to when I meet my mate Chrissie for a drink. You wouldn't think it to look at her, but Chrissie writes them hard-as-nails cop dramas for the telly. She looks more like one of them bleeding-heart social workers, with her wholemeal jumper and jeans. But Chrissie's dead sound, her and her girlfriend both. The girlfriend's a brief, but in spite of that, she's all right. That's probably because she doesn't do criminal stuff, just divorces and child custody and all that bollocks.

So I'm having a pint with Chrissie in one of them trendy bars in Chorlton, all wooden floors and hard chairs and fifty different beers, none of them ones you've ever heard of except Guinness. And I'm telling her about my little prob-lem. Halfway down the second pint, she gets that look in her eyes, the dreamy one that tells me something I've said has set the wheels in motion inside her head. Usually, I see the results six months later on the telly. I love that. Sitting down with Kimmy and going, 'See that? I told Chrissie about that scam. Course, she's softened it up a bit, but it's my tale.'

'I've got an idea,' Chrissie says.

'What? You're going to write a series about some poor fucker trying to go straight?' I say.

'No, a job. Well, a sort of job.' She knocks back the rest of her pint and grabs her coat. 'Leave it with me. I'll get back to you. Stay lucky.' And she's off, leaving me surrounded by well-meaning like the last covered wagon hemmed in by the Apaches.

A week goes by, with me trying to talk my way into setting up a little business doing one-day hall sales. But everybody I approach thinks I'm up to something. They can't believe I want to do anything the straight way, so all I get offered is fifty kinds of bent gear. I am sick as a pig by the time I get the call from Chrissie.

This time, we meet round her house. Me, Chrissie and the girlfriend, Sarah, the solicitor. We settle down with our bottles of Belgian pop and Sarah kicks off. 'How would you like to work on a freelance basis for a consortium of solicitors?' she asks.

I can't help myself. I just burst out laughing. 'Do what?' I go.

'Just hear me out. I spend a lot of my time dealing with women who are being screwed over by the men in their life. Some of them have been battered, some of them have been emotionally abused, some of them are being harassed by their exes. Sometimes, it's just that they're trying to get a square deal for themselves and their kids, only the bloke knows how to play the system and they end up with nothing while he laughs all the way to the bank. For most of these women, the law either can't sort it out or it won't. I even had a case where two coppers called to a domestic gave evidence in court against the woman, saying she was completely out of control and irrational and all the bloke was doing was exerting unreasonable force to protect himself.'

'Bastards,' I say. 'So what's this got to do with me?'

'People doing my job get really frustrated,' Sarah says. 'There's a bunch of us get together for a drink now and again, and we've been talking for a long time about how we've stopped believing the law has all the answers. Most of these blokes are bullies and cowards. Their women wouldn't see them for dust if they had anybody to stand up for them. So what we're proposing is that we'd pay you to sort these bastards out.'

I can't believe what I'm hearing. A brief offering me readies to go round and heavy the kind of toerags I'd gladly sort out as a favour? There has to be a catch. 'You're not telling me the Legal Aid would pay for that, are you?' I say.

Sarah grins. 'Behave, Terry. I'm talking a strictly unofficial arrangement. I thought you could go and explain the error of their ways to these blokes. Introduce them to your baseball bat. Tell them if they don't behave, you'll be visiting them again in a less friendly mode. Tell them that they'll be getting a bill for incidental legal expenses incurred on their partner's behalf and if they don't come up with the cash pronto monto, you'll be coming round to make a collection. I'm sure they'll respond very positively to your approaches.'

'You want me to go round and teach them a lesson?' I'm still convinced this is a wind-up.

'That's about the size of it.'

'And you'll pay me?'

'We thought a basic rate of two hundred and fifty pounds a job. Plus bonuses in cases where the divorce settlement proves suitably substantial. A bit like a lawyer's contingency fee. No win, no fee.'

I can't quite get my head round this idea. 'So it would work how? You'd bell me and tell me where to do the business?'

Sarah shakes her head. 'It would all go through Chrissie. She'll give you the details, then she'll bill the legal firms for miscellaneous services, and pass the fees on to you. After this meeting, we'll never talk about this again face to face.

And you'll never have contact with the solicitors you'd be acting for. Chrissie's the cut-out on both sides.'

'What do you think, Tel?' Chrissie asks, eager as a virgin in the back seat.

'You could tell Kimmy you were doing process serving.' Sarah chips in.

That's the clincher. So I say Ok.

That was six months ago. Now I'm on Chrissie's books as her research assistant. I pay tax and National Insurance, which was a bit of a facer for the social security, who could not get their heads round the idea of me as a proper citizen. I do two or three jobs a week, and everything's sweet. Sarah's sorting out Kimmy's divorce, and we're getting married as soon as that's all done.

I tell you, this is the life. I'm doing the right thing and I get paid for it. If I'd known going straight could be this much fun, I'd have done it years ago.